ECONOMICS
and Urban Problems

ECONOMICS
and Urban Problems

HEINZ KOHLER
Amherst College

Theodore Lownik Library
Illinois Benedictine College
Lisle, Illinois 60532

D. C. HEATH AND COMPANY
Lexington, Massachusetts Toronto London

330
.91732
K79e

Copyright © 1973 by D. C. Heath and Company.

All rights reserved. No part of this publication may be reproduced or transmitted in any form or by any means, electronic or mechanical, including photocopy, recording, or any information storage or retrieval system, without permission in writing from the publisher.

Published simultaneously in Canada.

Printed in the United States of America.

International Standard Book Number: 0-669-84566-3

Library of Congress Catalog Card Number: 73-1842

Preface

This book grew out of a course I taught at Amherst College in the fall of 1971 on the economics of urban problems. The students of that course had had little or no contact with the study of economics, and the writing is geared to that level. The book is therefore aimed at beginning students in economics or at the layman who is interested in this particular set of domestic problems.

As the title and table of contents reveal, this book for the most part ignores highly technical and advanced theoretical developments in the area of urban economics, however fascinating they may be. Thus there are no chapters on location theory, nor any mathematical models of urban growth. Instead, Part One offers a basic knowledge of the fundamental economic problem of scarcity and the resultant need for making choices and incurring opportunity costs. It develops the principle of rational behavior and shows how a market economy might coordinate the actions of large numbers of independent decision makers in such a way as to assure rational use of scarce resources. Finally, it provides a view of the nature of the city and its recent evolution.

Armed with this background and the most basic analytical tools, the reader is then immediately led to a consideration of the main economic problems besetting our urban areas. Part Two deals with issues that predominantly affect economic justice. It shows the nature of income distribution and poverty and considers policies that would affect the extent of poverty. These include redistributions of wealth, improvements in health, education, and employment, and redistributions of income. Part Three takes up problems associated with inefficient use of resources: housing, transportation, and pollution. Finally, Part Four concerns the fiscal crisis of urban governments and considers the proper division of labor among governments.

The problems so examined are the ones my students were most eager to investigate, and I owe my most important debt to their curiosity and concern. In addition, I am deeply indebted to dozens of my colleagues. While many are not personally known to me, they have shared their ideas on urban problems with the world, and so with me, through articles and books that have appeared in ever growing numbers, particularly during the last decade. To all, I wish to express my deep gratitude.

Numerous small portions of this book have been reproduced from earlier publications of mine. I wish to express my appreciation to The Dryden Press of Hinsdale, Illinois, for so readily granting permission to use these passages. Last but not least, I wish to thank Mrs. Dorothy Ives and Mrs. Eleanor Starzyk, both of whom typed drafts of this work, performing as usual, speedily and with perfection.

Heinz Kohler
Amherst, Massachusetts
March 1973

A Note to the Student

Economics has much to contribute to an analysis and eventual solution of urban problems. Although this book covers a truly vast area, it does not pretend to cover everything economists have to say about the subject. For those who wish to pursue these matters in greater depth, or to keep up to date as time passes, the following suggestions for finding further readings or statistical data will be helpful.

Finding journal articles. To find journal articles, consult the *Index of Economic Articles* (formerly *Index of Economic Journals*). The volumes of this index, which are prepared by the American Economic Association and published by Richard D. Irwin, Inc. (Homewood, Illinois), list all economics articles in the English language since 1886. A superb classification schedule allows the reader to find immediately selected articles on any subject, including the area of urban economics. To find articles of very recent date, consult the *Journal of Economic Literature*, published four times a year by the American Economic Association at Menasha, Wisconsin.

Finding books. The most comprehensive listing of books can be found in the *Library of Congress Catalog.* Available in every large library, this catalog lists books by author as well as by subject matter. Recent publications of economics books are also listed, and frequently reviewed, in the aforementioned *Journal of Economic Literature.* Finally, the U.S. Government Printing Office in Washington, D.C., puts out a *Monthly Catalog of U.S. Government Publications.* Many of the entries, such as the recorded hearings before Congressional committees, contain some of the most fascinating and up-to-date information on current urban problems.

Finding statistics. To find statistical data, consult the *Statistical Abstract of the United States.* It is published annually by the U.S. Bureau of the Census in Washington, D.C. Note in the *Abstract* also, besides actual data, the listing of statistical abstract supplements, the guide to sources of statistics, and the listing of recent censuses and of state statistical abstracts. These contain references to all the primary sources of statistics.

Another aid. Any serious student should become familiar with the above three aids to research. By using them, you can literally find anything that has been written on a subject that interests you. By using them repeatedly, you will eventually learn what types of publications are most likely to contain the information you are after. If you are particularly interested in statistics on poverty or on unemployment you may come to like, respectively, the *Current Population Reports* (Bureau of the Census) or *Employment and Earnings*

(Bureau of Labor Statistics). If you prefer studying the chances of black capitalism, the *Review of Black Political Economy* may be more to your liking. Others concerned primarily with ecology or with alternatives to our economic system may make *Environmental Affairs* or *The Review of Radical Political Economics* their favorite journal. All this comes with experience, and I urge you to gain it on your own. Nevertheless, for those who prefer more specific guidance than the above, selected readings have been listed at the end of each chapter of this book. These include a few books and articles I have particularly liked. But since your preferences may well differ from mine, do make use of the three general references mentioned above. To make it easier for you, the end-of-chapter selected readings include specific page numbers on which the *1972 Statistical Abstract* lists data or references concerning the material discussed in the chapter. They include, finally, specific classification numbers under which the *Journal of Economic Literature* and the *Index of Economic Articles* list articles concerning the chapter's subject matter.

Contents

Part One: Basic Concepts

Part Two: Matters of Equity

Part Three: Matters of Efficiency

Part One
Basic Concepts

We cannot hope to understand urban economic problems, or suggest solutions for them, without an awareness of the framework within which these problems occur. In particular, we must know about the nature of our economic system. This is necessary so we can judge whether our economic problems result from flaws in the very logic of that system, or from mere aberrations that might be corrected with the system itself maintained. Similarly, we must come to know about the nature of cities and their recent evolution. This is necessary so we can judge whether our urban problems are an inevitable part of any city's life, or merely a by-product of the recent history of cities that is amenable to correction without a complete return to rural living.

The purpose of Part One is to assure such overall understanding. The ground is thus prepared for the discussion of individual urban problems in the remaining parts of the book.

1 On the Rational Use of Resources

Every society has an economic system. In this chapter, we pose a simple question and try to answer it: What is an economic system supposed to do? We begin with fundamentals.

THE ECONOMIC PROBLEM

In every society, people have *economic wants*. Individuals and also groups of people harbor desires for a vast array of commodities and services: food and clothing, shelter and education, medical care and clean water, bombers and missiles, courthouses and highways. To simplify matters, we shall refer to this vast set of want-satisfying commodities and services as *goods*.

The really important thing to note, however, is this: *In every society, many economic wants cannot possibly be fulfilled*. This is so because goods are not made from thin air. Goods are made with certain ingredients that economists call *resources*. These include "labor"—shorthand for all types of human effort. They also include "land"—shorthand for all the gifts of nature in their original state, such as virgin soil, minerals, and timber. Finally, they include "capital"—shorthand for man-made ingredients in the productive process, such as buildings, machines, and producers' inventories (anything from raw materials to finished goods). Because the vast quantity of resources that would be required to make all the goods all the people want does not exist, every society faces *scarcity* as its ultimate economic problem. No matter what the society does, some of its economic wants simply cannot be satisfied. This is a basic fact of life.

There are two obvious solutions to this scarcity problem. One is the creation of a new kind of man who desires less. If people's economic wants could be reduced sufficiently, there might be enough resources to make all the goods all people desired. This approach, however, is being rejected almost universally. We ignore it in this book, too.

The logical alternative remains: People can strive to satisfy economic wants as much as possible by instituting a well-thought-out program of resource use. Such a program should first mobilize resources to produce the *largest possible set of goods*. That is, society should use all available resources fully;

and it should use them efficiently, never wasting a single opportunity to assure that resources are used as frugally as possible. After all, every bit of resources saved from the production of a given quantity of one good can be used to produce additional units of this good or other goods. (It is obviously from this need for economizing resources that economics gets its name.)

Second, society's program of resource use should assure that the total of goods produced is composed of the *right proportions of different goods.* If people preferred food to missiles under any and all circumstances, for instance, the largest possible collection of missiles produced would satisfy economic wants less than the largest possible collection of food. Thus resources must be directed toward the production of the largest possible set not of just any goods but of the most desirable goods.

Third, the society's program of resource use must assure that goods are *correctly apportioned among people* so that the greatest satisfaction may be gotten from these goods. There may well be occasions when giving goods to one family rather than another creates greater satisfaction than might otherwise be obtained.

Yet even when society proceeds to use its resources, and to apportion its output, as carefully as possible (according to the three goals just stated), there will be many economic wants that must remain unfulfilled. For this reason, the allocation of resources for various uses and the apportionment of goods among people involve a painful process of choice.

CHOICE AND OPPORTUNITY COST

Consider the allocation of resources to the production of goods. The process of choosing what to do with scarce resources in a situation in which there are obviously not enough to make all the goods people want is painful precisely because every use of resources for one purpose means forgoing the opportunity to use them for another purpose also desired. As economists are fond of putting it, every use of resources involves an *opportunity cost.* The opportunity cost of producing any one good is nothing but the quantity of another good that might have been made with the resources that were used to make the first. Figure 1.1, "The Production Possibilities Frontier," shows the principle by use of a graph.

Imagine a society that uses its technical know-how to produce, in the best ways known to man, nothing but military goods, such as bombers, missiles, or bullets. By using all its resources fully and efficiently, such a society would be able to produce some maximum quantity of such goods, that shown by distance *OA* in Figure 1.1. This same society could, of course, devote all its resources to making goods for civilian uses, such as cakes, dresses, or clean air. By using all its resources for this purpose instead, it would, with its existing technical knowledge, produce some other maximum quantity of goods, exemplified by *OB*. This society could also produce any one of the many combinations of military goods and civilian goods lying on line *AB*. This is its *production possi-*

Figure 1.1 **The Production Possibilities Frontier**

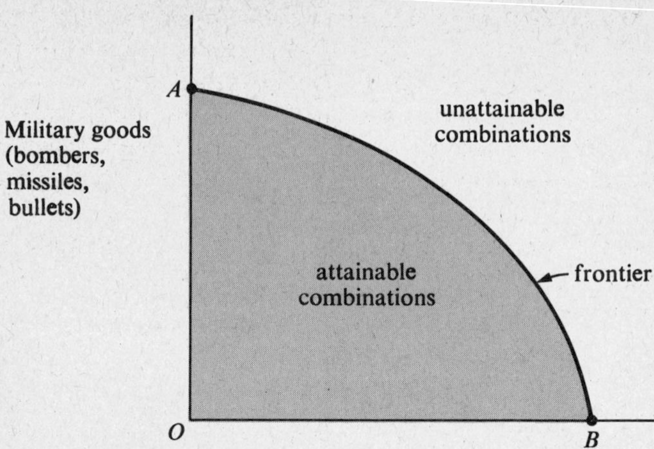

This production possibilities frontier shows all the combinations of two groups of goods that a society is capable of producing by using its resources fully and efficiently. Thus it divides the set of all conceivable combinations of goods into two: attainable ones (shaded) and unattainable ones.

bilities frontier. For the moment do not worry about the particular shape of this curve. There are good reasons to draw it in this way rather than as a straight line or curved the other way, but these reasons are not important to our present discussion. What is important is this: The existence of scarcity is illustrated by the fact that all combinations of goods lying above and to the right of line *AB* are unattainable, even though they may well be wanted by people. Combinations lying to the left and below the line are attainable, but would use fewer resources or less efficient production methods than the society has available.

It is now very easy to illustrate the concept of opportunity cost. If the society were to produce quantity *OA* of military goods, it would have to forgo quantity *OB* of civilian goods. Thus the opportunity cost of *OA* military goods would equal *OB* of civilian goods. Alternatively, if the society were to produce *OB* of civilian goods, it would have to forgo production of *OA* of military goods. The opportunity cost of *OB* of civilian goods would equal *OA* of military goods.

Historically, many a society has incurred heavy opportunity costs in order to carry forward certain national goals. Hitler urged his countrymen to forgo butter in favor of guns, and he presided over a massive national effort to cut the production of civilian goods in favor of military goods. Stalin, interested in rapid economic growth of the Soviet Union, drastically cut the production of consumer goods and greatly increased the production of capital goods. The increased quantities of buildings and machines produced then, he argued, would allow a much greater production of consumer goods later. The United States, in the 1960's, carried on a similar massive redirection of resources. Such tasks as the abolition of poverty and the cleaning up of the environment were slighted in order to carry forward the national commitment to fight a war in Vietnam and to land a man on the moon.

We as individuals must similarly incur opportunity costs, every day, wherever we turn. Just as the nation as a whole has limited *resources* to spend, each individual has a limited *money income*. When you spend your money on ice cream, you might have to forgo the opportunity of seeing a movie. Then the movie forgone is the opportunity cost of having ice cream. When a family spends its money on furniture, it might have to forgo a vacation trip. Thus the vacation trip forgone is the opportunity cost of having the furniture.

Similar costs are incurred by all of us as we allocate the limited *time* available to us. If we watch the evening news television program, we might not be able to watch the sunset. Not enjoying the sunset is the opportunity cost of seeing the news telecast. Whatever we do, because there are so many things we like to do and time is limited, we cannot help incurring opportunity costs. Right now, as you read this book, there is surely something else you could do now and would like to do. As long as you refrain from doing it, forgoing the other activity is the opportunity cost of studying economics.

THE PRINCIPLE OF OPTIMIZATION

The above discussion raises an interesting issue. How do we decide on the allocation of our time among the many activities we engage in? Or how do we decide on the allocation of our money income among the many goods we want? Even a moment's reflection reveals one interesting fact: Seldom, if ever, do we make all-or-nothing decisions. We never seem to spend *all* our time studying economics and *none* of it doing other things. We never seem to spend all our income buying apples and none of it buying other goods. Rather, we engage in a whole variety of activities in a day, just as we buy a large collection of different goods with our income. Societies do the same thing. They never use all their scarce resources for one purpose only. Hitler did not really choose *all* "guns" and *no* "butter" (combination A in Figure 1.1). Rather, he made Germany move along its production possibilities frontier from a combination near *B* (lots of civilian goods, few military goods, but some of *both*) to one nearer to A (lots of military goods, few civilian goods, but some of both). The choice is illustrated in Figure 1.2, "Moving along the Production Possibilities Frontier."

In short, we all realize this: Although we can never have all of everything we want, we can always have a little more of one thing by giving up a little of another. Clearly, then, if we are interested in maximizing our well-being, we must somehow continually compare the potential welfare gain from a little more of one thing with the potential welfare loss from a little less of another. Unconsciously perhaps, as we attempt to maximize our well-being, we all must

Figure 1.2 Moving along the Production Possibilities Frontier

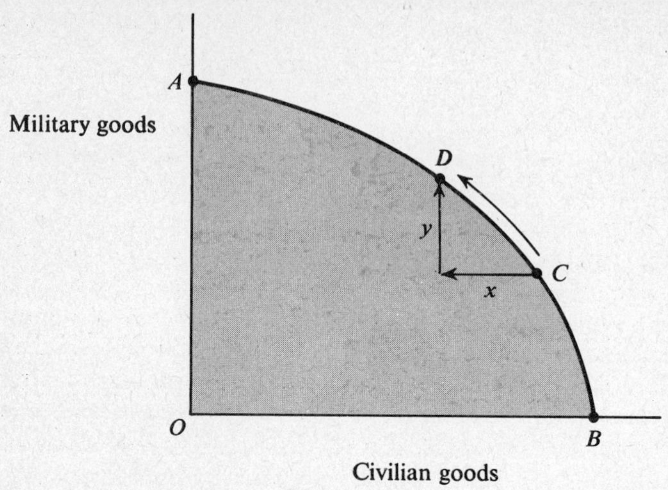

A society currently producing combination C of military and civilian goods could by giving up quantity *x* of civilian goods gain quantity *y* of military goods, thus ending with combination *D*.

engage in *marginalist thinking*, that is, thinking in terms of small changes in quantities. Most of the time, this leads us to do a combination of many things rather than one thing only. Let us pursue this thought in some detail.

The Law of Diminishing Marginal Effectiveness

Imagine yourself in a situation wherein you can spend your daily income on either food or clothing or any combination of both. Buying and consuming a first unit of food on this day will bring you a certain satisfaction or benefit, which we shall designate as quantity *a*. Buying and consuming a second unit of food on this same day will bring an *extra* benefit, or *marginal benefit*, which we shall designate as quantity *b*. At this point, your *total* benefit equals $a + b$. Similarly, you can buy and consume a third, fourth, fifth unit of food, and so on, until you run out of money. Each unit brings you a marginal benefit (*c*, *d*, *e*, and so on), an amount of extra satisfaction by which your total benefit increases. More likely than not, however, the marginal benefits will decline as the daily quantity of food consumed increases:[1] Whatever satisfaction you got from the first unit of food, the extra satisfaction from other identical units consumed on the same day is likely to get progressively less. After a while, you will

[1] For the sake of a simpler illustration, it will be assumed in this book that the marginal benefit begins to decline *immediately* after the first unit of consumption, rather than *eventually*, after an unspecified number of units have been consumed.

even be satiated (or become sick), and another unit of food will then add nothing to your total benefit (or will even decrease it). This is an example of the *law of diminishing marginal effectiveness*, which states: If the level of any benefit-producing activity is increased successively by equal units during a fixed time period (while the levels of other activities are held constant), the additional activity units will after some point lose effectiveness and produce declining marginal benefits (that is, successive units will raise the total benefit by less and less).

The terms *activity* and *benefit* used in this definition can refer to a great variety of things. For instance, *activity* can refer to the use of an input in the productive process. Then the benefit derived is the quantity of output produced. In that form, the above principle is frequently referred to as the "law of diminishing returns." But the term *activity* can also refer to the use of a good in the process of consumption, as in our example. Then the benefit is the quantity of satisfaction experienced by the consumer. The principle is illustrated in Figure 1.3, "The Law of Diminishing Marginal Effectiveness."

Now we should notice two things. First, that which has just been said about food could have been said about clothing as well. We can imagine the total and marginal benefit of clothing consumption as behaving similarly, according to the lines in Figure 1.3, as daily clothing consumption is increased. Second, if the marginal benefit declines with increased consumption, it must *rise* with *decreased* consumption. Refer once more to Figure 1.3, "The Law of Diminishing Marginal Effectiveness." Other things being equal, going from four units of food consumed per day to five units adds e units of satisfaction to the total benefit. The marginal benefit has dropped from *d* to e. Conversely, going from five units of food consumed per day to four units *subtracts* e units of satisfaction from the total benefit. The marginal benefit has *risen* from e to *d*. In short, the larger our original level of consumption, the less our total benefit is raised by an additional unit of consumption *and the less it is reduced by the loss of such unit*. To put it another way, the smaller our original level of consumption, the more our total benefit is raised by an additional unit of consumption and the more it is reduced by the loss of such unit. For example, while you may not value another apple very highly when it is offered to you after you have just eaten ten, you may value it very highly when you are offered one after having had none. Conversely, you may hardly care when getting ten apples rather than eleven, but care a great deal when someone suggests you eat none instead of one! How we feel about things depends very much on the circumstances in which we find ourselves. This brings us to an important point.

Marginal Opportunity Cost

We know that in a world of scarcity we can have more of one good only by giving up some of another. Therefore, given our money income, anytime we gain some satisfaction (say because we buy more clothing), we also lose some

Figure 1.3 **The Law of Diminishing Marginal Effectiveness**

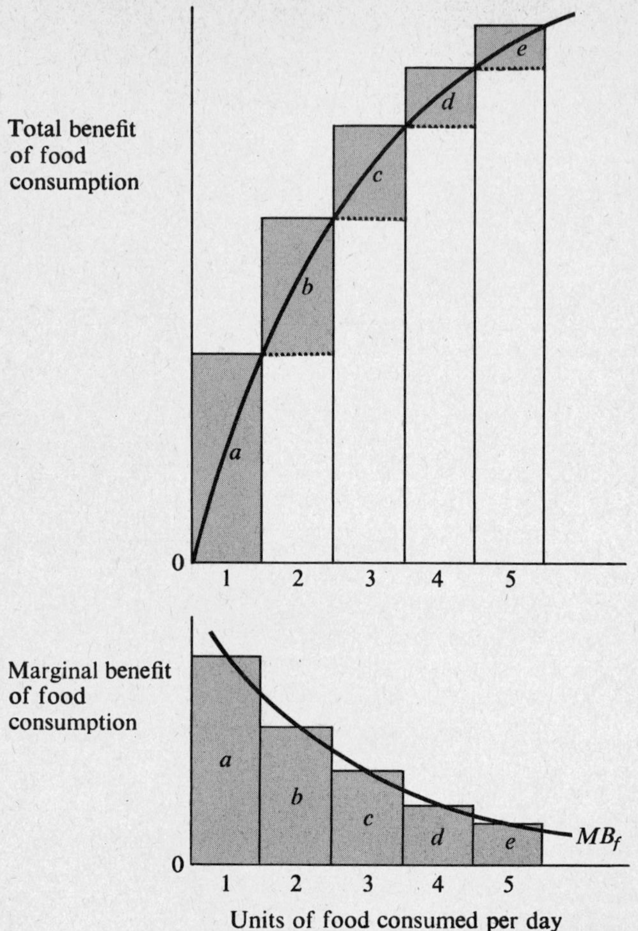

If the quantities of other goods consumed are held constant, as the units of food consumed per day increase, the marginal benefit of food consumption (MB_f) declines. Note blocks a through e in the lower graph, the height of which pretends to measure the marginal benefit. Or note the smooth declining curve drawn through the top of each block. The total benefit of food consumption in the upper graph—being nothing else but the sum of the marginal benefits—rises by less and less as food consumed increases by equal units. This illustrates the law of diminishing marginal effectiveness.

satisfaction (say because we must buy less food). The positive change in total benefit (marginal benefit) of more clothing then has come at an opportunity cost: the negative change in total benefit of less food. The latter is therefore called the marginal opportunity cost—or simply the *marginal cost*—of the extra clothing. This might be illustrated as in Figure 1.4, "Cost Is Benefit Forgone."

This graph is based on Figure 1.3. Assume each unit of food and clothing to be defined as "one dollar's worth" so that they can be exchanged one for one. Now assume sufficient money income to buy five units of one or of the other. Then a consumer might spend all his money buying five units of food. Or he might buy four units of food *F* and one unit of clothing *C*, or 3*F* and 2*C*, or 2*F* and 3*C*, or 1*F* and 4*C*, or 5*C*. Giving up the fifth unit of food (to get the first of clothing) involves loss of satisfaction equal to e (Figure 1.3). This is the marginal cost of the first clothing unit consumed (note quantity e in the lower graph, Figure 1.4). Similarly, giving up the fourth unit of food (to get the

Figure 1.4 **Cost Is Benefit Forgone**

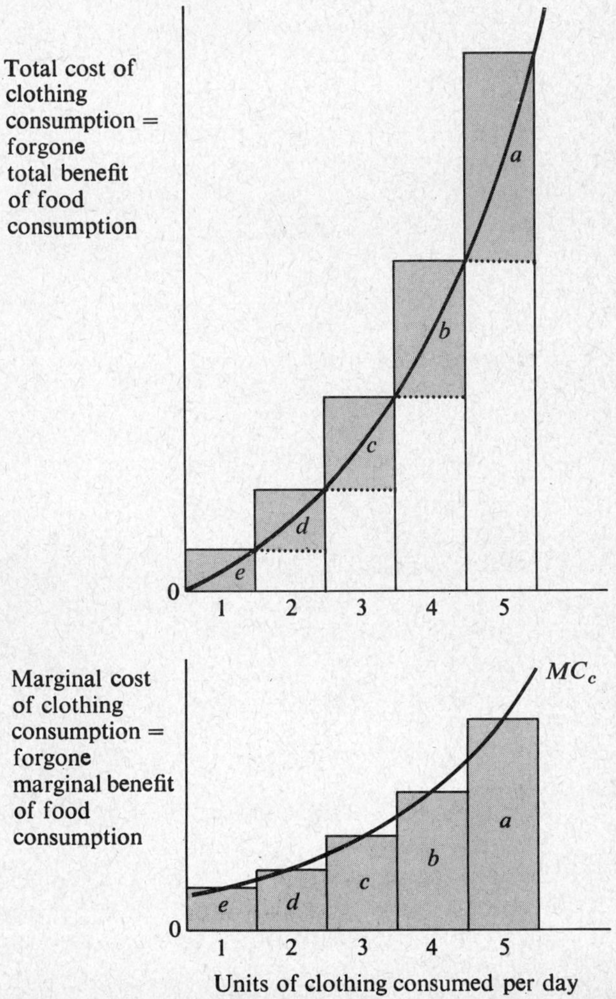

The declining marginal benefit of increased food consumption (Figure 1.3) translates into a rising marginal cost of increased clothing consumption if food has to be sacrificed for clothing.

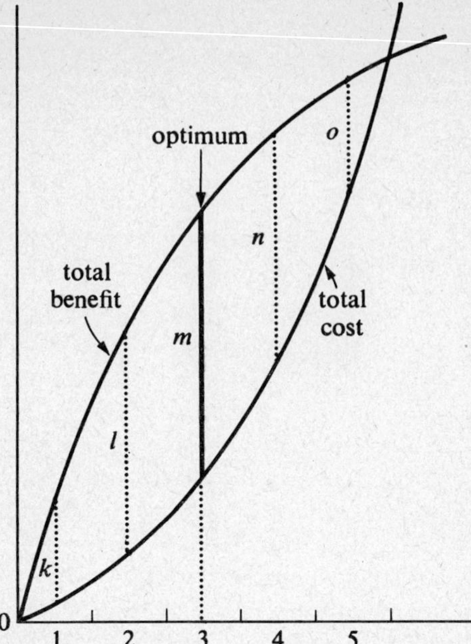
Total benefit
and total cost
of clothing
consumption
optimum
total
benefit
total
cost
k
l
m
n
o
0
1
2
3
4
5

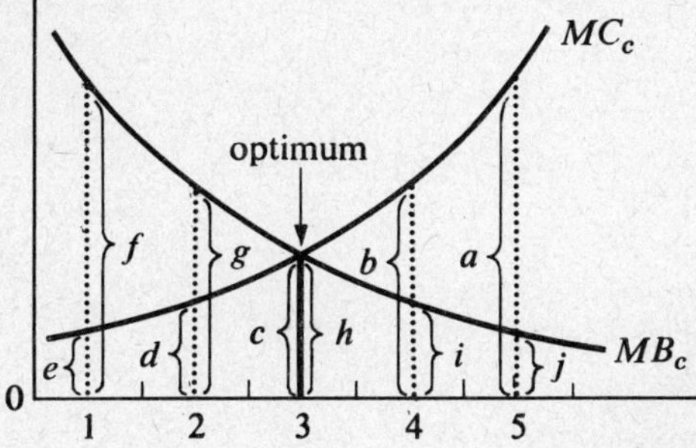
Marginal benefit
and marginal cost
of clothing
consumption
optimum
MC_c
MB_c
a
b
c
d
e
f
g
h
i
j
0
1
2
3
4
5

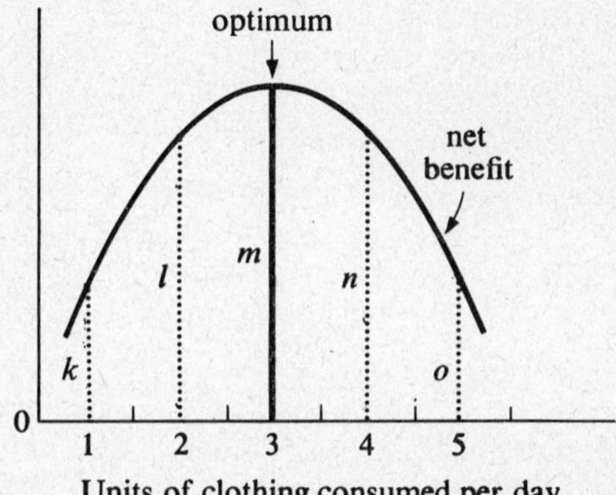
Net benefit
of clothing
consumption
optimum
net
benefit
k
l
m
n
o
0
1
2
3
4
5
Units of clothing consumed per day

second one of clothing) involves loss of satisfaction equal to *d* (Figure 1.3). This is the marginal cost of the second clothing unit consumed (note quantity *d* in the lower graph, Figure 1.4). At this point, the *total* cost of clothing consumption is e + *d* (upper graph). Similarly, you can proceed to derive the remainder of Figure 1.4.

Rational Behavior

Now consider a rational consumer, that is, one interested in getting the greatest possible total satisfaction from his limited income. In our example, it is but a short step toward determining the quantities of food and clothing such a person would elect to buy under the circumstances we have assumed. Take clothing. He would simply *compare the marginal cost with the marginal benefit* of clothing consumption.

If under given circumstances the marginal benefit of clothing consumption MB_c were to exceed the marginal cost of clothing consumption MC_c, or what is the same thing, exceed the marginal benefit of the alternative food consumption MB_f, he would increase clothing consumption. This is so because he would gain more satisfaction from consuming more clothing MB_c than he would lose from consuming less food, $MC_c = MB_f$. However, if circumstances were such that the marginal benefit of clothing consumption were to fall short of the marginal cost of clothing consumption, he would decrease clothing consumption. This is so because he would lose less satisfaction from consuming less clothing MB_c than he would gain from consuming more food, $MC_c = MB_f$. In either case, *total* satisfaction would go up. By implication, it would be maximized when the marginal benefit just equaled the marginal cost of clothing consumption. (At this point, since $MB_c = MC_f$ and $MC_c = MB_f$, the marginal benefit and marginal cost of food consumption would be equal, too.)

Figure 1.5, "Optimization," summarizes this discussion.

In the upper two portions of the graph, the smooth curves representing the total and marginal cost of clothing consumption in Figure 1.4, "Cost Is Benefit Forgone," have been redrawn. Added are a total and a marginal benefit curve for clothing consumption, analogous to those for food in Figure 1.3, "The Law of Diminishing Marginal Effectiveness."

Now it becomes immediately obvious what a welfare-maximizing consumer must do in the assumed circumstances. He must consume three units of clothing per day. If he consumes less, he will find the marginal benefit of clothing consumption MB_c exceeding the corresponding marginal cost MC_c.

Figure 1.5 Optimization

This graph illustrates the principle of optimization with an example about choosing the correct level of clothing consumption. Anyone desiring to maximize the net benefit of an activity should expand that activity up to the point at which the marginal benefit just equals the marginal cost of that activity. This optimum is reached at three units of clothing consumption in this example.

Note how distance *f* exceeds *e* and *g* exceeds *d*. In each case, by consuming more clothing at the expense of food, he would raise his total benefit (by *f* or *g*, respectively), but would raise his total cost by less (by *e* or *d*, respectively). Since the additional satisfaction from more clothing would exceed the loss of satisfaction from less food, the difference between his total benefit and total cost, or his *net benefit* would rise (from *k* toward *m*). Note how the net benefit is plotted separately in the lowest portion of the graph.

Similarly, our consumer would be foolish to consume more than three units of clothing per day. If he did, he would find the marginal benefit of clothing consumption falling short of its marginal cost. Note how distance *j* falls short of *a* and *i* falls short of *b*. In this case, by consuming less clothing, but more food, he would *lower* his total benefit (by *j* or *i*); but he would lower his total cost more (by *a* or *b*). Since the loss of satisfaction from less clothing would be exceeded by the additional satisfaction from more food, his net benefit would again rise (from *o* toward *m*).

Thus a simple rule emerges. It is a general rule of rational behavior and is called the *principle of optimization:*

> Anyone desiring to maximize the total net benefit of an activity should expand that activity up to the point at which the activity's marginal benefit (the increased satisfaction to be had from another unit of the activity) just equals its marginal cost (the decreased satisfaction resulting from the required reduction in another activity, which alone makes possible the additional unit of this activity).
>
> As long as the marginal benefit exceeds the marginal cost, the activity should be expanded. When the marginal benefit falls short of the marginal cost, the activity should be contracted. If one follows this principle, any divergence between marginal benefit and marginal cost tends to disappear, since marginal benefit tends to decline and marginal cost tends to rise with increasing levels of an activity (and the opposite). Thus one will reach the best possible (or optimum) position, where the *total* benefit exceeds the *total* cost by the greatest amount, yielding the maximum net benefit.

$MB > MC$ Expand activity.
$MB = MC$ Optimum level of activity.
$MB < MC$ Contract activity.

Conclusion

We can now go full circle and return to the issue raised at the beginning of this section. We make so few all-or-nothing decisions precisely because we are following the principle of optimization in much of our daily life. Rarely is it desirable to expand an activity to the maximum possible extent. Note how in the top graph of Figure 1.5, "Optimization," the total benefit of clothing consumption would indeed continue to rise beyond the optimum if our consumer purchased a fourth or fifth unit. But it is the *faster* rise in total cost that makes such action inadvisable.

If you go through life with open eyes, you will meet examples of this in your personal life, every day, wherever you turn. There is a logical stopping point to *any* activity, whether it is eating ice cream or playing tennis or even studying economics. All activities have marginal opportunity costs, all of which will eventually rise as the activity level is increased. All have declining marginal benefits also. Given your limited income, as you eat more and more ice cream, you have to forgo more and more apples, clothing, vacation trips, and so on. Eventually, long before you spend all your money on ice cream, you will decide that another dish of it just isn't worth it any more. This is a sure sign that the marginal cost of more ice cream exceeds the marginal benefit!

The same principle applies to playing tennis or studying economics. The further you push either of these activities in the week, the less likely you are to benefit from another hour of it. The marginal benefit is declining! The further you push these activities, the more you are likely to lose from giving up another hour of alternatives, such as swimming or studying physics. The marginal cost is rising! Eventually, you will say that "enough is enough." When the extra cost of losing an hour of time for studying physics just begins to outweigh the extra benefit of gaining an hour for studying economics, you have reached the logical stopping point for the latter activity.

This principle of optimization is universal for all who want to maximize welfare under conditions of scarcity. Society must apply it when deciding how to allocate its scarce resources and how to apportion the goods produced, just as you must apply it when deciding how to allocate your scarce money income or your scarce time. Instead of devoting all your money to ice cream or all your time to economics, you do well to do a little bit of many things—some economics, some physics, some tennis, and so on. Similarly for society; instead of devoting all its resources to expanding health care or education, to building better houses or more missiles, to constructing subways or cleaning up the environment, it is most likely to maximize people's economic welfare by doing a little bit of each. Remember: No matter how good, holy, or sacred any of these activities may seem, in a world of scarcity there is some logical stopping point beyond which an activity should be expanded no further. *This is the point at which the marginal cost and marginal benefit have come together.*

TASKS FOR AN ECONOMIC SYSTEM

Now we must consider a key issue. How can large groups of people—living in a world of scarcity—consistently apply the principle of optimization in their economic affairs? That is, how can they be sure to maximize social welfare when setting up and carrying out their program of resource use? How can they best decide what to produce (and what not to produce), the way in which to produce, and for whom to produce, *and do all this with the aim of maximizing the welfare of people?*

If all families were totally isolated from each other, there would be no problem. Each family would use the resources at its disposal for the production of the types and quantities of goods it deemed best. It would use the methods of production that seemed most effective in saving resources. It would naturally retain and consume all of its output. In making all these decisions, it would apply, perhaps unconsciously, the principle of optimization. If it perceived any divergence between the marginal cost and marginal benefit of any activity, it would change the level of that activity until the divergence was eliminated. And that would be that. But such is not the real world.

For rather obvious reasons, people in practically all societies—and certainly in the United States—do not wish to live in autarkic family units. They know they can increase their welfare by setting up a production program based on *specialization and exchange*. Such action allows the production of more and higher-quality goods from given resources than would otherwise be possible. A number of reasons apply.

For one thing, different people have different inherent talents and can concentrate on what they can do best. Even in cases in which this is not so already, skills can be created, for a division of labor among people reduces each person's work to a simple operation and increases the dexterity with which each participant produces his portion of society's output. "Practice makes perfect." This advantage is lost to the jack-of-all-trades. The division of labor also saves time that would be lost if a single individual carried on two operations, possibly in two places, with two different sets of tools, and had to pass often from one operation to the other.

Adam Smith enunciated the advantages of the division of labor 200 years ago, when he pointed out that a pinmaker could not produce twenty pins in a day if he himself had to do everything that was required—drawing out the wire, straightening it, cutting it, pointing it, grinding it for receiving the head, making the head, and so on. Yet, Adam Smith observed, ten people, only poorly equipped with machinery but with the proper division of labor among them, were able to make 48,000 pins in one day.

Further, specialization stimulates the invention of machines and makes their use possible. It also allows a few people to use relatively large units of equipment, so installation costs might be less than if many used smaller units. Also, a technology might be used that cannot be used on a small scale at all. If we all made our own cars, none of us could have the advantages of an assembly line!

Finally, resources can be saved because fewer transactions are needed, with many a specialized buyer or seller engaging in bulk rather than tiny exchanges.

This is why, as each person specializes in the production of one good or part thereof, total output from given resources is greatly increased. All of us can be richer! But there is a price we must pay for this: Since specialization without exchange makes no sense, specialization increases greatly our dependence on others. The individual bushman, personally embodying all of his society's technical knowledge and producing all he needs, could most likely survive in complete isolation from his fellow tribesmen. The individual American hardly could. He would not know how to grow food, how to catch game, how to clothe or house himself; much less would he know how to make or repair most of the tools surrounding him and used by him daily. He is rich only as long as he can count on a smoothly running system of specialization and exchange. Assuring such a smoothly running system is anything but easy. Typically, each family produces little, if anything, of what it consumes. Most likely, it exchanges most or all of its own output with others who similarly specialize. These others, furthermore, are apt to be not a few identifiable persons, but literally hundreds of thousands of unknown people who in one way or another help provide the goods any one family consumes. This is why in modern society the working out of a rational program of resource use (one that maximizes social welfare) requires a very special set of institutions to guide everyone's economic actions. These institutions are called the *economic system*. It must perform a number of tasks. Let us consider just three of these.

Economic Order

The economic system must, first of all, assure order, that is, *coordinate* the specialized activities of millions of people. Every single decision about the use of resources in the modern specialized economy automatically involves thousands of other decisions. Someone or something must assure, therefore, that any one decision fits in neatly with all other decisions. Otherwise, there would be innumerable instances of too much of one good and too little of another being produced until the entire complicated production process came to a grinding halt. To see what is involved, imagine that a relatively few people in Detroit decided to build one million cars. Would this affect only the workers and facilities in Detroit that are directly involved in car manufacture? Of course not. It would also affect steelworkers in Pittsburgh, rubber factories in Akron, glassworks in Toledo, paint producers in New York, and textile manufacturers in Atlanta. It would affect iron-ore miners in Minnesota, railroad workers in Michigan, bankers in Connecticut, machinists in Texas, typists in California—in short, a host of other people and productive facilities throughout the nation.

Nor have we touched on more than the surface of what is involved here. The decision to produce cars would have effects that spread ultimately to every region and occupation in the country. For instance, to produce the glass to make the cars, we might need highways and trucks and drivers to bring sand to Toledo glassworks. Hence we should need other resources to make highways and trucks and to teach people to drive the trucks. And we should need more resources to make tankers and harbors and pipelines and oil refineries to get the gasoline to run those trucks. As you will easily sense, there is no end to all this complexity. Every decision to use resources for one purpose in one way or another affects everything we do in the economy. All our economic decisions are intricately bound together. The decision to employ resources in one direction inevitably requires decisions to employ them in other directions as well, for each output, by requiring inputs, affects other outputs. The economic system must assure that such coordination takes place.

But society does not want just *any* program of resource use, however well coordinated. The economic system, therefore, must also assure that resources and goods are drawn away from less important uses and placed in more important uses whenever the principle of optimization is violated. This involves two types of consideration, in turn.

Economic Efficiency

One is a matter of *economic efficiency:* The allocation of resources among producers or of goods among people is considered economically efficient only if it is impossible to reallocate resources or goods and thereby make someone better off without making anyone else worse off. On the contrary, a situation is economically inefficient if it is possible to make someone better off without making anyone worse off. This would mean that a marginal benefit could be had at a zero marginal cost.

No one has to lose from the elimination of economic inefficiencies. Social welfare can be increased *with certainty.* Consider just two examples. Suppose each of two families owned quantities of fish and meat. Family A would indifferently exchange 1 lb of fish for 2 lb of meat, or vice versa. Family B would do likewise, but at a rate of 2 lb of fish for 2 lb of meat. That is, each family would consider itself equally well off if it made such an exchange at the stated rate. Clearly, though, this situation is economically inefficient: If Family A handed Family B 2 lb of meat and received 1.5 lb of fish in exchange, *both* families would be better off. This is so because Family A would have been equally well off had it received 1 lb of fish for 2 lb of meat (but it received 1.5 lb). Family B would have been equally well off had it given up 2 lb of fish for 2 lb of meat (but it only had to give up 1.5 lb).

Or suppose each of two producers supplied fish and meat. Producer X could refrain from producing 1 lb of fish and produce 2 lb of extra meat instead, or the opposite. Producer Y could do likewise, but at a rate of 2 lb of fish for 2 lb of meat. That is, both producers could change the composition of their output in the way stated by reallocating *given* resource quantities. Clearly, this situation would be economically inefficient too: If X produced 1 lb less of fish, he could produce 2 lb more of meat. If Y at the same time produced 2 lb less of meat, he could produce 2 lb more of fish. Overall, society would have 1 lb more of fish, and no less meat, than before, and all this from the *same* quantity of resources! Thus society was operating inefficiently *below* its production possibilities frontier. By correcting this error, and reallocating production tasks between the firms, some person could receive 1 lb more of fish (and no one needed receive any less meat)—clearly a gain in welfare.

Other examples could be given, but the point is already clear: A good economic system must make sure to eliminate each and every instance of economic inefficiency. In our illustrations it should provide incentives for

Family A to give up some meat (and get more fish), for Family B to give up some fish (and get more meat), for Producer X to take resources out of fish production (and put them into meat production), and for Producer Y to take resources out of meat production (and put them into fish production).

Economic Justice

Another task of the good economic system is to provide *economic justice*, or *equity:* the distribution of goods among people is considered equitable only where the potentiality no longer exists for a redistribution of the total goods during which some people are made better off to a greater degree than others are made worse off. The redistribution issue, of course, arouses great controversy. Note that getting rid of inequities (unlike getting rid of inefficiencies) involves deliberately making someone *worse off*. But this is justified by the alleged *greater* gain in someone else's welfare. That is, it is believed that a marginal benefit can be had at a positive, but smaller, marginal cost. The only trouble is that there is no objective way to compare the welfare of one person with that of another. If we took fish as well as meat away from Family A and handed both to Family B, we could never *prove* that the decreased welfare of Family A (the marginal cost of this action) was more than compensated for by the increased welfare of Family B (the marginal benefit). Still, the economic system must somehow decide on the distribution of goods among people, for all of them want more than they can possibly have.

In the next chapter we consider what kinds of specific institutions might tackle these important tasks of assuring economic order, economic efficiency, and economic justice.

Summary

1. Every society faces the same basic economic problem: Many of its economic wants cannot possibly be fulfilled. This is so because goods fulfill those wants, goods are made with resources, and there are not enough resources to make all the goods all the people want. The problem stems from the scarcity of resources.
2. The impact of the inevitable scarcity of goods relative to wants can be minimized, however. This requires a program of resource use that produces the largest possible set of the most desirable goods and assures their careful apportionment among people.
3. Naturally a painful process of choice is involved, for every use of scarce resources involves an opportunity cost. This is familiar to all of us from the need for allocating our limited money income or limited time. We can always buy or do a little more of one thing if we buy or do a little less of another. However, owing to the law of diminishing marginal effectiveness, declining marginal benefit of the activity being expanded and rising marginal benefit of the activity being contracted will result, with the latter being the former's marginal cost.

4. A rational person, aiming to maximize his welfare, would expand an activity only as long as the marginal benefit exceeded the marginal cost of doing so. He would contract an activity if the opposite held. He would find the optimum (welfare-maximizing) level of an activity by choosing a level of it that equalized marginal benefit and marginal cost. This is the principle of optimization. It applies also to society at large.
5. The need for an economic system arises precisely because it is very difficult to apply the principle of optimization consistently on a large scale. This difficulty is enhanced by the desirability of maximizing output via a system of specialization and exchange among families. This requires a mechanism to coordinate the specialized activities of millions. The rational use of resources requires further that such economic order is assured together with economic efficiency and economic justice.
6. Resources and goods are allocated efficiently when it is impossible, through any conceivable reallocation, to make any person better off without making another person worse off. Therefore, inefficiency always implies the possibility of an unambiguous increase in social welfare: someone then can be made better off without anyone being made worse off. A marginal benefit can be had at zero marginal cost.
7. Goods are allocated equitably when there is no potentiality for raising social welfare by making someone better off at the expense of someone else. There is then no way to get a marginal benefit at a smaller marginal cost. Since it is impossible to measure after a redistribution of goods by how much one person's welfare has gone up and another person's has gone down and then to see how the two measurements compare, it always remains debatable whether taking from Peter to give to Paul really raises social welfare.

Terms[2]

capital
economic efficiency
economic justice
economic order
economic system
economic wants
equity
goods
labor
land
law of diminishing marginal effectiveness
law of diminishing returns
marginal benefit
marginal (opportunity) cost
net benefit
opportunity cost
principle of optimization
production possibilities frontier
resources
satiation
scarcity
total benefit
total cost

[2] Terms and symbols are defined in the Glossary at the back of the book.

Symbols

MB *MC*

Questions for Review and Discussion

1. Explain to a layman why not everyone can have everything for the asking.
2. Suppose the people in a country decided to give up the "rat race" and be content with a minimum of economic goods. Illustrate their likely position on a graph of production possibilities.
3. What do you think is the opportunity cost of each of the following:
   (a) giving more foreign aid;
   (b) stepping up the arms race;
   (c) avoiding air and water pollution;
   (d) avoiding traffic congestion on urban expressways?
4. When people say "time is money," what can they possibly mean? Use the term *opportunity cost* in your answer.
5. "If the principle of diminishing marginal effectiveness did not hold, one could grow the world's annual crop of wheat in a single flower pot." Explain.
6. When Hitler told his countrymen that they had to choose between guns and butter, he was clearly thinking in terms of moving along the country's production possibilities frontier. How can a country possibly turn butter into guns? Why might larger and larger gun production require ever greater sacrifices of butter forgone?
7. What is the opportunity cost to a student of more extracurricular activities? Show why the marginal opportunity cost of enlarging such activities is the greater the more time is already spent in this way.
8. Explain the following statements.
   (a) "It may be wise for a household to stop the consumption of any good long before satiation is reached, and it would be stupid to increase consumption beyond satiation."
   (b) "It may be wise for a nation to stop putting more resources into education long before the extra benefits from such action have fallen to zero."
9. Consider your own activities during the past 24 hours. Why didn't you do more (or less) of each?
10. On what basis would a rational student allocate time among sleeping, eating, recreation, and studying? among studying economics, physics, and biology? among tennis, swimming, and going to movies?
11. On what basis would a rational nation allocate its scarce resources between private and public goods? between present consumption and investment for future consumption? between producing more personal consumer goods and cleaning up the environment?
12. "Without scarcity, the principle of optimization could be violated with impunity." Evaluate.

13. Do you think real-world households really attempt to maximize their economic welfare? If so, do you think they succeed? What might keep them from succeeding?
14. "The price of specialization, which brings us higher output, is not only interdependence. The worst of it is that it brings alienation. As Adam Smith observed, 'The man whose life is spent in performing a few simple operations . . . generally becomes as stupid and ignorant as it is possible for a human creature to become.' In short, specialization is apt to turn men into passive unreasoning robots and that is not worth the benefit of greater output." Discuss.
15. "There *is* a simple way to measure the degree of equity achieved: Any economic arrangement is equitable only if it is impossible to make anyone better off without making someone else at least equally much worse off." Evaluate.

Selected Readings

Fusfeld, Daniel R. *Economics*. Lexington, Mass.: D. C. Heath and Co., 1972. Ch. 2. On choice and opportunity cost.

Kohler, Heinz. *What Economics Is All About*. Hinsdale, Ill.: The Dryden Press, Inc., 1972. Chs. 1–3. More detail on scarcity, choice, opportunity cost, and the economy's interdependence.

National Urban Coalition. *Counterbudget: A Blueprint for Changing National Priorities, 1971–1976*. New York: Praeger, 1971.

Schultze, Charles L.; Fried, Edward R.; Rivlin, Alice M.; Teeters, Nancy H. *Setting National Priorities: The 1973 Budget*. Washington, D.C.: The Brookings Institution, 1972.

Both of the preceding books deal with an actual situation of choice under conditions of scarcity: how to allocate federal funds among the many competing uses, ranging from defense to health, from education to employment programs, from income support and crime prevention to housing and transportation, from the environment to fiscal relief for local government.

NOTE: The *Journal of Economic Literature* lists recent articles on social choice in section 025. The *Index of Economic Articles* catalogs them under 2.162.

2 *The Logic of the Market Economy*

The market economy is the type of economic system used in the United States. Our emphasis is not on describing the actual economy, but on showing how a market economy might go about the task of allocating resources and apportioning goods produced *under the best of circumstances* (which may not prevail in reality). Understanding the logic of the market economy helps to isolate some of the chief factors responsible for real world economic problems, for those can be traced directly to the divergence of our actual market economy from the ideal.

WHO SHOULD MAKE ECONOMIC DECISIONS?

Someone in society must make decisions about the proper use of resources. That is, someone must see to it that resources are used fully and efficiently. Someone in society must make decisions about the proper apportionment of goods. That is, someone must see to it that goods are distributed efficiently and equitably. Naturally, the decision maker involved must be exceedingly well informed on a number of things. First, he must know about the quantities of all resources available: whether these quantities are fixed (and at what levels) or whether they are variable (and if so, how). Second, he must know about technical matters of production: what quantities and combinations of resources can be turned into what types and quantities of goods. Third, he must know about people's preferences: what combination of goods any one family would consider best for its welfare, what overall quantities each family should get so as to maximize social welfare.

We can imagine the decision maker involved to be a single person; or a small group of persons might undertake the centralized direction of all economic activity. This "central planning board" might attempt to arrange the production and apportioning of goods in accordance with a central economic plan. Using the aforementioned information, it might determine in a central office the types and quantities of goods that ought to be produced, and the firms that should carry out this production, and the quantities and combinations of resources they should use when producing the assigned output quantities, and the quantities different families should receive. The central planning board would have to draw up a carefully coordinated plan of everyone's economic activity, making sure that the contemplated actions of all persons would mesh perfectly. This having been accomplished on paper, households and firms could simply be asked to follow instructions laid down for them. The central plan would guide all of economic life: Each enterprise manager would be told what and when to produce, how much, what types and quantities of resources to use, and where and when to deliver the goods. Each household would be told where and when to deliver specified types and quantities of resources, and each would receive a centrally planned set of goods in return. Everyone would carry out orders of an economic commander-in-chief!

However, it would be exceedingly difficult to follow this type of procedure. This is so because such planning would require a tremendous quantity of *centralized* information. Unfortunately for any would-be central planners, information on resource availability, production techniques, and family preferences is, in the first instance, not available in one place, but dispersed in the minds of millions of individuals. It would take an elaborate bureaucracy and a huge computer capacity to gather and digest widely dispersed masses of data on available resources, techniques of production, and people's preferences. The working out of a realistic, comprehensive, and coordinated plan on the basis of all this information would also be extremely complicated, requiring the use of additional high-speed electronic computers. The issuing of detailed "marching orders" to all firms and households and the supervision of the accurate execution of these orders would further swell the ranks of the bureaucracy. There is no doubt that a lot of resources would have to be tied up in the very process of planning and managing the economy. Yet such costs may be unavoidable no matter what kind of economic system society sets up.

There is another, more serious problem: Suppose the attempt to gather so much important information in one central place were less than successful. Suppose the central planning bureaucracy were unable to assemble sufficiently detailed information. As a result, mistakes would be made in formulating and executing the central plan—mistakes that would lead to unemployment or inefficient employment of resources or to inefficient or inequitable distribution of goods. For example, the economic plan might be internally inconsistent, when production plans might specify insufficient quantities of one good needed to produce planned quantities of another. This sort of miscalculation would lead to intermittent breakdowns in the production process, and thus to intermittent waste of resources through unemployment. Furthermore, insufficient information at the planning center might lead to inefficiency in the allocation of resources and goods, even if resource unemployment were avoided. Central planners, who could be less than omniscient, and administratively unable to cope with real-life complexities, might react to the lack of knowledge by imposing uniform treatment on many firms and households in circumstances wherein they would be better treated differently. Consider, for example, the allocation of resources to producers, say the case of distributing labor among farms. Instead of distributing the total of farm labor in such a way that farms where it would boost output most are given preference over other farms where it would boost output little (until the marginal benefit of labor use should be equalized everywhere), the central planning board might distribute labor *uniformly*, the same quantity going to each farm or to each acre. The board might simply not know enough about differences in the circumstances of individual farms to act otherwise. The result might be a very inefficient resource use, with labor on some farms adding quantities to output that are smaller than amounts that could have been produced had this labor been used on other farms that possessed perhaps more fertile soil, better climate, more machinery, and so on.

An analogous problem might arise when consumer goods are apportioned among households. For instance, if equal quantities of all consumer goods were distributed to all persons, a policy easily advocated when detailed knowledge on preferences is lacking, inefficiency would be sure to result unless all persons had identical tastes. (For proof of this proposition, recall the numerical example in the section on economic efficiency at the end of Chapter 1.)

In short, without complete and detailed information about the circumstances peculiar to every firm and household, a central planner might well fail in maximizing the total benefit society could realize from its scarce resources. Perhaps, people have argued, one could reduce the likelihood of mismanagement (leading to unemployment or inefficient employment of resources or to inefficient or inequitable distribution of goods) if management of economic activities were *decentralized*. Perhaps one could avoid the need for collecting and digesting so much information in one central place. This might be done by allowing the very firms and households who possess the knowledge relevant to proper economic decision making to make those very decisions. To return to our examples, each farmer, knowing his own circumstances best, might decide for himself what quantities of labor to employ. Each household, knowing its own preferences better than anyone else, might decide for itself what combinations of goods to consume. Indeed, the making of economic decisions by a multitude of individuals rather than a few is the central characteristic of the *market economy*.

In this type of economic system great value is placed on the freedom of individuals to make their own optimizing decisions. That is, each individual is expected to maximize his own net benefit from whatever economic activity he pursues. Each is considered the best judge of what contributes to his own well-being. No one is told by anyone else what to do or what not to do. However, everyone is free to cooperate with others in economic matters if he finds it beneficial. That is, people can buy or sell goods or resources if and as they please. The framework within which potential buyers and sellers of goods or resources make contact with one another for purposes of transferring ownership is called a *market*. That is why the economic system that emphasizes decentralized decision making by individuals operating in markets is called a market economy. It would be wrong to conclude, however, that government—the role of which would have to be so all-pervasive in a centrally planned economy—could be absent entirely in the market economy. On the contrary, government would have a number of important functions.

THE ROLE OF GOVERNMENT IN THE MARKET ECONOMY

It is not hard to imagine that the absence of government would create a state of anarchy, within which the strongest individuals or coalitions of them would maximize their own welfare at the expense of other people's welfare. By the use of brute power, they would appropriate whatever available resources or goods they desired, if necessary, taking them away from the weaker members of society without compensation. In order not to allow the law of the jungle to prevail, government must *establish and protect property rights.* In addition, since it is held desirable that people who wish to do so can participate in a large-scale division of labor without being subject to coercion by others, government must *assure unrestricted voluntary exchange* among individual decision makers. A government framework based on these undertakings could promote peaceful cooperation among people in working out a well-coordinated program of economic activity that assures full and efficient use of resources and also the efficient and equitable distribution of goods.

Establishing Property Rights

Before doing anything else, government must establish and define property rights in all scarce things. Recall that these are the things that are not available in sufficient quantities to give everyone whatever quantity he desires if he could just have the item concerned free for the asking. Actual governments do establish property rights; so much so that the existence of these rights is usually taken for granted. However, they are not God-given, but a conscious creation of man. Each society must decide, for instance, whether its scarce resources are to be privately or publicly owned. In some societies such as the United States, private ownership of land and capital predominates; thus these societies are called *capitalist.* In other societies such as the Soviet Union, public ownership of land and capital predominates; these societies are called *socialist.* But there are many exceptions in both cases.

In any case, establishing property rights means establishing *rights to exclusive use;* and it should surprise no one that the nature of property rights has a lot to do with the way decisions are made in an economy. It certainly makes a difference whether property rights are bestowed upon private individuals, on groups of people, or perhaps even on fictitious persons like private or public corporations. The moment it has been decided who has the exclusive right to the use of people, land, and capital, it has also been decided who has a great deal to say on the questions of resource allocation and output sharing.

The matter of property rights can be fairly complex. Rare is the case where the right to exclusive use is not subject to some restrictions. Suppose someone privately owns a house. Does he also own the minerals that may be found underneath it? Does he own the airspace above? May he use the house for *any* purpose? May he sell the house, rent it, burn it down? The answers to these questions are in no way self-evident. They require further decisions by society.

Most important are decisions on the *transferability* of property rights. Each society must decide on whether it wants to make property rights transferable, that is, whether private or public holders of such rights may give them to someone else, and whether the transfer may obtain forever (as in the selling of a house) or whether it may obtain for a limited time only (as in the renting of a house) or whether both types of transfer are allowed.

Take people. Universally we assume that people are privately owned and that, in contrast with the days of slavery, people can own only themselves. This implies that normally each person has the exclusive right to decide what use is made of him. This right, furthermore, cannot be transferred to someone else forever. Even if people want to, they may not sell themselves outright as slaves. Temporarily, however, the right to use oneself can be transferred. People may enter into a labor contract that allows others, for limited periods, to decide what use shall be made of them.

In addition, property rights in land and capital, whether private or public, may be transferable without limit, for short periods only, or not at all. For instance, in the United States, the property right in a privately or publicly owned factory or piece of land may usually be transferred either without limit (they may be sold outright) or for a limited time only (they may be rented instead).

Our main point, however, is this: *The logic of the market economy requires that transferable property rights be established in all scarce things.* Without this there can be no exchange of scarce resources or goods.

Protecting Property Rights

Having established property rights, government must assure that owners cannot be forced to give up these rights. Owners must be allowed to withhold the use of scarce things they own from all others or to use their property rights to engage in voluntary exchanges with others holding similar rights. Thus government must assure *internal order* by a system of laws, courts, and police. So that the physical coercion of one individual by another can be prevented, a government monopoly of force must be established. It forestalls the use of force by private parties. Laws of contract must set up the conditions ruling voluntary exchange. If necessary, courts must help arbitrate differing opinions on the meaning of contracts voluntarily made, and government must stand ready to enforce compliance with them.

Assuring Unrestricted Voluntary Exchange

When two people exchange scarce things and when the exchange is truly voluntary, neither party loses. One or both gain. If it were not so, the exchange would not take place voluntarily. Thus it is desirable to maximize the opportunities for voluntary exchange, for this maximizes the welfare that society manages to squeeze out of its scarce resources. Government must facilitate widespread exchange by *setting standards and norms*, such as providing a monetary unit and a uniform system of weights and measures. These, too, are matters we usually take for granted. If we were reduced to barter, our ability to participate in a large-scale division of labor would vanish. How could a teacher of economics who wanted three loaves of bread, a pair of shoes, and a haircut, ever hope to find a baker, a shoemaker, and a barber who were just dying to be instructed in economics? In short, without the existence of money as a convenient medium of exchange the myriad of voluntary economic transactions occurring daily in any modern economy would be unthinkable. We all would be the poorer for it. But if there is to be money, for obvious reasons a government monopoly of creating money and regulating the quantity thereof is indispensable.

As another condition for unrestricted voluntary exchange, government must *assure that all people have perfect knowledge of available opportunities for exchange*. That is, everyone must receive all the information necessary to make rational choices. Everyone must know about all the types and qualities of resources or goods that are being offered or sought, and in addition the terms (prices) at which exchange is possible. Clearly, through lack of such knowledge some people might be kept from maximizing their welfare. They might engage in one exchange, for example, while another (the possibility of which was not known to them) would have been preferred by them. Or instead, they might entirely miss an opportunity to make a beneficial deal. It is this kind of reasoning that has our actual government already involved in a variety of knowledge-spreading activities designed to inform everyone as fully and cheaply as possible of all the above factors relevant to engaging in voluntary exchange. Laws to prevent fraud fall in this category. Their purpose is to prevent people from making "voluntary" exchanges on the basis of insufficient or false information. If you voluntarily exchange money for meat that is represented as beefsteak but really comes from a horse, you are being forced in a subtle way to engage in an exchange you would not voluntarily have made. The same would be true if you were voluntarily to pay money for treatment to a "doctor" who, although you did not know, never had any medical training at all. Or consider the voluntary exchange for money of your labor services as a dishwasher in a laboratory. If the dishes you are washing are highly contaminated with radioactive materials and no one tells you, you would most likely be engaged in something that only appears to be a voluntary exchange.

Some people argue that the government is not needed for this knowledge-spreading activity. Sooner or later, someone will find out about the horse meat, and that firm will go bankrupt. Sooner or later, our "doctor's" reputation will go sour, and patients will stay away in droves. Sooner or later, workers in the laboratory will drop dead of a strange disease, and that will discourage others from taking a job there. Sooner or later, in short, all those engaged in fraud will be eliminated from the scene. Some go further and argue that discovery of these things does not have to be eventual but can be immediate. Buyers or sellers of anything should always make sure to find out what they are doing, and if they neglect finding out, let them suffer for their negligence! But this puts an extraordinary burden on individuals who don't care to be cheated. Clearly, government can become the instrumentality by which we do jointly what would be very hard and expensive for us to do severally. Instead of every buyer of meat investigating the operation of every supermarket prior to every purchase, a government agency does it and certifies to all that beef is beef. The cost per person is infinitely smaller than it would be if everyone started his private investigation. This is even more true for highly technical goods (like medical services), where the individual purchaser would not have the competence to investigate even if he tried. This role of government then justifies the existence of the Food and Drug Administration (responsible for guaranteeing clean and safe foods, drugs, and restaurants); the licensing of certain practitioners (like medical doctors and lawyers); the control of deceptive advertising, labeling, and packaging, carried out by the Federal Trade Commission; laws concerning working conditions; and so on. The public employment service, similarly, is an activity designed to spread information on available workers or jobs so as to maximize the chances for beneficial exchange based on full knowledge of alternatives.

Next, government can facilitate voluntary exchanges by *assuring the freedom of mobility to all potential parties to exchange.* This means that everyone must be free to buy at the going price any quantity of any resource or good and buy it from any seller. Similarly, everyone must be free to sell at the going price any quantity of any resource or good and sell it to any buyer. No man-made restraints against entering or leaving any market (the economist's term) can be put in the way of anyone. Obviously, if someone knew of a desirable exchange opportunity and were not *allowed* to exercise it, social welfare could not be maximized. In a subtle way, people would be forced into other, less preferred exchanges. Thus it is important that government restrain anyone who tries to prevent others from engaging in a particular type of voluntary exchange. In the real world, antidiscrimination laws serve such a purpose. They stipulate, for instance, that people able and willing to buy goods (such as housing or schooling) may not be excluded from the market or any part of it on account of their sex or race. Likewise, people able and willing to sell resources (such as labor) may not be excluded from the market for any similar reason. Nor may anyone be restricted from producing and selling any good or buying any resource that he is able and willing to sell or buy, respectively.

Finally, government interested in promoting the most widespread voluntary exchange must see *to it that no single market participant or small group of conspirators among them can fix the terms of exchange.* Exchange in each market must always take place at the objectively correct price—the price at which the overall quantities offered and sought are equal. No buyer must be allowed to intimidate any seller into selling for a price lower than this correct one. No seller must be allowed to intimidate any buyer into buying at a price higher than this correct one. The government policies concerning knowledge and mobility tend to facilitate the achievement of this goal: the policies help to maximize the number of exchange participants, which in itself reduces the chances of coercion. Where there are many sellers, for example, any one buyer is protected from coercion by a seller because of the existence of many alternative sources of supply. Where there are many buyers, any one seller is protected from coercion by a buyer because of the existence of many alternative sources of demand.

THE EMERGENCE OF MARKETS

If government pursues the policies just outlined, many people will desire to exchange the property rights to goods and resources held by them for rights to other goods and resources held by others. They will exchange to the extent that they believe their welfare can be enhanced by such exchange. Thus the pursuit of self-interest by individuals gives rise to the emergence of markets. These markets are called *perfectly competitive* when all market participants are fully informed on exchange opportunities and are perfectly mobile; there are so many buyers and sellers that none of them, acting alone, can influence the terms of exchange (that is, the price); and prices are perfectly flexible. Under such conditions, no individual can affect the fortunes of others. Therefore, perfect competition is impersonal. No buyer or seller has any rivals that have to be watched. Everyone knows that price in each market is set by the interaction of numerous buyers (who demand) and numerous sellers (who supply) in such a way that quantity demanded just equals quantity supplied. Only a change in total demand or supply can change that price.

In the real world, these conditions of perfect competition rarely obtain in any market, and as we shall see shortly, this is the very reason for many of our economic problems. Before we turn to this issue, however, let us consider the main features of a market economy without worrying about the degree of its perfection. Figure 2.1, "The Market Economy," provides an overview. It gives a simplified picture of the flow of goods and resources and their monetary counterflows in any market economy.

On the left-hand side of Figure 2.1, we find *households*, of which there are some 70 million in the United States. Each household contains one person living alone or several living together, whose total action in making economic decisions is usually with the aim of maximizing the well-being of all who compose the household unit. Toward the outside, households typically act as a

Figure 2.1 The Market Economy

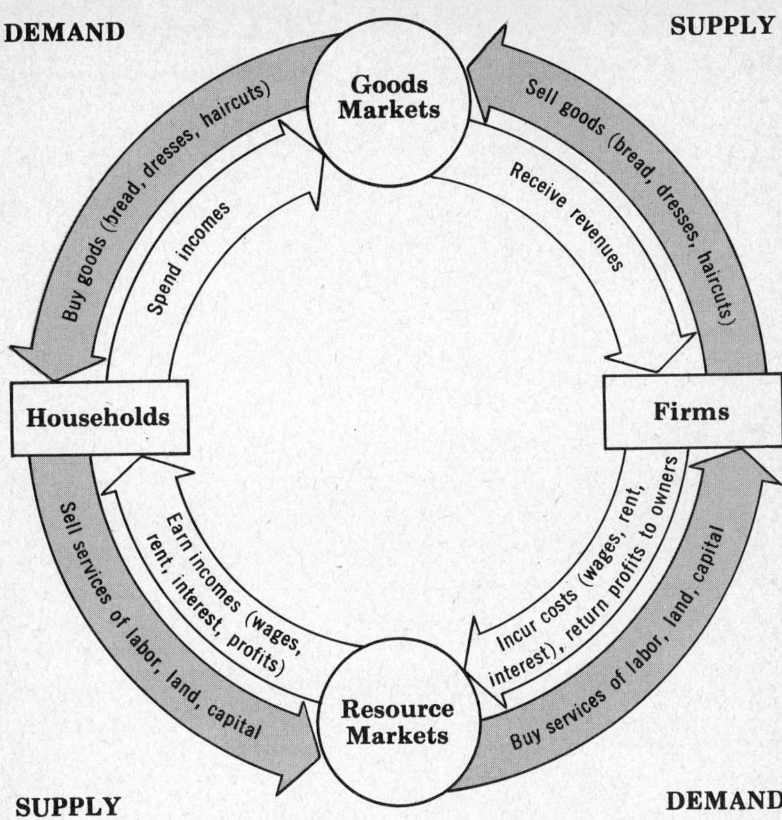

This circular-flow diagram is a simplified picture of the market economy. Households as owners of resources supply resources to firms, which demand them to produce goods. Goods are in turn supplied to and demanded by households (outer circle of real goods and resources). Put differently, firms incur costs, which (together with profits) become the incomes of households, and in turn are spent on goods bought from firms (inner circle of dollars).

single unit. It is for our purposes of no interest at this point how households are organized internally to arrive at decisions about selling resources and buying goods. We assume they somehow resolve their internal conflicts, decide what they want, and act accordingly.

In the United States, households face some 12 million business *firms;* these are pictured on the right of the figure. Each firm is established by one or more entrepreneurs, and run by them with the help of managers, people providing a special kind of labor that organizes the production of goods by combining other labor with land and capital. After all, resources do not get together by magic. Some person, or group of persons, must organize a firm in the first place. In contrast to hired managers, who can keep it running, the entrepreneur must continue to make nonroutine decisions. He must take leadership in introducing new products, new production methods, new forms of business organization, new markets in which to buy or sell. He must finally decide when to close down altogether. All the while, he must bear the risk of wasting his efforts and of losing his property. The expected does not always happen. Seemingly worthwhile ideas may turn out to be disastrous. Hoped-for profits may turn out to be losses. Naturally, for their organizing, innovating, and risk-taking activities, entrepreneurs hope to make as large a profit as possible. For our purposes it is of no interest at this point how firms are organized internally to arrive at decisions about buying resources and selling goods. Toward the outside, each firm, too, acts as a unit and aims, we assume, at maximum possible profits.

It is now clear that households face firms on two fronts, so to speak, with two kinds of markets intervening. There are, pictured on top of Figure 2.1, the markets for goods, or the outputs of the economy, and, pictured at the bottom, the markets for resources, or the economy's inputs.

It is now easy to picture households as owners of resources trying to sell the services of their resources for as much as they will bring. Someone who has only his labor to offer will naturally try to get the highest wage possible (lower left corner of Figure 2.1). Someone with entrepreneurial ability will try for the highest possible profit income. Someone who owns property will similarly strive for the highest possible rent and interest return for its use. Firms, on the other hand, will find it in their self-interest to buy any given quantity of nonentrepreneurial resource services at the lowest possible prices (lower right corner). In this way, firms minimize costs and hence maximize profits for their household owners. Thus, the interplay between the two parties will come to establish prices for the resources traded in the resource markets. We shall investigate this process in more detail shortly.

Similarly, households, as earners of money incomes, will try to buy goods they desire (and can afford) at the lowest possible prices in the many markets where goods are traded (upper left corner of Figure 2.1). This is what you are doing every time you shop around for the "best buy," regardless of whether you walk from store to store, scan a mail-order catalogue, or "let your fingers do the walking through the yellow pages" of your local telephone directory. On the other hand, business firms naturally will not maximize profits unless they sell any given quantity of goods for as much as they can get. This is, indeed, what they will attempt to do (upper right corner). The interaction of buyers and sellers in the goods markets will establish prices for all goods. This, too, we shall study in more detail shortly.

Notice how the diagram brings out the circularity of economic activity. There is the *real* (outer) flow of resources and goods. It shows how human sweat and thought and nature's gifts and man-made tools are turned into bread, dresses, haircuts, and all the other goods people want. Then there is the *monetary* (inner) flow of dollars of cost and income, expenditures, and revenues that simply *reflects* the more basic, real forces at work.

Because all relationships between households and firms take the form of competition for the "best deal" in either of the two markets pictured, you can easily see why our economy is also often referred to as a *market*, or *competitive*, *economy*. These terms are usually used in contrast to *command economy*, a system in which all economic transactions are guided by a central human authority, a possibility we noted above. Recall again that the competition of the market economy is peaceful. The inevitable conflicts of interest that arise in a world of scarcity, wherein not everyone can have everything, are in effect solved by saying: "You have something I want. Would you give it to me if I gave you something you want?"

Yet so far we have said nothing to indicate why such a system of voluntary exchanges, with each person seeking his self-interest, should produce order rather than chaos. And would it assure efficiency and equity? To these questions we now turn.

THE OPTIMIZING DECISIONS

To see the manner in which perfectly competitive markets would, indeed, create order in society's economic affairs, let us first consider the typical economic decisions that have to be made by households and firms, respectively. As a glance at Figure 2.1, "The Market Economy," quickly shows, there are four types of decisions involved: Each household must decide on the quantity of each good to be purchased and on the quantity of each resource to be sold. Each firm must decide on the quantity of each good to be sold and on the quantity of each resource to be purchased.

As we know, for the net benefit from an activity to be maximized, the marginal benefit and marginal cost have to be equated. This is the key to the behavior of households and firms.

Demanding Goods

Consider a household's decision on the best quantity of a good, say bread, to be bought. In the manner of Figure 1.3, "The Law of Diminishing Marginal Effectiveness," the marginal benefit of consuming bread can be expected to decline with additional units of bread consumed per day, a variety of other factors being equal, such as the household's taste, income, and so on. This is illustrated by the columns reaching up to the marginal benefit curve *MB* in part (a) of Figure 2.2, "Optimizing Decisions and Market Equilibrium." However, the exact size of marginal benefits is now measured not in units of satisfaction—for that is impossible—but in terms of money the household would be willing to part with to get additional units of bread. Presumably, if each additional unit of bread brings less extra satisfaction than previous units do, the household would only be willing to pay less extra money for successive units. While the household in the illustration would be willing to pay 40 cents for the first unit of bread per day, it would pay only 35 cents for a second unit, 15 cents for a sixth unit, and so on.

Figure 2.2 Optimizing Decisions and Market Equilibrium

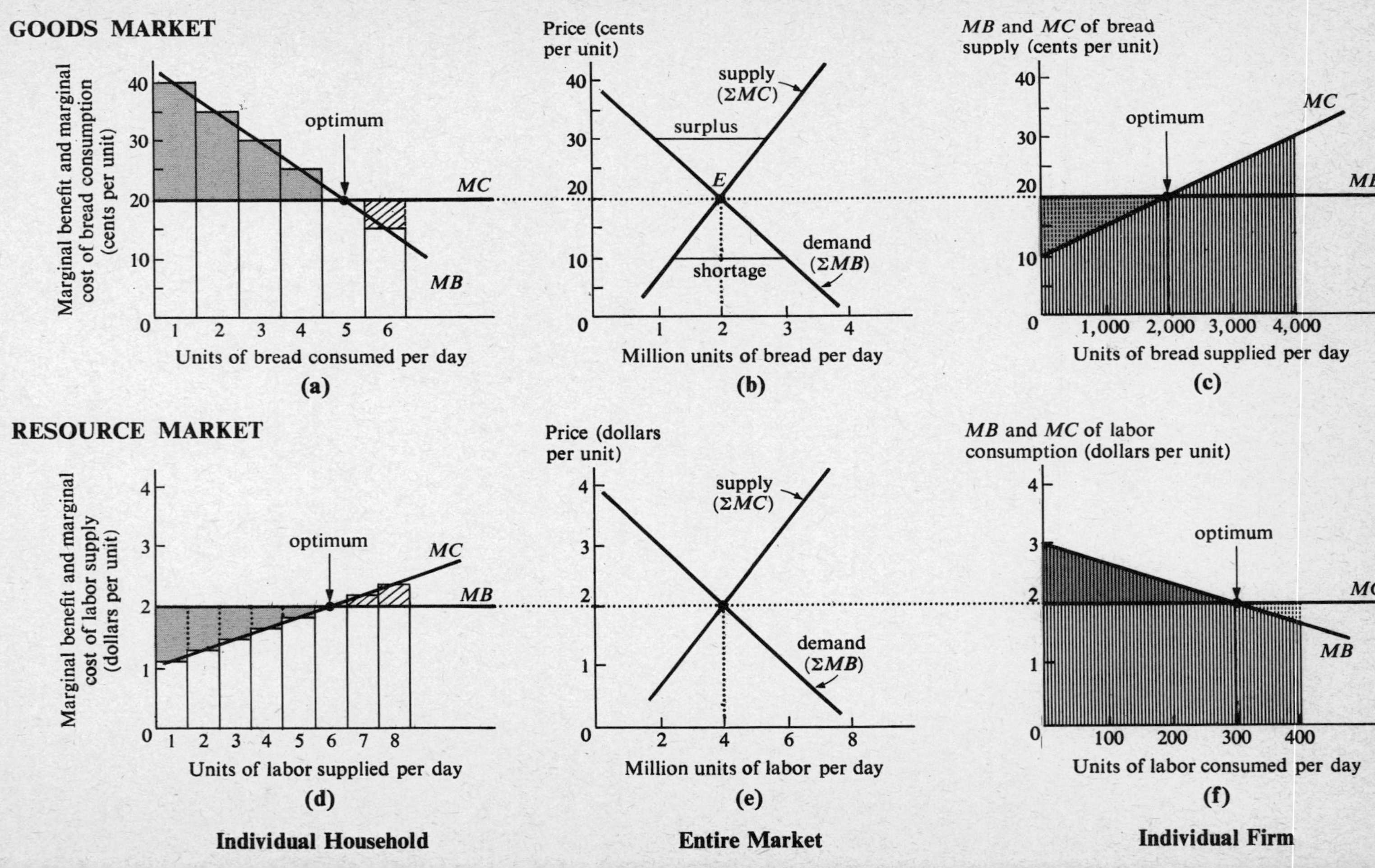

But in the case of perfect competition each household comes to believe that the actual amount it has to pay per unit (the market price) is fixed regardless of how much it buys. This market price can be called the marginal cost to the household of bread consumption. In our example, this price has been assumed to equal 20 cents per unit of bread. That is, no matter how much bread the household already consumes per day, it will always have to part with another 20 cents to get another unit of bread.

Now it is obvious that our household should buy five units of bread per day. The first unit bought costs 20 cents (*MC*) but brings satisfaction worth 40 cents (*MB*), or a marginal net benefit of 20 cents, shown by the shaded area in the first column. The second unit brings benefit of another 35 cents, still costs only 20 cents, thus brings a marginal net benefit of 15 cents, shown by the shaded area in the second column. So it goes, until the fifth unit bought adds 20 cents to benefit as well as cost, yielding no marginal net benefit. At this point, the total net benefit is maximized and equal to the total shaded area. Note how the household would be foolish to buy a sixth unit of bread. It would bring 15 cents of additional satisfaction, but 20 cents of additional cost, or a negative marginal net benefit of 5 cents (crosshatched area). Thus it would reduce the total net benefit below its maximum by this amount.

Supplying Resources

The decision on the best quantity of a resource, say labor, to be sold would be similarly made. The marginal benefit of this activity would be the income received per unit supplied.

In the case of perfect competition, the individual household rightly believes that it would receive the same reward per unit (the market price) regardless of how much it sold. This constant price then is the marginal benefit to the household of supplying labor. It has been assumed to equal $2 per unit of labor (note part (d) of Figure 2.2). Yet in order to supply labor, the household has to give up a precious thing: alternative uses of time, like recreation, sleeping, taking care of one's house or children, and so on. For the sake of verbal simplicity, let us refer to such unpaid uses of time as "leisure" time, recognizing full well that these alternatives may well involve more than mere recreation. Units of such leisure time can be expected to become increasingly precious to the household as less leisure is left. Thus—akin to the process illustrated in Figure 1.4, "Cost Is Benefit Forgone"—the increasing marginal benefit of leisure (as it becomes scarcer) turns into the increasing marginal cost of work (as more is supplied). This is illustrated by the rising blocks under the *MC* curve in part (d). The optimizing household would therefore supply six units of labor per day, reaping a total net benefit shown by the shaded area.

This graph provides a bird's-eye view of decision making in the goods market [(a) through (c)] and the resource market [(d) through (f)]. The optimizing decisions of individual households and firms determine market demand or supply and ultimately equilibrium price and quantity.

If it supplied less labor, the marginal benefit would exceed the marginal cost of supplying more, so it could improve its welfare by supplying more. If the household supplied more labor, the marginal benefit would fall short of the marginal cost (implying marginal losses of welfare shown by the crosshatched areas), so it could do better by supplying less.

Demanding Resources

The situation for the individual firm, which is assumed to strive after maximum profit, is analogous. Consider part (f) of our graph. Since the market price of all resources in a case of perfect competition would appear as given to the firm (as with the household), a firm facing a $2 price per unit of labor faces a constant marginal cost of consuming labor at that level. That is, no matter how many units of labor this firm has already bought, it believes that it can always get another unit for $2. The marginal benefit from using labor, however, can be expected to decline with increasing use of labor. As a firm adds additional units of labor to its production process (the quantities of all other inputs and its knowledge about converting resources into goods remaining constant), the physical additions to output will eventually decline. This phenomenon is simply another application of the law of diminishing marginal effectiveness. Since the actions of any one firm will not affect the price of output, the declining additions to output quantity (as more labor is used) translate into declining additions to output value (which is output quantity times price). Thus the additional *monetary* benefits from using additional labor will also eventually decline, a trend shown by the declining columns under the marginal benefit curve *MB*.

Thus our profit-maximizing firm will use 300 units of labor per day, reaping a total net benefit shown by the shaded area. If it used more labor, the additional cost ($2 per unit) would exceed the additional revenue, reducing total profit. If it used less, it would unnecessarily forgo additional profit.

Supplying Goods

A firm would in analogous fashion decide on the best quantity of a good to be supplied. In the case of perfect competition, the good's market price would be given to the firm, say, at 20 cents per unit of bread. This would be the marginal benefit of supplying bread. It is illustrated by the horizontal line in part (c) of Figure 2.2. No matter how many units of bread this firm has already supplied, it knows that it can always get 20 cents more revenue for another unit. The marginal cost of supplying bread, however, can be expected to rise when greater quantity is produced. The rise would be a consequence of the same forces that explain the declining marginal benefit in part (f) of the graph. If additional units of resources eventually yield smaller quantities of extra output (technology and quantities of other resources remaining the same), then equal additions to output would require ever larger additions of resources.

Given the constant price of resources, we must then infer that equal additions to output eventually require larger additions to cost, that is, rising marginal cost. The firm depicted in part (c) would maximize its profits by supplying 2,000 units of bread per day. If it supplied less, it would not be maximizing its profit, since an additional unit supplied would add to revenue 20 cents (marginal benefit) but would add to cost less (note the height of the rising columns under the marginal cost curve). Similarly, the firm would be foolish to supply more, for its profits would surely decline as each additional unit would add more to cost *MC* than to revenue *MB*.

Conclusion

We conclude about perfect competition, therefore, that if government performs its role and if individuals are given freedom of action, each household and firm can be expected to follow the principle of optimization in order to maximize its welfare. The performance uses two sets of information. One is made up of the *unique knowledge* each household and firm possesses. Each household knows best about its own tastes and the exact way diminishing marginal effectiveness applies to it. Each firm knows best about its own production possibilities, that is, its current quantities of land, buildings, heavy specialized machinery, and top management; the extent of its technical knowledge; and the way in which variable quantities of labor and materials applied to these will yield diminishing marginal returns. Graphically, this unique knowledge is shown by the declining marginal benefit lines in parts (a) and (f) and by the rising marginal cost lines in parts (c) and (d), respectively. The other set of information is *common knowledge*, but no less important. It concerns the market prices given to perfect competitors. These are illustrated by the horizontal marginal cost lines in parts (a) and (f) and by the horizontal marginal benefit lines in parts (c) and (d), respectively. These prices signal to each individual the social evaluation of all scarce things. Any potential user of scarce things can look at a price and know the social marginal cost of his activity. Users of bread (part (a), Figure 2.2), for instance, can look at the 20-cent price and be sure that it reimburses all who helped supply bread for their cost (part (c)). Users of labor (part (f)) can similarly look at the $2 price and be sure that it reimburses all of the actual suppliers of labor (part (d)) for the value they place on leisure forgone. Thus users see—by looking at a price—the social marginal cost of their activity; they can compare it with their own marginal benefit and then make a socially responsible choice.

Under influence of all these factors, the quantities of goods and resources demanded and supplied are uniquely determined. Naturally, any change in these factors would yield different results. In our example, an increased price of bread would clearly reduce the quantity consumed (part (a)) but raise the quantity supplied (part (c)). A decreased price of labor would lower the quantity supplied (part (d)) but raise the quantity consumed (part (f)). Similarly, changes in tastes (parts (a) and (d)), in the quantities of other inputs, or in technology (parts (c) and (f)) would change the outcome by changing the position of the optimum.

MARKET EQUILIBRIUM

We can now ask and answer a further question. What determines the overall quantity traded in a market and what determines the price at which this exchange takes place?

In discussing parts (a) and (c) of Figure 2.2, "Optimizing Decisions and Market Equilibrium," we simply *assumed* a price of 20 cents per unit of bread. Our household, given its particular circumstances (as reflected in the marginal benefit curve of part (a)), then chose to consume five units of bread per day. Presumably, we could determine similar quantities for all other households. Each might consume the same or more or less at this price depending on its circumstances (and thus the position of the *MB* curve in part (a)). The total figure consumed by all households might be 2 million units of bread per day at the 20-cent price. This is shown by point *E* in part (b).

Now note that the household depicted in part (a) would have consumed only four units of bread at a price of 25 cents, but five units at a price of 15 cents. We can assume that, similarly, other households would consume more at lower and less at higher prices. Thus the slope of the *market demand* curve for bread (part (b)) is similar to the marginal benefit curve of the individual household (part (a)). It is the horizontal summation of all marginal benefit curves ($\sum MB$) showing for each possible price how much all households *together* would consume.

In analogous fashion, we can derive a market supply curve for bread (part (b)) by the horizontal summation of the marginal cost curves of individual firms (part (c)). Just as our particular firm would supply more or less at higher or lower prices, other firms would do the same. Thus the *market supply* curve would have the same general shape as a single firm's marginal cost curve.

The price at which market demand just equals market supply is called the *equilibrium price*. The corresponding quantity is the *equilibrium quantity*. They are expressed in part (b) of Figure 2.2 as 20 cents per unit and 2 million units per day. They are called *equilibrium* price and quantity because they tend to stay at this level. Higher or lower prices would not. At a price of 30 cents, for instance, a *surplus* would develop. Households would buy less; and firms would supply more *and could not sell what they offered*. Competition among sellers would lower the price to the equilibrium level. In the opposite situation, at a price of 10 cents, a *shortage* would exist. Firms would supply less; and households would demand more *and could not buy what they tried to get*. Competition among buyers would raise the price to the equilibrium level.

In analogous fashion, market demand and market supply in each resource market would establish equilibrium price and quantity. Here, too, supply would be the horizontal summation of marginal cost curves, indicating for each conceivable price the total that would be supplied by all households together. Demand would be the horizontal summation of marginal benefit curves, indicating for each conceivable price the total that would be demanded by all firms together.

THE PROMISE OF PERFECT COMPETITION: ORDER

Through the process of peaceful competition the perfectly competitive market economy creates order in each market and in the whole system of markets.

The Individual Market

The age-old conflict between buyers and sellers is resolved in each individual market. Buyers always want lower prices, sellers always want higher prices. The market becomes the arbiter, telling both which price alone can be maintained under existing circumstances of tastes, technology, and resource availability. This is the equilibrium price, the only correct indicator of the degree of scarcity prevailing. Every buyer able and willing to pay that price can buy all he wants. Every seller able and willing to accept that price can sell all he wants. On the contrary, all those unable or unwilling to pay or accept, respectively, the equilibrium price *are excluded from the particular activity* for which the price is established. They are the ones who cannot buy and consume bread or labor (although they would like to at a lower price), who cannot produce and supply bread or labor (although they would be ready to at a higher price). Thus all potential buyers and sellers in each market are split into two groups, those that can participate in the particular activity and those that cannot. This is graphically illustrated in Figure 2.3, "How a Market Discriminates." Its caption makes it self-explanatory.

The System of Markets

The kind of order created in each market would—via the interdependence of markets—be created in the economy as a whole. And this overall order would be maintained in the face of changes in underlying tastes, technology, or resource availability.

Increased taste for bread: Short-run effects. Consider how an increase in taste for bread would affect the economy. If this increased taste for bread were typical of all households, market demand would rise, raising the price of bread. The increased price of bread, while somewhat dampening the increase in quantity demanded, would induce greater production of bread. In the *short run*, the bakeries involved, although their technical knowledge and the quantities of some of their inputs such as buildings and equipment were fixed, would expand output within the limits of their existing plant capacity. Perhaps they would use more labor and materials by introducing overtime operations. All

Figure 2.3 **How a Market Discriminates**

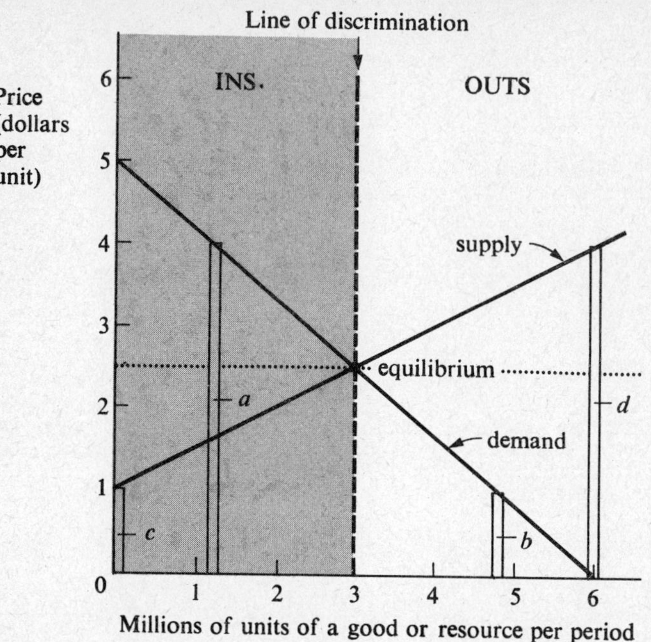

Demand and supply forces in this perfectly competitive market for a good or resource would establish a $2.50 equilibrium price and a 3-million-unit equilibrium quantity. It is possible to consider all potential buyers and sellers as would-be players in a game called exchange. We can imagine that those who want the good or resource are lined up on the horizontal axis according to the decreasing urgency of their demands. Someone most eager and therefore willing to pay $5 per unit would be first in line next to the vertical axis. Someone else (or the same person requiring another unit less eagerly) and only willing to pay $4 (or $1) would appear further to the right (at *a* or *b*, respectively). We can also imagine potential suppliers lined up horizontally according to the increasing size of their costs. Someone able to supply a unit for the least amount, say $1, would be first in line for this activity (*c*). Someone else (or the same person) able to provide another unit at higher cost only (say $4) would appear further to the right (at *d*), with less of a chance to participate in this activity. If we imagine a vertical line drawn through the equilibrium point, we see how the market discriminates among all potential market participants. Those buyers able and willing to pay the market price or more (such as *a*) are "in" (and pay the market price). Those unable or unwilling to pay that price (as *b*) are "out." Those sellers able and willing to accept the market price or less (such as *c*) are "in" (and receive the market price). Those unable or unwilling to accept that price (as *d*) are "out." All those lined up in the shaded area will trade (and at a clear gain); all others will not. In a world of scarcity, such discrimination concerning who can and cannot participate in an economic activity is inevitable. The higher-cost suppliers and less eager demanders alike are coerced into leaving the game. This avoids the anarchy that would result if everyone tried to do what cannot possibly be done. Note that among the "outs" there is not a single supplier who could cover costs even when getting paid the highest price an excluded demander offered to pay. So no *voluntary* exchange could get these people together.

this is shown in Figure 2.4, "Short-Run Effect in the Goods Market of an Increased Taste for Bread." This graph is based on parts (a)–(c) of Figure 2.2, "Optimizing Decisions and Market Equilibrium." It shows how a new equilibrium is reached in the short run. Increased taste for bread by the typical household (*MB* shifts to *MB** in part (a)) raises market demand (*D* shifts to *D** in part (b)). To eliminate the shortage (*ab*) that would now exist at the old 20-cent price, equilibrium price rises to a new, 25-cent, level (point *c*). As a result, households as a group reduce quantity demanded (movement from *b* to *c* along new demand curve *D**). Firms as a group, using existing plant capacity more intensively, raise quantity supplied (movement from *a* to *c* along unchanged supply curve *S*).[1] For the typical household (part (a)), the higher price becomes higher marginal cost of consumption (*MC** in part (a)). For the typical firm it becomes the higher marginal benefit of supplying (*MB** in part (c)). The household pictured here consumes more, although less than it would have at an unchanged price. (Higher taste moves it from the old optimum to *d*; higher price moves it from *d* to the new optimum.) The firm pictured here produces more, 3,000 rather than 2,000 units per day. As it moves from its old optimum at *f* to its new optimum at *g*, its profit increases by the amount depicted by area *ifgh*. It is easy to see why.

Profit: Normal and above-normal. Any firm's profit equals its revenue from selling output minus its cost applicable to producing the output sold. The profit can be divided into two parts, *normal profit* and *above-normal profit*. Normal profit is the minimum return necessary to keep the firm in existence in the long run. It represents the maximum amount the owner of the firm could earn in alternative pursuits from the resources he owns and uses in his firm. For instance, if a person works full time in his business, but could earn $5,000 a year in the best available job working for someone else, he would have to clear at least $5,000 a year in his business to keep it going. This would be his normal profit. If he were to earn less, he would close shop and work for someone else. Similarly, if this person had in addition put into his business ten acres of land (which he could have rented to someone else for at most $1,000 a year), his normal profit would rise to $6,000 a year. If he were to earn anything less, he would do better shutting down. Profit made above the normal amount is what every entrepreneur hopes for. Yet interestingly, in perfect competition, above-normal profit tends to approximate zero. This is so because everybody would immediately *know* where above-normal profits could be made, *mobility* would assure the influx of new firms hoping to reap it, and this would raise

[1] It is assumed here that the prices of variable resources do not rise even as many bakeries demand more of them. This assumption allows us to picture each firm as moving along an unchanged marginal cost curve rather than along one that is also shifting upwards. Thus the market supply curve is also unchanged. The assumption may be realistic under circumstances wherein the increased demand for resources by bakeries (as people demand more bread) is exactly offset by decreased demand for resources by firms in other industries (as people demand less of other goods now that they demand more bread). To the extent that resource prices do rise as bakeries demand more resources our example would yield different quantitative results, but it would still yield the same qualitative answers.

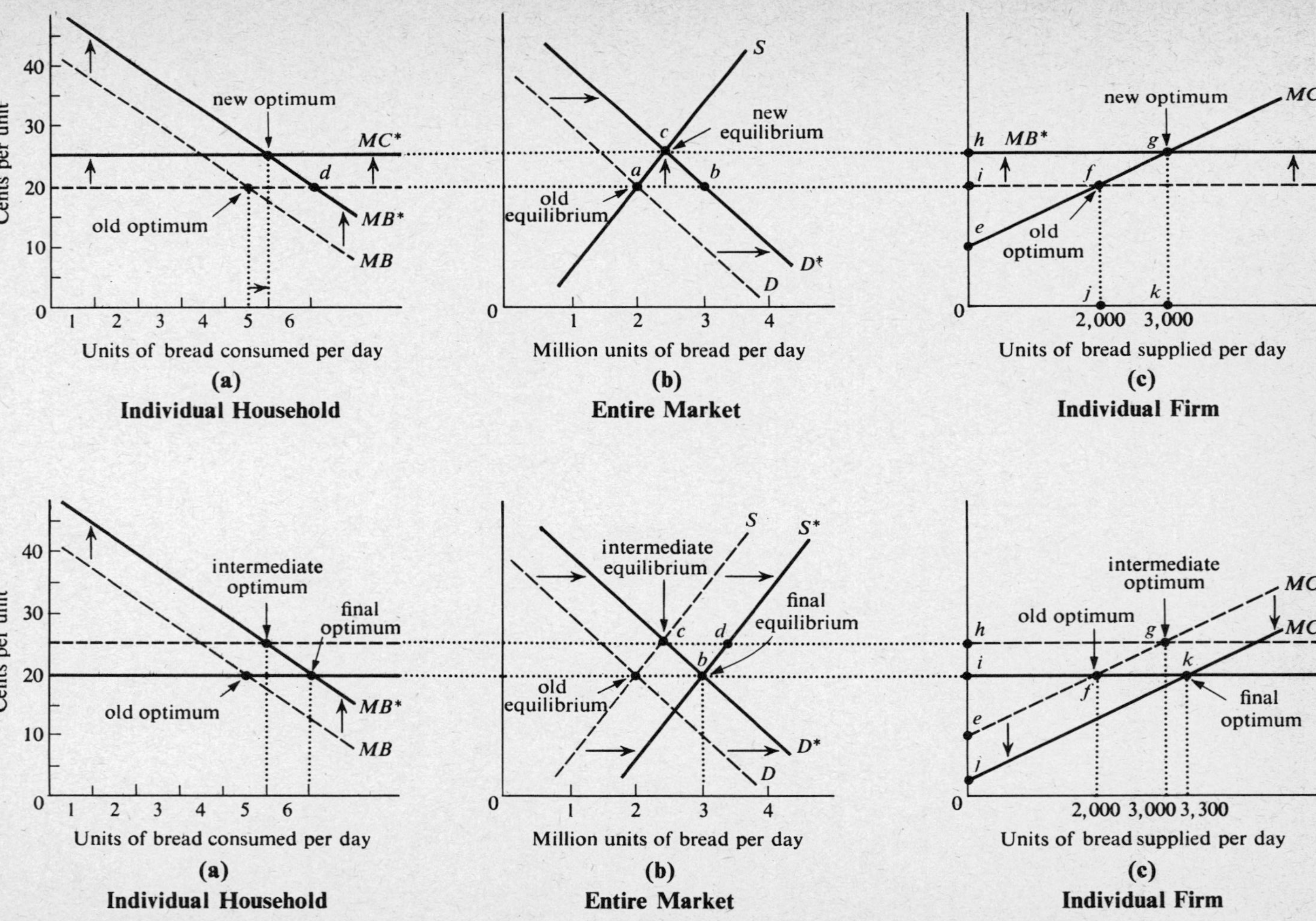
Cents per unit
40
30
20
10
0
1 2 3 4 5 6
new optimum
MC*
d
old optimum
MB*
MB
Units of bread consumed per day
(a)
Individual Household
S
new equilibrium
c
a
b
old equilibrium
D*
D
0 1 2 3 4
Million units of bread per day
(b)
Entire Market
new optimum
MC
h
MB*
g
i
f
e
old optimum
j
k
0 2,000 3,000
Units of bread supplied per day
(c)
Individual Firm
Cents per unit
40
30
20
10
0
1 2 3 4 5 6
intermediate optimum
final optimum
old optimum
MB*
MB
Units of bread consumed per day
(a)
Individual Household
S
S*
intermediate equilibrium
c
d
final equilibrium
b
old equilibrium
D*
D
0 1 2 3 4
Million units of bread per day
(b)
Entire Market
intermediate optimum
MC
old optimum
h
g
MC*
i
k
f
final optimum
e
j
0 2,000 3,000 3,300
Units of bread supplied per day
(c)
Individual Firm

market supply and depress price, lowering profits made. Only when profit has fallen to normal would this process come to a halt. Perfect competitors destroy the very thing they seek!

Cost: Fixed and variable. Cost, too, can be divided into two categories, *fixed cost* and *variable cost.* Fixed cost is independent of output volume and occurs even at a zero volume of output as long as a firm exists. It might represent such items as interest paid on borrowed money currently embodied in buildings and equipment or rent paid on buildings, equipment, and land leased for long periods; or property taxes; or the salaries of hired managerial personnel with lengthy contracts. Variable cost, on the other hand, is zero at zero output volume and then rises with quantity produced. It might represent such items as wages of workers or allowances for the wear and tear of equipment in use or raw-material costs. Variable costs for any output volume can also be measured as the sum of marginal costs for all units produced. From a basis of the fixed cost that is already present at zero output, the marginal cost of the first unit produced measures the variable cost of producing one unit. The marginal costs of the first plus second units measure the variable cost of two units, and so on. The sum of the marginal costs of the first 2,000 units measures the variable cost of 2,000 units. In part (c) of Figure 2.4 this is shown by area *Ojfe*. Since the total revenue from selling 2,000 units at 20 cents each equals area *Ojfi*, the triangle *efi* must equal that part of revenue covering fixed cost plus profit. It is the net benefit to the firm of producing a positive output volume rather than producing nothing (and incurring losses equal to fixed cost). Indeed, in a graph such as Figure 2.4(c), the triangle whose three sides are the vertical axis, the marginal benefit curve, and the marginal cost curve lying below it always represents fixed cost plus profit. This must be so, since it always equals total revenue minus variable cost.

Figure 2.4 Short-Run Effect in the Goods Market of an Increased Taste for Bread

In the short run, an increased taste for bread by each and every household (*MB* shifts to *MB** in part (a)) raises market demand (*D* shifts to *D** in part (b)). This raises the equilibrium price from 20 cents to 25 cents and induces each firm to produce more (part (c)).

Figure 2.5 Long-Run Effect in the Goods Market of an Increased Taste for Bread

In the long run, an increased taste for bread by each and every household (*MB* shifts to *MB** in part (a)) raises not only market demand (*D* to *D** in part (b)), but also market supply (*S* to *S** in part (b)). The latter reflects the expansion of productive capacity of old firms (*MC* to *MC** in part (c)) and the entry of new firms into the industry. Price may eventually return to its original level.

Increased taste for bread: Long-run effects. In our example, as the firm raises output to 3,000 units per day, revenue rises to 3,000 times 25 cents, or $750, shown by area *Okgh*. Variable cost rises to area *Okge*. Hence fixed cost plus profit becomes *egh*. Since fixed cost does not change with output volume, the new area *ifgh* represents an increase in profit, as stated above. If previous profit (contained in *efi*) was normal, the additional profit (*ifgh*) must be above-normal. This brings us to an exceedingly important point.

In perfect competition, this appearance of above-normal profit will have further consequences in the long run. First, existing bakeries will, as soon as it becomes physically possible, expand their previously fixed facilities. Second, as we just noted, the extraordinary profitability of baking bread will be widely known, and given the unrestricted entry into all markets, new firms will spring up in this industry. As a result market supply will rise; and product price will fall, possibly right back to its original level.[2] This will reduce profit back toward normal levels, and in turn put an end to the expansion of old firms or the entry of new ones. All this is shown in Figure 2.5, "Long-Run Effect in the Goods Market of an Increased Taste for Bread." This graph is based on Figure 2.4, "Short-Run Effect in the Goods Market of an Increased Taste for Bread." It shows the longer-run consequences. The above-normal profits of bakeries (such as *ifgh* shown in part (c)) lead them to expand their capacities. As they enlarge their plants, more and better equipment or better organization might allow greater additional output per extra unit of labor and materials. What is the same thing, additional units of output may cost less extra labor and materials. That is, marginal cost may fall as shown, from *MC* to *MC**. In short, old firms supply more at each price than before. This alone would increase market supply from *S* toward *S** in part (b), an effect that would be reinforced by the entry into the industry of entirely new firms. To eliminate the surplus (*cd*) that would now exist at the 25-cent price, equilibrium price falls to 20 cents (point *b*). We assume that at this price supply ceases to expand because no more above-normal profits can be made. As a result of the lower price, households as a group increase quantity demanded (movement from c to *b* along demand curve *D**). Firms as a group lower quantity supplied within their new, larger plant capacity (moving from *d* to *b*) along new supply curve *S**. For the typical household (part (a)) and the typical firm (part (c)) the lower price becomes the signal to seek the final optimum shown in parts (a) or (c), respectively, and to abandon the intermediate one reached in the short run.

For the firm, the period of above-normal profit is over. It is easy to see

[2] The entry of new firms by itself would raise the demand by the baking industry for resources and drive up their price. Thus the rise in market supply referred to in the text might be pictured as the net effect of two opposing forces: a shift of the supply curve to the right (because there are more firms) and a smaller shift of the supply curve to the left (because resource prices have risen). On the other hand, resource prices might also remain unchanged if the increased demand for resources by new bakeries is exactly offset by decreased demand for resources by firms going bankrupt in other industries (now that people demand more bread and, perhaps, less of other goods than before).

why. When it was producing 2,000 units of bread per day at the old 20-cent price, its profit plus fixed cost equaled *efi*. Now, as it produces 3,300 units in a larger plant, profit plus fixed cost equal *jki*. The difference, of *jkfe*, cannot be above-normal profit but must represent the new level of fixed cost plus normal profit. If it weren't so, further new firms would enter the industry, raising supply and depressing price and profit. But we assumed in drawing Figure 2.5 that such expansion of supply had come to an end.

Summary. Overall then, we can conclude that under perfect competition, increased demand for a good leads to higher price in the short run as well as some increased production within given plant capacities. Higher price, however, raises profit above normal. This leads in the long run to enlargement of existing firms and the building of new ones. This further raises quantities produced and supplied and depresses price and profit. When profit is back to normal, this process ends. Depending on how far market supply has risen relative to market demand by the time this happens, the final price can be above the initial one, equal to it, or even below it.

Further consequences. So far we have played down the effects of all this on the resource markets, but these, too, would be widespread. In the short run, the increased price of bread would, for instance, raise the marginal benefit of using labor to make bread (the *MB* in part (f), Figure 2.2, "Optimizing Decisions and Market Equilibrium"). This would increase the quantity of labor used at any wage (part (f)), a matter we already noted when considering the increase in production within given plants (part (c), Figure 2.4). This increased demand for labor by existing firms would eventually be swelled by additional demand from new firms. By itself this would raise the price of labor (part (e), Figure 2.2). Possibly though, the increased demand for labor by the bakery industry (reflecting people's increased demand for bread) might be exactly offset by the decreased demand for labor by other industries (if people buy less of other goods). In that case, the price of labor might not change at all; it would simply be a matter of workers losing their jobs in other industries and finding new ones—at the same wage—in the baking industry. Something like this may well be the long-run result, even if wages were to rise in the short run in the baking industry. Consider the reason.

In the longer run, any higher wages to be had in the baking industry than elsewhere would attract workers from other occupations as well as those newly entering the labor force. This would raise the supply of bakery workers (and lower the supply in other occupations). Wages in the baking industry would therefore drop (and other wages would rise), and the whole process would end when wages were again equalized in all occupations for the given quality of labor involved. Analogous statements could be made for other resources used by bakeries.

Nor is this all. Other markets would be affected, in turn, until in the end literally every economic activity would be affected at least in some small way.

We need not and cannot pursue all the repercussions. In any case, the main point is now clear: While the market economy has no central *human* authority at all, while it has no battery of computers to guide economic life, it has a central authority nevertheless.

The governor. We might say that the market economy is governed by the *price system,* by the totality of interdependent prices in goods and resource markets, to which self-seeking households and businessmen respond and which, in turn, continually respond to their actions. Price changes become the *signals* transmitting the need for further change throughout the economy whenever there is a change in the degree of scarcity. This occurs whenever wants or the ability to satisfy them change (tastes or technical knowledge and resource availability increase or decrease). It is exactly this kind of information that any human central planner simply could not get nor digest, but that, through price changes, is transmitted to all those of whom further action is required. Those sellers whose prices rise find their incomes rising. They are encouraged to expand their activity. Others are enticed to join them. Conversely, reduced prices (and incomes) discourage people from a line of activity.

Price change is the signal, higher income the carrot, and lower income the stick needed to bring about the adjustments required by a change of underlying scarcity conditions. Households and firms who follow the signals of the price system are rewarded with high income. Those who refuse to follow are punished with low income. Thus the price system is the invisible mysterious *governor* that guides all by disseminating information to just those parties of whom action is required.

This then is the mechanism that under perfect competition assures perfectly (and otherwise less perfectly) the consistent allocation of resources we wondered about earlier. As people buy more cars, they bid up car prices and in the very process give a simple, unambiguous signal for action to tens of thousands directly and indirectly involved in car manufacture. Without a single order having been issued at any central planning agency, car manufacturers begin to produce more cars, for it is more profitable to do so. In turn, greater purchases of steel, rubber, glass, paint, and fabrics are made by car manufacturers, raising the prices and profitability of those lines of endeavor as well. Other self-seeking producers respond in turn. All of the affected entrepreneurs, furthermore, begin to hire more labor, land, and capital, and the prices of these resources are driven up too. For instance, wages in these industries rise and so more people are induced to become autoworkers, steelworkers, rubber workers, and so on. Thus the price system acts like a system of telecommunications. The most essential information on what must be done is passed on just to those who need to know it.

True enough, firms are free to produce more cabbages even when households want more cars, but if they do, these cabbage producers will be eliminated from the scene by bankruptcy. Similarly, households are free to become farmers even though more steelworkers are needed, but if they do, they too will become "bankrupt," finding themselves out of work, on the welfare rolls, or employed intermittently and at perpetually low wages. With most people's preference for higher rather than lower income taken for granted, most people are likely to do what consistent resource allocation demands of them. All those who apply their resources to the wrong purpose—directly or indirectly helping to produce cabbages when cars are wanted—will be punished with low income. All those who apply their resources to the right purpose—directly or indirectly helping to produce cars when cars are wanted—will be rewarded with higher income.

At its best, the price system can do more than create order in a complex economic system without a human hand to guide it. Adam Smith, whose *Wealth of Nations* (1776) makes him the founder of modern economics, described the price system in these words:

> Every individual endeavors to employ his (resources) so that (their) produce may be of greatest value. He generally neither intends to promote the public interest, nor knows how much he is promoting it. He intends only his own security, only his own gain. And he is in this led by an *Invisible Hand* to promote an end which was no part of his intention. By pursuing his own interest he frequently promotes that of society more effectually than when he really intends to promote it.

This brings us to the next point.

THE PROMISE OF PERFECT COMPETITION: EFFICIENCY

A perfectly competitive price system also assures efficiency in the allocation of resources and of goods. We can easily show why by referring to the examples used in the section on economic efficiency at the end of Chapter 1. (However, what is concluded here would hold for other conditions of efficiency as well.) Family A, faced with prices of, say, \$2 per pound of fish and \$1 per pound of meat would consume quantities of these goods to the extent that the last pound of fish brought \$2 of marginal benefit and the last pound of meat brought \$1 of marginal benefit. (Recall the discussion of part (a) of Figure 2.2, "Optimizing Decisions and Market Equilibrium.") Thus it would be indifferent about exchanging in its consumption process 1 lb of fish for 2 lb of meat, since each quantity brought the same marginal benefit (1 lb of fish as well as 2 lb of meat add to satisfaction a quantity measured by \$2). In the case of perfect competition, however, Family B would face the *same* prices. This would be so because people would possess perfect market knowledge and perfect mobility. Hence the price of any one good or resource could not differ among sellers. Any seller who tried to sell above the market equilibrium price would have no buyers at all, since they could get identical units from his competitors at the equilibrium price (and people would know it and be able to take advantage of this knowledge). On the other hand, no rational seller would try to sell below the market equilibrium price, for he then would find that everyone tried to buy from him.

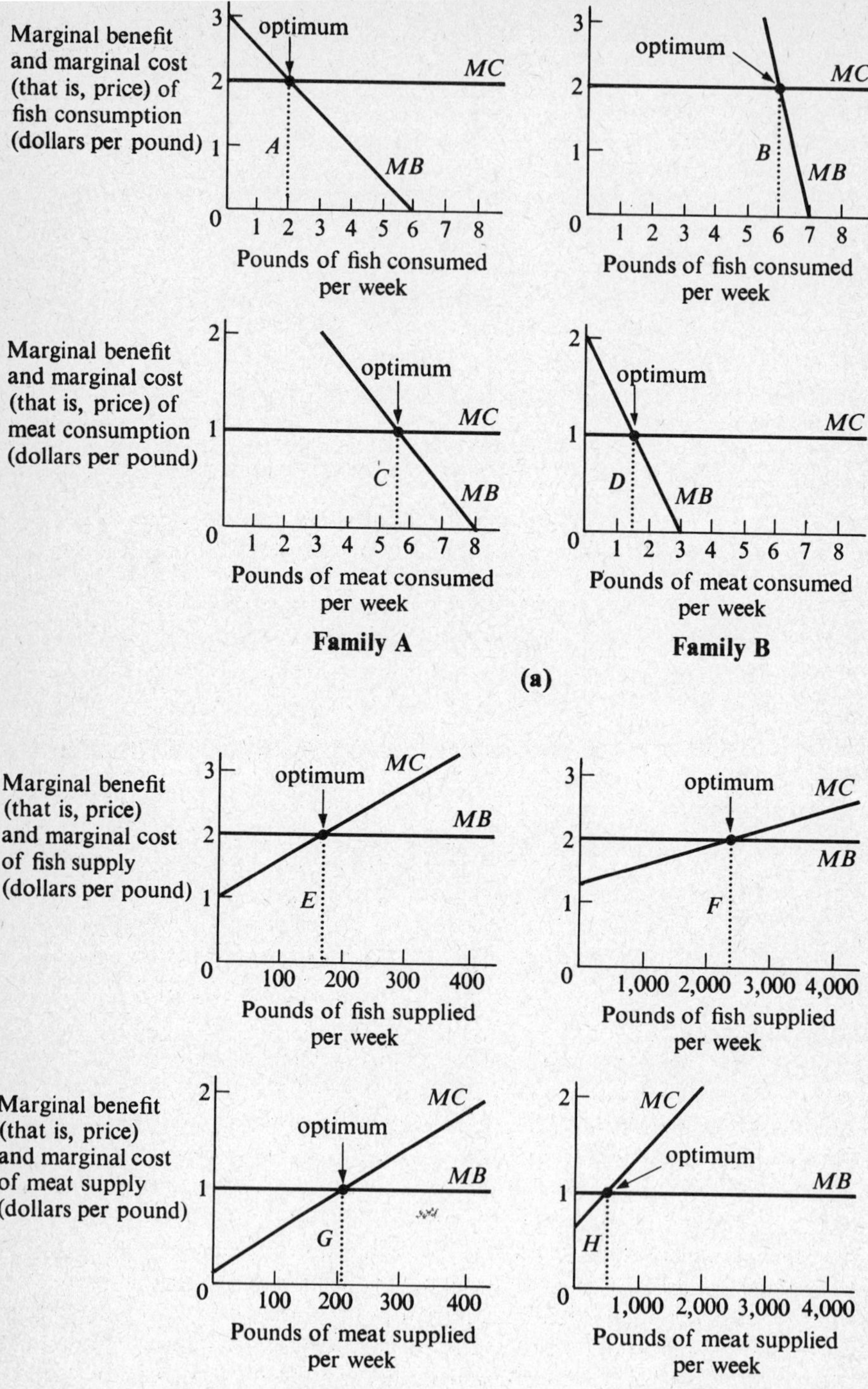
Marginal benefit and marginal cost (that is, price) of fish consumption (dollars per pound)
optimum
MC
MB
A
Pounds of fish consumed per week
optimum
MC
MB
B
Pounds of fish consumed per week
Marginal benefit and marginal cost (that is, price) of meat consumption (dollars per pound)
optimum
MC
MB
C
Pounds of meat consumed per week
optimum
MC
MB
D
Pounds of meat consumed per week
Family A
Family B
(a)
Marginal benefit (that is, price) and marginal cost of fish supply (dollars per pound)
optimum
MC
MB
E
100 200 300 400
Pounds of fish supplied per week
optimum
MC
MB
F
1,000 2,000 3,000 4,000
Pounds of fish supplied per week
Marginal benefit (that is, price) and marginal cost of meat supply (dollars per pound)
optimum
MC
MB
G
100 200 300 400
Pounds of meat supplied per week
optimum
MC
MB
H
1,000 2,000 3,000 4,000
Pounds of meat supplied per week
Producer X
Producer Y
(b)

He could not possibly accommodate all buyers in the market and would be forgoing revenue unnecessarily.

Thus Family B would indeed face the same prices as Family A. Following its self-interest, it would buy possibly different *total* quantities of fish and meat, but quantities such that the *last* pounds bought and consumed would bring marginal benefits of $2 (for fish) and $1 (for meat). Thus it would have in the process of consumption the *same* indifferent exchange ratio of fish for meat (1 lb for 2 lb) as Family A. Efficient allocation of goods would prevail because no exchange between the families could leave one better off without leaving the other worse off. Could a central planner have achieved this result?

The situation would be similar for our two producers discussed on page 16. Producer X, faced with the same prices ($2 per pound of fish and $1 per pound of meat) would produce quantities to the extent that the marginal cost of producing fish would equal $2 and the marginal cost of producing meat, $1. (Recall the discussion of part (c) of Figure 2.2.) Thus Producer X could cut fish production by a pound and save $2 of resources. These could produce 2 extra pounds of meat, the marginal cost of which is only $1 per pound. He could "exchange" 1 lb of fish for 2 lbs of meat in the process of production. In the case of perfect competition, however, Producer Y would face the *same* prices. Following his self-interest, Y would produce possibly different *total* quantities of fish and meat, but quantities such that the last pounds produced would cost $2 (for fish) and $1 (for meat). Thus he would have the *same* exchange ratio in production (1 lb of fish for 2 lb of meat) as Producer X. Efficient allocation of resources would prevail, because no alteration of production plans could raise output from given resources and thus make someone better off while making no one worse off. Could a central planner have achieved this result?

Figure 2.6, "Efficiency through Selfishness," summarizes this discussion.

PERFECT COMPETITION: EQUITY?

The question mark introducing this section is not a misprint. The perfectly competitive market economy would determine how goods are apportioned

---

***Figure* 2.6 Efficiency through Selfishness**

In the case of perfect competition, the pursuit of selfishness by all individuals leads, paradoxically, to the common good of maximum social welfare. This is so because each individual in each market is constrained in his optimizing decision by market equilibrium prices that are common to all. While their individual circumstances differ (the *MB* curves of households in part (a) and the *MC* curves of firms in part (b)), one end result of optimizing is the same: Once the optimum points of consumption or production have been chosen according to people's self-interest, any given good is valued the same at the margin by each family consuming it ($A = B$, and $C = D$), and any given good has the same marginal cost for each producer producing it ($E = F$, and $G = H$). Therefore, no reallocation of goods among households, or of production tasks among firms, can raise welfare.

among households. There is no way of telling, however, whether the apportionment would be a "just" one in some objective sense of the word, for the reason that there is no such objective sense. There is no objective measure of a person's welfare, nor is there a yardstick by which the welfare of one person can be compared with that of another. Hence all discussions of equity necessarily involve no more than opinion. When someone advocates that A be made better off at the expense of B to raise social welfare, he has already crossed the invisible borderline from matters of logic to matters of conscience.

Even though there is no way to prove that a perfectly competitive economy would or would not be an economically just society, many observations can clearly be made about it. In the case of perfect competition, goods would go to him who can pay for them, and how much any household can pay would essentially depend on its money income. The amount would be determined, in turn, by the pattern of resource ownership and the equilibrium prices established in the resource markets for the use of labor, land, and capital, respectively. The individual who has large quantities of resources to sell or whose resources command a high price would get a higher money income, hence a larger share of society's real output, than that individual for whom the opposites hold. We can expect that some would receive prizes in the lottery of life by accident of birth. Having inherited large quantities of land or capital, the services of which can be sold, they would receive a large share of real output—and they would receive it without exertion and independently of desert.

Others might be favored by accident of opportunity. Having inherited special talents or received good education or training and thence being endowed with a skill that just happens to be in great demand, they might become rich not without work but by work. Others still, with equally good genes and equally much education and training, may possess a skill in low demand, and they might be poor in spite of hard work. Even though a sufficient amount of bad conduct could ruin any amount of good fortune, no degree of good conduct could assure success in a perfectly competitive market economy without fortunate accidents. Hard work alone would not assure high income. And many people—the very young, the very old, the sick and disabled—cannot even work at all. Their income in a perfectly competitive market economy would be zero. Undoubtedly, income and goods might be distributed quite unequally in such an economy. Undoubtedly, some would advocate drastic government action—a determined Robin Hood policy, direct money transfers from the rich to the poor until all persons' money incomes should be *equalized*. In perfect competition, it might be argued, firms would use resources to make a profit: they would follow the path where "dollar votes" are heaviest. The rich could cast a lot of dollar votes in the market for goods. Thus, their desire for vitamins for their dogs and a Cadillac for themselves would be satisfied before the poor people's needs for vitamins and clothes for their children. Somehow income should be paid according to need, people might argue, to give everyone an equal chance to commandeer the use of resources by equipping everyone with an equal amount of dollar votes. Otherwise the economy would efficiently produce what some people's consciences tell them are the wrong things!

However, one could make a good case for retaining *some* inequality in incomes. For instance, differences arising from unequal effort put forth by people with equal opportunities might be justified. Note in particular that in a perfectly competitive economy, there would be no artificial barriers to equal opportunity except the initial distribution of property rights in capital and land, which might be unequal. In contrast with the real world, however, all people would be fully informed as to educational and job opportunities. They would enjoy unhindered entry (as to educational institutions, housing, and jobs).

Nor would there be *exploitation*, which is the receipt by someone of less than he contributes to production. In a situation of equilibrium, every resource would be paid exactly the value of its contribution to production. This would be the marginal benefit it produced for the user, the amount of which would be lost if a unit of this resource were to be withdrawn from use (see parts (d) through (f), Figure 2.2). Also, payment would be *nondiscriminatory*—equal pay for equal services. All suppliers (whether male or female, white or black, old or young) of a given type of labor would receive the same pay. Thus one might accept at least those income differences arising from unequal effort in a climate of equal opportunity.

One might even go further and justify the degree of inequality in money income that is clearly temporary, the result of sudden shifts in tastes, technology, or resource availability. This might be done in recognition that such differences are the very signals needed to bring about necessary redirections in resource use. By eliminating all such differences completely, one would paralyze the governor of the economy, which is the price system. Indeed, one would create chaos, unless a human central planner were readied to take over the price system's work!

Finally, one can show that income inequality is likely to be conducive to economic growth. For instance, if all families share income equally, there is less likely to be much investment in new capital goods than if income is very unequally distributed. Recipients of very large shares of income are more likely to invest in new capital goods than recipients of small income shares who are more likely to favor private consumption. If income is very equally distributed and distributed to private individuals, there are no recipients of very large income shares. Hence more private consumption, less capital formation, and less economic growth is likely. Thus there are opportunity costs involved even in choosing among broad economic goals. The price of more rapid economic growth may be less economic justice. The price of more economic justice may be less economic growth.

All this is not to say that *all* income differences likely to arise in a situation of perfect competition are morally acceptable. Undoubtedly the least defensible income differences would be those stemming from inheritance, natural and legal. Those who are poor because of mental or physical disabilities, as well as those who are rich for having inherited income-producing land or capital, might be the objects of governmental intervention. Such income differences due to inheritance might be mitigated or eliminated by redistributive government policy. As a result, the rich would buy fewer yachts, and the poor more meat. These changes in demand would change prices, and resources would be reallocated accordingly. But this is as one would expect. The price system is a mindless robot. Depending on how buyers cast their dollar votes, it can produce one set of goods in as orderly and efficient a fashion as any other set.

To conclude, it would be foolish to condemn the perfectly competitive market economy for reasons of inequity. Any apportionment of income and goods considered unjust can always be corrected by government without affecting the system's marvelous ability to create order and efficiency. Thus the promise of a decentralized economy wherein each individual can make his own self-interested decisions, yet wherein overall economic order, efficiency, and justice prevail—that promise can be realized *if government safeguards the preconditions of perfect competition and in addition redistributes income in ways considered socially desirable.*

SOME PROBLEMS WITH REAL-WORLD MARKETS

Many people would argue that our real-world market economy is not a society in which economic justice prevails. In addition, it is obvious to anyone that it is not peopled by fully informed and perfectly mobile buyers and sellers, all of whom may engage in any voluntary exchange to their liking at terms of exchange they are powerless to affect and none of whom is ever forced into an involuntary exchange. The existing inequities and inefficiencies can be traced to the failure of government to redistribute income sufficiently and to safeguard the preconditions for perfect competition. As it turns out, all our urban economic problems are problems of inequity or inefficiency or a mixture of both. All could be solved by proper behavior on the part of government.

Matters of Equity

We have just noted how the market economy is hard-boiled and impersonal. If you are born lucky, with lots of land and capital or special talents, you may get a lot of money income and you can cast a lot of dollar votes in the market for goods. All this, possibly, without the slightest need to work. If your neighbor is unlucky, owning no land and capital, having been born with low intelligence and poor health, he will get little or no money income even in the case of perfect competition. In the real world, all this may be reinforced by market imperfections. Lack of market knowledge, lack of mobility, or the fixing of prices by powerful groupings of people may deny some people access to health care, education, job training, jobs, or better-paying jobs. People denied such opportunities will have few dollar votes to cast in the goods market. Still, they might have to work 50 hours a week. Should we be surprised if they are tempted to get rich by crime?

Much of existing inequality does not square with our sense of fair play. Humanitarianism and a sense of justice demand that those without income and those with low incomes be helped by others more fortunate. That is the subject matter of Part Two of this book: Matters of Equity. Part Two concerns—within the context of urban life—the extent of poverty and policies likely to affect it. These are policies concerning a redistribution of land and capital, health care, education, employment, government money transfers, and crime. Since all these policies ultimately affect the way income and therefore goods are apportioned among people, they are most easily grouped under the heading of equity. This is not to deny that some of these issues also raise matters of efficiency.

Matters of Efficiency

All other urban problems are predominantly problems of inefficiency. Housing, transportation, and pollution problems are therefore grouped together in Part Three of this book: Matters of Efficiency. Some of these problems arise from the failure of government to safeguard the preconditions of perfect competition.

Failure to establish property rights. First, the government has failed to establish transferable property rights in *all* scarce things. This gives rise to involuntary exchanges and, naturally, much social tension. Most notably, government has failed to establish and enforce property rights—private or public—in parts of the natural environment, such as the air or bodies of water. As a result, many people making decisions in goods or resource markets make them on the basis of *price signals that are wrong*. In a perfectly working perfectly competitive society, the user of a good, for instance, would know that all those who have given up something to help make the good available to him have been properly compensated. If things are as they should be, he would know that by paying the price, he is paying for the social cost of production of the good. As we saw above (pp. 42–43), in a situation of long-run competitive equilibrium when the industry has no tendency to expand or contract (and market price has no tendency to change), the going price will produce just enough revenue to cover a firm's variable cost plus fixed cost and allow it to make a normal profit. Thus buyers pay for the effort of laborers and managers, for the use of someone's land and capital, and indeed, for any inconvenience the process of production places on others. The last would include such things as compensation of the owners of nearby air and water for any noise, foul gases, and liquid wastes the producing factory might emit. Yet if the government has failed to designate who has the exclusive right to the use of such air and water, the factory can emit all the noise, foul gases, and liquid wastes it wishes without having to compensate anyone for this. Such social costs would not enter its monetary cost accounting. Hence there will be neighbors who suffer. Their medical bills may be higher than in the absence of pollution, if bad air or water affects their health. They may have to spend money on air conditioners to preserve their health. Their taxes may be higher than in the absence of pollution, if municipal water works have to install new water purification devices. Their vacations may be costlier than in the absence of pollution, if they have to travel farther than otherwise to find safe swimming places. Their jobs may be lost if they made a living catching fish that die in foul, heated, or radioactive water. True enough, all of these people might have exchanged good air or water for bad air or water voluntarily, *but only for payment of a sum of money considered high enough to compensate them for the damages.* Without the help of the government's defining of property rights, however, no individual is able to charge factories (and ultimately their customers) for the suffering they cause. Nor is any individual able, by refusing to accept compensation, to keep a factory from polluting in the first place. Indeed, any self-interested producer would also use other resources, like labor and timber and minerals, by just taking what it needed if the government had not designated who has exclusive control over these resources. Since owners of labor, timber, and minerals have been designated, any factory must acquire the right to use them from their owners, who can withhold that right entirely or transfer it for a sum of money. So the cost of labor, timber, and minerals shows up in a firm's accounting. The cost of dumping things into the environment does not show up in this way. It does show up in the complaints of people suffering from pollution, who are rightly angry for being forced to exchange clean air and water and a quiet neighborhood for a filthy and noisy environment. Nobody forces them to exchange good leisure time for work without compensation. Why should it be proper, they ask, to coerce them into giving up equally valuable parts of the good life without compensation?

Figure 2.7, "Undefined Property Rights Spell Inefficiency," illustrates this discussion. The caption makes it self-explanatory. Note the obvious inefficiency involved if a firm's costs do not include pollution avoidance expenditures or compensation payments to pollution victims. In this example, if a 30-cent price per unit of paper prevailed and, say, a 20-cent price per unit of bread, welfare-maximizing buyers of the two goods would make sure to buy quantities such that the ratio of the marginal benefit of paper to the marginal benefit of bread equaled 3:2. Thus they would indifferently exchange a unit of paper for 1.5 units of bread. However, if the paper price is incorrect (if the social marginal cost of producing paper is 40 cents) while that of bread is correct (if the social marginal cost of producing it is 20 cents), society could produce 2 units of bread by not producing 1 unit of paper. This is so because it would save, by not producing a unit of paper, 30 cents' worth of resources in the paper mill and *another* 10 cents elsewhere (as in the provision of medical services, air conditioners or water purification devices, all of which would not be needed so much as pollution subsides). Thus it would be possible to make someone better off without making anyone worse off. For example, paper users could be given a unit less and 1.5 units of bread more (they would be equally well off) if resources in paper mills were shifted to bakeries. Pollution victims would be better off. Hence the original situation used resources inefficiently.

Failure to demand adequate amounts of pure public goods. We have just seen how the process of production can generate economic inefficiency if a producer can impose costs upon others who are unprotected by property rights. The process of consumption generates similar effects. Note the noise created by snowmobilers and the air pollution caused by auto drivers. There exists another interesting possibility: Producers and consumers might confer *benefits* upon others and be unable to collect revenues from them. In this case it is the producers or consumers rather than the outside parties affected who do the complaining. Indeed, if most of the benefit goes to others, private demand and subsequent production and consumption are strongly discouraged. The goods involved are *pure public goods.* These are goods that must be consumed by all if they are to be consumed by one. Unless government demands them, they may not be produced at all. National defense is an example. If even one person in the nation is to be protected from foreign enemies, all persons must be protected. The good in question is indivisible. Unlike oranges and most other goods, it cannot be withheld from him who does not pay. As a result, no rational and self-interested individual will *by himself* voluntarily spend money on such a good. Yet he would spend it if others did too. Without government initiative, he can always wait for others to do it first and thus be sure to get all the benefit without cost. Since all individuals reason likewise, there is no private market demand for pure public goods. Realizing this, people who agree that all would gain if the public good were produced can vote to have it procured by government, with payment being exacted simultaneously from all through taxation.

The provision of internal order by an adequate system of laws, courts, and police is also clearly a pure public good. Yet all too frequently, government provision of this good is inadequate. Note how property rights are eroded by inadequate laws, or inadequate enforcement of laws, concerning fraud and deception in the provision of consumer goods (hence the attention received by "Nader's raiders"). Note how the entire criminal justice system is so poorly financed and organized that crime is reinforced rather than suppressed: the treatment of the accused is often a function of their income, trials are lengthy, and prisons are schools for crime rather than centers of rehabilitation.

Failure to assure full information. Third, governmental efforts to bring full market information to all potential buyers and sellers are frequently less than adequate. In the resource market, for instance, the numbers of job openings and numbers of qualified job seekers often coincide, but the two parties do not know of each other. This leads to unnecessary unemployment. Young people going to school receive totally inadequate guidance as to career planning. As a result, they may train for jobs in low demand, programming themselves for unemployment or low-wage employment. Consumers are

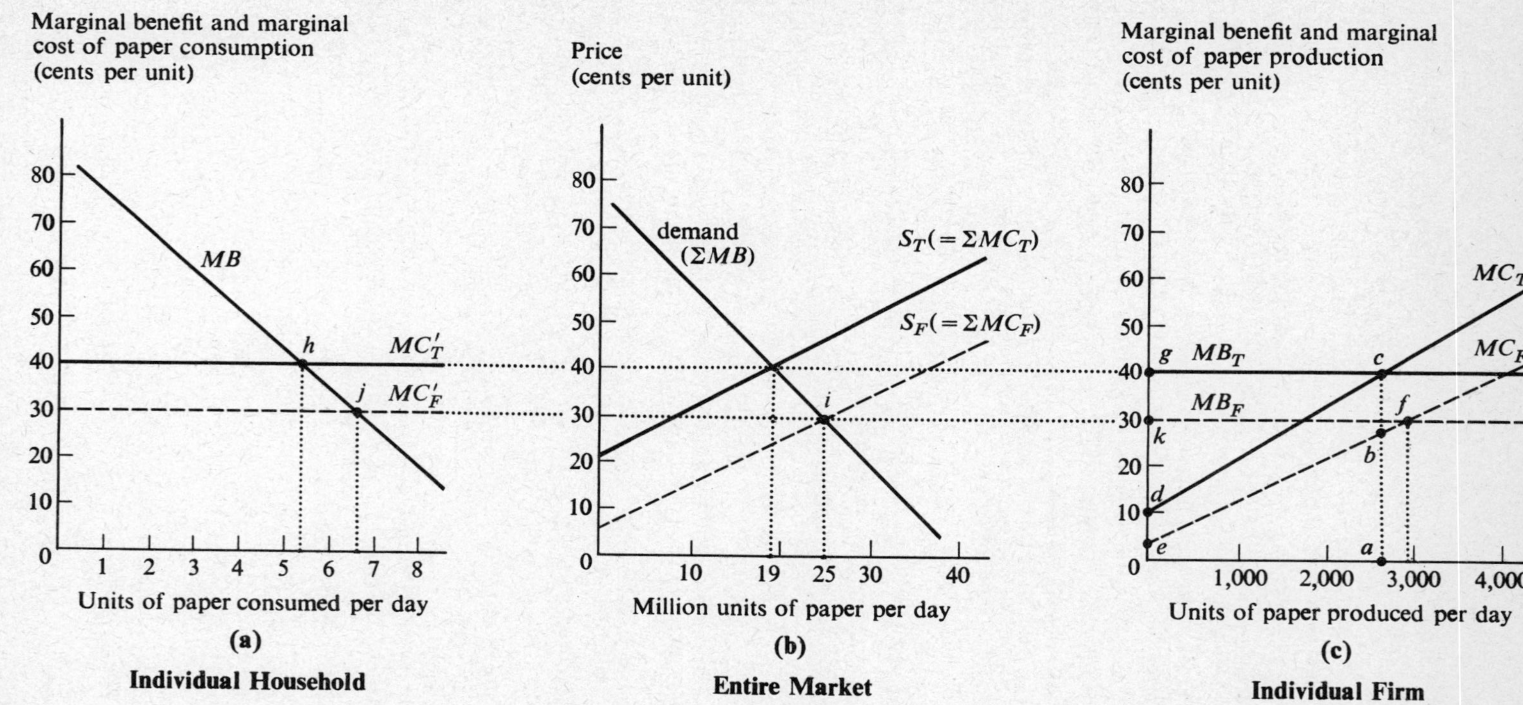

Marginal benefit and marginal cost of paper consumption (cents per unit)
80
70
60
50
40
30
20
10
0
MB
h
j
MC'_T
MC'_F
1 2 3 4 5 6 7 8
Units of paper consumed per day
(a)
Individual Household
Price (cents per unit)
demand (ΣMB)
S_T(=ΣMC_T)
S_F(=ΣMC_F)
i
10 19 25 30 40
Million units of paper per day
(b)
Entire Market
Marginal benefit and marginal cost of paper production (cents per unit)
MC_T
MC_F
g
MB_T
MB_F
c
f
k
b
d
e
a
1,000 2,000 3,000 4,000
Units of paper produced per day
(c)
Individual Firm

frequently unaware of the range of goods available and of their qualities. Indeed, government frequently allows private parties to *restrict* the flow of information, as by deceptive advertising, packaging, and labeling. Thus consumers miss many opportunities to enhance their well-being. Note how private organizations such as Consumers Union have become successful because of the great demand for better market information.

Failure to assure full mobility. Fourth, government often allows private parties to restrict the scope of voluntary exchanges by hampering the degree of mobility in the economy. Frequently, government itself is an active participant in such schemes. As a result, economic inefficiency appears. People are less well off, as shown by the fact that they are cajoled or forced into

---

Figure 2.7 Undefined Property Rights Spell Inefficiency

If government fully defined property rights in all scarce things (including, for example, the scarce capacity of the natural environment to absorb wastes), the true marginal cost of paper production might be MC_T for the firm pictured in part (c). The market supply would then be S_T. Together with market demand, a correct price of 40 cents per unit of paper would be established under perfect competition. It would appear as the true marginal cost of consumption (MC'_T) to each household and as the true marginal benefit (MB_T) to each firm. This price would compensate fully all those having given up something for the sake of paper production. For the firm pictured in part (c), variable cost would equal *Oacd*, of which the portion *ebcd* would equal compensation payments to those hurt by pollution or expenditures to avoid pollution. Fixed cost plus normal profit would equal *dcg*. The household pictured in part (a) would optimize at intersection *h*, consuming a little over five units of paper per day. The firm pictured in part (c) would optimize at intersection c, producing about 2,600 units of paper per day. Altogether (part (b)), 19 million units would be produced and consumed per day.

Now suppose those who contribute to paper production by giving up clean water for dirty water are not compensated for their sacrifice, owing to lack of definition of property rights. Each firm's marginal cost of production would then drop to a false level, MC_F in part (c). The quantity supplied on the market at each price (part (b)) would rise. S_F would replace S_T. Market price (intersection *i*) would become 30 cents per unit of paper. This false price signal (MC'_F, part (a)) would move the household's optimum from *h* to *j*, raising its daily paper consumption to nearly seven units. This false price signal (MB_F, part (c)) would move the firm's optimum from c to *f*, raising the daily output of the firm to nearly 3,000 units. Its fixed cost plus normal profit (*efk*) would be the same as before (*dcg*), but variable cost now would not contain any pollution compensation or avoidance expenditures. Altogether, 25 million units would be produced and consumed per day. Inefficiency would prevail because social welfare could be increased by producing less paper with pollution side effects and more of other goods without such side effects. Confronted with false price signals, however, neither firms nor households have any incentive to change their behavior. They are not aware of the true opportunity costs of their decisions to produce and consume this much paper.

making exchanges that are clearly less preferred than alternatives they would make if they enjoyed full mobility. For instance, often private people are not allowed to produce and sell certain goods *at all.* These include narcotics, gambling services, services of prostitutes, and mail delivery. Unless government then provides those goods, they tend to be produced illegally, giving rise to a large industry called organized crime.

In other cases, government allows only *a few* designated sellers to produce certain goods. In some cases, this is easily explained—competition, although possible, may be deemed undesirable for technical reasons or reasons of public safety. These are called cases of *natural monopoly.* Examples are in the fields of water supply, electric or gas power production, and telephone service. The duplication of water and gas pipes, or of power and telephone lines, if several firms could compete (let alone many), would clearly represent a great public nuisance. It would also represent technical inefficiency because most of the equipment of most of the competitors would not be used most of the time. Many electric power producers, for instance, can obtain lower average costs the larger the scale of operations, up to enormous capacities. In 1970, these technically most efficient plant sizes were in excess of 300,000 kilowatts for conventional steam plants (generating about four-fifths of electric power in the United States). Atomic power plants now being built promise further cost savings of 30 percent per kilowatt-hour with one-million-kilowatt plants. Some of the hydroelectric stations have optimum plant sizes of millions of kilowatts. Because one million kilowatts is enough to meet the total power needs of many a large American city, it is clear that perfect competition among technically efficient power producers is out of the question. This explains how government got into the business of helping some private firms keep other private firms out of markets. Unfortunately, the very existence of regulatory agencies left room for other alert and aggressive firms to befuddle or bribe regulators. Before long, government activity *against* perfect competition had mushroomed.

Consider how the government grants, for the sale of many a good, *exclusive franchises* to one firm or a few in fields that are clearly *not* natural monopolies: buses, taxis, and airlines, for instance. Consider how the government grants *production quotas* (as for corn) to some farmers, thereby preventing others from entering certain occupations (such as corn growing, or cattle raising based on corn production). Consider how the government grants *patents,* thereby preventing some would-be producers from using certain production processes. Consider how suburban governments pass *zoning laws and building codes,* thereby preventing the production of apartment buildings or cheap single-family houses in their area. By restricting competition in all these fields, government helps reduce the quality or availability and helps raise the price of goods. As a result it *creates* such problems as these: Some people (the central-city poor) remain poor because they cannot get to jobs for lack of affordable housing near jobs (in the suburbs) or lack of affordable transportation (mass transit to the suburbs). Other people (the affluent suburbanites) for lack of mass transit facilities commute to their jobs (in the cities) in private cars causing traffic congestion and pollution. Since some goods are kept artificially scarce, all people pay more than necessary for these goods (such as cereal and beefsteak made with corn and shoes produced with patented machines).

In the resource market, too, some potential sellers are prevented from operating in the market. *Social custom* or *employer discrimination* or *labor union rules* that deny certain people (females, the elderly, racial or ethnic minorities) access to certain occupations or job categories are examples. Governmental *licensing of professions* (broadly defined to include not just doctors and lawyers, but also barbers, yacht salesmen, and even egg graders!) more often than not goes beyond the desirable, which is the certifying of professional competence, and includes arbitrary restrictions on the numbers who may enter the "profession." Whatever the device used to restrict artificially the number of people acquiring and selling a skill, the result is the same: Those allowed entry have relatively high incomes, those kept out have relatively low incomes, and the competitive market's tendency to equalize the differences is paralyzed. No doubt poverty associated with perpetually low incomes of women, blacks, and Spanish-speaking people is in part explained by this circumstance.

Failure to assure price flexibility. Fifth, government is the chief culprit when it comes to fixing prices above or below their perfectly competitive equilibrium levels. Price fixing creates problems even if full knowledge and mobility exist. Setting highway tolls, for instance, below their correct equilibrium levels and below the true marginal cost of production of road services misinforms potential users of the true state of affairs and leads them to demand an excessive quantity of such services. Without physical restrictions to road entry, traffic congestion is the natural outcome.

Fixing housing rentals below their equilibrium levels has similar consequences. The false price signal misinforms buyers and sellers about true scarcity conditions. Quantity demanded goes up, quantity supplied goes down. Housing congestion results.

Government is equally active in resource markets. It fixes interest rates. It fixes wages, or it helps labor unions do the fixing. As a result, some workers are priced out of jobs.

The reason. This recounting of anticompetitive behavior by government is by no means exhaustive. Is this role of government surprising? Not really, except to the naive. Some people think of government as the impartial servant of the public good. They see it as the instrumentality of achieving "the national interest." Yet a nation does not have interests; people do. Within the nation, there are many people, and invariably they have conflicting interests. Much of public policy is directed toward promoting the *special* interests of some people at the expense of the interests of other people.

Just imagine you were a producer of, say, housing under conditions of perfect competition. Suppose you were making a normal profit. Here are two reasons why you might ask for government help:

Case 1: Market demand rises, price rises, and above-normal profit appears. As we showed above in the section on profit, the entry of new competitors can be relied on to raise market supply, depress price, and thus compete away your above-normal profit. Is it difficult to see why you might seek government help (perhaps in the guise of "assuring professional competence") to keep new competitors out? If successful, this could turn your *temporary* above-normal profits into permanent ones! Why should you care that people get less housing and at a higher price than otherwise? *Your* income would be higher.

Case 2: Your competitors discover a way to produce housing much more cheaply (perhaps by mass production techniques). Their cost curves are down, they supply more housing, market price drops, and your normal profit disappears or turns into losses. This is upsetting to your entire life style! You must either get out of this business or conform and also use the new technology. How much nicer if you didn't have competitors because, say, governmental codes outlawed mass production methods! You could have *a nice quiet life*, keeping any technological breakthroughs a secret or refusing to introduce them. Why should you care that people get less housing and at a higher price than socially necessary? *Your* profit would be normal, and your life would be peaceful!

It might be instructive for you to reread the last two paragraphs by substituting another good for housing, such as medical care. To emphasize our point: Even though people as a group lose, the distortion of prices away from the perfectly competitive outcome can always help a few mightily. Indeed, in our actual market economy, many a well-organized minority has succeeded in gaining political support for programs that clearly help a few people a great deal while ignoring the interests of the many.

CONCLUSION

One conclusion clearly emerges. Many of our economic problems could be solved *within the framework of the market economy*, if government remedied its sins of omission as well as commission. Redistributing income to promote equity would be involved. Promoting efficiency by fully defining property rights, arranging for the adequate production of pure public goods, ceasing all government actions, and countering all private actions, restrictive of the flow of information to and of the mobility of market participants, and eliminating price fixing—all would be involved. The logic of the market economy does not necessarily create problems of inequity and inefficiency. The market economy is fundamentally capable of producing a system of communications and incentives for orderly and efficient resource allocation that is unlikely to be duplicated by central economic planning.

Summary

1. Basically two ways exist for allocating resources and apportioning goods. One involves central economic planning, a method that requires a great amount of centralized information initially available only in decentralized form. For this reason, the feasibility of producing and executing a perfectly coordinated plan from a single center is doubtful. Many resources would certainly be tied up in the planning bureaucracy, waste through unemployment or inefficient use of resources would be likely, and the distribution of goods would probably be inefficient or inequitable.
2. The market economy is an alternative to central planning. It stresses decentralized decision making by a multitude of individuals. Each has to make his own optimizing decisions. Government has the role of setting up a framework promoting widespread and voluntary exchange among individuals.
3. Government must establish and define transferable property rights in all scare things. It must protect these rights by assuring internal order. It must assure unrestricted voluntary exchange among individual decision makers. Widespread exchange can be facilitated by setting standards and norms, increasing the flow of information on available exchange opportunities, safeguarding the mobility of all potential market participants, and preventing price fixing.
4. Under such conditions, markets will emerge. When all market participants are fully informed, perfectly mobile, and individually unable to influence the terms of exchange, and prices are perfectly flexible, perfect competition is said to exist.
5. In each category, goods as well as resource market, the independent optimizing decisions of households and firms determine market demand or supply and ultimately equilibrium price and quantity. In making these decisions, each household uses knowledge only it possesses (the marginal benefit of consumption and the marginal cost of resource supply). Each firm uses similarly unique knowledge (the marginal benefit of resource use, the marginal cost of production). Both compare their unique knowledge with the market price that is common to all and indicates the *social* evaluation of the scarce item. As a result, the selfish optimizing decision is constrained to be a socially responsible choice. No one can gain unless he reimburses others for any loss.
6. The establishment of the equilibrium price neatly divides all potential market participants into two groups: those that can and those that cannot engage in the particular activity for which the price is established. Such

division is inevitable in a world of scarcity wherein it is impossible for everyone to do everything.

7. The system of equilibrium prices, furthermore, might be termed the governor of the perfectly competitive market economy. These interdependent prices link all markets. They provide the information and the incentive for millions of independent decision makers to act in just the way needed for consistent resource allocation. For instance, under perfect competition increased demand for a good leads to higher price in the short run as well as some increased production within given plant capacities. Higher price, however, raises profit above normal. This leads in the long run to enlargement of existing firms and the building of new ones. In turn, production and supply are raised and price and profit depressed. When profit is back to normal, this process ends. Depending on how far market supply has risen relative to market demand by the time this happens, the final price can be above, equal to, or even below the initial one.
8. The system of perfectly competitive equilibrium prices has one important side effect: It guides society to economic efficiency. This is so because each self-interested household and firm adjusts quantities bought or sold to the identical set of prices. As a result, no matter how different their circumstances otherwise, *at the margin* all market participants value any good or resource alike. Even though they may consume different total quantities, for instance, each household consuming a good gets the same marginal benefit from this good as any other household consuming it. Even though firms producing the same good may turn out different total quantities, each firm has the same marginal cost. There is then no possibility of an unambiguous increase in welfare by reallocating goods for consumption or production. Other conceivable efficiency conditions would similarly be fulfilled in perfectly competitive equilibrium.
9. The perfectly competitive economy does not assure equity in any objective sense of the word. It would apportion money income and therefore goods on the basis of resource quantities supplied and their equilibrium prices. However, any income distribution considered unjust can be corrected by government intervention without destruction of the system's ability to create order and efficiency in resource allocation. For many reasons, however, a completely equal apportionment of incomes among people would never be desirable.
10. Many people argue that economic justice does not prevail in the real-world market economy. Everyone agrees that inefficiencies abound. Problems can be traced to an inadequate performance of essential government functions: The government does not adequately redistribute income. It fails to establish transferable property rights for *all* scarce things. It fails to demand adequate amounts of pure public goods. It fails to assure full information and mobility. It fails to assure price flexibility.
11. The real-world economic problems associated with matters of equity and efficiency could be solved within the framework of the market economy if government remedied its sins of omission and commission listed above. Since the promise of the market economy is so great, a try would be well worthwhile.

Terms[3]

above-normal profit
capitalism
centrally planned economy
command economy
competitive economy
equilibrium price (quantity)
exclusive franchise
exploitation
firm
fixed cost
household
internal consistency (of resource allocation)
long run
market
market demand
market economy
market supply
mobility
natural monopoly
normal profit
perfect competition
price fixing
price system
production quota
property right
pure public goods
shortage
short run
socialism
surplus
variable cost

Symbols

Σ

Questions for Review and Discussion

1. "One of the assumptions underlying the perfectly competitive market economy is this: People know best what is good for them, therefore their tastes, as expressed in their demand, should determine how resources are used. But this leads to overemphasis on material gratification. Resources would be better allocated if a governmental panel of cultured experts decided what is really good for people." What do you think?
2. "Government should keep hands off the economy." Discuss in light of this chapter, bringing out arguments in favor and against.
3. "In ordinary discourse, competition refers to personal rivalry. Yet economists define *perfect competition* as exactly the opposite situation, in which personal rivalry is completely absent. Perfect competition, they argue, provides an important curb on the bargaining power of any individual, and that, in turn, makes for a more peaceful world. The more competition there is, the more

[3] Terms and symbols are defined in the Glossary at the back of the book.

peaceful the exchanges are likely to be. The less competition there is, the more likely that bitterness and violence will arise." Do you agree? Consider the type of competition and bargaining at the stock market; between a labor union and a corporation; and at an international conference. Cite cases of competition from your own experience.

4. "Government should not really allow all people free entry into all markets. It quite properly forbids cigarette and liquor sales to minors, sale of dope to anyone, prostitution, and so on." Discuss.
5. Suppose an ice age unexpectedly arrives. To protect "the freezing children of poor families" the government freezes the existing price of gloves. What consequences would you expect?
6. What do you think is the consequence of setting below-equilibrium maximum interest rates on loans to college students ("to protect them from usury")?
7. Consider Figure 2.6, "Efficiency through Selfishness." Can you show how a central planner would create great inefficiency if he assigned the same *total* quantities to each family or firm in the face of these divergent marginal benefit curves of families and marginal cost curves of producers? Why might he do it nevertheless?
8. Draw a graph like Figure 2.2, "Optimizing Decisions and Market Equilibrium." Can you show for goods and resource markets the effects of
   (a) artificial restrictions to market entry placed in the way of some willing buyers;
   (b) artificial restrictions to market entry placed in the way of some willing sellers;
   (c) government price fixing above equilibrium;
   (d) government price fixing below equilibrium?

   Who would be helped by each of these actions? Who would be hurt? Why would the resultant situation be inefficient?
9. Show, with the help of one of the efficiency conditions discussed in this chapter, how racial, age, or sex discrimination worsens the potential welfare of everyone, not just those who are discriminated against, but also those who impose the discrimination.
10. Government imposes tariffs, quotas, and other restrictive regulations on the import or export of goods or resources. Foreigners can then not easily sell the good or resource in the domestic market, and citizens have difficulties selling abroad. Can you show, perhaps by using one of the efficiency conditions discussed in the chapter, how restrictions to the international exchange of goods or resources may worsen the welfare of all nations, including the one imposing the restrictions?
11. MR. A: Government grants patents for the exclusive use of a machine or technological process that is necessary for the production of a good. Other sellers are then effectively prevented from entering that market. Typically, this is true even in the long run. Although patents are valid for a limited period only (presumably to encourage innovation), they usually have the effect of giving a firm an impregnable market position by the time the patent expires. Therefore patents

should be abolished for they limit competition and eonomic efficiency.

MR. B: Patents should be granted, for without them an inventor could not reap all the benefits he gave society. A swarm of imitators would reap most of the benefits. Since the private gain from invention would fall short of the social gains, too few resources would be allocated to research and development.

Who is right?

12. Advertising is big business. In 1969, over $19 billion was spent for that purpose in the United States. In some cases (as in the soap industry) as much as 10 percent of sales revenue was used for advertising. Much of it, to be sure, is informative and therefore useful in spreading information needed for effective competition. Some of it, however, is meaningless and purely persuasive, and gives no hard information at all. It only serves to build prestige for the firm concerned by linking its product in people's minds with favorable circumstances. ("Blondes have more fun.") What then should government do about advertising?
13. "Economic efficiency is impossible. For example, it requires that the marginal costs of all producers of a given good be equal. Since firms come in all sizes, it is absurd to think that all producers of a given good could ever have identical marginal costs." True or false? Why?
14. "The trouble with the market economy is this: If demand changes from cameras to skis, prices in the ski industry rise, and so will output and employment, profits and wages. The opposite happens in the camera industry. As a result, income is redistributed as in a blind lottery. Everyone in the ski industry, whether hard-working or lazy, wise or foolish, honest or dishonest, finds a pot of gold in his lap. Everyone in the camera industry, regardless of desert, is punished. This is unfair." Discuss.
15. "Many governmental policies that are destructive of perfect competition (and economic efficiency) are pursued with the goal of affecting the income share going to a particular group of people. Therefore, it would be very difficult, if not impossible, to change these policies." Evaluate by considering the types of governmental policies mentioned in this chapter.

Selected Readings

Fusfeld, Daniel R. *Economics.* Lexington, Mass.: D. C. Heath and Co., 1972. Chs. 5, 21–26, 30–33. A simple but excellent analysis of the perfect and imperfect market economy.

Kohler, Heinz. *Economics: The Science of Scarcity.* Hinsdale, Ill.: The Dryden Press, 1970. Chs. 16, 17, 23, 25. On centrally planned and market socialism as alternatives to the capitalist market economy.

———. *What Economics Is All About.* Hinsdale, Ill.: The Dryden Press, 1972. Chs. 4–5. More detail on the nature of the market economy and the economic role of government.

Leftwich, Richard H. *The Price System and Resource Allocation,* 3rd ed. New York: Holt, Rinehart and Winston, 1966. A detailed technical analysis of all aspects of the market economy.

NOTE: The *Journal of Economic Literature* lists recent articles on microeconomic theory (section 022), welfare theory (024), the capitalist system and comparisons with other economic systems (051 and 053), industrial organization and public policy toward monopoly and competition (610), and urban economics (931).

The *Index of Economic Articles* catalogs, in sections beginning with the indicated numbers, articles on the theories of the household and firm, demand and supply, markets, prices, and welfare economics (2.1), and on government in the economy (3.0), capitalism (3.1), business organization (14), and market structure (15).

3 *The Rise and Fall of the American City*

We now turn our attention from the nature of the economic system to the nature of the city. We ask why people live in cities, what makes cities grow, and what forces are responsible for their decline. As we focus on these questions, we come to recognize certain trends in the recent history of most American cities—trends that go a long way in explaining why the failures of government that we have so far isolated have their most serious consequences in the urban areas of our land.

THE BROAD SWEEP OF HISTORY

Cities have existed for almost 6,000 years if we count settlements of 10,000 people or more. Naturally, they have not always been what they are today. Their size alone has undergone remarkable change. Even the largest cities of antiquity—Babylon, Athens, Alexandria, Rome, Constantinople—had well under a million people in population. In contrast, in 1972, there were 11.5 million people living in the New York standard metropolitan statistical area alone.[1] The government at this time had identified within the United States 263 such areas (called SMSA's for short). Each SMSA is a county (in New England, a township), or a group of contiguous counties, containing at least one central city (or twin cities) with at least 50,000 people. In 1970, 69 percent of the U.S. population lived in such areas, but another 5 percent lived in smaller urban areas (with more than 2,500 people). Thus only 26 percent of all Americans lived in rural areas or in small towns (below 2,500 people). Five percent of Americans lived on farms. In 1790, when the first census was taken, it was the other way around: 5 percent of Americans lived in *urban* places.

Indeed, the process of urbanization in the United States, as in the rest of the world, is a very recent phenomenon, which began with the industrial revolution and has accelerated most notably since the early years of this century. The outlook is for more of the same. Even the most conservative estimators

[1] The statistical data used throughout this chapter come from U.S. Bureau of the Census, *U.S. Census of Population, 1970* (or earlier) and *Current Population Reports*, series P-20, P-23, and P-25.

of population growth predict the existence of at least 50 million more Americans by the end of this century. Most of these will be born in cities. By the year 2000, as growing cities become contiguous, an interlocking chain of urban complexes will have come into being. Note Figure 3.1, "Megalopolis: Urban Sprawl in the Year 2000." More likely than not, there will be over 20 metropolitan regions with over 1 million people in each. The largest of these, according to the U.S. Department of Housing and Urban Development, is expected to be the Atlantic seaboard region, with 67 million people. It will have practically merged with the Lower Great Lakes region and another 59 million people. California, with 43 million people, will be next in size, followed by 13 million people on the Florida peninsula. Other urban areas shown in Figure 3.1 will contain anywhere from 1 to 5 million people each. These will include—in the mid-South—the Southern Piedmont, north central Georgia, north central Alabama, and Memphis. They will include—in the Pacific Northwest—the Puget Sound and Willamette Valley areas. And they will include a number of smaller areas, such as the Salt Lake Valley, St. Louis, Louisville, and the others labeled in Figure 3.1.

So far, the growth of American cities has been essentially unplanned and unregulated by government. It has rather been the outcome of the inde-

Figure 3.1 **Megalopolis: Urban Sprawl in the Year 2000**

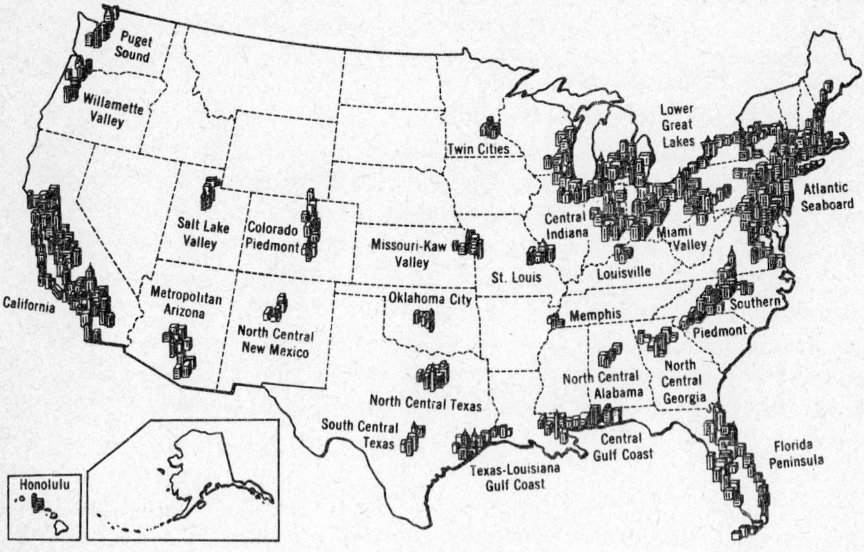

Source: Jerome P. Pickard, Dimensions of Metropolitanism *(Washington, D.C.: Urban Land Institute, 1967), p. 33. Reprinted with permission.*

More likely than not, there will be over 20 metropolitan regions with over 1 million people in each in the year 2000. They will contain over three-quarters of the U.S. population.

pendent decisions of millions of households and firms. If we want to understand what makes cities grow, we must inquire into the forces behind these decisions.

WHY CITIES EXIST

All cities have one characteristic in common, and that is *spatial concentration* of people. For some reason people choose to be close to each other rather than spread out evenly over the landscape. These reasons have undoubtedly differed over time. In ancient times, people walled themselves in in cities for purposes of defense against aggression by other people. In the modern days of missiles and bombs, defense is the worst possible reason for spatial concentration. In ancient times, people chose to live in close proximity because it allowed them to communicate more effectively with each other, indeed, to communicate at all, and so it is now. Thus cities have been and still are centers of religion, science, education, politics, and "culture." City living is valued by residents as a consumer good capable of satisfying wants relating to these activities. People often prize cities for the vast array of opportunities for personal development, for the excitement and stimulation they find there. In all times, however, the dominant reason for the dense agglomeration of people in cities has been an economic one: *The spatial concentration of the economic activities of many people helps preserve and enlarge the advantages of the division of labor.* A division of labor among people assures greater and higher-quality output from given resources. For instance, each American family could—as the Chinese have tried—produce its own steel in tiny backyard furnaces. If instead some families concentrated entirely on mining coal, others on mining ore, others on transporting these to a central place where others built and still others operated giant blast furnaces—the same number of families might get considerably more and higher-quality steel. We noted the reasons earlier: the increased proficiency of each specialized worker, now freed from time-consuming interchanges of location and tools; the use of equipment when none was used before; and the use of larger units or new types of equipment. *Yet these results depend on a fairly reasonable proximity in space of specialized activities.* If the coal were mined in Pennsylvania and the iron ore in California, and blast furnaces were readied in Florida, the same number of families might *not* get higher steel output, for too many of them would have to be busied keeping open the lines of transportation and communication among the cooperating parties. Obviously, the closer in space all the specializing families could be to each other, the smaller the *transactions cost* involved (that is, the cost of arranging for transportation and communications), and the greater the chance of reaping substantial advantages from the division of labor. No wonder then that households and firms in a market economy find it desirable to carry on their activities of production, exchange, and consumption in a few selected places where potential partners to the exchange of goods or resources are close at hand or from which they can most cheaply be reached. In short, the clustering of economic activities in particular places is a matter of economizing resources, of fighting scarcity to the utmost by not wasting resources unnecessarily in the very process of getting together with all those engaged in activities related to one's own.

Optimization Revisited

Exactly *where* economic activities will come to cluster will depend in the market economy on the many locational decisions made independently by households and firms. Rarely, if ever, will a potential businessman find, for instance, that his suppliers and customers are conveniently located in the same spot. Suppose a potential steel producer were to find that coal was located in Pennsylvania (and nowhere else), iron ore could be gotten in California (but also in Minnesota and off ships arriving from Sweden at Eastern seaports), while most buyers of steel were operating in Florida. Where should he build those blast furnaces? Locating at the source of any one input clearly would bring the benefit of not having to ship that input somewhere else, but it would involve the cost, equally obvious, of having to ship other inputs to the place of manufacture and the product to the place of demand. Any other locational choice (such as locating where customers are) would have similar advantages and disadvantages. A profit-maximizing businessman would find himself in something like a tug-of-war with respect to his locational choice. Some potential benefits would lure him in one direction (to the coal fields of Pennsylvania or the iron ore mines of Minnesota or the seaports of the East). Others (like the location of his customers) would lure him in another. Naturally, he would consider the marginal benefit and the marginal cost of moving away from any arbitrary potential location. As long as the marginal benefit of moving to another location exceeded the marginal cost of doing so, a move would be indicated. For example, by saving $10 million a year in transporting coal (the marginal benefit) while spending an added $6 million a year on transporting steel to market (the marginal cost), the firm's profit would be up by $4 million (the marginal net benefit). Even if competition eventually forced the firm to pass on this gain to customers via lower prices, its new profit might reappear for other reasons (perhaps, again, temporarily): If lower price raised quantity demanded significantly, the firm might in the long run use a different method of production, yielding significantly lower average costs and thus higher profit even at lower prices.

In any case, each firm must consider the benefits and costs of alternative locations and can be expected finally to choose that actual (optimum) location from which any potential move is considered to yield no net benefit. Firms are free to make locational choices on the basis of other considerations (locating, perhaps for noneconomic reasons—in the entrepreneur's home town or near his mother-in-law), but if they do, and the market economy works well, such high-cost producers will be eliminated from the scene by bankruptcy. They could not, in the long run, meet the competition of lower-cost competitors with optimal locations. As a result, most real-world firms in an industry make locational choices of a type similar to each other, and this is all that is needed to give birth to cities!

Firms in so-called *weight-losing* industries (that use bulky raw materials to make less bulky products) tend to locate near raw material sources. The iron and steel industry is one example. Firms in *weight-gaining* industries (producing bulky products, such as beer, by adding huge quantities of some ubiquitous material, such as water, to small quantities of other inputs) or firms producing perishable products (frozen foods) or fragile products (glassware) often prefer to minimize transportation of the final product. They locate near customers. Firms producing highly variable products (high-style clothing or toys, weekly magazines, advertising, investment banking services) try to do both at the same time, that is, locate near suppliers and near customers.

Frequently, such firms spring up only in large cities—for the reason that they operate under great uncertainty. One month, after a successful space venture, people are "crazy" about outer space. They are demanding clothing imitating space suits, want to play with toy rockets, want to read articles about rocket fuel and neutron stars, and look for advertisements exploiting the new interest in space. Then suddenly the president visits China. The space craze evaporates overnight, only to be replaced by an overwhelming appetite for things of Chinese motif. People want to wear Chinese-style clothes; buy Chinese dolls for their children; read about the Great Wall, ancient Chinese history, acupuncture, and modern Chinese painting; use advertisings with a Chinese theme; and perhaps even invest in joint U.S.-Chinese business ventures. Obviously, no firm operating in such a volatile environment can be prepared for all conceivable circumstances. Our dressmaker or magazine or investment banker friends, for instance, cannot have equipment or inventories on hand or people on their staffs who can deal with every one of a million unforeseeable exotic demands. Yet they do want to be able to change their products swiftly when new opportunities appear. So they locate where they can have not only a constant eye on their competitors but also immediate access to specialists. That is, fashion design houses do not care to store or to produce all types of materials, but they do care to be near someone who can provide—at a moment's notice—buttons with space designs today and with Chinese characters tomorrow. Magazine publishers do not staff themselves internally with specialists on everything, but they want to be able to reach a specialist and use his services at a moment's notice. While they need someone knowledgeable about rocket fuel today, they need someone else who knows about ancient Chinese history tomorrow. Similarly, investment bankers must be able to get advice from a specialist on Houston real estate today and from an expert on Far Eastern trade and merchant ships tomorrow.

Thus the general theory of rational behavior developed in Chapter 1 is once more seen to explain real-life phenomena: the clustering of economic activities leading to the formation and growth of cities.

A Look at Actual Locational Choices

A look at the location of actual cities will strengthen our thesis. Although there are historical accidents, such as the location of Salt Lake City, founded by the Mormons, most cities have been located in a particular place because of a particular characteristic of a piece of land that promised many people an economic advantage in comparison with locating elsewhere. The presence of coal or mineral deposits, rivers, or natural harbors are obvious lures. The city of Pittsburgh, for instance, was founded in its particular location because steelmakers could most cheaply assemble there local coal and limestone and Lake Superior iron ore.

When the dominant *mode of transportation* was ships, cities were founded along the coast or large rivers: Boston, New York, Philadelphia, Charleston, New Orleans, St. Louis, Cincinnati. In such locations, firms recognized ideal transshipment points and, before long, ideal places of production. To the extent that raw materials were not locally available but were shipped in, or products were made for people living elsewhere, such location assured the cheapest transportation costs. Frequently, these cities were also connected with their hinterland by a system of canals and steamboats.

In the nineteenth century, after railroads were invented and built, railroad lines began to rival rivers in importance for urban establishment. Where railroad lines met, or where the railroads met rivers, cities arose, and as city maps show, they expanded along the railroad lines. Within cities, firms tended to cluster around the nodal points of the transportation system, that is, the central railroad terminals and harbors. The shipment within the city of bulky raw materials and finished goods by horse and wagon—an expensive proposition—could thus be minimized.

The dominant *technology of production and communication* also made firms prefer central city locations. When waterwheels provided the major source of power, firms were clearly tied to rivers. When steam power set them free from the river's edge, the need for bulky coal transportation still made locations near rivers, harbors, or railroads preferable. The need to exchange ideas and information—on matters of productive technique, styles, quality, prices, matters of law, finance, or management—at a time when the messenger boy or personal meetings were the best means of doing so made central location imperative. Everyone who was engaged in the productive process saw a clear advantage in being as close as possible to everyone else.

The resultant great demand for certain locations by business tended to raise the prices of such parcels of land. Such increase in cost could be countered by buying small parcels only and operating out of multistory facilities. Similarly, workers settled in high-rise buildings to save on rent, or in row houses adjacent to the trolley lines to save on commuting costs.

We conclude: American cities were formed because self-interested households and firms realized an advantage in carrying on specialized economic activities in close proximity to others similarly specializing. In view of the dominant modes of transportation (water and rail), production (steam power), and communication (personal meetings), the transaction costs of a large-scale division of labor were minimized by carrying out that division of labor in spatially concentrated fashion.

HOW CITIES GROW

It is fairly easy to guess how a city might grow. Quite likely, it would pass through a number of stages in the process.[2]

The Stage of Export Specialization

Originally, a single firm might recognize the locational advantage of a particular parcel of land. This might be a meeting of two large rivers, associated with nearby deposits of ore and coal. It simply is cheaper to make steel there than anywhere else. Other firms in this business, if they wish to compete anywhere near this place, must settle there, too. Before long, the steel industry dominates the area. A one-industry town comes into being, full of miners and steelworkers and a few others serving their needs. Most likely, this population exports (sells beyond the city limits) most of what it produces. Most likely it imports (buys beyond the city limits) most of what it consumes. The town is in the stage of *export specialization*. As is true for any area, the level of income, of output, and of employment in the city will depend on the level of aggregate demand Y in the city. This demand will be the sum of household consumption C_H, such as food, and investment I_H, such as houses; of business investment I_B, such as machines; of government consumption C_G, such as typewriters, and investment I_G, such as school buildings; plus the net spending by people living outside the city. The latter would be the city residents' exports minus imports $X - M$. Thus

$$Y = C_H + I_H + I_B + C_G + I_G + X - M.$$

In the event that households, businesses, and government buy everything they consume or invest from nonresidents,

$$C_H + I_H + I_B + C_G + I_G = M,$$

and therefore

$$Y = X.$$

That is, the city's level of income, of output, and of employment is totally dependent on its ability to sell outside the city. If city exports grow,

[2] The discussion of stages in city growth is based in part on Wilbur R. Thompson, *A Preface to Urban Economics* (Baltimore: Johns Hopkins Press, 1968), Ch. 1.

so does the city's economy. As different exports grow at different rates, so different cities relying on such exports grow differently. It will never be completely the case that exports equal aggregate demand. Nevertheless, in the early life of many a city, exports do play a crucial role, for a very large percentage of city residents' expenditures are then directed toward outsiders and much of their income comes from outside.

Note how many cities are nicknamed after their export sector. Pittsburgh becomes the "steel capital" and Detroit the "auto capital"; Rochester becomes noted for cameras, Hartford for insurance, New York for clothing, Seattle for aircraft, and Los Angeles for movies.

This is not to say that a city with the original advantage must end up as the sole producer and exporter of a good. The further away a good is sold, the more the transportation cost adds to its price and the greater the likelihood of the original cost advantage's being wiped out. At the point in space at which this occurs, other higher-cost producers can successfully compete, and a new city can spring up. Thus steel gets more expensive the farther you ship it from Pittsburgh, and higher-cost West Coast steel producers have no trouble competing out West with Pittsburgh steel. The lower the cost of transporting the output, the fewer the centers of production to be found outside the lowest-cost locality.

The Stage of Diversification

Once an export industry has begun to flourish in a city, a new stage in the city's growth is likely to follow. This stage occurs when the industry's important customers and suppliers find it advantageous to locate in the city. Again, the wish for an improved ability to compete due to a lowering of transportation costs will play a significant role in bringing this about.

Where there is mining and basic steelmaking, those who produce and service mining and steelmaking equipment will tend to settle. So will processors and users of steel. In time, these will attract others in turn; for each of the new industries also has customers and suppliers. Although many of the newcomers will do much business within the city, their activities will not be confined to this one place. Some will export, in turn. Then the city export sector will broaden; this would mean, in our example, a range from steel and machine tools to vehicles and household durables. The city's economy has turned into a *diversified export complex*.

This association of various industries, which economists call the process of agglomeration, is easily cumulative. Again and again, some customers and suppliers find it advantageous to move close to their source of purchase or sale. Before long, the whole range of economic activities can be found in the city.

The Stage of Maturation

Eventually, activities that are supportive of many types of industries will find a rich market in the city and will settle there. There will come the makers of packaging and the wholesalers, the producers of advertising and financial services; there will come lawyers and management consultants, and the private and public providers of consumer goods: food, clothing, shelter, recreation, roads, education, sanitation, and police protection. More and more of local production will be locally consumed, more and more of former imports will be locally produced. Less and less will the growth of the city's economy depend on the demand by outsiders. While typically two-thirds of employment in a city of 10,000 depends on export demand, this percentage steadily declines to about one-third in a city of 10 million. Somewhere along the road, perhaps when half of its output is locally sold, the city is said to have reached *maturation*.

By virtue of having been the first to arrive at this stage, the city may even become one of regional or national eminence, eventually trading diversified commodities and services on a large scale with other cities, and also consuming a large proportion of its output locally.

Do all cities mature? Although a city's growth process may stop and even reverse on the way to maturation, there seems to be some critical size in a city's economy, perhaps in the neighborhood of supporting a quarter million population, beyond which it never contracts except in catastrophic circumstances. There are a number of reasons.

First, at this stage local industries are so diversified—containing a random blending of young, mature, and declining occupations—that almost automatically the average rate of national growth is maintained.

Second, at this stage the city's electoral strength in state and federal government will be such that it cannot be ignored when government expenditures are allocated.

Third, at this stage the accumulation of capital in the form of housing, school, transport, and business facilities is so vast and the local market is so large that new industries are continually tempted to locate there, at the very least establish branches in the area.

Fourth, new industries are more likely to be born there because the supply of entrepreneurial leadership is steady. This is only in part the result of entrepreneurial genius being attracted to a large city from elsewhere. It is also a matter of probability that such genius appears more often in a large mass of people. If a Henry Ford is born just once in 10,000 births, then a city of 50,000 with 1,000 births a year may expect one such genius in ten years (and he may wander off to a larger city). A city of 500,000, however, with 10,000 births a year, may get one such person every year.

The Role of Migration

We have seen how a city may grow because of some initial local economic advantage that is compounded many times by the growing number of firms and people that are attracted to the initial situation and then to each other. A natural question arises: Where do these new settlers come from? For any one city, there are three answers. Some arrive due to natural causes, that is, an excess of births over deaths. Some are won through intercity competition, wherein one city gradually wins out over others and realizes an excess of immigrants over emigrants. That is, the growth of one city can be fed at the expense of other cities.

Yet another, the third, reason is most significant. The great urbanization of the twentieth century cannot be explained by the growth of some cities at the expense of other cities. Nor can it be explained by natural increases in urban populations. Its cause lies, paradoxically, in events in the countryside. First, there were unprecedented improvements in agricultural technology. Farm output per man, which grew at 1 percent per year in the 1920's, has outstripped by far the productivity in manufacturing and has grown at over 5 percent a year since World War II. The demand for food and fiber, however, unlike the demand for manufactured goods and services, has grown much less. Thus a significant decline in the demand for agricultural labor appeared at the very time that demand for labor soared in manufacturing and services. Second, the rural birthrate has greatly exceeded the urban birthrate. Thus the supply of labor rose least where the demand rose the most (in urban areas). It rose most where the demand rose least (in rural areas). This led to significant differences in wages between rural and urban areas. Not surprisingly, these rural-city wage differentials (and to some extent differences in welfare benefits) set off one of the greatest migrations of people in U.S. history—the move from the farms to the cities. The most recent effects of this migration are shown in Table 3.1, "U.S. Population by Residence and Race." In the few

Table 3.1 **U.S. Population by Residence and Race (In Percentage of Totals)**

Residence	Total		White		Nonwhite	
	1950	*1970*	*1950*	*1970*	*1950*	*1970*
SMSA[a]	62.5	68.6	63.0	67.8	58.6	74.0
Central cities	35.5	31.4	34.6	27.8	42.7	56.4
Suburbs	27.0	37.2	28.3	40.0	15.9	17.6
Other nonfarm areas	22.2	26.6	22.8	27.3	17.8	21.8
Total nonfarm	84.7	95.2	85.8	95.1	76.6	95.8
Farm	15.3	4.8	14.2	4.9	23.4	4.2

[a] Covers 243 standard metropolitan statistical areas as defined in 1970.

Source: *U.S. Bureau of the Census.*

Since World War II, urbanization has proceeded at a rapid pace for all Americans, but more so for nonwhites than for whites. Note how blacks and other nonwhites have become concentrated in central cities, while whites have become suburbanized.

years since 1950 alone, the farm population has declined from just over 15 percent to just under 5 percent of the U.S. population.

Census data from 1870 to 1970 show us the major paths taken by internal migrants. During these one hundred years, a net average of 464,000 people per decade moved out of the South. (That is, while more people may have moved out than shown, others moved in.) The net figure covers an average net inmigration of 148,000 whites per decade and an average net outmigration of 612,000 blacks per decade. In this geographic area, the East South Central states (Alabama, Mississippi, Tennessee, and Kentucky) experienced continuous net outmigration by whites and blacks during the entire one hundred year period. The largest net exodus from any part of the United States during a single decade came in the 1950's when 1,466,000 people left. Another source of migrants, mostly white, have been the West North Central states (the Dakotas, Minnesota, Nebraska, Iowa, Kansas, and Missouri). Net outmigration since late last century has accelerated to an average of 710,000 per decade since 1920.

The major recipients of these internal migrant flows have been the Western, North Eastern, and East North Central states. Thus the Mountain and Pacific states of the West received since 1870 a net average of 1,748,000 people per decade, of whom 105,000 per decade were black. The Middle Atlantic and New England states (which include Pennsylvania, New York, and the states to their north and east) received during the past one hundred years a net average of 835,000 people per decade, of whom 249,000 per decade were black. Finally, the states of Illinois, Indiana, Ohio, Michigan, and Wisconsin (East North Central) received a net average per decade of 264,000 whites and 211,000 blacks.

It is important to note that all these data are averages for decades and that they refer to net migration flows among large regions. The gross migration flows in particular years and smaller areas, such as individual cities, have often been even more impressive than these overall data might indicate. For instance, the movement of a family from a farm in Georgia to the city of Atlanta would not show up at all in the aggregate data, since both places are within the same census division. Similarly, the movement of a family from Atlanta to Philadelphia and back two years later would be netted out from the statistics. One should not be surprised, therefore, that in recent times as many as one million people *per year* have been migrating from the countryside into metropolitan areas.

Who have these people been? Typically, they have been younger persons, and typically, in both places of origin and destination, above average in education and training. They have been whites from Kansas moving to Seattle, Phoenix, or Detroit and others from Appalachia streaming into the cities of Ohio; they have been blacks from Florida going to Boston and others from Mississippi going to Chicago; they have been Mexican-Americans from Louisiana and Texas going to Los Angeles. This vast movement of people intensified, in unprecedented fashion, the growth of urban areas in general. Yet, strangely enough, for many newly arrived migrants, the higher incomes that lured them into the cities of the North, East, and West have not materialized. Other forces have been at work—little noticed at first, but slowly gathering momentum until only the blind and deaf could ignore them—forces that spell the end of the city of old. *These forces are taking away some of the reasons for the spatial concentration of economic activity in central city locations.* Together with the simultaneous arrival of rising numbers of poor rural migrants and certain actions by more affluent urban dwellers, they provide the ingredients for disaster.

THE DECLINE OF CENTRAL CITIES

In the early days of American cities, the combined forces of transportation, production, and communications technologies prompted firms to seek out central city locations. During the past few decades, all these fields have experienced significant technological change. As a result, the traditional reasons for locating in central cities have been weakening.

Technological Changes

Take *transportation.* The significant change here is the invention and large-scale introduction of the automobile earlier in this century. As trucks and passenger cars became generally available and as a superb network of highways was built, the monopoly of the railroad and the trolley car was broken, just as they had once broken the monopoly of ships, horses, and buggies. Businesses suddenly found themselves able to move raw materials and finished goods within and among cities cheaply and flexibly, indeed, between any two points of their liking. Householders found that they could live at any spot outside the city, enjoying cheap land, space, and privacy, as well as the proximity of salt water beaches or mountain ski slopes, while easily commuting to city jobs. Thus a new world emerged: a firm could settle anywhere and still count on being able to assemble a labor force easily and ship materials and products cheaply. Naturally, they began to turn their backs on high-priced and crowded locations near harbors, rivers, and railroad terminals and began to look at the cheap open spaces outside the city limits.

Developments in air transportation only served to reinforce this trend, since the main airports were located away from city centers. The railroads, too, accepted the inevitable by introducing "piggyback" transport, that is, the carrying of truck trailers on railroad flatcars specially designed for this purpose.

Changes in *production technology* provided a strong incentive to leave city centers and make use of the locational freedom that had arrived with the automobile. Electrification and the assembly line were the two great innovations. Prior to the advent of atomic power, electric-power stations still were tied to places where huge quantities of coal could be most cheaply assembled, that is, near water or rail lines. All users of electric power, however, in contrast with the situation in days of steam power, were free to move anywhere. Moving became desirable as the cost savings in the use of continuous-flow methods of mass production became apparent. For that, businesses needed spacious single-story plants. As householders showed their preference for country living, firms needed large parking lots also. In short, businesses needed space—the very opposite of what was provided by the cramped, multistory factories built in city centers at the turn of this century.

Advances in the *technology of communications*, finally, removed the last reason for central location of manufacturing plants. Consider how the need for personal meetings has been obviated by the telephone, which allows immediate ties between any two persons. Consider the introduction of television, which allows the immediate transmission of images—in color, if desired—as well as their recording and delayed playback. Consider the development of computers, incredibly efficient in processing, storage, retrieval, and transmission of data. Computers allow white-collar workers such as managers, accountants, advertisers, lawyers, and researchers to guide, from any location, purchasing, production, and sales activities that are widely dispersed. Modern communications allow everyone to be linked with everyone else with near-zero time lags.

More likely than not, the continuing spread in the future of direct telephone ties, combining visual and audio messages, or the use of closed-circuit TV, the Xerox machine, and computer tie-ins by firms as well as households, will even strengthen the resultant trend toward dispersal and away from concentration. Indeed, additional whole fields such as education are likely to experience radical changes. Just as the cultural monopoly of the central city theatre, opera, museum, or concert hall has been broken by movies and television, it may well become unnecessary to leave one's home to go to school.

The Great Exodus

Technological change has thus brought upon the city a *crisis of function:* the magnetism of central location has greatly weakened. This has given rise to a great exodus of firms and households from the central city. But in both cases the outmigration has been a selective one, that is, not all types of firms and households have been leaving. Firms engaged in manufacturing and trade were among the first to leave. With a few exceptions such as Kansas City, Los Angeles, and Portland, Oregon, the central cities experienced an exodus that became a national pattern. From 1948 to 1958, the central cities of the 40 largest metropolitan areas lost half of their manufacturing, a third of their wholesaling, and three-quarters of their retailing jobs. In the 1960's this trend continued unabated.

At the same time, many families have also been abandoning the central city. While this outward migration occurred at a rate of 500,000 a year from 1950, it jumped to 900,000 a year after 1965. Note the relative loss of population in central cities and the comparable increase in the suburbs between 1950 and 1970, as indicated in Table 3.1, "U.S. Population by Residence and Race."

However, those who have left for the suburbs have been *white, relatively young families in the middle and higher income brackets.* In the typical city, the families in that 5–10 percent earning more than $20,000 a year have come to pick the choicest residential locations around the city: wooded or hilly terrain, lakefronts, or the seacoast. Typically, these people are white Protestants, but there is likely to be among them a sprinkling of white Catholics and Jews. The same types of families dominate the middle-income ranges (from $7,000 to $20,000 a year). They are likely to make up 70 percent of the metropolitan area population and can be found in ever greater proportions living in the endlessly sprawling new suburbs. Many of these people have followed blue-collar jobs to the suburbs; the white-collar workers among them are most likely to commute to central city jobs.

Not surprisingly, the exodus of the types of firms and people just described has adversely affected the chances of many to make a living in the central city: lower-skill service jobs are harder to come by; the downtown retail business is in the doldrums. Look at any central city and note how big department stores have opened branches in suburban shopping centers (where they do the bulk of their business), while the older downtown store languishes. Note how restaurants and movie houses close, together with all those ma-and-pa grocery stores along the old trolley-car streets. That neighborhood bakery, fish store, or candy store—once flourishing in the city—gets to be more of a museum piece with every passing year.

What Is Left Behind

In the typical city, therefore, left behind predominantly are firms outside manufacturing and trade, such as those providing administrative, financial, and governmental services. These kinds of firms, which are supplying a highly variable product in a highly competitive market, are among those that continue to find central city locations attractive. They are watching their volatile market continually (and the way in which their competitors are responding to it); and they must have immediate access to a large array of specialists as the need arises. For them changes in transportation and production technology have not been significant, and even changes in communications technology have (so far) been of minor importance. What often matters for success in such businesses is still old-fashioned face-to-face contact: a chance remark exchanged casually over lunch may disclose unsuspected opportunities; the shop talk of technical experts may stimulate new ideas; personal favors may be important (and the request for them cannot be entrusted to the telephone any more than the letter); designers must actually see and touch various materials (rather than ordering by phone via a catalog number); lawyers and bankers may require personal contact for reasons of confidentiality; when speed is of the essence, authors might have to be present to read proof; and so on.

When it comes to residents, what has predominantly been left behind in central cities are lower-income families, typically black Protestants, Latin

Catholics (their ranks being continually increased by immigration), and white Protestants who are advanced in age. These people find it difficult or impossible to earn a good living, for a number of reasons. Overall, there has been no increase in central city jobs corresponding to the increase in the labor force. To make things worse, there has been a loss in the very types of jobs (manufacturing, wholesaling, retailing) that have traditionally gone to the least educated and trained, who make up the bulk of the families left behind. These people lack the literacy or technical or professional knowledge indispensable for those jobs that have gained in importance (general and government services). Even in manufacturing itself, automation has devalued the premium once put on physical strength or manual dexterity, while appreciating the value of specialists.

Nor can these people follow the jobs that have migrated to suburban locations. The reason may be that they lack the necessary information about available jobs; that public transportation is inadequate; or that housing in the suburbs is not available to blacks, Spanish-speaking whites, and older people. The housing problem arises from racial and ethnic discrimination, lack of income, or both.

The results of this situation are predictable. The central cities become the depositories of low-skilled, poor, or old people. Members of racial or ethnic minorities inhabit the blighted parts of the city that ring the old industrial areas and inhabit them under conditions of involuntary segregation. These areas are the *ghettos*. Old people—most of them white—tend to inhabit the *gray areas* between the ghettos and the noose of white suburbs surrounding the cities. These are typically areas of aging and unattractive but nonslum housing. They are the suburbs of the past, built in the first three decades of this century and now obsolete. Built under a policy of maximum site coverage, they have no room for lawns and shrubs and trees and wide open spaces. Typical are two-family row houses, frame walkups, and four- to six-story apartment houses. Decades ago when they were built, these areas were served by brand new transit systems (railroads and streetcars), and they were eagerly sought after by the first generation of children of the pre–World War I wave of immigrants from abroad. Now their children have in turn left for the newer suburbs of single-family homes, leaving the old people behind, who are least able or willing to move.

What is left behind in central cities, then, is all too often a permanently depressed economy that has ceased to share or share fully in the national rate of economic growth. Net investment is likely to be lower than average. Even though in many central cities the construction of luxury apartments for the very rich has increased in recent years, more often than not the area's total capital stock (industrial plant, housing, streets, and public buildings) is allowed to deteriorate. Private, as well as public, per capita consumption is low and—as in the early days of any city—most of what is consumed in this area is imported from the outside. Imports are paid for from the export of labor services (in low-wage occupations) and with governmental transfer payments (such as welfare, unemployment, and old age benefits). Some individuals escape the depressed economy, but others drop into it. A pervading spirit of frustration exists, strengthened by the unprecedented material prosperity of the suburbs, which for everyone is in plain view but not in reach.

Statistics

All our remarks are borne out by statistics. Take population growth (combining data on net migration and the excess of births over deaths). From 1960 to 1970, 81 percent of all white population growth occurred in the new suburbs, in which young white families are concentrated and to which they are moving from central cities. But 84 percent of all black population growth occurred in central cities, in which the blacks are segregated and to which they are moving from rural areas. Ironically, earlier in this century, cities were inhabited by whites almost exclusively. Over 90 percent of all blacks lived in the rural South. Now the twelve largest cities alone account for one-third of the black population in the country. In 1950, 12 percent of the population of central cities was black. By 1970, the percentage was 21. Four cities (Atlanta, Gary, Newark, and Washington, D.C.) even had black majorities.

Now consider jobs. Table 3.2, "How Jobs Have Shifted to the Suburbs," is most instructive. During the 1960's, considering the nation's fifteen largest metropolitan areas as a group, absolute employment levels in central cities not only ceased to grow but actually declined. As shown in column 1 of Table 3.2, this was true for nine of the fifteen areas individually, with Detroit making the worst showing. Four central cities barely held their original position in terms of absolute employment figures. Only two (Dallas and Houston) made significant employment gains (but less so than their suburbs). On the other hand, every suburb gained in absolute employment (column 2). As a result, with one minor exception (Pittsburgh), the share of central cities in metropolitan area employment fell significantly.

RECIPES FOR DISASTER AND FOR SANITY

Many economic problems we are considering are not exclusively urban in nature, but they are aggravated by spatial concentration of people and firms. Recall the discussion, in the previous chapter, of the failure of government to perform the crucial tasks assuring a properly working market economy. These tasks number failure to redistribute incomes adequately, failure to establish property rights in all scarce things, failure to demand sufficient amounts of pure public goods, failure to assure full market knowledge and mobility, and failure to maintain price flexibility. It is fairly easy to see why such failures might have more serious social consequences in urban areas than in rural ones. Indeed, given the crisis of function our central cities are now experiencing, one can hardly think of a better recipe for social disaster than these types of governmental failure. By implication, one can also see where the solution must lie.

The concentration of acute poverty in the cities could greatly be alleviated

Table 3.2 **How Jobs Have Shifted to the Suburbs**

Standard Metropolitan Statistical Area	**1960–1970 Percentage Change in Number Employed**		**Central City's Percentage Share in Area Employment**	
	Central City (1)	*Suburbs* (2)	*1960* (3)	*1970* (4)
1. New York	− 9.7	+ 24.9	71.2	64.1
2. Chicago–Gary–Hammond	−13.9	+ 64.4	67.8	52.5
3. Los Angeles–Long Beach	−10.8	+ 16.2	52.2	45.7
4. Philadelphia	−11.3	+ 61.4	63.0	48.2
5. Detroit	−22.5	+ 61.5	56.7	38.6
6. San Francisco–Oakland	+ 0.4	+ 22.7	55.1	50.0
7. Washington, D.C.	+ 1.9	+117.9	63.8	45.1
8. Boston	− 8.6	+ 20.2	44.5	37.8
9. St. Louis	−15.2	+ 80.4	60.7	42.0
10. Pittsburgh	+ 4.4	+ 2.5	36.0	36.3
11. Cleveland	−15.3	+ 82.5	71.7	54.0
12. Baltimore	− 5.6	+ 76.6	65.9	50.1
13. Houston	+49.2	+164.2	84.3	75.6
14. Minneapolis–St. Paul	+ 0.2	+126.2	76.4	58.9
15. Dallas	+37.6	+ 73.5	75.6	71.0
Total	− 6.9	+ 43.6	63.0	52.4

SOURCE: *U.S. Bureau of the Census.*

During the decade of the 1960's, employment in the 15 largest metropolitan areas (here ranked by 1970 employment) rose from 19.1 million to 21.4 million people. But in the central cities it fell from 12.1 million to 11.2 million while rising in the suburbs from 7.1 million to 10.2 million. As a result, the central cities' share of total employment in the metropolitan areas fell from 63 percent to 52.4 percent.

in the long run by the assurance of widespread, voluntary exchange. In particular, this assurance could come by the opening up of equal opportunities in the markets for health services, education, housing, and jobs. Poverty could be alleviated in the short run by a determined redistribution of income from the affluent to the poor.

Similarly, the solution of other urban problems we shall take up requires determined governmental action. The incorrect pricing of transportation services, for instance, might not matter in rural areas where road space is less scarce than in cities. It matters very much in urban areas, where people are tightly packed together in space. Within the framework of a market system, only a correction of the basic problem (which is a false price signal) can get rid of traffic congestion. The lack of definition of property rights in the environment also does not matter in rural areas, where the absorptive capacity of the air or water to receive wastes is larger than the demand for it at a zero price.

Yet in urban areas, where households and firms are concentrated, such abundance is unlikely to exist. So governmental negligence in defining those rights leads to improper price signals and inevitable pollution.

The approach taken in the remainder of this book will be this: No economic system other than the market economy has scored comparable success in creating widespread material well-being. It is therefore undesirable to abandon the whole system for an unproven alternative. This is all the more true because each of the urban economic problems of our day could be solved by nothing more than the determined performance by government of functions that would assure a perfect working of the market economy. Ultimately, the correction of our urban problems will depend on the ability of our political system to generate the necessary government action. Whether this ability can be realized is certainly an important question that economists are not professionally qualified to answer. What economists can do, however, is to point out which alternative courses of action are available to the policy maker and what the likely implications of these alternatives are.

Summary

1. In 1972, there were 263 standard metropolitan statistical areas in the United States. Each contained one central city (or twin cities) with at least 50,000 people. About 70 percent of the U.S. population lived in such areas, but another 5 percent lived in smaller urban areas. The process of urbanization is expected to continue during the rest of this century.
2. The chief characteristic of cities is spatial concentration of people. The dominant reason for such development has often been economic: spatial concentration of the economic activities of many people helps preserve and enlarge the advantages of the division of labor through minimization of transaction costs (those of transportation and communication) among those who specialize.
3. Profit-maximizing firms can be counted on to find the particular optimum location at which the marginal benefit of moving just equals its marginal cost. In some cases, this may mean locating at the source of an important raw material; in others, where customers are; and so on. Most likely, similar firms make similar locational choices. The formation or growth of cities is an inevitable result.
4. The particular location of actual cities bears out this truth. Some are located at the source of raw materials. Others, when the dominant mode of transportation was ships, sprang up along the coast or big rivers. Later the railroads had a similar influence on location. Originally, the technologies of transportation (ships, railroads), of production (waterwheels, steam power), and of communication (personal contact) combined to create advantages to central city locations, which were irresistible to all engaged in economic activities.
5. Once established, a city is likely to pass through a number of growth stages—export specialization, diversification, and maturation. Although any one city

could grow at the expense of other cities, the simultaneous growth of all American cities during the twentieth century has been fed by an unprecedented movement of people from the countryside to urban areas.

6. Recently, however, the economic fortunes of America's central cities have taken a turn for the worse. This can be traced to technological changes in transportation (the rise of the automobile), in production (the assembly line, electric power), and in communications (the telephone, TV, computers). All these changes have created the possibility and the incentive for firms and households to disperse from central city locations. As a result, the central city is in a crisis of function. The former magnetism of central location has greatly weakened.
7. This has given rise to an outmigration of firms and people, but a selective one, notably by businesses in manufacturing and trade and middle- and higher-income white households. On the other hand, firms providing services or requiring face-to-face contact with suppliers or customers, as well as lower-income families, have been left behind or number among those who continue to move into the central city. The lower-income group includes, in disproportionate numbers, blacks, and Spanish-speaking and older white families.
8. For a variety of reasons, these people cannot earn a good living in the central city: there are not enough jobs; they are not suited to do the jobs left behind; and they have difficulty commuting to or moving to the suburbs. So the central cities have become depositories for low-skilled, poor, or old people, who inhabit the ghettos and gray areas and are being frustrated by a permanently depressed economy.
9. The failure of government to perform the functions assuring a properly working market economy has its most serious consequences in urban areas. At the same time, the proper performance of these functions holds out the greatest hope for the solution of urban economic problems.

Terms[3]

diversification stage
export specialization stage
ghetto
gray area
maturation stage
piggyback transport
standard metropolitan statistical area
transaction costs
weight-gaining industry
weight-losing industry

Symbols

C
I
M
SMSA
X
Y
subscripts *B*
G
H

[3] Terms and symbols are defined in the Glossary at the back of the book.

Questions for Review and Discussion

1. "Although there were cities 5,500 years ago, they were small, surrounded by a rural majority of people. Before 1850, no society on earth was urbanized. Even by 1900, only one was (the United Kingdom). Today, all industrial nations are urbanized. In 1970, over a third of the world population lived in cities. In 1990, over half of it will." Can you explain this trend?
2. Considering Figure 3.1, "Megalopolis: Urban Sprawl in the Year 2000," ask yourself this: Should some agency of government take a firm hand and plan future urban growth? If so, how?
3. What do you think determines the location of industries in the country? of barbers within a city?
4. Why, do you think, did the auto industry get its start in Detroit?
5. "Since the level of unemployment varies with the level of aggregate demand, there is a simple way for a city government to reduce poverty. It can just spend more, thereby reducing local unemployment." Evaluate.
6. Using data from Table 3.1, "U.S. Population by Residence and Race," show how nonwhites are more urbanized than whites and how whites are more suburbanized than nonwhites. Can you explain these facts?
7. "Small inventions can have enormous consequences. Many centuries ago, the invention of the horse collar freed the serfs. In this century, the invention of the automobile destroyed the city." Discuss.
8. "Cities are anything but melting pots. Rather, they harbor a number of distinct cultures with different attitudes and value systems, and their differences are strengthened by residential segregation. As a result, there is less chance for harmony than for antagonism and strife." Explain.
9. Why, do you think, do different income, racial, and ethnic groups in cities hold such disparate views on religion, the family, the role of education, and of political authority?
10. Using supply and demand curves, indicate why barriers to the mobility of racial or ethnic minorities that force them to seek jobs in a limited number of occupations only or to seek housing in a limited space only will lower their wages and raise their rents. What would such barriers do to those outside the realm of discrimination?
11. "There is one bright hope for cities: Even though they are losing at least some of their economic reason for being, they can become centers of politics, education, culture, and recreation. This is all the more true since automation continually gives people more leisure time, and they will want to spend it with other people in noneconomic pursuits." Do you agree? Why or why not?
12. Can you think of anything that is likely to revitalize America's central cities? Or should we just throw them away?
13. "City governments are political creatures of state governments. As a consequence, their tax sources are assigned and regulated by the state. If it weren't so, city governments would have no fiscal problem." Evaluate.
14. Mayors have claimed that their attempt to alleviate poverty from local revenues

is likely to increase the incidence of poverty in central cities. Why may this well be true?

15. "It is doubtful that anything but a complete reform of the political system will ever solve our urban economic problems." Discuss.

Selected Readings

Edel, Matthew, and Rothenberg, Jerome. *Readings in Urban Economics.* New York: Macmillan, 1972. Part 1 presents readings on location theory and metropolitan growth, Part 2 on intraurban location and land use. Excellent lists of important writings in these fields are also given.

Fusfeld, Daniel R. *Economics.* Lexington, Mass.: D. C. Heath and Co., 1972. Ch. 42 discusses the economics of cities.

Gordon, David M. *Problems in Political Economy: An Urban Perspective.* Lexington, Mass.: D. C. Heath and Co., 1971. Pp. 1–56. Presents different views (conservative, liberal, radical) about the role government should play with respect to urban problems.

Hirsch, Werner Z. *Urban Economic Analysis.* New York: McGraw-Hill, 1973. Chs. 1, 2, and 6–9. Presents intermediate to advanced analysis of urban problems; both microeconomic and macroeconomic tools are presented and applied (for example, in dealing with the spatial characteristics of markets or the process of urbanization).

Thompson, Wilbur R. *A Preface to Urban Economics.* Baltimore: Johns Hopkins Press, 1968. Part 1. Discusses the urban economy in great detail, including determinants, processes, and stages of growth and patterns of economic instability.

Ullman, Edward L., and Dacey, Michael F. "The Minimum Requirements Approach to the Urban Economic Base." *Papers and Proceedings of the Regional Science Association,* 1960. Discusses the relationship between export demand and city employment and how it varies with city size.

U.S. Bureau of the Census. *Statistical Abstract of the United States, 1972.* Washington, D.C., 1972. Lists some statistics on the location and migration of population and businesses (Sections 1 and 33) and—more important—sources to other statistics: Note the listing of statistical abstract supplements (p. v); and the guide to general sources of statistics (pp. 910–12, 936–37, 942–43), to recent censuses (pp. 955–59), and to state statistical abstracts (pp. 961–64). Suggestion: Look at the detailed census data for your hometown and assemble a statistical portrait of its population and businesses and of recent trends in numbers and composition of people and jobs.

NOTE: The *Journal of Economic Literature* lists recent articles on U.S. economic history (section 042), industry studies (630–35), population, labor force, and jobs (800–50), and the urban economy (931).

The *Index of Economic Articles* in sections beginning with the indicated numbers catalogs articles on location theory (2.1337, 2.15), economic history (5.4), industry studies (15.5), regional economics (22.2), industrial dispersion (22.23), and population size, composition, and migration (16.3, 18).

Part Two
Matters of Equity

We live in a world of scarcity. Not everyone can have all the goods he wants. No wonder that people end up "fighting over the pie." Each person knows that he can get a larger share of goods by holding on to what he has and by trying to get more at someone else's expense. But how much *should* each person get? That is what the equity question is all about. In this part of the book, we deal with issues that predominantly concern matters of equity. We deal, that is, with poverty and a number of policies that would, if undertaken, have their most significant impact on the way goods are shared among people. These are policies concerning a redistribution of wealth; concerning health care, education, and employment; and concerning income transfers, either through government or through private activities that can be charitable or criminal in nature.

4 The Dimensions of Poverty

Judged by his income, the average American is exceedingly rich compared with the overwhelming majority of mankind. And he is becoming richer all the time.[1] The 1970 median money income of families of two or more persons was $9,867. In terms of 1970 dollars, the median money income had been only $5,269 as recently as 1947. This picture, however, is easily misleading. Not every American is an average American. Not every American enjoys a money income close to the median that would enable him to buy a large share of the goods produced each year. Whether we look at Americans individually or by family groupings, the income of many is considerably below the national median, and these people are poor. Many others are considerably better off than the national median suggests. The national median only tells us that in 1970 half of *all* American families earned at least $9,867 (and another half earned less). But now consider particular types of American families. In the same year of 1970, half of all black families earned less than $6,279, and half of all female-headed families earned less than $5,093. On the other hand, half of all white families earned at least $10,236, and half of all male-headed families (with working wives) earned at least $12,276. Even within these groupings the incidence of poverty or luxury was highly uneven, varying with such factors, often interrelated, as place of residence, years of schooling completed, age and work experience, and occupation.

Wherever one looks, one finds inequalities. In terms of income, people on farms and in small towns are generally worse off than residents of other areas. People in central cities are generally worse off than residents of the suburbs. And within any area, nonwhites are generally worse off than whites, females worse off than males, the uneducated worse off than the educated, and the young and old worse off than those of middle age.

THE LORENZ CURVE

A simple device, the *Lorenz curve*, gives us an immediate picture of the extent of income inequality within any group of people. Let us look at all American

[1] Most of the statistical data used throughout this chapter come from U.S. Bureau of the Census, *Current Population Reports*, Series P-60.

households as a group, including among them unattached individuals, as well as families of two or more persons. We draw a square, as in Figure 4.1, measuring percentage of total money income received on the vertical axis and the percentage of households on the horizontal axis. Households are arranged from left to right from the one with the lowest to the one with the highest income.

Perfect Equality

Now imagine drawing a straight line from the bottom left corner at O to the top right corner at e. This line could be called the *line of perfect equality*. You can easily see why. If all households in a country shared total income equally, it would be true that 20 percent of the households shared 20 percent of total income (we would be at *a*), that 40 percent of all households shared 40 percent of total income (we would be at *b*), and so on, until 100 percent of all households shared 100 percent of total income (at e).

Figure 4.1 **The Lorenz Curve**

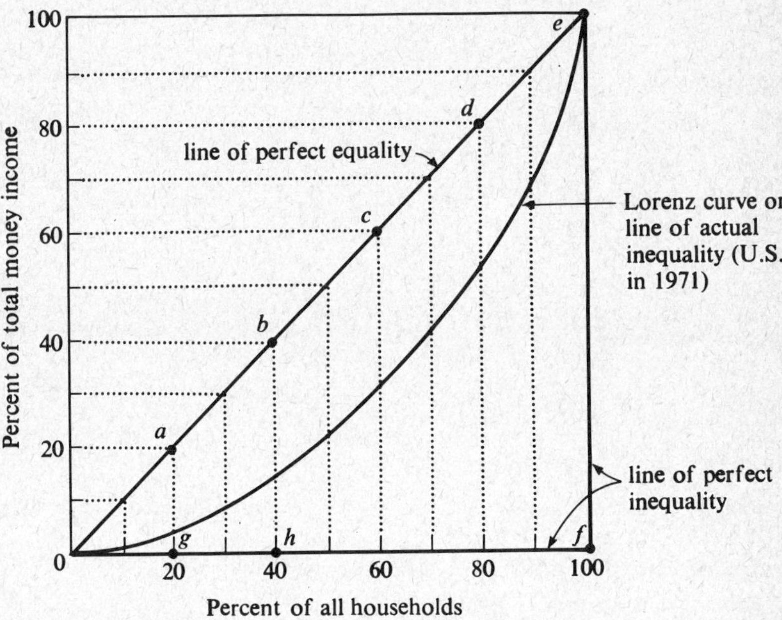

SOURCE: *Table 4.1, columns 4 and 5.*

The Lorenz curve is a graphical representation of the extent of income inequality within any group of people, such as all households in a country. If all shared money income equally, any given percentage of households would share the same percentage of total money income. If inequality exists, the 10, 20, 30, 40, etc. percent lowest-income households will share less than 10, 20, 30, 40, etc. percent of income.

Perfect Inequality

Imagine, at the other extreme, that one household received all the income, whereas all the others received none of it. If we arranged the households on the horizontal axis as before on the basis of income, we should find that the poorest 20 percent of all households received 0 percent of total income (we should be at *g* rather than at *a*), that the poorest 40 percent of all households similarly shared 0 percent of total income (we should be at *h* rather than *b*), and so on. Even 99 percent of all households would still share 0 percent of total income (we should be just a little bit to the left of *f* rather than to the left and below *e*). Yet when we considered *all* households, including the one having all the income, we should find that 100 percent of households had 100 percent of income (we should be at *e*). Thus, we could call the line *Ofe* a *line of perfect inequality*.

Actual Inequality

As you might expect, reality is somewhere in between these two extremes. Money income in the United States is distributed neither perfectly equally (as would be pictured by the line of perfect equality) nor perfectly unequally (as shown by the line of perfect inequality). If we arrange all households in ascending order, starting with the one with the lowest annual money income and going to the one with the highest, we get Table 4.1, "The Distribution of Money Income in the United States, 1971." In 1971, there were 69.6 million households in the United States, if we add 16.3 million unattached individuals to 53.3 million families of two or more persons. These households received a total of $861 billion of personal income. This refers to wages, rents, interest, dividends, unincorporated business profits, and transfer payments, all before personal income taxes. Most of this personal income was received in the form of money, and we now look at its distribution. The 2.4 percent of the poorest households (referring to income), as column 2 tells us, received only 0.1 percent of total income—column 3. Under perfect equality, they should have received 2.4 percent of the total. They all received less than $1,500 in that year. Next come households receiving between $1,500 and $1,999 annually. They comprised another 1.6 percent of the total number of households and received only 0.3 percent of total income. And so it goes. You can easily interpret the remainder of columns 1 to 3.

We can, however, also calculate from this information the data needed to draw the *line of actual inequality* for the United States in 1971. For this purpose, we have added cumulatively in columns 4 and 5, respectively, the data of columns 2 and 3. If the 2.4 percent poorest households received 0.1 percent of total income—row 1, columns 2 and 3—and if the 1.6 percent next poorest received 0.3 percent—row 2, columns 2 and 3—then $2.4 + 1.6 = 4.0$ percent of poorest households must have received $0.1 + 0.3 = 0.4$ percent of total income. This is shown in row 2, columns 4 and 5. Thus, the data of columns 4 and 5 are exactly the ones needed to draw the Lorenz curve. These data are plotted

Table 4.1 The Distribution of Money Income in the United States, 1971

Income Class (1)	Percent of Households in Class[a] (2)	Percent of Total Income Received by Households in Class (3)	Percent of Households in Class or Lower Ones (4)	Percent of Total Income Received by Households in Class or Lower Ones (5)
Under $1,500	2.4	0.1	2.4	0.1
$1,500–$1,999	1.6	0.3	4.0	0.4
$2,000–$2,499	2.0	0.4	6.0	0.8
$2,500–$2,999	2.2	0.5	8.2	1.3
$3,000–$3,499	2.5	0.7	10.7	2.0
$3,500–$3,999	2.3	0.7	13.0	2.7
$4,000–$4,999	5.4	2.1	18.4	4.8
$5,000–$5,999	5.7	2.7	24.1	7.5
$6,000–$6,999	5.6	3.1	29.7	10.6
$7,000–$7,999	6.2	4.0	35.9	14.6
$8,000–$8,999	6.0	4.4	41.9	19.0
$9,000–$9,999	6.3	5.1	48.2	24.1
$10,000–$11,999	12.6	11.8	60.8	35.9
$12,000–$14,999	14.4	16.6	75.2	52.5
$15,000–$24,999	19.5	31.2	94.7	83.7
$25,000 and over	5.3	16.3	100.0	100.0

[a] A household is two or more persons living in the same dwelling unit and related to one another by blood, marriage, or adoption or a single person (other than an inmate in an institution) unrelated to the other occupants in the dwelling unit or living alone.

SOURCE: *U.S. Bureau of the Census*, Current Population Reports, *Series P-60.*

in Figure 4.1, "The Lorenz Curve." Like a loose string fastened to points O and e, this line hanging below the line of perfect equality (Oe) and above that of perfect inequality (*Ofe*) provides a visual representation of actual income inequality in the United States. Any increase in equality would shift it toward Oe, any decrease toward *Ofe*. In fact, federal personal income taxes in the United States have the effect of reducing after-tax income inequality somewhat, although not appreciably so.

INCOME INEQUALITY VS. POVERTY

Incomes can be very unequal, yet there may not be any poverty. If with present price conditions and the size of American households today, the American household with the lowest income received $10,000 a year, and many other households many times that amount, we could hardly call anybody poor, although there would be inequality. Columns 1 and 4 of Table 4.1 show us, however, that 10.7

percent of all American households—almost 7.5 million—received less than $3,500 in 1971. Most people would agree that these households were poor (unless they owned large assets on which to live). Many people would go further and argue that "one should do something about poverty." In his 1964 State of the Union Message, President Johnson committed the nation to a war on poverty. The Congress, in passing the 1964 Economic Opportunity Act, made it "the policy of the United States to eliminate the paradox of poverty in the midst of plenty." The issue has remained before the public ever since.

Defining Poverty

It is difficult to define what is to be meant by poverty, and not everybody will agree with any definition chosen. Yet such a definition is needed if we are to measure the extent of poverty. This certainly is a prerequisite for abolishing it. There is considerable disagreement over whether poverty should be defined on a relative or an absolute basis. An *absolute* definition of poverty specifies a certain dollar household income as the poverty line without regard to the actual distribution of income among households. For example, if the specified figure were $3,500 a year, any household earning less than $3,500 would be regarded as poor, all others as nonpoor. This would be so regardless of what size incomes were earned by people not poor. The *relative* definition of poverty, on the other hand, stresses a poverty line that stands in a specified relation to above-poverty incomes. It might say, for instance, that all households earning less than 80 percent of the median household income in the country are poor, regardless of how high this figure is. If the median income were $10,000 a year, the poverty line would be $8,000; if the median were $20,000, the poverty line would be $16,000, and so on.

The U.S. government counts the poor with the help of an absolute definition. This involves figuring out some minimum annual dollar amount needed by a household and comparing such a figure with the dollars available to that household. However, this is easier said than done.

The meaning of "need." What things are to be included when one considers a household's "needs"? If one were to include all the household's wants, the total of needs could never be satisfied. One is tempted to classify some wants as "true needs" and others as "luxuries," and to go about it "scientifically," establishing first a minimum adequate diet required to keep a person alive. For a moderately active man, such diet may involve the annual consumption of the following:[2]

370 pounds of wheat flour
57 cans of evaporated milk

[2] This interesting piece of information is taken from George J. Stigler, "The Cost of Subsistence," *Journal of Farm Economics*, May 1945, pp. 303–14. This diet contains the optimum amounts of calories, protein, minerals, and vitamins established by the National Research Council. Thus it is a physiological minimum and leaves out of account such "luxuries" as variety and palatability of diet.

111 pounds of cabbage
23 pounds of spinach
285 pounds of dried navy beans

One might then proceed to evaluate this minimum adequate diet. At Amherst, Massachusetts, in March 1973, it cost $140.86 to purchase the above quantities. The average American household—in 1971 almost three persons—might, therefore, "need" $423 for food annually. Experience shows that households typically have to devote at least twice as much money to other purchases besides food, such as clothing and shelter. Thus one might triple the figure, giving a minimum necessary spending of $1,269 per year per average household. Any household of average size having this dollar amount or less available may then be called poor. Over time, the figure may have to be adjusted with changes in prices and attitudes. For instance, the meaning of *need* is bound to change. Luxuries of today have a habit of becoming the needs of tomorrow.

Available means. The dollars available to a household will, however, also be a difficult figure to establish. Surely this figure should include earned money income, such as wages, rent, interest, and profits. It should also include money transfers that are not received in return for services currently rendered, such as pensions, unemployment relief, and welfare payments. But what about a household's access to credit? What about assets in its possession?

A household with no money income at all but a million dollars of bank accounts, stocks, bonds, and real estate and ample opportunity to borrow can hardly be called poor compared with one with an annual income of $1,000 and none of the former's advantages. Unfortunately, data on assets and credit availability are hard to come by, and most estimates of poverty in the United States are based on comparisons of household money income alone.

The U.S. definition. During the early 1960's, the U.S. government listed all families with a money income below $3,000 per year as poor, all others were counted as above the *poverty line.* The $3,000 figure was calculated to assure a family's minimum need in the way of food, clothing, medical care, and shelter, the latter including such "luxuries" as heat, a refrigerator, cold and hot water, an indoor flush toilet, a bed for every person, electric lighting, and enough furnishings to have a common meal. The government's argument was similar to ours. In 1959, argued the Department of Agriculture, a minimum nutritional meal cost 22.8 cents per person.[3] With the average family size known to be 3.65 persons per family, a bare daily minimum of food was considered to cost about $2.50, or somewhat below $1,000 per year per average family. This figure was then tripled.

[3] For more recent estimates of the minimum price of nutritionally good diets as defined by the U.S. Agricultural Research Service consult U.S. Bureau of the Census, *Statistical Abstract of the United States: 1972*, p. 85. The same source (p. 350) also lists estimates of complete budgets for urban and other families compiled by the U.S. Bureau of Labor Statistics.

According to Table 4.1, "The Distribution of Money Income in the United States, 1971," this definition of poverty, when applied to families and unrelated individuals in 1971, would place about 8 percent of American households, or almost 6 million of them, below the poverty line. These were the households who received money income below $3,000 in 1971 and who together shared 1.3 percent of total income. Notice, however, how inadequate this kind of figure is bound to be.

First, increases in prices since 1959 have by now eroded the purchasing power of the $3,000 annual figure.

Second, as we have already pointed out, household asset holdings are neglected. To the extent that some of these households have large assets, they should not be classified as poor. This may be especially true for some of the older people. It has been estimated that the measured incidence of poverty among the old would fall by a third were we to count their ability to draw on their assets. But the incidence of measured poverty among all people may fall by only 3 percent when we take assets into account.

Third, concentration on annual income alone may cause distortions if incomes fluctuate. A family having a temporary $1,000 income will be classified as poor, even though it has had $25,000 for years before, similar high prospects for the future, and easy credit access. There is considerable turnover among the poor. Only 69 percent of the poor in 1963 were poor in 1962. The U.S. Department of Commerce has suggested for this reason that the average income for two years be used for the purposes of establishing the incidence of poverty.

Fourth, much income in kind is left out of consideration. Some households may grow large amounts of fruits and vegetables on their own land, receive milk, butter, cheese, and eggs from their animals, and live in a house to which they hold clear title. Their cash needs are lessened by the value of such income in kind. If they receive cash income of $2,900 in addition to income in kind, we might not want to classify such households as poor along with others less fortunate. This is especially important for urban vs. rural comparisons, and also for regional comparisons. (Any household in Southern California needs less cash for heating than any household in Maine.)

Fifth, the $3,000 criterion doesn't account for the actual circumstances of different households. Old people may need less food (hence cash) than young ones; sick people may need more cash (for drugs) than others; and a family of twelve has greater needs than a family of three. The latter point is likely to lead to especially bizarre cases. A single person with $2,900 a year of money income will be poor, but a family with *any* number of children and $3,100 a year will be above the poverty line. Unless other factors mentioned above make up for it, this would hardly satisfy our sense of reasonableness.

To overcome these difficulties the government has used a more sophisticated definition of poverty in recent years. The Social Security Administration (SSA) in 1964 defined, and the Federal Interagency Committee in 1969 redefined, poverty income lines for over 100 household types with different required cash needs for each. This accounts for differences in income in kind, family size, sex and age of head, but not yet for asset holdings and temporary income fluctuations.

The SSA also has defined a somewhat higher income line for the near-poor. It is one-quarter higher than the poverty line. That is, if you are at or below the poverty income line, you are classified as poor. If you are above it, but at or below the near-poverty line, you are near-poor. Table 4.2, "Poverty Income Lines, 1971," shows some of the definitional limits used in 1971. These limits are adjusted annually with changes in the consumer price index.

Counting the Poor

Once poverty is defined, the poor can be counted. This is not so difficult, for the U.S. constitution requires that a population census be taken every ten years to allocate among the states the seats in the House of Representatives in proportion to the states' populations. The census takers attempt to reach every American during the census. The census yields detailed information as to who is poor by the official definition and how many poor there are. In between, other methods are used to estimate the numbers involved. Figure 4.2, "Number of Poor Persons and Incidence of Poverty," gives the available postwar data for the United States. The top line shows the number of poor persons (not of households); refer to the left-hand scale. As you can see, the number has declined from 43 million in 1947 to 24.2 million in 1970. Then, in 1971, a nine-year downward trend was reversed, and the number of poor persons rose to 25.6 million by 1972. The broken lower line refers to the percentage of poor

Table 4.2 Poverty Income Lines, 1971

	Poverty Income Line			
	Nonfarm Residence		Farm Residence	
Household Characteristics[a]	*Male Head*	*Female Head*	*Male Head*	*Female Head*
1 member	$2,136	$1,978	$1,783	$1,669
Under 65 years	2,181	2,017	1,853	1,715
65 years and over	1,959	1,934	1,666	1,643
2 members	2,641	2,581	2,224	2,130
Head under 65 years	2,731	2,635	2,322	2,195
Head 65 years and over	2,450	2,437	2,081	2,089
3 members	3,246	3,127	2,749	2,627
4 members	4,139	4,116	3,528	3,513
5 members	4,884	4,837	4,159	4,148
6 members	5,492	5,460	4,689	4,656
7 members or more	6,771	6,583	5,749	5,516

[a] Households are defined here as the total of families and unrelated individuals.

SOURCE: *U.S. Bureau of the Census,* Current Population Reports, *Series P-60.*

Figure 4.2 **Number of Poor Persons and Incidence of Poverty**

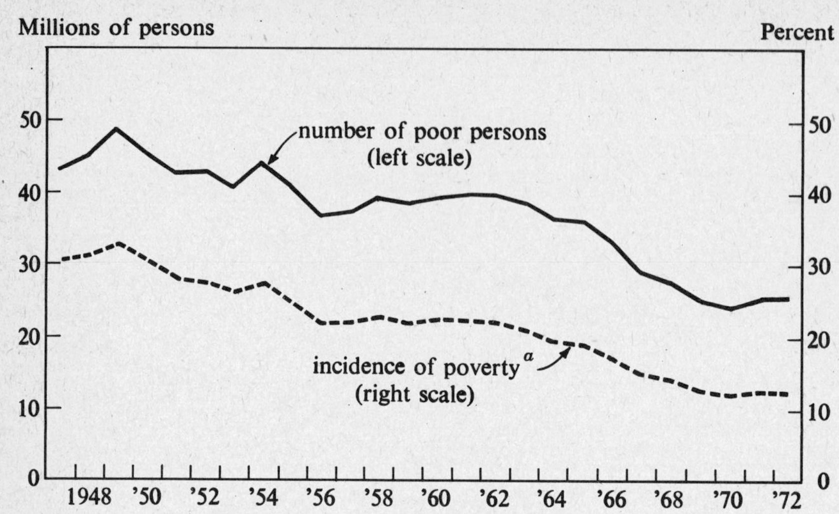

[a] Poor persons as percentage of total noninstitutional population.
NOTE: Poverty is defined by the Social Security Administration poverty-income standard.
SOURCE: *U.S. Bureau of the Census,* Current Population Reports, *Series P-60.*

Except for periods of recession (1954, the late 1950's, the early 1970's), the occurrence of poverty in the United States has been declining since 1949.

persons in the population; refer to the right-hand scale. This percentage has also declined, from 30 in 1947 to 12.2 in 1970, but it rose to 12.5 by 1972. Clearly, percentage figures are much more revealing of the seriousness of the problem than absolute numbers are. Even so, overall figures never tell the whole story. From 1960 to 1972, for instance, the numbers and percentage of poor in *metropolitan* areas declined much less (by 2 million, or 14 percent) than in all areas (by 13 million, or 34 percent). At the same time, poverty among urban whites declined more than among urban nonwhites, and while that among urban male-headed families declined, that among urban female-headed ones actually rose. It pays to look at the detail.

Who Are the Poor?

Indeed, census data do give us more than totals. Consider the overall picture first. In early 1972, some 25.6 million of all Americans were poor. Some 383,000 of these were Orientals, American Indians or Eskimos; all others were white or black. Table 4.3, "Selected Characteristics of Poor Persons in the United States, 1972," presents selected data on the 25.2 million whites and blacks classified as poor. These data go a long way in suggesting the reasons for the poverty of these people. Consider the first row of the table. Note how

Table 4.3 Selected Characteristics of Poor Persons in the United States, 1972

Characteristic	Number in 1,000's Whites	Blacks	Percentage of All White and Black Poor Persons
Under 14 years of age	5,177	3,046	32.7
Age 14 and above	12,603	4,350	67.3
employed part time only	3,630	1,445	20.1
keeping house	3,444	785	16.8
ill or disabled	1,569	718	9.1
going to school	1,071	706	7.1
employed full time[a]	1,330	405	6.9
retired	1,155	112	5.0
unemployed year-round	220	113	1.3
other	184	66	1.0
All ages	17,780	7,396	100.0

[a] Includes 82 thousand young males in the armed forces.

SOURCE: *U.S. Bureau of the Census,* Current Population Reports, *Series P-60.*

almost a third of all poor persons were children under 14 years of age. They certainly had no control over their poverty status. Then consider the composition of the remaining two-thirds of poor persons, all aged 14 and above. About 20 percent of all poor persons were at least 14 years of age and could only find part-time work. In fact, 60 percent of this group worked part time for fewer than 27 weeks in the year, the other 40 percent worked part time anywhere between 27 and 52 weeks.

Another 17 percent of all poor persons—all female—were at least 14 years of age and stayed home keeping house. Of these women, 36 percent were 65 years of age or older. Undoubtedly, a large percentage of the 64 percent younger women in this group were tied down with small children.

We note next that 9 percent of all poor persons were at least 14 years of age and either ill or disabled. Some 46 percent of this group were 65 years of age or older.

Slightly over 7 percent of all poor persons were at least 14 years old and still going to school. Over 93 percent of this group were under 22 years of age. Another 7 percent of all poor persons were at least 14 years old and fully employed during the entire year. Yet their pay was so low as to keep them below the poverty line.

Of the remaining poor who were 14 years old or over, 5 percent were retired (and almost 99 percent of these were 65 years or older), 1.3 percent could not find any work (although they looked for it), and 1 percent could not be classified in any of the groups listed so far.

Another way of looking at the data involves noting the *incidence of poverty*, that is, the percentage of persons that were poor in a group with otherwise common characteristics. As we noted, some 25.6 million of all Americans were poor in early 1972. Since there were some 204.5 million Americans, one can also state that 12.5 percent of all Americans were poor. It is most revealing to go beyond absolute numbers and to consider the incidence of poverty for smaller groups of Americans. This shows whether these smaller groups were hit by poverty in greater or smaller proportion than all Americans as a group. In this case, any subgroup of Americans of whom more (or fewer) than 12.5 percent were poor in 1972 could be said to have been affected by poverty more (or less) than proportionately.

For instance, in early 1972, 69.6 percent of all poor persons in the United States were white, but a larger percentage of all Americans—whether poor or not—was white. Hence the incidence of poverty among white Americans was only 9.9 percent—less than the overall incidence of 12.5 percent. This is noted in the first and last rows of Table 4.4, "The Incidence of Poverty for Selected Groups in the United States, 1972."

Table 4.4 The Incidence of Poverty for Selected Groups in the United States, 1972

Group	Poor Persons in Group as Percentage of All Poor Persons (1)	Incidence = Percentage in Group Who Were Poor (2)
White Americans, all ages	69.6	9.9
under age 14	20.3	11.6
males, age 14–21	4.8	9.3
females, age 14–21	5.6	10.8
males, age 22–64	9.9	5.7
females, age 22–64	14.9	8.2
males, age 65 and over	4.1	13.8
females, age 65 and over	10.0	24.3
Black Americans, all ages	28.9	32.5
under age 14	11.9	41.8
males, age 14–21	2.4	32.5
females, age 14–21	2.8	34.7
males, age 22–64	2.9	16.6
females, age 22–64	6.5	30.3
males, age 65 and over	0.9	33.5
females, age 65 and over	1.6	43.7
Other Americans, all ages	1.5	16.1
All Americans	100.0	12.5

SOURCE: *U.S. Bureau of the Census,* Current Population Reports, *Series P-60.*

We note similarly in column 2 how the incidence of poverty was more than proportionate to their numbers for blacks (32.5 percent) and for members of other nonwhite races (16.1 percent). Incidentally, the incidence of poverty among Spanish-Americans who made up 9.2 percent of the poor and are, of course, included among the whites in Table 4.4—was 25.6 percent.

It is easy to interpret the remainder of Table 4.4. In 1972, poverty hit disproportionately all nonwhites, regardless of age, and the aged among whites. Most severely affected were black women aged 65 and over; least affected were white men, aged 22 to 64. Within any age group, females were affected more than males; within any racial group, the young and old more than those of middle age.

Who Are the Urban Poor?

We also have data on the geographic distribution of the poor. They show us that in 1972 poverty was by no means an urban phenomenon exclusively. Only 57 percent of all poor persons lived in metropolitan areas, while 43 percent lived in small towns and rural areas.

However, rural poverty, being spread out, is more easily hidden. Urban poverty, being concentrated, is easier to see. Since only 57 percent of all poor persons lived in metropolitan areas, while a much larger percentage of all persons lived there, the incidence of poverty was somewhat less in metropolitan areas (10.4 percent) than in nonmetropolitan areas (17.1 percent). However, metropolitan areas contain central cities as well as suburbs. The incidence of poverty was much less in the suburbs (7.2 percent) than in the central cities (14.2 percent). In both places, it was much less for whites (6.3 percent in suburbs, 10.6 percent in central cities) than for blacks (23.8 vs. 27.9 percent). These figures reflect the distribution of the population: only 22 percent of all poor persons (26 percent of whites and 13 percent of blacks) lived in suburban areas, while 38 percent of the total of all persons lived there. At the same time, 34 percent of all poor persons lived in central cities (29 percent of the white poor and 49 percent of the black poor), while 30 percent of the total of all persons lived there.

Table 4.5, "Selected Data on Poor Persons in United States Metropolitan Areas, 1972," provides some further detail that allows us to speculate on the causes of urban poverty. Note in column 3 how 37.5 percent of the urban poor were children under 16 years of age. What can we say about the urban poor aged 16 and above? Another 16.4 percent of the urban poor—not explicitly shown but listed among the remaining household heads or family members in the table—were 65 years of age or older. Most likely, poverty came to them as a result of ill health, age, and retirement from jobs. Still another 10.5 percent of the urban poor were household heads working full-time year-round and remaining poor, nevertheless.

Many of the reasons for poverty cited in Table 4.3, "Selected Characteristics of Poor Persons in the United States, 1972," undoubtedly apply to the

Table 4.5 Selected Data on Poor Persons in United States Metropolitan Areas, 1972

Characteristic	Number in 1,000's Whites (1)	Blacks (2)	Percentage of All Metropolitan Area White and Black Poor Persons (3)
Central city poor residents			
Under 16 years of age	1,670	1,670	23.2
Age 16 and above	3,508	1,942	37.9
male household heads	1,031	416	10.1
female household heads	1,592	899	17.3
others	885	627	10.5
Suburban poor residents			
Under 16 years of age	1,589	470	14.3
Age 16 and above	3,031	504	24.6
male household heads	875	133	7.0
female household heads	1,182	172	9.4
others	974	199	8.2
All metropolitan area poor residents	9,798	4,586	100.0

Source: *U.S. Bureau of the Census,* Current Population Reports, *Series P-60.*

remaining 36 percent: Some must have been mothers tied down with children. (There were 3.1 million children under 16 in poor urban female-headed households.) Some must have been going to school. Some must have been ill, disabled, or unable to find full-time work.

Data on the incidence of poverty among urban groups are even more revealing. Table 4.6, "The Incidence of Poverty for Selected Urban Groups in the United States, 1972," speaks for itself. As was true for the United States as a whole, the incidence of poverty in urban areas was higher for blacks than for whites, higher for females than for males, higher for the aged than for all persons. Most severely hit were persons in households headed by black females, least affected those in families headed by white males.

ON ELIMINATING POVERTY

Before we can reasonably entertain various proposed methods for eliminating poverty, it is worth while to pause and look at the big picture. Whatever method one may eventually choose, can it succeed? Can we lift everyone out of poverty *at the same time?* Or can we only make the poor rich by making the rich poor? Is poverty perhaps inevitable, at least for some people? If "the

Table 4.6 **The Incidence of Poverty for Selected Urban Groups in the United States, 1972**

Group	Incidence = Percentage in Group Who Were Poor: Whites		Blacks
Central city residents			
all persons	10.6	14.2	27.9
persons in male-headed families	5.5		12.5
persons in female-headed families	30.7		51.7
unattached males	20.1		33.0
unattached females	31.6		48.3
all persons 65 years and over	17.3		30.5
Suburban residents			
all persons	6.3	7.2	23.8
persons in male-headed families	3.6		12.6
persons in female-headed families	24.7		54.6
unattached males	15.0		37.1
unattached females	30.3		54.9
all persons 65 years and over	15.1		39.3
All metropolitan residents	8.0	10.4	26.9

SOURCE: *U.S. Bureau of the Census,* Current Population Reports, *Series P-60.*

poor are always with us," isn't it useless to try to do anything about poverty? Throughout history, some people have considered certain groups in the population as doomed to poverty.

However, more often than not, history has proved them wrong. In the United States at least, the incidence of poverty has declined remarkably. This trend was illustrated by the broken line in Figure 4.2, "Number of Poor Persons and Incidence of Poverty." Poverty in the United States is not inevitable; this is true for particular groups of people, and also for the population as a whole. Poverty in the United States could be eliminated if we cared to do so. This happens to be a lucky circumstance. It is certainly not a statement one could make about every country in the world. Even if the total income of China or India were distributed with absolute equality, poverty could not be eliminated. Even if all of their GNP consisted of consumer goods (as it does not), an absolutely equal distribution would give goods less than $100-worth to each person per year. Quite the contrary holds for the United States. Take 1972. Even if we left the major divisions of GNP untouched (22 percent for government, 16 percent for investment, 62 percent for consumption), we should be left with $721.1 billion of consumer goods, or $3,454-worth per person. For the average household, there was over $10,000 of consumer goods available.

Thus, it would have been possible to redistribute consumer goods from the rich to the poor so that no family or individual remained below the poverty line. This shows that something *can* be done about poverty. Whether it *should* be done (and if so, by what method) is another question and one each person must decide for himself. However, we can narrow down the choices by considering a number of alternative ways of attacking poverty. This is done in the remaining chapters of Part Two.

Summary

1. Although the average American is rich compared with most individuals of other countries, not every American is an average American. Incomes in the United States are unequally distributed.
2. The extent of inequality can be measured by the Lorenz curve. In recent years in the United States, the 25 percent lowest-income households received only 8 percent of total income, but the 25 percent highest-income households received 48 percent of total income.
3. Income inequality does not necessarily imply poverty. However, there is general agreement that poverty exists in the United States. The U.S. Congress has pledged to "eliminate the paradox of poverty in the midst of plenty."
4. It is difficult to agree on the meaning of poverty, because it involves a comparison of two slippery concepts, "needs" and "means." The U.S. government originally used a family income of $3,000 a year as the "poverty line." In recent years, a more sophisticated definition has been in use, taking account of different cash needs for different household types. This definition placed 25.6 million Americans (12.5 percent of the population) below the poverty line in 1972.
5. Over the long run (since 1949), poverty in the United States has declined. There have been reverses during recessions, however.
6. A detailed look at statistics on poor persons in 1972 shows that about a third of them were children under 14 years of age. Twenty-seven percent of the poor were working, but frequently only part-time. The remaining poor did not work, being tied down with small children, sickness or disability, going to school, and being retired or unemployed. The incidence of poverty fell disproportionately on nonwhites and, among whites, on the aged and Spanish-Americans. Within any group, females were affected more than males; the young and old more than those of middle age.
7. Statistics on poor persons in 1972 also show this: 57 percent of all the poor lived in metropolitan areas. The incidence of poverty in these areas as a whole was smaller than the national average, but it was much smaller in the suburbs and larger in the central cities. In any place, it was smaller for whites than for nonwhites, for males than for females, and for middle-aged than for young or old persons. Thus urban poverty statistics confirm the country-wide evidence: The chances of being poor are greatest for nonwhites, females, children, and the aged.

8. In the United States at least, poverty is not inevitable. This is so because per capita GNP is so high. A more equal sharing of income could bring everyone above the poverty line at the same time.

Terms[4]

absolute definition of poverty
incidence of poverty
line of actual inequality
line of perfect equality
line of perfect inequality
Lorenz curve
poverty line
relative definition of poverty
transfer payments

Questions for Review and Discussion

1. Take the data on the next page for 1935–36 U.S. households and draw a Lorenz curve in the graph. Was income distribution more unequal or less unequal in 1935–36 than in 1971? (HINT: Redraw the 1971 line on the same graph, using the data of Table 4.1.)
2. Draw a Lorenz curve for the world as a whole using the following 1965 data:

Percentage of World's Population	*Percentage of World's GNP*
55	9
65	13
71	18
86	42
100	100

   Using the U.S. 1971 data given in the text for comparison, determine where income distribution is more unequal, in the U.S. or in the world as a whole?
3. "If we were to draw a Lorenz curve for different occupations, we should find the curve for lawyers out further from the line of perfect equality than that for doctors. That for doctors, in turn, would be out further than that for college teachers, and that for college teachers out further than that for army officers." Try to explain.
4. "The Lorenz curve has to be interpreted with caution. Just imagine how it would look in any one year in a society in which everyone's *lifetime* income was absolutely equal, while the income of the young and old always was much lower than that of middle-aged people." Explain.

[4] Terms are defined in the Glossary at the back of the book.

Income Class	*Percentage of Households in Class*	*Percentage of Total Money Income Received by Households in Class*
Under $2,000	77.7	45.4
$2,000–$2,999	13.1	19.5
$3,000–$3,999	4.4	9.2
$4,000–$4,999	1.7	4.5
$5,000–$7,499	1.6	5.8
$7,500–$9,999	0.6	3.2
$10,000 and over	0.9	12.4

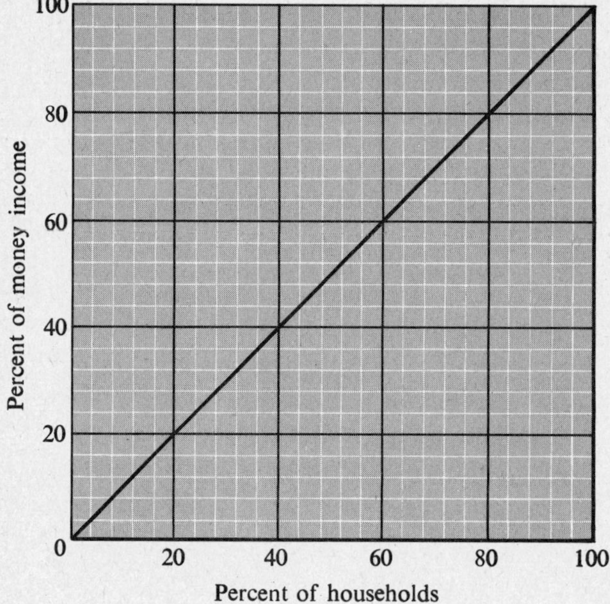

5. Do you think an impecunious graduate student who soon will earn $25,000 a year from medical practice should be counted as poor? Justify your answer.
6. Define *poverty*. Would it have been defined in the same way in 1920? Why or why not?
7. Take a look at Table 4.2, "Poverty Income Lines, 1971." Using the definitions shown there, consider your family and all your acquaintances. Are any of them poor? On the basis of your determinations, do you consider the definition reasonable? Why or why not?
8. "Consider Figure 4.2, 'Poverty Income Lines, 1971.' Compared with the national median income (over $10,000 for all households) the poverty lines are drawn ridiculously low. They should be set equal to the median." Discuss.

9. Between 1947 and 1970, the median income of nonwhite families, as a percentage of the median income of white families, grew from 51.1 percent to 61.3 percent. Yet the absolute difference in the median incomes also grew, from $1,543 to $3,957. Have nonwhites become better or worse off?
10. "Since 70 percent of poor American families in 1972 were white, it is absurd to argue that poverty hits the nonwhite more." Evaluate.
11. If slightly *more* than half of all poor persons lived in metropolitan areas in 1972, how can the incidence of poverty in these areas have been *less* than the national average?
12. "There is one sure way to eliminate poverty: giving jobs to all the poor." Using data presented in this chapter, show why this statement is *false*.
13. "The U.S. experience shows clearly that poverty in this world can be eliminated by nothing else but a proper redistribution of income." Discuss.
14. MR. A: An equal distribution of income is only fair.
    MR. B: It would be a catastrophe. Nor would it be fair.
    Discuss.
15. If you think that our country's income distribution is unjust, what would you suggest to improve it? What would be the cost of your policy?

Selected Readings

Fusfeld, Daniel R. *Economics*. Lexington, Mass.: D. C. Heath and Co., 1972. Chs. 3, 36, and 37 discuss income, poverty, and wealth.

Gordon, David M. *Problems in Political Economy: An Urban Perspective*. Lexington, Mass.: D. C. Heath and Co., 1971. Pp. 223–44. Presents conservative, liberal, and radical views on thc definition of poverty, and also historical data on its extent. Note also the excellent poverty bibliography on pp. 268 ff.

Herriot, Roger A., and Miller, Herman P. "The Taxes We Pay," *The Conference Board Record*, May 1971. Discusses the distribution among families of *total* income, defined as the sum of net national income plus adjustments for underreporting plus realized capital gains.

U.S. Bureau of the Census. *Statistical Abstract of the United States: 1972*. Washington, D.C., 1972. Lists some recent statistics on income, poverty, and wealth (Sections 11 and 33) and—more important—sources to other statistics: Note the listing of statistical abstract supplements (p. v); and the guide to general sources of statistics (pp. 915–17 and 940–43), to recent censuses (pp. 955–56), and to state statistical abstracts (pp. 961–64). Suggestion: Look at the detailed data for your home town in the 1970 Census of Population and study the distribution of income revealed therein. Draw a Lorenz curve.

NOTE: The *Journal of Economic Literature* lists recent articles on the economics of poverty in section 914. The *Index of Economic Articles*, in section 21.

5 On Redistributing Wealth

We have noted how the sharing of goods in a market economy depends essentially on the way money income is distributed among people. That, in turn, depends on the pattern of resource ownership and the equilibrium prices established in the markets for resources. Thus it can be made clear why some people remain poor even in the midst of a prosperous economy. They hold a position within the United States very much like that of the underdeveloped countries in the world at large. Relative to other people, they have few, if any, resources that can be sold at high enough prices to assure above-poverty level incomes. For instance, many of the poor own little or no land or capital. Some do not even have labor to sell. Think of the disabled or old people forced into retirement by failing health. Others are prevented from offering labor for sale. Consider women tied down with small children, or old but healthy people subject to enforced retirement at a given age. Still others cannot find a buyer for labor services they do offer, or they earn little even if they do find a buyer. Think of all those involuntarily idle, all or most of the time, because they cannot find a job; and consider those remaining poor despite full-time work.

Some people like to stress the first of these factors when explaining the existence of poverty. "Income-producing wealth—that is, land and capital—is so unequally distributed," they say, "that those who have it have high incomes and are rich, while those who don't, have low incomes and are poor." As they see it, a more equal distribution of such wealth would eliminate poverty. Let us explore that argument.

THE UNEQUAL DISTRIBUTION OF WEALTH

It is certainly true that wealth is very unevenly distributed in the United States. It is also true that most of the very rich can trace their high incomes in no small part to the ownership of wealth. The top 5 percent of income recipients, while earning 10 percent of all wages, get more than two-thirds of all dividends and half of all other property income. However, it is not true that most of those owning negligible quantities of land and capital are poor. Most of these people earn above-poverty incomes even though they sell nothing but labor.

As a result, money income in the United States is distributed much less unequally than wealth.

Unfortunately, precise and recent data on the distribution of the ownership of land and capital are not available, but good substitute data (on the distribution of household *wealth* at the end of 1962) are available. They are presented in Table 5.1, "The Distribution of Wealth in the United States, December 31, 1962." Data on wealth (assets of households minus liabilities secured by these assets) include other things (such as money and private cars) besides the ownership of land and capital, but there is every reason to believe that land and capital ownership is highly correlated with wealth as here defined. As the table shows, in late 1962 the least fortunate quarter of households owned only 0.5 percent of total wealth, while 17.4 percent of households at the other extreme owned 73.8 percent of it. The luckiest 0.3 percent of households held 21 percent of total wealth. These things do not change rapidly, and most likely more recent data would show the same.

The data in columns 4 and 5 are what we need to draw a Lorenz curve and gain a real picture of the distribution of wealth. This is done in Figure 5.1, "Lorenz Curves of Income and Wealth." For purposes of comparison, the Lorenz curve on income (Figure 4.1, "The Lorenz Curve") has been redrawn

Table 5.1 **The Distribution of Wealth in the United States, December 31, 1962**

Size of Wealth (1)	Percent of Households in Class[a] (2)	Percent of Total Wealth Held by Households in Class (3)	Percent of Households in Class or Lower Ones (4)	Percent of Total Wealth Held by Households in Class or Lower Ones (5)
Under $1,000	25.3	0.5	25.3	0.5
$1,000–$4,999	18.7	2.4	44.0	2.9
$5,000–$9,999	15.7	5.5	59.7	8.4
$10,000–$24,999	22.9	17.8	82.6	26.2
$25,000–$49,999	10.7	18.2	93.3	44.4
$50,000–$99,999	4.3	14.4	97.6	58.8
$100,000–$199,999	1.2	7.7	98.8	66.5
$200,000–$499,999	0.9	12.5	99.7	79.0
$500,000 and over	0.3	21.0	100.0	100.0

[a] A household is two or more persons living in the same dwelling unit and related to one another by blood, marriage, or adoption or a single person (other than an inmate in an institution) unrelated to the other occupants in the dwelling unit or living alone.

SOURCE: *Dorothy S. Projector and Gertrude S. Weiss,* Survey of Financial Characteristics of Consumers *(Washington, D.C.: Board of Governors of the Federal Reserve System, 1966).*

Figure 5.1 Lorenz Curves of Income and Wealth

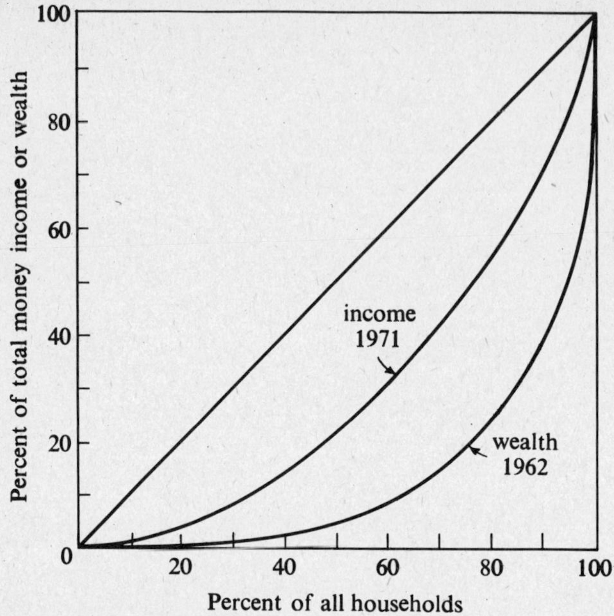

SOURCE: *Tables 4.1 and 5.1.*

In the United States, wealth (and probably the ownership of land and capital) is much more unequally distributed than income.

here. It is striking how wealth is so much more unequally distributed than income. Nevertheless, even though failure to own land and capital does not condemn most people to poverty, it may be true that a more equal sharing of land and capital would eliminate poverty. Some argue that this could best be done by establishing socialism; others would prefer to expand the private ownership of land and capital to groups now excluded from it. Let us consider both of these arguments.

THE CALL FOR SOCIALISM

Land and capital as such have little value to someone who is poor. Imagine, if you will, a poor family of seven—father, mother, grandpa, and four children—crowded into a dilapidated apartment in an urban ghetto. Suddenly someone presents a fancy certificate stating that this family now owned two acres of orange groves in central Florida, as well as ten turret lathes in an auto plant in Pontiac, Michigan. You can easily see why this sharing in the nation's land and capital would not automatically transport our family into a state of bliss. Our family would not be housed any better. It would not be clothed any better. And if it cared to be fed any better it would have a tough time, indeed, getting its own oranges from central Florida onto its kitchen table! To really gain from its newly acquired wealth our family would have to do one of two things. First, it could, ironically, *get rid of* this wealth by selling the two acres and the ten turret lathes, perhaps right back to their original owners. Indeed, this would probably be the first thought expressed at the family council table. The end result would be no redistribution of land and capital at all, but rather a one-time money transfer from owners of land and capital to the poor. This money transfer could also be spread out (in smaller amounts) over time. For example, the old owners of capital and land might borrow the money required for repurchase from the banking system and pay forever an annual interest charge for the amount borrowed out of their future income. Our poor family, on the other hand, could deposit the money received in the banking system and forever receive interest from the banks in future years. This shows the net effect of this whole procedure: an annual income transfer from the rich to the poor (via the banks).

Second, our family could hold on to its new wealth and see to it that those acres and those lathes were used in the process of production. That is what their former owners did. They could not feed, clothe, and shelter themselves with orange groves and turret lathes, either. But they saw to it that these were used, together with other resources, to produce oranges and cars, respectively. They also saw to it that part of the revenues from selling oranges and cars was paid to them for having contributed resources to the making of these goods. Under some fancy name, such as *rent* or *interest* or *profit*, the owners of land and capital thus received *money income*, and *that* they converted into goods they cared to consume. To own land and capital—and be better off because of it—our poor family would have to do the same. *It would have to get an income from the use of wealth.*

Obviously, though, our family and the many others like it who would be beneficiaries of a general redistribution of land and capital, could not very easily use the wealth personally (as by camping in the orange grove), nor could they supervise the proper use by others of small and scattered portions of the nation's land and capital. That is why advocates of this approach often call for *socialism:* "Everyone," they say, "should share equally in the ownership of land and capital. The best practical way of doing this would be through socialism. All land and capital would be jointly owned by everyone, but the government would manage the use of it in public enterprises. The rent, interest, and profit income received by these firms would be evenly divided up among all owner-citizens. This equal distribution of nonlabor income would put a quick end to poverty."

WOULD SOCIALISM END POVERTY IN THE UNITED STATES?

The crucial question to be answered is whether it is true that socialism would end poverty. We have already noted how fallacious this thesis would be for most countries of the world. Socialism has not made the Chinese rich; they simply do not have enough land and capital to allow the labor force to produce a large quantity of goods per person. Their traditional poverty has not been owing to private ownership of property. They have remained poor even after the advent of socialism. Yet there is a kernel of truth in the argument. The Chinese GNP is much more equally distributed now than ever before. There are no more private wealth holders who receive high nonlabor incomes. Now everyone is poor, but all the poor are just a bit less poor than they used to be!

It is very tempting to imagine that a United States experiment in socialism—owing to the large quantity of goods produced per person in this country—would have much more favorable results for the poor than the Chinese experiment did. One could imagine that the high productivity of land and capital here would result in high money income from their use so that an equal distribution of it would lift everyone above the poverty line. Let us pursue that thought.

Suppose an act of Congress bestowed all property rights in land and capital directly on the federal government—thus creating socialism—with the proviso that the nonlabor income derived from this public wealth would be distributed equally among all citizens. How much income from wealth would everyone get? To answer this question we must look at the *functional* distribution of income in the United States.

The Functional Distribution of Income

The functional distribution of income shows how much of our gross national income is payment to labor, and how much payment for the use of capital and land. Consider the data shown in Table 5.2, "The Functional Distribution of U.S. Gross National Income, 1970."

Economists in past centuries were most eager to get the kind of information contained in Table 5.2. They thought that most people had only one type of income: that one gets only labor income, or only rental income from land ownership, or only interest and profit income from the ownership of capital and the running of businesses. If this were true, the functional distribution of income would tell us how GNP is divided among "classes" in society. Much of the work of Karl Marx was based on reasoning along this line. He saw GNP divided among masses of poor proletarians on the one hand (who received wages) and a handful of rich landowners and capitalists on the other (who received all the rents, interest, and profits). Marx argued that eventually conditions for the poor would become unbearable and the struggle among the classes would end in revolution, the expropriation of the rich, and a socialist society in which all would share equally the income from land and capital. Let us study the U.S. data and consider the chances of eliminating poverty by this method.

Inspection of Table 5.2 reveals that in 1970, $601.9 billion of gross

Table 5.2 The Functional Distribution of U.S. Gross National Income, 1970

	Billions of Dollars	Percent
Wages, salaries, and supplements	601.9	61.8
Net indirect business taxes	86.7	8.9
Business transfer payments	3.9	0.4
Capital consumption allowances	87.6	9.0
Rental income of persons	23.3	2.4
Net interest	33.0	3.4
Proprietors' income	66.9	6.9
Corporate profits, including inventory valuation adjustment	70.8	7.2
Gross national income	974.1	100.0

SOURCE: *U.S. Department of Commerce,* Survey of Current Business.

national income was earned in the form of *wages, salaries, and supplements* thereto. (The supplements include employer contributions to such items as social security, unemployment and health insurance, retirement funds, employer compensation for injuries, and so on.) Thus, at first sight, labor income appears to have been 61.8 percent of gross national income. Hence it is tempting to conclude that the remaining 38.2 percent must have been property income and would have allowed a socialist government to distribute $372.2 billion cash equally among all citizens. It is quite wrong to conclude this, however. There was no $372.2 billion of cash that could have been distributed among all had socialism existed in 1970.

For one thing, in 1970, government collected $86.7 billion *net indirect business taxes.* This included mainly collections of sales, excise, and property taxes, plus a small current surplus of government enterprises minus a small amount of government subsidies to private businesses. Obviously, government would have continued to exist under socialism. It would have continued to commandeer some resources for its own purposes. This would have required continued taxation as a means of forcing private households not to direct all resources toward consumer goods production. Thus we could expect that a socialist government in 1970 would have continued to collect those $86.7 billion in indirect taxes. This would have left—at most—$285.5 billion of nonlabor income for general distribution in our hypothetical pool of cash.

Yet, in 1970, *businesses* had already made *transfer payments* of $3.9 billion. That is, businesses gave up that amount of income in favor of others, either voluntarily (as in the form of corporate gifts to nonprofit organizations) or due to coercion (the amounts involved were stolen, usually by means of consumers incurring debts that proved later to be uncollectable). We can expect that this would also have continued under socialism. Thus we should have left—at most—$281.6 billion of nonlabor income for distribution.

But this is still illusory. In 1970, $87.6 billion of income was used by business to make up for the wear and tear of structures and equipment used in 1970 production. Obviously, capital would have continued to wear out under socialism. Socialist managers, too, would have had to replace it. Otherwise, the capital stock would have started to depreciate in use until it disappeared. Output and income from the use of capital would have become zero. This would have defeated the entire purpose of having introduced socialism in the first place, namely, to capture that output and income for the benefit of the population as a whole, rather than let a few lucky capitalists get it all. Thus under socialism in 1970, an amount of gross national income equal to *capital consumption allowances* could not have become available for general distribution, either. Which would have left for general distribution—at most—$194 billion, the sum of rental, interest, and profit income.

Now consider the meaning of *rental income* in the U.S. national accounts. It includes not only earnings from renting real property (including natural resources), but also the imputed net rental returns to owner-occupants of nonfarm dwellings, and royalties from patents and copyrights. The imputed net rental returns to owner-occupants of nonfarm dwellings in 1970 equaled $13.7 billion. It is an amount of income that was not actually paid to or earned by anybody in cash. Rather it is an estimate of the net amount nonfarm homeowners could have earned (after depreciation, taxes, interest) had they rented out their homes at current rates rather than lived in them. Thus this amount could not possibly have been distributed under socialism, unless all homeowners had been expropriated and forced to pay rent to the government for living in their former homes. A closer look at patent and copyright incomes reveals them to be mostly income from *labor*, involving all kinds of inventions and designs; the composing of books and articles, and dramatic and musical works; and the making of maps, drawings, photographs, prints, motion pictures, and all works of art. This income amounted to $1.6 billion in 1970. Thus $15.3 billion of the $23.3 billion of personal rental income could not have been considered distributable nonlabor income: it either was not cash at all or was really labor income. This would have brought the possible total for such nonlabor cash income down to a maximum of $178.7 billion.

Next consider *net interest*. In the U.S. national accounts it equals the net interest payments to Americans by U.S. businesses and foreigners plus imputed interest. The latter equaled $32.8 billion of the $33 billion total. That is, this amount was not actually paid in cash to anybody. Rather it is an estimate of four items. The first item estimated is how much interest owner-occupants of nonfarm dwellings would have earned had they lent the money invested in their homes to someone else rather than sinking it into their own homes. They were estimated to have earned interest "from themselves" of $16.5 billion in 1970. Second, a similar estimate was made for money invested by owners of institutional buildings in those buildings and hypothetical interest earned thereon: $0.7 billion. Third, $0.4 billion was estimated to have been earned by owner-occupants of farm dwellings from their own money. Finally, it was estimated that financial intermediaries had provided $15.2 billion of free services to customers, which was really paid by underpaying customers on interest. (For example, banks are paying no interest on checking accounts, but are providing a variety of services free to customers. This can be viewed as the net result of two actions: paying interest and then immediately charging an equal amount for services rendered.) In short, most of the net interest contained in the gross national income was not received in cash. It could not have been distributed by a socialist government, unless the government had forced, first, all owners of residences and institutional buildings to pay interest *to the government* on money invested in these buildings, and second, all financial institutions to pay interest on their customers' money *to the government* in all cases where no interest is currently paid at all. This being a highly unlikely occurrence, our distributable pool of cash would have shrunk to a maximum of $145.9 billion.

Now consider the $66.9 billion item labeled *proprietors' income.* Investigation reveals this to be the income of professional people working for themselves and of unincorporated businesses and farms. Of the $15.8 billion of farm income included in the 1970 total, $1.1 billion was no cash income at all, but the imputed net rental returns to owner-occupants of farm dwellings (the net amount they could have earned, after depreciation, taxes, and interest, had they rented out their homes at current rates rather than lived in them) plus the imputed value of food and fuel produced and consumed on farms (the amount they could have earned had they sold, rather than personally used up, such food and fuel). Clearly, unless a socialist government had forced farmers to pay rent to the government on their own homes and to pay the government cash for food and fuel produced and consumed on the farm, this $1.1 billion would not have been distributable to anyone. We shall assume that it would not have been.

The remaining $65.8 billion of proprietors' income was received in cash. Yet surely a great portion of it was *labor* income. The income of sole proprietorships, partnerships, and producers' cooperatives, which is included here, is without doubt in part a return to land and capital used by the owner, but just as surely it is in part a return to his own labor in his own business. (On this point recall the discussion of normal profit in Chapter 2.) It would be absurd to consider all the income of doctors, lawyers, grocers, retailers, and farmers as nonlabor income. Indeed, the opposite assumption (that all this is labor income) is likely to be much closer to the truth, since many of these types of unincorporated businesses operate in declining industries or hold the high-cost positions in otherwise expansionary industries. Hence they are likely to have a lower-than-average return on land and capital. Indeed, one can estimate the portion of the $65.8 billion that is probably a return on land and capital as follows: In 1970, the net worth of unincorporated businesses was at most $382 billion. Assuming a 5 percent return on this investment, returns to land and capital were $19.1 billion. Hence $46.7 billion of the total nonimputed proprietors' income was labor income. This can hardly be exaggerated, for there were well over 10 million single proprietorships and partnerships, and this estimate would assign on the average to each single proprietor or partner a labor income of under $4,300 a year. Deducting the estimated amount of labor income, we are led to the conclusion that the total of distributable nonlabor income available to a socialist government would have shrunk further to a maximum of $98.1 billion.

Now we must have a closer look at *corporate profits*. (The inventory valuation adjustment is of no concern here. It is in any case a small figure and represents the national income accountant's attempt to eliminate apparent profits or losses that result not from any producing or selling activity of the corporation, but from the valuation of inventories at changing prices.) The important thing to note for our purpose is this: Fully $34.1 billion of 1970 corporate profits was taxed away by government. Arguing, as we did earlier, that a socialist government would have continued to levy taxes, the cash amount available for distribution would have shrunk further to $64 billion.

This $64 billion figure broke down as follows: Of their after-tax profits, corporations retained $11.7 billion. Cash receipts of individuals, which were returns to capital and land owned, came to $25 billion of corporate dividends, and as we noted earlier, $8 billion of rents, $0.2 billion of interest, and probably $19.1 billion of unincorporated business income. Yet on all these amounts received by individuals, *personal income taxes* were levied. Only retained corporate profits escaped such taxes. We can assume these personal taxes to have taken at least 20 percent of the $52.3 billion total, or $10.5 billion. (The average 1970 tax bite on personal income was 14.4 percent, but the recipients of the above income types were almost certainly in the higher tax brackets. The poor as a group received less than one-tenth of 1 percent of this.) Thus accounting for personal income taxes, our distributable nonlabor income total shrinks once again, to $53.5 billion. All this is summarized in Table 5.3, "Components of U.S. Gross National Income, 1970."

Evaluating the Prospects

Now assume that a socialist government had really appropriated the $53.5 billion in 1970 and distributed it among all. In a 204.8 million population, $261 would have gone to each person. This is roughly the amount by which the poor could have become richer by socialism, and it is the only amount the formerly rich recipients of nonlabor income could have retained. Would such a policy have been a wise one? One can seriously doubt it, and for a number of reasons.

A first and most obvious objection is that this policy would improve the lot of the poor by so little. Although the amount involved is hardly negligible, it is much smaller than most proponents of socialism would expect. Looking at *billions* of corporate profits, they are typically dreaming of thousands of

Table 5.3 **Components of U.S. Gross National Income, 1970 (In Billions of Dollars)**

Official Designation	Income (Before Personal Income Taxes) Total	From Labor	From Property: *Nondistributable*	From Property: *Distributable*
1. Wages, salaries, supplements	601.9	601.9	...	...
2. Net indirect business taxes	86.7	...	86.7[a]	...
3. Business transfer payments	3.9	...	3.9[b]	...
4. Capital consumption allowances	87.6	...	87.6[c]	...
5. Rental income of persons	23.3	1.6[d]	13.7[e]	8.0
6. Net interest	33.0	...	32.8[f]	0.2
7. Proprietors' income	66.9	46.7[g]	1.1[h]	19.1[i]
8. Corporate profits, incl. inventory valuation adjustment	70.8	...	34.1[a]	36.7
Gross national income	974.1	650.2	259.9	64.0
Personal income taxes		105.4	...	10.5
Net income: total		544.8	...	53.5
Net income: per capita (dollars)		2,660	...	261

[a] Nondistributable, on the assumption that a socialist government would have to collect the same amount of taxes as its capitalist predecessor.
[b] Nondistributable, on the assumption that business gifts and thefts from businesses would continue at the same rate in socialism.
[c] Nondistributable, on the assumption that capital would be replaced at the same rate in socialism.
[d] Includes royalties from patents and copyrights concerning all inventions, designs, the writing of books and articles, dramatic and musical compositions, and the making of maps, drawings, photographs, prints, motion pictures, and all works of art.
[e] Nondistributable, on the assumption that a 100 percent tax on the imputed net rental returns to owner-occupants of nonfarm dwellings is undesirable.
[f] Nondistributable, on the assumption that a 100 percent tax on imputed interest (on the equity of owner-occupants of houses and institutional buildings and on checking accounts) is undesirable.
[g] Includes an average annual return of $4,300 to the labor of owners of unincorporated businesses (doctors, lawyers, grocers, retailers, farmers).
[h] Nondistributable, on the assumption that a 100 percent tax on the imputed net rental returns to owners of farm dwellings and on the value of food and fuel produced and consumed on farms is undesirable.
[i] Estimated as a 5 percent return on the net worth of unincorporated businesses.

SOURCE: *U.S. Department of Commerce.* Survey of Current Business *and unpublished data.*

dollars coming to each person. They would be bitterly disappointed. The same data used above to derive the $261 per person figure suggest a much better policy: a more equal distribution of *labor* income. Counting wages and salaries ($601.9 billion) as well as the labor components of rental income and proprietors' income discussed above ($1.6 billion and $46.7 billion, respectively), labor in 1970 received $650.2 billion before taxes. After taxes, this came to $544.8 billion. Distributed equally, this would have given $2,660 to each man, woman, and child in the United States. Such a policy is even more appealing when one realizes that payments to labor, as used here, include payments to all types of human effort, not only to the janitor and assembly-line worker, but also to the corporation executive and the president of the United States. Thus, one can hardly draw any meaningful conclusions about returns to various economic classes from this aggregate figure.

Second, there are positive dangers to the type of socialist distribution contemplated above. We must not ignore further consequences of such a policy. Interest, rent, and profit, after all, serve a function. They are in many cases the reward for risk-taking and enterprise. Property owners take risks, and they innovate in the hope of getting some margin of income beyond what other people get. Sometimes they do. At other times they even lose. In addition, property owners save a large part of their income. Instead of buying consumer goods and just replacing their existing capital stock as it wears out, they expand the capital stock. In 1970, corporations alone retained and invested almost a third of their net profits. Unincorporated businesses, professional people, and farmers often do likewise with their net income from property. But what do you think would happen if all land and capital were publicly owned and everyone in the country got an equal and relatively small share of the net property income derived therefrom? The private incentive—and the means—to take risks, to innovate, to be thrifty and invest would be gone. Why take risks, innovate, or be thrifty and invest if any new capital is *everybody's* property and if in any case my income will be the same as anybody else's? As a result, the growth of the capital stock and the rate of technical advance would slow down. The country's production possibilities would cease to expand! As population would grow, but real GNP would not, real GNP per head would fall. That nice $261 per person in 1970 would become $251 per person in 1971, and $241 per person in 1972, and eventually disappear altogether. Like children's fighting over a pie and ending up with less than they could have had (as they spill a third of it on the floor), our insistence on getting a certain share of GNP may lower what we can get!

Nor have we considered the entire problem. Not only would socialism and absolute property income equality affect GNP growth by discouraging private effort, innovation, and investment; it would do so also by interfering with the price system. As we noted in Chapter 2, business income differences in a market economy are needed as a signal to channel resources in the direction demanded by consumers. If consumers want more cars and fewer buggies, businesses would ordinarily begin to earn more if they were to use resources more in the production of the former than of the latter. This would cause resources to shift until the right kinds of goods are being produced. There is no reason, however, for any private or public manager of resources to shift resources in response to shifts in demand if his income will be like every other's, no matter what he does.

Of course, one can and would have to do something about this. *Government* could take over the role of private entrepreneurs, of private savers and investors, and of the price system, too. Government could levy *extra* taxes on the $261 property income everyone received. It could use the proceeds to finance new capital formation and technological advance. It could use them to set up an elaborate central planning mechanism to take over the work of the price system of channeling resources in the right directions. In this way, perhaps production possibilities would continue to expand. As population grew, per capita GNP might be prevented from falling. It might even rise. But we cannot be certain that government would succeed where private property owners did. Consider the East European and Chinese experience in central planning.

In the short run, therefore, the gain to the poor of establishing socialism would be absolutely negligible. Unless we want to court disaster, they could not even keep that $261 per person discussed above. In the long run, everyone might lose if socialism is a failure. There is no reason to expect that it would do better than capitalism. Eradicating poverty by socialism would be a most inefficient way of going about it.

Finally, in the United States, this method would be totally impractical. The poor after all (in contrast with the poor in many other countries) are a minority. The majority of the American electorate would never buy this approach. A violent revolution on this issue would, in turn, have no chance of success.[1]

MINORITY CAPITALISM: AN ALTERNATIVE?

Some people have suggested an alternative. Instead of taking income-producing wealth from those who now have it, they propose giving the racial and ethnic minorities in this country, who are bearing such a disproportionate burden of poverty, a chance to acquire their own property. "Let us have lots of minority-owned businesses, employing, buying from and selling to members of minority groups," they say, "and poverty among the minorities will become a thing of the past. Instead of having socialism for all, let us have capitalism not just for English-speaking whites, but also for blacks, Puerto Ricans, American Indians, Oriental Americans, and so on." Statistics show that in 1971, minority groups in the U.S. made up 15 percent of the population but owned less than 3 percent of businesses, and these were invariably small. For example, the forty-six black insurance companies *together* were smaller than the sixtieth ranking white insurance company. The largest black bank in the country (Freedom National Bank of Harlem) was not even among the nation's 1,000 largest banks. Altogether, black businesses held less than 0.5 percent of business assets. To evaluate the possibilities for minority capitalism let us consider one aspect of it, the chances of black capitalism. A brief look

[1] If you would like to pursue this subject, you are urged to read Barrington Moore, Jr., "Revolution in America?" *New York Review*, January 30, 1969.

at history will help. Except for history, what is said here about the chances of black businesses in the future can be said about other minorities as well.[2]

A Look at History

Some blacks have been in business for a long time. Ever since emancipation, blacks have had free access to commodities. If they had the money, they could buy any commodity that was for sale (with the notable exception of houses). But blacks have not enjoyed open access to services. Whites simply would not sell certain services to blacks. Others they would sell only at exorbitant prices. Life insurance companies would charge blacks triple the rate charged whites (although such discrepancy was not justified by differences in mortality rates). By their actions, whites opened up a fertile field for black businessmen. Late last century, hundreds of black-owned insurance companies were formed. And blacks opened barber shops, beauty parlors, hotels, restaurants, and undertaking businesses. They had no competition from whites. And they had a captive market: other blacks. Segregation also provided specialized advantages to some black manufacturing firms. They supplied the above-mentioned service establishments. And also owing to segregation, there arose a group of black professionals (doctors, lawyers, teachers) who served a black market only. Given the small income of the black community, all these businesses remained relatively small. In 1960, there were 50,000 of them. And the 1960 census revealed an interesting fact. The average income of all blacks in the United States was about 50 percent that of whites. But the income of black businesses and professionals serving the captive black market was 80 percent that of whites in similar jobs.

But during the 1960's, the effects of the 1954 Supreme Court decision against segregation began to be felt. For the black business and professional class the effect was disastrous. They had operated behind a protective wall, free from competition of white-owned businesses. The Supreme Court decision and the changing mood of the country toppled that wall. Large national corporations began to look at the black market. They began to compete with the small black businesses. (Have a look at who advertises in *Ebony!*) Of 200 black-owned insurance companies, more than three-quarters became defunct. Black-owned cosmetics companies went out of business as national cosmetics firms began to offer special cosmetics for the black market. Other white-owned companies introduced African-motif garments, jewelry, and greeting cards, and even "soul food" preparations. Black-owned restaurants and hotels closed as blacks began to use white facilities.

It is against this background that we must judge the chances for black capitalism. We cannot reverse the trend of established white-owned national corporations competing with black-owned small businesses. Is this the time to create more of the latter? Is this the time, as some blacks urge, to create an entire spectrum of black-owned businesses serving the black market?

[2] The remainder of this section is based in part on Andrew F. Brimmer, "The Trouble with Black Capitalism," *Nation's Business*, May 1969, pp. 78–79.

The Chances for New Black-Owned Ghetto Businesses

First of all, we must consider the technological realities. As we move from service businesses to retailing to wholesaling and to manufacturing, the optimum size of the firm rapidly increases. Thus it becomes increasingly difficult financially for any prospective black businessman to enter fields from which blacks have traditionally been absent. The path of least resistance would be the traditional one, but is it a good idea for blacks to set up more *service and small retail establishments?* It certainly is *possible*, for these firms require relatively little capital. But these firms also have the lowest profit margin (maybe 3 percent) throughout the economy. Are we going to cure black poverty by pulling blacks into the most marginal of businesses? This is like creating an urban equivalent of subsistence agriculture!

"Well," some people say, "blacks should form community action groups and jointly establish *large shopping centers*, in the city ghettos perhaps." Blacks have done so in a number of cities across the nation, ranging from Hartford and Buffalo to Philadelphia and Washington to Harrisburg and Cleveland to Chicago and Minneapolis to Phoenix and Los Angeles. What are these ventures like? Consider the much publicized case of a 1968 Los Angeles "ghetto conglomerate," Action Industries, Inc. It is tightly controlled by area residents, mostly black and Mexican-American. It features, or plans to feature, a supermarket, two service stations, a home and commercial maintenance company, subcontracting of bench assembly work, a catering service, a doughnut shop, a "soul food" restaurant, an auto diagnostic center, an arts and craft shop, an employment agency, and a real estate development. Yet, in late 1968, it was only employing 200 persons.

Another black-owned shopping center opened in Philadelphia in 1968, partly financed by a Ford Foundation grant. It rented space to the A&P, the Bell Telephone Company, and the old black-owned North Carolina Mutual Insurance Company. It established a number of small black businesses: dry cleaning shop, pharmacy, book store, card and gift shop, hardware store, furniture store, and apparel shops.

What has been the experience of this type of venture in a dozen cities studied? There have been a few successes, notably Progress Plaza in Philadelphia and Willie Naulls Plaza in Los Angeles. *Yet there have been many more failures*. Uniformly, the experience was this: Sales volume rose significantly in the early months of operation and then fell precipitously, burying hopes of profitable operations. Invariably, operating costs were higher than in established white-owned businesses outside the ghetto, so prices had to be higher. Alternatives being available, these new black-owned businesses did not have a captive market. Customers went elsewhere. Why, finally, were operating costs higher? For many reasons: lack of entrepreneurial experience, higher land prices and taxes, smaller average purchases from low-income customers, slower turnover of perishable items, increased pilferage and vandalism, higher insurance rates, and greater wage costs. (Because employees were recruited from the culture of poverty, their absentee rate was exceedingly high. Three people might have to be hired to ensure two on the job.)

How about the chances of black-owned *manufacturing plants?* Again we must look beyond proud dreams and face realities of financing, costs, and profits.

First, truly large plants cost hundreds of millions of dollars. Although some blacks announced in 1971 that they would seek help from the World Bank, the United Nations, the Soviet Union, or Japan, if necessary, it can be doubted that such financing can be obtained.

Second, many manufacturing operations are not suitable for the areas where blacks live. One cannot put up an oil refinery in the midst of an urban ghetto. After all, it is a residential area. Indeed, the location of factories in central cities runs counter to the general decentralization trend in industry that was discussed in Chapter 3. Establishing new plants in city centers is *asking* for trouble. Higher land prices, taxes, and insurance rates, higher transportation costs in congested areas, insufficient space for horizontal plant layout, an inadequate supply of skilled labor—all these combine to put the new plants at a marked competitive disadvantage. Their construction, furthermore, owing to the lack of vacant urban space, usually requires the razing of dwellings and thus leads to a worsening of housing problems.

Third, even if one were to overlook these problems of financing and costs, the possibilities of establishing enough black-owned new plants to make a dent on black poverty are clearly limited. From 1958 to 1963, for example, the annual rate of all new manufacturing plant formation in the United States was 3,500. Of these, only 2,600 were suitable for the areas where poor blacks live. But only 500 of these employed more than twenty people. In addition, there is no reason to believe that all new manufacturing plants in the country can be owned and operated by blacks and located near black residential areas. Even if blacks succeeded in getting ownership of just 11 percent of all businesses (the black population share) and if employment per black firm equaled the average of all existing firms, only an additional 776,000 jobs would be created. If all these jobs went to blacks, blacks could be expected to employ at best 7 percent of all blacks. Thus the chances of blacks to get out of poverty by establishing, right where blacks are living, an entire spectrum of black-owned businesses are truly negligible.

The Chances for Help from White-Owned Businesses

What about white-owned firms coming to black neighborhoods and eventually sharing ownership or management with local residents? The Congress of Racial Equality (CORE) has promoted the idea. However, the thought of locating in ghetto areas has hardly been sweeping white businesses like wildfire. It is easy to see why. The cost disadvantages of locating in central cities rather than suburbs are large nowadays, and they apply to whites as well as blacks. In addition, although they are reluctant to talk about it, white businessmen see disadvantages that may not apply to all black businessmen. They fear the "get-whitey" attitude of black ghetto residents: It results in above-average shoplifting losses and pilferage on the job, in looting and firebombings, in vandalism (such as the continual disappearance of shrubbery and even grass and the breaking of windows), in nightly break-ins leaving holes in walls and roofs, and in neighborhood muggings scaring away high-income customers and employees alike.

Still, and surprisingly so, some white companies have recently located in ghetto areas. Partly on their own and partly after government prodding, they have begun to go into poor neighborhoods and agreed to forget about high school diplomas, prison records, age, sex, race, and similar barriers to employment. Examples are the Control Data Corporation's new plant in the North Side slum of Minneapolis, the Avco Corporation's new commercial printing plant in the Roxbury section of Boston, and the Aerojet plant in Watts, Los Angeles. Yet the record so far has not been a pleasing one.

The Aerojet Corporation in Watts, Los Angeles, for example, received a federal subsidy of $1,300 per employee for training area poor. Its actual training costs turned out to be $5,000 per employee. It planned to hire 500 poor people. It had to hire 1,200 in order to have an average of 500 present. Many could not handle the training program. Employment dropped to 300.

Another example is the fate of black car dealerships. In 1967, when it was discovered that there was one black among 28,000 new car dealers in the nation, the auto companies began to set up black car dealerships in the city ghettos. By 1970 there were thirty of them, but not one of them had yet made a profit. Some of the reasons: Most of their customers were bad credit risks and could not get credit from banks; the dealers themselves were the constant targets of tool thefts, auto parts thefts, and vandalism, which raised insurance costs greatly; there are few large spaces in central cities, hence car lots are scattered and security costs are much greater; and the new dealers lack management experience.

The Role of Government and of Foundations

The federal government has encouraged white business to operate in the ghetto. The Economic Development Administration of the Commerce Department was giving subsidies in the late 1960's for training the unskilled and chronically unemployed in slum-based plants. The Office of Economic Opportunity offered "success insurance" (initially insuring businesses in four cities against losses incurred in private job training of 4,000 persons) and insured loans to private persons to upgrade their skills. But there are limits to what the government can do. For example, Senator Robert Kennedy introduced a bill in the Ninetieth Congress designed to lure firms to poverty areas by providing a richer set of incentives for this type of operation.[3]

[3] *Congressional Record*, July 12, 1967; reprinted as Robert F. Kennedy, "Industrial Investment in Urban Poverty Areas," in John F. Kain, ed., *Race and Poverty* (Englewood Cliffs, N.J.: Prentice-Hall, 1969).

Nothing ever came of the bill, but it is instructive. It had the most generous set of tax incentives ever devised: A firm locating in the area and employing more than fifty poor people would be able to deduct from its tax bill 7 percent of plant construction costs, 10 percent of machinery costs, and 25 percent of wages paid to the poor. The Department of Commerce estimated that this would save firms $91,000 on a $1 million investment. It also estimated that the types of firms likely to take advantage of the incentive program would be found exactly in those industries already found in poverty areas (textiles and leather, for example). These industries then were paying an average wage of $3,000 per year. In short, the richest set of incentives ever devised would bring to the poor the kind of firms paying poverty wages! Over a ten-year period, estimated the Department of Commerce, $770 million in wages might be generated (from 250,000 new jobs). The cost to the government: $500 million. Surely, there must be better ways of doing things.

Still, promoting ghetto economic development is fashionable. Private foundations have also entered the picture. In a significant policy shift, the Ford Foundation announced in 1968 that it would engage in ventures aiding the poor and minority groups, looking only for "high *social* yield." Traditionally, the foundation had looked for high money yield, using the income from its financial investments for charitable purposes. In a shift away from safe philanthropy, the foundation has supported bold projects designed to calm social tensions. Among the first of these were a black business development, racially integrated and low-income housing, grants to test community control of schools and promote voter registration, and the purchase of land for aesthetic, recreational, and scientific purposes.

The Nixon administration has taken a number of steps to promote minority business prospects. (After a 1969 National Congress of American Indians and the call for "red capitalism" by 105 tribes, the term *black capitalism* has been quietly changed to *minority capitalism.*) In 1969, it established a new Office of Minority Business Enterprise in the Commerce Department. Its aim was to help blacks, and also Mexican-Americans, Puerto Ricans, and American Indians, to get jobs and business ownership in new "industrial complexes" to be created in the urban ghettos with federal aid. In 1969, the office initiated Project Enterprise to finance minority businesses. Large national companies were urged to set up, within a year, 100 Mesbics (Minority Enterprise Small Business Investment Companies), each of which was to have a minimum private endowment of $150,000. The Mesbics were to be licensed and regulated by the Small Business Administration, which would match their funds 2:1 for a total of at least $450,000 (or 3:1 for a much larger private endowment). This could, in turn, be used to secure at least another $1.8 million of government-guaranteed private bank loans. Thus each Mesbic might potentially finance $2.25 million or more of minority business needs. It was hoped that $500 million of funds would be found in this way by mid-1970. In 1970, the Ford Foundation pledged $2.5 million to Mesbics in nine major cities and two rural areas (Georgia and Oklahoma) to generate a total of funds ten times that amount. In spite of all these efforts, success has been slow in coming. At the end of 1971, only 39 of 100 planned Mesbics actually existed. In 1971, the Mesbic that was pushed as a model (the Arcata Investment Company in California) failed when more than half of its loans went sour. This is not surprising for many new minority enterprises have serious problems producing unfamiliar products with inexperienced workers and finding customers. To alleviate this problem, the government has encouraged assistance to the new businesses from "big brother" companies, which would provide managerial and technical consultants and even absorb early losses. The federal government itself awarded some $138 million in contracts by mid-1971 at an estimated 11 percent higher cost than might be obtained in competitive bidding. (In 1970, the federal government let $14 million of such contracts for such items as detergents, boxes, mail bags, typewriter covers, and auto repair services.) To oversee all these programs, a presidential committee urged in 1970 the establishment of an Agency for Expanded Ownership (to merge the Office of Minority Business Enterprise with the Small Business Administration and the Economic Development Administration).

Conclusions

All in all, the findings of a 1968 study by the Brookings Institution still stand. It stated that the possibilities of developing "ghetto industry" and thereby eliminating inner-city unemployment and poverty "were strongly limited." The study showed that much publicized moves by big companies to set up ghetto plants were giving jobs to only a handful. And to suggest that black entrepreneurship can produce much more than a token number of new jobs, even for a long time to come, was called "pure romanticism."

Indeed, the most successful minority enterprises have turned out to be those of the Cubans in the Miami area. Yet in late 1970, 6,000 such businesses had only a total of 1,500 employees. This is not to deny that minority capitalism is very important for the minorities, at least symbolically. Many of them believe that integration with the dominant white English-speaking society is not the optimum solution for them. They would prefer economic independence over economic integration, even if the latter were based on equal opportunity. However, there is little to support the belief that such independence could be an economic success, much less be successful in eliminating the poverty of minorities.

If one rejects socialism or minority capitalism as poor ways of eliminating poverty, an obvious alternative emerges. One can concentrate on improving labor rather than nonlabor income. One can stress the maintenance and development of human capital rather than the redistribution or development (in the hands of the poor) of nonhuman capital. That is, one can push action in areas of health, education, job training, and employment. These matters are discussed in the following three chapters.

Summary

1. Some people remain poor even in the midst of a prosperous economy. These poor have, relative to other people, few if any resources that they can sell at high enough prices. For instance, many of the poor own little or no land and capital. Some people argue, therefore, that a redistribution of wealth would eliminate poverty.
2. However, failure to own land and capital does not automatically bring poverty. Most people have only labor to sell, yet are nonpoor. As a result, income in the United States is distributed much less unequally than wealth.
3. In 1962, the least fortunate quarter of households owned only 0.5 percent of total wealth (but the quarter of poorest households in 1971 earned 8 percent of total income). In the same year of 1962, the most fortunate 17 percent of households owned over 73 percent of total wealth (while the richest 17 percent of households in 1971 earned 36 percent of total income).
4. While some would prefer to eliminate poverty by establishing socialism, others would rather expand the private ownership of land and capital.
5. Under socialism, all land and capital would be jointly owned by everyone. The government would manage their use in public enterprises, and it would distribute equally to all owner-citizens the nonlabor income derived from this use. However, this can eliminate poverty only when the per capita quantity of goods produced with land and capital is large.
6. A study of the functional income distribution in the United States allows an estimate of the nonlabor income each citizen could expect to get under socialism. Based on 1970 data, the following emerges: Each citizen could have received $261 of nonlabor income under a socialist regime. This calculation is based on a number of assumptions:
   (a) that a socialist government would have continued to levy the same amount of indirect business taxes, corporate taxes, and personal income taxes to finance general government activities as its capitalist predecessor;
   (b) that socialist enterprises would have been subject to making transfer payments and to replacing worn out capital at the same rate as their capitalist predecessors;
   (c) that it would have been undesirable to tax away the imputed net rental returns to owner-occupants of dwellings or to tax away imputed interest income or the imputed value of food and fuel consumed on farms; and
   (d) that all income from patents and copyrights and much of the income of unincorporated firms (doctors, lawyers, retailers, farmers) would have been treated as labor income, whatever the official name given to it.

   If one were to drop *all* of these assumptions, each citizen could have received $1,817 in 1970.
7. However, in the long run, even a distribution of as little as $261 per person per year could not have been maintained. This is so because the socialist government would have needed *extra* taxes to carry on the formerly private activities of innovation, adding to the capital stock and managing enterprises and to replace the governing functions of the price system with a human bureaucracy of central planners. Since this might not be successful, eradicating

poverty by socialism seems a most inefficient way of going about it. And it would be impractical, too.

8. The alternative, of abolishing poverty by expanding capitalism to include new groups of people among owners of wealth, is little more promising. Consider the chances of new minority-owned ghetto businesses. Historically, black service businesses and black professionals, for example, have served a captive market of blacks, who were excluded by white businesses. These black entrepreneurs, however, have suffered greatly in recent years as a result of integration. The chances of expanding black ownership in these fields are therefore slim. Equally slim are chances for setting up successful black-owned shopping centers or manufacturing plants in urban ghettos. They all run into great difficulties with obtaining financing and with keeping operating costs at levels competitive with white-owned businesses outside the ghetto. In addition, the rate at which blacks could possibly acquire business ownership under the best of circumstances would be too slow to eradicate black poverty.
9. The chances for help from white-owned businesses are little better. Such businesses suffer from the same cost disadvantages in central city locations. They suffer from additional racially motivated problems when locating in ghettos.
10. Government and private foundations have, however, encouraged minority capitalism in a variety of ways. These include the provision of training subsidies and success insurance, the establishment of Mesbics, the arranging of big brother company assistance, and preferential letting of government contracts.
11. All in all, the redistribution of wealth does not appear as a promising and practical approach to eliminating urban poverty.

Terms[4]

assets
black capitalism
business transfer payments
capital consumption allowances
corporate profits
functional income distribution
gross national income
imputed food and fuel income
imputed interest income
imputed rental income
income-producing wealth
inventory valuation adjustment
liabilities
Mesbic
minority capitalism
net indirect business taxes
net interest
net worth
proprietors' income
red capitalism
rental income of persons
success insurance
wage supplements
wealth

[4] Terms are defined in the Glossary at the back of the book.

Questions for Review and Discussion

1. Consider Table 4.1, "The Distribution of Money Income in the United States, 1971" and Table 5.1, "The Distribution of Wealth in the United States, December 31, 1962." Where does your family fit in? Do you think its position is deserved? Why or why not?
2. "Most of the very rich in the United States can trace their position to inherited ownership of limited natural resources (oil, urban land) or industrial capital. For instance, of 75 persons recently identified with a net worth exceeding $75 million, 45 became rich through oil, autos, chemicals, or aluminum. We should stop all inheritances." Evaluate.
3. Explain why socialism is not necessarily a sure-fire cure for poverty.
4. "The standard of life of a family does not improve by owning land and capital unless it allows others to use such wealth." Evaluate.
5. The text section entitled "The Functional Distribution of Income" argues from 1970 U.S. data that each citizen under socialism could have received only $261 of nonlabor income. Yet this is based on a number of assumptions (see Summary, item 6). Would you accept each of these assumptions? If not, why not?
6. Suppose you had the power and the will to establish socialism in the United States. Using 1970 data, how much money would you distribute to each citizen? Draw up a complete list of the necessary executive orders to make this possible. How popular would this list be?
7. Do you earn any imputed income? What is it? Do you think it ought to be taxed the same way as money income?
8. Evaluate the argument that it would be smarter to distribute labor income equally than to distribute nonlabor income equally.
9. "Why equalize the receipt of *nonlabor* income? What is needed is an equalization of *income*, whatever its source." Evaluate.
10. "The ghetto economy is nothing but the economy of an underdeveloped country. It can be helped in the same ways rich countries help underdeveloped ones." Look at any standard economics text and read the chapter on underdevelopment. Then decide what the quotation means and whether you agree with it.
11. "In 1968, a group of black leaders and Philadelphia banks, in cooperation with the Economic Development Administration of the Department of Commerce, established the Job Loan Corporation. Its aim: to help the disadvantaged start or expand their own businesses. Typically, minority ghetto dwellers have little money of their own and cannot get loans, having no collateral, no business experience, a bad credit rating, and possibly even a police record. The Job Loan Corporation does not make loans itself. It processes loan applications, favoring blacks and Puerto Ricans. It looks only at motivation and success prospects, not at the applicant's past. Applicants approved by it are guaranteed to get a loan from one of the participating banks. Loans are for five years, unsecured, at interest rates below those charged for the best customers. Any loss is spread among the participating banks. In addition,

the new businessmen get aid from the Philadelphia Bar Association, the Philadelphia Institute of Certified Public Accountants, and the Greater Philadelphia Chamber of Commerce. Most of the loans made in the first half year were for less than $5,000. Ninety percent went for retail and service establishments: rubbish collection, jewelry repairs, service stations, beauty shops, dress shops, paint businesses, luncheonettes. Obviously here is a model plan for abolishing poverty in the United States." Discuss.

12. "The best way for blacks to get a piece of the action, that is, to become businessmen, is to be franchised by larger companies, for example, to head automobile dealerships or gasoline stations. This way they are outfitted by the larger company, need less capital, and have a greater chance of success than going it alone." Evaluate.
13. "The attempt to build up a viable spectrum of minority-owned businesses in the ghetto ("gilding the ghetto") is an attempt (by whites) to beautify and thus maintain the shameful situation of residential segregation." Evaluate.
14. The poor (often black) feel that they are exploited by store owners (often white). A Federal Trade Commission study in Washington, D.C., revealed this about furniture and appliance stores: In the ghetto, prices averaged $255 per $100 wholesale cost. In the rest of the city, prices averaged $159 per $100 wholesale cost. Does this prove exploitation? (HINT: The *net* return of ghetto retailers was lower than that of stores in the other areas.)
15. "The alternative offered to gilding the ghetto (namely ghetto dispersal by the outmigration of ghetto residents) is an attempt (by whites) to break up the political power base of residents within the ghetto. It should be resisted by members of minorities." What do you think?

Selected Readings

Edel, Matthew, and Rothenberg, Jerome. *Readings in Urban Economics.* New York: Macmillan, 1972. Pp. 307–25. Discusses ghetto development vs. dispersal as approaches to fighting ghetto poverty.

Fusfeld, Daniel R. *Economics.* Lexington, Mass.: D. C. Heath and Co., 1972. Chs. 6–7, 34, 36–38, and 42. Discusses GNP accounting, the distribution and redistribution of income and wealth, and the economics of the ghetto.

Gordon, David M. *Problems in Political Economy: An Urban Perspective.* Lexington, Mass.: D. C. Heath and Co., 1971. Pp. 138–46. Discusses black capitalism. Note the bibliography on pp. 162 and 269.

Lampman, Robert T. *The Share of Top Wealth-Holders in National Wealth: 1922–1956.* Princeton, N.J.: Princeton University Press, 1962. Historical data on the distribution of wealth.

Terrell, Henry S. "Wealth Accumulation of Black and White Families: The Empirical Evidence," *The Journal of Finance,* May 1971. Presents recent trends in wealth distribution.

U.S. Bureau of the Census, *Statistical Abstract of the United States, 1972.* Washington, D.C., 1972. Lists some statistics on income, wealth, and minority businesses (Sections 11 and 17) and—more important—sources to other statistics: Note the listing of statistical abstract supplements (p. v); and the guide to general sources of statistics (pp. 910–12, 915–17, 940–41), to recent censuses (pp. 955–56), and to state statistical abstracts (pp. 961–64).

NOTE: The *Journal of Economic Literature* lists recent articles on national income accounting (section 221), national wealth (224), and social indicators (225). The *Index of Economic Articles* catalogs, in sections beginning with the indicated numbers, articles on income distribution (2.2) and national income and wealth (8.2).

6 *Ensuring Good Health*

Many people own neither land nor capital, yet they are not poor. They earn good incomes though selling nothing but their labor services. Some people, however, are not so lucky. They are barred from working for reasons of poor health. Consider the victims of physical infirmities and mental breakdown. They may have been born crippled or mentally retarded. They may have been disabled by war or accidents in later life. Or their strength may have been sapped by chronic diseases. Some of these abnormalities come with age (like arthritis or cardiac disturbances), others are self-inflicted (like alcoholism or drug addiction). Afflicted people are necessarily found in any society. They have to rely on others entirely to enjoy even a bare minimum of food, clothing, shelter, and medical care.

While it is fairly clear to everyone that some people are so old or ill or disabled that they cannot work at all (19 percent of the poor in 1972), it is frequently overlooked that there are great differences in health also among all those other people who are physically able to work. Just as it would be a mistake to consider all machines that can still run as equals, it would be wrong to so consider all persons who are physically employable. Some machines can develop but little power; others a great deal. Some are defective and break down a lot; others are in first-class running condition. There are corresponding differences among people. Some have great physical strength and mental vigor; others have little stamina and lack vitality. Some are always healthy and well fed; others catch every disease that comes along, and are malnourished. Not surprisingly, some of those who do have labor to sell (and nothing else) can work intermittently only or they perform labor of low quality for reasons of poor health. They compare to the worst and least desirable of all functioning machines! They end up being poor.

But why are some people physically and mentally so well off, while others are not? Only in small part can it be explained by personal differences in genetic endowment. Mostly, it is the consequence of the unequal distribution of income, together with serious imperfections in the markets for medical care. These cause many people to be in poor health because they get neither adequate diets, clothing, and shelter, nor access to first-class medical care. This ultimately leads them, in turn, to be less productive and therefore less desirable workers, and thus to be poor. This chapter examines this issue by focusing on the lack of nutrition and medical attention as causes of poverty.

HUNGER IN AMERICA

The poor health of many people is caused by nothing more mysterious than malnutrition. Some Americans are literally starving to death. In 1968, the Department of Agriculture estimated that 5 million Americans were chronically hungry. Ten million more were undernourished. The Senate Select Committee on Nutrition and Human Needs made a similar estimate in 1969. The largest nutritional survey ever made in the U.S., which was released in 1971, showed many millions of people seriously deficient in vitamins A, B_2, and C, and anemic to the point of requiring medical attention.

Who are these people? You will not find them in the all-white suburbs. You find them living in tarpaper shacks in eastern Kentucky, the migrant labor camps in Florida, the Mississippi delta, the Mexican-American slums of San Antonio, and the Indian reservations throughout the country. There you find conditions resembling those of the worst spots in the underdeveloped world. People have marasmus (calorie starvation: loose flesh hangs on spindly arms and legs). People have kwashiorkor (protein deficiency leading to irreversible brain damage). People have rickets (vitamin D deficiency, leading to soft and deformed bones). People are plagued with intestinal parasites. And people die. But *why*? In part, this may be caused by inadequate knowledge. People just don't always know enough to provide themselves with a proper diet. More likely, though, it is a matter of inadequate funds. It was no accident when the Department of Agriculture found that 63 percent of families earning less than $3,000 a year had highly inadequate diets. This was not true for higher-income families.

HELPING PROVIDE ADEQUATE NUTRITION

There are two obvious ways by which people on inadequate diets can be helped by government. They can be given food directly, or they can be given money they are free to spend on food, if they choose, or on something else instead. In the United States, the former approach has been taken. Government-directed programs to combat insufficient or improper diets include commodity distribution, food stamp, and several child nutrition programs. Table 6.1, "Major Government In-Kind Assistance Programs Providing Nutrition," shows the dimensions of current programs in these fields.

Few observers interested in eliminating the roots of poverty are, however, content with either the size or type of current food programs. For one thing, the *child nutrition program* is not restricted to the poor. It involves direct commodity distribution, a special milk program, and cash subsidies for school lunch programs from which many nonpoor children benefit. The other two programs listed in Table 6.1 are restricted to the poor, but do not reach all of

Table 6.1 **Major Government In-Kind Assistance Programs Providing Nutrition, United States, Fiscal 1971**

Program	Total Federal Outlays (Millions) (1)	Number of Beneficiaries (Thousands) (2)	Average Annual Outlay per Recipient (3)
1. Commodity distribution	$346	6,797	$51
2. Child nutrition	905	50,574	18
3. Food stamps	1,522	10,567	144

SOURCE: Statistical Abstract of the United States, 1972, pp. 85–87.

them (note column 2). Finally, those who are reached find the aid inadequate. Note how the average annual outlay per recipient is extremely low (column 3).

The oldest of these nutritional programs, a program of free *commodity distribution* (item 1 in Table 6.1), was introduced in the 1930's. It still operated in 36 states in 1971. Under this program, 22 basic farm commodities are distributed, including canned meat, processed cheese, beans, flour, and dried prunes. However, the program provides a bland, monotonous diet and fails to meet nutritional requirements (it includes no vitamin D–fortified milk, for instance). Some people suspect a simple reason: It is a program to get rid of particular farm surpluses and to shore up farm prices more than one to help the poor.

More recently (in the 1960's), the *food stamp program* was instituted (item 3, Table 6.1). The idea was this: People would either receive "free" (for a 50-cent fee) or buy from the government so-called food stamps. These could be exchanged for a variety of food items in regular stores. To qualify for free stamps in May 1969, a family of three or less had to be certified at a monthly income of less than $20; a family of four or more, at less than $30. As a result, the bulk of poor people had to buy their stamps. However, they also were helped, for people who bought stamps would receive, in stamps, perhaps double the money they paid; in 1971, $2.28 of stamps were issued for a $1 payment on the average.

All over the country, however, recipients have criticized the stamp program. First, it forces the values of the nonpoor administrators onto the poor. The poor are not allowed, for instance, to buy foreign-grown food (except coffee, tea, sugar, cocoa, and bananas). As a result, some people could not buy hamburger, as it contained some Argentine beef. Food stamps cannot be used for alcoholic beverages, cigarettes, dog food, laundry products, mops, or crayons, and similar items sold in grocery stores.

Second, participants are unanimous that the monthly allotment runs out in two or three weeks.

Third, they charge outright abuses in administration. In many a county, the political machine dominates the administration of the program. Local officials do not always follow the spirit of the federal law. A 1970 White House investigation revealed the program in many counties to be "a paper program with absurdly low participation rates" of those legally eligible. Poor people may be rejected illegally (but they do not know their rights of appeal). Or poor people are invited to buy stamps, but for a minimum of $50 only (and they never have that much cash). Hundreds of families in one Mississippi county did not even have 50 cents to get the "free" stamps. Some poor people cannot afford transportation to the county seat where stamps have to be claimed in person. Or they are physically unable to go. In one Georgia county (Glascock), the sheriff even ran the welfare representatives out of the county, declaring that a food program would "just mean a lot of niggers lined up." Some counties managed to keep college students and hippie-type communes out of the program. Or take Collier County, Florida. Officials rejected the program (for migrants), stating that they could take care of their own "worthy" poor. Direct federal intervention (which is authorized by law in low-income areas) was impossible however, because the county's average income (swelled by a booming tourist business) was high.

President Nixon, quite aware of these criticisms, has raised federal spending on the programs listed in Table 6.1 from $1.1 billion in fiscal 1969 to $4.1 billion in fiscal 1973. The coverage of the programs has been expanded greatly, with the proviso that all recipients register for work and accept it when offered unless this jeopardizes their health. All counties in the nation are to have food programs and use uniform eligibility standards, based on family size and income. Starting in 1972, the 900,000 poorest of the poor (earning less than $30 a month) could get totally free stamps even without the fee. (They received $108 of stamps per month for a family of four.) Also, 5,000 persons were hired in 1969 by the Cooperative Extension Service to help the poor serve more nutritious meals, that is, to fight hunger associated with ignorance rather than lack of funds. So far, none of these programs have eliminated hunger in America.

UNRESTRAINED SICKNESS AND BIRTHS

The provision of medical care in the United States involves a giant industry. It covers the activities of professionals, such as doctors, dentists, nurses, and related personnel. They operate in a great variety of places: in homes and offices, in hospitals and sanitariums, in nursing homes and laboratories, in public health departments and universities. It also covers the activities of many others, such as ambulance drivers and producers of drugs and appliances, insurance men and construction workers. Is it any wonder that Americans, in fiscal 1972, spent over $83 billion on health? This amount equaled 7.6 percent of the GNP. While spending $394 per person, in constant dollars twice the amount spent per person in fiscal 1950, Americans had the highest per person health expenditure of any country in the world.[1] The 1972 total includes not only private and public personal health care expenditures for hospital and nursing home care (43 percent), for the services of physicians, dentists, and other medical practitioners (27 percent), and for such things as drugs, eyeglasses, and appliances (12 percent), but also spending on medical facilities construction (5 percent), medical research (2 percent), and a variety of other categories. The latter include government public health activities (other than for pollution control, sanitation, water supply and sewage treatment) and in-plant health services provided by industry; they do not include expenditures for medical education.

Of the $83 billion total, 55 percent was paid directly for medical services and commodities by private consumers or private insurance companies on their behalf, 26 percent was paid by the federal government, 14 percent by state and local governments, and 5 percent by others (private medical facilities, industry, and philanthropy).

Evaluating the Success of the Medical Effort

How successful has this giant effort been in providing medical care for Americans? This question can be answered in at least two ways, and in both cases the answers are discouraging.

First, we can concentrate on the big picture. We can look at Americans in general and compare chief health indicators with other countries or over time. When we do, we find that in 1970 the life expectancy of U.S. males was eighteenth in the world, of females, eleventh; and the U.S. ranked seventh in preventing maternal mortality and thirteenth in preventing infant mortality. This was worse than a decade earlier.

Death rates from many diseases are higher in the U.S. than elsewhere; such diseases include tuberculosis, diabetes, arteriosclerotic heart disease (including coronary hypertensive heart disease), influenza, pneumonia, and bronchitis. Over time, comparing 1900 with 1965, we find the U.S. life expectancy to have increased by almost twenty-one years at birth, but by less than three years at age 65. That is, the U.S. medical system has greatly cut infant and child death rates, but not learned to deal with the degenerative diseases of old age. Furthermore, to a significant extent, increases in life expectancy have been increases in expected years of bed disability and institutionalization, not in years of expected healthful life.

Second, and more important, we can look at various groups of Americans and ask whether they all enjoy *equal* access to medical care. Whatever is true for the average American, is it also true for every American? In short, the question is whether all Americans can expect to receive medical care imme-

[1] Most of the statistical data used in the remainder of this chapter come from U.S. Public Health Service, *Vital Statistics of the United States* and *Health Resources Statistics* or from U.S. Social Security Administration, *Social Security Bulletin* or from U.S. Bureau of the Census, *Current Population Reports,* Series P-60.

diately when it is needed and receive it in good facilities, from well-trained personnel who render care cheerfully and with true concern for the patient. Unfortunately, this is not so. Many Americans, notably the poor, cannot expect to receive medical care at a moment's notice, nor can they count on the best in facilities and personnel. This uneven access to medical care for different people may well account for the bad international comparisons cited above.

Why Some People Do Not Get Adequate Medical Care

Lack of income. The most obvious reason for the state of affairs just described is differences in income. Those who have less income than others will get less of many goods, including medical care.

Lack of insurance. Nor does private insurance make up for the lack of income. Such insurance serves the purpose of pooling the risks of incurring high medical expenses and concomitant loss of income. While the costs of illness are totally unpredictable and can be catastrophic for any one family, they are quite predictable for a large group of people and can be shared among them. Thus getting insurance means exchanging the uncertainty of having either zero or catastrophic expenses for the certainty of smaller expenses (the insurance premium). Those with low incomes may not have the money to pay the premiums. In addition, many insurance schemes are linked with employment and thus not available to those without steady jobs. Predictably, low-income people have the least insurance. At the end of 1968, found the Public Health Service, while about three-quarters of the total civilian population had some private health insurance, only a third of the poor did. Among all persons under 65, about 35 percent of those with annual incomes below $3,000 had hospital and surgical insurance, but over 90 percent of those with incomes of $10,000 or more had such insurance. Furthermore, most people are only partially covered, even with insurance. Few are protected against income loss. As to medical costs, at the end of 1968, among all persons under 65, 80 percent had some surgical coverage, only 46 percent had some coverage for office visits and drugs, and only 3 percent for dental expenses. It should be noted that most coverage is subject to limitations, such as thirty days in the hospital per illness, a monetary maximum, or the exclusion of preventive or psychiatric care.

Lack of physical access. There is another important factor that explains why some people cannot get adequate medical care. Many people, even if able to pay, find themselves physically without access to medical services, since the production of medical services tends to be distributed very unevenly geographically. This reflects in part the residential choices of active medical personnel. They like to locate where life is pleasant and patients are prosperous. In 1970 there were 171 physicians per 100,000 persons in the United States as a whole. Yet this rate ranged from 68 in Alaska to 238 in New York. The corresponding rate for U.S. dentists was 47, ranging from 26 in Mississippi to 68 in New York.

The 1970 U.S. rate for nurses was 345; in 1966 it had ranged from 133 in Arkansas to 536 in Connecticut. Another revealing fact is this: In 1971 there were 200 physicians per 100,000 persons in the suburbs, but only 50 in the central cities. Indeed, in some inner-city and rural areas doctors simply cannot be found. (In 1971 there were 130 counties with no private doctors at all.)

Similar discrepancies can be found in the availability of medical facilities. For example, in 1970 there were 417 short-term hospital beds per 100,000 persons in the United States, ranging from 192 in Alaska to 650 in North Dakota. All other states were in between. This is especially serious in an age wherein the best medical treatment requires more than the family doctor and his black bag. Modern medicine at its best is delivered by platoons of specialists using intricate machinery, and these are typically located far away from inner-city and rural areas, in sprawling medical centers connected with medical schools.

In general, rural and inner-city residents have the most difficulties with physical access to medical service, both because the manpower and facilities are located elsewhere and because transportation to such facilities is either unavailable or too costly for them.

The Effects of Inadequate Medical Care

Since inadequate medical care is closely related to lack of funds and rural or inner-city areas (where the poor are concentrated), it is no wonder that it affects the poor the most. Surveys show that families visit general practitioners, and consult specialists, less frequently the lower their income. It is no accident, therefore, that in 1970 the life expectancy of American Indians was 42 years, of blacks 65, and of whites 72, while at the same time Indians and blacks were disproportionately hit by poverty. Nor is it an accident that chronic diseases affecting employability are four times as prevalent among the poor as among the nonpoor.

So, not receiving medical attention or adequate diets creates bodies that are ill, that cannot provide steady labor services, and that are thus doomed to remain ill and malnourished for lack of income—a vicious circle. There is another contributing factor, however.

Medical attention can be directed at controlling disease and also at restraining births. For the poor it tends to do neither very well. While lack of funds and inaccessibility of medical personnel or facilities make it impossible for many people to regain their health when they meet with disease or accident, the same factors cause others to lose their health when they cannot plan the number and spacing of their children. In 1971 well over 5 million women could not afford to purchase birth control information and devices available to the more affluent. Women in this category have about half of all unwanted babies. However, other women, who are not hampered by lack of funds, are often faced with other obstacles. These range from religious scruples and embarrassment at consulting a doctor to archaic laws (concerning sex education, voluntary sterilization, and abortion) to inaccessibility of trained medical personnel to deliberately obstructive administrative practices by hospitals (based on the age and marital status of patients).

Between 1960 and 1968, the Department of Health, Education, and Welfare found, 20 percent of all children born in the United States were not wanted by one or both parents. Thus there were over 7 million unwanted children in this period. While 42 percent of the babies of the poor were unwanted, only 17 percent of those of the nonpoor were unwanted. Yet only 20 percent of poor women of childbearing age received family planning services by 1969. Interestingly, in March 1972, the average number of children under 18 was 2.23 for all families, but it was 2.81 for all poor families. If we count the number of children per 1,000 women aged 15–44, we find this for 1972: while all women taken as a group had 241 per 1,000, poor women had 363. Poor white women had 340, all white women 232. Poor black women had 406, all black women 304. For both races the number of children was smaller than these figures in the central cities and larger in the suburbs. In all cases did the poor have substantially more children than the nonpoor.

Studies show, however, that the poor *want* fewer children. Although the actual fertility rate of the poor was 55 percent higher in 1969 than for the nonpoor, surveys showed the poor to prefer smaller families. There are good reasons. Obviously, the physical and mental health of the mothers concerned is involved, but so is the mental health of the father and other members of families into which too many children are born. Ultimately, a family's economic fortunes are seriously affected by too many children. To begin with, there is less income per head. This is so not only because there are more heads, but also because mothers of young children typically have to withdraw from the labor force or at least choose different careers or working habits than otherwise. The following, therefore, should not come as a surprise: In 1972, 8.4 percent of all three-person families were poor, and this ranged from 4.2 percent for those headed by a white male to 47.1 percent for those headed by a black female. At the same time, 23.9 percent of all seven-person families were poor, and now the range went from 15.1 percent for white male-headed families to 68 percent for black female-headed ones.

The poverty of large families, furthermore, tends to be passed on to the next generation. With every extra child in the family per capita expenditures on health care, good food, and education drop. The more children, the less attention each receives. Their mental development is held back. In addition, the incidence of mental retardation is higher after the third child. Also, children from large families leave school earlier. (The percentage of youngsters who complete high school falls sharply with a rise in the number of siblings.)

HELPING PROVIDE ADEQUATE MEDICAL CARE

Those without income or insurance adequate to buy sufficient medical care have by no means been left entirely to their own devices. A number of government programs have aimed at bringing medical attention to them.

Major Government Assistance Programs

In a sense, all governmental *income assistance* programs increase the ability of the recipients to demand medical services. Think of social security benefits, aid to families with dependent children or unemployment insurance benefits, to name just a few. These programs are discussed further in Chapter 9. We shall not discuss them here because there is no way of telling how much of the money received is actually used for medical care by the recipients.

It is similarly uncertain who is aided by the *tax system* in connection with medical expenses. Since medical expenses in excess of 3 percent of gross income are deductible from gross income before taxable income is figured, families with large enough medical expenses and incomes high enough to pay taxes can get a rebate on their medical expenses in the form of lower taxes. (In fiscal 1971 the federal government lost $3.2 billion in potential tax revenue through this device.) This tends to help the nonpoor much more than the poor.

It is a different matter, however, with a number of *in-kind assistance* programs. Here the recipients do not receive cash or save taxes. They receive direct medical services or commodities, while the government pays the providers of these services. Among these programs are Medicare, Medicaid, and many others. Their dimensions in fiscal 1972 are shown in Table 6.2, "Major Government In-Kind Assistance Programs Providing Medical Care."

Legislation for the Medicare and Medicaid programs was enacted in 1965 as amendments to the Social Security Act (Titles 18 and 19, respectively). The federal Medicare program provides health services mostly to those over 65 years of age. In fiscal 1972, 64 percent of Medicare funds were paid to hospitals, 23 percent to physicians, and most of the remainder to others who provided health services directly to the aged covered by the program. Since mid-1973 certain younger people who suffer from acute kidney disease or who are eligible for Social Security disability benefits can also join Medicare. For a $4-a-month premium—matched by the federal government—Medicare initially paid all hospital expenses in excess of $50. It also provided for the payment of outpatient medical services (in excess of $50) if supplementary insurance was purchased (at $5.60 per month, later $5.80). These rather generous provisions may be tightened, however, for in fiscal 1972 premiums only covered 14 percent of Medicare expenses. In his budget message for fiscal 1974, President Nixon proposed that Medicare patients be made to pay the first day's full cost of hospital room and board plus 10 percent of all costs on other days. He also proposed that the supplementary insurance (at $6.30 per month) only cover 75 percent of those outpatient costs in excess of $85 and that this $85 deductible be raised over time at the same rate as Social Security benefits. Thus Medicare is less and less likely to eliminate the medical money worries of the aged poor. Note also that the program undoubtedly helps many who are not poor. According to an estimate by the Office of Economic Opportunity, only $5 billion or 30 percent of the $16.7 billion of *federal* spending on in-kind health assistance

Table 6.2 Major Government In-Kind Assistance Programs Providing Medical Care, United States, Fiscal 1972

Program	Outlay in Millions		
	Total	Federal	State and Local
1. Medicare	$8,819	$8,819	...
2. Medicaid[a]	7,465	4,090	$3,375
3. General hospital and medical care	4,235	446	3,789
4. Veterans hospital and medical care	2,256	2,256	...
5. Defense Department hospital and medical care (incl. military dependents)	2,188	2,188	...
6. Selected public health activities	2,100	823	1,277
7. Workmen's compensation medical benefits	1,200	30	1,170
8. Maternal, child, and school health services	794	235	559
9. All others	430	320	110
Total[a,b]	$29,487	$19,207	$10,280

[a] State payments of $138 million from Medicaid funds of Medicare premiums for old age supplementary medical insurance have been counted under Medicare and deleted from Medicaid.

[b] The total equals the government portion of the $83 billion national health expenditure figure cited in the text, except for government spending on medical research and medical facilities construction. Medical education expenditures are neither included in this table nor in the $83 billion figure.

Source: *U.S. Department of Health, Education, and Welfare,* Social Security Bulletin, *January 1973.*

in fiscal 1971 went to benefit poor persons directly. In that year, the percentage for Medicare alone was 24, for Medicaid alone it was 68.

Medicaid is designed for low-income families not covered by Medicare. It involves large federal grants to the states. The states, in turn, pay the providers of medical services and commodities. Of the total shown in Table 6.2, 41 percent went to hospitals, 24 percent to nursing homes, 13 percent to physicians, dentists, and other professionals, 7 percent to druggists, and the rest to others. Critical statements aver, however, that low-income families receive "free" medical services under demeaning circumstances. Also, the program reached at most only a third of its potential clientele even so far along as 1971, and in 1973 President Nixon moved to cut costs by eliminating federal payments for adult dental care coverage from Medicaid.

The third largest in-kind assistance program, general hospital and medical care, involves mostly the provision of state mental hospitals. Their services, as all the others listed in Table 6.2, are not restricted to the poor.

The public health activities included cover programs for American Indians, for seamen, in neighborhood centers, and others. They do not include pollution control, sanitation, water supply, and sewage treatment activities.

One of the most significant new in-kind programs (hidden in the maternal, child, and school health services category) concerns birth control. The 1970 Family-Planning Services and Population Research Act provides that family-planning services (counseling and contraceptive devices) be made available on a voluntary basis through a new Center for Family-Planning Services to any or all of 5 million women too poor to pay for them. In addition, the Center for Population Research of the National Institutes of Health receives research support to find "an effective, safe, inexpensive, reversible, and self-administered contraceptive device" and to study human behavior with a view to formulating correct policies encouraging the use of contraceptives. In 1971 the Office of Economic Opportunity even initiated a voluntary sterilization program for men and women in Appalachia. Medical expenditures by the Office of Economic Opportunity for medical vocational rehabilitation and temporary disability insurance medical benefits are grouped under the "all others" category in Table 6.2.

Lessons from the Recent Medical Care Price Inflation

The injection of large amounts of government money on the demand side of the markets for medical care has led in recent years to a highly undesirable and unanticipated consequence: a spiraling of medical care prices with little concurrent or subsequent increase in the real supply of medical services. In a properly functioning market, this is not what should have happened. Under perfect competition, an increase in demand would lead to a higher equilibrium price in the short run; in the long run, an increase in demand would stimulate an increase in supply and depress the price until a larger quantity should be supplied, perhaps at the original price.[2]

As it turns out, between 1950 and 1972, while consumer prices in general rose 74 percent, medical care prices rose 147 percent. Near the end of this period, in 1971, a typical bill for a terminal cancer patient in a New York City hospital was $18,339 for 110 days!

Interestingly, the divergent behavior of consumer prices in general and medical care prices in particular began around 1955, and was due to increases in hospital charges and in fees for professional services, not to increases in prices of drugs and appliances. There are a number of explanations.

While drugs and medical appliances are produced in a fairly competitive, profit-oriented market, medical manpower and facilities are produced in an environment lacking competition and profit orientation. Pharmaceutical com-

[2] You might wish to review the discussion of this mechanism in Chapter 2 above, notably in the text dealing with Figures 2.4 and 2.5.

panies, makers of eyeglasses, and so on, respond to increased demand with rapid increases in supply, thereby holding price increases down. The supply of professional and hospital services is much more sluggish in response to demand.

Consider medical manpower. The number of medical students trained, for instance, is strictly regulated by the American Medical Association (AMA), but certainly not with regard to the current demand for medical services. Ever since Dr. Flexner wrote his famous report in 1910 on the then deplorable status of medical schools in the United States, the AMA has followed his advice about medical education, stressing advanced biological research in laboratories, combined with clinical experience gained at university medical centers, as a prerequisite for *any* type of medical practice. By accrediting only medical schools that followed this prescription, and by licensing only doctors so trained, this approach quickly eliminated quackery in the medical profession. But the emphasis on the above two pillars of medical education had other effects besides high-quality doctors. It also limited severely the *number* of doctors. Originally, this was so because a sufficient number of high-quality applicants could not be found who could be expected to go through the required course of rigorous training. In recent years, however, such restrictions as to numbers have been maintained, even though medical schools have been swamped with high-quality applicants. Some suspect a rather selfish reason on the part of the AMA: artificial restrictions to the number of doctors trained reduces competition among practitioners, leads to higher equilibrium prices for doctors' services, and assures the receipt of higher incomes by them. (Refer again to the section preceding the Conclusion of Chapter 2 on failure to assure full mobility.)

Emphasis on the production and licensing of *highly trained* specialists has had another effect: deemphasis on the training and licensing of *lesser trained* allied health personnel (such as physical therapists, dental hygienists, and all types of medical assistants). This was done for fear of encouraging quackery. Yet the end result has been a further roadblock to a rapid rise in the supply of medical services; the training of the very people who could be trained the fastest is neglected, and full-fledged doctors and dentists—already in short supply—have to do work others could do just as well.

All in all, the faithful application of the Flexner model has created an institutional setup wherein increases in the demand for professional medical services do not lead to rapid increases in their supply. They are primarily met by higher prices. When private and public funds became more plentiful around 1965 and the demand for medical services consequently rose, doctors and dentists simply eliminated the shortage by raising fees. No one started a crash program to raise more trained personnel. (In terms of Chapter 2's discussion, increased demand led to the expected short-run effect depicted in Figure 2.4, while the long-run effect, shown in Figure 2.5, failed to materialize.)

Hospital administrators acted in a corresponding fashion. Not being profit-oriented (most hospitals are nonprofit institutions) and being in charge of localized monopolies, they did not think in terms of expanding facilities or constructing new ones in response to higher demand. (They would rather do that in response to philanthropic gifts that appear at irregular intervals.) As demand rose, they just raised fees. They were originally prodded into doing so in the 1950's by increased unionization of hospital workers and the introduction of new costly technology (like open heart surgery). The latter is another effect of the Flexner philosophy: Where emphasis is placed on highly trained specialists, one must provide highly elaborate facilities for their use and one must update them as fast as new knowledge is gained. In the process, one is likely to forget about the creation of less fancy facilities away from giant medical school-hospital complexes, to be located perhaps in remote rural areas or in city ghettos.

Another factor that has contributed to the raising of professional and hospital service fees has been the knowledge on the part of doctors and hospital administrators that private or public insurance was increasingly paying for the services provided. Thus higher fees would have no immediate effect on the financial position of any one patient. (In the long run, of course, insurance premiums or taxes would go up to pay for costlier programs.) Nor had any one patient an incentive to resist higher fees since they were paid by a third party. Unlike buyers in other markets, medical service buyers (whether private individuals or those who supply them with funds) are extremely ignorant and uncertain about what they are buying or the alternatives available. By themselves, they cannot make a rational choice. They must allow the seller to decide for them on what is bought: the type of treatment and tests performed, the need for hospitalization, the frequency of visits to the doctor, and so on. It has been asserted that doctors tend to choose fancy over less fancy care (by ordering unnecessary surgery, for example), thereby raising demand and prices (and their incomes) artificially.

We conclude, therefore, that increases in the demand for medical services cannot be relied on to bring forth corresponding increases in their supply. This is so because the medical service markets are highly imperfect, being characterized by consumer ignorance, artificial restrictions to the entry of new suppliers, and inefficient use of existing manpower and facilities.

The lessons learned from the recent inflation experienced in connection with the medical services industry can be used to good advantage. They can be used to formulate better policies to give more people access to medical care and a road out of poverty.

Increasing the Overall Supply of Medical Resources

The overall supply of medical manpower and facilities might be increased, and in a number of ways. The most obvious one involves increased training of doctors, dentists, nurses, and allied health personnel, and also increased facilities construction. A 1970 report of the Carnegie Commission on Higher Education, for instance, recommended a 50 percent increase in the number of medical students and a 20 percent increase in the number of dental students. Other groups such as the Surgeon General's Consultant Group on Medical Education and the National Advisory Commission on Health Manpower have come to similar conclusions.

Quite possibly, this can only be achieved by breaking the monopoly of the American Medical Association in accreditation of medical schools and licensing of medical personnel. Government could use its powers of the purse to overcome possible resistance. All levels of government spent $1.8 billion in fiscal 1972 for medical research, $1.4 billion for medical facilities construction, and several hundred million dollars on training medical personnel. These funds could be increased *and allocated with strings attached:* To encourage the training of *greater numbers* of general medical personnel (or of particular types) federal grants to medical schools might be made not in a lump sum but as so many dollars per graduate, with no limit on the total provided. To encourage *faster* training, a shorter-than-usual number of years to graduation may be specified as a condition for such grants. (Both of these provisions were contained in the Comprehensive Health Manpower Training Act of 1971.) Finally, the government could itself undertake to train and license health personnel (as the Department of Labor did recently with allied health professions).

The government could at any time fund the construction of new medical schools or hospitals, as it has since 1946 under the Hill-Burton Facilities Construction Act. (In 1972, Congress did vote to create nine new federally funded medical schools, one linked with the Pentagon, eight with the Veterans Administration. On the other hand, in 1973, President Nixon proposed to eliminate the Hill-Burton subsidies, which have aided 11,000 hospitals to the tune of $3.8 billion since 1946.)

More Efficient Use of Medical Resources

Not less important than increasing the overall supply is a stimulation of the more efficient use of old or new medical manpower and facilities. In many ways, our high-quality doctors do the wrong things as seen from the standpoint of society. They locate in the wrong places. They waste their time doing things lesser-trained assistants could do just as well. They provide some important services while neglecting others at least as important. Medical facilities, similarly, are often of the wrong type and in the wrong place. These matters, too, could be changed by an alert government.

So that the supply of doctors in neglected inner cities and rural areas would increase, doctors being paid under any governmental insurance scheme might be offered bonuses over regular fees if they would locate their offices in such areas. Or for the same goal to be achieved, if doctors had their education financed with federal loans, outstanding debts might be forgiven if they located in places where doctors are needed most. Beginning in 1972, federal medical personnel (in the National Health Service Corps) have been placed in shortage areas under the Emergency Health Personnel Act of 1970.

To change the *types* of things doctors do might require nothing less than changing the basic philosophy of the U.S. medical system. Under the Flexner model, the U.S. health industry has become a *sickness system* that is designed for a small number of highly qualified specialists with elaborate facilities and that responds to catastrophe after it occurs. Yet one might concentrate less on sickness and more on health. That is, an alternative to this system of *crisis care* would be the introduction of a *health maintenance system* wherein the emphasis would be on *continuous and preventive care.* Much sickness could be forestalled, and what is important, much of that could be done by large numbers of paraprofessionals working under the supervision of doctors and using less elaborate but more numerous facilities.

Consider the smoking, drinking, eating, and living habits of Americans. These often lead to sickness that doctors must then treat; but such treatment would be unnecessary if health education were more widespread (and such education need not be given by fully trained medical doctors). Similarly, dentists would be less busy if there were more dental technicians. Psychiatrists would be less overburdened if there were more mental health workers providing preventive care. All kinds of preventive medical care—the screening of those in need of doctors, and indeed the treatment of minor problems—could be carried out by physicians' assistants and neighborhood health aides. In 1971, there were 550,000 nurses who had dropped out of the labor force, many of whom could surely be recruited for such purposes. There also were numbered at that time thousands of veterans having medical skills that could be used and upgraded where necessary. By being obsessed with getting the highest possible quality care, Americans have doomed some of their own number not to get any care at all.

It is fairly easy to see how such changes might be brought about with the proper economic incentives. To replace crisis care with preventive care, the medical insurance system could be changed to discourage crisis care in the hospital and encourage preventive care outside the hospital. This might require shifting the emphasis from private to public insurance and changing the method of paying doctors.

Private insurance companies, for instance, avoid coverage of preventive care outside the hospital. They do so because this strategy, although wise in the long run for the insured and the insurance industry alike, seems unwise for any one company. If it considers the short run, it can foresee high initial costs of uncovering many treatable conditions. These high costs would have to be paid by the company and probably bring it losses. If it considers the long run, it can foresee that the initial investment in preventive medicine may have a payoff in healthier and longer lives for the insured and in profits for the insurance industry (as its need to pay out benefits is reduced drastically in the future). But there is no guarantee that the same people in whom company A made the initial investment will continue to buy insurance from company A. Possibly company B will reap the benefits (steady premium income, low expenses over many years), the foundation for which was laid by A. Unwilling to bet on the long run, private insurance companies shy away from covering preventive medicine. Governmental insurance could more easily take a long-run view.

Private insurance companies also pay doctors and hospitals on a *fee-for-service* basis. This is equivalent to paying workers on a piecework basis. The more sick people doctors treat, the better off doctors are.[3] Much is to be said for paying doctors on a *capitation* basis instead. By this method, they agree in advance to provide, for a fixed fee, all medical services a person might require over a given period. This sets up the incentive to keep the person healthy. The doctor's income increases not with the number of days a person is sick, but with the number of days he is *not* sick. In short, this would revive an old Chinese custom whereby doctors were paid only when a patient was not ill. This would stimulate thinking along lines of *cost effectiveness*: How can a group of patients be kept healthy at minimum cost? Quickly, doctors would break down their skilled job into components requiring less skill. They would come to stress comprehensive *preventive* care with use of cheaper, paramedical personnel and automated testing equipment whenever possible. They would join in group practice to cut costs by sharing buildings, instruments, and receptionists; by centralized record keeping, accounting, and purchases; and so on.[4]

The maldistribution of medical facilities, by type or geographically, could be similarly corrected by attaching conditions to government funding. As a long-run solution to the unavailability of care in rural and inner-city areas, new medical or dental schools and associated hospitals could be located in such areas by varying construction grants by location. In the same way, the use of traveling facilities such as mobile multipurpose clinics could be greatly increased. Selected outpatient clinics now existing in scarcity areas could be upgraded and expanded. Special transportation services to outlying medical facilities might be set up.

From all this might develop, in the long run, a new three-tier system of medical facilities. First, *neighborhood clinics* might provide basic preventive outpatient services, using much paramedical personnel and new types of equipment. Such services may include vaccinations, dental care, family planning,

[3] The fee-for-service system has also encouraged the recent rise in medical prices, as doctors and hospitals are encouraged to *itemize*. Instead of charging $6 per visit, they might charge $2 for diagnosis, $2 for treatment, $3 for urinalysis, $2 for blood count, and $1 for administrative expense, making a $10 total.

[4] One program of this type (the Kaiser Plan in California, Hawaii, and Oregon) has worked quite well. During 1950–65, for instance, when hospital charges rose 50 percent in the U.S., they rose only 15 percent in the participating hospitals. The hospital use rate under the Kaiser Plan was 30 percent below the California average. This is explained by greater outpatient care and a reduction in unnecessary hospitalization, which often occurs in other plans as patients whose insurance coverage excludes outpatient services try "to get their money back" by being hospitalized. Other group prepayment plans have had similar experiences. These include—besides the Kaiser Foundation Health Plan—the Health Insurance Plan of Greater New York, the Community Health Association of Detroit, the Group Health Association of Washington, D.C., and the Group Health Cooperative of Puget Sound. They served about half of the 8 million people covered by such plans in 1972.

occupational therapy, social work, and routine physical exams. However, such exams (of apparently perfectly healthy people) may be much more thorough than heretofore. They might concentrate on picking up early warning signals. Exams might include the blood serum test that can single out probable emphysema victims as much as forty years before the first symptoms appear. They might include microphotographs of the back of the eye, which can help in the diagnosis of incipient glaucoma and in the estimation of the likelihood of diabetes ten years in advance. They might include thermography, the infrared scanning of, say, a person's forehead, which can show by the indication of temperature differences even the slightest restriction of the blood supply and thus indicate the likelihood of a future stroke. They might include use of the bicycle cardioergometer, which measures heart performance under stress, as well as routine examinations of a person's life style, to single out people prone to heart attacks. From all this might result specific recommendations, ranging from suggestions on diet (less sugar, less fat, less smoking) to suggestions on life style (more exercise, more leisurely meals, less staggering work load, more time for family and friends, different occupation, different geographic location) to advice on the taking of drugs (anticoagulants to forestall that stroke).

At a second level, people found sick might be referred to *cooperating specialists and basic hospitals*. The latter could specialize in general in-patient care. Third, more difficult tasks (open heart surgery, X-ray therapy, organ transplants) could be left to *specialized regionalized facilities*.

Increasing the Demand for Medical Services

Once measures have been taken to assure the responsiveness of the supply of medical services to demand, further increases in demand by those now insufficiently served need not be feared. And in recent years, the call for broader insurance coverage provided by government has become louder. Gone are the days when national health insurance plans (like that of President Truman not so many years ago) were rejected out of hand as socialistic. A 1971 Harris poll showed Americans 2:1 in favor of the idea of cradle-to-grave coverage. This would cost somewhere between $100 billion and $200 billion a year, and most actual proposals are more modest, adding to present annual health expenditures anywhere from $4.5 billion to $70 billion. The cheapest proposal is that of the American Medical Association, called *Medicredit*. At an annual extra cost of $4.5 billion, the federal government would pay health insurance premiums for the poor and grant income tax credits for the payment of private insurance premiums to the affluent. Next comes the National Health Care Act, proposed by the Health Insurance Association of America and costing an extra $15 billion. It closely resembles Medicredit, but places the administration in the hands of the states.

President Nixon proposed a National Health Insurance Partnership Act. It would require employers to provide health insurance for all employees. Employers would pay 75 percent of the premium, employees the rest. This insurance would provide uniform benefits federally set, covering visits to doctors' offices and hospitalization. Each family would pay the first $300 of bills a year plus 25 percent of the rest, with insurance paying the remainder. Low-income families without an employed adult would receive different benefits, financed from taxes, under a family health insurance plan that would replace Medicaid. Americans would join health maintenance organizations stressing preventive care. The extra cost would be $11 billion a year.

The National Health Insurance and Health Services Improvement Act, proposed by Senator Javits, would cost an extra $48 billion a year. It would involve extending Medicare from the elderly to all citizens. (Introduced in 1965, Medicare provides hospital insurance for all over 65 at a $4-a-month premium matched by the federal government, plus additional voluntary medical insurance coverage.)

Finally, the Health Security Act, proposed by Senator Kennedy and organized labor, would cost another $90 billion a year by 1974. It would provide for all health expenditures of all citizens, to be financed half and half by general taxes and payroll levies. Each year, Congress would approve a national medical care budget. It would be allocated to ten main regions, then to one hundred areas within each, and finally to each hospital and practitioner (on a capitation basis). Patients would be covered for everything and pay nothing.

Whatever method of funding demand for medical care is finally agreed upon, there are good reasons for allowing patients to make use of these funds in as flexible a way as possible and for not presenting any one doctor or hospital with a captive market. For example, a policy that would enable patients to choose among many doctors or hospitals, with these in turn *competing* with each other, would tend to keep medical costs down. For example, *health vouchers*, similar to food stamps, might be given to people, who would be free to spend them on any type or combination of medical services they chose. At the same time, the AMA cartel agreement among doctors and hospitals not to compete by price might be made illegal.

Summary

1. Most people earn above-poverty incomes by work. Some cannot do so for reasons of poor health. Their poor health can be explained only in small part by differences in genetic endowment. Most likely it is caused by such factors as inadequate diets and lack of medical care. This, in turn, is the result of inadequate income and certain market imperfections.
2. In 1968, for instance, 5 million Americans were chronically hungry, 10 million more were undernourished. Of families earning less than $3,000 a year, 63 percent had inadequate diets.
3. Government programs to combat insufficient or improper diets include direct food distribution, food stamps, and several child nutrition programs. These

programs, however, do not reach all the poor. Some of them also reach the nonpoor. Those who are reached find the aid inadequate.

4. When it comes to medical care, the U.S. is the highest per capita spender in the world ($394 per person in fiscal 1972). Yet, compared with other countries, it ranks far from the top in results if measured by life expectancy, death rates, and incidence of disease. This may well be due to the fact that not all Americans have equal access to good medical care.
5. Some people do not get adequate medical care because they lack income or insurance coverage. Many do not have physical access to medical manpower and facilities, owing to a geographic maldistribution. Noticeable shortages exist in rural and inner-city areas where the poor are concentrated.
6. As a result, chronic diseases affecting employability are four times as prevalent among the poor as among the nonpoor. Another result is that the poor have less of a chance to control births. Poverty is thereby accentuated in a number of ways.
7. A number of government programs tend to increase the medical attention received by the poor. Among them are all types of cash assistance programs, and also certain provisions of the tax laws allowing medical deductions. More directly, they include in-kind programs, such as Medicare for the elderly, Medicaid for the poor, and family planning services. These reach many nonpoor and by no means all of the poor. Nor is the aid sufficient for those who are reached.
8. In recent years, the injection of large amounts of government money on the demand side of the markets for medical care has led to a rapid inflation of medical care prices rather than a rapid expansion of the supply of real medical services. This points to serious imperfections in the markets for medical services.
9. These imperfections include artificial and unnecessary restrictions regarding the numbers and types of medical personnel trained. They include an unresponsiveness of the supply of medical facilities (usually nonprofit) to the numbers and types demanded. They include lack of knowledge on the part of medical service buyers, resulting ultimately in inefficient use of existing manpower and facilities.
10. By the use of proper economic incentives, government could do much to assure an increase in the supply of medical services. It could, first, encourage training of additional personnel and construction of additional facilities. It could, second, encourage more efficient use of medical resources, for example by influencing the location of personnel and facilities and the types of services they perform.
11. More efficient operation might involve moving from a sickness system (wherein highly qualified specialists with elaborate facilities respond to catastrophe after it occurs) to a health maintenance system (wherein a host of paraprofessionals, using less elaborate facilities, would be guided by specialists to prevent catastrophe). Such a new system might reach more people for any given resource expenditure than the old one. It could be encouraged by greater emphasis on public insurance and the payment of doctors on a capitation basis.
12. Once measures have been taken to make the supply of medical manpower and facilities responsive to the quantity and types demanded, it would make

sense to give more money to those persons now insufficiently served, thereby enabling them to demand more medical services. A large number of demand-raising programs have recently been proposed, ranging from tinkering with present programs to instituting a comprehensive national health service.

Terms[5]

capitation system
child nutrition programs
commodity distribution program
fee-for-service system
food stamp program
health maintenance organization
health vouchers
Medicaid
Medicare

Questions for Review and Discussion

1. "Adequate medical care ought to be made available to all. After all, this involves a matter of life and death. It is positively immoral to ration medical care via the market system in the same way as TV sets." Do you agree? Why or why not? How about substituting "food" for "medical care" in the above statement? or clothing? or housing?
2. "The President's Commission on Population Growth and the American Future estimated that an all-inclusive national program to prevent unwanted pregnancy and improve child health care could cost over $8 billion a year. Obviously, it would be worth it." Discuss.
3. "Emphasis on use of birth control in poverty programs is dangerous, for it adds tension to race relations. Some blacks tend to see the suggestion of whites that blacks as well as whites ease poverty by limiting their families as perhaps an unconscious attempt of the whites to eliminate black people. This may seem unduly paranoid, but is it really? In 1968, a Delaware state senate committee recommended legislation that would provide for sterilization of women who use welfare funds to support more than two illegitimate children. The dangers involved here are obvious." What do you think?
4. A mid-1972 study by the Planned Parenthood organization for the Presidential Commission on Population Growth and the American Future showed that a third of all women were using ineffective birth control methods or none at all. The Commission recommended that abortion laws be liberalized and abortion (and also other birth control methods) be available to all regardless of age, income, or marital status. This was rejected by President Nixon. Do you agree with the president? Why or why not?
5. In 1968, the American Public Health Association urged that, as in Japan and the Soviet Union, safe, legal abortions be made available to all women as a

[5] Terms are defined in the Glossary at the back of the book.

matter of right. In the same year, the pope issued an encyclical, "On Birth Control." He said: "We must once again declare that the direct interruption of the generative process already begun, and, above all, directly willed and procured abortion, even if for therapeutic reasons, are to be absolutely excluded as licit means of regulating birth. Equally to be excluded . . . is direct sterilization. . . . Similarly excluded is every action which . . . proposes . . . to render procreation impossible." What do you think?

6. Recently a number of states, notably California, Kansas, and New York, have liberalized abortion laws to provide a backup for failed contraception. Should they have? Monsignor McHugh, director of the U.S. Catholic Conference's family bureau, answered this way: "If the child can be killed in his mother's womb any time she decides he isn't wanted, what prevents us from killing the aged, the sick, the mentally or physically disadvantaged, or members of objectionable minority groups when their lives become a burden to others and they are—at least to some degree—unwanted?" What do you think?
7. Critics of the 1970 birth control bill mentioned in the text scoff at promoting *voluntary* birth control by making contraceptive devices and information available to those who want them. They say this will never avert the eventual overpopulation chaos. For one thing, such a voluntary birth control program is not perfect. It does not reach all people. Furthermore, even 100-percent-sure contraceptives widely used will not slow population growth unless people's *motivation* is affected. What we need, they say, is a clearly defined maximum population goal and a system of incentives to achieve it. This may include *compulsory* sterilization, free abortions, legal postponement of the marriage age, true equality in education and jobs for women (to allow them to develop interests competing with marriage), and economic levers (taxing single people less than married ones, paying bonuses for not having children, eliminating tax exemption for children, levying a tax on children). What do you think of these proposals?
8. It has been proposed, as a means of controlling population growth, that each baby receive at birth one "birth stamp." This would allow it (legally) to have one child. Upon marriage there would then be two birth stamps available per couple, allowing them (legally) to have two children. These stamps could be freely traded, their price being set by demand and supply, like the price of General Motors stock. Unmarried persons and couples not wishing to have children would be able to sell their stamps. Couples wishing to have more than two children would have to buy stamps. Having more than two children without the necessary stamps would result in a permanent doubling of the couple's income tax. What do you think of this proposal as a way of fighting poverty?
9. "President Nixon has found the best way to stop inflation in the medical service industry, comprising 300,000 doctors, 20,000 nursing homes, and 7,000 hospitals: In 1971, he froze all wages and prices for 90 days. Then he put controls on wage and price increases. Specifically, the Price Commission ruled in December 1971 that: (a) noninstitutional health care providers (such as doctors) could raise fees by no more than 2.5 percent a year, if justified by cost increases; (b) institutional health care providers (such as hospitals) could raise fees by 2.5 percent a year any time, by 6 percent a year, if justified by

cost increases and so proved in a written report, by more than that only with government approval." Do you think this is the best way? Why or why not?

10. It is often argued that health practitioners should have the freedom to conduct their practice where and as they wish, and that patients should have the freedom to choose practitioners. Do you agree? What if this freedom conflicts with the goal of assuring access to health services for all people?
11. "Health insurance—private or public—is a mistake. When no such possibility existed to spread risk, that is, when each family had to pay on a fee-for-service basis, each family would economize. It would be keenly aware of how each extra prescription or procedure or day in the hospital would add to its bill. So it would make sure that health services were used only when unavoidable. Health insurance, by removing this incentive to save, can only lead to waste." Discuss.
12. "The American health care system's reliance on independent solo practitioners is stupid. It means forgoing the innumerable advantages of a division of labor in the health industry." Considering the advantages of specialization enumerated in Chapter 1, what do you think this statement could mean?
13. "The Chinese have it all over us in medical care. They invented acupuncture and the capitation system. More recently, they created the barefoot doctors—essentially laymen narrowly trained in some one aspect of medicine—who in huge numbers can perform preventive and minor sickness care." What do you think? Should one sacrifice quality for quantity in medical care?
14. Mr. A: Any national health insurance program is a bad idea because it allocates resources to health care through a collective decision. If the total money so spent were divided up equally among all citizens, they would probably spend less on health care and more on other goods, proving the economic inefficiency of the system.

    Mr. B: If people were given cash and then acted as Mr. A assumes, this would only show consumer ignorance about the relative marginal benefit of health care versus other goods. So this is actually a point *in favor* of a national health insurance program. It would force each individual to spend on health care what is in his best interest (whether he knows it or not). Furthermore, it protects the individual from excessive unpredictable health expenditures by providing a pooling of risks.

    Who is right?
15. "There are other reasons besides nutrition and medical attention that explain the poor health of many: inadequate clothing, inadequate shelter, and inadequate education." Try to elaborate on this statement.

Selected Readings

Gordon, David M. *Problems in Political Economy: An Urban Perspective*. Lexington, Mass.: D. C. Heath and Co., 1971. Pp. 315–54. Presents conservative, liberal, and radical views on the health care system and provides an excellent bibliography.

U.S. Bureau of the Census. *Statistical Abstract of the United States, 1972.* Washington, D.C., 1972. Lists some recent statistics on nutrition and health (Sections 2 and 33) and—more important—sources to other statistics: Note the listing of statistical abstract supplements (p. v); and the guide to general sources of statistics (pp. 923, 926–30, and 953–54), to recent censuses (pp. 955–56) and to state statistical abstracts (pp. 961–64).

NOTE: The *Journal of Economic Literature* lists recent articles on the economics of health (section 913) and the health service industry (635).

The *Index of Economic Articles* catalogs, in sections beginning with the indicated numbers, articles on health insurance (9.43, 21.7), nutrition (21.31), and medical care (21.7).

7 *Providing Skills*

The last chapter concentrated on the condition of the human body. A person's mind, however, is equally important for one's ability to work and earn a good income. Just as machines can be designed to perform either highly complicated tasks or only simple operations, so human beings can similarly be designed for a variety of occupations. Even if all people were equally healthy and equally well-nourished, there could be great differences among them in education and training. This would make prospective employers prefer one over another. Indeed, the majority of the employable poor are shunned by employers, because they have had only a minimum of education, training, and work experience. Why are so many people insufficiently skilled, and what can be done about it?

LACK OF SKILLS MEANS LACK OF GOOD JOBS

Consider the *education of family heads* who are over the age of 25 in the United States.[1] In 1972, in the population as a whole, 25 percent of them had had only elementary school education (not necessarily complete). For the heads of poor families among these, the percentage was double, or 50 percent. Among poor family heads, it was 40 for white females, 40 for black females, 54 for white males, and 67 for black males. If we include high school dropouts among the insufficiently educated, we find that in 1972, 42 percent of all U.S. family heads over the age of 25 had not completed high school. However, the percentage was 71 for all heads of poor families as a group. This was, essentially, the weighted average of these percentages: 62 for white females, 70 for white males, 73 for black females, and 85 for black males.

Another illuminating fact is this: While in 1972 all family heads over 25 as a group had had a median schooling of 12.3 years, the poor among them

[1] Most of the statistical data in this chapter come from U.S. Bureau of the Census, *Current Population Reports*, Series P-20 and P-60, from U.S. Bureau of Labor Statistics, *Special Labor Force Reports* and *Employment and Earnings*, from U.S. Office of Education, *Biennial Survey of Education in the United States* and *Digest of Educational Statistics*, and from U.S. Manpower Administration, *Manpower Report of the President*.

had had a median schooling of only 9 years. Clearly, when you are poorly educated in an economy wherein the demand for educated labor is relatively high, your chances of being unemployed, underemployed, or employed in low-paying jobs are excellent, indeed.

Consider the *recent work experience of family heads* in the United States. Among the population as a whole, 85 percent of 1972 family heads had been employed in 1971 (including service in the armed forces). But only 54 percent of the heads of poor families had been so employed. Among the heads of poor families, 69 percent of black males had been employed, 64 percent of white males, 40 percent of black females, and 36 percent of white females. To put this another way, while among all family heads 15 percent had been (voluntarily or involuntarily) unemployed, among poor family heads 46 percent had been so unemployed.

Now consider the *length and type of employment*. Let us define part-time work as any work taking less than 50 full-time weeks per year. Then, among all 1972 family heads who had been employed in 1971, 24 percent had worked part time. Yet among the employed heads of poor families, 60 percent had worked part time (51 percent of white males, 53 percent of black males, 79 percent of black females, and 85 percent of white females in this group).

What kinds of jobs did they hold? Among all 1972 family heads who had been employed in 1971, 31 percent were professionals, managers, or officials. For the poor as a group, this percentage was only 20 (and it was 30 percent for white males, 9 for black males, 8 for white females, and 6 for black females). Among all 1972 family heads who had been employed in 1971, 35 percent were craftsmen, foremen, or clerical and sales workers. For the poor as a group, however, this percentage was only 23 (and it was 31 for white females, 26 for white males, 17 for black males, and 8 for black females). Finally, among all 1972 family heads who had been employed in 1971, 32 percent were operatives, household workers, other service workers, or laborers. Yet among the poor as a group, this percentage was 55 (and it was 86 percent for black females, 72 for black males, 61 for white females, and 40 for white males). Those employed family heads not listed in one of the three categories of jobs were in the armed forces.

Thus we can conclude that those people who have had little education and training have the least chance to get and hold full-time or skilled jobs. They have the greatest chance of getting part-time or unskilled jobs and thus of being poor. Table 7.1, "Education and Income," illustrates dramatically the relationship between education and income for American males 25 years of age and over. In 1968, for American males, the difference between finishing elementary school and finishing high school meant $92,000 in lifetime income on the average. The difference between finishing high school and finishing college spelled another $236,000. Even though the figures differ among the races or between the sexes, it is always true that more education translates into more income.

Table 7.1 Education and Income, United States, 1968

Educational Level of Males, 25 Years and Older	Average Annual Income	Lifetime Income	Additional Lifetime Income by Reaching Next Educational Level
Elementary school			
Less than 8 years	$ 3,981	$196,000	. . .
8 years	5,467	258,000	$ 62,000
High School			
1–3 years	6,769	294,000	36,000
4 years	8,148	350,000	56,000
College			
1–3 years	9,397	411,000	61,000
4 years or more	12,938	586,000	175,000

SOURCE: Statistical Abstract of the United States, *1972, p. 114.*

WHY SOME PEOPLE REMAIN UNSKILLED

A natural question arises. Since most people know, at least vaguely, how education translates into income, why are so many insufficiently prepared for skilled jobs, and thus programmed for poverty?

The Role of Inherited Intelligence

There are some who will give you a simple answer. "It is all a matter of heredity," they say. "Some people are simply born with inferior intelligence and endowed by nature with a generous dose of laziness in addition. They *cannot* be educated." As if to prove their point, they point out simultaneously how lack of education and poverty are more frequent among nonwhites than among whites. There is no evidence, however, to support such racist "explanations" of poverty. For one thing, although poverty hits a greater percentage of nonwhite than of white people, in 1972, 70 percent of all poor persons were white. In addition, no one has yet devised a way of measuring a person's genetic intellectual potential. If one were to try to prove the existence of inborn racial differences in intelligence, one would have to test the embryo at the time of conception, and it is very hard even to imagine this being done. After conception, environmental factors begin to play a role. Potential native intelligence can, so to speak, become eroded during pregnancy by any malnutrition, emotional stress, and lack of medical care on the part of the mother, all of which could be the result of discriminatory treatment of the mother by society. Interestingly, in the United States in 1963 only 0.4 percent of all white mothers went through pregnancy and birth entirely without medical help, but the figure was 10 percent for nonwhites. In 1968, infant mortality was for nonwhites almost twice that for whites. Maternal deaths were almost four times as frequent for nonwhites as for whites. Life expectancy at birth was over seven years shorter for nonwhites.

It is also a well-established fact that without adequate prenatal health care the likelihood of brain damage in the newborn is much greater. American psychiatrists find the incidence among children of mental deficiency and neuropsychiatric disorders resulting from inferior medical care of expectant mothers to be significantly larger among blacks than whites. Hence, tests in later life that purport to show lower intelligence for blacks than for whites may well be a measure of discrimination that started before birth rather than of any genetic differences.

Furthermore, scientists distinguish two meanings of *intelligence*. One is intellectual potential. It is determined at conception by the genes you inherit. It cannot be measured. The other is the development of this potential after conception. It is determined by the environment: the mother's before birth, the child's afterward. We can attempt to measure the degree of actual intellectual development later in life with the help of intelligence tests that evaluate comprehension and performance. Clearly there *are* inherited physical differences among people. That is why all girls do not become movie stars and all boys do not become famous athletes. More likely than not, there are inherited mental differences also. But we can never look at a black boy's IQ score of 80 and a white boy's score of 100 and conclude anything about their genes, about where both might have gone had both been equally nourished by a friendly environment. Indeed, the black boy may yet end up with an IQ of 140 unless physical damage to his brain has occurred since conception. The intelligence quotient can measure only the degree of development of the potential, not the potential itself; it is not an unchanging figure.

One other thing should be noted. Even where the development of intelligence has proceeded equally for all, many IQ tests still score higher for whites than for blacks. This is because some tests are "culturally biased." One intelligence test for children aged 5, for instance, contains sketches of two women. Both are white. But one is the Hollywood stereotype, straight-nosed, thin-lipped. The other is flat-nosed and thick-lipped. The child is asked to choose the prettier face. The child is not supposed to choose the (white) face with Negroid features. But which will be picked by black children? Another question asks children to distinguish maples, oaks, and pines. How well are you likely to do if you have never seen anything but pavement? As a result, IQ test scores do not necessarily indicate either intellectual potential or actual intellectual development!

The Culture of Poverty

We have shown that we cannot blame the lack of education of the poor on genetic inferiority. But we also saw that the development of intellectual potential may well be stunted. This deserves a few additional comments. There is a vicious circle about poverty. Many of the poor are poor not because they were born "naturally dumb," but because their parents were poor. And this childhood environment predisposes them to becoming poor in turn. Poor children tend to grow up in densely packed, dirty, and dreary neighborhoods. Houses are dilapidated and structurally unsafe; even basic plumbing is lacking. Their father may be the victim of discrimination in his job. (In the United States, the income of black men, for example, was on the average in 1969 less than two-thirds of that for white men with the same level of education and the same area of residence.) The father's job is likely to be of low status as well as low-paying. (In the case of black people, this reflects a long history of injustices and brutality going back to slavery.) Or the father may be unemployed. Perhaps there is lots of friction in the home. There is little hope and much despair. Maybe the father just takes off one day and never comes back. Indeed, many of the poor grow up in fatherless homes. For example, only a minority of black children reach 18 having lived with both parents all along. In part this is explained by divorce rates. (In 1972, 25 percent of all and 38 percent of poor black women and 8 percent of all and 20 percent of poor white women who had ever been married were divorced or separated.) In part, the record is explained by behavior associated with illegitimacy. In 1970, for example, 90 percent of illegitimate children were kept by a family member in black families, as against only 33 percent in white families. As a result, 29 percent of black families were female-headed as against 9 percent of white families. In families with income below $3,000, only 24 percent of black and 44 percent of white children were living with both parents. (For all families, the percentages were 67 and 91 for blacks and whites, respectively.)

Now consider a child in such a fatherless and poor family. Possibly it is neglected, perhaps ill-treated. There is no intellectual stimulation: no skillful adult conversation, no music, no books, no paper, no crayons, few toys, no exposure to travel. Children are slow in developing powers of observation, expression, and muscular control.

The authority of the father is undermined or nonexistent owing to his absence. For long periods, the family probably scrapes by on welfare. (A majority of black children are on welfare at some point during their childhood.) The child has no one to look up to. It grows up without a feeling of security, without sufficient love, and without discipline. It does not learn to be reliable or honest, or to enjoy learning or working. On the contrary, it picks up socially disapproved behavior. And there is so much to be picked up! The rates of illegitimate pregnancies and delinquency are much higher among the poor than among the nonpoor. In 1969, in poverty areas, the number of murders equaled that of U.S. war deaths in Indochina. Other crimes of violence were on the rise. A study found narcotics and gambling revenues in three New York slums to exceed state welfare payments to these areas. In such an environment, a child grows up without aims and ambitions for itself.

It is in early childhood that we learn characteristic patterns of behavior. We learn to feel in certain ways about the world and ourselves. Children from destitute homes enter school not only with little developed intelligence, but also with an attitude of indifference, or even hostility, not conducive to intellectual achievement. Their unstable home environment, itself the result of poverty, becomes the prime determinant of their own future. The attitudes, beliefs, customs, habits, and morals pervading such an environment are referred to as the culture of poverty. This culture of poverty cripples those who come in contact with it because it shapes their behavior in such a way as to program them in turn for a lifetime of poverty.

Shall we believe the racists and call the children of today's poor "naturally lazy and shiftless"? That would be grossly unfair. But people *are* this unfair. That is why we must again issue a word of warning. The facts cited above, like the unthinking comparison of IQ test scores, can easily be twisted to substantiate a (mistaken) view of inferiority of the poor. A discussion of the family instability of the poor can easily be used to justify prejudices. But we must take this risk of being misunderstood. We must look at the culture of poverty and all its ugliness of family disruption, lack of love, and deprivation. We must not hide it, for we are here uncovering an important mechanism that helps us explain what causes poverty. This is a first and necessary step for abolishing it. Describing how people live is not the same thing as pointing an accusing finger at them. We cannot hold people responsible for conditions clearly beyond their control.

Inadequate General Education

The above-described problems feed on themselves. Imagine now what happens when a child from the culture of poverty enters school. He may be apathetic or wildly undisciplined. He may make a bad showing on IQ tests because he never was stimulated intellectually. He may be inattentive—perhaps because he gets little sleep at home with seven people in one room, perhaps because he is sick and has no medical care, perhaps because he is hungry and cannot afford to pay even 15 cents for the school lunch, perhaps because he cannot relate the stories, and music, and even the very language he meets in school to anything he knows of the real world from which he comes. Finally, he may be dressed shabbily and even dirtily most of the time. In short, he may not be particularly lovable, especially when compared with those well-behaved, bright, attentive, well-dressed, and clean middle-class children in the other school down the street! Many teachers, perhaps unconsciously, will make that comparison.

The self-fulfilling prophecy. Teachers will expect that little can be achieved by "the slum kids." This prophecy on the part of the teacher is likely to be self-fulfilling. Psychologists tell us that people have a vested interest in being right. People hate to be wrong. And teachers are people. The teacher, expecting nothing, will (perhaps unconsciously) make sure that nothing occurs! He will pay little attention to the child, will challenge it little. And the child's intelligence will continue to be stunted rather than developed.

Inferior schools. A 1970 study by the Carnegie Foundation charged that U.S. public schools in general were oppressive and joyless. With schools being dominated by the interests of teachers, the interests of children were being suppressed. Curricula were followed mindlessly, without serious thought about the purposes and consequences of what was being done, the report concluded. Most likely, all this is worse for the poor, for the children of the poor are being educated in school facilities and by teachers incredibly inferior to those available to the children of their more fortunate fellow citizens. The schools of the poor, compared with those of the more affluent, are likely to be more crowded (and disorderly), and to have less well-stocked libraries, simpler curricula (lacking advanced science and language courses), and less modern equipment (such as closed-circuit TV, language labs, and computers). They are more likely to have low-skilled or substitute teachers or teachers dissatisfied with their jobs who talk down to students and assign busy work. Such extremely unequal endowment with resources is, in part, the result of the long-standing U.S. tradition of "separate but equal" education for the races.

Segregated schools. Racially segregated education in itself lowers the value of education to the poor, some psychologists think. That is, segregation itself is seen to have an adverse effect on performance, equality of teachers and physical facilities notwithstanding. Psychologists find that fellow students have a greater effect on a pupil's academic achievement than the quality of his teacher does or the physical facilities of his school. Well motivated and bright students with a highly developed IQ tend to pull others up to their level of performance, for instance. To the extent that minority students have low motivation and little developed intelligence, it is in their interest, therefore, to have contact—in integrated schools—with fellow students whose intellectual performance is superior and, hopefully, "catching." Yet in recent years, more than 60 percent of black first-graders entered schools that were more than 90 percent black.

The result. Thus the poor are already handicapped and continue to be handicapped by the culture of poverty when they get to school. Their health and nutrition are bad, and so is their mental development. They are behind the nonpoor when they get to school. The school does not help them catch up. (Studies such as the 1966 Coleman Report show that the intellectual difference between racial-minority children and others is greater at the end than at the beginning of schooling.)

In short, it simply is not enough to provide all youngsters with free access to *some* school and then to tell them that it is their own responsibility to achieve. Many children are much too crippled by the culture of poverty to take advantage of whatever opportunities are offered them. All too often, bad and segregated schools offer little, indeed.

Is it any wonder that even motivation to learn fails to get instilled? The bad school perpetuates what has started in the home. It further stunts intellectual development. It becomes a place of defeat, of humiliation, a place to drop out of. And so they drop out. The dropout rate among the poor is vastly greater than among the nonpoor. So are truancy rates. Thus the poor have fewer years in school and fewer days of attendance when in school, and they learn less than the more affluent. As a result, in 1970, while 20 percent of U.S. children failed to obtain a literacy level and math performance skills required for available employment, the percentage was over 75 in most poverty areas. Low skills spell unemployability in an era wherein even the simplest jobs require the ability to read a technical manual, write reports, or perform some calculations. Therefore, by giving up on education prematurely, the poor, in effect, give up on escaping poverty. This is evidenced by the fate of the 25 percent high school dropouts. In the big cities in 1971, their unemployment rate was well over 50 percent (for those aged 16–21). In an era when demand for unskilled labor is generally declining, high school dropouts must compete against each other for the remaining unskilled jobs. Their unemployment rate nationally, in 1971, was 21 percent. And it was 19.5 for males, 23.7 for females, 19.5 for whites, and 26.7 for nonwhites. Interestingly, among high school dropouts in this age group, only 61 percent were in the labor force, as against 79 percent for graduates. This might indicate that many of them had given up hope and were not even looking for work.

Inadequate Career Preparation

Even if a youngster overcomes the possible barriers of a poor home environment and of poor elementary and secondary schools, a high school diploma does not guarantee bliss either. It does not assure access to higher education, for instance. In 1970, 40 percent of the college-age population went to colleges or universities, but many others wanted to. If they were unqualified intellectually, there was no one to help them catch up. If they were so qualified, there were often other barriers: inability to obtain funds or inability of colleges to provide enough slots for all applicants. Not surprisingly, almost half of all college students came from the 25 percent highest-income families, and only 7 percent came from the 25 percent lowest-income families.

Nor does a high school diploma guarantee immediate access to a job, even though it helps. For many students high school curricula are on the wrong track. They prepare students for one thing only: to go to college. Those that do not go to college (and this is still the majority) are unprepared for the next step in life. Nobody has shown these youngsters how their talents relate to the field of work. They are frustrated as they face the labor market without any knowledge of how it works and without any competence for jobs. What has gone wrong?

Most probably, youngsters have received little if any expert guidance on career preparation. Parents in general, and more so those steeped in the culture of poverty, know practically nothing about career counseling. Unfortunately, many high school counselors do not, either. The typical high school curriculum contributes little to the exploration of career alternatives while youngsters are still in school. There is precious little chance for students to engage in realistic vocational training, that is, in areas for which they have an ability and a liking, and wherein future labor demand can be expected. To be sure, 10 percent of high school instruction in 1971 was vocational-technical in nature. Yet over half of this was related to home economics or agriculture, hardly the correct fields to train for in the late twentieth century, at least not if the goal is the acquisition of *salable* skills. (In 1971, less than 5 percent of the civilian labor force had jobs in agriculture.) Also, vocational education courses are typically staffed with teachers of little education and with minimal experience. The whole enterprise is considered "low status," compared with the academic curriculum, by teachers, students, and parents alike.

Nor are there chances for youngsters to be placed in work-related adult activities outside the school during their school years in order to learn first hand, as they must sooner or later, about employer expectations, the workings of the labor market, and the types of educational preparation required for various jobs. No wonder that a 1971 study revealed that half of all high school graduates had not received assistance to choose and enter an occupation consistent with their abilities, aspirations, and the cold hard facts of the real world. No wonder that in the large cities just about half of high school graduates aged 16–21 were unemployed, too. (Nationally, in 1971, the percentage rate was 11.3, but it was 11.8 for males, 11.1 for females, 10.1 for whites, 21.7 for nonwhites.) All these matters were confirmed in 1972 by the report of the Fleischmann Commission on New York City's secondary schools. It concluded that most youngsters graduated from high school "with neither the prospect of continued study nor a marketable skill."

Inadequate Training on the Job

Most workers in the United States pick up their skills informally on the job. Yet it is very difficult, especially for high school dropouts, to pick up a good skill on the job. There are a number of reasons why job training cannot be expected to do what formal schooling has not done. Formalized hiring procedures of businesses discriminate against people with little education, lack of work experience, and arrest records. Union rules discriminate against young people and assure jobs first to older and experienced union members. Add to this informal outright discrimination against women and racial minorities in union apprenticeship programs, and you can figure out the chances of a high school dropout (or graduate) from the culture of poverty ever learning a decent skill on the job.

And again be careful. Don't say: "It was all his own fault." Was it his fault that his mother was malnourished during his prenatal life? Was it his fault that no one cared for him when he was very young? Was it his fault that he never knew a real home, but life taught him all too well the meaning of unanswered hunger and untreated sickness? Was it his fault that he was so "unlovable" in first grade that teachers and fellow students turned on him and made school a place of permanent humiliation? Was it his fault, finally, that he became "tough" and sought solace in drugs and sex and riots and just dropping out?

Conclusion

Undoubtedly, *some* of the poor lack the skills demanded in the labor market because they could not or would not acquire skills. They may have been born with an inferior intellectual potential, or they may have been too lazy to take advantage of educational opportunities open to them. Yet it would be a great mistake to assign much importance to such conceivable explanations for the lack of skills, as some people are fond of doing. Much more likely to be true is this: Many people who do not own income-producing property, who are in fairly good health, and who are willing and eager to provide labor services remain poor because the labor they have to offer is of low quality. Having grown up in the culture of poverty, and having found schools and jobs ill-suited to develop their potential, they have never acquired many skills. Affected by the relatively low demand for low-skilled labor, they have had determined for them a life of unemployment, underemployment, and low-wage employment—in short, a life of poverty.

IMPROVING THE SKILLS OF THE POOR

Once more it seems that there is a fertile field in which government can set things right. Government can make sure that all people have a chance to pay for at least a reasonable quantity of services that provide general education and job training. It can assure market mobility, that is, see to it that the educational industry responds to people's monetary demand (producing the types of services that people want) and that no one is constrained from buying those services wherever he chooses.

This freedom of purchase and mobility is not an actuality. Although general education and job training is hardly a pure public good, government at all levels is deeply involved in the field of education, considerably more so than in the health field. In 1971, 86, 89, 93, and 78 percent, respectively, of students aged 5 to 34 going to kindergartens, elementary schools, secondary schools, or higher educational institutions went to *public* schools. In the 1971–72 school year, Americans spent $86.1 billion, or 8.2 percent of their GNP, on education; and 81 percent of this total of national school expenditures was spent on public schools. Table 7.2, "Major Federal Grants Supporting Education," shows the dimensions of federal spending on education in 1971–72. The table is pretty much self-explanatory with the exception of a few items. "Assistance for deprived children" involved funds for the schooling of poor children (under Title 1 of the 1965 Elementary and Secondary Education Act) and also other aid programs, as for the physically handicapped, for bilingual education and dropout prevention. "Impact aid" was supporting school districts near federal installations, as in the vicinity of military bases. "Other" programs included aid to school libraries, provided films for the deaf, supported civil rights tech-

Table 7.2 Major Federal Grants Supporting Education, United States, School Year 1971–72

Program	Outlays: Millions	Outlays: Percentage of Total
Elementary and secondary education	$ 4,018	34.6
assistance for deprived children	1,622	14.0
economic opportunity and Indian education	701	6.0
impact aid	517	4.5
vocational education	293	2.5
others	885	7.6
Higher education	$ 5,330	45.9
training grants, fellowships and scholarships	3,349	28.8
basic research aid	1,295	11.2
facilities and equipment aid	686	5.9
Vocational, technical, and continuing education	$ 2,262	19.5
Total	$11,610	100.0

SOURCE: *U.S. Office of Education,* Digest of Educational Statistics.

nical aid, funded the teacher corps, schools for dependents abroad, veterans education, special area projects (as for the Cuban refugees), and more. In addition, to these federal expenditures, state and local governments in 1971–72 spent well over 50 billion additional dollars on education.

All this reflects one basic fact: Our society has a strong preference for a procedure that collects taxes from all, turns these funds over to public officials, and lets them provide some minimum of education to all via "free" elementary and secondary schools. Additional education is then offered below cost in heavily subsidized higher educational institutions. The obvious alternative of giving each family with children an equal share of these tax funds and letting them buy educational services produced privately in a free market has seldom been considered seriously. As a result, all but the very rich (who can afford to buy private schooling even after having paid general school taxes) are constrained to take whatever educational services are provided by a local monopoly. If that monopoly provides services inferior to those that people want or if it provides services on a discriminatory basis to different families, the "buyer" has no recourse whatsoever. It is as if all the money Americans spend on food each year were collected in taxes, handed over to "grocery store boards" who run retail food stores and provide food "free" to each family via a particular store to which it is assigned. If these stores then stock beans (even though people prefer carrots) or if they provide different quantities or qualities of food to different families, any one family can do very little about it. Having lost control over the money, it has lost mobility. It cannot punish one producer for providing the wrong things, nor reward another for doing the right things, by switching its allegiance from one to the other. An improvement in the educational conditions of the poor requires, therefore, more than the appropriation of additional public funds for increased in-kind assistance. Much thought must also be given to the way things have been done in the past. Changes therein may be just as important as increases in the overall size of educational programs.

Early Education

Fifty percent of a person's full intellectual development occurs in the first five years of life, that is, typically, prior to being placed in a planned learning environment. What is learned in these years is a necessary precondition for later intellectual development. If the opportunity of these years is wasted, future opportunities are destroyed with it. Considering the disastrous effect of the culture of poverty on the intellectual growth of many children, high priority might be given to improving the early childhood environment of children. This can be done by improving their home life or by providing an antidote to a nonstimulating home. To a considerable extent, the poor themselves have recognized early educational needs.

Improving home life. Among blacks, certain aspects of the black power movement reveal such recognition. This may seem surprising on the surface, since the obvious aim of the movement is to increase the political power of blacks. Considering how adherents of the movement are promoting fond but hopeless dreams of black capitalism (or black socialism), how they are known to substitute on occasion rhetoric for analysis, how they often confuse defiant gestures with political action, one may wonder what all this could possibly have to do with the early home environment of children. But on that account, there is much reason to welcome the movement. A group cannot cooperate on an equal basis with others without having first developed a sense of its own distinctiveness and of its own worth. In the development process, the blacks may escape the culture of poverty that holds them back. Just consider the effect of the strict rules of behavior laid down by the Black Muslims. Followers are encouraged to hold on to their jobs and their families, to forgo "loose" living. Women are told to be subservient to their husbands. If you know anything about the history of blacks, you can see the importance of this. White slave masters in North America never showed any respect for the integrity of slave families. Fathers were separated from their wives and children. As a result, children tended to grow up in a mother-centered household. After emancipation, this tendency continued. Given society's cruel treatment, the black male was of little use for the family. He was a bad provider. This has continued to the present, with black men being unemployed, underemployed, or employed at low wages disproportionately to their numbers. This has contributed to continued dominance of black female-headed households, doomed to poverty and dooming children to the same. The Muslim creed may reverse this tendency, mainly by changing *attitudes* so as to make black families more stable units, units that have aspiration and hope, that are ready to use educational opportunities offered them rather than paralyzed in the face of them. The offering of such opportunities becomes more likely if blacks have a voice in government. Black power can help channel funds for bettering schools of the poor. It can, through busing or neighborhood control of schools, enforce higher quality education.

Preschool programs. Governmental attempts also have been made in recent years to counter the influence of bad home environments. Most noticeable among these is the *Head Start program.* Head Start, for which $369 million was budgeted in fiscal 1973, is to give poor youngsters a better start on education. It provides for better child nutrition, health care, and parent involvement, as well as an academic program. Additional preschool programs are provided under Title 1 of the 1965 Elementary and Secondary Education Act. In fiscal 1973, they provided an added $93 million of federal funds.

However, the worthwhileness of the Head Start program was questioned in 1969. A study by the Westinghouse Learning Corporation of Ohio (contracted by the Office of Economic Opportunity) had tested 2,000 disadvantaged children nationwide in the first three grades of school. It found that summer Head Start programs had left no noticeable impact on the children's linguistic abilities, mathematical skills, or attitudes. Year-round programs had made a marginal difference only between Head Start participants and equally disadvantaged children not in the program. Congress and the president, however, were determined to push the program. They criticized the report for having presented nationwide figures. (Possibly, the averages covered up superb results in some places with failures in others.) They argued that possibly good results had been frittered away afterward by bad teaching. They figured that in any case the severe damage done to the children of the poor from early infancy on cannot be expected to be erased in one summer or even a single year of part-time attention; that over time, effects would show, both on children and parents. They therefore urged that the program should start earlier and continue longer (that Follow Through programs be instituted). President Nixon reduced the 1969 participants in the summer program but raised enrollees in the year-round program. Still, the number of poor children reached to date is exceedingly small. In the population as a whole in 1970, 80 percent of five-year-olds attended kindergarten, while 23 percent of four-year-olds, 9 percent of three-year-olds, and no younger children attended prekindergarten. Most of these enrollees, however, came from nonpoor backgrounds. Head Start and Title 1 (both of which are aimed at the poor) supported less than 5 percent of these three- and four-year-olds. Thus one might argue for a more determined effort to make preschool available to all on a voluntary basis.

Another vehicle for early education might be day care programs. Programs for welfare mothers in job training, for instance, spent an additional $507 million in fiscal 1973 on preschoolers. Indeed, there is much pressure for the provision of public day care facilities from women in general, not just the poor. This reflects the long-standing trend of women's entering the labor force. This is only in part the result of women having fewer children nowadays than in past generations. Even the percentage of *mothers* in the labor force is continually rising: from 22 percent in 1950 to 42 in 1970 overall, from 14 to 32 for those with children under a year, and from 33 to 52 for those with children aged 6–17. These women want to work because of changes in attitudes and changes in technology in the home and on jobs: The women's liberation movement encourages them to make use outside the home of their high educational achievement; modern child-rearing techniques favor the social interaction children get in kindergarten; there is less to do in the home (canning? weaving?); and outside jobs are physically easier. As a result, 37 percent of all children under 15 in 1971 had working mothers. However, most of the child-care arrangements involved custodial care in someone's home only, not child development programs in day care centers. These might involve full day care (up to twelve hours) for children of working mothers. They might involve part-time care (up to four hours a day) for all others. In 1971, the cost per person per year of such child development and day care was $1,750, that of part-time care $500.

Since fewer than 5 percent of mothers seeking day care are able and willing to pay more than $1,000 per year for day care (as was noted in hearings before the Senate Finance Committee in 1971), some have called on government to foot the bill. Indeed, in 1970, the Senate Finance Committee proposed the establishment of a federal corporation that would contract with businesses and nonprofit groups for the care of children of welfare mothers. However, the Revenue Act of 1971 authorized income tax deductions of up to $400 a month for expenses in the carc of children under fifteen. Meanwhile, also in 1971, President Nixon vetoed a bill for establishing a national system of comprehensive child development and day care. He argued that family-centered approaches to child rearing are preferable to communal ones.

In any case, more than monetary demand must be generated. In order to succeed, such a program must be supported by an increased supply of preschool teachers capable of supplying more than custodial care. At the 1970 elementary school pupil to teacher ratio of 25:1, the 15 million children aged 2–5 and those 1.5 million younger ones with working mothers could have used 660,000 preschool teachers. In the same year, only 100,000 such teachers existed and 5,000 such teachers graduated. Thus there is much opportunity to train several hundred thousand professional or paraprofessional preschool teachers.

Elementary and Secondary Education

One important way to improve elementary and secondary education involves increased overall expenditure on school facilities construction (including teacher-training schools) and on training and hiring high-quality teachers. Other ways involve spending present funds so as to assure all students of an equally good education. This might be done in a number of ways.

Equalizing per-student expenditures. School expenditures per pupil in the white suburbs, for example, have greatly exceeded those in most nonwhite central city schools. Audits by the U.S. Office of Education frequently find $500 per pupil annual differences. In the state of New York, in 1968–69, per-pupil expenditures even ranged from $1,093 in Buffalo to $1,943 in Great Neck (with $1,330 in New York City). Such differences might be eliminated. A series of court decisions—first by the California Supreme Court in 1971, then by others in Arizona, Kansas, Michigan, Minnesota, New Jersey, Texas, and Wyoming—have challenged school discrimination based on wealth. They noted as unconstitutional the existing property tax finance of schools. This allows, argued the courts, wealthy districts to raise large funds per pupil even at low tax rates, while poor districts raise small amounts per pupil even at high tax rates. Thus the children of the poor are denied equal protection of the laws. In 1972, when it was expected that the U.S. Supreme Court would eventually decide the issue of property-tax-financed schools, four states (California, Colorado, Michigan, and Oregon) put the issue before voters in statewide referenda. In each case, a change in the status quo was rejected. In 1973, the U.S. Supreme Court rejected it too, arguing that the U.S. constitution does not guarantee the right to equal educational opportunity. The New Jersey constitution does, however; and the New Jersey Supreme Court struck down that state's school financing system just two weeks after the U.S. Supreme Court's ruling.

Favoring schools of the poor. If there are to be differences in per-pupil expenditures, one can make a good case for *reversing* the present tradition and giving the poor not inferior, but superior facilities and teachers. This would recognize that poor children enter school with handicaps and that the school, not the child, has responsibility for assuring educational achievement. The successful school would then be the one that reduces the child's dependence on his social origin, that allows it, in the end, to compete on an equal basis with others. As some have put it, "Equal access to schools is irrelevant. We must assure not just a right to compete. We must give to all an honest chance to win. Equal *outcome* is what matters."[2]

Indeed, a recent federal ruling can be expected to have this effect. The intent of the 1965 Elementary and Secondary Education Act, Title 1 of which supplies *extra* funds to be used for disadvantaged students, has been ignored in two-thirds of the 16,400 school districts receiving aid under the act. The aid

[2] You may wish to read James S. Coleman, "Equal Schools or Equal Students?" *The Public Interest,* no. 4 (Summer 1966):70–75; and "The Concept of Equality of Educational Opportunity," *Harvard Educational Review,* Winter 1968, pp. 7–22.

funds were used to finance the regular activities of the schools of the poor, the savings in local and state funds being channeled to other schools. A federal ruling banned such supplanting of funds and required that *state and local* school funds be equalized among the schools of the poor and the more affluent by mid-1972. Thus the spending of *federal* funds for the poor was to give them greater per pupil expenditures overall. By early 1973, however, there was a question whether there would be any federal funds at all. President Nixon proposed to dismantle some 32 federal educational grant programs, including assistance for deprived children and impact aid and vocational education. He proposed a $2.5 billion a year special educational revenue sharing program (that would channel funds to state and local governments) and tax credits for parents sending their children to parochial and other private schools.

Busing for integration. Instead of changing expenditures on poor pupils by changing the overall size or distribution of expenditures, one can reach the same result by switching the poor to different schools. One can, indeed, it is argued, achieve *better* results because the mixing of children from different economic, racial, or ethnic backgrounds helps all of them to learn living in a mixed society and helps the disadvantaged pick up skills from more advanced peers. This is one of the goals of busing pupils for integration. Since the U.S. Supreme Court outlawed school segregation in 1954, some progress has been made in changing the racial composition of schools. Among the successes in this sense are the voluntary busing programs of Berkeley and Riverside, California; Hartford, Connecticut; and Evanston, Illinois. Still, much of the road to integration lies ahead. Consider these 1968 data for students in elementary and secondary schools: Of minority students in 32 northern and western states, 44 percent (and in 11 southern states, 77 percent) were attending schools with 95 percent or more minority students. Only 28 percent in the North and West (and only 18 percent in the South) attended schools where minorities made up less than half of the student body. Similarly, of white students in the North and West, 70 percent (and 52 percent in the South) attended schools with 95 percent or more white students. Only 2 percent in the North, West, and South attended schools where whites made up less than half of the student body. By 1970, these figures, interestingly, were unchanged in the North and West. In some cities, such as Boston, racial separation had increased, while it had significantly decreased in the South. Over 39 percent of minority students there now attended schools in which minorities made up less than half the student body.

However, there is still uncertainty about what integration itself accomplishes. The result of a 1972 study of school integration by Harvard's Professor D. J. Armor was surprising to many. In six cities across the nation (Ann Arbor, Boston, Hartford, New Haven, Riverside, and White Plains) it found these *short-run* results: no improvement in academic achievements, aspirations, or self-esteem of black students; no improvement in race relations, but increased separatist desires.

The public at large shows general disapproval not of school busing as such (for that is an old tradition) but of busing *for integration*. The boycotts, court fights, fistfights, and bus bombings have been directed not at the two-thirds of students who ride buses, but at the fewer than 3 percent of students who ride them for the express purpose of achieving racial balance. Critics in the South have stressed "freedom of choice"; critics in the North, the "neighborhood school" concept, in this fight. While affluent whites often fear the impact of the culture of poverty on their children, poor blacks have other fears, notably that integration could hamper the development of pride and self-confidence in their children and the teaching of matters relevant to the life of minorities (such as black history). Oftentimes, blacks would prefer segregated schools, provided that they are under black community control.

It is no wonder, therefore, that by 1972 busing had become a big issue in the presidential campaign, and it kept Congress and the courts alike busy. In Denver, Detroit, Indianapolis, and Richmond, federal courts ordered wide-ranging busing programs between central city and suburban schools to eliminate racial imbalance. The biggest of these orders (Detroit) involved two-way busing of 310,000 students between schools in the central city (65 percent black) and fifty-three white suburbs.

In 1972, Congress got into the act also. The House passed a bill forbidding categorically the use of federal funds for busing, forbidding federal officials to urge the use of local funds for this purpose, and delaying all court-ordered busing until all appeals were exhausted. At the time of this writing, this bill had not yet been reconciled with a milder Senate-passed version. It forbids the use of federal funds for busing unless requested by local authorities, and if students' health, safety, or education is impaired by it, and it delays busing across school-district lines until 1973.

Meanwhile, President Nixon called in 1972 for a moratorium on new federal court-ordered busing. In 1973, the U.S. government joined the state of Virginia in its court fight to kill the Richmond busing order. In the U.S. Supreme Court, Virginia won. And in some places busing has been discontinued for economic reasons. For example, a three-year experiment in Washington, D.C., was ended in 1971 when the annual cost of busing children from 95-percent-black inner-city schools to 2-percent-black suburban schools turned out to be $1,870 per student!

Curricular reform. Perhaps the most important change that can be made at the elementary-secondary level of schooling involves the curriculum. In a 1970 message on educational reform, President Nixon proposed a new national institute of education to research, experiment, and innovate in the field of education in order to raise the return we get from educational expenditures. In view of the delicate relationships in all school districts among boards of education, administrators, teachers, teachers' unions, and parents, this is by no means an easy matter. How can schools be made more joyful and less oppressive? How can one assure that all school graduates have (1) sufficient communication and mathematical skills to participate in the economy, and (2) information and experience to wisely select a career that is consistent with their abilities and aspirations? What is quite possibly needed is a system of economic incentives to break the monopoly now held by school boards on curricular matters. To encourage experiments with abandoning the status quo and to reward beneficial purposeful change, there are at least two approaches that might be taken.

First, the tax dollars now spent on education might be handed not to school boards, but to parents in the form of *educational vouchers.* Akin to food stamps, these could be spent by them on any kind of education they might find most beneficial for their children. They might make contracts with any one of many *competing* private or public educational companies, for instance. Soon superior schools would be in heavy demand, flourish, and expand, while inferior ones would be in low demand and be forced to improve or go bankrupt. Experiments are under way. In 1973, the Office of Economic Opportunity initiated a statewide voucher experiment in New Hampshire. In San Jose, California, educational funds for 1972 were distributed via vouchers to parents, and children could attend any of six participating schools in the city. On presentation of the vouchers, their children were enrolled, and public school funds were channeled to individual schools in proportion to the vouchers in their possession. In addition, the Office of Economic Opportunity contracted to provide one-third additional funds for schools receiving vouchers from poor families, thereby making the children of the poor most desirable rather than least desirable. In Gary, Indiana, an entire school in a black inner-city district was turned over for four years to a private educational service company. It was completely responsible for hiring teachers, selecting materials, and setting the curriculum. It guaranteed reading and math performance skills of students at the national norm and was under contract to return fees otherwise. During the 1970–71 school year, the percentage of students reaching or exceeding the norms rose from an initial 25 percent to 73 percent, indicating a phenomenal success. Second-year tests proved inconclusive, however, and the experiment was scrapped at the end of 1972. Nevertheless, such successful features as individualized instruction, ungraded classes, and the use of teacher's aides were continued.

Other experiments have been even less encouraging. The Office of Economic Opportunity announced in 1972 that similar *performance contracting* by six companies teaching 23,000 students in poverty districts of 18 cities had achieved no better results than the conventional teaching of control groups.

Nevertheless, the idea is intriguing to many. In 1972, New York City's Fleischmann panel, for instance, recommended that eleventh- and twelfth-graders who wish to drop out of public school be given vouchers representing their share of public school funds. These could be used by them to go to any private vocational or technical school that provides labor market skills that will be needed in the future according to Labor Department projections.

Second, the federal government, which in 1971–72 paid for 8 percent of elementary-secondary education, could allocate its funds so as to reward successful curricular innovation. Title 1 funds, for instance, were distributed simply on the basis of a formula reflecting the geographic distribution of school-age children from low-income families. There was no specification of a program goal; and no significant impact on student performance had been made by 1971. Yet such funds could be distributed in accordance with the *achievement* of specified reading and math objectives. Schools in which students do not pass federally administered evaluation tests would simply lose federal funds that might then go to parents as educational vouchers. Thus schools would have the incentive to succeed, through experimentation, if necessary. If they do not succeed, they could be liquidated like a bankrupt firm, and parents could channel funds to competitors.

Similar incentives could be set up in high school to encourage genuine career preparation and placement programs (including post-graduation follow-up). Undoubtedly, doing the right thing at this stage would be cheaper in the long run than training or retraining unemployed adults with families. President Nixon's proposed $2.5-billion-a-year special education revenue-sharing plan could easily be constructed to include the above-mentioned incentives.

Education beyond High School: College

So that the opportunities of those completing high school might be improved, colleges and universities might be enabled and encouraged to expand admissions, and prospective students might be enabled to gain admission without discrimination and to pay for higher education. To achieve the former, the federal government could increase its institutional aid for buildings and personnel. It could also use the economic lever of present and extra aid to encourage colleges and universities to use existing facilities more efficiently (for example, through full-year and full-day use of buildings and through audiovisual aids to assist teachers). It could encourage an increase, through more active recruiting, of the enrollment of those groups to whom college has been closed in the past. It could encourage a variety of structural changes, such as the offering of three-, two-, and even one-year degree programs and of more adult programs and better vocational programs, combined with the opening of colleges to all high school graduates as a matter of right. Already things have been happening along these lines.

Open admissions. The enrollment of minority students had risen to 10.5 percent by 1970, that of blacks being 6.9 percent. Integration has also proceeded. Whereas in 1964 less than 50 percent of black college students went to schools with white majorities, 75 percent did by 1970.

The idea of open college admission (admitting any high school graduate of whatever quality) has been tried in a number of places, notably in California, Hawaii, Kansas, Montana, New York, Ohio, and Wyoming. Criticism of universal college education has, however, been widespread. People argue that the dream of equality come true is an impossibility because it ignores the "natural aristocracy" of intellectual competition. They complain that "unqualified students are being swept into colleges on the wave of the new socialism" bringing with them a nightmarish decline in academic quality. The experience in general has been that most students with bad high school records do not take advantage of the free admission policy (or flunk out in their first year). However, in some places, ill-prepared students take remedial courses on the side or receive tutorial guidance. One such place is the City University of New York, which admits to one of its seventeen campuses any student graduating from a New York City high school. In 1970, 26 percent of admitted students would not have been eligible by earlier standards (a high school average of 83 for senior colleges and of 75 for two-year community colleges). Yet admission does not guarantee success: 36 percent of these flunked out in their first year.

Providing funds. In 1970, estimated the U.S. Office of Education, half a million qualified students could not go to college because of lack of funds. Their desires could be translated into ability to pay for college spaces in a variety of ways. Students from low-income families could be subsidized through scholarships, work-study grants, living allowances, or subsidized or guaranteed loans. None of this is new.

Under a variety of laws, as the National Defense Education Act and the 1965 Higher Education Act, the federal government provided $3.3 billion in training grants, fellowships, and scholarships to college students during the 1971–72 school year. In addition, the federal government made $540 million in low-interest student loans, and it guaranteed further loans made to students by private banks.

But the size of such programs could be increased. This was the aim of the proposed 1972 Higher Education Act. It envisioned $18.5 billion of aid to colleges, universities, and students, supplemented by a new National Student Loan Marketing Association. This organization was to be formed by selling its own stock to foundations and educational and financial institutions. It was then to operate by selling federally guaranteed bonds and using the proceeds to purchase student loans from other lenders, such as banks and universities, enabling them to make additional loans. The loans (principal and interest) were to be repaid like mortgages, by the students over a fixed number of years after graduation; or students might have obliged themselves to pay a fixed percentage of future income. Such an arrangement already exists at a number of places, like Duke, Yale, and the Ohio state colleges. It should be noted that when anyone can with assurance obtain funds for study, the sponsoring universities are also freed from any constraints to charge tuition covering full costs. This enables them to provide additional spaces as required. Nor is there any question that higher education could be so financed. It pays off well financially. If human slavery were allowed, it would pay any financial investor more handsomely to buy a share in a promising youngster rather than in the most profitable of American businesses. By paying say $10,000 for a high school graduate's college education, the investor would cause this person's annual earnings to rise on the average by $4,790 over what they would otherwise have been (see Table 7.1, "Education and Income"). This sum the investor might then appropriate, thus receiving a return of 47.90 percent *per year!* Because this form of slavery is not allowed, such profitable investment opportunity may remain unused in the case of poor families, unless government in one way or another helps disadvantaged individuals to "invest in themselves."

As an alternative way of subsidizing students, the federal government could also undertake to pay the full tuition for all Americans wishing to go to college. (In 1972, this might have cost $40 billion.) The method of payment might be by the granting to students or their parents full tax credits for educational expenditures (charging low-income families negative taxes, perhaps).

In fact, however, government action is likely to be more restrained. In his budget message covering fiscal 1974, President Nixon addressed the issue, promising to "bring higher education within reach of every qualified student in America." He proposed a new $1 billion federal scholarship program of "basic educational opportunity grants." These would be available to college and university students, to students of post-secondary vocational institutions (such as secretarial schools) and even to those taking home study courses. Each student might receive up to $1,400 a year, but never more than 50 percent of the cost of tuition, fees, room and board, commuting, and so on. The size of the grants would be reduced where parents can contribute. This would, in turn, be determined by a formula relating family income and assets, family size and number of children in post-secondary education, and other factors. The Nixon plan would abolish other federal aid for higher education, except the private bank loan guarantees.

Education beyond High School: Job Training

Even if college admission were guaranteed and funds for that purpose freely available, not all youngsters would go to college. Some do not complete high school. Others do, but don't care for college. But they surely can be helped also.

Financial aid. During high school, financial aid may be given to ensure their staying in school. Many poor teenagers face a bitter choice: drop out and help provide for the family or stay in school and starve. To tell them that "free" schooling is theirs for the taking is a cruel hoax. Helping them financially, to obtain literacy training, job skills, and motivation through work experience, is a good investment for society. It reduces the social costs of drug addiction, delinquency, crime, and continued poverty. One may go even further than this.

Professor James Tobin of Yale has proposed the creation of a federal government endowment to encourage *all* types of education beyond high school. The plan proposes paying everyone $5,000 at age 19 if it will be used for higher education or training. The amount would be repaid in full or in part after age 28 from the higher income realized. As we noted above, the monetary returns to education are truly staggering. Furthermore, such a program would be only fair. In many ways many youngsters are subsidized going to universities. Why not help all? Why not also subsidize the education of those *not* engaged in university training, but who could benefit from vocational education and job training?

Thus all the policies discussed above for promoting college education might be expanded in coverage to similarly promote the continued education of others not in college. Here, too, a number of programs are already in existence.

Public training programs. Most direct training programs by the federal government are relatively new, for until recently the old system of employment offices was about the only type of manpower program in existence outside the regular school system. Table 7.3, "Enrollment in Federally Aided Vocational and Work Training Programs" shows the numbers enrolled in fiscal 1971 in federally aided vocational and work training programs. About 10 million persons were affected in 1971.

Vocational training has experienced a boom in recent years. Prior to 1963, it was based on the Morrill Act of 1862 (granting land to state colleges) and the Smith-Hughes Act of 1917 (granting money to states). It promoted education in agriculture, trades, and industry, but the numbers trained were small for many years. However, training enrollments have rapidly risen from 3.8 million persons in 1960 to 10.4 million in 1971. The impetus to this rise was given first by the Vocational Training Act of 1963, which was a step geared to fight chronic unemployment. More recently, laid-off white collar workers and college dropouts have joined in large numbers the housewives and high school dropouts who used to dominate the scene. Federal aid has risen from $12 per person enrolled in 1960 to $44 in 1971. Yet all these programs have a serious fault. As in 1918, when federal concern with vocational education started, they stress traditional areas of home economics and agriculture to the extent of almost 40 percent of the trainees, quite the opposite of what the changing patterns of the economy require! Nevertheless, the percentage used to be much higher, and such office occupations as data processing, such trades as refrigerator and engine repair, paramedical specialties, truck driving, and restaurant cooking, and such industrial arts as laser technology are beginning to grow in importance. They have outdone such old favorites as fashion design and photography. Indeed, in recent years, 85 percent of public vocational school graduates have found jobs in the fields they trained for. In 1971, while 16 percent of teenagers were unemployed, only 5 percent of those with vocational training were.

The Manpower Development and Training Act of 1962 was also designed to cope with chronic unemployment. It made funds available for training and

Table 7.3 **Enrollment in Federally Aided Vocational and Work Training Programs, United States, Fiscal 1971**

Program	Enrollment (Thousands) (1)	Expenditures per Trainee (2)
Vocational programs[a]	8,794	$ 172
home economics	2,570	74
agriculture	853	139
office occupations	2,111	118
trades and industry	1,906	185
other	1,354	476
Manpower Development and Training Act	228	$1,474
institutional training	156	1,769
on-the-job training and JOBS optional program	72	833
Neighborhood Youth Corps	740	$ 576
in school	120	483
out of school	53	2,170
summer	567	446
Job Corps	50	$3,220
JOBS Program	93	1,817
Concentrated Employment Program	94	1,777
Operation Mainstream	22	3,273
Public Service Careers and New Careers	47	1,957
Work Incentive Program (WIN)	112	571
All programs	10,180	$ 281

[a] Enrollment for fiscal 1970; expenditures per trainee as of fiscal 1969.

SOURCE: *U.S. Office of Education,* Vocational and Technical Education *and U.S. Manpower Administration,* Manpower Report of the President.

retraining people and for maintaining their families during this time. (The act also required the secretary of labor to submit to the president and Congress an annual manpower report. This has been done since 1963.) However, at first, the typical trainee was a white male high school graduate. Only one-third the trainees were from the disadvantaged groups, which form the bulk of the chronically unemployed. In the late 1960's, efforts were being made to raise to two-thirds the proportion of the disadvantaged in the program: older workers displaced by technological change, persons in correctional institutions, handicapped workers, the paroled, the illiterate, and the young. By 1971, slightly more than half of the trainees came from poor families. In that year 63 percent were male, 40 percent were nonwhite, 38 percent were under 22 (and 9 percent over 45), 14 percent had less than a ninth-grade education, and 51 percent had at least a twelfth-grade education. Of the 1971 enrollees, only 53 percent completed the program and only 41 percent obtained employment.

The Neighborhood Youth Corps Program emerged as part of the Economic Opportunity Act of 1964. Its aim was to provide basic education, training, and work experience. It was from the start aimed wholly at the disadvantaged. Since 1967, training has been given to youths (from 16 to 21 years of age) in residential job corps camps, and to others in neighborhood youth corps centers. When first enrolled, 50 percent of job corps participants failed to read at the fifth-grade level, and 30 percent could not read a simple sentence. The neighborhood youth corps program reaches annually several hundred thousand needy students who receive a modest amount of aid from in-school and summer programs helping them to continue in school. It also trains youths no longer in school. In fiscal 1971, some 740,000 poor persons were involved in programs (ranging from pollution clean-up to training teachers' aides) designed to serve the participants and their neighborhoods simultaneously. Of 1971 participants, 55 percent were male, 61 percent nonwhite, 100 percent under 22 years of age, 21 percent had less than a ninth-grade education and only 4 percent had at least a twelfth-grade education.

In 1968 a program entitled Job Opportunities in the Business Sector (JOBS) was initiated. It was designed to bring the "flexibility and imagination of the private sector into full partnership with the government." With the federal government contributing funds, private industry was to train and hire 500,000 of the hard-core unemployed by mid-1971. (The goal was later raised to 614,000.) The government was to identify and locate the unemployed; private companies were to train them and offer them jobs. Under the arrangement, the private employer would pay normal training costs, and the government would pay any additional expenses. These would, for instance, involve costs for individualized teaching of reading and writing, for the correction of special health problems, for transportation, and for counseling on all kinds of matters ranging from personal care to work proficiency and follow-up assistance to assure that the newly trained would keep their new jobs. To do the business part of the program, a National Alliance of Businessmen was formed in late 1967. The government part of the program was carried out as part of a new Concentrated Employment Program of the Labor Department aimed at employing the disadvantaged in poverty areas through federal, state, local government, and private cooperation. Other programs were mushrooming in the late 1960's—Operation Mainstream, New Careers (and later Public Service Careers), and the Work Incentive Program (WIN). All these, in one way or another, were aimed at helping the unskilled and chronically unemployed.

In 1971 the characteristics of trainees in these programs ranged from 38 percent male (WIN) to 74 percent (Job Corps); from 36 percent nonwhite (Operation Mainstream) to 73 percent (Job Corps); from 5 percent under 22 (and 40 percent over 45) in Operation Mainstream to 100 percent under 22 in the Job Corps, and from 16 percent with less than a ninth-grade education (and 40 percent with at least a twelfth-grade education) in the Concentrated Employment Program to 45 percent (and 25 percent) in Operation Mainstream.

The federal government in its role as employer has also entered the act. The Department of Transportation trains workers, half of them nonwhites, for skilled highway construction jobs. The armed forces have long had specialized training programs. Some 2,000 courses, from auto repair to aerospace technology, are available. The Armed Forces Institute allows members to receive the equivalent of a high school diploma. In 1966, Project 100,000 was added, an attempt to make military service a path to a productive career by accepting and training a third of the 300,000 persons annually labeled unfit for service by previous standards.

Evaluation. The fond hopes of many advocates of these programs have not been realized. For one thing, the size of programs is too small. Note (Table 7.3) how in 1971 the average annual training expenses were only $281 per person. Studies have shown that to really train people without successful schooling and without work experience to the point where they have a skill that can land them a job *that they can expect to keep* costs at least $4,000 a year per trainee. (This incidentally, is very worthwhile, since a twenty-year-old now doomed to lifelong part-time employment may earn $2,500 a year without training, but easily $7,500 a year with training. This amounts to a $225,000 return by the time he retires.) It is no wonder, therefore, that the failure rate in current programs is very high when measured by actual employment. Programs typically provide only modest skills that in no way assure getting a job.

As a result, many who have found employment have ended up with jobs paying no more than their former welfare checks. (The National Welfare Rights Organization in 1971 advised its members not to enter WIN, for it would provide "just jobs to scrub, cook, and clean." Only 20 percent of WIN trainees, who received day care, medical care, and transportation aid while training, ever got a job; fewer kept one.) Even those finding good jobs, as in the auto and aerospace industry under the JOBS Program, have in large numbers been disappointed as the 1970 recession made them the first to be laid off. As a result, the JOBS Program has not reached its target.

Thus one can easily think of improvements. In addition to an increase in training effort per person, the geographic distribution of training programs and their subject matter could be greatly improved. For instance, too many Job Corps centers were started in rural areas (and 60 such centers were closed), too few near urban centers (where only 9 of 30 promised centers were open by early 1971). Similarly, the type of training given is often not very imaginative. It centers on fitting people to jobs, while often jobs could be created to fit people. The great need, referred to above, for paraprofessionals such as aides to doctors, nurses, and teachers could be met from the pool of people entering these training programs.

President Nixon, in his fiscal 1974 budget message, signaled the end of direct federal involvement in vocational education and most work training programs, except for the JOBS Program (for hardcore unemployed), the Job Corps (for disadvantaged youths), the Work Incentive Program (for employable welfare recipients), and certain veteran training and retraining programs. He urged adoption of a special manpower training revenue-sharing program that would put the responsibility for job training and employment services, together with federal funds, in state and local hands. Part of his proposed special educational revenue-sharing program would, in addition, be earmarked for vocational education.

Private training programs. Besides promoting training of its own, government has also attempted to open wide the doors to private on-the-job training by *counteracting discrimination* in selecting people for such programs. The federal government has used its vast power of the purse for this purpose. Citing the Civil Rights Act of 1964, the Nixon administration in 1969 proposed the "Philadelphia Plan." It called on employers in Philadelphia who had federal contracts exceeding $500,000 to make a "good faith effort" to increase minority employment on federal construction projects. Contractors and unions were urged to meet with minority community representatives and agree voluntarily on specific minority "hiring goals." This was aimed at the long-standing practice of building trades unions of excluding blacks from learning skills on the job.

In 1969, although 30 percent of the local labor force was nonwhite, fewer than 2 percent of the members of the six building trades unions were. (The unions were those of the ironworkers, plumbers, steamfitters and pipefitters, sheetmetal workers, electrical workers, and elevator construction workers.) Since workers are referred to construction jobs through union hiring halls and not hired directly by employers, failure to become a union member means failure to get a job and on-the-job training. Discrimination in this field had led to civil disorders and tense confrontations in several cities. The Nixon executive order, however, stirred up opposition not only of contractors and unions, but also in Congress and within the administration. For example, Senator Sam J. Ervin, Jr. (D., North Carolina), criticized the plan as in effect promoting hiring quotas based on race, in violation of Title 7 of the Civil Rights Act of 1964. Elmer B. Staats, the controller general, agreed. By law, the controller general pays the bills of the federal government and may refuse to make payments he considers to be illegal. He promised to block payment to the first Philadelphia contractor who had agreed to the plan. He also charged that the plan violated the Civil Rights Act of 1964 by requiring racial quotas, and thus all contracts under the plan should be considered void. Nevertheless, these internal squabbles were ironed out. Goals for hiring, argued the proponents of the plan, did not set a ceiling to the employment of any minority group, nor were they mandatory (as long as a good faith effort was made to reach them), hence they were not quotas.

Outside the government, things went even less smoothly. When no voluntary agreement worked out, the federal government *imposed* its own "affirmative action plan": by 1970, 4 percent of the Philadelphia construction labor force would have to be black; 9 percent by 1971; 14 percent by 1972; and 19 percent by 1973, or all federal funds would be withheld. This was followed in 1971 by labor department quotas for nonwhites in federally registered apprenticeship programs. The Contractors Association of Eastern Pennsylvania sued, but in 1971, the U.S. Supreme Court upheld the legality of the Philadelphia Plan. The Building and Construction Trade Department of the AFL–CIO vowed to resist, since "racial quotas, under any guise are repugnant to all Americans." Complaining that the plan "inundates [apprenticeship] programs with unqualified short-term dropouts at the expense of dedicated future craftsmen," the union labeled "this attempt at social engineering . . . a poorly disguised effort to restructure our economic society to the whims of a handful of federal mandarins."

Yet at that time the government persisted. In 1971, when it became evident that unions and contractors had avoided placing more blacks by just switching all black employees to the federal construction sites, the Philadelphia plan was extended to cover the *private* work of federal contractors also.

Philadelphia-type voluntary plans were planned for over a hundred other cities, including Atlanta, Boston, Buffalo, Chicago, Cleveland, Denver, Detroit, Miami, Newark, New Orleans, New York, Pittsburgh, San Francisco, Seattle, St. Louis, and Washington, D.C. By 1971, only thirteen had come up with voluntary plans; two others (San Francisco and Washington, D.C.) also had plans imposed on them.

Since early 1972, the federal government has also threatened federal contractors *outside* the construction industry with loss of contracts unless specific hiring goals are set up for women and minorities and a good-faith effort is made to reach them. This ruling affected all firms supplying more than $50,000 worth of goods per year to the federal government. One of the early fruits of this new policy was an agreement with the American Telephone and Telegraph Company.

In general, though, these affirmative action plans have been plagued by litigation, delays, and sabotage. The Chicago Plan called for placement of 4,000 blacks or Spanish-Americans within one year, but only 855 had been placed in apprenticeships and 75 in jobs 18 months after the plan went into effect. In 1971, the federal government threatened to impose its own plan. By 1972, a new Chicago Plan called for the hiring of almost 10,000 minority construction workers within four years. In Philadelphia itself only 200 blacks had been placed by late 1972 (as opposed to the planned 3,200). The Pittsburgh agreement to place 1,250 blacks in four years was signed only after all federal funds were withheld and construction had stopped for over a year.

In general, the numbers of minority members placed in private on-the-job training programs have been minute. Insufficient federal manpower has made it impossible to work out, impose, and enforce reasonable placement goals and timetables in most places. By 1973, officials in the Office of Federal

Contract Compliance found themselves continually overruled by higher government officials when they attempted to cancel contracts for violations of affirmative action agreements. The entire effort seemed to have come to a standstill.

Summary

1. People who are poorly educated and trained in an economy wherein the demand for educated and skilled labor is relatively high, have excellent chances of being unemployed, underemployed, or employed in low-paying jobs. They are programmed for poverty.
2. There are many reasons why some people remain unskilled while others do not. Probably least important are personal differences in inherited intelligence. Much more important are differences in early home environment. The culture of poverty, for instance, is likely to cripple the intellectual development of those who come in contact with it. Not less important are quality differences in general education resulting from diverging teacher expectations and from differently endowed and segregated schools. These tend to reinforce the effects of home environments.
3. As a result, many children from disadvantaged backgrounds learn less in school and drop out of school earlier than their more affluent peers. Even those who do finish high school are unlikely to be prepared for careers. High school curricula are college-oriented. They ignore the needs of the majority: to discover their talents and how they relate to the field of work. Nor is it easy to pick up good skills on a job.
4. To improve matters and provide skills for the poor, more public funds might be allocated to the educational enterprise. At the same time—and perhaps more important—things might be done differently than in the past. Early education might be fostered through improving the home life of the poor or through special preschool programs, like Head Start or provision for high-quality day care. Elementary and secondary education might be improved by equalizing per-student expenditures among schools, by favoring the schools of the poor financially, by busing students for integration, and by curricular reform.
5. Curricular reform might be accomplished by handing tax dollars presently spent on education to parents in the form of educational vouchers. This might create a competitive market for educational services in which bad schools would be eliminated through bankruptcy. Or it might be accomplished through the allocation of federal funds in such a way as to reward successful curricular innovation.
6. Post–high school education could be improved by a variety of college reforms and of manpower training programs. The former might include nondiscriminatory and open admissions, more efficient use of existing facilities, and better financing arrangements. The latter might be accomplished via financial aid to trainees, the offering of public training programs, and the opening of private ones to all on a nondiscriminatory basis.

7. Public training programs have been mushrooming since the 1960's. They enrolled over 10 million people by fiscal 1971, but spent only $281 per year per trainee on the average. Attempts to open private training programs to the disadvantaged include the Philadelphia Plan and similar schemes in other cities. Their overall impact has been minimal.

Terms[3]

affirmative action plan
culturally biased IQ tests
culture of poverty
educational vouchers
open admissions
performance contracting
self-fulfilling prophecy

Questions for Review and Discussion

1. The Armed Forces mental test measures the ability to perform at eighth-grade level. Fifty-six percent of blacks fail it. This is four times the rate of failure among whites. Can you explain this?
2. An intensive study has been made of so-called identical twins. (They have an identical genetic inheritance.) Two types of cases have been examined: those reared together in their parents' homes and those separated in early infancy and brought up in different environments.[4] Measures of intelligence of these two groups were compared with measures of intelligence of nonidentical twins, of siblings reared together, of siblings reared apart, and of unrelated children reared together. In all these cases, genetic endowment differs and increasingly so as you go down the list. It was found that intelligence scores were increasingly different the more the genetic endowment varied. The differences between identical twins reared together and those reared apart were small. Thus it was concluded that "individual differences in intelligence . . . are influenced far more by genetic constitution, or what is popularly termed *heredity*, than by postnatal or environmental conditions." What do you think? Justify your answer. Do you wish to reconsider your answer to Question 1? Why or why not?
3. Studies show consistently that children in families where the father is present have a higher IQ than in fatherless families. Can you explain this?
4. "There is an unusually high incidence of consensual marriages (people living together without being legally married) as well as of abandonment of (legal) wives and children among the poor. This proves they are inferior people." Discuss.
5. Do you think it is true that school segregation by itself has an adverse effect

[3] Terms are defined in the Glossary at the back of the book.
[4] Cyril Burt, "The Genetic Determination of Differences in Intelligence: A Study of Monozygotic Twins Reared Together and Apart," *British Journal of Psychology* (1966), pp. 137–53.

on pupil performance? Think of all-black schools, all-white schools, all-Jewish schools, all-Catholic schools, all-girl schools.

6. "Ghetto schools have been anything but a failure. Their obvious role is to prepare a minority for lower-class jobs, not to teach cognitive abilities. This is done by instilling the ideology and personality traits required for capitalism: the wish and ability to work persistently, to conform, to respond to incentives, to defer gratification." Discuss.
7. "Summer Head Start programs are a waste. They give nothing but recreation to the children and (quite unearned) money to some teachers. They do not improve the children's readiness for school." Discuss.
8. Do you think the government should subsidize day care programs for working mothers? Consider the costs and benefits from the standpoint of the children, mothers, and taxpayers involved.
9. In a recent year, posh Beverly Hills, California, spent $1,232 per elementary school pupil, while taxing itself only 2.38 percent of assessed property value. Nearby Baldwin Park, meanwhile, taxed 5.48 percent, yet per pupil spending was only $577. Can you explain it?
10. "It is short-sighted to sponsor equal per pupil expenditures everywhere in the hope of assuring equal education. One reason is this: The purchasing power of the dollar differs in different places. Land costs differ. School construction costs differ. Teachers' salaries must differ (they need combat pay in central cites). Maintenance costs differ (heating and snow removal in the North, vandalism in the city, transportation in rural areas)." So, if equal expenditures can't be the yardstick, how would you assure "equal education" for all?
11. "It is silly to equalize expenditures per pupil in central city and suburban areas. Children go to school for education, not for money. Equal money misses the point." Evaluate.
12. "There are many reasons for the existence of racially segregated schools—maintenance of official dual school systems, gerrymandering of school district lines, selective abandonment of school buildings and careful selection of new school sites, and the operation of purely economic forces leading to segregated housing patterns." How would you deal with each of these? Is busing always the best answer?
13. In mid-1972, the Carnegie Commission on Higher Education recommended that undergraduate schools cut their programs from 4 to 3 years. This could be done by cutting required courses, increasing independent work, and lengthening the academic year, and (if high schools cooperate and teach more advanced material) by advanced placement of new students. Critics have argued that this is a bad idea for it would surely cut general education in favor of specialization and this is the last thing one should do at a time when admissions of unprepared students are rising rapidly. What do you think? What other costs of such action can you see? What are the benefits?
14. In 1972, the Presidential Panel on Nonpublic Education proposed a tax credit for parents of the 5.2 million children (83 percent Catholic) attending elementary and secondary nonpublic schools. It urged a reduction of these parents' annual federal taxes by $400 or half the tuition, whichever was lower.

Do you think this is a good idea? How about using this idea for converting all public schools into private ones?

15. It has been proposed that "tutorial stamps" be issued to the poor. These could be given by the poor to any approved college or high school student for special tutorial services to be rendered to the children of the poor. The tutors then could turn in the stamps to the federal government for cash. What do you think of this proposal as a means of abolishing poverty? (Consider the effect on the children of the poor, on the tutors' ability to earn money for their own education, and also on others, say potential high school dropouts, who could then stay in school thanks to the existence of part-time employment opportunities previously taken by the tutors.)

Selected Readings

Gordon, David M. *Problems in Political Economy: An Urban Perspective.* Lexington, Mass.: D. C. Heath and Co., 1971. Pp. 85–90, 117–37, 161–222. Presents conservative, liberal, and radical views on the role of education and job training, and contains excellent bibliographies.

Moynihan, Daniel Patrick. *The Negro Family: The Case for National Action.* Washington, D.C.: U.S. Department of Labor, 1965. Discusses how the childhood environment of some people predisposes them to poverty later in life.

U.S. Bureau of the Census. *Statistical Abstract of the United States, 1972.* Washington, D.C., 1972. Lists some statistics on education and job training (Section 3) and—more important—sources for other statistics: Note the listing of statistical abstract supplements (p. v); and the guide to general sources of statistics (pp. 918–20 and 954), to recent censuses (pp. 955–56), and to state statistical abstracts (pp. 961–64).

NOTE: The *Journal of Economic Literature* lists recent articles on education and training (sections 811 and 850), the economics of education (912), and the economics of discrimination (917).

The *Index of Economic Articles* catalogs, in sections beginning with the indicated numbers, articles on human capital (2.214, 2.3431), the economics of discrimination (2.1335, 15.342), labor markets, training and retraining (19.2), and the economics of education (21.8).

8 Securing Well-Paying Jobs

There are some people who are healthy, and perhaps even skilled, and still they remain poor. Their poverty problem is based on other factors than health or skills. Some of them may be prevented by a variety of circumstances, and for periods of varying lengths, from taking a job at all. They are involuntarily unemployed. Others may be working full time, but earn so little as to remain poor.

For example, in 1971, 5.9 percent of the civilian labor force was officially listed as involuntarily unemployed.[1] However, in the nation's standard metropolitan statistical areas (1960 definition) the 1971 unemployment rate was 6.3 (5.7 percent for whites and 10.2 percent for nonwhites). In the poverty neighborhoods of those SMSA's having a quarter-million inhabitants or more, the unemployment rate was 9.7, and here it was 8.0 percent for whites and 12.4 percent for nonwhites. Within these poverty areas, 20 percent of white and 38 percent of nonwhite teenagers were counted as unemployed; among those aged 20 and above, 7.1 percent of white males, 6.6 percent of white females, 10.2 percent of nonwhite males, and 10.0 percent of nonwhite females were unemployed. This type of detail concerning geographic, sexual, and racial differences is not sufficient to paint the full picture of the job situation.

Consider how these statistics are defined. Involuntary unemployment data are obtained by the Bureau of the Census through a monthly sample survey of about 50,000 households. These households are interviewed, and interviewers use the following guideline: The bureau considers anyone sixteen or above who is not working *at all* during the week in which statistics are gathered as involuntarily unemployed if he is currently available for work (even if perhaps temporarily ill) and if he (1) has looked for work in the preceding four weeks or (2) has not looked for work because he is (a) temporarily laid off subject to recall or (b) scheduled to begin a new job within thirty days. "Looking for work," furthermore, can take many forms, such as going to the employment service, applying to an employer in person, answering a want ad, being registered on a union or professional listing, and so on. A person sixteen

[1] Most of the statistical data in this chapter come from U.S. Bureau of Labor Statistics, *Employment and Earnings, Handbook of Labor Statistics,* and *Monthly Labor Review* and from U.S. Bureau of the Census, *Current Population Reports,* Series P-60.

or above who has worked even one hour for pay or profit during the survey week is regarded as *employed.* So is a person who has a job or business but is not working because of illness, vacation, labor-management dispute, bad weather, or personal reasons (such as hunting for another job). And so is a family member who has worked at least fifteen hours a week in a family enterprise without pay.

Two important facts should be noted. First, official statistics on involuntary unemployment do not count people who are working only *part time*—even though they want full-time jobs. They are counted among the employed and account for about 10 percent of persons documented as employed. Second, official statistics on involuntary unemployment also do not count *discouraged* workers, that is, persons who want a job, but have stopped looking because they consider finding work as hopeless. They have experienced so much rejection that they refuse even to search for work. They are counted among the voluntarily unemployed, as many retired people or children in school are, for example. Thus, you see how important it is to understand the meaning of our statistics. Even when the official tally of involuntary unemployment reads zero, we may still have a great problem if many discouraged workers are hidden among the genuinely voluntarily unemployed, or if many of the "employed" are only working part time although they would rather be employed full time. A 1969 Labor Department survey of slum areas in large cities is revealing. By the official definition, involuntary unemployment there was 5.1 percent. With the addition of discouraged workers to the labor force, and the counting in of discouraged as well as involuntary part-time workers with the other involuntarily unemployed, the rate rose to 17.3 percent. A 1970 survey, taken as part of that year's census of population, confirmed this inadequacy of official unemployment statistics. It covered 13 million people in fifty-one urban poverty areas. (Half of these people were blacks, 36 percent English-speaking whites, 12 percent Spanish-speaking whites, and 2 percent belonged to other races.) The surveyed New York City areas were typical: By the official definition, involuntary unemployment among the people surveyed there was 8.1 percent (while the rate for the city as a whole was 4.4 percent). However, adding discouraged workers to the labor force and then counting discouraged workers with the other involuntarily unemployed raised the unemployment rate to 11 percent. Also counting the involuntarily part-time employed raised it further to 13.3 percent. Finally, 25.9 percent of those in the New York survey area (and 30.5 percent in all of the fifty-one survey areas) were either involuntarily unemployed (official definition), discouraged workers, involuntarily part-time employed, or fully employed at less than $2 per hour (easily a poverty line wage).

All this fits in well with independent data on poor persons. Recall Table 4.3, "Selected Characteristics of Poor Persons in the United States, 1972." It is easy to calculate from the data given in this table that 47.1 percent of white and black poor persons over the age of thirteen who were not going to school were either unemployed year-round or employed part time only or working full time. This kind of problem, inability to find enough work or to find well-paying work, will now concern us.

TYPES OF INVOLUNTARY UNEMPLOYMENT

There is something else we should note about unemployment statistics. Not all of those counted as involuntarily unemployed are in the same kind of trouble. In November 1972, for instance, 50 percent of the unemployed had been unemployed for less than five weeks. At the other extreme, 9 percent had been unemployed for over twenty-six weeks. This portrays that there are different types of involuntary unemployment. As we shall see, each of these requires a different type of countermeasure, in turn.

Frictional Unemployment

When the numbers and types of job openings and job seekers roughly coincide, but the two are temporarily mismatched, one talks of *frictional unemployment.* Such unemployment may persist due to *insufficient information.* Jobs requiring certain skills may be available in Pennsylvania, while people possessing the requisite skills may be looking for such jobs in Virginia. Unless potential employers and employees come to know about each others' existence, no labor contract will be struck. Until it is struck, the workers concerned may be involuntarily unemployed—and poor. Frequently, people just entering the labor force find themselves in such a position, such as students who have completed high school, vocational training, or college, or housewives who have finished rearing their children. They just don't know where the jobs are, even though such jobs may exist. Existing placement services are frequently very ineffective. They stress waiting. They leave people under the illusion that the type of job they are looking for will eventually turn up in just the location it is being looked for. More often than not, the reality is that people for a job like that in that locality will never be wanted. Realistic information about job opportunities must be brought forcefully to the individual. He must be told where he is *not* wanted, as well as where he is wanted.

Another type of frictional unemployment occurs because people are *mobile*: they quit jobs or are laid off or fired from them. Think of the people laid off annually owing to seasonal factors; think of people who quit because they want to improve their status; think of those who are discharged because their employer is going out of business or moving away. Even if they have another job to go to, they will be unemployed for a period lasting from a few days to a few months. These people account for a significant percentage of all unemployed. In November 1972, 15 percent of official unemployment was connected with voluntary quitting, 13 percent with new entry, and 32 percent with reentry into the labor force.

There is another possibility. Some people, living in Virginia, possessing skills demanded in Pennsylvania, and knowing about it, may be *unwilling* to move. Psychologically, they may be tied to a particular geographic location or group of relatives or friends whom they are unwilling to leave behind. They are unemployed because they are *immobile*. Their unemployment or underemployment will then become chronic. But other conditions of *chronic unemployment*, wherein the types of job openings and job seekers are seriously mismatched, are more likely.

Chronic Unemployment

Often people cannot find work in the type of job they are best capable of performing for reasons of *discrimination*. For reasons of race, sex, age, religion, or national origin, employers may not want to hire *particular persons* even though they be qualified for the job. If employers would rather hire no one than hire a black person, a woman, a person over 60 (or under 20), a Jew, or a Puerto Rican, all the skills in the world won't help these people to lift themselves out of poverty by work.

Examples of discrimination in hiring or subsequently in promotion or dismissal abound. This leads to people remaining unemployed or remaining low-paid in spite of having skills. Little else can explain why a smaller percentage of nonwhite male high school *graduates* than of white male high school *dropouts* end up with skilled and semiskilled jobs. Little else can explain the fact that in 1970 minority citizens (blacks, Spanish-Americans, Orientals, and American Indians) who held 20 percent of all federal government jobs, held 53 percent of GS 1 jobs (the lowest pay scale in the General Schedule), and only 2 percent of GS 16–18 jobs (the three highest-paying categories). Little else can explain why in 1971 only 20 percent of college and university faculty members were female and of these 35 percent were instructors (only 16 percent of men held this rank) and only 9 percent full professors (while 25 percent of men were). As a result, 63 percent of female faculty members earned less than $10,000 a year (while only 28 percent of their male colleagues did).

More systematic statistics bear this out also. Not only do women as well as nonwhites tend to be crowded into a few occupations, but they earn less than white males in any given occupation and at any given educational level.

It is very easy to see how this sort of result occurs if mobility in the labor market is restricted artificially. Consider Figure 8.1, "The Dual Labor Market." Part (a) depicts, let us assume, the overall market demand for jet pilots and the supply, at alternative annual wages. In a perfectly working market, 20,000 of all licensed pilots would find employment at the $10,000-a-year salary. Some licensed pilots (depicted on the supply curve to the right of equilibrium point *E*) would not be willing to work for as little as $10,000 and would seek work elsewhere. Some employers (depicted on the demand curve to the right of *E*) would not be willing to hire for as much as $10,000 and would also stay out of the market.

Now suppose, however, that the market is split artificially in two: 90 percent of employers (perhaps the *major* airlines specializing in carrying passengers) hire only male pilots, 10 percent (perhaps other operators

Figure 8.1 The Dual Labor Market

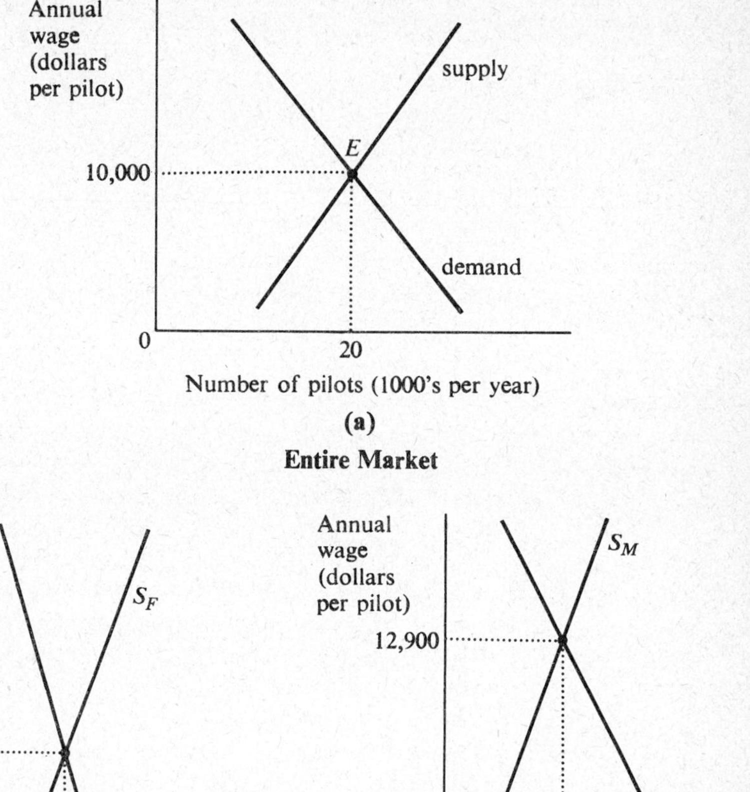

When a fraction of workers having a certain skill is crowded into a (different) fraction of the labor market, differences in pay arise among people with identical skills.

specializing in carrying *freight*) want only female pilots. The demand curve from part (a) reappears split in two in parts (b) and (c). Curves D_F (demand for females) and D_M (demand for males) add (horizontally) to total demand in part (a). If female pilots cannot enter the male market (and the contrary), the supply has to be split, too. Thus S_F (supply of female jobs) and S_M (supply of male jobs) add to total supply. Unless the supply just happens to split in the same way as demand, differences in pay will emerge. We suppose that half of licensed pilots are male and half are female. In that case, 50 percent of pilots (females) are crowded into 10 percent of the market, and their pay is low ($5,700 a year). Another 50 percent of pilots (males) share 90 percent of the market, and their pay is high ($12,900 a year). Thus the dual labor market, which confines some people to some types of jobs for no relevant reason (sex is irrelevant, skill is not), results in some people (males) gaining at the expense of other people (females) *who are equally skilled.*

In a perfectly working market this could never happen. Informed and mobile females would bid for the (here) male-only jobs, raising the supply (and lowering the wage), compared to what it now is in part (c). At the same time, the supply in the (here) female-only jobs, as in part (b), would fall (and the wage rise). This would continue until the situation depicted in part (a) would prevail: people with equal skill would get equal pay.

In reality, such mobility is frequently lacking. Females or minorities are often restricted (for reasons unrelated to their skills) to certain occupations or job categories within these occupations. As a result, some people, having the same skills as other people, end up getting lower pay in given jobs than other people. This may go hand in hand with lower status, unpleasant or exhausting duties, little or no chance of advancement, uncertainty of job tenure. For example, our 7,500 female pilots in part (b) may be flying freight (low-status), at night (unpleasant), without hope of advancing to company vice president, and subject to frequent layoffs (as the freight business responds to business conditions). Indeed, some people having the same skill as other people may end up with jobs requiring altogether lower skills (as licensed female pilots end up as flight-service weather briefers instead). This sort of thing is widespread and by no means confined to such an exciting occupation as piloting jets. Why do some people with high school diplomas end up as low-status janitors (doing unpleasant things at *low* pay, without hope for advancement), while others with the same education have more pleasant jobs with *higher* pay? More often than not, artificial barriers to labor market mobility (added to previous barriers to equal educational opportunity) are to blame. In a perfect market, just the opposite result would be expected: unpleasant jobs would get *higher* pay than pleasant ones because people would move among jobs until this was true.

The methods used to split labor markets artificially are usually very subtle. Employers always come up with "good" reasons for their behavior. Some blame their customers. Retail store owners argue that they would lose all their white customers were they to employ *black* salesmen. Airline companies argue that no one would fly with them were they to use *female* captains and *male* stewards. Television stations argue that only *youthful* announcers attract a large audience. Owners of snack bars claim their business would collapse unless *teenage girls* tend to it.

Employers may also blame their workers or the unions to which they belong. Contractors often argue that all their white employees would walk off the job were they asked to work side by side with blacks. They may cite collective bargaining contracts to hire union members only, but (alas) certain groups of people may not be members of this union. Unions, in turn, may keep out of their ranks certain groups of people by charging high initiation fees that certain people cannot pay or by administering entrance tests they are likely to fail. In 1971, the steamfitters union required applicants for its apprenticeship program to relate (among other things) Shakespeare with *Othello*, Dante with *Inferno*, Dali with painting, and Walt Whitman with poetry, and also to explain *modiste, debutante, myth,* and *verity*. Since the test was based on white middle-class education and experience, less than 20 percent of whites but 67 percent of nonwhites failed it.

Professional associations may similarly screen out of their ranks certain groups of people, as the American Medical Association does by its control over medical school accreditation and the types of licensing tests required.

Employers themselves also cite placement tests of their own as reasons for not hiring or promoting. Yet few of these tests are really objective, or indeed relevant for the job to be performed. A test used in 1971 to promote common laborers to coal miners required an explanation of B.C., *adept*, and *adopt!* The federal government seems to be using similarly biased tests. In 1970, the Civil Service Commission tests for *college graduates* seeking federal jobs paying between $7,000 and $10,500 a year, passed 42.1 percent of white applicants, but only 8.6 percent of blacks.

Employers can also cite laws as justification for discrimination in hiring. State laws license perhaps as many as eighty separate occupations, ranging from taxicab operator to tree surgeon, from psychologist to potato grower, from egg grader to beautician. Licensing is done ostensibly to guarantee high-quality services to the public. However, very often the type of licensure tests administered keep some groups of people from ever being licensed in some occupation. Thus they cannot legally be hired. Many states also have "protective" laws for workers that, in effect, keep certain groups of workers from getting jobs. Thus women are often not allowed to work more than a set number of hours a week, to work overtime, or to work at night. In Ohio, they are barred from lifting more than 25 pounds in a job and from holding certain jobs at all. (These include bellhopping, pinsetting, meter reading, shoeshining, and truck driving.) In other states, they may not mine coal or be a bartender. The federal government won't hire them for border patrol or as criminal investigators.

To make things difficult for the objective observer, there usually is a kernel of truth in the arguments used by those who discriminate. Yet often their *real* reason for discrimination is not the stated one. Equally often, the real reason for discrimination can be shown to be groundless. For instance, many employers simply hate to hire, much less promote, women because they believe them to remain in the labor force only for a few years, to hold a job less long than men, and to be absent more often while they hold it. Yet 1970 statistics do not bear this out. Past experience shows that the average single woman, aged 35, will work for 31 more years (more than can be said for men of the same age). The average married woman, aged 35, can be expected to work for another 24 years. In addition, women are *less* likely than men to leave a given employer. In 1970, 8.6 percent of women but 11 percent of men changed jobs. Finally, women were absent from their jobs 5.3 days in the year on the average, which was slightly better than the men's record.

The end result of all this is the existence of significant differences in pay among various groups of people. Thus the hopes of those who have been educated to realize the full returns from their schooling can be frustrated by discrimination. A 1969 study by the Equal Employment Opportunities Commission showed that only one-third of the black-white income differences can be explained by differences in education and training. The rest must be blamed on racial discrimination. Just as blacks earn less than whites even in the same occupation, so women earn less than men. At least a fifth of the sex differential in pay, noted the President's Council of Economic Advisers in 1973, cannot be explained away by differences in hours worked, work experience or education. In 1971, women earned anywhere from 47 percent of the average man's salary (in sales) to 72 percent (in teaching). Indeed, both black and white women with some college education earned on the average less than the average black man with eight years of education. In short, by subtly keeping others out of certain jobs entirely, or if they enter, by keeping them in the lower ranks of these jobs, white non–Spanish-speaking males have monopolized well-paying jobs. In 1971, they held 96 percent of all jobs paying more than $15,000 a year. The other 4 percent had to be shared by all others: females in general, and blacks, Spanish-Americans, and American Indians in particular.

Unemployment, or low-wage employment, of skilled people can also be caused by other factors. Discrimination *outside* the labor market could be one factor. Discrimination in housing, for instance, might make it impossible for some people to move to a place near a potential job site. Lack of adequate transportation may make it impossible for them to commute from their existing residences. In such cases, their unemployment—and poverty—may become chronic.

Skilled people can also have other problems, unrelated to discrimination. *Mothers tied down with small children* may be incapable of going to work, even though they have salable skills that are in great demand. They just cannot get away if they cannot find someone to care for their young ones. In 1972, 40 and 62 percent, respectively, of all poor white and black women with some children under six and others between six and seventeen were also family heads. Only 6 percent of them were fully employed. A 1968 study by the Department of Health, Education, and Welfare showed nationally 45 percent of welfare mothers employable, except for having to care for children. (The percentage was even 65 in New York City and 56 in Chicago.) These had more than a twelve-year education and they had work experience in skilled jobs. These facts point out the difficulties of working mothers: while 4 million mothers with children under six were working in 1970, only 640,000 licensed day care spaces existed. Therefore, over three-quarters of the children involved were cared for by relatives or friends, 13 percent by the mother during work, and 8 percent were not cared for by anybody. Quite likely, many of the employable welfare mothers not working were trying to avoid the last-named situation.

Another reason for chronic unemployment may lie in *structural changes in the economy*. As it must happen in a dynamic economy, as time passes people's tastes and technology change. Some occupations, industries, and geographic areas become increasingly important; and some completely new industries appear; whereas other industries live a long life of attrition and finally die out. As a result, many a skilled craftsman may find one day that his skills have become obsolete. Thus locomotive repairmen, coal-mining engineers, and airplane designers find themselves out of a job as people abandon the railroads for private cars, and substitute oil for coal and private for defense spending. The business accountant, the flight engineer, and the foreman in the manufacturing plant find themselves in the street as new and fancy automated equipment is installed that can do their job and can do it better and faster. All these people may become chronically unemployed, too, and join the ranks of the poor, unless they are willing and able to retrain or relocate. Time has passed them by. This is again reflected in our statistics. Certain regions such as the textile towns of Massachusetts, the isolated coal towns of Appalachia or cities having lost big defense contracts are suffering from above-average rates of unemployment, even among the highly skilled.

General Unemployment

Last but not least, overall spending in the economy may decline (or its growth may slow), for any one of a thousand possible reasons. This may create a *generalized* fall in (or slowdown in the growth of) the demand for labor. In such times, many people of all skills, all races, all ages, all religions, all origins, and both sexes, and living in all places may find themselves unemployed—and poor—at the same time. The total number of job openings is too small for the total number of job seekers. This sort of thing happened in 1970–71, when a general economic slowdown spread poverty beyond the city ghettos into the land of suburbia. While 3.5 percent of all civilian workers had been unemployed in 1969, the figure became 6 percent by December 1971. The 12.2 percent unemployment rate for teenagers in 1969 became 17.3 by December 1971. During the same period, the rate for male Vietnam veterans (aged 20–29) jumped from 4.5 to 8.4 percent, that for women (20 years and over) from 3.8 to 5.8, that for men (20 years and over) from 2.0 to 4.3, that for whites from 3.1 to 5.4, that for nonwhites from 6.4 to 10.4, that for blue-collar workers from 3.9 to 7.5, and that for white-collar workers from 2.1 to 3.6 percent. Thus, even in a period of general unemployment, young, female, nonwhite, and unskilled workers were affected in greater proportion than older, male, white, and skilled workers, respectively.

ABOLISHING INVOLUNTARY UNEMPLOYMENT

All of the many types of involuntary unemployment have persisted in our economy for as long as we can look back into our history. Yet, if you have carefully pondered the lessons of Part One, the existence of unemployment in a market economy, *except as a temporary phenomenon,* might strike you as somewhat of a paradox.

The Unemployment Paradox

Consider the market for any type of labor, say high school social science teachers. Imagine that we made a survey of all school boards in the country and asked each how many high school social science teachers they planned to employ next year. Obviously, this would depend on many things, but all other factors being equal, the answers we receive will undoubtedly vary with the salary that we assumed to exist. The salary is the price that has to be paid to get this type of labor. Suppose we find that at a price of $12,000 per year, school boards decide not to offer any positions to social science teachers at all, but that at correspondingly lower salaries more and more boards decide to add the subject to their curriculum. If they could get away with paying no more than $2,000 a year, they would hire 600,000 teachers.

We can similarly imagine interviewing all potential teachers. We could ask them under what circumstances they would teach social science in high school next year. Again, this would depend on many things. Let us assume most of those things as fixed; let us only vary the potential salary paid. We should undoubtedly find that the number of people willing to teach in high school can vary. This will be so even though the number trained to teach social science may be rather fixed in any one year. At $2,000 a year, these people may prefer to do nothing or to offer themselves for other jobs. Quantity supplied is zero. At $12,000, there may be 600,000 people looking for this kind of job. At $20,000, even college professors will become available for high school jobs.

Now note that our interviews would have yielded the demand schedule and the supply schedule for high school social science teachers. The answers given by school boards would be the demand schedule. The answers given by potential teachers would represent the supply schedule. By graphing these two, we could derive Figure 8.2, "The Market for High School Social Science Teachers." The information gathered from school boards would appear as the demand curve *D*. The information gathered from their potential employees would show up as supply curve *S*.

We can now use the graphical illustration of the market for this type of labor to predict what would happen next year, with perfect competition existing among all market participants. (True enough, real-world markets for high school teachers may not be perfectly competitive, but let us assume for a moment that they are.) We can predict that such a competitive market would tend to establish a $7,000 salary figure and that 300,000 people would be employed. Only at intersection c do we find equilibrium. There would be no unemployment, because all who want to work in this occupation at this wage would be employed.

At any higher annual wage, there would be a surplus, that is, unemployment. For example, at $10,000, only 120,000 people would be hired (point *a*),

Figure 8.2 The Market for High School Social Science Teachers

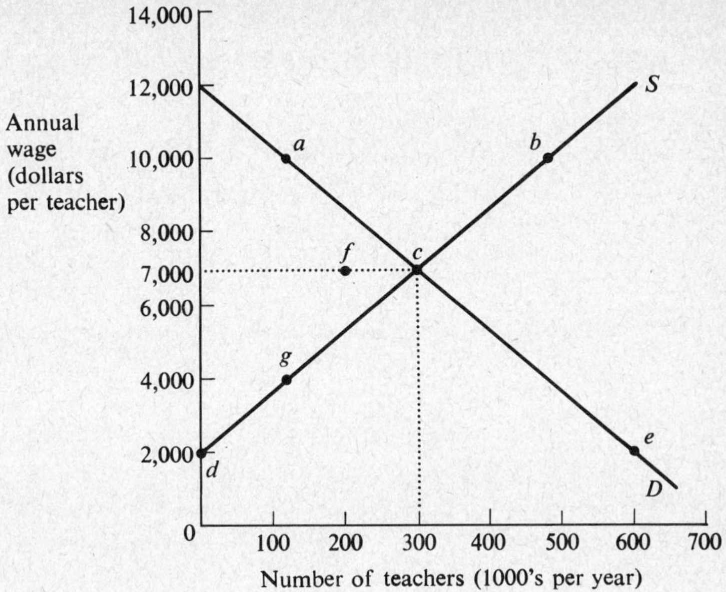

In a perfectly competitive market, demand and supply would establish equilibrium price and quantity for any resource, even the services of high school social science teachers. In this example, their annual salary would be $7,000, and 300,000 of them would be employed. There would be no unemployment. At any higher wage, there would be a surplus of teachers; at a lower one, a shortage. At $10,000, for instance, only 120,000 would be hired (point *a*), but 480,000 would seek employment (point *b*). The surplus 360,000 would be unemployed. At $2,000, on the other hand, nobody would willingly work (point *d*). School boards would in vain try to hire 600,000 teachers (point *e*).

but 480,000 seek employment (point *b*). The horizontal difference of 360,000 would represent unemployment (*ab*). A fall in the wage to $7,000 would eliminate it, for two reasons. First, quantity demanded would rise by 180,000 along *ac*. Second, quantity supplied would fall by 180,000 along *bc*. As school boards become readier to hire (because of the lower salary), some potential teachers decide not to work at all or to work at other jobs (also because of the lower salary).

At a lower-than-equilibrium wage, there would be a shortage. At $2,000, nobody could be had. But the shortage (of *de*) could be eliminated by a rise in pay to the $7,000 equilibrium. Again the reason is twofold: quantity demanded would fall by 300,000 along *ec*; quantity supplied would rise by 300,000 along *dc*. As more and more school boards decide to forgo the luxury of social science instruction, more and more potential teachers offer themselves for the job, leaving voluntary unemployment or other jobs behind.

Now we come to the main point. What has been said about social science teachers could have been said about labor in general. It could have been said about capital. It could have been said about land. In a perfectly competitive market economy, movements in prices eliminate surpluses and shortages. Thus, they can also be expected to eliminate the particular surplus, commonly called unemployment. Our analysis leads us to expect that unemployment in a market economy, if it exists at all, will be rather short-lived, being eliminated through the price system!

But this is hardly what we see happening in real life. Why this paradox? What has gone wrong with the market economy? We only need remind ourselves of an assumption we made when discussing Figure 8.2, "The Market for High School Social Science Teachers." We assumed a market economy that was perfectly competitive. This allowed us to study the principle of the invisible hand in all its purity, without being detracted from the main idea. But clearly, in the real world, which we have been studying earlier in this chapter, competition is not perfect. Suppose some of those potential high school social science teachers, who are pictured in line *S* of Figure 8.2, lack the full knowledge and mobility ascribed to all market participants under perfect competition. Or, suppose teachers band together in unions and enforce above-equilibrium salaries, thereby destroying the price flexibility that would exist in perfect competition due to the great number of competing buyers and sellers. Using Figure 8.2, we can easily perceive the consequences.

At a $7,000 equilibrium salary, perhaps only 200,000 teachers are hired (point *f*) because 100,000 of them (distance *fc*) are unaware of the openings available. This would be a clear case of frictional unemployment due to lack of knowledge on the part of teacher-sellers or school board–buyers.

Or, suppose school boards discriminate against nonwhite or female social science teachers. So far as the boards are concerned, the supply might be represented by another line *S′*, lying parallel to the left of *S* and going, let us suppose, through point *a*. You might wish to draw in such a line and imagine it represented the supply of white male teachers only. In that case, $10,000 would become the salary paid to some 120,000 white males, but another 360,000 nonwhite or female teachers (distance *ab*) would in vain seek such employment. This would be a clear case of chronic unemployment due to lack of mobility on the part of teacher-sellers.

Finally, suppose a general recession occurs. As incomes (and tax revenues) fall, the budgets of school boards are slashed. Among other things, the demand for social science teachers falls. You might want to draw a new demand line parallel to the left of *D* in Figure 8.2, cutting supply *S* at point g. In a perfectly competitive market, salaries would drop to $4,000 a year, and the employment figure for social science teachers would become 120,000. But suppose a strong teachers' union prevented any salary adjustment below the original $7,000 a year figure. Then school boards would hire no one, while 300,000 teachers looked for jobs (point c). If such a situation were generalized throughout the economy, we might call this a case of general unemployment due to the lack of funds on the part of buyers of labor, such as our school boards, to buy all that is offered at current (nonequilibrium) prices.

In short, the unemployment "paradox" is no paradox at all when labor markets are imperfect. Clearly then, some real-world involuntary unemployment can be removed by restoring the conditions of perfect competition in labor markets, or if this proves impossible, by countering the effects of imperfections.[2] To these possibilities we now turn.

Improving Labor Market Information

The extent of frictional unemployment could undoubtedly be reduced by improving informational services. In 1966, the National Commission on Technology, Automation, and Economic Progress proposed to the president a "nationalization" of the present state-federal unemployment service via a computerized national job availability service matching workers and jobs. (The West European success in depressing the level of unemployment has been attributed to an excellent employment service, among other things.) A 1968 law, in fact, authorized the development of a comprehensive system of labor market information using electronic data processing and telecommunications equipment for up-to-the-minute contacts among recruitment, job-training, and placement agencies. An experimental computerized *job bank* at the Maryland State Employment Service in Baltimore was a great success. (It increased the placement of minority job seekers by 25 percent, mainly because the system eliminated the effect of residential segregation on coming to know about jobs in the suburbs.) A similar one had been installed in over 100 metropolitan areas in 43 states by the end of 1971. These job banks covered 60 percent of the labor force. In each case, job counselors can feed into the computer a job-seeker's occupation, salary preference, and location. This can be weighed against 20,000 job openings within minutes, and the computer points out the five openings coming closest to filling the bill.

Also with federal help, a statewide matching system was working in Utah when President Nixon took office; the president has announced plans to make this a nationwide system by 1976. By mid-1970, statewide systems were operating also in California, New York, and Wisconsin, and ten additional states were planning to introduce them. As an alternative to providing such service itself, government could also subsidize private employment agencies, perhaps by allowing job seekers to deduct agency fees from taxable income.

Improving Labor Market Mobility

Improved labor market information would quickly reveal that the involuntary unemployment of some people in some places is matched by appropriate job

[2] Lest the reader be misled, it should be noted that under certain conditions unemployment *dis*equilibrium may persist even in a perfectly competitive world. These conditions are spelled out in detail in Gardner Ackley, *Macroeconomic Theory* (New York: Macmillan, 1961).

openings in other places. To the extent that such geographic mismatching of jobs and workers persists because of workers' inability to pay moving or transportation expenses, *relocation allowances or transportation subsidies* could be instituted. Under a 1965 amendment to the Manpower Development and Training Act, the federal government has given an average of $750 of relocation assistance to thousands of workers who moved out of economically depressed areas. The Uniform Relocation Assistance and Real Property Acquisition Policies Act of 1970 made another step in that direction. It provided for aid to persons displaced by federal projects, paying homeowners up to $15,000, and businesses and farms up to $10,000, and tenants $2,000 for down payment on a home or $1,000 per year rent supplements up to four years, as well as $300 moving expenses.

Much more serious are other kinds of barriers to mobility, notably the practices of discriminatory hiring and promotion. To eliminate chronic unemployment on that account, *antidiscrimination policies* concerning hiring and promotion might be pursued. A number of actions have been taken in this regard.

Under the authority of the Civil Rights Act of 1964 (which in Title 1 bars racial discrimination, and in Title 7, sex discrimination), the federal government has, as we noted in Chapter 7, demanded from federal contractors "affirmative action plans" to eliminate discrimination in on-the-job training. The same authority has been used to assure nondiscriminatory hiring, compensation, promotion, and discharge of those already skilled.

In addition, in 1967, President Johnson issued a general ban of discrimination against women in federally aided jobs for which contracts exceed $50,000 and more than fifty persons are employed. In 1970, this was expanded to eliminate male-female distinctions in newspaper job ads, except where sex (as for actors or models) is a bona fide occupational requirement. Also banned were penalties to women for having children, sex distinctions in seniority rules, and restrictions of job classifications to one sex. (Indeed, the U.S. Supreme Court in 1971 voided the state protection laws for women. It also ruled that women may not be excluded from any job for having children, nor may they be excluded for any other reasons unless men are excluded for the same reason.)

Age bias has been outlawed since 1967, making it illegal to lay off or refuse to hire and promote persons because of their age.

A 1970 presidential order asked each federal government agency head to undertake "affirmative actions" against all forms of discrimination, but no quotas were set. (In 1970, although 10.7 percent of federal employees were black, fewer than 2 percent were in the top seven grades.) In 1971, the U.S. Supreme Court ruled that the content of employment tests must pertain to the job at stake: "It must measure the person for the job, not the person in the abstract." For example, any pencil and paper test (which obviously requires reading and writing ability) is illegal unless reading and writing ability is essential for the job. Some progressive employers have therefore turned to oral tests and tests of work sampling, wherein workers are placed in an actual work situation and tested on how they handle it. For nonfederal employment, the Equal Employment Opportunities Commission, set up as part of the Civil Rights Act of 1964, has been ready to receive complaints from individuals employed in private firms with 25 employees or more. (By mid-1973, the commission had a backlog of 70,000 cases waiting for investigation.) However, the commission has been refused by Congress the power to issue cease-and-desist orders against unions and employers (including state and local governments) in discrimination cases. Until 1972, it could only attempt a reconciliation of the parties involved. Failing that, individuals had to bring private suits. Some have scored successes. For instance, an agreement was reached in 1971 between the federal government and the University of Michigan to improve employment opportunities for women. A federal court in 1971 ordered a construction union to pay blacks compensation for depriving them of jobs.

Since 1972 and the passage of the Equal Employment Opportunities Act, the commission itself can sue also. Along with other federal agencies, suits have been filed against a number of private and public employers. A number of breweries (which supply beer to the military) have been sued for racial discrimination. (In St. Louis, the federal government found in 1970 that 37 percent of the population were black, but 60 percent of the residents around the Anheuser-Busch brewery were black. While 80 percent of the brewery job applicants were black, blacks comprised only 2 percent of its employees and only 0.4 percent of brewery union members.) The city of Boston has been sued for racial and ethnic discrimination. (In 1973, 20 percent of the population were black or Spanish-speaking, but only 0.9 percent of Boston's firemen were. Most firemen were Irish or Italian.) The Greyhound Bus Lines were sued for age discrimination. Among others sued for racial or sex discrimination were the cities of Montgomery, Alabama, and Los Angeles, and U.S. Steel, Bethlehem Steel, and Libbey-Owens-Ford (with the United Glass and Ceramics Workers), and General Motors and Chrysler (with the auto unions), and AT&T. (In early 1973, AT&T made a multimillion-dollar settlement for having excluded women and minority males from well-paying installation, maintenance, and repair jobs, and it pledged to place more men as operators and clerks.)

Yet some people, like Harvard's John Kenneth Galbraith, have argued for a much stronger stand against discrimination. It would assure not only nondiscriminatory hiring, but also nondiscriminatory promotions. Galbraith proposed a "minorities advancement plan." Under it, legal quotas would be set for all employers having over 2,000 employees and for all job categories paying in excess of $15,000 a year (except the top three positions in each firm or government). Quotas would assure that blacks, American Indians, Orientals, Spanish-Americans, and females are represented in the same proportions as in the full-time labor force. (The exclusion of firms with fewer than 2,000 employees was designed to minimize political resistance and was in recognition of the lesser flexibility smaller firms have in hiring and carrying out training programs. The $15,000-a-year floor was set to avoid tangles with labor unions.) Under the plan, each affected employer would file with a Minorities Advancement Commission a timetable for compliance, with full compliance scheduled in ten to thirteen years, depending on the firm's size. Firms not holding to the timetable would be fined an amount larger than the wages women and minorities would have earned had they been properly represented.

Others believe that nothing short of a constitutional amendment can eliminate discrimination. For example, the National Women's Party (which won the female vote in 1920) promoted a constitutional amendment that "equality of rights under the law shall not be denied or abridged by the U.S. or by any state on account of sex." The House passed this twenty-seventh amendment to the U.S. Constitution in 1971, and the Senate in 1972. By March 1973, the amendment had been defeated or "buried" by 11 states, ratified by twenty-eight of the required thirty-eight states. Many legislators oppose the amendment and argue that it would take protection from women in such matters as property settlements, child custody, and alimony in divorce cases; maternity leaves in employment; or combat duty in the military.

People's ability to freely enter various labor markets can be promoted in other ways than by countering discrimination. Among these are *day care and training programs.* Day care programs would serve the dual purpose of child development and freeing mothers for work. (The 1971 Revenue Act encourages this, at least for families that pay taxes. It allows working wives to deduct from taxable income up to $400 a month for child care expenses as long as annual family income is below $18,000. It allows lesser deductions for incomes up to $27,600.) The multitude of training programs discussed in the previous chapter can provide people with skills for the first time as well as providing them with new skills should their skills become obsolete. Indeed, there has been a boom in *adult* retraining in recent years. In 1971, 13 million adults were pursuing part-time formal training: roughly half in colleges (such as the New School for Social Research, America's first university for adults), a quarter in business job-training programs, and another quarter in a variety of private tutorials, correspondence courses, and courses offered by community organizations (libraries, museums, and so forth). A few governmental retraining programs for adults were also available in 1971, but they were small and ineffective in bringing employment to more than a handful. Among these was a U.S. Office of Education program to retrain 1,500 black teachers from the South who had lost jobs in the wake of school desegregation. They were being trained as job counselors and for special education projects (handicapped, early childhood, vocational). Another program was training scientists, engineers, and technicians with aerospace-defense backgrounds for work in urban planning and environmental control.

Raising Aggregate Demand

Programs of improving labor market information and mobility may not be sufficient to assure full employment, especially if wages and salaries are inflexible in the downward direction. However, the unemployment-creating effect of such market imperfections can be countered by always maintaining a high-enough level of aggregate demand, that is, of spending on new American goods by households, businesses, and governments. Through proper monetary and fiscal policy, the government can always raise aggregate demand to any level desired. In our earlier example, this might raise the school boards' demand for social science teachers sufficiently from our assumed recession level to employ everyone looking for work at the union-enforced salary of $7,000.

Recent history. The enormous impact the level of aggregate demand has on the incidence of poverty can be judged from the experience of recent years. It suggests that one can reduce poverty greatly through an all-out effort to promote full employment and economic growth. The maintenance of a fully employed and growing economy can by itself be a powerful force in the reduction of poverty for this reason: In a market in which demand for labor is strong relative to the supply, the chances of the poor unemployed, partially employed, and low-skilled are enhanced as employers have greater incentive to seek out and train workers.

The 1969 *Economic Report of the President* reviewed the issues involved here. It showed that all the progress in reducing the number of poor persons was made in periods of prosperity. From 1949 to 1953, 1954 to 1956, and since 1961, the number of poor persons has declined on the average by well over 2 million per year. On the other hand, the short recession of 1954 wiped out half the gain of the preceding four years. Similarly, the sluggish economic growth of the late 1950's set back the fight against poverty by seven years. We can now add that the recession of 1970–71 had the identical effect. (You can verify all this by studying the top line in Figure 4.2, "Number of Poor Persons and Incidence of Poverty.")

Who were the poor people helped most? They were male family heads of working age. The number of poor people in this category changed not at all from 1959 to 1961. It declined by 400,000 per year from 1964 to 1966. The tight labor market increased their wages if they were employed. It reduced the incidence of unemployment and part-time work. Businessmen, who could not find skilled workers to hire, increasingly turned to the chronically unemployed and the poorly educated, and they trained them on the job.

Interestingly, the prosperity of the 1960's did not help poor families headed by females of working age. Why? Because women are less likely to look for work. Many have children to take care of, and there may be no day care centers. Or they are hired last, because of sex discrimination or because they have even less prior job experience on the average than men do. And even when women are hired, they are put in different categories of jobs, are paid lower wages, and have less steady employment, as compared with men (hence they are less likely to escape poverty).

Another group of poor people helped by prosperity in the 1960's were the aged. The incidence of poverty among them declined substantially. In part, this was owing to a 21 percent increase in social security benefits (which would probably not have been voted in a recession). In part, it was owing to the fact that old people were allowed to work beyond normal retirement age, again because of the great demand for labor. To the extent that these people would have had poverty incomes otherwise, this is reflected in less poverty among those aged 65 and over. A period of prolonged prosperity can, furthermore, reduce the number of poor in this group by giving people a greater chance to accumulate higher pension rights.

The percentage of poor persons who were ill and disabled also fell in the 1960's. Like people with low education and no work experience, they are more likely to find well-paying jobs when labor is hard to get.

Finally, the 1960's brought a substantial decline in the number of near-poor. Most of these are employed, but employed at low wages. The decline in this category is significant. Because most of the poor who ceased to be poor became near-poor, it means that more people moved out of the near-poor category than entered it.

The specter of inflation. Some argue that raising aggregate demand to raise employment (and reduce poverty) is not worth pursuing, as it creates a worse disease: inflation. These critics argue that a little bit of recession is a good thing because it prevents inflation. And inflation, we are told, hurts the poor more than anyone else. The poor have relatively fixed incomes: low hourly wages, fixed pensions, fixed welfare payments. As inflation proceeds, they can buy less and less with their money. Not so with the nonpoor, we are told. Middle-class auto workers force up wages. Doctors raise fees. If the price of oranges goes up, the middle-class housewife just switches to strawberries. The poor cannot do that; they are stuck with buying beans.

This is a serious argument. Does it stand up to analysis? It is quite true that a policy that continually pushes aggregate demand to the limit of our productive potential will accelerate inflation.

But a careful study by investigators at the Institute for Research on Poverty revealed this: During inflation, the prices paid by the poor rise less rapidly than the prices paid by the nonpoor. In other words, the price of beans may rise less than that of oranges or strawberries. But more important, the money income of the poor rises much *faster* during inflation than that of the nonpoor: Social security benefits are not fixed. (During the 1960's, they were continually raised by deliberate policy decision; since then they have been automatically raised with increases in the consumer price index.) And above all, the poor get more income from work during prosperity. They have higher wages, more steady work, and full-time work instead of low wages, part-time work, and no work at all. The harm done to the poor by inflation during prosperity is more than offset by the gains that prosperity brings for them. In other words, it is better to earn $3,000 a year when prices rise at 5 percent than to earn $500 with prices rising at 1 percent. The recent U.S. experience confirms this.

As Figure 4.2, "Number of Poor Persons and Incidence of Poverty" so vividly shows, recessions and sluggish growth *raise* the number of the poor.

True enough, more unemployment is a remedy for inflation. But so far as the poor are concerned, this would hurt them more than inflation itself. The very methods used to promote full employment and growth could profitably pay special attention to the lot of the poor.

Selective increases in aggregate demand. If, for instance, it is necessary to raise aggregate demand to reach full employment, this may be done by providing additional income to the poor rather than to the rich. An unemployed steelworker can be put to work just as well by increasing the demand for steel to make refrigerators or schools or hospitals for the poor as by increasing it to make yachts for the rich. A tax cut could, for instance, easily discriminate in favor of the poor. There is nothing to prevent us from cutting taxes of the poor to below zero by giving them tax refunds for taxes they have never paid. Similarly, increased government spending could be in areas and on projects helping the poor directly, and not just indirectly by giving them jobs through the multiplier chain of additional induced spending. Examples of such policies in the past are government spending on regional development.

The Area Redevelopment Act of 1961 (slated for extinction according to President Nixon's fiscal 1974 budget message) concentrated government spending in areas of chronic unemployment. Funds were to finance community projects and private undertakings that employed the chronically unemployed. They were also to help the displaced to train for new jobs in the industries of the area. Another example is the Appalachia Program of 1965, which was initiated to develop employment opportunities in 350 counties and 12 states from New York to Alabama. This is a huge economically depressed area. The program is paving the way for private industrial development through the public construction of roads and health facilities, as well as land erosion control and the restoration of water and timber resources.

Nor is government restricted to spending funds near the unemployed in the hope that they will somehow be hired. It can hire them directly. In 1966 the National Commission on Technology, Automation, and Economic Progress proposed to the president that the federal government become an "employer of last resort," providing at least 500,000 full-time public-service jobs for those unable to find work. Presumably the poor unemployed (and perhaps even a specified subset of them, like the handicapped or like mothers) could be hired for the construction, maintenance, and repair of public structures and parks, and as nonprofessional aides in schools, hospitals, welfare offices, and even fire and police stations. Indeed, the Emergency Employment Act of 1971 was the first public employment law operating along these lines since the Works Project Administration of the 1930's. Its aim was to find permanent employment at the minimum wage for 150,000 recent veterans, welfare recipients, and unemployed professionals living in high-unemployment areas (defined by a national unemployment rate over 4.5 percent and a state and local rate over 6 percent). Local governments had to do the hiring but the federal government contracted to pay 90 percent of the wage bill for two years. However, by 1972, the intent of the act had frequently been thwarted, as local governments laid off their original full-time employees, only to rehire them with the federal funds. Even where this was not the case, those with the greatest labor market difficulties (high school dropouts, older workers, women, the long-term unemployed) were typically slighted in favor of those with the greatest chances of finding work on their own (adult male high school graduates with recent work experience). By early 1973, President Nixon indicated that the entire program would be phased out of existence.

COUNTERING LOW-WAGE EMPLOYMENT

Some people argue that additional measures must be taken to assure people not only of jobs, but of *well-paying* jobs. They point to the working poor and argue that only one thing can help here: the setting of minimum wages above levels currently paid. For instance, it has long been a strongly held view of organized labor that a higher minimum wage is one of the keystones in any effort to eradicate poverty. This attitude has been supported by government. When Willard Wirtz was secretary of labor in 1969, he proposed a $2-an-hour minimum and urged that the new minimum apply to every worker in the U.S., with no exceptions of any kind. He pictured his minimum-wage proposals as an effective weapon to help push forward "the new national purpose to eliminate poverty." Wilbur Mills made the identical proposal in 1971 "to ease welfare costs." President Nixon endorsed the idea and in 1973 called for a $2.30-an-hour minimum by 1976.

Actually, the setting of minimum wages above market equilibrium levels goes back to the 1930's. The Fair Labor Standards Act of 1938 set a minimum wage of 25 cents an hour, but it did not by any means cover all workers. Over the passage of time, the minimum level has been raised and the coverage of the law has been expanded greatly. The hourly minimum was raised to 75 cents in 1950, to $1.00 in 1956, to $1.15 in 1961, to $1.25 in 1963, to $1.40 in 1967, and to $1.60 in 1968. In 1973, the federal minimum wage was still $1.60 an hour. However, there were still workers who were not covered by the law or were subject to exceptions. Employees of state and local governments, many farm workers, and household workers were not covered at all. Some agricultural workers (on large farms) were subject to a $1.30 minimum. Congress was in the process of raising the minimum and extending coverage, however. Yet there is reason to believe that this kind of interference with the price system causes more problems than it solves.

Likely Effects of Minimum Wages

Economic theory does not provide any *certain* answers to the question about the likely effects of imposing minimum wages. To a large extent, what happens depends on whether markets are perfectly competitive or not.

Perfect competition in resource markets and goods markets. Consider the case wherein perfect competition prevails originally in the markets for resources as well as goods. This type of situation was depicted in Figure 2.2, "Optimizing Decisions and Market Equilibrium." Market supply and demand for labor established an equilibrium price (part (e)). Everyone who looked for work at this wage was employed and received the value of his contribution to production, the *marginal value product MVP*. If any one worker were to withdraw from employment, his employer would lose the marginal value product. It equals revenue equal to the worker's *marginal physical product* (that is, the output he had added) evaluated at its market price. Graphically, this *MVP* was measured by the marginal benefit at the optimum point in part (f). The employer would save an equal amount in wage cost (the marginal cost *MC*) if a worker were to withdraw from employment. Now consider Figure 8.3, "Minimum-Wage Effect in Perfect Competition." It corresponds to parts (e) and (f) of Figure 2.2. We assume that originally a perfectly competitive market establishes an equilibrium wage of $3,200 per year, leading to the employment of 400,000 workers (point e in the graph). The individual firm, pictured in part (b) finds its optimum at the point at which its $3,200 per year marginal cost just equals the workers' marginal value product. It hires 170 workers. A minimum wage of $5,000 a year is now imposed. As a result, more people are attracted to looking for work in this occupation and locality. The quantity of labor supplied rises along *eb* to 600,000 workers. At the same time, however, the quantity demanded *falls* along *ea* to 200,000 workers. This is so because at the higher wage, with the price of output as it is, each employer finds a new optimum where fewer workers are employed and their marginal value product rises to the new and higher marginal cost of employment *MC′*. Naturally, actual employment is determined by demand, at point *a*. Those lucky enough to remain employed are considerably better off, getting $5,000 rather than $3,200 a year. But many of their potential fellow workers suffer for this. They are now unemployed, having lost their previous jobs or newly entered the labor force (distance *ab*).

Perfect competition in resource markets but not in goods markets. Even if the resource markets were perfectly competitive, resource buyers who are imperfect competitors in the goods market would behave differently in the resource market than if they were perfect competitors in goods. As we know, any firm hires labor up to the point at which the marginal cost of hiring it equals the marginal benefit of using it. As we just noted, in part (b) of Figure 8.3, "Minimum-Wage Effect in Perfect Competition," under perfect competition the former is given to the firm by the market and is identical with the wage. The latter is eventually falling and is identical with the marginal value product. Yet if the user of labor is an imperfect competitor in the goods market, the marginal benefit of using labor is *not* the marginal physical product of labor multiplied by product price (which is marginal value product). Rather it is the *marginal revenue product*, or the marginal physical product of labor multiplied by the *marginal revenue* from selling the product. The marginal revenue

Figure 8.3 **Minimum-Wage Effect in Perfect Competition**

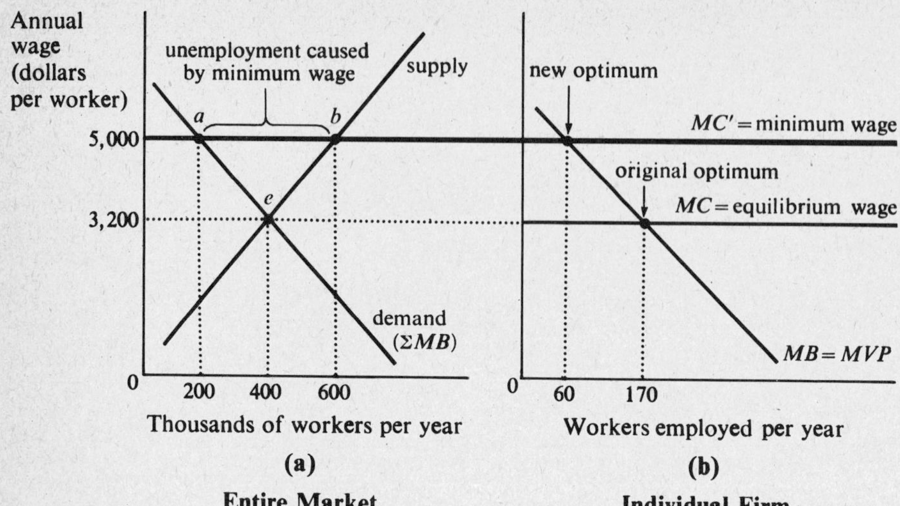

In a perfectly competitive labor market, the imposition of an above-equilibrium minimum wage causes each firm to find a new optimum position at less employment. It causes households to supply a greater quantity of labor. Overall, this creates unemployment (distance *ab*) and reduces the level of employment. Thus some workers gain (those remaining employed), while others lose (those becoming unemployed).

product, furthermore, is always lower than the marginal value product because marginal revenue is lower than price.

An example will illustrate the point. If there is perfect competition in the labor market, the marginal cost of hiring another man equals the market wage of, say, $2,700 a year. Say, the annual marginal physical product of a man is 1,000 tons of aluminum. Suppose aluminum is currently selling at $3 a ton. It seems that it would pay to hire the man (comparing $2,700 with $3,000). Yet an imperfect competitor in the aluminum market may well decide against it. Since he supplies a large percentage of the market total, he has to figure thus: "Without the extra man, my total output is (let us suppose) 20,000 tons and price is $3 a ton. With the extra man, my total output would be 21,000 tons *and this could be sold only at a lower price of, say, $2.95 a ton.* Thus the extra man would produce extra value (a marginal value product) of 1,000 × $2.95, or $2,950. But marginal revenue to my firm would be less, since I would acquire the opportunity to sell another 1,000 tons not only at the added wage cost of $2,700, but also at the cost of forgoing 5 cents of revenue on each of 20,000 tons. To my firm the $2,950 gain in revenue would in part be offset by a $1,000 loss in revenue. Net revenue gain, or marginal revenue product, would be $1,950 (implying a marginal revenue per ton of $1,950 divided by 1,000 tons, or $1.95 per ton). It would not pay to shell out $2,700 in wages to gain $1,950 in revenues."

To maximize his profit, any producer holding a monopolistic product market position would hire labor only up to the point where falling marginal revenue product equals the wage, even though falling marginal value product would be above it. All this is illustrated in Figure 8.4, "Minimum-Wage Effect in the Presence of Monopolistic Exploitation." Consider part (b) of the graph first. For reasons just shown, labor's marginal revenue product *MRP* is always below its marginal value product *MVP* if the user of labor holds a monopolistic position in the goods market, requiring him to lower product price in order to sell more. In our example, when *MVP* was $2,950, *MRP* was only $1,950. The profit-maximizing firm in part (b) naturally looks to the marginal revenue product as the marginal benefit from employing labor. Thus market demand (part (a)) is the sum of marginal revenue product lines rather than the sum of marginal value product lines. If the number of people looking for jobs varies with the wage as shown by the market supply curve of labor, perfect competition in the labor market establishes an equilibrium wage of $2,700 per

Figure 8.4 **Minimum-Wage Effect in the Presence of Monopolistic Exploitation**

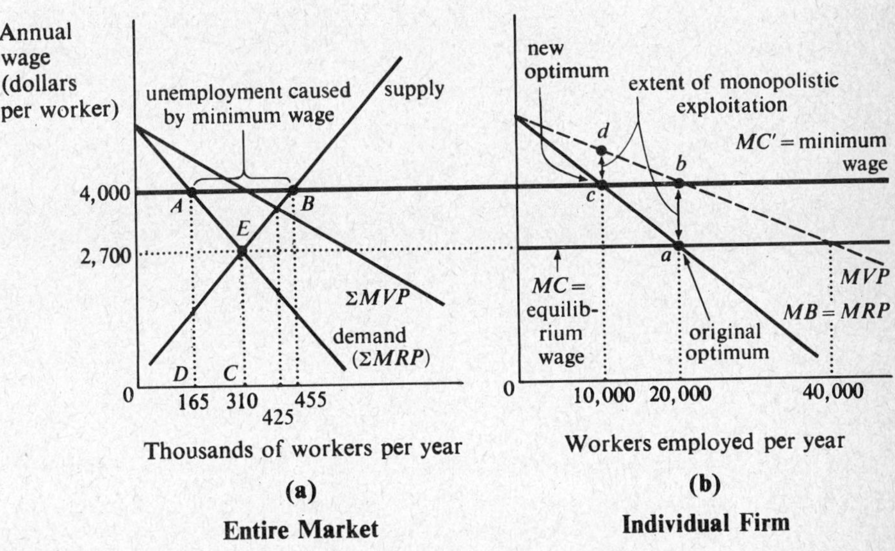

When a minimum wage is imposed on a situation of monopolistic exploitation, unemployment is created (distance *AB*), and the level of employment drops (distance *CD*). Thus some workers gain (those remaining employed), while others lose (those becoming unemployed). Monopolistic exploitation, as shown by the divergence of marginal value product from marginal revenue product, continues (distance *cd* rather than *ab*).

year, and 310,000 workers are hired (point *E*, part (a)). Our firm finds its optimum and hires 20,000 workers (point *a*, part (b)). Since the marginal worker receives a wage below the marginal value product, *monopolistic exploitation* of labor is said to exist. Its extent (distance *ab*) is indicated in part (b) of Figure 8.4. Note how, compared with perfect competition in goods markets (when each producer can count on selling additional output at unchanged prices and a firm's demand for labor equals the marginal value product), employment is reduced. Our particular firm hires 20,000 rather than 40,000 workers. Overall, 310,000 rather than 425,000 workers are employed. These employment reductions are the result of imperfections in the goods market.

The imposition of a minimum wage at, say, $4,000 a year only worsens things. Our individual firm finds a new optimum and only employs 10,000 workers. In the entire market, quantity demanded drops along *EA*. Quantity supplied rises along *EB*. Actual employment ends up at 165,000 workers (point *A*), with 290,000 being involuntarily unemployed.

Imperfect competition in all markets. We can now go a step further and introduce imperfection into the labor market as well. Let us consider the buyer's side of the market first and assume that our imperfectly competitive seller of goods also happens to be a *monopsonist* in the labor market who is facing numerous unorganized suppliers of labor. This means he is the *only buyer* of labor, perhaps in the proverbial "company town." The people living there may be tied to the town emotionally, or because of friends or ignorance of alternatives; or because moving is costly or they fear the unknown. Thus the one employer is employing practically the whole labor force in the relatively isolated community. We are making this extreme assumption only for illustrative purposes, however. The results so reached remain intact when less stringent conditions are imposed on the labor market.

The foremost consequence of this monopsonistic situation is that the labor supply curve with which our individual firm is confronted is not the now familiar horizontal marginal cost curve just used in parts (b) of Figures 8.3 and 8.4. That is, even in the absence of minimum-wage legislation, our firm cannot buy any quantity of labor it wants at a *given* market-determined price. Rather, it is confronted with the entire *rising market supply curve*. The firm must choose any one of the many price-quantity combinations on it. It can set the wage anywhere it wishes, but must then accept whatever quantity of labor is forthcoming. It can get more people to work for it only by raising the wage paid. This draws in more people into the local labor force, either from other localities or from the previously voluntarily unemployed. The supply curve to it is identical with rising market supply. The firm may, for instance, buy per day 8,000 hours of labor at $1 each, spending $8,000. It could, perhaps, buy 10,000 hours of labor only by offering $2 per hour, spending $20,000. To buy 2,000 hours more, it has to offer a higher price on *all* units. Then each additional hour, although bought for $2, increases purchase costs by

$$\frac{\$20{,}000 - \$8{,}000}{2{,}000} = \$6.$$

The marginal cost of acquiring labor now *exceeds* the wage. In short, just as the marginal revenue from selling more output is below output price for the monopoly firm, the marginal cost of buying more input is above input price for the monopsony firm. Since the rational firm only buys a quantity of labor where marginal cost equals marginal benefit, a monopsonist-monopolist buys a quantity where labor's marginal value product is above its price for two reasons: the marginal cost of acquiring labor exceeds labor's wage, and marginal value product from using labor exceeds marginal revenue product (which is set equal to marginal cost by the rational firm). This is illustrated in Figure 8.5, "A Firm's Optimum Labor Force in the Presence of Monopolistic and Monopsonistic Exploitation." Due to the firm's monopoly position in the goods

Figure 8.5 A Firm's Optimum Labor Force in the Presence of Monopolistic and Monopsonistic Exploitation

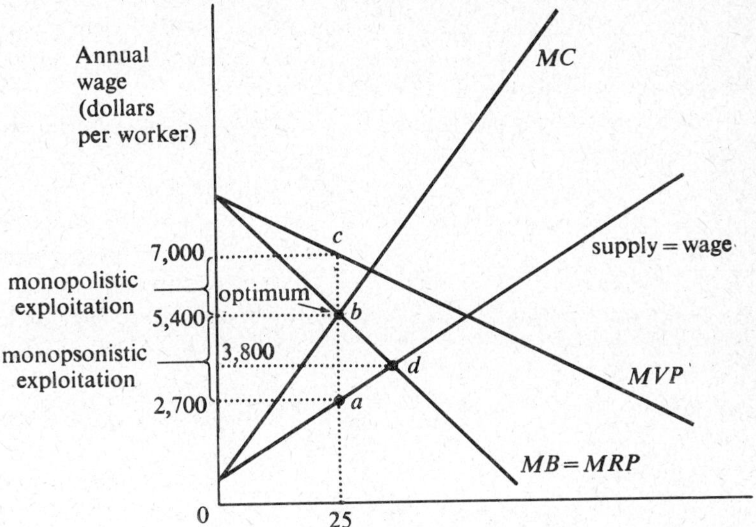

Any employer optimizes the quantity of labor hired by equating the marginal benefit of using labor *MB* with the marginal cost of hiring it *MC*. For an employer who is a monopsonist in buying labor, the marginal cost is above the wage. If he is also a monopolist in selling goods, the marginal benefit is below the labor's marginal value product. The employer pictured here finds the optimum at point *b*, corresponding to 25,000 workers. According to the supply curve, these can be hired at \$2,700 a year. Thus monopsonistic exploitation exists (*MC* above wage), and so does monopolistic exploitation (*MVP* above *MRP*).

market, the firm's marginal benefit from using labor is labor's marginal revenue product *MRP*, and it is always below labor's marginal value product *MVP*. Due to the firm's monopsony position in the labor market, the marginal cost of acquiring labor *MC* is always above the wage that has to be paid to acquire it (as shown by the supply curve). Our firm finds its optimum employment volume where a $5,400 marginal benefit equals marginal cost (at point *b*). As indicated by the supply curve (point *a*), it has to pay $2,700 a year to acquire 25,000 workers. The difference between the marginal cost of $5,400 and the wage of $2,700 measures the extent of *monopsonistic exploitation.* Of course, the value of the marginal worker's contribution to production is higher still ($7,000, shown by point *c*). The difference between the marginal value product of $7,000 and the marginal revenue product and marginal cost of $5,400 measures, as before, the extent of *monopolistic exploitation.*

Now imagine that a minimum wage is introduced above the $2,700 a year level currently paid. Graphically, the imposition of a minimum wage shows up as follows: The upward sloping labor market supply curve becomes irrelevant to the firm below the level of the minimum wage. It simply cannot hire labor below that new wage, although it remains free to hire labor at a higher wage. Thus the labor supply curve and marginal cost curve become a horizontal line and coincide at the level of the minimum wage up to their point of meeting the market supply curve. At larger labor quantities, however, the old (separate) supply and marginal cost curves prevail.

The effects of this on employment and unemployment, however, now differ depending on the *extent* of the minimum-wage hike:

If the minimum-wage hike is *small,* involving a new wage anywhere between the original level ($2,700 in Figure 8.5) and the level corresponding to the intersection (at *d*) of the marginal benefit and supply curves ($3,800 in Figure 8.5), the result will be *higher* employment and *no* unemployment.

If the minimum-wage hike is *moderate,* involving a new wage anywhere between the level of the intersection (at *d*) of the marginal benefit and supply curves ($3,800 in Figure 8.5) and the level of the intersection (at *b*) of the marginal benefit and marginal cost curves ($5,400 in Figure 8.5), the result will be *higher* employment and *some* unemployment.

If the minimum-wage hike is *large,* involving a new wage above the intersection (at *b*) of the marginal benefit and marginal cost curves ($5,400 in Figure 8.5), the result will be *lower* employment and *much* unemployment. All this is shown in the following three graphs.

Consider Figure 8.6, "Effect of a Small Minimum-Wage Hike in the Presence of Monopolistic and Monopsonistic Exploitation." The imposition of a minimum wage (here at $3,300) wipes out the portion of the supply curve below the minimum. It also wipes out the corresponding portion of the (higher) marginal cost curve for acquiring labor. In this case, the imposition of a $3,300 minimum wage changes the supply curve as well as the marginal cost curve, to a horizontal line up to a quantity of 31,000 workers. That is, up to a yearly supply of 31,000 workers, our firm is now in the state of a

Figure 8.6 **Effect of a Small Minimum-Wage Hike in the Presence of Monopolistic and Monopsonistic Exploitation**

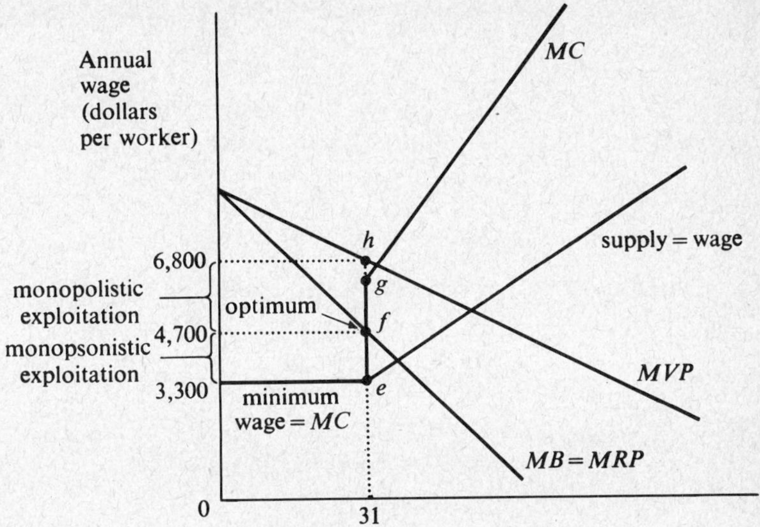

A small minimum-wage hike can bring higher employment, while avoiding unemployment. Note how (compared with Figure 8.5) 31,000 rather than 25,000 workers are employed when a $3,300-a-year minimum wage prevails. Note that all those who want to work at this wage (as shown by point e on the supply curve) find employment. Monopsonistic and monopolistic exploitation are still present.

perfect competitor in the labor market. Wage is given to it by law at the $3,300 level. This won't change no matter how many workers it hires (up to 31,000 a year). Thus its marginal cost of acquiring labor equals this wage. Beyond 31,000 workers, however, the firm is again in the position of a monopsonist. Even though the first 31,000 workers (who were willing to work for less than $3,300) gladly accepted the minimum wage, more workers can be had only for higher wages. Marginal cost at e jumps to g and joins the original curve. Beyond 31,000 workers, marginal cost and wage (along the supply curve) again diverge.

Under the circumstances, it is clear what our firm will do. It must abandon its old optimum at *b* (Figure 8.5), where it hired 25,000 workers for $2,700 each. It will seek its new marginal benefit–marginal cost equality, and find it at f (Figure 8.6). Thus it will hire 31,000 workers at $3,300 each! *It hires more workers than before, and pays each more than before!* There is no involuntary unemployment.

Now consider Figure 8.7, "Effect of a Moderate Minimum-Wage Hike in the Presence of Monopolistic and Monopsonistic Exploitation." As in the previous example, the portion of the supply curve lying below the minimum

Figure 8.7 **Effect of a Moderate Minimum-Wage Hike in the Presence of Monopolistic and Monopsonistic Exploitation**

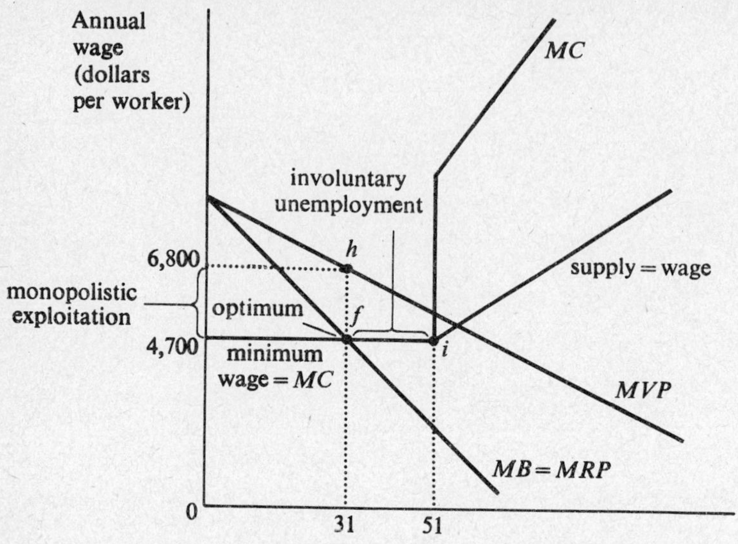

A moderate minimum-wage hike can bring higher employment, while simultaneously creating some unemployment. Note how (compared with Figure 8.5) 31,000 rather than 25,000 workers are employed when a $4,700-a-year minimum wage prevails. Yet another 20,000 workers (distance *f i*) who also want to work at this wage cannot find jobs. Monopsonistic exploitation has been wiped out; monopolistic exploitation is still present.

wage has been wiped out as illegal. So has the corresponding portion of the (higher) marginal cost curve. The firm abandons its old optimum at *b* (Figure 8.5). It finds a new one at the new marginal benefit–marginal cost equality at *f* (Figure 8.7). Thus it hires 31,000 workers at $4,700 each. *It hires more workers than before, and pays each more than before. Yet unemployment appears.* At the $4,700-a-year wage, 51,000 workers wish to work (as shown by point *i* on the supply curve). Note that monopsonistic exploitation has been completely wiped out, while monopolistic exploitation (distance *fh*) continues.

Finally, consider Figure 8.8, "Effect of a Large Minimum-Wage Hike in the Presence of Monopolistic and Monopsonistic Exploitation." In this case, the firm finds a new optimum at *j*, hiring 14,000 workers at $7,000 each. *It hires fewer workers than before; much unemployment is created.* At the $7,000-a-year minimum wage, 74,000 workers wish to work (as shown by point *k* on the supply curve). Again, monopsonistic exploitation has been wiped out, but monopolistic exploitation (distance *jl*) continues.

Thus we conclude: In the presence of monopsonistic and monopolistic exploitation, the imposition of minimum wages above current wage levels may,

Figure 8.8 **Effect of a Large Minimum-Wage Hike in the Presence of Monopolistic and Monopsonistic Exploitation**

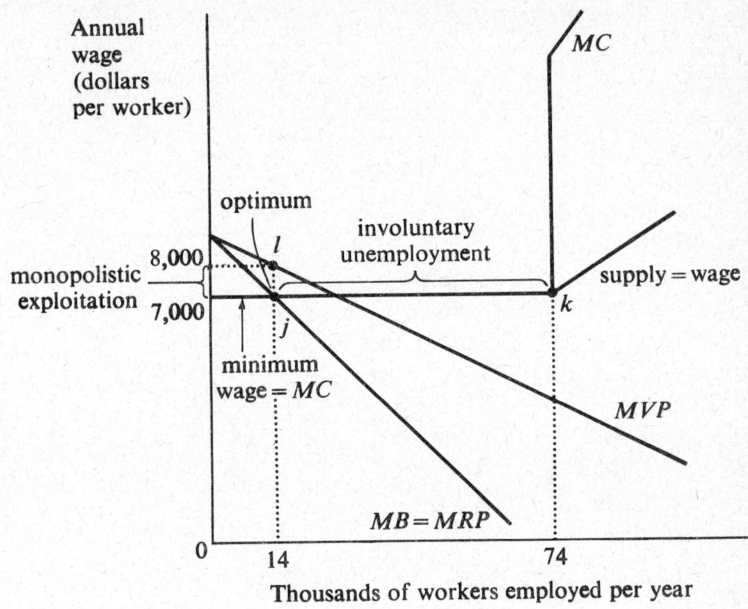

A large minimum-wage hike results in lower employment and increased unemployment. Note how (compared with Figure 8.5) 14,000 rather than 25,000 workers are employed when a $7,000-a-year minimum wage prevails. Yet another 60,000 workers (distance *jk*) who also want to work at this wage cannot find jobs. Monopsonistic exploitation has been wiped out, monopolistic exploitation is still present.

depending on the extent of the wage hike, raise or lower employment and avoid or create unemployment. Lowered employment and higher unemployment are more likely the larger the wage hike.[3]

The Historical Experience

The above theoretical conclusions are confirmed by historical experience. The fate of the Mississippi Delta cotton workers is an example. Their labor market as well as the market for their product operated in circumstances that come as close to perfect competition as one can hope to find in reality. In 1960, there were 30,510 of these workers receiving at most $3.50 a day, often less. When the federal minimum wage raised their pay to $10.40 for an

[3] It should be noted that this assumes given marginal benefit curves. The results would have to be modified if the marginal benefit of using labor should change as a consequence of the minimum-wage imposition. In the long run, this may happen. For example, total income might change (as it clearly does in our examples). This may affect the demand for and price of the very product here produced, hence the *MB* curve might shift, offsetting or reinforcing the results we noted. Similarly, firms affected by minimum wages may introduce new labor-saving technology, again causing the *MB* curve to shift.

eight-hour day, their numbers rapidly shrank, to just a handful by 1970. Chemicals and machinery took their place. In 1960, farmers had spent per acre $46.80 on labor and $13.50 on chemicals. After the imposition of the minimum wage, they spent per acre $13.50 on labor and $24 on chemicals. Instead of plowing one row at a time, they now ride mammoth tractors and cultivators sweeping across the fields at five miles per hour, turning eight rows at a time and shooting weed-killers into the soil as they go. The unemployed watch.

Of course, this story proves little. Although minimum wages have been imposed and raised on several occasions in recent U.S. history, it is by no means easy to assess their effect from this historical experience. It is not easy because employment and price levels are influenced by many factors besides minimum wages. Wages have risen consistently for at least a hundred years. Employment in the long run has also risen, although there have been short-run declines. We can expect this general trend to continue with or without minimum-wage legislation. Thus it is difficult to sort out the effects of minimum wages from the events that would have occurred anyway. If employment after raising the wage goes up, would it have gone up anyway? Might it have gone up by more? If employment goes down following a minimum-wage imposition, we can similarly wonder: Would it have gone down anyway for other reasons? Might it have been unchanged or even risen otherwise? Which part of the observed effect was really due to minimum wages alone?

All this gets even more complicated because the coverage of the minimum-wage law is not complete. If minimum wages imposed on a certain occupation lower employment in it, the people affected may well find employment in noncovered occupations where wage rates adjust with supply and demand. For instance, agricultural workers becoming unemployed may move to nearby cities and seek employment there. Possibly they end up as common laborers, although not until they have lowered wages in such occupations by swelling the supply. Thus, our unemployed Mississippi cotton workers may migrate to California and Michigan and find employment as porters and domestics and laundry workers. Possibly, they may end up earning more than the $3.50 a day they made in the Delta, but they may not. The likelihood that there will be a great improvement in their lot is small indeed. There is some solid evidence that minimum wages do more harm than good. First of all, we must realize that minimum wages in the United States have been set relatively low, roughly at half the level of average manufacturing wages. Thus the great majority of workers have always had wages exceeding the minimum and thus been unaffected by changes in the minimum. We should expect, therefore, that unskilled workers have been affected most strongly by the imposition of minima. Among the most unskilled are teenagers.

A study by Yale Brozen compared unemployment among teenagers in the month before an increase in the statutory minimum and in the month the increase took effect.[4] From 1950 to 1968, each time an increase took effect,

[4] Yale Brozen, "The Effect of Statutory Minimum Wage Increases on Teen-Age Employment," *Journal of Law and Economics*, April 1969, pp. 109–22.

unemployment rose, in January 1950, for instance, from 15.2 percent of the teenage labor force to 17.7 percent; in February 1968, from 12.6 percent to 13.3 percent. Since unemployment rose only in half the months otherwise studied over a twenty-year period, this persistent rise in unemployment after a minimum-wage hike could not be explained by chance. Furthermore, over time, teenage unemployment, relative to unemployment of all groups, has risen. In January 1950, the teenage unemployment rate was 2.2 times the general rate. By 1968, it was 3.6 times the general rate.

Brozen's study noted that minimum-wage statutes have increased the incomes of a few workers at the time of their imposition, namely of those workers who did not lose their jobs. These increases would have come anyway within two to five years. This is evidenced by studying the wage rates of non-covered workers such as private household and agricultural workers. These have been rising 4 percent per year since 1949 despite the depressing effects of additional workers looking for jobs in this sector after having been forced out of jobs covered by minimum wages. Apparently, successive amendments to the minimum-wage statute have jumped wages in the first year in the affected occupations, with very slow rises occurring thereafter. The total increase in the long run has differed little in covered and not-covered occupations. Brozen concluded:

> If all that happened as a result of the minimum-wage statute was a change in the timing of wage rate increases, there would be little to concern us. However, in the interval between the time that the minimum wage is raised and the time that productivity and inflation catch up with the increase, thousands of people are jobless, many businesses fail which are never revived, people are forced to migrate who would prefer not to, cities find their slums deteriorating and becoming over-populated, teenagers are barred from obtaining the opportunity to learn skills which would make them more productive, and permanent damage is done to their attitudes and their ambitions. This is a large price to pay for impatience.

Conclusion

Thus we can conclude that there must be better ways of attacking poverty arising from low-wage employment than setting minimum wages. To the extent that anybody gains from minimum wages, it is likely to be disadvantaged workers gaining at the expense of other disadvantaged workers. Much more promising are other policies discussed earlier: assuring that aggregate demand is high and that sellers of labor are healthy, well educated, well informed, and as mobile as is humanly possible. Too many of those remaining poor in spite of full-time work do not have these advantages. Even when they are healthy and skilled (as many are not), they are facing slack labor markets crisscrossed with barriers to mobility, and they face these markets in ignorance. Naturally, when nonwhites and females are crowded into some occupations no matter what their education, their wages will come to be relatively low.

Large supply, relative to demand, always lowers price. By the same token, when white males artificially restrict other occupations to themselves, their wages will come to be relatively high. Small supply, relative to demand, always raises price. The abolition of barriers between high-wage and low-wage markets is infinitely more likely to help the poor than setting minimum wages in low-wage markets. The *abolition* of minimum wages might be more helpful to the poor (such as teenagers) by opening up employment opportunities.

Summary

1. Some people remain poor because they cannot get a job at all. Others, however, remain poor because they cannot get a full-time job or because they cannot get a job that pays well. Official data on involuntary unemployment, therefore, tell only part of the story. People working part time are counted as employed, and so are people working full time and remaining poor. People discouraged from looking for work are even counted as outside the labor force, as children or the retired are.
2. It must also be noted that there are different types of involuntary unemployment. Each requires a different type of countermeasure. Frictional unemployment exists when the numbers and types of job openings and job seekers roughly coincide, but are temporarily mismatched. It arises most often when people first enter the labor force, reenter it after a period of voluntary unemployment, or voluntarily leave one job for another. It tends to persist only because of insufficient labor-market information. Chronic unemployment, in contrast, spells a more serious mismatching of job openings and job seekers. It is caused by discrimination (when employers refuse to give jobs to some potential employees), by the inability of workers to leave home (when mothers are tied down with small children), and by structural changes in the economy (when people come to possess obsolete skills). General unemployment, finally, spells a general lack of job openings relative to job seekers.
3. The existence of involuntary unemployment in a market economy may at first glance appear as somewhat of a paradox. One would expect forces of supply and demand to equilibrate the resource markets, thereby eliminating unemployment, which would appear as surpluses in these markets. Clearly, this is not happening in reality. One reason is simple to comprehend: Our market economy is not perfectly competitive. Labor-market participants lack full information and mobility, and wages are sticky downwards. To the extent that involuntary unemployment is caused by such factors, it can be removed by restoring to labor markets the conditions of perfect competition or by countering the effects of imperfections.
4. The extent of frictional unemployment could be reduced by improving informational services, for example by computerized job banks. Chronic unemployment can be fought with antidiscrimination policies concerning hiring and promotion, with the provision of day care programs for the children of mothers

who want to work, and with retraining programs. The elimination of general unemployment calls for high levels of aggregate demand.

5. Aggregate demand can be raised to any desired level by proper monetary and fiscal policies. Recent U.S. history confirms that such policies reduce poverty by giving more and better-paid jobs to the poor. Nor is it a good idea to refrain from such policy for fear of creating inflation. The best ways to raise aggregate demand involve measures helping the poor directly, as well as indirectly, such as tax cuts for the poor or government spending in depressed areas or on public service employment of the poor.
6. Some people argue that additional measures should be taken to counter low-wage employment, as by setting minimum wages above equilibrium levels. Labor unions and government are agreed on the desirability of this approach. Economists are more cautious.
7. The effects of imposing above-equilibrium minimum wages depend on the initial conditions prevailing in markets. Economic theory predicts an increase in involuntary unemployment under the majority of conceivable conditions. If the wage increase is small or moderate, however, a simultaneous increase in employment is conceivable under conditions of monopsonistic exploitation. In all other cases, those disadvantaged workers remaining employed are likely to gain at the expense of other disadvantaged workers who lose their jobs or cannot find jobs.
8. It is difficult to interpret the effects of actual minimum-wage impositions in U.S. history. However, available evidence tends to confirm the theoretical predictions. One can conclude, therefore, that the imposition of minimum wages is a poor approach to eliminating low-paying jobs. Policies assuring high aggregate demand on the one hand, and health, skills, market knowledge, and mobility of job seekers on the other, are eminently preferable as methods to eliminate low-wage employment.

Terms[5]

aggregate demand
chronic unemployment
discouraged workers
dual market
fiscal policy
frictional unemployment
general unemployment
involuntary unemployment
job banks
marginal physical product
marginal revenue
marginal revenue product
marginal value product
minimum wage
minorities advancement plan
monetary policy
monopolist
monopolistic exploitation
monopsonist
monopsonistic exploitation
voluntary unemployment

[5] Terms and symbols are defined in the Glossary at the back of the book.

Symbols

D

MC

MRP

MVP

S

Questions for Review and Discussion

1. Thomas Dernburg and Kenneth Strand made a study of the discouraged-worker hypothesis, the belief that perhaps many involuntarily unemployed are hidden in the statistics of voluntary unemployment simply because they have given up looking for work. (See their "Hidden Unemployment 1953–1962: A Quantitative Analysis by Age and Sex," *American Economic Review*, March 1966, pp. 71–95.) They added estimated numbers of such discouraged workers to official labor force and unemployment totals. As a result, the overall unemployment rate in 1962 (officially at 5.6 percent) jumped to 8.5 percent. The unemployment rate for men jumped from the official 5.3 percent to 7.0 percent. The unemployment rate for women jumped from the official 6.2 percent to 11.3 percent. Similar results were reached for 1953–61. In light of this, would you think it worth while to change official data-gathering procedures? If so, how? What about all those part-time workers now counted as *employed*?
2. "The fact that the unemployment rate for teenagers is significantly above the national average proves that people hiring workers discriminate against teenagers." Do you agree? (HINT: What if teenagers enter and leave the actual labor force more often than other people because they only desire to work intermittently? What if young people in general have a healthy propensity to change jobs voluntarily to test their aptitudes and opportunities?)
3. "The fact that the unemployment rate among blacks is significantly above the national average proves that people hiring workers discriminate against blacks." Discuss. (HINT: What if blacks are currently less skilled than others, have a harder time getting transportation out of inner-city ghettos, and have a different age composition from that of the population on the average?)
4. "Employers have often been accused of using 'arbitrary hiring standards' (for example, a high school diploma, no record of arrest). This keeps many people from ever getting a good job. Employers should simply look at people's innate ability, their motivation, not their past." What do you think? Isn't it inevitable for any employer to discriminate when hiring?
5. "Just as the United States has 'separate but equal schools' based on race and wealth, it has 'separate but equal occupations' based on race and sex. In both cases, the 'equality' alluded to is a myth, and in both cases the result is poverty for one of the separated groups." Explain.
6. "Automation has us by the throat. If it is true that national productivity rises at 3.2 percent per year, any child can figure out what it means: The *same* workers can produce 3.2 percent more output each year—or (and here comes the rub) we can produce the same output with *fewer* workers. Now just look-

ing around shows what we *are* doing: one would have to be blind not to notice how those fancy servomechanisms are replacing elevator operators, telephone operators, even office workers and assembly line workers. If we stopped automation, job openings would sprout like dandelions." Discuss.

7. "If there is general unemployment, it does not help us to cure the causes of frictional and chronic unemployment." Discuss.
8. "The very expression calling government an 'employer of last resort' betrays a value judgment, namely, that the best possible use of labor is to be found in the private sector of the economy. This is wrong. The need for more employees in the public sector to produce health and educational services, for example, is vastly greater than in the private sector to produce trinkets. Government should formally guarantee the right to work to every citizen and become the employer of *first* resort." What do you think?
9. President Nixon, proposing a *nationwide* computerized job matching program, said, "Modern technology can serve human needs. If computers can match boys and girls for college dates, they can match job-seeking men with man-seeking jobs." Do you agree? (Consider that a computer cannot make the subtle judgments a skilled interviewer can make about an applicant's abilities and interests, that a nationwide system would cost $180 million, that most people maybe would not want to move to jobs further than their immediate area.)
10. President Nixon has stressed "volunteerism" for curing chronic unemployment. He has emphasized the limits of governmental power and the larger role private enterprise must play. He said, "Private enterprise, far more effectively than the government, can provide the jobs, train the unemployed . . . offer the new opportunities which will produce progress." What do you think?
11. "According to the text, a minimum wage can offset monopsonistic exploitation of workers in the labor market. In the process, the level of employment may rise (if the wage hike is moderate) or fall (if it is not). All this, of course, assumes *unchanged* marginal revenue product. However, if workers as a group have higher income and raise the demand for the firm's product significantly, the marginal revenue product may be raised and all results correspondingly be altered." Evaluate.
12. Mr. A: Students should be allowed to work below the minimum wage.

    Mr. B: It is unfair and unreasonable to pay young people less than the minimum wage. Youngsters doing an adult's work should get an adult's pay.

    Evaluate these contrasting positions.
13. "Government should pay a subsidy to employers, if necessary, so that everyone could be employed at minimum wages. This would be cheaper than having millions on welfare." Discuss.
14. What do you think would be the effect of a *nationwide* minimum wage covering all workers? What about a *city-wide* minimum wage covering all workers in New York only? Explain your answers.
15. The minimum wage prescribed by the Fair Labor Standards Act and its amendments aims at preventing exploitation of employees by employers. It may

make the employees worse off and create business monopolies. Here is an example: In 1965, when the minimum wage went to $1.25, crabmeat packers and fishermen in North Carolina had to cease operations. They had been supplying Washington, Baltimore, Philadelphia, and New York. Now they could not continue to compete with similar plants and fishermen further north. They could not pay $1.25 plus transport costs and still meet the northern competitors in northern cities. So the poor southerners who were to be helped ended up unemployed. What would you do about this? (Do you think there should be a lower minimum wage for the South?)

Selected Readings

Council of Economic Advisers, *Economic Report of the President.* Washington, D.C., 1973. Pp. 89–112, 155–59. Discusses the economic role of women, the discrimination they face, and the degree to which women are represented in about two hundred occupations.

Fusfeld, Daniel R. *Economics.* Lexington, Mass.: D. C. Heath and Co., 1972. Chs. 4, 8–20, and 35. Discusses the role of aggregate demand in the economy and how it can be influenced, and also the role of labor unions.

Gordon, David M. *Problems in Political Economy: An Urban Perspective.* Lexington, Mass.: D. C. Heath and Co., 1971. Pp. 57–85, 90–117, 181–90. Presents conservative, liberal, and radical views on employment, unemployment, the dual labor market, racism, and exploitation. Note also the excellent bibliography on pp. 158–62 and 272.

Hirsch, Werner Z. *Urban Economic Analysis.* New York: McGraw-Hill, 1973. Ch. 5. Discusses national, urban, and neighborhood labor markets and policies concerning market inefficiencies, unemployment, poverty, and racial discrimination.

U.S. Bureau of the Census, *Statistical Abstract of the United States, 1972.* Washington, D.C., 1972. Lists some statistics on the labor force, employment, unemployment, and earnings (sections 8 and 33) and—more important—sources to other statistics: Note the listing of statistical abstract supplements (p. v); and the guide to general sources of statistics (pp. 933–35), to recent censuses (pp. 955–56), and to state statistical abstracts (pp. 961–64).

NOTE: The *Journal of Economic Literature* lists recent articles on macroeconomic theory (section 023), stabilization theory and policies (133), inflation (134), monetary theory and policy (310–15), fiscal theory and policy (321–25), labor markets and public policy (820–26), and the economics of discrimination (917).

The *Index of Economic Articles* catalogs, in sections beginning with the indicated numbers, articles on labor force, wages, and unemployment (2.22, 2.343), discrimination (2.1335, 15.342), wage flexibility and employment (2.318), minimum wages (2.224, 19.3), monetary policy (2.3, 9.9), fiscal policy (10.2), employment policies (12.3), and all aspects of labor economics, including occupational mobility, unemployment, labor force composition, the public employment service (19.2), wage differentials (19.3), labor unions (19.4–19.5), and labor market regulation (19.7).

9 *Giving Money to the Poor*

Programs designed to bring good nutrition, health care, education and training, and ultimately jobs to the poor will alleviate much of poverty. Public opinion surveys show that this is the path out of poverty that most of the poor, as well as most other Americans, would prefer to any other alternative. But such programs, however preferred, will not eliminate poverty overnight, nor will they reach all the poor, even in the long run. Some people will remain poor in the transition period during which they receive health care and education and training, and are placed on a job. Some may remain poor even after having found a job, if it pays low wages because market demand for their skill is low relative to the supply. Some may remain poor, at least temporarily, if the programs of health, education, training, and job placement work less than perfectly. And some will remain poor because these programs cannot possibly alter their lot: those with irreversible disabilities, physical or mental, or those too old or not old enough to be trained for a job and to be put to work.

Thus one can make a good case for one additional type of program: assuring some minimum of money income to all the poor as long as other programs have not yet enabled them to earn it on their own. Yet such proposals are much more apt to be resisted by the nonpoor than programs of health, education, and employment. The latter programs have broad support because just about everyone pays taxes willingly for something that can help *everyone* (not just the poor). But welfare programs (at least on the surface) only benefit *a select group* (namely, the poor), and they do so at the expense of the nonpoor. A society that makes welfare payments to the poor plays Robin Hood. It attempts to redistribute the existing total of income by robbing rich Peter to help poor Paul. If this is to be done, an important question arises about the best way of doing it. This chapter and the next deal with that issue.

PRIVATE VS. PUBLIC CHARITY

A great many income transfers occur *voluntarily* within families, as between the productive family members, on the one hand, and the children, the elderly, and the sick, on the other. We are not concerned with such voluntary intra-family transfers here.

There are also a number of voluntary *interfamily* transfers (via the churches, Red Cross, and the like), but these are not of great significance in alleviating poverty. They involve altogether a tiny fraction of 1 percent of GNP. In 1970, for example, all forty-five Christian churches in the United States contributed together $764 million in benevolences, or 0.08 percent of GNP. However, they spent much more than this amount on new construction, and four times this amount on all congregational expenses. In the same year, the United Fund Campaigns raised almost the identical amount of $817 million. Not all of these amounts, however, went to Americans (church benevolences include foreign missions) or to American poor families. Even if they had, this would have equaled only 14 percent of their aggregate income.

Without question, any *serious* income redistribution must be a system of *involuntary interfamily* transfers through governmental taxation of the well-to-do and welfare payments given to the poor. This is bound to be resented, and partly at least for good reasons. It is not always true that those with high incomes have them undeservingly from having inherited a great deal of income-producing property, or being the lucky owners of a skill that just happens to have come into great demand, or having had better opportunities. Even among those with *equal* opportunities, some families end up with higher incomes than others because they work harder, or have been thriftier or worked harder in the past. Most of us would consider it unfair if they got penalized by higher taxes designed to equalize incomes. Thus every society must decide how far it should carry a program of involuntary transfers.

The Desirable Extent of Transfers

No society has created absolute income equality. Some people such as the (academic) socialists frequently argue for a *complete* equalization of money income by government. Failure to do so, they fear, will allow some rich people (with large money demand) to commandeer resources toward the production of such luxuries as private airplanes and summer houses by the sea, while there are still poor people (with lower money demand) in need of such necessities as refrigerators and children's furniture. "Everybody," they say, "should have an equal number of *dollar votes* in the market, and then we can be sure that the whims of some do not get satisfied before the crying needs of their brothers."

This argument is attractive to many, especially to those who favor political democracy, a system that (ideally) also gives an equal vote to each person. It is equally attractive to others for religious reasons, because they believe that every person is equally precious in the eyes of God. Yet, an equal distribution of income may seriously affect incentives (and has for this reason not been introduced in any socialist country). Thus one can make a good case for not carrying income equalization too far. In the United States, poverty can be eliminated easily with only *minor* redistributions of income, while retaining substantial inequality. For instance, we might look at the difference between the actual income of the poor and the income needed to place them above the poverty line. In 1972, this difference was $12 billion. It has been called the "poverty income deficit," and one might set out to tax the "rich" only to the extent required to fill this gap.

There is even a less painful way. As the President's Council of Economic Advisers noted in 1969, on the average, the real per capita income of Americans grows at about 3 percent per year. We could simply redistribute this growth dividend. Suppose we taxed the nonpoor (of whom there are so many) just enough to cut their annual real income increase to 2.5 percent. If we give this to the poor (of whom there are fewer), their real income could rise at 12 percent per year. As a result, the poverty gap would be closed in four to eight years.

THE PRESENT WELFARE SYSTEM

Already the various levels of government in the United States are engaged in a great number of money transfer programs designed to alleviate poverty. Let us look at the payments side first.

Benefits Paid

Table 9.1, "Major Government Cash Assistance Programs," lists the principal programs in effect. They amounted to $76.2 billion for 1971, or 7.3 percent of GNP. This does not count the food, health care, education, and training expenditures, as discussed in previous chapters, that were made directly by government and given to people in kind or from which people benefited indirectly. Just as the benefits from government health and education expenditures went to many nonpoor, so government cash transfers to persons were only in part payments to the poor. Some of the cash transfers, however, must have helped to alleviate poverty, especially that associated with old age, disability, youth, and unemployment. Yet it is important to note one thing. The programs listed in Table 9.1 were enacted at many different times, without any master plan. One may have been enacted in response to the exigencies of the Great Depression, another to mitigate dissent and unrest within a particular group of people. There is no overall coordination of this multitude of programs. Many of the poor are not reached by any of them. Those that are reached are not helped enough.

The oldest cash assistance program (for veterans who served and were disabled in a war) goes back to the Revolutionary War. A military retirement program was added after the Civil War, and the federal civil service retirement program in the 1920's. All other programs listed in Table 9.1 were born in the 1930's.

Social insurance programs go back to the 1935 Social Security Act. It has been amended on many occasions since to change coverage, financing procedures, and benefits. In 1973, the act provided protection against wage loss resulting from old age, prolonged disability, death, or unemployment and protection against the cost of medical care in old age.

Table 9.1 Major Government Cash Assistance Programs, United States, 1971

Program	Total Outlays (Millions) *(1)*	Number of Beneficiaries (Thousands) *(2)*	Average Annual Outlay per Recipient *(3)*
Assistance to those 65 years and over	$50,182		
Social security retirement and survivors benefits	33,591	23,962	$1,402
Old-age assistance	1,888	2,053	920
Retirement (military, civil service, railroad)	12,952	3,589	3,609
Veterans' pensions	1,751	2,329	752
Disability programs	$12,183		
Workmen's compensation	2,350	n.a.	n.a.
Veterans' compensation	4,258	3,235	$1,316
Social security	3,580	2,798	1,279
Aid to the blind	101	81	1,247
Aid to the permanently and totally disabled	1,189	1,002	1,187
Temporary disability benefits (state employees, railroad)	705	n.a.	n.a.
Aid to families with dependent children	$6,203	10,156	$ 611
Unemployment insurance	$6,231	7,428	$ 839
Others (general assistance, emergency assistance, intermediate-care facilities)	$1,430	1,209	$1,183
Total	$76,229		

NOTE: Some of the data in this table are preliminary and estimated. n.a. = not available.

SOURCE: *U.S. Department of Health, Education, and Welfare,* Social Security Bulletin *and its* Annual Statistical Supplement, *and U.S. Manpower Administration,* Unemployment Insurance Statistics.

The old-age, survivors, disability, and health insurance (OASDHI) program provides monthly cash benefits to retired or disabled insured workers and their dependents and to the survivors of an insured worker. Within the specifications of the law, retirement benefits are payable to an aged insured worker; to his aged spouse or his spouse at any age caring for his child who is under age 18 or totally disabled; and to his child who is under age 18, totally disabled, or a full-time student of age 18 to 21. An aged worker becomes eligible for full benefits at age 65, although he may elect reduced benefits up to three years earlier; his spouse is under the same limitations. Special benefits are also provided the aged-72-and-over who do not meet the insured status requirements. Under certain conditions, survivor benefits are payable to some dependents of an insured worker, including his aged or disabled widow or his widow at any age caring for his child who is under age 18 or totally disabled; his child who is under age 18, totally disabled, or a full-time student of age 18 to 21; and aged parents. Disability benefits are payable to an insured worker under age 65 with a prolonged disability that meets the definition in the act and to his dependents on the same basis as dependents of retired workers. A lump sum benefit is also payable on the death of an insured worker.

Beginning July 1966, health insurance has been provided under two coordinated plans for nearly all people of age 65 and over: A hospital insurance plan that covers hospital and related services and a voluntary supplementary medical insurance plan that covers physicians' services and related medical services, as was noted in Chapter 6.

By 1971, well over 90 percent of the labor force was covered by social insurance, as compared with the original coverage of less than half of the labor force. (Still excluded are railroad workers and many government employees, but special social insurance programs exist for their benefit.) The size of monthly benefits varies with previous earning levels, thus turning poor workers eventually into poor beneficiaries. In 1972, the minimum monthly benefit for a single retired person was $84.50, the maximum was $259.40, and the average paid was $156. For a retired couple, the corresponding figures were $126.80, $389.10, and $271. The figures were considerably less for surviving family members. Since 1972, automatic adjustments in benefits are made whenever the Consumer Price Index increases 3 percent or more.

Benefits were typically smaller under other social security programs. Take *workmen's compensation*. All states have programs providing protection against work-connected injuries and deaths. Federal workmen's compensation laws cover federal government employees, private employees in the District of Columbia, and longshoremen and harbor workers. In addition, the Social Security Administration administers a "black lung" benefits program for coal miners disabled by pneumoconiosis and for specified dependents. Most state workmen's compensation laws exempt such employments as agriculture, domestic service, and casual labor; about half of these laws exempt employers who have fewer than a specified number of employees. Occupational diseases, or at least specified diseases, are compensable under most laws.

In most states, total payments to injured workers or to survivor families are limited as to time, amount, or both. All compensation acts require that medical aid be furnished to injured employees; in one-fifth of the laws, there are either duration or cost limitations—or both—on the amount of medical benefits provided. Payments are also low in other programs, financed in part by federal funds, but all administered by the states and localities, that provide *public assistance* to the aged, the blind, the permanently and totally disabled. Each state establishes the conditions under which needy people may receive assistance and it determines how much they shall receive.

Aid to families with dependent children also goes back to 1935. It is also a joint federal-state program. The program was established for widows and orphans only, but at a later time, separated, divorced, and unmarried mothers were included. (In 25 states, on a small scale, women and children have recently become eligible for aid even with the presence of a man in the family, provided that he was involuntarily unemployed.) The numbers aided have risen very rapidly since World War II, from under 2 million in 1955 to 11 million in 1972. Payments have varied considerably from state to state (going, in 1971, from a monthly low of $55 per family in Mississippi to a high of $288 in New York).[1] Of the 1971 beneficiaries, 57 percent lived in central cities, 18 percent in suburbs, 25 percent in rural areas. Just about half were white and half were nonwhite. In 76 percent of the cases the father was absent from home; in 14 percent, incapacitated or dead; in 6 percent, unemployed. Eighteen percent of recipients had been such for at least five years; 35 percent, for less than one year. Only 18 percent of the mothers were employed or in training, not always full time.

The program of *unemployment insurance* is also a joint federal-state program. The federal government fixes minimum benefits and payment periods. Both unemployment insurance and the public employment (placement) service are administered through the Manpower Administration of the Department of Labor and each state's employment security agency. State agencies also administer unemployment compensation for eligible ex-servicemen and federal employees, and cash allowances to persons being trained under the Manpower Development and Training Act.

State unemployment insurance laws pay benefits to unemployed covered workers who meet the qualifications in the state law. Until the present, many workers were excluded from such insurance, including employees of very small firms, agricultural processing workers, state and local government workers, Americans working abroad, and employees of nonprofit organizations (state hospitals, colleges). The excluded made up 18 percent of the labor force in 1969. Those just mentioned are to be included by 1973. Remaining excluded from coverage will be the railroad industry and most workers in agriculture and domestic service. Even among those in covered occupations, payments cease after a given period. As a result, 64 percent of all unemployed did not receive benefits in 1968.

In most states, a waiting period of 1 week must be served before payments begin. Benefits are payable for a maximum number of weeks, ranging from 26 to 39 weeks among the states (most frequently 26 weeks). From 1972, under the provisions of the 1970 Employment Security Act and the 1971 Emergency Unemployment Compensation Act, workers can receive an extra 13 weeks of benefits when the national unemployment rate has exceeded 4.5 percent for 3 months and a state's average unemployment plus benefit exhaustion rates add to at least 6.5 percent or when the state rate exceeds 4 percent and is 20

[1] Most of the statistical data used in this chapter come from the sources to Table 9.1 and from U.S. Social and Rehabilitation Service, *Public Assistance Statistics*.

percent higher than the average rate in a corresponding 13-week period during the 2 preceding years.

Benefits paid equal a percentage of wages received in the previous week or quarter, a percentage that ranged from 31 in Alaska to 61 in Hawaii in 1969, but there is a maximum cutoff point. Maximum weekly benefits without dependents' allowances range from $45 to $105. Nine states and the District of Columbia augment their allowances for dependents. Maximum augmented weekly benefits range from $65 to $129. The mid-1972 average payment was $56 a week.

Taxes Levied

It is important to note, however, that the small amounts paid under these welfare programs (note Table 9.1, column 3), even when adjusted downward to exclude payments to the nonpoor, greatly exaggerate the net gain to the poor. The net gain to the poor is exaggerated by the payments data because the poor as well as the rich pay taxes that provide the funds for government transfers. They may benefit not at all or much less than the data seem to imply. For example, as of 1973 retirement, survivors, disability, and hospital insurance benefits are paid for by the "contributions" of workers, employers, and the self-employed on earnings up to $10,800 (originally $3,000). Workers and their employers each pay 4.85 percent (originally 1 percent), and the self-employed pay 7.0 percent of covered wages for retirement, survivors, and disability insurance. The special benefits for noninsured persons of age 72 and over are financed from general funds. For hospital insurance, all workers and employers, and the self-employed each pay 1 percent. For persons 65 and over currently not insured under social security, the hospital benefits will be financed out of federal general revenues. The voluntary medical insurance plan is financed by a $6.30 a month (effective July 1, 1973) premium paid by persons of age 65 and over who choose to enroll in the plan, and by an equal contribution by the federal government from general revenues. The money collected is deposited in federal trust funds, from which benefits are paid.

Public assistance is financed in part from federal funds granted to states under the Social Security Act. The states may also receive grants for medical assistance to persons not able to take care of their medical bills themselves. The Social and Rehabilitation Service handles the federal aspects of these programs. (Aid to other needy persons is furnished mainly through general assistance, toward which the federal government makes no contribution.)

Or consider unemployment insurance funding. The standard rate of contributions payable by employers in all but 9 states is 2.7 percent of the taxable payroll. However, employers with favorable unemployment experience may be assigned a lower rate (except in Puerto Rico); in 1971, the average contribution rate under state laws was estimated at 1.5 percent of the taxable payroll. In most states, the contribution is based on the first $4,200 paid to a worker during the year. In a few states, the rate applies to wages above $4,200. Contributions are deposited to state accounts in the federal unemployment trust fund, from which states withdraw amounts needed for benefit payments.

A 3.2 percent federal tax is levied on the payroll of employers of one or more workers in industries covered by the act and is used to finance the federal-state program. Employers subject to the federal law are allowed a credit of 2.7 percent of taxable payrolls for contributions paid to state agencies under state unemployment insurance laws; the federal government retains 0.5 percent of the tax, out of which the Congress appropriates funds each year to cover employment security administrative costs and to finance the federal share of the extended-benefit program.

There is no question that all these taxes, *even if not officially* levied on the poor, are in part paid by them. A look at the theory of tax incidence can help show why.

The Theory of Tax Incidence

Even though the government has decided on the type of tax and who should pay it at what rate, someone else may end up paying it nevertheless. It is one thing to say who should pay a tax, but quite another to determine who really bears its burden ultimately. This is so because the payer of the tax can often *shift* it onto others. He might shift the tax burden to people from whom he buys something by paying them less than before. He might shift the burden to people to whom he sells something by charging them more than before. Then we say that the true burden of the tax, the *tax incidence*, rests with these other people.

Take the case of the market for shoes depicted in Figure 9.1, "The Incidence of a Sales Tax." Curves *D* and *S* represent the demand and supply curves for this hypothetical competitive market in the absence of any government intervention. Equilibrium price is $15 a pair. Equilibrium quantity is 6 million pairs per year. Just follow the dotted lines from the *D-S* intersection at point *a*.

Now suppose a government levies a stiff $3 sales tax per pair of shoes. The law specifies that the *seller* must pay the tax. What is the result? Sellers will naturally try to shift this burden onto buyers. They will offer any given quantity of shoes only if they can receive $3 per pair more than before. Graphically, the tax shifts the supply curve from *S* to *S**. The present equilibrium quantity of 6 million pairs, for example, is offered by them for $18 per pair rather than $15. Point *d* lies above point *a* by this amount. The same is true for any other hypothetical quantity. Sellers always want $3 per pair more than before (for example, distance *cb* equals *ad*).

Can we now expect that 6 million pairs are sold at $18 each? In other words, will the entire tax be shifted onto buyers? Not in this case. The demand curve has not changed. Buyers neither know nor care that sellers must pay a new tax. But as the demand curve tells us, buyers would only take

Figure 9.1 The Incidence of a Sales Tax

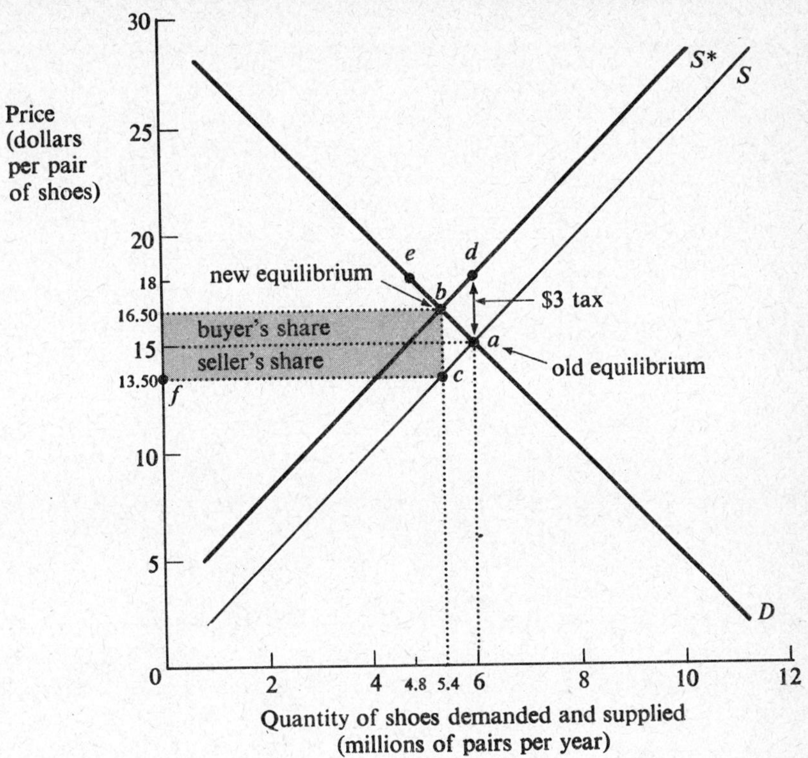

This graph illustrates how a sales tax levied on sellers may be partially shifted onto buyers. Without being aware of the reason, buyers suddenly find a lower supply at any given price (S* replaces S). Equilibrium price rises (a to b). Buyers end up paying part of a sales tax imposed upon sellers.

4.8 million pairs at a price of $18 per pair (point e). If suppliers still supplied 6 million pairs, there would develop a surplus of 1.2 million pairs (distance ed). Thus price cannot rise to $18. It can only rise to the new equilibrium at point *b*, at which *S** and *D* intersect. At this new equilibrium price of $16.50 per pair, buyers willingly take and sellers willingly offer 5.4 million pairs per year. Just follow the dashed lines from the *D-S** intersection at point *b*. Sellers who previously would have offered this quantity for $13.50 (point c) now sell it for $16.50 (point *b*). Thus it appears as if the entire tax has been shifted to buyers, even though it is still the sellers who make out the check to the government. The tax being $3 per unit (distance *bc*), we can multiply this unit tax by quantity sold (distance *fc*) to get the total amount of tax collected (the shaded box).

Closer inspection shows, however, that sellers have not shifted the entire tax burden. Compare the present situation with the original one. Buyers used to pay $15 per pair. Now they pay $16.50. This is $1.50 more, or only *half* the tax. Sellers used to get $15 per pair. Now they get $16.50, give $3 to the government, and end up with $13.50. They too pay half the tax, getting in effect $1.50 less than before. As indicated in the shaded box, in this example the ultimate incidence of the tax rests half with buyers, half with sellers, even though sellers make the actual tax payment to the government. However, one must not conclude that this is always a necessary result. It is also possible that the entire tax is shifted or none of it is. Consider the case where demand is so great that people are willing to pay *any* price rather than go without or with less of the good. This would graphically show by a vertical demand curve going through points *a* and *d*, let us say. (You may wish to pencil it in.) If you now superimpose our hypothetical tax, you will find the new equilibrium at point *d*. Price does indeed rise to $18 and quantity remains unchanged as *S* shifts to *S**. In this case, buyers bear the entire burden of the tax. This is typical whenever someone is very eager to buy or sell. Whoever is completely inflexible will end up bearing the tax! He who insists on buying no matter what the price will be taken advantage of by sellers. He will end up paying (even though indirectly) the taxes imposed on the seller. He who insists on selling no matter what the price will be taken advantage of by buyers. He will end up paying (even though indirectly) the taxes imposed on the buyer. What do you think would happen if new taxes were imposed on an employer, and his employees offered to continue working for him no matter what he paid them? They would be paid less, thereby in effect bearing the burden of the employer's tax!

Thus it is not at all obvious who *ultimately* pays how much in taxes in the United States. Just looking at the tax laws and the signatures on tax payment checks is not enough. This lack of clarity obviously complicates any determination of net gain from existence of the welfare system.

Tax Incidence in the United States

In the United States in 1970, 33 percent of *all* governments' tax receipts came from the federal personal income tax. Another 35 percent came from other federal taxes (corporate taxes, 12 percent; social security taxes, 15 percent; indirect business taxes, 8 percent). The final 32 percent were levied by state and local governments (property and sales taxes bringing in 23 percent and corporate and personal income taxes the remainder of the grand total). We can make a number of general as well as specific observations about the incidence of these taxes. Income, estate, gift, and inheritance taxes were typically *progressive*. That is, they took a larger *percentage* of higher than of lower incomes. (A tax taking the same percentage of all incomes is called *proportional*; a tax taking a smaller percentage of higher than of lower incomes is termed *regressive*.) Property taxes, customs, sales, payroll, and excise taxes tended to be regressive.

If we relate the amounts of taxes paid—property, customs, sales, payroll, and excise—to the *incomes* of the taxpayers (rather than to property value, sales value, and the like), most of these taxes turn out to be regressive. In the case of customs, sales and excise taxes it is true because these taxes tend to be shifted in full to buyers via higher prices, because the poor tend to save less (and saving is untouched by such taxes), and because the poor spend a much larger proportion of their income on taxed items than the rich. So they end up paying a greater portion of their low incomes for such taxes. In the case of property taxes the same effect occurs because they are shifted by businesses (including landlords) to buyers (including renters) via higher charges. Such payroll taxes as social security taxes, which are levied as a certain fixed percentage of income below a certain ceiling, are also regressive, because not everyone's income is completely below that ceiling. Suppose that the tax rate is 3 percent on income up to $7,000 a year. Then a man with a $5,000 income will pay $150, or 3 percent, but a man with a $10,000 income will only pay 3 percent on $7,000, or $210, that is, 2.1 percent on his income. The employer portion of social security taxes, furthermore, is likely to be shifted to others via higher prices or lower wages. Again, the poor pay more because most of their income is wage income and they spend most of it. Corporate profit taxes are shifted partly to consumers via higher prices, partly to stockholders via lower dividends. Thus, due to the shifting of taxes, many people pay quite different types of taxes and quite different percentages of their incomes from what merely looking at the tax law might make one believe.

Many studies have been made to determine the combined impact of all taxes and transfers. In the last analysis, who really pays or is paid? What is the percentage of *all* taxes paid, directly *and indirectly*, and of all transfers received by various income groups in the United States? The best and most recent answer is given in a study by two Bureau of the Census experts.[2] Using data for 1968, they defined a concept of *total income* equal to the net national product (adjusted upward for underreported money income) plus realized capital gains. Then they figured what percentages of all taxes ultimately fall on each income group and what percentages of all transfers they received. The results are shown in Table 9.2 and Figure 9.2. Overall, families (including unrelated individuals) paid 31.6 percent of their income in taxes and received 6.9 percent back in transfers. Thus the net tax burden was 24.6 percent of total income. Although some taxes, such as the federal income tax (column 5), were progressive throughout the income range, the total tax structure (column 1) showed little progressivity, except at the very highest level. Indeed, the total structure was regressive at the lower end. The proportion of income eaten up by taxes *dropped* from 50 percent for families with incomes under $2,000 to 29.2 percent for those at the $8,000–$10,000 income level. Families with incomes from $4,000 to $50,000 paid almost exactly the same proportion

[2] Roger A. Herriot and Herman P. Miller, "The Taxes We Pay," *Conference Board Record*, May 1971, pp. 31–40.

Table 9.2 Government Tax and Transfer Rates as a Percentage of Family Income: United States, 1968

	Total			Federal Taxes				State and Local Taxes		
Adjusted Money Income Levels	Taxes (1)	Govt. Transfer Payments (2)	Taxes Minus Transfer Payments (3)	Total (4)	Income Tax (5)	Corp. Profit Tax (6)	Social Security Tax (7)	Total (8)	Property Tax (9)	Sales Tax (10)
All Levels	31.6	6.9	24.6	21.7	9.5	4.7	5.1	9.9	3.7	2.8
Under $2,000	50.0	106.5	−56.5	22.7	1.2	6.0	7.6	27.2	16.2	6.6
$ 2,000–$ 4,000	34.6	48.5	−13.9	18.7	3.5	4.3	6.5	15.7	7.5	4.9
$ 4,000–$ 6,000	31.0	19.6	11.4	19.0	5.3	3.6	6.7	12.1	4.8	4.1
$ 6,000–$ 8,000	30.1	8.6	21.5	19.4	6.5	3.2	6.8	10.7	3.8	3.6
$ 8,000–$10,000	29.2	5.5	23.7	19.1	7.4	2.9	6.2	10.1	3.6	3.3
$10,000–$15,000	29.8	3.9	25.9	19.9	8.7	2.9	5.8	9.9	3.6	2.9
$15,000–$25,000	30.0	3.0	27.0	20.7	9.9	3.9	4.6	9.4	3.6	2.4
$25,000–$50,000	32.8	2.1	30.7	25.0	12.9	7.5	2.5	7.8	2.7	1.8
$50,000 +	45.0	0.4	44.7	38.4	19.8	15.4	1.0	6.7	2.0	1.1

NOTE: Family income is defined as a family's share of net national income (that is, all the incomes other than capital consumption allowances as listed in Table 5.2), adjusted for underreporting, plus realized capital gains.

SOURCE: Roger A. Herriot and Herman P. Miller, "The Taxes We Pay," Conference Board Record, *May 1971, p. 40.*

in taxes—about 30 percent. Only for the above-$50,000 group did the proportion rise significantly, to 45 percent.

All this was the result of the regressive impact of corporate profit taxes (except at the upper end), of social security taxes, and of all state and local taxes (columns 6–8). In 1968, families with incomes below $2,000 paid 27.2 percent of their incomes in state and local taxes. But this percentage dropped steadily throughout the range of incomes to as little as 6.7 percent for families with incomes in excess of $50,000. The regressivity of these taxes outweighed the progressivity of the federal income tax.

The Net Effect

The above picture of the true incidence of tax payments must be augmented by a look at the impact of transfer payments. The poorest families (income below $2,000) received 106.5 percent of their income in transfers (column 2), and this percentage steadily declined to 0.4 percent for the richest (income above $50,000).

Thus the *net* effect of taxes and transfers was remarkably progressive (column 3): Families with under $2,000 augmented their money income by 56.5 percent when transfers as well as taxes are taken into account. Families with incomes from $2,000 to $4,000 augmented their income 13.9 percent. Net tax rates rose progressively from 11.4 percent at the $4,000–$6,000 income level to 44.7 percent at the level of $50,000 and over. Figure 9.2, which is self-explanatory, summarizes our discussion. Note that it shows only the net effect of the tax and transfer system. It leaves out of account the impact on real-income distribution of government spending *on goods*. The benefits of government spending on goods also affect different income groups differently, thereby reinforcing or offsetting the redistributional impact of taxes and transfers.

THE CALL FOR WELFARE REFORM

That poverty persists is truly proof that existing welfare programs have not been able to abolish poverty. This inability persists in part because the programs were not exclusively designed for that purpose, and in part because they are financed by taxes that partially or wholly offset the intended effect. Still, in 1968, the tax and transfer system raised the incomes of the poorest families (incomes below $2,000) by 57 percent over what they would otherwise have been. On the other end of the scale, it took almost 45 percent of the income of the richest ($50,000 and above). In 1965, the system reduced the number of poor by 30 percent below what it would have been otherwise. Yet 31 percent of welfare recipients remained poor despite help. And 54 percent of the poor received no welfare payments at all. Should we reform welfare to make it do a better job?

Taxes as Percent of Family Income

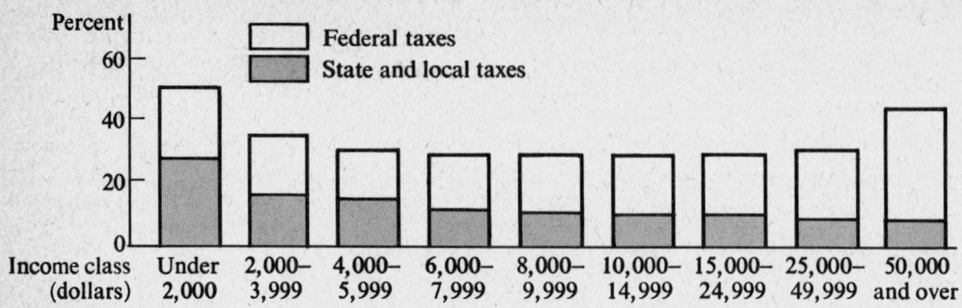

Transfers from Government as Percent of Family Income

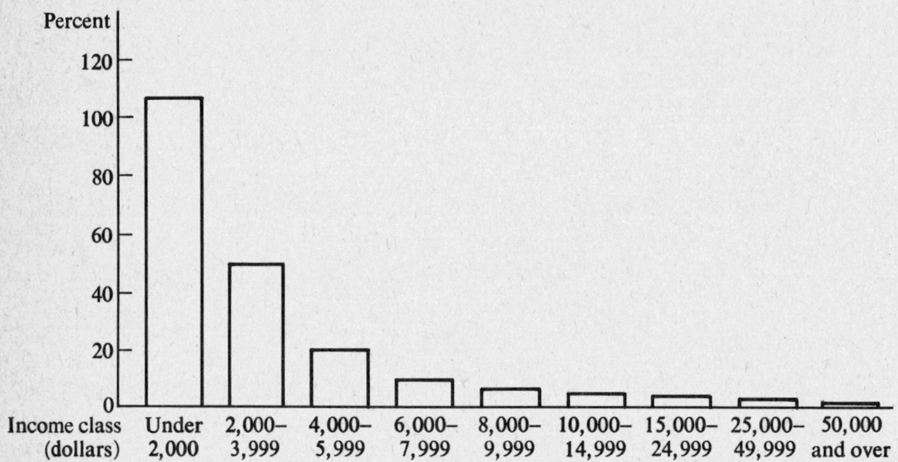

Taxes Less Transfers as Percent of Family Income

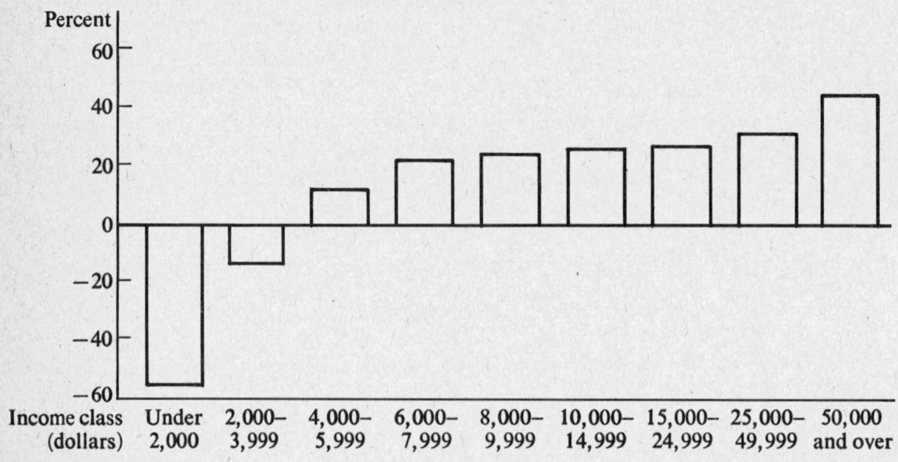

SOURCE: *Table* 9.2.

Improving the Present System

To judge the chances for improvement, we must realize that in the United States, as in other countries, much welfare legislation has been influenced by the *Puritan ethic.* According to this, the poor themselves are responsible for their condition: "They are shiftless and lazy (why else would they have so little education?). They are shortsighted (why else would they have saved so little, have such large families, and be so stubborn about moving away from their depressing environment?). Therefore, poverty is well deserved. Help them we may, but we should help as few as possible as little as possible lest we reward their undesirable behavior." So went the argument.

Nowadays, we are more inclined to see poverty as a result of social deficiencies (lack of aggregate demand, technological change, discrimination). Hence, we tend to believe that society should remove what it has created. Thus, we might argue for expanded coverage and benefits as well as a decrease in red tape.

Expanding coverage. Many of the poor are not reached by welfare programs. Workmen's compensation and unemployment insurance, for instance, do not give blanket coverage to the poor. Until 1972, millions of domestics, agricultural workers, small business employees, and state and local government employees were excluded from their benefits. Many of these categories will continue to be excluded after certain changes have gone into effect in 1973. Even those "covered" are usually not paid for more than 26 weeks in any one year. Thus many recipients exhaust their benefits.

Aid to families with dependent children is another example. Although federal law allows such aid to go to families with unemployed fathers, many states refuse to extend benefits to families with males present. States also try to reduce coverage by setting residency requirements. Under such laws, poor families are denied all public assistance until they have been residents of the state for a minimum period, and they are given funds to return to their previous residence. (Such one-year requirements were set in Colorado, Connecticut, Hawaii, New York, Rhode Island, Utah, and West Virginia, but later overturned by the U.S. Supreme Court.)

Increasing benefits. Look at column 3 of Table 9.1, "Major Government Cash Assistance Programs." In spite of the total cash assistance of close to

---

Figure 9.2 Taxes and Transfers from Government as Percentage of Total Income (Excluding Transfers), by Income Class, United States, 1968

Because the poor not only receive transfers but also pay taxes, the net gain to them of transfer payments is reduced. Only those with incomes under $4,000 per year have any net gain at all.

$80 *billion*, the average monthly benefits (item 1c excluded) never exceed $117 per recipient (just divide the annual column 3 entries by twelve). Benefits often are substantially lower than that, since they are anything but uniform among the states or among different types of welfare programs. All this reflects the Puritan ethic. These programs are often designed to save money, not to save people. We could save more money in the long run by spending more now, some people argue.

Yet quite the opposite from spending more has been happening. In 1971, nineteen states, from Alabama to New York to Kansas to California—plagued with ever increasing welfare rolls—sharply *decreased* welfare benefits. (A Colorado county even dropped all welfare programs completely. The state of Nevada repealed its own welfare law. The state of Texas made no welfare appropriations for 1972.) Twenty other states required additional appropriations, often at the expense of education budgets (New Hampshire, Oregon, Vermont). All were considering cutting budgets. Some hoped to do so by eliminating suspected widespread fraud and cracking down on "overly liberal" welfare offices (Massachusetts). Others (California, Illinois, New York) tried to put welfare recipients to work in community projects for 20 hours a week at current wages, thereby letting them *earn* their aid. They have punished refusal with no benefits. All states have urged the federal government to simply take over the whole burden of payments. They are unlikely to get a favorable response. In 1973, President Nixon announced measures to "strengthen the management" of federally aided welfare programs, notably the controversial program giving aid to families with dependent children: The federal government would reduce its contribution to encourage the states to eliminate an alleged 7 percent ineligible families from the program and to cease overpaying yet another alleged 14 percent. Such crackdown on ineligibles and such tightening of administrative procedures was to restore public confidence in welfare programs.

Reducing red tape. Some people disagree with the federal encouragement of tighter administrative procedures. They urge just the opposite. They note how many welfare programs subject recipients to a great deal of humiliation. Their affairs are investigated meticulously and continually. Should they be found to earn any amount, their welfare aid is reduced by an equal amount. Their homes are searched. They are continually treated as untrustworthy, promiscuous, and lazy. They are "pushed around" in a hundred different ways, and they "better be quiet, or else." Bureaucratic supervision has helped to enhance the breakdown of the family among the poor. Families with an able-bodied man present (whether he is the legal father or not) have been denied aid for dependent children. But aid has been granted to the mother in the absence of a man. An unemployed father, or one who could not earn enough even if working, has a choice: desert the family to put them on welfare or stay home and see them starve. Such insane pieces of legislation can and must be changed. In addition, supervision is costly, taking on the average 10 percent of welfare funds. In spite of such arguments, the U.S. Department of Health, Education, and Welfare in 1973 criticized twenty states for insufficient "quality control" in welfare programs, notably for their reliance on written self-declarations by would-be welfare recipients. States were threatened with loss of federal funds unless verification procedures by questioning and requiring of documentation were reinstituted.

The Negative Income Tax

Considering all its faults, one can make a good case for abolishing the entire existing patchwork of welfare programs in favor of a radically new approach, using the existing federal income tax system. As was shown in Table 9.2, column 5, the federal income tax system is already a progressive one. This feature could be greatly enhanced by making tax rates much bigger at the upper end and much smaller, that is, substantially *negative*, at the lower end. As a result, taxes minus transfers could be so much more negative at the lower end (and so much more positive at the upper end) of the income distribution that no person or family would remain below the poverty line. Such a program would be exceedingly simple to administer, since the Internal Revenue Service is already in existence.

How it might work. It might work like this. Every American, every year, files an income tax return. He sums up all his income, which quite possibly is zero. He then, as the tax law provides, subtracts any exemptions and deductions. If the resultant figure is negative or very low, as it would be with a zero or very low income, the individual gets a check *from* the government. He "pays" a *negative* income tax. The negative tax could be set at such a rate as to bring every American family's income above the poverty level. It could abolish low after-tax incomes overnight.

Such a program would automatically reach all the poor, even the working poor. It would be irrelevant to inquire into the causes of poverty, whether permanent or temporary. A poor person would automatically get help, whether he were white or black, farmer or engineer, old or young, working or unemployed, healthy or disabled. The program would make unnecessary the present crazy patchwork of welfare programs. There would be no necessity for establishing "need." The poor would receive help as a matter of right. And that help would be uniform nationwide for people in identical circumstances. Objective rules would be followed rather than the discretionary power of local administrators, a feature that has created such a great potential for abuse in present welfare programs. To be sure, the negative income tax program would be a radical innovation and a politically difficult one. But, as it has been said so often, "people will act wisely only after all other alternatives have been exhausted." Many people believe this time has come.

What would be the extra cost of a negative income tax package? Would it cost just another $12 billion (in addition to making up for present welfare payments), as indicated by the poverty income deficit? No, it would cost substantially more than this.

For simplicity, assume we wanted to give every family an annual income of $4,000. A family earning nothing would receive a negative tax of $4,000. Suppose the father finds a job and earns $2,000. Should we reduce the negative tax by $2,000, leaving his total income unchanged? Of course not. This is exactly what many present welfare programs do. Present programs often discourage the poor from seeking income-earning activities by reducing welfare payments by a dollar or almost that for every dollar of earned income received. It is easy to see why people then lose all incentive to work. Why work for a year if your income remains the same as if you had not worked at all? This gives rise to much social tension. Some families work full time, and they earn the same income as others not working. They do not like this at all.

Therefore, reducing welfare or negative tax payments by a dollar for every dollar earned (which is equivalent to slapping a 100 percent tax on earned income) is the last thing we want to do to the poor. We want to encourage them to become educated and trained and to work.

We must tax their own earnings less. It is important that the negative tax should be reduced by a lot less than earned income rises, so that a poor person can increase his income by working rather than being idle. Suppose we reduce negative taxes by 30 cents for every dollar earned. Then our man will find this: If he earns $2,000, he loses $600 in negative taxes. His total income rises from $4,000 to $5,400. It pays him to work!

How much will our man have to earn before he loses all his negative tax revenue? Four thousand dollars divided by 30 cents, or $13,333. If he earns $13,333, he is taxed (at 30 cents on the dollar) exactly $4,000. At this point, his negative taxes disappear. They are offset by the positive taxes he has to pay on his earned income.

The formula is simple. Divide the official poverty income level (our assumed $4,000) by the tax rate on earned income (our 30 cents per dollar), and you find the exact income level at which net taxes paid are zero. People below this income level will get more taxes than they pay. People above it will pay more taxes than they get.

But note what this implies. It implies (in our case) that everyone who earns less than $13,333 receives a net amount of money from the government. As Figure 9.2 shows, this is hardly the case at present. Thus, the government will not only lose a great amount of tax revenue, but it will also have to pay large sums to people who are not even poor! It must do this, we noted, in order not to discourage the recipients of negative taxes from working at all. For this reason, the negative income tax would cost a great deal more than $12 billion. It may well cost $30 billion or even more. It is up to each of us to decide whether abolishing poverty is worth this price.

Note also that there is no real way out of this incentive-cost dilemma. Consider once more our formula

$$\frac{\text{Desired minimum family income level}}{\text{Tax rate on earned income}} = \begin{array}{l}\text{Family income level at which}\\\text{net positive tax payments begin.}\end{array}$$

Reducing the income level at which net positive tax payments begin (and thus reducing the overall cost of the program) can be achieved in two ways: (1) We can lower the desired minimum family income level. But then we may not be able to get rid of poverty! (2) We can raise the tax rate on earned income. But then we ruin people's incentive to work! A presidential commission on income maintenance studied this very problem. It proposed a minimum income level of $2,400 for a family of four, and a 50 percent tax rate on earned income. Table 9.3, "How a Negative Income Tax System Might Work," shows the effect of such a proposal.

First steps. A first step in the direction of a negative income tax system was taken in 1969. President Nixon announced plans to abolish, by 1971, aid to families with dependent children and establish a new Family Security System applicable only to families with children. Regardless of residence, an American family would be guaranteed $500 a year each for its first two members and $300 for each additional one. Thus a family of four would be guaranteed annually a minimum federal payment to bring its income to $1,600. Other earnings of recipients would be taxed after they exceed $720 a year, at a rate of 50 cents on the dollar. Thus, the negative tax was to be eliminated when regular earnings reach $3,920 a year. The program was expected to cover over 22 million persons and cost $4 billion in the first year. In return, the recipients (except the disabled and mothers with preschool children) were to be required to register with the employment service. If capable, they were to work in or train for a "suitable" job. Additional training allowances and day care centers for half a million children were also planned.

But things did not work out this way. The House passed a slightly amended Nixon bill in 1970, but the Senate did not. There was much opposition to introducing what was seen as the first step to a "megadole," a system that would "demoralize honest working people" and "destroy the fabric of society by establishing a permanent nonworking class." Recipients under the act were seen as "quitting work en masse, going on a spending spree." The Senate voted instead a number of experiments to see how such a system would work.

Three careful three-year experiments have been in progress since 1968 under the auspices of the Office of Economic Opportunity. About 1,400 male-headed families in New Jersey's six largest cities were receiving cash grants in an assessment of the impact of guaranteed income on the poor. Seven different combinations of income guarantee (ranging from zero to $4,352) and tax rates on earned income (ranging from 30 to 70 percent) were tested. Preliminary findings showed that the families in the program worked slightly less but earned more on their own than similar families that were not aided. Other experi-

Table 9.3 How a Negative Income Tax System Might Work

Earned Annual Income (Dollars) (1)	50% Tax on Earned Income (Dollars) (2)	Minimum Guaranteed Income Level (Dollars) (3)	Tax Collected (Dollars) (4) = (2) − (3)	Effective Tax Rate on Earned Income (Percent) $(5) = \frac{(4)}{(1)} \times 100$	After-Tax Income (Dollars) (6) = (1) − (4)
0	0	2,400	−2,400		2,400
600	300	2,400	−2,100	−350.0	2,700
1,200	600	2,400	−1,800	−150.0	3,000
1,800	900	2,400	−1,500	− 83.3	3,300
2,400	1,200	2,400	−1,200	− 50.0	3,600
3,000	1,500	2,400	− 900	− 30.0	3,900
3,600	1,800	2,400	− 600	− 16.6	4,200
4,200	2,100	2,400	− 300	− 7.1	4,500
4,800	2,400	2,400	0	0	4,800
5,400	2,700	2,400	300	5.6	5,100
6,000	3,000	2,400	600	10	5,400

In a negative income tax system, net positive tax payments begin at an earned income level equal to the guaranteed minimum level (here $2,400) divided by the tax rate on earned income (here 0.5), or at $4,800 in this example. There is no need for the minimum guaranteed income to be as low as shown here. Nor must the tax rate on earned income be constant. It might be varied from a low rate at low earnings to a higher rate at high earnings, since taxes might discourage people more from working in low-paying types of jobs than from working in high-paying types.

ments were being conducted with 800 rural families, whites in Iowa and blacks in North Carolina. In 1971, further tests were under way with 2,300 families in Seattle and 3,000 families in Denver with particular emphasis on the effects of job training and child day care.

In 1971, the House passed another, more generous negative income tax bill. It was to cover 35 million persons and cost $11.5 billion in the first year. However, it provided that all able-bodied recipients (including mothers with children over 2) would have to accept *any* job offered (unless it paid less than 75 percent of the minimum wage). While the Senate debated the bill, President Nixon requested a delay of the Family Security System so that it would not become effective before mid-1973 (if passed). By late 1972, however, a hopelessly deadlocked Senate rejected the bill. Instead, it approved further experiments with three versions of the Nixon proposal, but a Senate-House conference junked those plans as well. (On almost the same day, a British government "green paper" proposed the adoption of a negative income tax for Great Britain.)

The outlook. There can be no doubt that for political reasons alone the negative income tax system will be long in coming in the United States. Observers believed that the 1972 rejection has caused an inevitable five-year delay in this type of project. Even if a version of the Nixon bill had been passed, it would only have been a first step to a more determined system of income redistribution. For one thing, the Nixon proposal excluded single persons and childless couples, among whom many of the aged poor can be found. The guaranteed-benefit level of the 1971 House bill was $2,400 for a family of four, but the official poverty-level income for such an urban family was over $4,000 and can be expected to be over $6,000 by 1976. Finally, the tax rate on earned income (set at 50 percent) was really higher where aided families lose in-kind assistance (food stamps, public housing aid, Medicaid) as their earned income rises. Thus any negative income tax system that is comprehensive, guarantees a fairly high minimum income, and preserves incentives by setting a fairly low tax rate on earned income is bound to be very costly indeed.

The potential costliness would not endear such a program to a Congress pervaded by the Puritan ethic. Nor is Congress likely to reach for the most obvious source of funds available for financing such a program, namely the closing of *tax loopholes*. Nevertheless, it is instructive to consider the possibilities.

Everyone knows that Congress does not tax all types of income alike. Some forms of income are exempt from federal taxation, either in whole or in part: The appreciation over time in the value of, for example, land, buildings, and stocks, called *capital gains*, is never taxed, unless these items are sold during the holder's lifetime. If sold, they are taxed at half the usual rate. Interest earned on state and local government bonds or life insurance policies is not taxed. Income earned from oil, gas, and mineral ventures tends to escape taxation. So does income spent on state and local taxes, mortgage interest, charities, and big medical bills. The income of married couples is taxed at lower rates than that of single people. And so it goes.

It is interesting to note what would happen if Congress abolished all these tax preferences and exemptions and taxed all types of income alike, regardless of who earns it, how it is earned, and what is done with it. A computer analysis of a sample of 90,000 federal income tax returns of 1966, together with data from a 1967 Survey of Economic Opportunity, was made at the Brookings Institution by Joseph A. Pechman and Benjamin Okner. It brought this surprising result: Without loopholes, 1972 federal tax revenues would have been $77.3 *billion* higher. Furthermore—and here comes the important point—it would have mostly been the rich who would have paid these extra taxes.

This can be seen by considering Table 9.4, "Family Tax Savings from Tax Loopholes." On the average, lower-income families saved negligible amounts from tax loopholes. By the closing of tax loopholes in 1972, the 6 million poorest families would have had to pay $92 *million* in additional federal taxes. The 3,000 families with incomes over $1 million alone would have paid $2.2 *billion* more. Thus a theoretical possibility emerges: to finance a costly negative income tax program (which would favor low-income people) by closing tax loopholes (which would hurt high-income people). Whether such a scheme would be politically feasible is another question.

***Table* 9.4 Family Tax Savings from Tax Loopholes, United States, 1972**

Annual Family Income	Annual Family Tax Savings	Total Tax Savings of Income Group (Millions)
Under $3,000	$ 16	$ 92
$3,000–$4,999	148	1,014
$5,000–$9,999	339	6,583
$10,000–$14,999	651	11,420
$15,000–$19,999	1,181	12,383
$20,000–$24,999	1,931	9,565
$25,000–$49,999	3,897	17,392
$50,000–$99,999	11,912	7,449
$100,000–$499,999	41,480	7,835
$500,000–$999,999	202,751	1,314
Over $1 million	720,490	2,210
Total	$1,096	$77,257

SOURCE: *Joseph A. Pechman and Benjamin Okner, "Individual Income Tax Erosion by Income Classes," Reprint 230, The Brookings Institution, Washington, D.C., 1972, pp. 33 and 36.*

Children's Allowances

Those who have despaired of the political difficulties with a comprehensive negative income tax system have proposed an alternative: a system of *children's allowances*. These are systematic payments by government to *all* families with children. This would be a birthright, *independent of family income*. The United States is the only Western industrialized nation that does not have such a program. The proposal rests on the knowledge that three-quarters of poor youths come from fatherless families or families with five or more children. These allowances might greatly enhance family stability and cut into the vicious circle of poverty breeding poverty. It has been found abroad, furthermore, that such allowances do *not* encourage more births (as some critics fear) and that they *are* spent on the better health and education of children. Unlike the negative income tax, this plan is politically attractive. Public opinion hesitates to support "the lazy poor," but is enthusiastic about "investing in the future of children."

There are two main drawbacks to this system. It would require substantial payments to families now not poor. Hence, it would be a costly and highly inefficient way of helping the poor. Almost certainly the cost of such a program would exceed even the cost of the negative income tax. Also, childless adult poor would not be helped at all.

In 1971, even an annual allowance of only $600 per child would have cost $43 billion, or $28 billion if the child exemption for income tax purposes were eliminated.

Summary

1. Some people can never be helped out of poverty by programs of health, education, training, and job placement. Those who can potentially be helped cannot be helped overnight. Thus one can make a good case for additional programs of money transfers to the poor as long as they remain poor for any reason.
2. Theoretically, such interfamily income transfers could be voluntary just as intrafamily transfers are. Any serious income redistribution must involve an involuntary program using the taxing powers of government. There is no reason why such redistribution should equalize family incomes, however. There are good reasons not to go that far but only perhaps to close the poverty-income deficit.
3. The present welfare system already makes a great effort at income redistribution. In 1971 it provided close to $80 billion of cash assistance (and additional billions of in-kind assistance) through a multitude of uncoordinated programs.
4. The main cash assistance programs aid the elderly, the disabled, families with dependent children, and the unemployed. However, many people who are

not poor receive benefits, many poor people receive no benefits, and those who do get aid receive small amounts.

5. Furthermore, recipients of benefits often help finance the programs by paying taxes—directly or indirectly. The latter point is of particular importance. As the theory of tax incidence shows, a tax may be officially placed upon one party but be shifted by it to another party, who ultimately comes to bear its burden. This fact complicates any determination of the net gain to the poor from the welfare system.
6. Careful studies of the ultimate impact of all taxes in the United States show that they are not very progressive. Indeed, the total tax structure is regressive at the lower-income end. The proportion of income eaten up by taxes drops from 50 percent for families with annual incomes under $2,000 to 29 percent for those at the $8,000–$10,000 income level. Only above incomes of $50,000 does progressivity take hold.
7. The net effect of taxes and transfers is remarkably progressive, but only families with annual incomes under $4,000 have any net gain from the system.
8. Some people call for welfare reform to assure that the system abolishes all and not just part of poverty. This might be done by expanding the coverage of present programs, increasing their benefits, and reducing red tape. There has been a tendency for the opposite to happen.
9. Welfare reforms might also involve entirely new approaches, such as a negative income tax system or children's allowances. Under the negative income tax system, the family income level at which net positive tax payments begin equals the desired minimum family income level divided by the tax rate on earned income. This imposes a dilemma: Any attempt to provide all families with a high-minimum guaranteed income and also strong work incentives (via a low tax rate on earned income) brings many nonpoor under the system. The scheme then becomes exceedingly costly.
10. The prospects of high budgetary costs, together with the prevailing Puritan ethic, have so far prevented any negative income tax program from passing Congress. One can also doubt the willingness of Congress to grasp an obvious financing possibility: the closing of tax loopholes, which in a recent year would have yielded over $77 billion of additional revenue. Possibly, a system of children's allowances, although costly, would be more palatable politically.

Terms[3]

capital gains
children's allowances
dollar votes
negative income tax
poverty income deficit
progressive tax
proportional tax
Puritan ethic
regressive tax
tax incidence
tax loopholes

[3] Terms are defined in the Glossary at the back of the book.

Questions for Review and Discussion

1. "Unless people have equal incomes, they are not political equals." Evaluate.
2. "No matter what the U.S. government says, poverty is a *relative* matter. As long as some people have less money to spend than others (no matter *how much* they have), there is poverty. Absolute income equality is what we need. This can only be achieved by getting rid of the market economy and once and for all recognizing that people's activities as producers (which determine their income in the market economy) have nothing to do with their needs as consumers (which require them to spend money in a market economy)." Evaluate.
3. "You will never eliminate poverty by giving money to the poor any more than you will get rid of the use of marijuana by subsidizing it. What we should do is *tax* the poor." Evaluate.
4. MR. A: Income maintenance programs do not cure poverty. They only cover up symptoms.
   MR. B: You are quite wrong. Poverty today breeds poverty tomorrow. Cover up poverty today and it will die out tomorrow.
   Who is right?
5. "The elderly should not receive income support. Most of them have large assets on which to live. In 1962, for instance, couples aged 65 and over held median assets of $11,180." Evaluate.
6. "The easiest way for dealing with poverty would be for government to give money to the poor. This money could be newly created and would cost no one anything." Evaluate.
7. What do you think of the wisdom of a law that reduces welfare cash benefits dollar for dollar as a welfare family's earned income rises? What about a law that reduces cash benefits by only 33 cents for each dollar earned, but makes welfare families ineligible for in-kind assistance (food stamps, medical care, public housing) as their income rises?
8. In 1971, President Nixon signed a bill requiring all able-bodied recipients of welfare aid under the aid for dependent children program to register for work or training by mid-1972 as a condition of continued eligibility. Excluded from this requirement were the ill, the elderly, children under 16, mothers with children under 6, and persons caring for the disabled. Do you think this is a good law? Consider the costs and benefits.
9. "Transfer payments only encourage laziness." Discuss.
10. In mid-1969, Congress put a "freeze" on aid to families with dependent children (AFDC): It forbade federal financing for any claims resulting from any increase in the percentage of deserted or illegitimate children. It ordered that AFDC mothers who are offered child day care facilities must accept work when offered. Do you think Congress has acted correctly? (Does Congress have a right to moralize and to force mothers to leave their children?)
11. "Many existing welfare programs, such as social security and unemployment benefits, are more designed to protect the middle class against income insecurity than to protect the poor against low income. They block the return

to poverty of those who 'made it.' They do not help people to leave a poverty condition." Discuss.

12. "The disincentive problem always discussed in connection with the negative income tax is overstressed. You can easily get away with taxing people 90 percent on earned income. People in this country *love* to work. Why else do wives work in addition to husbands? Why else do people work overtime? Why else do people 'moonlight' during vacations?" What do you think?
13. "A negative income tax system would be unworkable for this reason: Knowing full well that the government stands ready to make up the difference between people's actual earnings and a decent income, employers would raise their profits by cutting wages. Thus the general taxpayer—by supplementing low-wage incomes—would be supplementing the profits of rich businessmen." Evaluate.
14. What do you think would be the effect of the negative income tax on the migrations of people and businesses discussed in Chapter 3?
15. Mr. A: It is absurd for the government to allow deductions for medical expenses from taxable income, but not to allow deductions for the purchase of other consumer goods.

    Mr. B: It is absurd to allow *any* deductions.

    Evaluate.

Selected Readings

Boulding, Kenneth E., and Pfaff, Martin. *Redistribution to the Rich and the Poor: The Grants Economics of Income Distribution*. Belmont, Calif.: Wadsworth, 1972. A fascinating discussion of explicit and implicit grants that sometimes increase and at other times decrease income equality. Includes a study of the distribution among households of the benefits and burdens of governmental spending on goods rather than of government taxes and transfers.

Fusfeld, Daniel R. *Economics*. Lexington, Mass.: D. C. Heath and Co., 1972. Chs. 36 and 38. Discusses the distribution and redistribution of income.

Gordon, David M. *Problems in Political Economy: An Urban Perspective*. Lexington, Mass.: D. C. Heath and Co., 1971. Pp. 244–72. Presents conservative, liberal, and radical views on income redistribution, including an excellent bibliography.

U.S. Bureau of the Census. *Statistical Abstract of the United States, 1972*. Washington, D.C., 1972. Lists some statistics on social insurance and welfare programs (sections 10 and 33) and—more important—sources to other statistics: Note the listing of statistical abstract supplements (p. v); and the guide to general sources of statistics (pp. 929–30 and 948–50), to recent censuses (pp. 955–56), and to state statistical abstracts (pp. 961–64).

Note: The *Journal of Economic Literature* lists recent articles on welfare programs (section 911), the economics of poverty (914), and social security (915).

The *Index of Economic Articles* catalogs, in sections beginning with the indicated numbers, articles on tax incidence (2.1338, 2.243, 10.42–10.44), taxation (10.4), and transfer payments, including social security (21.2), negative income tax and family allowances (21.3), old age assistance (21.4), veterans' benefits (21.5), and unemployment assistance (21.6).

10 The Link Between Poverty and Crime

In 1968, James Tobin, an eloquent advocate of the negative income tax, said:[1]

> The war on poverty is too crucial to be relegated to the status of a residual claimant for funds that peace in Asia and the normal growth of tax revenues may painlessly and gradually make available. When asked to make sacrifices for the defense of their nation, the American people have always responded. Perhaps some day a national administration will muster the courage to ask the American people to tax themselves for social justice and domestic tranquility. The time is short.

This sounds ominous, and for good reasons. Poverty is costly, not only to the poor. Just think of crime—born and flourishing in an atmosphere of disease and ignorance, of deprivation and despair. People who are deprived of material comfort, human dignity, and lives of fulfillment have little to lose. If society does not help them, it is a short step for them to take matters into their own hands and attempt to enforce a redistribution of income—on their own terms.

MUCH OF CRIME IS ECONOMICALLY MOTIVATED

Nor can there be any question that much of crime is economically motivated. Consider the statistics on "serious crimes," as collected by the FBI. Recent data are given in Table 10.1, "Rates of Serious Crimes, United States, 1971." It should be noted that these data refer to crimes per 100,000 people in the population. They were collected under the FBI's Uniform Crime Reporting Program. Under the program, in 1971, over 6,500 local, county, and state law enforcement agencies, serving over 92 percent of the population, reported, on a voluntary basis, the number of offenses known to them. However, in 1969 the President's Commission on the Causes and Prevention of Violence believed that the 5 million crimes *reported* in that year represented only half of the number actually committed.[2] Probably the same can be said of the 6 million reported crimes of 1971.

[1] James Tobin, "Raising the Incomes of the Poor," in Kermit Gordon, ed., *Agenda for the Nation* (Washington, D.C.: The Brookings Institution, 1968), p. 116.

[2] For this reason, the Law Enforcement Assistance Administration has recently persuaded the Bureau of the Census to initiate an independent regular crime survey. It will be based on a twice-yearly survey of 150,000 households and businesses.

Table 10.1 Rates of Serious Crimes, United States, 1971

Population Group	Total (1)	Crimes of Passion: Murder (2)	Crimes of Passion: Rape (3)	Crimes of Passion: Aggravated Assault (4)	Economically Motivated Crimes: Robbery (5)	Economically Motivated Crimes: Auto Theft (6)	Economically Motivated Crimes: Larceny (7)	Economically Motivated Crimes: Burglary (8)
United States	2,907	9	20	177	187	457	909	1,148
SMSA's	3,547	10	24	201	255	600	1,074	1,382
6 cities, over 1,000,000	5,779	21	42	388	862	1,177	1,199	2,089
21 cities, 500,000–999,999	5,406	20	52	357	525	1,143	1,313	1,997
30 cities, 250,000–499,999	4,759	14	35	277	359	901	1,224	1,950
98 cities, 100,000–249,000	4,383	11	27	240	226	739	1,350	1,790
200 cities, 50,000–99,999	3,223	6	17	151	126	499	1,180	1,243
509 cities, 25,000–49,999	2,798	5	12	131	95	397	1,117	1,042
1,224 cities, 10,000–24,999	2,244	4	10	123	51	251	924	880
2,810 cities, less than 10,000	1,829	4	8	128	31	173	763	722
Rural areas	1,032	7	11	101	15	70	344	485
Suburbs[a]	2,411	4	14	117	70	306	924	975

[a] Also included in above city groupings.
NOTE: The figures in this table are offenses known to police per 100,000 population. Detail may not add to total because of rounding.
SOURCE: *Federal Bureau of Investigation,* Uniform Crime Reports, *1971.*

The seven crimes rated as "serious" by the FBI and listed in Table 10.1 can be divided, somewhat arbitrarily, into crimes of passion and economically motivated crimes. The former include murder, rape, and aggravated assault. Murder statistics include all willful felonious homicides, and exclude suicides, accidental deaths, deaths caused by negligence, and so-called justifiable homicides. Rape data refer to forcible rapes and attempts. Aggravated assaults include assaults with intent to kill, but not "simple" assault and battery. In 1971, these three crimes of passion made up only 7 percent of all serious crimes.

In short, fully 93 percent of serious crimes were economically motivated. Robbery includes the taking or attempted taking of anything of value by force or threat of force. Auto theft includes all cases of motor vehicles driven away and abandoned. Larceny includes theft (other than auto theft) of property in excess of $50 value without the use of force, fraud, and violence. Thus it excludes theft through burglary, embezzlement, "con" games, forgery, worthless checks, and so forth. Burglary, finally, includes any actual or attempted unlawful entry regardless of whether followed by a felony or a theft.

CRIME AS AN URBAN PROBLEM

There is something else we should note. Serious crime is predominantly an *urban* problem, whether we look at offenses in terms of numbers or of rates. In 1971, of 424,000 reported crimes of passion, 81 percent were committed in standard metropolitan statistical areas (SMSA's), but only 10 percent in rural areas. Of 5.6 million economically motivated crimes in 1971, 87 percent were committed in SMSA's, 6 percent only in rural areas. This shows also in crime rates. As can be seen clearly in Table 10.1, with minor exceptions only, crime rates for every type of serious crime were higher the bigger the city under consideration. Note how, in cities with over a million people, the rate for robbery compared with the rural rate was 58 times larger, for auto theft 17 times larger, for larceny 4 times larger, and for burglary 4 times larger also. Differences between central cities and suburbs were smaller, but still substantial. Thus, statistically, the chances of being a criminal or a crime victim are considerably greater for a central city resident than for suburban or rural residents.

How Poverty Breeds Criminals

It is no accident that crime is rampant in central cities where so many of the poor are concentrated under conditions of residential segregation. The city ghettos are teeming with people who are poor, unemployed, and quite aware of the affluence around them. This means that their pockets are empty, they have nothing productive to do, and they have lost faith in social justice. Especially among the young, such frustration is more likely to erupt in violence than in quiet resignation. As the chieftain of a Chicago youth gang put it in 1970: "It's getting really bad. A lot of guys are out of work, and you know what the lion does when the lion gets hungry. He goes out and gets what he wants by force. And there will be a whole lot of lions out in the streets this summer."[3]

So the cities erupt like volcanoes, as Watts did in 1965, Newark and Detroit in 1967, and a whole string of cities in 1968 following the assassination of Martin Luther King, Jr. On occasion, open rebellion with riots (and looting) is replaced by a kind of guerrilla warfare: a multitude of small-scale snipings, brick-throwings, and firebombings directed against the symbols of "the system." And always, there is the mounting wave of "serious crimes," pushed onward and upward—by the young or the nonwhite in considerably greater proportion than by the old or the white.

It can be doubted, however, that most of these criminals are social misfits acting irrationally. More likely than not, those who commit economically motivated crimes are making a perfectly *rational* response to the circumstances of their environment. Given limited opportunities to earn money in legitimate pursuits, they can often provide best for themselves and their families by violating the law.

Consider a simple example of two individuals, Opulent and Pauper, contemplating an armed bank robbery. If each individual were rational, he would compare the benefit to himself of committing such an act with the cost to himself. Possible benefits or costs accruing to others would be neglected. The data of Table 10.2, "Hypothetical Benefit-Cost Analysis of a Bank Robbery," illustrate the type of thinking a rational person would have to make. First of all (line 1a), the prospective criminal would estimate the amount of money the bank robbery would yield. We suppose the haul is expected to be $30,000. Second (line 1b), the rational criminal would add a dollar estimate of the psychic benefit he receives from committing the crime. That is, the criminal might derive pure pleasure from the excitement of it all, but we refrain from any such estimate here.

Next come the costs. Any prospective criminal hopes that they will be zero, but a rational person must consider the probabilities. Suppose that the probability of being arrested is 0.5 (line 2a), that is, that there is a 50-50 chance of being caught or getting away with it. Arrest does not mean conviction, however. Suppose that the probability of being convicted as charged is also 0.5 (line 2b), that is, that there is a 50-50 chance of being convicted or acquitted should arrest occur. Next one must consider (line 2c) the likely time spent in jail should conviction occur. Suppose a 15-year sentence is likely, with the possibility of parole after 8 years. Thus actual jail time is expected as 8 years. Since, however, the probabilities of arrest and conviction are 0.5 each, their combined probability is 0.5 times 0.5, or 0.25. Therefore, the probable actual jail term from any one bank robbery is 0.25 times 8 years, or 2 years (line 2d).

What do our friends have to lose from a probable two-year hitch in jail? Opulent, let us suppose, holds a $25,000 a year job, Pauper is unemployed most

[3] *Wall Street Journal*, June 23, 1970, pp. 1 and 24.

Table 10.2 Hypothetical Benefit-Cost Analysis of a Bank Robbery

	Opulent		Pauper	
1. Private benefit				
a. Monetary		$30,000		$30,000
b. Psychic		.....		.....
2. Private cost				
a. Probability of arrest	0.5		0.5	
b. Probability of conviction if arrested	0.5		0.5	
c. Expected actual jail term if convicted	8 yr		8 yr	
d. Probable jail term from this robbery (d = a × b × c)	2 yr		2 yr	
e. Annual income	$25,000		$1,000	
f. Probable income loss from this robbery while jailed, undiscounted (f = d × e)	$50,000		$2,000	
g. Probable income loss from this robbery while jailed, discounted at 5 percent		$48,810		$ 1,952
h. Probable income loss from this robbery after being paroled, discounted		$50,000		0
i. Probable other costs		$ 2,000		0
3. Net benefit of committing crime		−$70,810		+$28,048

of the time and makes $1,000 a year in the numbers racket. Both would lose these incomes for two years (line 2f), but the *discounted value* of this loss would be somewhat less (line 2g).[4] In addition, Opulent might never get his well-paying job back after coming out of jail, but Pauper, who runs the numbers, could count on his job. Thus Opulent would have to consider an additional loss from lowered earnings later in life. The amount is simply estimated (line 2h). Last, but not least, our friends might incur other costs if they commit the crime, and some of these might be incurred regardless of arrest or conviction. These costs might be monetary, like legal defense costs. They might be psychic, like guilt feelings, the monetary value of which would have to be a wild estimate. It has been assumed that Opulent would have probable defense costs of $2,000 per robbery, while Pauper would receive free legal counsel (line 2i).

[4] A sum of money to be received in the future is worth less now than in the future. For instance, if the current interest rate is 5 percent, a dollar to be received in a year is now worth the same as 95.238 cents, for 95.238 cents invested at 5 percent for a year yields $1. Thus future money is "discounted" to yield its present money equivalent. Hence next year's $25,000 salary is only worth $23,810 now.

This brings us to the grand conclusion (line 3). It would be perfectly rational for Pauper to rob the bank! It would be equally rational for Opulent to stay home and work. Poverty does, indeed, breed criminals!

The Victims of Crime

This is not to say that economically motivated crime is an efficient way of redistributing income. If the poor tend to commit crimes more often, they are also more often the victims of crime. Tellingly, a disproportionate number of the victims of serious crimes (other than larceny) are black. Among the 1965 victims of serious crimes other than murder, about a quarter had incomes under $3,000 a year and about three-quarters had annual incomes under $10,000.[5]

In addition to direct victims, crime claims many indirect ones, too. The costs of crime go far beyond lost lives and limbs, mental anguish, income forgone, property destroyed, and large hospital bills for the immediate victims. As with taxes, the ultimate incidence of these costs might be widely dispersed from the point of impact. Affected businesses, for example, will try to recoup losses from customers through higher prices or from employees through lower wages. They will buy more insurance, again passing on the cost of premiums, at least in part, to those from whom they buy or to whom they sell.

Indeed, one can make a good case for generalizing the costs of crime and making society at large, rather than selected individuals, the victims of crime.[6] This might be done by compensating individual victims for their losses from general tax revenues. This idea is an ancient one, going back at least 4,000 years to the Babylonian Code of Hammurabi. At that time, a robbery victim could prepare an itemized statement of loss and be compensated by the governor in whose jurisdiction the crime had been committed. In seventh-century England a similar custom prevailed, and everything had its price, from murder to adultery to the loss of an eye.

Since that time, the *compensation principle* has lain dormant. Societies preferred to imprison, multilate, or kill offenders, while granting victims the right to sue their attackers for damages. Obviously, that is of little help most of the time. In the 1960's, however, the compensation principle was revived, first in New Zealand and the United Kingdom, then in a number of states in the U.S. California now compensates victims and those ("good Samaritans") who are hurt while helping to avert a crime or capture an offender. However, the persons involved must be poor, and they cannot collect more than $5,000. New York state pays medical expenses without limit and even reimburses lost income up to $15,000. Hawaii, Maryland, Massachusetts, and Nevada have similar statutes, and Congress has considered a federal bill on the subject ever

[5] Most of the statistical data used in this chapter come from the President's Commission on Law Enforcement and Administration of Justice, *The Challenge of Crime in a Free Society* (Washington, D.C.: Government Printing Office, 1967), and from U.S. Bureau of the Census, *Current Population Reports*, Series P-60, *Governmental Finances and Public Employment*, and *Expenditure and Employment for the Criminal Justice System*.

[6] See Duane G. Harris, "Compensating Victims of Crime: Blunting the Blow," *Federal Reserve Bank of Philadelphia Business Review*, June 1972, pp. 14–20.

since 1965. Most people, of course, would prefer to stop crime rather than compensate its victims.

HOW TO STOP CRIME

Some people see criminals as individual aberrations from the social norm. They believe that crime can best be stopped by stepping up efforts to apprehend, convict, and isolate offenders until society can be sure of their good behavior. They see the best hope in a stronger system of law enforcement. They suggest spending more public funds, as through the Crime Control and Safe Streets Act of 1968 or the special law enforcement revenue-sharing plan President Nixon proposed in 1973. This is designed to raise the private cost of crime as it is affected by items 2a–c in Table 10.2.

To *raise the probability of arrest*, advocates of this approach would improve police operations. They would make available more officers and patrol cars, more gadgets, ranging from riot guns to tear gas, from powerful walkie-talkies to night-vision devices, and to computerized intelligence systems. They would provide funds for paying informers or bathing city streets in light when the sun has set.

To *raise the probability of conviction*, they would improve the whole court system so everyone can be quickly tried and appeals can be handled immediately.

To *raise the deterrent effect of the justice system*, they would deny bonds for people awaiting trial, mete out stiffer penalties, make prisons less pleasant, and tighten parole regulations.

All this has been tried, with little observable effect. Between 1960 and 1970, the spending of all governments in the United States on the criminal justice system rose from $3.3 billion to $8.6 billion. Of the 1970 funds, 64 percent were local, 25 percent state, and 11 percent federal. Of the total, 59 percent went for police, 20 percent each for the courts and prisons.

Yet while the spending against crime rose by 156 percent at current prices (and by obviously less in real terms), the FBI's serious crime count for the nation as a whole rose from 2.0 million in 1960 to 5.6 million in 1970, or by 176 percent. This does not prove the ineffectiveness of anticrime measures taken (for without them crime might have risen even more), but it does show that crime was not stopped, even though a serious effort was being made at doing so.

Some think they know why there has been so little success in stopping crime. They believe that the strict application of more massive police power is the wrong way of going about it. It not only threatens everyone (by eroding civil liberties), but actually raises the likelihood of *violent* crime. To offset any increase in the probability of arrest and conviction, a criminal might kill rather than gag witnesses, for example.

Critics of stronger law and order policies also question whether stiffer sentences are a deterrent. For one thing, individuals contemplating a crime may discount long sentences (What's the difference, they may say, between a 20- and a 30-year term?). Secondly, jails as now run have proven to be excellent *schools* for crime. Through contact with other more experienced inmates, many a first offender acquires new criminal skills, raising the private benefit (line 1a, Table 10.2) to be expected from a new crime. As a result, 35–55 percent of convicted criminals repeat their crime. Studies show the incidence of repeating crime to rise with the length of sentences. It is least for those receiving probation.[7]

The way to stop crime, these critics assert, is to raise the private cost of crime not by stiffer law and order policies (affecting items 2a–c, Table 10.2), but by raising the opportunity cost of being in jail (items 2e and 2f, Table 10.2). That is, one should convert Pauper into Opulent! This might be done by changing prisons from places of maintenance (where the emphasis is on *confining* undesirables) to places of rehabilitation (where the emphasis is on *providing skills* usable in legitimate labor markets). Any potential criminal who could earn $25,000 a year in a legitimate pursuit, like Opulent, would think twice before committing a crime.

The opposite has been done so far. Only 5 percent of total prison costs have in recent years been devoted to rehabilitation. Other policies, as they were discussed in Chapters 5–9, of nutrition, health care, education, training, job placement, and generous income maintenance would, similarly, keep those people who are outside prisons from turning to crime for income support. In short, it is argued that eliminating urban poverty means also eliminating most of urban crime.

URBAN CRIME IN PERSPECTIVE

Although most people hearing the term *urban crime* think of the types of crime discussed so far, it is worth while to note that crime so defined constitutes only a small portion of total crime. There are other types of crime, equally serious, also economically motivated, but frequently outside the focus of public attention. These are *organized crime* and other crimes not accounted for in the FBI's index of seven "serious" crimes. We might just refer to them as *non-index crimes*. They, too, are committed for the sake of redistributing income. Their economic impact dwarfs the importance of those seven index crimes. The President's Commission on Law Enforcement and the Administration of Justice (noted in footnote 5) estimated the economic impact of crimes during fiscal 1965. The annual amount of losses to victims or of income transfers from victims to criminals was $600 million for the four economically motivated crimes contained in the FBI index (and another $815 million for the three crimes of passion). But the figure was believed to have been $7.925 *billion* for four types of organized crime alone (narcotics, loan sharking, prostitution, and gambling). Note that the gambling component does *not* include the

[7] One such study is based on 10,000 offenders in 20 jurisdictions. See Martin A. Levin, "Policy Evaluation and Recidivism," *Law and Society Review*, August 1971.

total amount gambled but only the amount retained by organized crime, and that no estimate is made for the very large annual sums transferred additionally through extortion and blackmail. Other nonindex crimes (ranging from shoplifting, employee theft, and embezzlement to fraud, forgery, arson, and vandalism) took another estimated $3.332 billion.

Interestingly, many of these crimes are not necessarily committed by people who are poor, but poor people are often the victims. Much of organized crime involves nothing else but the production and sale of goods that are demanded but the supply of which has been declared illegal—a classic case of restriction to market entry. In some cases, organized crime obviously does a lot of harm (murder, extortion, blackmail) that no possible benefit can offset, but in others it is doubtful whether any harm is done to society that differs from that done by certain goods legally produced. For instance, the production and sale of a drug like marijuana can hardly be said to be much different from the production and sale of alcohol. Nor do illegal gambling services differ from official state lotteries—except that one activity is illegal while the other is not.

A 1972 study by the Fund for the City of New York (a nonprofit organization established by the Ford Foundation to conduct research on social issues affecting the city) recommended, as the Knapp Commission had earlier, that criminal laws against gambling be repealed. Shortly thereafter, a New Jersey legislative study commission made the same recommendation. The New York study noted that in New York City $1.7 billion a year was being grossed by illegal gambling operators; of this $1 billion in sports betting, $600 million in numbers betting, $150 million in horserace betting, and $35 million in pool card betting. A survey showed that one in four New York adults played the numbers. Obviously, those who do engage in this and other types of organized crime do so because they hope for better income than is attainable by them in conventional jobs, and this is usually true because of the artificial restrictions to entry in this industry.

Employee theft of cash and merchandise or shoplifting by customers are believed to amount to perhaps 2 percent of total retail sales. Often they are not reported, and so they do not show in official police statistics. The impact of all types of fraud is similarly understated. Businesses that sell useless but expensive nostrums for incurable diseases, builders that sell thinly disguised substandard housing as high quality, repair shops that do shoddy work but claim otherwise, corporations that get together and contrive to set artificially high prices, all of them are attempting to redistribute real income in their favor. Most of them, most of the time, are violating some law. Consider just one famous example.

The Electrical Equipment Industry Conspiracy

Early in 1961, the newspapers headlined one of the biggest pieces of business news in many years. A federal judge in Philadelphia, claiming that the survival of the free-enterprise system was at stake, had imposed fines totaling $2 million on twenty-nine electrical equipment industry firms and dozens of their employees after they were convicted of conspiracy to fix prices and rig bids. Seven prominent executives of the electrical equipment industry, coming from such renowned firms as General Electric, Westinghouse, and Allen-Bradley, were convicted of the same conspiracy and were sentenced to jail. All defendants had pleaded guilty or no defense. Here is what had happened.

In addition to such common items as refrigerators, washers, and electric motors, which were sold to millions, these firms were producing gigantic pieces of apparatus such as power transformers, switchgear assemblies, and turbine-generator units, built to specification for relatively few customers. Such items, understandably, had no common price and were sold, mostly to private electric utility companies and to various levels of government, in sealed bids, with the lowest bidder getting the business. The prices involved were gigantic, too. A 500,000-kW turbine generator, producing electricity from steam, cost $16 million, for instance. As a result, the economic position of many a firm in this field was one of feast or famine: either there were large orders for the giant and expensive pieces of equipment or there were none at all.

Naturally, the executives of the industry were less than enthusiastic about this situation. Their anxiety was reinforced by the marked overcapacity with which the industry had come out of World War II. The industry was equipped to meet peak government demands of the war, but that demand had vanished and was not yet replaced by growing private needs. No wonder they all wanted to appropriate for themselves whatever private demand there was for these products. This urgent desire led in 1955, and again in 1957, to price wars among the firms involved. In a famous "white sale," prices of some equipment were cut in successive rounds by as much as 50 percent, that is, by millions of dollars! As you might expect, that was no solution. Profits throughout the industry plummeted. There was red ink in some cases.

While all this was going on, the executives of the firms involved saw one another frequently. They had common interests. They met at industry association meetings and technical conferences. Some were personal friends and met socially. Naturally, they talked about their mutual desire to ensure their firms' survival.

What each needed was secure minimum prices and a minimum share of the market. They did not need to be told that their past behavior had been mutually destructive. Was it difficult to formulate the idea of a common response to a clearly recognized common danger? Of course not.

Before long, beginning in 1956 and continuing into 1959, the executives exchanged information on costs, prices, and intentions. They decided to fix prices and divide markets so that everyone could "get along." Nominally sealed bids were rigged in advance so that each company would be assured a certain percentage of the available business. To preserve the secrecy of the operation, the executives referred to their companies by code numbers in their correspondence. They made telephone calls from public booths or their homes rather than from their offices. They also falsified expense accounts for their meetings to cover the fact that they had all been in a certain place at the same time.

Yet, as so often happens, there is no honor among thieves. An employee of a small conspirator company told all to federal officials in 1959. As a result, two years later, the American business community had the exhilarating spectacle of watching some of the nation's most highly paid (and impeccably dressed) executives being marched off to jail! Some watched in horror, others with glee. Meanwhile, customers were suing the convicted companies for hundreds of millions of dollars' worth of damages for having paid "artificially high" prices. This type of illegal behavior by businesses, whether corporate or not, is much more prevalent than it is prosecuted. It easily involves the theft of hundreds of millions of dollars each year. Yet many people tend not to regard such actions as "true" crime at all, even though the economic impact greatly overshadows crime in the streets of our cities.

Summary

1. There is a link between poverty and crime. If society does not help the poor, it is a short step for the poor to take matters into their own hands and attempt to enforce a redistribution of income—on their own terms.
2. Statistics on "serious crimes," as collected by the FBI, reveal that 93 percent of crimes were economically motivated in 1971. They also reveal such crimes as an urban problem. Over 85 percent of serious crimes were committed in SMSA's, and crime rates generally were higher the greater the population of a settlement.
3. Poverty breeds criminals. It creates groups of people—often concentrated in city ghettos—whose pockets are empty, who have nothing productive to do, and who have lost faith in social justice. In frustration, they turn to open rebellion, guerrilla warfare, or everyday crime. This is particularly true for the young.
4. The criminal behavior of the poor can be shown to be a perfectly rational response to the circumstances of their environment. Given limited opportunities to earn money in legitimate pursuits, they can often provide best for themselves by violating the law.
5. The poor, however, not only have more reasons to commit crime, they also are more often its victims—both directly and indirectly. For this reason one can make a good case for compensating crime victims with public funds.
6. Most people would prefer stopping crime to compensating its victims. Some would like to do so by becoming tough, that is, by stepping up efforts to apprehend criminals and isolate offenders. This has been tried in the 1960's, but with little observable effect.
7. Other people would prefer to go after ultimate causes and raise the opportunity cost of criminal activities. This would involve rehabilitation of prison inmates

through meaningful job training. It would involve meaningful antipoverty policies for the population in general.

8. Urban crime, however, must be seen in perspective. Its economic impact is dwarfed by the impact of other types of crime such as organized crime and crimes not accounted for by the FBI index of crimes. Considering the total picture, it is still true, however, that economic motivations are of overriding importance in crime. Ultimately, much of crime stems from people's unwillingness to accept the fact of scarcity and from their attempt to grab for themselves a larger share of goods at the expense of other people's share.

Terms[8]

aggravated assault
burglary
compensation principle
crime of passion
crime rate
discounted value
economically motivated crime
larceny
organized crime
robbery
serious crimes

Questions for Review and Discussion

1. The National Commission on the Causes and Prevention of Violence warned in 1969 that American cities were on their way to becoming a mixture of "places of terror and fortresses." The commission envisioned how in a few years the well-to-do would live in privately guarded compounds (complete with burglar alarms, iron bars on the windows, and armed guards), and would travel in armored vehicles through "sanitized corridors," while radical groups would possess tremendous armories and be capable of terrorizing the rest. Does this look like a realistic vision to you? How would you avoid its coming true?
2. "You cannot blame criminals for their actions. It's the fault of their environment." What do you think?
3. MR. A: Criminal behavior can always be explained by one simple fact: poverty.
   MR. B: No, not necessarily by poverty, but certainly by irrationality. Emotionally balanced and rational people would not commit crimes.
   Evaluate.
4. If people commit crime because they want to be richer, do you think crime can ever be stopped?
5. In 1972 the U.S. Senate passed a bill providing for the compensation of crime victims and of persons who help them. The bill covered federal crimes, but

[8] Terms are defined in the Glossary at the back of the book.

also provided for grants to the seven states who had shortly before passed similar bills. The Senate bill covered medical and burial expenses, loss of earnings, therapeutic costs, and child care expenses. It excluded compensation for property losses except for "good Samaritans," but even there it set a $100 deductible and a $50,000 limit. Do you think this is a good bill? Would you change it? Explain.

6. In 1968 Congress provided for federal aid to cities in the Crime Control and Safe Streets Act. Why should a taxpayer in Arizona help pay for police in Chicago?
7. "The smart way to fight street crime in our cities is to set aglow all those dark streets, parks, and alleys at night with high-intensity sodium vapor lights. Cities across the land that follow "operation golden light" score successes in cutting the crime rate: Owensboro, Kentucky; Wilmington, Delaware; Gary, Indiana. Other cities, such as Newark, which continued to rely on old-fashioned incandescent lamps, find crime continues to rise." What do you think?
8. New York University Professor Oscar Newman has argued (*Defensible Space*, Macmillan, 1972) that crime in public housing of big cities is linked to *architecture*: the higher the building, the higher the crime rate. For example, in New York City in 1969, while the number of felonies per 1,000 families was 30 in 3-floor walkups, it was 41 in 6- to 7-floor mid-rise buildings, and 68 in 13- to 30-floor high-rise buildings. Studying the location of these crimes, it was found that crime rates differed little among the three types of housing with respect to crimes committed inside apartments or on outside grounds. They differed greatly for crimes committed in interior public spaces, such as elevators, lobbies, corridors, stairs, and roofs (5.3 in walkups, 16.5 in mid-rise, and 37.3 in high-rise buildings). The reason was believed to be differences in "defensible space." In walkups, these public spaces, like well-peopled streets, are continually surveyed: they are shared by people who know each other, they are within calling distance of people in apartments. In high-rise buildings, on the contrary, these public places become a sparsely used no-man's-land, in which corridors serve so many apartments that residents cannot tell neighbors from strangers.

   What would you conclude from all this? Do you think that crime can be prevented architecturally, for example, by reducing the numbers of apartments per hallway, and per building? Could such measures prevent premeditated crime?
9. In 1972 the National Urban Coalition (an association of business, civic, and city government officials) sharply criticized the federal Law Enforcement Assistance Administration. It noted that in almost four years of operation roughly $1.5 billion had been spent against street crime but mostly for computerized data banks and police hardware, while the real need was for innovative projects reforming the police, court, and correction systems. How would you have spent the money?
10. In 1969 a Manhattan judge sentenced an affluent white defendant to a $30,000 fine and a suspended jail sentence (for a $20-million illegal stock deal). He also sentenced an unemployed black man to one year in jail (for a $100 theft of a TV set). Was that justice?

11. The way to stop crime is to reform our system of justice. Here is what I mean:
    (a) The police are racist. Why else were 550 blacks, but only 27 whites per 100,000 youths aged 10–17, arrested for robbery in 1967?
    (b) Judges are inconsistent. Why else were average sentences on identical narcotics charges 44 months in Connecticut and 90 months in Texas in 1968?

    So, if racism and inconsistencies were eliminated, criminals could respect the law, and there would be less crime." What do you think?
12. A 1972 decision by the U.S. Supreme Court made millions of poor defendants eligible for free counsel when facing possible jail terms on misdemeanor charges. State and local governments must foot the bill, which can run into hundreds of millions of dollars each year. Do you think such generosity is justified? Isn't it a sellout to criminals?
13. "The FBI's crime index is no good. It just counts numbers of offenses, but does not measure the level of damage and anxiety caused by them. The act of a teenager who steals his schoolmate's lunch money is equated with a vicious mugging." What would you do about this?
14. "The FBI's index of so-called serious crimes is a whitewash. It conveniently forgets about all the crimes committed disproportionately by the affluent and white community. It ignores corporate crimes of price fixing and pollution, of unsafe production processes, and of unsafe consumer goods. It ignores, similarly, organized crime that flourishes among Italian communities. Organized crime robs the poor in a variety of ways. They are seduced into squandering their money on gambling, prostitution, and narcotics. When they are addicts, they cannot earn income and must steal $75 of goods a day to get $15 of cash to support their habit. Also the poor are tricked by loan sharks into borrowing at 20 percent a *week*. They are made to buy in (legal) businesses at prices that are high because the organization has taken them over or extorts them by selling expensive labor and materials to them. *These* are the serious crimes." What do you think?
15. "For the ghetto, organized crime is actually a good thing: the legitimate labor market offers nothing but unemployment or low-wage and dead-end jobs to ghetto dwellers. It's different running the numbers or pushing drugs. You always have a job, you have a good income, and you can advance just as far as your potential will let you." Evaluate.

Selected Readings

Gordon, David M. *Problems in Political Economy: An Urban Perspective*. Lexington, Mass.: D. C. Heath and Co., 1971. Pp. 273–314. Presents conservative, liberal, and radical views on crime and crime prevention, including street crime, organized crime, and corporate crime, and also an excellent bibliography.

U.S. Bureau of the Census. *Statistical Abstract of the United States, 1972*. Washington, D.C., 1972. Lists some statistics on crime (sections 5 and 33) and —more important—sources to other statistics: Note the listing of statistical abstract supplements (p. v); and the guide to general sources of statistics (p.

936), to recent censuses (pp. 955–56), and to state statistical abstracts (pp. 961–64).

Note: The *Journal of Economic Literature* lists recent articles on the economics of crime under section 916.

Part Three
Matters of Efficiency

Almost every issue that receives the professional attention of economists involves matters of equity. Since economists deal with scarcity, this is not really surprising. On the other hand, there are problems that would persist even if everyone, let us say, had the identical money income to bid for the limited quantity of goods the economy can provide. The improper operation of markets can cause serious problems of inefficiency that are quite independent of the equity issue. When government does not perform its proper role in facilitating widespread voluntary exchange, as when it fails to assure potential market participants full information and mobility, when it fails to assure the establishment of correct prices for all scarce things—then price signals will come to be distorted. Actions taken on their basis will then cause and perpetuate rather than solve and eliminate problems. The housing, transportation, and pollution problems discussed in this part of the book are of this nature. They do involve, in part, matters of equity (just as matters of efficiency were involved in the discussion of, say, the medical care markets in Part Two). Predominantly, though, the problems discussed here derive from imperfections in real-world markets.

11 The Housing Problem

In 1970 there existed 68.6 million dwelling units in the United States. All but one million of these were available for year-round occupancy. Each of these dwelling units was a group of rooms or a single room intended for occupancy as separate living quarters. Each had direct access from the outside or through a common hall. Each had complete kitchen facilities for the exclusive use of the occupants.[1] At the same time, there were 62.9 million households in the country, counting both families and unrelated individuals. Thus for the country as a whole the housing problem was certainly not one of physical shortage of dwelling units. The same was true for smaller regions, such as the central cities or the suburbs, taken as a group. Indeed, in terms of sheer numbers, matters have been improving for decades, since the creation of new dwelling units has proceeded faster than population growth. From 1960 to 1970, for example, the number of all dwelling units rose by 17.7 percent, population rose by only 13.3 percent. The corresponding figures for metropolitan areas were 20.4 and 16.6; for nonmetropolitan areas, they were 12.4 and 6.5. Within central cities, dwelling units grew by 10.5 percent, population by 5.3 percent; the suburban figures were 31.4 and 28.2, respectively.

Statistics on the number of dwelling units, however, cannot give an accurate picture of the satisfaction their occupants derive from their use. It certainly is important to know how many rooms a dwelling unit contains and how large these rooms are. Indeed, the census bureau goes part way and collects separate data on whether dwelling units are *crowded*, which is said to be the case if there is more than one person per room.

The physical condition of a dwelling unit is equally as important as its size. One dwelling unit may have been built with stone or brick, another from scrap lumber or even tin. One may be well designed, another almost unfit for human living. One may be well maintained; another may have holes in its foundation, cracks in its walls, sagging floors, a leaking roof, and a

[1] Transient accommodations, barracks for workers, and institutional-type quarters were not counted in these data. Most of the statistical data used in this chapter come from U.S. Bureau of the Census, *1970 Census of Population and Housing, Current Population Reports*, Series P-60, and *Construction Reports*, Series C-20, from U.S. Department of Housing and Urban Development, *HUD Statistical Yearbook*, and from the President's Commission on Urban Housing, *A Decent Home* (Final Report, 1968).

furnace that does not work. One may have inside hot and cold piped water, a flush toilet, and bathtub or shower for the exclusive use of the people in the unit; another may have none of these conveniences. Indeed, the census bureau gathers separate data on dwelling units that are dilapidated or lack plumbing facilities. These are called *substandard* because they "do not provide safe and adequate shelter and in their present conditions endanger the health, safety or well-being of their occupants."

Finally, the well-being that people derive from a dwelling unit is bound to vary with the environment in which it is placed. When choosing a home, people also look for beauty, and a chance to relax or to interact with others. Such matters as the size and landscaping of the lot on which the dwelling unit is placed; peace and quiet; clean air; the availability of nearby recreational facilities, stores, and schools; the quality of governmental services (fire and police protection, garbage collection); access to jobs; congenial neighbors—all these help to determine the value a household places on a particular dwelling unit.

One might devise a theoretical *housing service unit* containing a bundle of satisfaction derivable from each and every one of the above factors. An uncrowded, well-built, well-maintained, well-equipped, and favorably located dwelling unit may yield a certain number of such housing service units, say 100 per month. An identical house or apartment—equally uncrowded, equally well built, equally well maintained, equally well equipped, but very unfavorably located—may yield considerably fewer of such units, say 70 per month. This is the kind of comparison prospective buyers or renters of dwelling units make. They look beyond the size and quality of the unit and consider the total environment in which it is set. All else equal, for example, they prefer a unit in a spacious, beautiful, quiet, and clean setting to one in a cramped, ugly, noisy, and filthy environment.

THE NATURE OF THE PROBLEM

This leads us directly to identifying the nature of the housing problem. *Even though the number of dwelling units may be adequate, the number of housing service units provided by them to their occupants may not be.* That is, even though everyone who at current prices wants to occupy a separate dwelling unit may do so, the supply of housing service units may fall short of the demand for them. This is the case in the United States.

Let us consider some of the information gathered in the last census. Of the 67.6 million year-round dwelling units then existing in the United States, 6.2 million were occupied by blacks, most of the remaining 61.4 million by whites. Of the black-occupied units, almost 62 percent were in the central cities and almost 15 percent in the suburbs of SMSA's; only 23 percent were in nonmetropolitan areas. Of the dwelling units occupied by whites (and the other nonblack races), only 30 percent were in central cities, but slightly over 37 and 32 percent, respectively, were in the suburbs and nonmetropolitan areas.

Now consider Table 11.1, "Selected Data on Crowded and Substandard Year-Round Dwelling Units, United States, 1970." As the entry in the first row and first column shows, some 9.1 million households in the United States lived in crowded or substandard dwelling units in 1970. Therefore, 13.5 percent of year-round dwelling units were either crowded or substandard (owing to the lack of some or all plumbing facilities) or both. In addition, an unknown percentage of uncrowded and standard dwelling units were undoubtedly located in highly objectionable environments. If we ignore this aspect (as we must for lack of data), the incidence of bad housing, section 1 of Table 11.1 tells us, was much greater outside than inside metropolitan areas (20 versus 10 percent), and it was slightly greater in central cities than in suburbs (11 versus 10 percent). Note also (sections 2 and 3 of Table 11.1) how the incidence of bad housing was much less for whites than for blacks. For the United States as a whole, 11.7 percent of all white-occupied dwelling units were crowded or substandard, but 31.7 percent of all black-occupied units fell into this category.

Sections 4 through 7 give further detail on the exact type of problem encountered. The numbers and percentages in sections 4 and 6 add to those in section 2; the numbers and percentages in sections 5 and 7 add to those in section 3. Thus for the United States as a whole, 5.8 percent of all white-occupied dwelling units were bad solely owing to crowding, another 5.9 percent were bad owing to insufficient plumbing and, perhaps, crowding, too. This accounts for the 11.7 percent figure cited earlier. Similarly, while 14.8 percent of all black-occupied dwelling units were bad solely owing to crowding, another 16.9 percent were bad owing to plumbing defects. These percentages add to the 31.7 percent figure cited above.

The noted differences among the races in the incidence of bad housing, which is observable for every geographic area in the country, points to an aspect of the housing problem arising from the prevalence of racial segregation in the housing market. *In general, nonwhites get fewer housing service units per dollar spent than whites do.* In 1960, for instance, 57 percent of black central city residents paying between $50 and $79 for small apartments lived in substandard units. Only 25 percent of whites paying this amount for identically sized apartments in the same cities fell in this category.[2] For identical housing, in most urban areas, blacks pay between 5 and 10 percent more than whites.[3]

To sum up, the housing problem is not one of inadequate numbers of dwelling units; it is one of inadequate provision of housing services by an adequate number of dwelling units, with the added complication that blacks and other minorities suffer disproportionately for that reason. This chapter examines the reasons behind this state of affairs, as well as an array of actual and proposed policies that might deal with it.

[2] Chester Rapkin, "Price Discrimination against Negroes in the Rental Housing Market," in John F. Kain, ed., *Race and Poverty* (Englewood Cliffs, N.J.: Prentice-Hall, 1969), p. 119.
[3] John F. Kain and John M. Quigley, "Housing Market Discrimination, Home-Ownership, and Savings Behavior," *American Economic Review*, June 1972, p. 263.

Table 11.1 **Selected Data on Crowded and Substandard Year-Round Dwelling Units, United States, 1970**

Characteristics of Crowded or Substandard Units	United States	Metropolitan Areas: *Total*	Metropolitan Areas: *Central Cities*	Metropolitan Areas: *Suburbs*	Non-metro-politan Areas
1. All bad units occupied by all races					
number (1,000's)	9,145	4,832	2,526	2,306	4,312
as percentage of all units in area	13.5	10.4	11.2	9.7	20.2
2. All white-occupied bad units					
number (1,000's)	7,178	3,724	1,717	2,007	3,454
as percentage of all white-occupied units in area	11.7	9.0	9.2	8.8	17.4
3. All black-occupied bad units					
number (1,000's)	1,967	1,108	809	300	858
as percentage of all black-occupied units in area	31.7	23.3	21.1	32.6	59.3
4. White-occupied crowded units with all plumbing facilities					
number (1,000's)	3,551	2,440	1,113	1,327	1,111
as percentage of all white-occupied units in area	5.8	5.9	5.9	5.8	5.6
5. Black-occupied crowded units with all plumbing facilities					
number (1,000's)	916	764	623	142	152
as percentage of all black-occupied units in area	14.8	16.1	16.2	15.4	10.5
6. White-occupied substandard units					
number (1,000's)	3,627	1,284	604	680	2,343
as percentage of all white-occupied units in area	5.9	3.1	3.2	3.0	11.8
7. Black-occupied substandard units					
number (1,000's)	1,050	344	186	158	706
as percentage of all black-occupied units in area	16.9	7.2	4.8	17.1	48.8

NOTES: 1. Crowded dwelling units are units having more than one person per room. Substandard units lack some or all plumbing facilities; they may or may not be crowded.
2. White-occupied dwelling units include all races other than black.
3. Detail may not add to total due to rounding.

SOURCE: *U.S. Bureau of the Census,* 1970 Census of Population and Housing.

HOUSING DEMAND AND IMPERFECT MARKETS

We noted in Chapter 3 the great migration of Americans into and out of central cities. New York City is typical. During the decade of the 1960's, there was a net outmigration of 955,519 whites, a figure only slightly smaller than that of the 1950's (994,000). Among whites remaining in New York City, however, births exceeded deaths by 338,392. Thus the white population declined by the difference, or 617,127. Clearly, there was a corresponding decrease in the demand for housing.

Yet there also was, during the 1960's, a net *in*migration of nonwhites into New York City of 435,840, a figure substantially higher than that of the 1950's (176,000). In addition, births exceeded deaths in this population group by 267,063. Thus the nonwhite population rose by 702,903. There must have been a corresponding increase in the demand for housing.

Increased Housing Demand in a Competitive Market

As it did in New York City, the demand for housing in recent years has gone up in other central cities also. The effect of such demand on the housing market—if it were perfectly competitive—can be easily perceived. All we have to do is once more apply the lessons learned in Chapter 2 where we discussed the short-run and long-run effects of an increased demand for bread. We apply this lesson to housing.

The short run. In the short run, the additional people would have to bid for the fixed supply of existing central city housing. The effect is shown in part (a) of Figure 11.1, "How the Perfectly Competitive Housing Market Responds to Rising Demand." It would at first be nothing else but a rise in the rental of existing dwelling units. If the existing supply were fixed at 3 million units (S_1), a rise in demand from D_1 *to* D_2 would in this hypothetical example open up a shortage of *ab* at current rents. This would raise monthly rents per original dwelling unit from \$100 to \$150. Any one family could maintain its old housing expenditure by moving into smaller quarters. They would undoubtedly be obliged by landlords who would subdivide existing dwelling units to create a greater number of smaller ones. Thus the supply of standard size units (S_1) would remain constant in terms of square feet, even though each unit might be divided into two or more separate and smaller quarters. Alternatively, some families would double up with other families and share the higher rent. (This is what often happens. New immigrants from the rural South or from Puerto Rico have tended to move in with relatives and acquaintances.)

The long run. However, under perfectly competitive conditions, this would not be the end of the story. In our example, landlords would have 50 percent higher revenues. Quite possibly, their costs would be higher too. The subdividing of standard-size apartments costs money. The very presence of more

Figure 11.1 **How the Perfectly Competitive Housing Market Responds to Rising Demand**

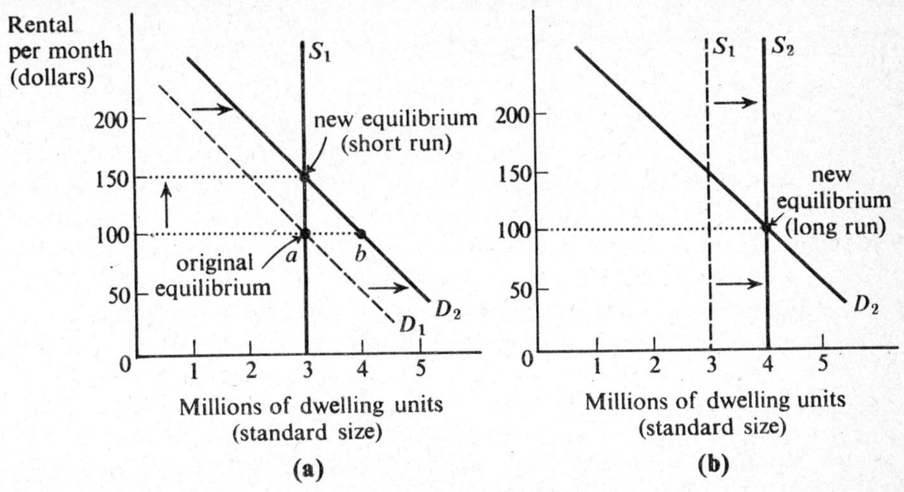

In the short run (part (a)), an increased demand (D_1 to D_2) for a fixed supply of 3 million dwelling units (S_1) raises the rental, as from \$100 to \$150 per month. In the long run, supply adjusts, possibly yielding (part (b)) the original rental of \$100 once 4 million units exist (S_2).

people (using more water and electricity, producing more garbage and breakage) would likely raise operating and maintenance costs. Yet it is also likely that profits (revenues minus costs) would be up in this line of activity. This would provide the incentive to some people to invest in the construction of new dwelling units. In the long run, therefore, as shown in part (b) of Figure 11.1, the supply of standard-size dwelling units might rise to 4 million (S_2). This would bring down the rental to its original level of \$100 a month and by this very fact eliminate the incentive for *further* new construction. At this point, everyone demanding a standard-size dwelling unit at the \$100 a month rental would find one. The short-run overcrowding would be eliminated.

The Effect of Rent Controls

In reality, things have worked out somewhat differently. For one thing, the price system's governing function has been paralyzed by government intervention. Rentals have often not been allowed to rise. Thus they have not been allowed to signal to prospective landlords that increased construction was in order. City governments have imposed *rent controls*. That is, they have set legal ceilings above which rents were not allowed to go. Although such laws were usually enacted to protect the poor from "profit-hungry landlords," it can be doubted that such policies have helped the poor.

Consider once more our hypothetical example in Figure 11.1. Suppose a government set maximum rents at $100 a month for standard-size apartments. As demand rose from D_1 to D_2, a shortage of *ab* would open up, but now it would not be eliminated by the process described above (wherein higher rents and overcrowding in the short run would lead to sufficient new construction to accommodate everyone in standard-size dwellings in the long run). Instead, as we contemplated above, overcrowding would develop *and no new construction would be initiated to eliminate it.* Indeed, the very opposite would be likely to happen. The supply of standard-size (subdivided) dwelling units (S_1) would *decline* over time, worsening overcrowding. This would be so because landlords' revenues would be unchanged, but their costs for creating and maintaining these units would be up. So profits would be down. In a market economy this would be a clear signal to raise revenues, cut costs, or get out of this line of activity. Unable to raise revenues, landlords would try to cut costs by cutting corners on operating and maintenance expenses. Before long, dwelling units would become dilapidated, as well as overcrowded. Many landlords would even abandon them altogether.

Nor is this just a fanciful hypothetical story. All too often, it is exactly what has been happening in our central cities. In New York City, increased demand for housing has gone hand in hand with a steady drop in private housing construction. While private construction of 48,500 dwelling units was initiated in 1961, the figure dropped steadily year after year to a mere 6,000 in 1970. This is not surprising, for landlords' profits have been squeezed between fixed-rent-controlled revenues and rising costs. Some of these higher costs, associated with the presence of more people, were referred to above. Others, ironically, have resulted from the attempt to cut costs. Consider how attempts to cut costs by undermaintenance have frequently backfired.

Undermaintenance. Poor maintenance of electrical wiring has turned buildings into firetraps and caused more accidents, so insurance rates have gone up. So have city taxes for fire protection.

Or landlords tried to save on janitorial services. As a result, their overcrowded tenants who must use multiple toilets and water facilities often use dirty ones. They sleep in vermin-infested, badly ventilated quarters. Their children get lead poisoning from eating peeling paint. Everyone gets sick from breathing garbage processed by inefficient incinerators. Everyone freezes in winter when old furnaces break down and go untended. In anger, residents have turned to vandalism. Thus the landlords' repair bills and insurance rates have gone up some more. Tenants have turned to crime and delinquency, and the landlords' taxes have gone up for police protection. Residents have turned to elected officials who have enacted laws against air pollution—and landlords' costs have gone up again as they had to buy new incinerators or burn more expensive types of fuel.

All this has been reinforced by the wave of businesses leaving the central cities, a matter discussed in Chapter 3. As taxable business property has shrunk in the city and unemployed and poor residents have been concentrated in it, city governments have tried to finance mounting welfare expenditures by raising taxes on residential property. In addition, any landlord who improved his property—perhaps in response to a citation for building code violations—quickly got the attention of the tax assessors, who once more raised his property taxes.

Abandonment. It is no wonder that many private owners have turned to outright abandonment of their inner-city property. Often this has occurred at a rate exceeding new construction. In New York City in 1970, while the construction of 6,000 new dwelling units was privately initiated (down from 8,000 a year earlier), and another 24,420 were started under public auspices, 52,000 units were abandoned (up from 33,000 in the previous year). This was far from exceptional. In early 1970, there were 24,000 abandoned buildings in Philadelphia, 7,500 in Houston, 6,000 in New York, 1,300 in Detroit. Most of these in due time fall victim to vandals, who strip them of heating, plumbing, electrical installations, windows, paneling, flooring, and stairways. Before long, they are littered with garbage, blackened by arsonists, and damaged beyond repair. Cynics tend to believe that those mysterious fires in the night are started by landlords themselves to collect insurance and thus liquidate their property. Be that as it may, more often than not the charred rubble becomes inhabited by dope addicts and alcoholics or families of urban squatters who have no other place to go. Or it becomes the "playgrounds" of children, a hangout of criminals, or just a place to abandon anything from old cars or dead dogs to broken furniture.

Slum formation. The undermaintenance of some buildings and the abandonment of others has become infectious. Even landlords not subject to an inordinate profit squeeze have found it not in their interest to maintain their property in the midst of deterioration. This was so because the value of any one piece of property depends not only on its own condition, but also on the neighborhood in which it is situated. A landlord who maintained his property in the midst of a deteriorating neighborhood may well find its value falling just as much as if he had not maintained it. And thus *slums* are born, entire areas wherein overcrowded and dilapidated housing predominate over other better units. Ironically, slum residents are likely to pay a much larger amount per housing service unit than other people outside the slum for similarly sized dwelling units. Even though both pay, say, $100 a month for the unit, those who live in the slum get fewer service units than those who live outside it. The former group gets shelter in a dilapidated dwelling lying in an undesirable environment, yielding, say, 100 housing service units per month. The latter group gets shelter in an identically sized well-maintained dwelling lying in a desirable neighborhood. This yields, say, 300 housing service units per month. Thus the slum dweller gets one, but the non–slum dweller three service units per dollar spent, even though both are subject to the same rent control law.

Slums also have a tendency to spread. Consider the gray areas (discussed in Chapter 3), that surround the inner cities. They are typically inhabited by older and moderate- to low-income families. These people expect that the slums will inevitably expand and slowly swallow up block after block of the gray area. Their expectations include visions of crime, higher insurance rates, and a mass exodus of their neighbors. They no longer have the will to maintain property, and the expected deterioration begins.

Racial Segregation

The housing situation in the suburbs has been totally different. Relatively high-income people have demanded single-family dwellings on spacious lots; these the contractors have provided, gobbling up land but also producing good-quality housing at an unprecedented rate. Overcrowding and dilapidation have remained children of the inner city. If one is to speak of a problem, the problem of the suburb is rather one of indiscriminately using up valuable space and—like the inner city—of failing to provide a truly beautiful living environment. Natural beauty has been replaced by endless expanses of look-alike tract houses on treeless lots. Consider the commercial strips with their garish signs, flapping pennants, and circus colors. Close your eyes and picture those ever present golden arches of McDonald's, the beaming face of Colonel Sanders of Kentucky Fried Chicken fame, the Dairy Queens, the Burger Chefs, the A&W Root Beer stands, the endless strings of gas stations, motels, shopping malls, movie theatres, and parking lots. Nevertheless, many inner-city residents would prefer present-day suburban to central city living environments. By a variety of means such as restrictive zoning practices, suburban residents have prevented selected inner-city residents from exercising such choice. And those excluded from the suburbs have not been the poor as a group, as one might think, but rather the racial and ethnic minorities *whether poor or not*. Data clearly show that poor *whites* are not excluded from the suburbs. In 1972, while of white metropolitan residents 61 percent of the nonpoor and 47 percent of the poor lived in the suburbs, only 25 percent of nonpoor and 21 percent of poor black metropolitan residents lived there.

Since racial segregation confines urban nonwhites to a fraction of the total housing stock that is smaller than their share in demand, they pay more for identical housing than whites do. Figure 11.2, "The Effect of Racial Segregation in Housing," illustrates the point with a hypothetical example. In a combined and color-blind housing market (part (a)), supply S and demand D might establish a $100-a-month rent per dwelling unit. Now suppose a third of the dwelling units are labeled "for blacks only," while two-thirds of them are reserved for whites. This is shown by S_B and S_W, respectively, in parts (b) and (c). If this does not correspond to the relative sizes of the demand for housing by black people and white people, price differences for identically sized dwelling units are bound to arise favoring one race or the other. If the fraction of the housing stock reserved for blacks is

Figure 11.2 The Effect of Racial Segregation in Housing

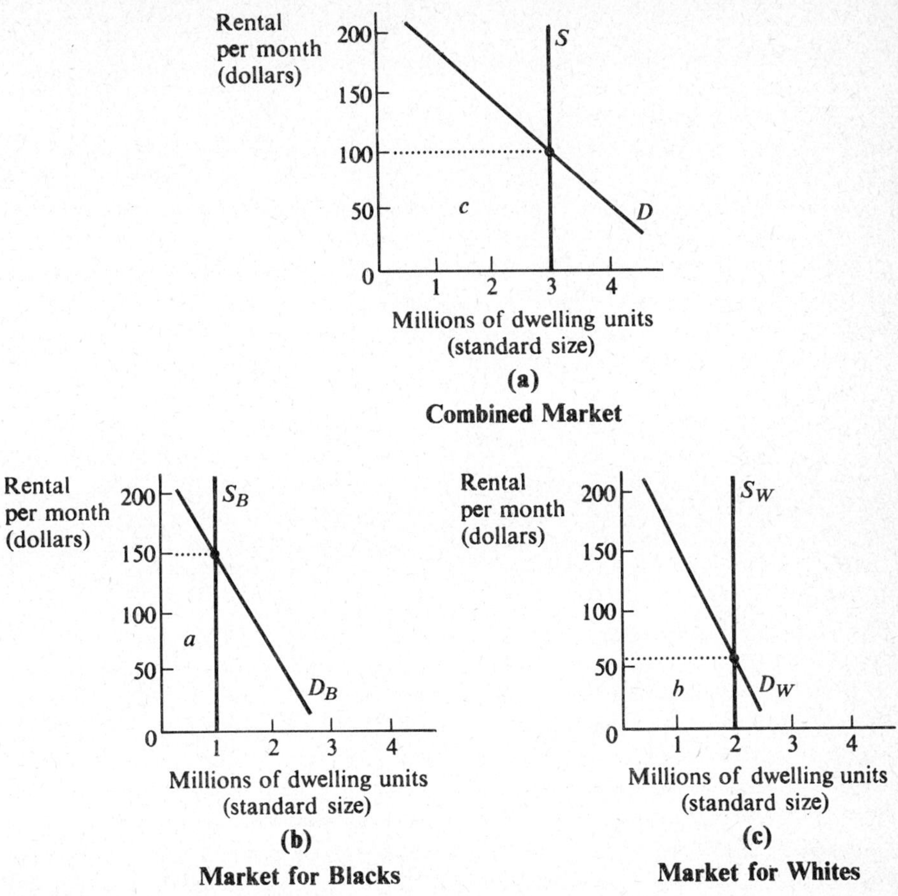

If buyers are segregated according to race and each group constrained to bid for a fraction of the total housing supply, each may end up paying different prices for identically sized housing. In this example, everyone would pay $100 a month per dwelling unit in a combined market (part (a)). Yet if half the demand came from black people D_B who were confined to bidding for a third of the housing stock S_B, in part (b), while half the demand came from whites D_W confined to the remainder of existing housing S_W, in part (c), both races would pay different prices ($150 and $60, respectively). Note that $D_B + D_W$ add to D, while $S_B + S_W$ add to S. Note also the similarity of this situation with that of segregated labor markets discussed in Figure 8.1, "The Dual Labor Market."

smaller than their fraction of demand, they will pay more than whites. If the fraction is larger, the opposite will occur. In this example, it has been supposed that blacks and whites each provide half the demand, labeled D_B and D_W, respectively. In that case, blacks end up paying more per dwelling unit

(\$150) than whites do (\$60). Interestingly, the total revenue taken in by landlords under segregation (areas $a + b$) is less than the total in a combined market (area c). We can expect something like this to have happened in reality. This requires one final comment. If segregation by race has the effect of raising the price of housing paid by racial or ethnic minorities relative to that paid by whites, members of these minorities would be more likely to be affected by rent control. In our example (parts (b) and (c), Figure 11.2), a \$100-a-month rental ceiling would not affect whites at all, but would set in motion the process described above of overcrowding, dilapidation, and slum formation among blacks only. What might be done about the continued existence of bad housing—and its concentration among minorities—is discussed in the remainder of this chapter.

RAISING THE PRIVATE DEMAND FOR HOUSING

A study commissioned by the president's Commission on Urban Housing and performed by TEMPO, General Electric's Center for Advanced Studies, found that millions of urban families could not afford to pay for adequate housing even if it were available in central cities or they were free to move elsewhere where it was available. Projecting data into the future, the study predicted that 3.4 million urban white families and 1.1 million urban nonwhite families will be in this predicament in 1978. These whites (half of them over 65 years of age) will represent 7.7 percent of all urban white families, while these nonwhites will make up 18.3 percent of all urban nonwhite families. Thus at least in part the housing problem is an income distribution problem and one might attack it as such. The housing policies favored by government so far have been those designed to raise the private demand for housing, presumably in the belief that this would stimulate private construction. Indeed it has, but mostly the construction of single-family housing for moderate- to high-income families living outside central cities. This is not to say that low-income families have not also gained. Their gain has come through the process of *filtering*, the passing on of well-maintained, but older housing to them as it was vacated by families moving into newer quarters. This gain to poorer families, furthermore, should not be discounted. It accounts for the fact that most of them live in standard rather than substandard housing. However, reliance on the process of filtering to provide housing to lower-income families also has its negative aspects. Older housing is located where people have settled first, namely in central cities and their old suburbs, the gray areas. Newer housing is being built in the new suburbs. Thus the process of filtering, whereby poorer people get old housing and richer people get new, has the same effect as an explicit law that segregates families geographically by income. To the extent that jobs have been moving to the newer suburbs (note Table 3.2), the filtering process predestines lower-income people to live where they are least likely to earn a good living and are most likely to sink into poverty.

The argument used by government to support policies relying on filtering usually involve the relative size of required subsidies. If the demand for good new housing is to be stimulated, it is said, moderate- and high-income families require only a small subsidy, low-income families require a much larger one. Since the latter can move into the standard housing vacated by the former, policies helping the upper half of the income distribution really help everyone, and this is said to be the cheapest way to help everyone. However, there are many more nonpoor families than poor ones, and these policies have not turned out to be cheap at all. Consider what they involve.

Tax Breaks

Provisions of the federal income tax law allow *deductions from gross income of mortgage interest paid and of property taxes* before taxable income is figured. A family earning $10,000 in wages, for instance, and paying $2,500 for mortgage interest and property taxes, would pay federal income tax on only $7,500 (ignoring other possible deductions). At a tax rate of 15 percent, it would pay not $1,500, but $1,125 in taxes. It would save $375, thus receiving through lower federal taxes a subsidy on housing. In 1972, these tax provisions cost the federal government $4.5 billion.

Most of this subsidy helps middle- and upper-income families. This is so for two reasons. First, most low-income families are renters. Although they may, in the last analysis, *bear* property taxes and mortgage interest through higher rents, it is not they, but the landlord who *pays* them and is entitled to the deduction. It is uncertain how much of this gain, if anything, he passes on in lower rents. It is equally uncertain whether renters are helped in part by the federal treatment of depreciation in rental housing. According to an *accelerated depreciation* rule, landlords may deduct depreciation from gross income at a rate greatly exceeding real depreciation. After the rental property is sold, the deduction process can be started all over again by the new owner. This tends to increase considerably the profitability of rental property and may in part be reflected in lower rents.

Second, even those low-income families who are owners of homes are subsidized by the tax system to a lesser extent than higher-income families are; low-income families typically take the standard deduction rather than choose itemization. Thus they gain no tax break on mortgage interest and taxes. Even if they do itemize, being in a low tax bracket makes the deduction worth less to them than to a high-income family. Indeed, it has been shown that in 1969, if a ceiling had been placed on deductions of mortgage interest (of $500) and of property taxes (of $300), the federal government would have collected another $1.5 billion in taxes, while the poor would have been unaffected.

Another federal subsidy to home owners comes from the *failure to tax at all net imputed rent*. That is, if home owners had to report as income the gross rental value of their homes minus depreciation and minus maintenance, insurance, interest, and tax payments, considerable taxes would be collected. Our above family, for example, might report, in addition to its $10,000 wage income,

$6,000 in rental income minus $4,500 in depreciation, maintenance, insurance, interest, and taxes, or a net imputed rental income of $1,500. This might be taxable, together with the full $10,000 of wage income. At a 15 percent tax rate, it would pay not $1,500 in taxes, but an additional $225 for a total of $1,725.[4] Since this is not done, and our family would in fact pay $1,125, as noted above, it can be said to be receiving a $600 subsidy over a non-home-owning family with equal income and wealth.

To put this another way, imagine two families with $20,000 in wealth. One invests this sum in a savings account, receives $1,500 interest and pays $225 in taxes thereon. The other invests this sum in a house, receives $1,500 in net imputed rent and pays no taxes thereon. Indeed, it avoids further taxes of $375 by making mortgage interest and property tax deductions from its $10,000 wage income. Compared with the other family, it has received a $600 bonus for home ownership. The difference may be even larger if the differential treatment puts these families in different tax brackets or if after-tax interest income is spent and becomes subject to sales tax. Net imputed rental income, which is automatically "spent" on housing, is not subject to any such tax. Again, however, it is upper-income families who gain most from this arrangement because renters are not helped at all, while among home owners the upper-income families have the greatest equity in their homes. In 1972, the federal government lost revenues in excess of $5 billion by not taxing imputed rent. A total of $9.6 billion was not collected by its decision to allow mortgage interest and property tax deductions and to exempt net imputed rent from taxation. Interestingly, this revenue loss by far exceeded the entire budget of the Department of Housing and Urban Development ($3.5 billion in fiscal 1972).

Mortgage Insurance or Guarantee

In the 1930's, one third of the entire U.S. population lived in substandard housing, that is, in units that were dilapidated or lacked full plumbing. At that time (in 1934) the Federal Housing Administration (FHA) was set up to promote better housing among Americans. The agency's purpose was to *insure* mortgages that were written on terms considerably more generous than common at the time. In addition, a number of GI bills authorized the Veterans Administration (VA) to *guarantee* mortgages of veterans. This revolutionized the mortgage markets.

In the 1920's, for instance, private home ownership required considerable savings prior to acquisition of housing. This was so because conventional mortgages that were offered mostly by local savings and loan associations required down payments of at least 50 percent and payment of the rest within five years. The FHA insurance and the VA guarantee took the risk out of the mortgage business and therefore attracted many more lenders and increased the flow of

[4] Note that the proposal to tax net imputed rental income discussed here is not the same as the socialist proposal, rejected in Chapter 5, of expropriating that income. The difference in this example is one between taking $225 or taking $1,500.

funds into housing. By standardizing mortgage provisions nationally, these programs also increased the geographic mobility of funds, leading, for instance, eastern banks to acquire mortgages in western states. Finally, these programs initiated the practice (which is now also followed by conventional lenders) of paying down 10 percent or less and repaying principal and interest in a constant monthly amount over a period of 25 years or more.

This has allowed a greatly increased demand for housing, since eligibility for mortgages has been extended beyond those with large savings to all with good steady income prospects. From 1967 to 1971, almost a quarter of new private housing units were constructed with FHA or VA aid. However, the programs have been of no help to families in the lower half of the income distribution. In 1969, when the average price of single-family homes mortgaged under FHA or VA arrangements was $20,000, and when down payments were well below 10 percent, terms were well above 25 years, and interest rates only 6 percent, the average monthly housing cost for these families was still $205. This included mortgage payment, insurance, taxes, utilities, heating, and upkeep. Since no family can afford to pay much more than 25 percent of its income for housing in the long run, this implies that single-family homes were unavailable for families with incomes below $9,840 a year, which was just about the median family income. This conclusion still held in 1973. It has been correctly noted that these programs have financed the move of the middle class to the suburbs.

Nor have the FHA-VA programs been of great help to renters. True enough, in 1960, 40 percent of mortgaged property with 1–4 units in metropolitan areas and 10 percent of mortgaged apartment houses were FHA- or VA-connected. Yet in Detroit in 1967, the monthly rent in FHA-aided two-bedroom apartments was $227 on the average. This would imply a required annual income of $10,896. Most likely, the rental and required tenant income in 1967 was larger in bigger cities than in Detroit; certainly they would be larger everywhere today.

Public Borrowing and Relending

Another method used by government to stimulate the demand for housing involves the following: Governmental units borrow funds in the open market in their own name. These can be obtained for lower rates than private borrowers have to pay, since the risk of default is nil and since purchasers of state and local government bonds escape federal income taxation on interest income. The borrowing governments then relend the funds so obtained to individual families or builders at the lower rates available to government. In fiscal 1970, 58 percent of all mortgages were financed in this way.

At the federal level, such activity has been carried out since the 1930's by the Federal National Mortgage Association (FNMA, or Fannie Mae). It has used its borrowed funds to buy up FHA-insured mortgages, thereby replenishing the funds of original lenders, who would pay FNMA at the same low rates at which it borrowed in the market. In addition, the Emergency Home Finance Act of 1970 authorized the FNMA to buy, with approval of the Department of Housing and Urban Development, conventional mortgages. However, the FNMA was berated in 1971, for "racism, sexism, elitism, and youthism" in implementing this new policy. The agency had issued guidelines for the types of conventional mortgages it would buy: "The mortgaged property must be located in a well-maintained neighborhood, not in certain central city areas; borrowers may not spend more than 25 percent of income on housing and must have excellent credit ratings; borrowers' incomes are defined to exclude earnings from part-time work, overtime, bonuses; working wives' income may only be counted half; and the borrowers' age plus the length of the mortgage must not exceed 80 years." It is easy to figure out why this would discriminate against minorities, blue-collar workers, women, and old people.

Since 1968, the operations of the FNMA have been supplemented by the Government National Mortgage Association (GNMA, or Ginnie Mae). It has specialized in buying up *subsidized* mortgages (to be discussed below) on houses valued at $24,500 or less. And since 1970, the Federal Home Loan Mortgage Corporation has entered the scene. It has specialized in buying up *conventional* mortgages, not FHA-insured or VA-guaranteed.

This type of program has not been restricted to the federal government. The state of California has had a program akin to Fannie Mae's since 1921. Since World War II, other states and even cities have imitated this. For example, under the city-state Mitchell-Lama program, operating since 1955 in New York, a nonprofit builders organization can receive funds raised by 50-year state and city bonds. These funds are lent at 2 percent below private borrowing rates and must be used for the construction of apartment housing. Low-interest construction costs, together with an exemption from property taxes, have under the program produced rents on the average 40 percent lower than otherwise. (In 1972, Mitchell-Lama rents ranged from $65–$95 per month per room as opposed to $110–$180 in unsubsidized New York City housing.) Earnings determine eligibility to live in the projects—a maximum of six times the rent for families of three or fewer, and of seven times the rent for larger families. Still, as in all other public borrowing and relending programs, middle-income families have gained the most. There have also been abuses. In 1973, the Scott Commission report berated New York's 108 Mitchell-Lama projects as "vehicles for subsidized luxury housing," since some tenants were found to earn $60,000 a year.

It must also be noted that the cost of such programs is not zero, even ignoring administrative costs. Although government does relend at the *same* interest at which it borrows, programs like this raise the demand for loanable funds in the government securities markets and thus raise interest rates above what they would otherwise have been. This raises the cost of all government projects, from federal roads to state hospitals to local schools. Alternatively, if extra funds flow into the government securities markets and rates there are accordingly left unchanged, they drain from other markets and raise the interest rates borrowing individuals and firms would otherwise have had to pay. The federal government also lost $1.2 billion in 1972 taxes by not taxing state and local bond interest. The hidden costs just referred to could be made obvious if government paid private borrowers direct cash subsidies on interest payments. To such programs we now turn.

Cash Subsidies to Reduce Interest Costs

In order to bring interest costs even below those paid by a borrowing government, the housing acts of 1959, 1961, 1965, and 1968 provided for direct interest subsidies. The 1959 act (Section 202) provided for federal loans of up to 50 years to nonprofit sponsors of *apartment houses*. The program was restricted to housing for the elderly and handicapped and eventually brought down the effective annual interest payments to 3 percent. In one city (Detroit, 1967) the typical rent for a two-bedroom apartment resulting under the program was $166 a month (requiring a tenant to have close to an $8,000 annual income).

In 1961, the program was expanded (Section 221) by loosening eligibility requirements for both sponsors and tenants and by authorizing the FNMA to buy up mortgages at 3 percent interest.

However, the 1968 act replaced the earlier program. It reduced effective interest to 1 percent for both prospective *home owners* (under Section 235) and *rental housing* (Section 236).

Prospective home owners would privately arrange for the construction or rehabilitation of single-family homes, as well as an FHA mortgage at market interest rates. They would pay mortgage interest as if the rate were 1 percent, with the government paying the rest. A similar arrangement was made for limited-profit or nonprofit sponsors constructing or rehabilitating rental housing. To be eligible for aid, prospective home owners had to have incomes no larger than five times the mortgage cost, tenants in subsidized apartment houses incomes no larger than four times the rent. Since the average rent turned out to be $147 a month for a two-bedroom apartment (Detroit data), the program has focused on families with incomes of about $7,000 a year. (The somewhat higher income limits for home owners were to cover their additional expenses for utilities and repairs.) Thus the 1968 act has tended to help families *near* the poverty level, most of them blue-collar whites. It has not reduced housing costs sufficiently to aid poor families.

In addition, the administration of the act has been severely criticized. These programs have been found subject to the most widespread abuses in the history of U.S. housing programs. Applications have been found falsified on matters concerning intermediaries, buyers, and properties. As a result, lawyers, title companies, and insurers have collected exorbitant closing costs and kickbacks. Aid has not been given on a racially neutral basis. A study released in 1971 by the U.S. Commission on Civil Rights charged that aid under Section

235 (which affected 130,000 houses from 1968 to 1970) had been given on a racially segregated basis, typically to help whites gain new homes in suburbs and to help blacks rehabilitate old homes in cities.

In addition, other investigations have shown, there have been inadequate controls over the quality of housing aided under the programs. New housing (90,000 houses from 1968 to 1970) has often been of such poor quality that it could not survive the life of the mortgage. Often it has turned into "instant slums." Rehabilitated housing (40,000 houses from 1968 to 1970) has often been formerly condemned housing provided with a "cosmetic paste-up" by real estate speculators. A 1972 federal survey showed 26 percent of homes newly constructed and 43 percent of homes rehabilitated under Section 235 to be of deficient quality. In one documented "fast-buck operation," an old row house was purchased by a speculator for $750 and superficially repaired. After being appraised at $6,000 by a crooked private appraiser hired by the FHA, the house was sold for that sum shortly thereafter. Thus buyers or renters of new or rehabilitated homes have frequently found them uninhabitable. As ceilings cave in, the roof leaks, the cheap paint peels off the walls, and the furnace breaks down, the new and relatively poor owners have little choice. They cannot afford repairs, so they simply move out and stop paying their mortgage. In the case of rental housing, the landlords do the same when rents cease coming in due to tenant dissatisfaction with the quality of housing. Indeed, in early 1972, 26 percent of apartment houses aided under Section 236 were in default on mortgage payments. The federal government held defaulted mortgages on 36,000 central city units, but estimated that it would hold some 240,000 units within a few years. Sooner or later, the federal government ends up owning these rapidly decaying dwelling units, together with the continued obligation to pay many billions of dollars each year to original lenders (an estimated $7.5 billion annually by 1978). In late 1972, the federal government owned 10,000 housing units in Detroit (where 12,000 poor families had gotten homes under the program but many were driven out either by poor housing quality or by loss of jobs). It owned another 3,000 units in New York (mostly in Brooklyn and Queens), 1,700 in Philadelphia, and many more in Chicago, Dallas, Indianapolis, St. Louis, Seattle, and Los Angeles. Foreseeing an eventual (and totally unintended) federal takeover of city slums, together with a $100 billion expenditure, congressional leaders recoiled from this "nightmare of bureaucratic abuse, corruption, and inefficiency that had become a bonanza for all except those intended to be helped." Largely as a result of this state of affairs, President Nixon cut Section 236 funds from $200 million in fiscal 1972 to $150 million in fiscal 1973. The number of dwelling units authorized for construction was cut from 239,000 to 174,000 in an effort to emphasize "quality over quantity." By early 1973, the president announced an eighteen-month moratorium on any new federal commitments to subsidize housing. Housing Secretary Romney in late 1972 had even recommended the complete abolition of all federally subsidized housing projects (along with most of his department) in favor of two simple direct subsidy programs: to poor families in the form of rent supplements and to public housing authorities in the form of operating subsidies.

Rent Supplements

A rent supplement program is aimed at providing housing funds specifically for the poor. However, government has shied away from giving cash assistance in the belief that extra cash income would be disproportionately spent on extra consumer goods other than housing. Thus the rent supplement program, initiated in 1965, is an in-kind program.

To be eligible, families must have incomes below the limit set for public housing in their community, usually $2,000 or less, and they must have few assets, and be elderly, handicapped, displaced by government action or natural disaster, or currently living in substandard housing. They must pay 25 percent of their income in rent; the federal government adds whatever is required to meet the rent charged by the landlord and pays the landlord this difference directly. This legislation has been hailed by its sponsors for a number of reasons.

Advantages. First, the subsidy is tied to the family, not to a particular housing project. Thus it allows a family to move to better housing wherever located should it become available and accessible. For instance, large poor families might in this way move into large *unsubdivided* apartments in the gray areas or even find housing in the newer suburbs.

Second, the size of subsidies under this program can be fine-tuned to the needs of families. Families with different income levels can live in the same house or area, some receiving and others not receiving the subsidy. Also any given family can remain in its quarters as its income changes. It would simply pay a different dollar amount for its housing (always a maximum 25 percent of income) and the size of the subsidy would change correspondingly. Thus the program promotes integration by avoiding the residential segregation of the poor typically found in public housing projects, which are always located in poverty areas and adopt rules forcing tenants to leave as their income rises.

Third, under this program the responsibility for constructing and operating housing units rests with private enterprise. This makes it all administratively easier, since no governmental machinery is needed.

Problems. Yet the rent supplement program has not been too popular in Congress. The size of the subsidies given has been resented (they have often been double those given in public housing programs). Indeed, it has been realized that the cost of really succeeding with this program would be exceedingly high as long as one attempted through it to improve housing under private auspices *within the central cities.* Only a manifold increase in present rent levels could produce the profitability required to induce any voluntary large-scale private investment in central city housing. Construction costs would be exceedingly high for a variety of reasons. There is little vacant land and it is expensive. Usually land can be found only by first demolishing existing structures. This must be done on a fairly large scale, since investors shy away from putting up an individual building in the middle of an otherwise squalid neighborhood. Any large-scale land assembly is costly because of the highly fragmented ownership of slum housing. Central city construction on high-cost land must mean high-rise construction, involving higher costs per apartment unit than garden apartments or row houses, which can be put up with different materials and methods.

All this is not what the program's sponsors had in mind. They would have liked to encourage central city housing construction and rehabilitation, but they would have been even happier with poorly housed people moving out of slums and gray areas into new construction *in the suburbs*. The suburbs, of course, have blocked apartment construction for fear of central city problems being transplanted to their areas. Suburban congressmen have therefore resisted the rent supplement program and its strong tendency to promote racial integration (as it enables people with very different incomes to live in the same building or area). Thus Congress has been reluctant to appropriate funds and has increased restrictions, for example, by limiting subsidies to a two-year period for any one family, by requiring that aided families pay at least 30 percent of the rent, and by setting limits on rents themselves.

Experiments. The Department of Housing and Urban Development, however, has been eager to escape the entangled and cumbersome bureaucracy of other programs and to expand rent supplement programs. Under the authority of the 1970 Housing Act, after its pretesting in Kansas City, the department initiated a three-year program involving 1,000 poor families in each of six metropolitan areas. These families seek their own rental or owned housing, contribute 25 percent of their income to the cost, and receive cash or vouchers from the federal government to make up any difference from actual costs. (In 1973, President Nixon exempted these experiments from his subsidy moratorium.)

In any case, letting housing prices find their equilibrium levels and supplementing the housing payments of the poor are policies only recently adopted and certainly not on a wide-enough scale to make any appreciable difference. They are more in the nature of experiments than full-scale attacks on the housing problem. Yet the discussion so far also suggests in what directions any successful policy would have to move. Whatever it does to the demand side of the housing market, it would have to assure an increase in the *supply* of good-quality housing to those who now do not enjoy it. As in the case of medical services (discussed in Chapter 6), there is no guarantee in the imperfect housing market that mere increases in demand bring forth corresponding increases in supply, as would be the case in a perfectly competitive world.

RAISING HOUSING SUPPLY THROUGH PUBLIC CONSTRUCTION

One obvious way of assuring good housing for all would involve direct construction of such housing by the government itself. This has indeed been tried, and over a long period.

Public Housing

The Housing Act of 1937 provided funds for government construction and management of multifamily housing projects for the poor. Under the act, local public housing authorities were formed. They raised funds by issuing long-term tax-exempt bonds. They used these funds to construct public housing units. The local housing authorities were reimbursed by the federal Housing Assistance Administration for the payment of interest and principal on the bonds. Each authority was expected to defray operating costs from rents. However, even here help was provided. The federal government was authorized to provide $120 per year for elderly, displaced, very poor, and very large families. Local governments typically relieved public housing from property taxes in whole or in part. Only tenants below certain income limits were admitted to the projects. They had to move out if their income rose above that limit. However, public housing has been somewhat less than a great success. By 1950, only 202,000 units were available for occupancy. Around that time Congress was stirred to act.

The promise of 1949. The 1949 Housing Act promised "realization, as soon as feasible . . . of a decent home and suitable living environment for every American family." It provided a federal subsidy for low-rent public housing and for urban renewal of gray areas (as well as a program of cheaper mortgage credit). The act promised construction of 800,000 public housing units in six years. The plan did not work out this way.

Insufficient construction. For one thing, too few units were built. Only 212,000 were built during the 1950–55 period (whereas 800,000 had been promised) and fewer than 600,000 units were built in twenty years. During that time, a greater number of low-cost housing units were *demolished* by public action!

Yet hope springs eternal. In 1968, a Housing and Urban Development Act was passed in the realization that the 1949 goal had not been accomplished. The new act promised private or public construction or rehabilitation of 26 million dwelling units over ten years. This goal was exceedingly ambitious, since its achievement required a doubling of the average annual construction activity since 1949 such that *each* year's construction would be 42 percent higher than the highest level ever achieved in U.S. history. It also required 6 million low- and moderate-income housing units, necessitating a tenfold increase in the annual production of such units. Despite the large number, the goal was later revised upward to 28.2 million units. Of these, 13.5 million were to house new families (who are being formed at a rate of 1.5 million a year), 3.5 million each were to replace deteriorating units and provide secondary units (used for recreation), 2 million were to make up for expected demolition and fire losses, 1.8 million were to replace dilapidated units, 1.2 million were to replace mobile homes, and 2.7 million were to be rehabilitated.

The 1969 goal of 2.6 million units produced was "met" by changing the goal and including mobile homes produced. When the president in mid-1972 reported that the nation was 8 percent ahead of the path charted toward the 28.2 million goal, his statement depended on the inclusion of mobile homes. The country's 1972 all-time record high production of almost 3 million units included about 600,000 mobile homes.

So far as public housing goes, by 1971 there were 993,000 units available for use, less than 2 percent of all housing units. At least 125,000 of the publicly owned units had not been newly constructed, but purchased or leased by public housing authorities. Almost 100,000 units had been constructed under state and city programs, mostly in New York.

The lack of success of all these public housing plans can be attributed to a variety of factors: congressional reluctance to appropriate funds, local squabbling over the location of public housing (suburbs trying to keep it in the city, city governments being reluctant to perpetuate segregation of the area's population by race and income), and inability to find contractors able to produce housing within federal cost limits (in 1971, $4,200 per room).

Forgetting the poorest. Nor has public housing reached the poorest of the poor. In New York City in 1967, the monthly apartment subsidy in public housing was on the average $55, the rent $64. In Detroit, the rent on two-bedroom apartments was $97, requiring roughly a tenant income of $4,656 per year. Thus the poorest families could not afford to live in public housing.

Failures. In addition, public housing has been a failure in human as well as financial terms. To be sure, public housing projects generally have provided adequate shelter. Seldom have they provided pleasant surroundings. To keep construction costs low and to minimize land taken away from the property tax base, public housing authorities have typically opted for the construction of high-rise buildings requiring small plots of land. To placate community opposition (and keep the poor out of sight), these projects have often been placed in bad locations, such as near junkyards or factories, in former lake beds, next to power lines, and isolated from schools, playgrounds, recreational facilities, stores, and jobs. Tenants have frequently felt the design of these tall structures to be positively inhuman, likely to imprison and oppress people and to take away their sense of community. Crime and vandalism in these projects, which have concentrated 3 million of the poor in small areas, have mushroomed.[5] For all

[5] Note the discussion of this in Question 8, Chapter 10.

these reasons, public housing projects—though providing physically adequate housing—have been shunned by those they were designed to help. Their reputation has been worse than that of slums. In mid-1969, 40 percent of the public housing in St. Louis was said to be vacant because people did not want to live in such a stigmatized environment. In late 1970, the St. Louis authority boarded up 26 apartment buildings built only in 1956. The eleven-story buildings had housed 12,000 people. By 1973, the St. Louis authority threatened to hand over other projects housing 25,000 people to the federal government. Lacking funds (its welfare tenants were paying less than $30 a month, federal subsidies were not coming), the authority had ceased to perform basic housekeeping functions. Dirt was piling up, elevators were not running, pipes were freezing and bursting, and vandalism was rampant. Nor was this atypical. In mid-1972, found the House Appropriations Subcommittee, 59 major public housing authorities had "serious financial problems" and 7 of them (Chicago, Detroit, Kansas City, Newark, New York, San Francisco, and Washington, D.C.) were "verging on bankruptcy."

To some extent, this outcome was foreseen. Attempts were made to avoid it.

Rescue attempts. Since 1964, some housing authorities have followed the "used house" approach, leasing or purchasing existing housing for occupancy by low-income families. This had the advantage of scattering the poor, but has resulted in higher operating expenses for the same reason. In 1968, the federal government even went further. It initiated *Project Turnkey* to "privatize" public housing. Under this program, 100,000 single-family homes (included in the 993,000-units public housing figure cited above) have been turned over by 1971 to poor families at bargain rates under the condition that they do their own maintenance and pay for utilities. Tenants pay $56 a month rent for the house, $19 of which goes into a "purchase" fund. After 18 years, they receive title to the house. The federal government pays the remainder of the cost.

Urban Renewal

The 1949 act also initiated widespread efforts at *urban renewal.* Under Title I of the act, a further subsidy was provided for land assembly in blighted areas in preparation for urban renewal. Each local government could establish an urban renewal agency. It designates *redevelopment areas* and acquires all real property therein, either by negotiation or eminent domain. An independently appraised fair-market value is paid. The agency then relocates any occupants to "decent, safe, and sanitary" housing. (The 1969 Housing Act requires cities to provide "low-income" housing for all displaced.) Thereafter, the agency clears the land and adds improvements, such as streets, lights, and sewers. It then transfers the land at much lower cost (about 25 percent of agency expenses) to a public housing authority or to private developers. The federal government pays two-thirds of the loss, as well as rent supplements to displaced households and cash grants to small businesses to aid relocation. Federal expenditures on this have amounted to $5.5 billion from 1949 through 1971.

The goal. The goal of this procedure has not necessarily been to increase the number of dwelling units supplied but rather to improve a neighborhood by completely changing land use in an area. This has also been emphasized by the most notable amendment to the 1949 Housing Act, the Demonstration Cities and Metropolitan Development Act of 1966, also called the Model Cities Act. The Model Cities Act was to help demonstrate how a blighted neighborhood could be renewed, physically and in the quality of life, by concentrating federal and local programs in a few places with a high degree of local resident control. The participating cities were asked to set up a comprehensive "workable program," including plans for education, health, recreation, crime control, manpower training, and transportation, and also the rehabilitation of buildings, outright clearance of others, and the substitution of new residential, commercial, industrial, or educational structures. In early 1969, 150 cities had received grants to prepare such plans and 46 began to implement them.

Evaluation. Overall, by 1968, the housing supply had *decreased* as a result of urban renewal, since the land had typically been used for commercial, cultural, or industrial purposes, or perhaps for the construction of fewer, high-quality housing units. The supply of low-income housing had definitely declined everywhere under urban renewal. This explains the unpopularity of the projects among the poor. Indeed, urban renewal projects have had the tendency to force the poor into playing a game of "musical houses." The highest-density slum area is typically selected for urban renewal; the poor are "bulldozed" out of the area and spill over into surrounding territory. They are turned into a kind of urban gypsy, raise densities elsewhere, making other areas, in turn, prime targets for urban renewal. Many critics have therefore urged that more emphasis be given to rehabilitation rather than new construction. This would preserve the social ties of existing neighborhoods, as well as their architectural merits (human-size buildings rather than high-rise "concrete jails"). This approach of providing housing may also take less time. On the other hand, rehabilitation is at least as expensive as new construction because it is so labor-intensive. It also cannot overcome many of the faults of older housing such as bad room layout, inadequate ventilation and lighting, and high maintenance costs.

New policies. Not surprisingly, the 1968 act set new priorities for urban renewal: (1) to create residences; (2) to make at least 20 percent of residential construction under urban renewal low-income and at least 50 percent low- or moderate-income housing. Thus Congress made it clear that it intended residents of blighted areas to be beneficiaries of renewal, not victims.

The 1968 act also increased relocation aid to the displaced. This was further expanded by the 1970 Uniform Relocation Assistance and Real Property Acquisition Policies Act. It provided for persons displaced by urban renewal or other federal projects rent supplements of $1,000 for four years (or a $2,000 down payment on a home); and damages up to $15,000 for home owners, plus $300 moving expenses; and up to $10,000 for businesses and farms.

Finally, the 1968 act initiated the Neighborhood Development Program. It is aimed at supporting small-scale projects (such as parks, neighborhood city halls, training centers, or playgrounds), to be completed within a year, possibly located in noncontiguous areas, and designed to improve existing neighborhoods.

A 1969 Housing Act went further: for every moderate income housing unit removed, it ordered another low- or moderate-income unit built *in the same area.* Under the provisions of this act, one of the nation's largest urban renewal projects, the Yerba Buena project in San Francisco, was halted in 1970. It was to demolish originally a 12-block section with 43 run-down residential hotels, 92 other residential structures, and a variety of cheap restaurants, pawnshops, and seedy bars. All this was to give way to a convention center, a sports arena, a high-rise luxury hotel, 6 office towers, a 4,000-car garage, an Italian cultural center, and an airline terminal. Four thousand dwelling units housing elderly and minority families were to be destroyed, 276 new ones were to be built. (In previous years, 6,000 such units had been destroyed, 662 built in *other* areas.) Low-cost public housing had a five-year waiting list and vacancies of private housing below $100 a month rent did not exist. Thus a city government's attempt to push *nonresidential* renewal (as a means of reversing the trend of businesses leaving the city) was thwarted.

By 1973, city after city was deeply involved in urban renewal: From Philadelphia's Society Hill and Independence Mall to Pittsburgh's Market Square and Gateway Center, from Cincinnati's Fountain and Riverfront Stadium to Oklahoma City's Myriad gardens and convention center, from the towering Market Street sports arena in Indianapolis to the Skyline Project in Denver—everywhere downtowns were struggling for a comeback. Federal government involvement in all this, however, has become increasingly uncertain. President Nixon has ordered a freeze, as of mid-1973, on new urban renewal, model cities, open space, neighborhood facilities, and similar grants. He proposed an urban community development special revenue-sharing plan that would give local governments $2.3 billion in fiscal 1975 and more thereafter.

RAISING HOUSING SUPPLY BY REMOVING MARKET IMPERFECTIONS

There is, finally, a third possibility. Government could use its powers to remove all barriers to perfect competition in the housing market. This could be expected to raise the supply and lower the cost of decent housing, thereby allowing the present occupants of low-quality or segregated housing to acquire standard housing under nonsegregated conditions. Government could start by eliminating one of its own sins.

Rent Decontrol

It is tempting to suggest that city housing problems would go away if the housing market were freed from rent controls and the strong housing demand be allowed to push rents up to equilibrium levels. Where necessary, low-income people could be aided sufficiently to demand high-rent housing by a system of rent supplements, or better yet, by the policies suggested in Part Two of this book. This would so raise the profitability of city housing that the private housing industry would respond, one might think. Maintenance, repair, renovation, and new construction would follow as a matter of course. And there are plenty of precedents. France, for instance, had practically no residential construction during nationwide rent controls from 1914 to 1948 but a vigorous boom since their abandonment. To some extent, the response would undoubtedly be true also in America's cities. Some policy steps have already been taken in this direction.

Freeing rents. For example, in mid-1970, shocked by endless waiting lists for apartments, an extremely low vacancy rate (less than 1 percent in New York City compared with 4.6 percent nationally), near-zero private housing construction, and accelerated abandonment of houses by landlords, New York's city council instituted the "maximum base rent program." Its purpose was to allow some rent increases to ensure a profitable return to landlords. A study of the profitability of New York City's apartments (93 percent of which were rent-controlled) showed the following: In order that owners might be allowed to make even a small profit, rents would have to be increased by over 45 percent on 46 percent of all units and anywhere from 23 to 45 percent on another 33 percent of all units. Under the new program, a fair maximum rent for each apartment was established. This rent was to be reached through fixed annual increases for each tenant. If a tenant moved out before that figure was reached, the next tenant would immediately pay the full maximum base rent. However, the program was superseded in 1971 by New York State's Vacancy Decontrol Law. This law also was passed for the express purpose of encouraging renovation and new construction. It allowed rent increases without limit when apartments were voluntarily vacated and at a rate of 7.5 percent a year otherwise. It promised no future state or municipal controls. (However, a 90-day federal rent freeze went into effect six weeks after the new law.) Nevertheless, within three months (July–September, 1971), private housing starts rose 237 percent over the corresponding period of the previous year. The starts of that quarter (5,183) almost matched those of the entire previous year (6,000). Housing starts (as measured by building permits issued for the private or public construction of apartments and single-family homes) rose steadily from a low of 17,600 in 1969 to a nine-year high of 33,563 in 1972. Previously, such building activity in New York City had been declining ever since 1962 when about 73,000 permits were issued.

Abolishing Restrictive Zoning

Government can also increase mobility in the housing market by abolishing restrictive zoning practices. This would widen the access to new housing, especially in the suburbs. It would supplement the Fair Housing Act of 1968, which gave minorities legal access (as of January 1, 1970) to 54 million of 68 million existing dwelling units in the country. That act covered housing units constructed with federal aid, apartments and homes sold by their builders for the first time, and single-family homes sold by their owners through real estate brokers. It still allowed discrimination in private sales without brokers and advertisements. However, even such discrimination was voided by a 1968 Supreme Court decision ruling out discrimination in *all* sales and rentals of real estate. Yet the abolition of legal discrimination has had few results so far as the housing situation of poor minorities is concerned because *zoning ordinances* have been keeping them out of the suburbs. Zoning laws, for instance, reduce the supply of land for any given use, such as apartment houses. Reduction of land supply raises the price of land that is zoned for such purposes, because the demand has to concentrate on a portion of the land area. Consequently, the price of housing built on such land is raised and keeps low-income people out. Zoning laws were first introduced some fifty years ago to ensure that adjacent land uses would not be incompatible. For example, they might be used to keep a noisy, smoky, and smelly factory from locating in the middle of residences. Thus zoning laws could assure, over the long run, a harmonious overall pattern of development. But then it was discovered that zoning could also be used to enhance the fiscal position of towns.

Fiscal zoning. Since local governments rely heavily on the property tax as a revenue source, the types of land uses within the town determine the value of land and buildings and hence the tax revenue yielded by a given tax rate. Land use also determines the quantity and type of government expenditures required. For instance, a town might, first, zone for "clean industry" (such as research laboratories or offices). This land use brings in tax revenue, while requiring few public services. Second, a town may exclude apartment dwellings and mobile homes. Such land use would bring in low tax revenue, while requiring a great deal of public services (notably schools for the hordes of children of apartment and mobile home dwellers). Third, a town may restrict residential construction to single-family homes erected on large lots. This decreases the supply of lots and raises their price. As a result, fewer and more expensive homes are erected, which is good for the tax yield. (In 1971, in Westchester County, outside New York City, about 94 percent of the land was zoned for residential uses and 99 percent of that for single-family homes, one-eighth with minimum lot sizes of four acres. In the U.S. as a whole in 1969, 99 percent of undeveloped land earmarked for housing was zoned for single-family homes.) Fourth, even when apartment construction is allowed, many a town specifies a high percentage (say, 80 percent) of one-bedroom apartments and no units larger than two bedrooms. All this translates into lower town expenditures (small apartments, like widely scattered single-family homes, means fewer children, fewer schools).

Challenging zoning power. It is clear how the site costs of new housing could be reduced by eliminating fiscal zoning. For example, if the exclusion of apartment housing or mobile homes, limits on their numbers or sizes, and minimum lot requirements could be outlawed, there would be an increased availability of lots of all sizes and for all purposes in the suburbs. This would tend to decrease the land cost of apartment and small-lot home construction, which has so far been confined to a fraction of the total land area. It would also increase the movement of poor families (mostly racial and ethnic minorities) to the suburbs. This is a touchy political issue and has led to battles between residents of affected communities and all branches and levels of government. Some have suggested that zoning powers be taken from local governments and invested in county or state agencies, which would presumably show interest in all the residents of a metropolitan area, including those trapped in inner cities. To forestall such moves, nine states (California, Colorado, Iowa, Mississippi, Montana, Oklahoma, Texas, Vermont, and Virginia) have passed laws requiring a public referendum for zoning changes that would allow low-income housing into an area. In California alone, half of all such petitions were turned down by voters since 1950. When challenged, these state laws requiring public referenda prior to residential zoning changes have been held illegal in lower courts, since no such referenda were required prior to the construction of highways, hospitals, or colleges. However, in 1971, the U.S. Supreme Court upheld these laws.

Others have suggested that states and the federal government use the carrot or the stick (as needed) to limit the uses local governments make of their zoning power. For instance, the federal government has to some extent helped work out voluntary easing of zoning restrictions. Examples are "fair share" plans to disperse federally subsidized apartment housing throughout the suburbs, as in Dayton, Ohio (1970), or Washington, D.C. (1972). The federal government could also accompany verbal persuasion with economic incentives. Thus it could decrease the local desire for fiscal zoning by increasing grants to localities for school expenditures. The U.S. Congress in 1971 did consider a bill creating a metropolitan housing agency in each city with the right to locate subsidized housing throughout the metropolitan area. The affected communities would have been given grants up to $3,000 per dwelling unit over a ten-year period to cover any additional expenses for community services. Thinking along the same lines, Housing Secretary Romney in 1971 gave priority consideration for federal grants for community development (water and sewer) to those communities allowing construction of low-income housing near jobs and avoiding concentration in one area. However, President Nixon spoke out against the withholding of funds entirely from communities for the purpose of forcing integration. (In 1973, the water and sewer grants were frozen along with other housing and renewal subsidies.)

Governments and private individuals have also gone to court over the zoning issue. The United States sued a St. Louis suburb (Black Jack) when it incorporated itself for the purpose of zoning out integrated housing. The state of Pennsylvania sued Upper Saint Clair Township (a Pittsburgh suburb), and the city of Cleveland sued one of its suburbs on the same issue. And the courts have generally ruled against restrictive zoning practices. The Supreme Court of Pennsylvania in 1970 ruled that high-density housing may not be zoned out solely to avoid the burden of municipal services. In 1971, it defined a three-acre minimum-lot requirement as unreasonable. The New Jersey legislature authorized nonresidents of a community to challenge its zoning laws in the courts. A New Jersey court in 1971 struck down an entire county's one-acre minimum-lot zoning ordinance for ignoring the "desperate housing needs" of urban New Jersey. The New York State Urban Development Corporation, with the paper authority to override local zoning laws, was embroiled in 1972 in a bitter court battle with the United Towns for Home Rule, nine Westchester County towns it had ordered to accept 100 subsidized apartments each. The Massachusetts legislature passed an "antisnob" zoning law allowing anyone denied a building permit in a municipality with less than 1.5 percent of its land zoned for low-income housing to appeal to a state housing appeals committee. However, the spirit of this law has been generally circumvented. Some localities have now zoned *exactly* 1.5 percent of their land for low-income housing. Others have forestalled low-income housing construction by a multitude of devices. These include the "slow motion procedure," an interminable line of witnesses brought before the appeals committee (as in Newton), the "sledgehammer blow," the taking by eminent domain for "conservation" of land desired for low-income housing (as in Chelmsford), and the "engineers attack," claiming that technical problems, such as excessive ground water, make construction on certain desired sites impossible (as in Concord).

Abolishing Restrictive Building Codes

What zoning laws can do, building codes can do, too. Building codes have also been introduced for a worthy purpose, namely, to guarantee minimum quality of construction. Yet many existing building codes are seriously out of step with the times. They may outlaw the use of new materials and techniques. Typically, codes require the use of specific materials (such as two-inch plaster walls) that at some moment in the past met certain performance characteristics (such as fire resistance). Yet new and cheaper materials (say, half-inch plastic boards) may have the very same characteristics while being totally illegal to use. Thus, in 1967, 48 of the 52 largest cities banned the use of plastic pipes for drainage systems in houses. In addition, many codes require minimum interior floor areas that often are in excess of what is reasonable for purposes of health or safety. This translates, in effect, into a requirement for minimum construction costs (of $45,000 for a single-family home in one actual case). Codes also prohibit the similarity of exterior design among neighboring residential structures, thereby eliminating cheap apartment complexes. Finally, most codes require not only that specified materials be used but that they be used by *licensed* workers (for example, master craftsmen). But lesser-trained workers may be able to do the work for much less.

In addition, building codes are usually diverse. They differ from town to town. This makes it impossible for any contractor to operate on a large mass-production scale. Again, building costs are higher than necessary.

Bringing about change. The solution is obvious. Building codes should be revised to allow the use of cheaper (but equally effective) materials and labor. They should be made uniform on a state or national level. This would allow mass-production techniques. It would allow the assembly of prefabricated shell houses that could be finished not by hired craftsmen but the tenants themselves. (Remember many of the poor have little money, but a lot of time and a good pair of hands.)

Change in this area is difficult. It runs into the vested interests of the building-trade unions (who want to keep plasterers employed), of material producers (who want to keep producing plaster), and of contractors (who want to keep things running smoothly in their accustomed track).

As might be expected, building codes have been challenged in the courts along with zoning laws. Their power, too, has been eroded. A New Jersey court, for instance, held minimum construction costs to be illegal.

A number of experimental programs have been initiated since 1967 allowing untrained people to build their own homes or cooperatively build apartments. On Long Island, in Washington, D.C., and in Indianapolis, poor people have been allowed to use their labor as down payment for dwelling units and have this "sweat equity" matched with mortgage loans to buy materials, such as precut, color-coded lumber.

Encouraging Mass Production

The challenge to zoning laws and building codes can be expected to reduce the costs of supplying good housing by reducing costs for land, for material, and for labor. There are additional ways of doing so. One of these involves the very organization of the construction industry itself. The U.S. construction industry has been notorious for its slow growth of productivity. Measured as real national income created in the industry per employee, productivity since 1950 has risen 1 percent per year in construction while rising 2.5 percent in the rest of private industry. At the same time, construction costs, like medical prices, have risen considerably faster than the consumer price index as a whole. There are a number of reasons for this. There is a lack of large-scale operations in the industry. Instead of mass production, production methods older than a millennium predominate among a preponderance of 50,000 small contractors and 200,000 subcontractors. Most of these have fewer than 4 employees and buy materials in small quantities. The typical firm puts up 8–10 houses in a year and operates only during good weather. Even the country's 50 largest construction firms account for less than 15 percent of annual production in their industry. The two largest producers (National Homes and Levitt and Sons) produce 11,000 and 5,000 units per year, respectively. There is also a terrific turnover of firms and workers. This tends to go hand in hand with a general prevalence of noninnovative management steeped in archaic thinking. The federal government has tried to do something about this.

Operation Breakthrough. In 1969, the federal government launched Operation Breakthrough. It called for demonstrations that complete houses could be mass-produced. The endeavor was undertaken in the hope of finally altering the long history of technological backwardness in the U.S. housing industry. In particular, advanced European techniques of prefabricating high-rise housing were considered worthy of imitation: casting whole concrete walls and floors in factories near the construction site, then hoisting the concrete slabs, complete with electrical conduits, heating ducts, plumbing, and carpeting, into place and joining them together.

The Department of Housing and Urban Development received 550 proposals to demonstrate the feasibility of mass production in housing, using semiskilled labor only and a variety of materials ranging from concrete to pressed dirt and sprayed resin. In 1970, HUD selected 22 builders to build at eight separate sites (Indianapolis, Jersey City, Kalamazoo, Macon, Memphis, Sacramento, St. Louis, and Wilmington) 2,000 prototype units for a variety of income levels. In 1971, the first *modular house* came off the assembly line in Battle Creek, Michigan. By year end, 52,000 factory-produced units had been produced in the U.S. and 90,000 more were produced in 1972. A 1972 study by Audit Investment Research, Inc., found, however, that well over half of 83 new companies in the factory housing field were either bankrupt or closing down to avoid bankruptcy, or were seriously considering giving up. Some had made costly errors, as when insufficient factory quality control yielded pieces that would not fit together at the construction site. All had run into unexpected logistical problems, like laws against nighttime transportation of modules, or daytime traffic jams that delayed delivery to the site and thereby negated any cost savings from factory mass production. Indeed, most were hampered in producing at sufficiently large volumes by zoning laws and building codes. In time, some of these problems can undoubtedly be overcome. For instance, the building codes of over 40 percent of cities, found the National Commission on Urban Problems in 1967, banned the use of preassembled plumbing systems and wiring units. By 1972, however, in anticipation of widespread factory production of houses, 20 states had enacted laws exempting state-certified factory housing from local building codes.

Among the states were California, Connecticut, Colorado, Georgia, Hawaii, Indiana, Maryland, Michigan, North Carolina, Ohio, South Carolina, Washington, West Virginia, and Virginia. Some people even called for the enactment of a *national* building code. Meanwhile, some building-trade unions agreed to moderate their long-standing hostility to industrial techniques, and to do factory work and site installation at (lower) industrial wage rates in light of the fact that workers for these operations can be trained in six weeks and work is unaffected by weather. This brings up another issue.

Removing Barriers in Construction Labor Markets

In 1970, the average hourly manufacturing wage was $3.36. The average hourly construction industry wage was $5.22. By 1971, the two figures were $3.63 and $6.39, respectively. In 1971, building laborers earned $4.91 an hour, painters $6.11, plasterers $6.56, carpenters $6.64, bricklayers $7.00, and electricians and plumbers $7.20. In part, such rates are due to the strong unions in the construction industry. We have already noted how building-trades unions have restricted the supply of labor into the construction industry. By insisting that construction work be done by skilled union craftsmen only, that it be done by age-old methods, and that relatively few apprentices be trained, construction workers have assured a relatively high demand for the skilled labor of relatively few. This has assured them high wages and has unnecessarily raised the cost of housing.[6] In part, however, the high wages result from the application of the Davis-Bacon Act of 1931, which requires contractors on federal projects to pay the highest union wage scales existing in the area. Thereby the highest union contract is spread throughout the industry if a lot of federally aided construction occurs.

In 1971, the government moved to hold down construction labor costs. At first, President Nixon appealed to management and union leaders in construction to devise a voluntary plan that would "seriously modify the wage-price spiral" in the industry. Then he suspended the Davis-Bacon Act. Finally, he used the authority of the Economic Stabilization Act of 1970 to set wage-price guidelines for construction via executive order. Wage increases were to be held to 6 percent (the 1961–68 average), violations being punished by injunction, $5,000 fines, and withdrawal of government contracts. In the future, all contracts were to be reviewed by craft dispute boards and a 12-member stabilization committee. This procedure was retained under Phase III of the Nixon anti-inflation program when most other price and wage controls were removed.

Challenges to racial discrimination by unions[7] and challenges to building codes can also be expected to moderate construction industry wages by raising the supply of construction workers.

[6] Note the obvious parallels to the medical profession discussed in Chapter 6.
[7] Discussed in the last section of Chapter 7.

Removing Barriers in Capital Markets

The construction of dwellings is a highly capital-intensive process. Large amounts of funds must be tied up during the period of construction and thereafter as well. If such funds are prevented from freely flowing into the construction industry, the supply of housing can be just as restricted as if all workers went on strike. Typically, the availability of housing funds is increased greatly by general monetary ease. On the other hand, this flow of funds into housing typically dries up completely in a period of monetary restraint, as was most recently evidenced in 1966 and from 1969 to 1970. The shortage occurs because many states have usury laws that set maximum interest rates chargeable on mortgages. The federal FHA and VA programs also set such maximums. When interest rates in general exceed these mortgage maximums, lenders cease to lend for this purpose and channel their funds into equivalent long-term investments like high-grade municipal bonds or Aaa corporate bonds that are not subject to maximum rates. Thus the housing industry tends to take the brunt of monetary restriction. (During the 1966 "credit crunch," housing starts fell by 314,000 from the previous year, during 1969–70 they fell by 76,000.)

In addition, in high-interest periods, demanders of housing funds tend to hold off, since mortgage contracts fix rates for extremely long periods, and it pays a borrower to make a contract when rates are low. There are also institutional restraints to financing some *types* of housing, such as factory-built housing. Normally, lenders have a first lien against land and a house in progress on the land. They lend at intervals as construction of a new house progresses on the site. Partial or finished factory housing not yet delivered to a final site, however, is treated as factory inventory. Financing for this type of housing has been very difficult to arrange, since the primary claimant in case of default has not been clearly established.

All these barriers could be removed. There is no need for setting maximum interest rates any more than for setting minimum wages. Indeed, in 1969, twelve states and the federal government raised mortgage maximum rates. The complete abolition of this barrier would forever eliminate the differential treatment of the housing market during periods of monetary restraint. Other institutional barriers could also be overcome. As in Europe, mortgage contracts could, for instance, specify rates that vary with the state of loanable funds markets.

A Final Note

In 1970, the median price of a new house was $27,000. Half of all families could not afford to pay more than $15,000. Can we expect that the policies discussed in this section—by tending to decrease the cost of land, materials, labor, and borrowed funds used in construction—will assure all families of decent housing?

In 1968, noted a presidential commission on urban housing, construction costs broke down as follows: 20 percent labor, 40 percent materials, 40 percent land, overhead costs, and profit. Housing occupancy costs are typically double what construction costs would indicate, because of maintenance, repair, utility, and property tax expenses. Thus even an unusually large cost saving per house of, say, 30 percent on labor, 30 percent on material, and 30 percent on other items (such as land, interest, and profit) could decrease occupancy costs by only 15 percent, not enough probably to bring a decent home to all. However, such gain from a more efficient operation of the housing market—*together with* a determined antipoverty policy, as discussed in Part Two—can be expected to make a standard quality home (in an environment of their choice) affordable by all families. This is so because antipoverty policies would give the present occupants of crowded, substandard, or segregated housing more money to spend, while policies to improve efficiency would give them the chance to demand housing in any location and the assurance that someone would supply decent housing at an affordable price.

LAND USE PLANNING

The operation of free markets can have unexpected and undesirable consequences, unless all market participants are made fully aware of and responsible for the costs of their actions. Such awareness is often lacking in housing markets. Individual decisions to buy or sell—each of which appears to be perfectly rational when made—can over time create overall consequences everyone deplores. They are produced when some costs of individual decisions have not been taken account of by the decision maker because they did not affect him personally at the time. They are *external* costs.

Undesirable Externalities

Consider the long-run effect of individual decisions to settle in the outlying areas of cities. Once-idyllic settings of small farms, vineyards, orchards, meadows, and woods are swallowed up by the inexorable march of ugly houses, complete with utility lines, TV antennas, and roaring lawn mowers. New highways serving these new settlements, like the touch of Midas, transform natural beauty into precious real estate, and before long into ugly commercial ribbon developments. There is no sense of community, just a dull sense of sameness everywhere. There is no downtown, just a random scattering of industrial, educational, medical, and government facilities. There must have been, people suddenly say, a better way.

Such things are bound to happen to some extent, for there are inevitable conflicts among people's economic, social, cultural, and aesthetic needs. But many conflicts could also be resolved by public *land-use planning*, by making people keenly aware of long-run consequences of their actions so that they make changes deliberately and for the better.

The Curse of Political Fragmentation

Such planning must necessarily be areawide. It cannot succeed as long as the political fragmentation of central city and suburban governments is not overcome by cooperation. Similar cooperation between city, state, and federal governments is needed. For example, planners at the local level must have power to use funds as they see fit. They cannot succeed as long as state or federal agencies prescribe how funds are to be used. A study revealed, for instance, that in 1970 the mayor of Oakland, California, had no control over 85 percent of federal funds being spent in his city.

Because of such problems, experiments were begun in 1970 in the model cities program in about a dozen cities: In some cases, the program was made city-wide rather than focused on a single poverty area, and was put completely under the control of the mayor. In other cases, mayors could set up programs in a specific area without advance federal approval; or mayors were given veto power over federal programs that did not fit well with the city's master plan.

Indeed, a master plan for the coordinated development of housing, business, and cultural opportunities throughout the ghettos, gray areas, and suburbs is a must if metropolitan areas are to be pleasant places to live. For instance, the suburban sprawl cannot be stopped—especially when antipoverty policies and a more efficient housing market cease to trap people in the ghettos—unless inner city living is made attractive. This certainly requires government action to provide greatly improved educational, cultural, and recreational facilities to everyone throughout the metropolitan area. Many metropolitan areas have developed master plans involving the *centers strategy.* Such a plan clusters offices, colleges, hospitals, shopping, and cultural facilities in a few planned centers of architectural distinction, located in both inner city and suburbs. They are to be endowed with common parking or mass transit facilities. Housing facilities are then to be developed all around each of these centers so as to make one such center easily accessible to everyone. To implement any such overall plan, however, a metropolitan *area* government would have to exist and be able to tax the entire population of the area. Yet the required cooperation among present governments has often not been forthcoming. Recent political reapportionment has made this ever more unlikely. Just as legislatures in the past were controlled by rural interests hostile to urban interests, they are now increasingly controlled by suburban interests hostile to inner-city interests. The "cornstalk brigade" has been replaced by the "crabgrass brigade." Quite possibly only a *federal* policy using economic incentives could overcome this problem.

Public Ownership and Renting of All Urban Land

The most drastic method might involve the assumption by the federal government of the ownership of all urban land. This land could then be leased for payment of a ground rent. Leases could be set for relatively short periods (perhaps twenty years) to allow changes in land use. Rents could be varied, for example, by charging more for the type of use the government wants to discourage, less for the type of use it wants to encourage. If a proposed land use imposes external costs, these could be made obvious to the user by an appropriately higher rent. If a user is willing to pay this, the use can be allowed, and the parties damaged by this can be reimbursed out of the rental payment.

Variable Taxes and Subsidies

The same control over urban land uses could be achieved by a system of taxes and subsidies imposed on present land owners, whether private or public. Undesirable land uses would be taxed, highly desirable ones would be subsidized. This would induce private or public land users to make adjustments in the type and location of their activities so as to get the best possible tax-subsidy deal. Again, the funds raised through taxes on undesirable uses could be used to compensate damaged parties. The funds needed to subsidize desirable land uses could be raised from benefited outside parties.

As a result, people would think twice about holding on to empty lots in an area plagued by severe housing shortage. They would think twice about squandering scarce inner-city land on huge cemeteries. A highway department would think twice before running a road through a park or historic buildings. Suburban governments would think twice about zoning in single-family large-lot homes and zoning out apartment houses. Developers would think twice about leapfrogging tracts of raw land to find cheaper lots while imposing additional costs on government for extending systems of sanitation and transport to ever more remote areas. All these undesirable land uses would be allowed, but they would be subject to heavy taxation.

Similarly, those engaging in desirable activities, such as putting up apartment housing in suburban locations near jobs, or renovating inner-city housing, or creating urban parks would be rewarded through subsidies.

This sort of thing is not entirely new. It has been tried, but only sporadically. For example, the federal government has been subsidizing the creation of urban parks to be created on "rooftops, vacant lots, school grounds, and streets." Some states and cities (such as New York) have granted property tax exemptions or partial rebates for some housing (such as low-income public housing and single-family homes). Some cities (for example, Pittsburgh) have put heavier taxes on empty lots. Others have put heavier taxes on old and dilapidated buildings (for example, Southfield, Michigan).

Toward a National Land Use Policy

The types of policies just described would run into a hornet's nest of vested interests. One might therefore raise one's sights beyond existing metropolitan areas. These, after all, contain only 10 percent of the U.S. land area, although they do contain 69 percent of the population. In 1970, 49 percent of the

U.S. was still farmland, but contained only 5 percent of the population. By the end of this century, however, as many as 100 million new people might arrive on the scene. There is no need for them to live in present-day cities, and one might give thought to the construction of completely *new cities* in the *nonmetropolitan* areas of the present.

New cities. In 1969, the National Committee on Urban Growth (consisting of senators, representatives, governors, mayors, and county commissioners) proposed the building of 100 new cities for 100,000 people each and of 10 new cities for 1 million people each to accommodate about a quarter of the population growth expected by the end of this century. It referred to the creation of 28 "new towns" in Great Britain since 1945. It asked for long-term federal loans and grants to engage in similar *planned* endeavors.

Both Britain and Sweden have built "balanced" new cities to accommodate the growth of London, Glasgow, and Stockholm. The closest to this in the United States has been the construction of Columbia between Washington, D.C., and Baltimore. This racially and economically integrated new town had 20,000 residents in 1972 and hoped to have 105,000 by 1980. It is being financed by some $80 million of private funds coming from such companies as Connecticut General Life, the Teachers Insurance and Annuity Association, and the Chase Manhattan Bank. Columbia has avoided the wholesale bulldozing so common in other developments, avoided the tight grids of look-alike tract houses, even banned above-ground utility lines, TV antennas, and individual mailboxes—not to mention billboards and McDonald's golden arches.[8] Instead, one downtown plus seven villages of 15,000 people are being developed, each with stream valleys, stately trees, open space, new lakes, walkways, and neighborhood clustering around a meeting hall, grade school, day care center, pool, and small shops. To repeat such ventures throughout the country, however, governmental prodding seems essential.

Federal inducements. The federal government could encourage such ventures by making grants for new towns on public lands, similar to the old land grants to the railroads. It could entice people to settle on undeveloped or federal surplus land (such as abandoned military installations).[9] This might be done via an "urban homestead act" similar to the one that won the West (giving public land free to families who settle on it). The government could also entice businesses to such places by channeling federal contracts on a priority basis to new cities. In 1970, the U.S. government took the first step toward

[8] Notice the opportunity cost involved here: the construction of aesthetically pleasing housing, as by avoiding look-alike tract houses, would presumably also mean higher construction costs. This would run counter to the desire by some—referred to above—of encouraging lower construction costs by revising building codes that outlaw look-alike housing.

[9] It has been suggested that "new towns in town" be developed at such places as New York's Brooklyn Navy Yard, Washington's Fort Lincoln, Salt Lake City's Fort Douglas, or San Francisco's Fort Funston.

developing new cities when it agreed to guarantee loans for beginning new towns near Minneapolis (Jonathan), near Dallas (Flower Mound), near Little Rock (Maumelle), in Illinois (Park Forest South) and in Maryland (Saint Charles). Jonathan is to have a population of 50,000 in 1990. This commitment (for $21 million) was the first under the New Communities Section of the 1968 Housing Act, which authorized such guarantees up to $250 million.

The 1970 Housing Act authorized the establishment of *community development corporations.* They are to guarantee up to $500 million of loans provided by private lenders to private or public community developers. (For private developers, 80 percent of the land cost and 90 percent of other costs can be guaranteed; for public developers, 100 percent.) These corporations can also make $24 million in direct 15-year loans to cover interest payments of private borrowers, according to the act (Congress did not appropriate funds, however). These corporations are further authorized to make grants (of $36 million in 1971, $66 million each in 1972 and 1973) to new communities for constructing public facilities (mass transit, schools, libraries), plus additional grants for public hiring (of teachers, nurses, policemen) and for community planning. Finally, the corporations can build new towns as demonstration projects on federal land.

In 1971, the federal government announced a national land use policy. It urges the states to develop land-planning and conservation programs by mid-1974. Each program would inventory, designate, and control (1) land of critical environmental concern, such as shorelands and river floodplains, and (2) land with key facilities, such as airports, highway exchanges, and parks. Thereby all prime commercial property would come under state control. Each program would also assure that local regulations do not restrict regional land-use plans, and it would control large-scale developments, such as in and around new towns. To provide incentives for such programs, states with federally approved plans are to receive in 1975 and thereafter 7 percent of federal highway, airport, and conservation funds that would be withdrawn from states without plans. This redistribution is to increase each year up to a total of 35 percent.

The effect. By 1971, additional new towns were being developed on the Pocono plateau in northeastern Pennsylvania (for 250,000 people), in Kentucky (Midland for 100,000), in North Carolina (Soul City for 50,000), in Lucas County, Ohio (for 50,000), and also near Minneapolis (Cedar River), and near Buffalo, Rochester, and Syracuse in New York. Meanwhile, the states have increasingly diminished the zoning powers of local governments, which mostly received them in the 1920's from the states in a series of "zoning enabling acts." By 1972, Colorado, Florida, Hawaii, Maine, Oregon, and Vermont had state zoning laws affecting large developments (in Vermont "anything over ten acres or above 2,500 feet elevation") and developments bound to have significant environmental impact. This would include developments of shorelands (like Florida's keys or cypress swamps), scenic areas (like

San Francisco Bay, Lake Tahoe, and New York's Adirondack Park, all of which are regulated by regional commissions), and big commercial undertakings (like Florida's 27,500-acre Walt Disney World or the 17,000-acre Dallas–Fort Worth jetport).

Summary

1. Data from the 1970 census do not reveal a physical housing shortage. The number of families and unrelated individuals fell short of the number of existing dwelling units overall, as well as in central cities and suburbs taken separately.
2. Nevertheless, a housing problem existed. This is so because some dwelling units were crowded or dilapidated or lacked plumbing or were situated in undesirable environments. Thus not every dwelling unit provided the same number of housing service units. Many people received an inadequate number of such units. In addition, racial minorities suffered disproportionately from this state of affairs.
3. The demand for housing in cities has been rising. If housing markets were perfectly competitive, increased demand would raise housing prices in the short run, but by this very fact increase housing supply in the long run. This process has frequently been short-circuited by the imposition of rent controls and the existence of other market imperfections.
4. These conditions have set in motion a process of low construction, overcrowding, undermaintenance, and finally dilapidation, abandonment, and slum formation. In addition, racial discrimination practiced by suburban residents has trapped racial minorities in these undesirable dwelling units and forced them to pay more than whites for equal-quality housing or to pay the same for lower-quality housing.
5. The housing policies favored by governments have so far involved raising the private demand for housing, presumably in the belief that increased demand would stimulate private construction. It has, but mostly the construction of single-family homes for moderate- to high-income families outside the central cities. The gain to low-income families has come through the process of filtering. Thus the policy of raising private demand has strengthened residential segregation by income.
6. The main demand-raising policies involve tax breaks (allowing deductions from gross income of mortgage interest and property taxes, accelerated depreciation provisions, and failure to tax imputed rent), mortgage insurance or guarantees, public borrowing and relending, cash subsidies to reduce interest costs (all of which increase the availability and lower the cost of loanable funds), and rent supplements.
7. There is no guarantee in the imperfect housing market that mere increases in demand bring forth corresponding increases in supply. The government has, therefore, supplemented demand-raising with supply-raising policies such as public housing construction and urban renewal. Neither has been very successful.

8. Another supply-raising strategy involves removal of market imperfections. Rents could be decontrolled, restrictive zoning and building codes abolished, mass production encouraged, and barriers in construction labor markets and in capital markets removed. Such moves would decrease the cost of land, materials, labor, and borrowed funds used in construction and thus raise the quantity of housing supplied at any given price.
9. The operation of unrestrained markets in housing, together with antipoverty policies, can be expected to eliminate the housing problem. It can also, however, have undesirable long-run effects if housing market decisions involve benefits or costs external to individual decision makers. To guard against such undesirable consequences of private decisions as the indiscriminate gobbling up of beautiful countryside by ugly suburbs, government can bring these consequences to the attention of people.
10. A remedy can be effected via metropolitan areawide planning by cooperating governments, involving master plans and the use of economic incentives inducing people to conform to such plans. Such incentives might be based on public ownership and renting of all urban land (with rents being adjusted according to land use) or on a system of variable taxes and subsidies.
11. An alternative strategy for avoiding undesirable social consequences of private decisions might involve a national land use policy encouraging the planning and construction of new cities and also the planning of land use outside cities. A number of such new cities are under development.

Terms[10]

building codes
centers strategy
community development corporations
crowded dwelling unit
dilapidated dwelling unit
dwelling unit
externalities
filtering process
fiscal zoning
housing service unit
modular house
new towns
political fragmentation
rent controls
slum
substandard dwelling unit
urban renewal
zoning laws

Symbols

FHA
FNMA
GNMA
HUD
VA

[10] Terms and symbols are defined in the Glossary at the back of the book.

Questions for Review and Discussion

1. In 1966 among central city residents, only 5 percent of whites lived in dilapidated housing, while 30 percent of nonwhites did. At the same time, whites spent less than 25 percent of their income on housing, while a third of the nonwhites spent more than 35 percent. Can you explain this?
2. In a special message to the Massachusetts state legislature, Governor Sargent in 1970 called for the enactment of an "emergency" measure authorizing towns and cities across the state to legislate rent controls. The Connecticut general assembly voted a similar measure in 1969. On the other hand, a mayoral committee in New York City reported in 1969 that the rent control system was partly to blame for the housing shortage and slum formation. It proposed that government subsidize higher rents to give owners the ability to maintain houses better. Whose advice should we follow?
3. The Civil Rights Act of 1968, the federal open-housing law, says, "It shall be unlawful, for profit, to induce or attempt to induce any person to sell or rent any dwelling by representations regarding the entry or prospective entry into the neighborhood of a person or persons of a particular race, color, religion, or national origin." This was to stop the practice of blockbusting, the exploitation of fears of a racially changing neighborhood in order to sell real estate. For minority groups, though, isn't blockbusting a good idea? It gives them housing that wouldn't otherwise be available.
4. "Federal government tax laws and FHA and VA programs help middle- and upper-income families accumulate wealth in the form of housing by providing low-interest loans, tax breaks, and a disciplined savings program coupled with a low-risk investment. In 1969, for instance, when the average price of homes mortgaged under the programs was $20,000, the lucky families involved could count on owning assets worth $20,000 some 25 years hence. All they had to do was make their monthly payments. Given appreciation over time, they could expect to own $40,000 or more. Families not owning their homes got no such help. Even if they saved the same amounts per month for 25 years, they were less likely to get as far ahead because other types of investment require more knowledge and sophistication on the part of the investor and were not favored by the tax laws. This is unfair." Evaluate.
5. "That the federal government is coming into ownership of so much decaying housing in inner cities should be applauded rather than lamented. If such land is accumulated in large plots, it could be used for creating parks, new communities, new homes." Evaluate.
6. "The federal government should become the 'houser of last resort,' building houses directly wherever private industry fails to provide decent housing for all." What do you think of this contention and what are your reasons for so thinking?
7. Mr. A: Urban renewal should be used as a tool to stop the racial and economic separation of citizens, to help exorcise the specter of increasing apartheid, where the blacks and the poor live in urban centers and the white and well-to-do in the suburbs.

   Mr. B: That is indeed what urban renewal has done. It should be called

> "Negro removal" and it should be resisted. Attempts to get blacks to scatter all over the suburbs are really attempts to break up the political power blacks are acquiring in central cities.

Evaluate.

8. "There is no guarantee that urban renewal is carried on to an optimum degree. The opposite is more likely to happen, because local governments make decisions on the basis of comparing *all* the benefits with *one-third* of the costs of projects (since the federal government makes them a gift of two-thirds of the cost)." Do you agree? How would you find the optimum? (Review Chapter 1 on the principle of optimization.)
9. In recent years, racial and ethnic minorities have begun to move to the suburbs. This has been the result of zoning changes, higher incomes, and enforcement of the Fair Housing Act. The arrival of the first blacks in the suburbs has been greeted in a variety of ways, ranging from harassment (in Detroit) to riots (in Philadelphia) to qualified success (in Willingboro, N.J., where developers provided free appliances to whites moving next to blacks). Everywhere whites have feared for their property values. To their surprise, housing values in integrated suburbs have risen and *more* than the national average. Can you explain it?
10. "The government could easily maintain the flow of funds into housing even in periods of monetary restraint and in the presence of maximum interest rates. It could simply require pension funds and mutual funds to invest a minimum percentage of their portfolios in residential mortgages. Or it could *induce* them to do so by making mortgage-interest income tax-exempt." Evaluate this proposal.
11. "There are externalities to private housing market decisions, for example, the effect on the value of a house by its neighborhood that may make an owner decide not to improve a dwelling. Urban renewal is a way of dealing with these externalities." Explain.
12. Housing Secretary Romney proposed Operation TACLE (Total American Community Living Environment) to spur metropolitanwide planning. The federal government would channel high-priority financing to winners of a national competition of planning for social and economic urban problem solving. The president, however, did not buy the idea. Would you? Why or why not?
13. The text suggests the public ownership and renting of all urban land as a method of coping with undesirable land uses. How might such a policy stop inner-city decay? or suburban sprawl?
14. "The government should hold all undeveloped land in reserve for later use. This would eliminate totally unnecessary windfall gains to private holders which make later uses costly. For instance, in Philadelphia, the city could have acquired land at $1,350 per acre in 1945. Had it held the land for 17 years, it could have sold it for $3,250 per acre and recovered an annual 5 percent holding cost. Land in 1962 sold for $10,250 an acre. No wonder the provision of proper schools, housing, parks, and transport facilities is too costly." Discuss.
15. Congress mandated in 1970 that the president prepare a biennial report to

assist in the development of a national urban growth policy. Yet in 1972, President Nixon played down the desirability of such a report, stating that he was against any policy "dictating where and how citizens will live and work." Evaluate the president's attitude. Isn't there a difference between dictating to people and providing economic incentives that cajole them into behaving in socially desirable ways? Isn't the very distinction between a centrally planned economy and a market economy one of coercing people either by the stick method or by the carrot method, coercion itself being inevitable?

Selected Readings

Case, Frederick E., ed. *Inner-City Housing and Private Enterprise.* New York: Praeger, 1972. Discusses the housing problem in nine selected cities: Atlanta, Baltimore, Fresno, Indianapolis, Los Angeles, Memphis, Newark, Oakland, and San Diego.

Edel, Matthew, and Rothenberg, Jerome. *Readings in Urban Economics.* New York: Macmillan, 1972. Parts 3 and 4. Discusses housing problems, with special emphasis on technical studies, as on filtering, segregation, redevelopment benefits, property values, and race. Note the bibliography on pp. 177, 249, and 250.

Gordon, David M. *Problems in Political Economy: An Urban Perspective.* Lexington, Mass.: D. C. Heath and Co., 1971. Pp. 355–407. Presents conservative, liberal, and radical views on housing problems, programs, and redevelopment, and also an excellent bibliography.

Hirsch, Werner Z. *Urban Economic Analysis.* New York: McGraw-Hill, 1973. Ch. 3. Discusses frameworks and models of household residential location, housing market imperfections, and policy approaches to combat neighborhood degradation, racial segregation, and sprawl.

U.S. Bureau of the Census. *Statistical Abstract of the United States, 1972.* Washington, D.C., 1972. Lists some statistics on housing and the construction industry (Sections 27 and 33), and—more important—sources to other statistics: Note the listing of statistical abstract supplements (p. v); and the guide to general sources of statistics (pp. 914–15), to recent censuses (p. 956) and to state statistical abstracts (pp. 961–64). Suggestion: Find out all you can about your home town from the 1970 Census of Housing.

NOTE: The *Journal of Economic Literature* lists recent articles on financial markets, including mortgage markets (sections 313 and 315), the construction industry (634), the economics of housing (932), land use (717), and the economics of discrimination (917).

The *Index of Economic Articles* catalogs in sections beginning with the indicated numbers articles on mortgage markets (9.48), property taxes (10.43 and 22.5), rent control (13.42, 13.75, 15.442), the construction industry (15.55), land use (17.3), consumer housing expenditures (20.23), zoning and redevelopment (22.3), and the economics of housing, including demand, supply, and government policies (22.5).

12 *The Transportation Problem*

Since World War II veritable miracles have been wrought in American transportation. In particular, interstate highways and the jet have revolutionized transportation among cities. By 1972, only 4,962 miles of a planned 42,500-mile network of superhighways were not yet under construction, while 33,796 miles of the system were complete. Part of this vast project is Interstate 95, a planned 1,866-mile "Main Street" of the East Coast, reaching from Maine to Florida. Although started in 1956, by 1970 the construction of this road was stalled at 16 large cities, including Boston, Philadelphia, Baltimore, and Washington, D.C. The delay was no coincidence, for the cities themselves are literally choking in traffic and its associated problems. City governments, which have spent more than $3 billion a year on urban highways in the 1960's, have become disenchanted with inviting more traffic and more of its associated problems by spending more still. More traffic is exactly what building more highways brings, experience has shown. Take the most obvious problem, *road congestion.* It is a situation in which there are so many cars on a road at any one time that average speed has to drop, and then the number of cars traversing the road in any given time period falls below its possible maximum. The construction of highways in and around cities appears to invite a situation of road congestion. The moment a highway is finished, it seems to lure people into living even farther out in the countryside. It is as if the supply of a new highway instantaneously created its own demand by creating another wave of suburbanites who crowd the new highways beyond capacity from opening day.

There are many reasons why such new emigrants come back to the city. Many still have jobs there. Suburban wives go shopping. Families visit the city for recreation. *And they come in their own cars.* The more highways are built, and the more people move, the more serious the traffic of people coming back into the center for relatively short periods of time. Before you know it, traffic congestion develops. This gets particularly bad where various types of traffic meet, as at airports. The Civil Aeronautics Board reported in 1969 the "complete saturation" of five airports: John F. Kennedy International, Newark, and La Guardia (serving New York), plus Washington National and Chicago O'Hare International. A similar state was predicted for 1975 for airports in

Atlanta, Boston, Miami, Los Angeles, and San Francisco. The congestion problem involves in this case saturation by planes of airspace, runways, taxiways, aprons, and parking areas, as well as insufficient parking for cars and inadequate highway approaches.

In the city centers, mammoth parking problems also appear together with mammoth traffic flows. In New York City in 1970, for example, 1.5 million vehicles entered the city on the average day from the outside to join 1.7 million vehicles stationed within. Some 45 municipal parking facilities and 5,000 private parking lots and garages were overflowing. Parking violations, ranging from double and triple parking to defacing "No Parking" signs with spray paint, ran up to 150 million a year. However, only 4 million tickets were issued and only 104,000 cars were towed for lack of both police manpower and storage facilities. A Traffic Action Committee noted the same conditions in late 1972.

Nor can people escape road congestion by abandoning cars for mass transit. It often is not available where it is wanted. Even though in the 1960's more than $200 million a year was spent on urban mass transit and thousands of new buses and subway cars replaced almost all older fleets as a result, dissatisfaction continues widespread. In city after city, year after year, bus, subway, and commuter railroad companies find the numbers of passengers dwindling, operating costs rising, and deficits becoming a way of life. So they curtail or even end service or they fail to improve its quality.

THE NATURE OF THE PROBLEM

An important aspect of the urban transportation problem is the prevalence of congestion.

Congestion

Consider the congestion of roads and parking places. Too many people are trying to use these facilities at the same time, for too many people choose use of the automobile over mass transit. Consider the typical surface travel patterns in urban areas. More than 90 percent of all vehicular travel occurs by private car. The remainder of vehicular travel—the overall importance of which shrinks in comparison—involves private or government-run *public transport*, mainly taxis and mass transit (buses, subways, streetcars, and railroads). In analyzing this unequal use of private cars and other means of transport, we find that private cars and other means compete with each other, but not for all people and all purposes.

Some people, notably low-income central city residents, if they travel at all, have no choice but to use public transport facilities. They provide a captive market. Other people, notably middle- and higher-income urban residents, could and do use either private or public transport.

The choice made by middle- and higher-income people depends entirely on the purpose of travel. As it turns out, for trips not related to work, they use private cars almost exclusively. This is not surprising, for such trips are concentrated neither in time nor in direction. A flexible means of transport is required for nonwork-related trips, and the private car has a technical advantage over any type of rigidly routed mass transit. Nonwork trips include trips from the city to suburban and rural locations and back for purposes of shopping and recreation. These trips tend to be spread over the typical day and over a large area and cause congestion only when they bunch up, as on weekends and holidays or in summer vacation time, when people go swimming or skiing or camping, attend ball games or special shows, or turn into tourists.

Only for trips to and from work by nonpoor residents do private and public transport compete actively. While in urban areas only 1 percent of nonwork-related trips are made on public transport facilities, 20 percent of work trips are so made (even 50 percent in New York City). Furthermore, these trips tend to be concentrated in a *few hours* each day, and they tend to be made along a *few routes*, as from the suburbs to the central business district, where every auto commuter tries to park in the same place. Considerable congestion ensues—work trips account for more than half of urban travel, and transport facilities (whether roads or rail) are simply not large enough to accommodate *rush-hour* traffic. As a result, things slow down, and urban auto commuters must pay extra fuel costs and are robbed of precious leisure. They spend, as the Department of Transportation found in 1969, 13 percent of their waking hours in traffic. Thus we conclude that one aspect of the urban transportation problem is the congestion of roads and mass transport facilities *at certain times* of the day, week, or year. Not only roads, railroads, subways, and buses are affected, but also other facilities such as airports and parking places. There are many times of the day (or night) when even the busiest airport or parking garage becomes deserted. Thus congestion is not an ever present phenomenon. Nor is it the only transportation problem.

Externalities

The massive use of private cars in and around cities creates many other problems. Most important, such use imposes costs on many who are not even using private cars; and car users escape the responsibility of paying all of these costs.

Accidents. In 1970, motor vehicles caused 55,000 accidental deaths and injured an additional 5.1 million people in the United States. Society is thereby forced to divert resources to the furnishing of medical, legal, and insurance services. Victims incur huge losses of health, property, and income. In 1967, for instance, the average fatal accident imposed $2,281 in medical bills and property loss plus an additional $87,242 in loss of expected future income. Certainly, no one reimburses the families of fatal accident victims for income loss; much less can anyone assuage the mental anguish they have to bear alone. Also in 1967, the average total loss for seriously injured auto accident victims was $8,290.

Neighborhood breakup. The construction of urban highways also creates serious barriers to social interaction. First of all, consider the obvious physical obstacle such a highway may place in the middle of a neighborhood. Partition reduces many of the social contacts that create neighborhood cohesion by reducing seriously the accessibility of some homes and businesses. Even where across-highway movement is possible between the two severed sides (as where highways are elevated or where pedestrian bridges are part of their design), the highway forms a visual and psychological barrier between people on the two sides.

Additional injury may be caused by the drastic change in traffic patterns after a highway is completed. Entire streets full of small stores and cafés may suddenly turn into a depressed area. Or they may turn into feeder streets for the big highway, with enormous increases in traffic load. This change, too, becomes a barrier between people living there. The stores and cafés where they used to meet are going bankrupt, the sidewalks on which they used to walk are inundated with noise and fumes. So people stay home.

Finally, many people's homes and businesses are physically destroyed by highway projects. They have to leave the old ncighborhood altogether and may never find another job. In recent years, an average of 60,000 people were so displaced. Three-quarters of these lived in urban areas, and most were middle- and low-income people, often of racial and ethnic minorities. Their numbers reflect the efforts of highway planners who route new roads through old, dilapidated neighborhoods rather than expensive newer ones where upper-income families are likely to live or do business. In addition, highway planners love to route roads through parks, along rivers or lakefronts, or through historic or cultural buildings. This avoids residential displacement, but imposes on people the additional burden of having to exchange the very few recreational areas left in cities for ugly highway structures. (As a result, in late 1972, an unusual coalition of wealthy whites and militant blacks existed, who in 32 federal lawsuits were battling the continuation of interstate highways into cities. Among the affected areas were Overton Park in Memphis, Brackenridge Park in San Antonio, Shaker Lakes in Cleveland, the Hudson River Expressway in New York, the Three Sisters Bridge in Washington, D.C., and the French quarter of New Orleans.)

Environmental damages. We just noted the noise and fumes created by increased traffic in a neighborhood. These factors affect entire urban areas and indeed rural areas far beyond. Their impact on property as well as on plant, animal, and human life is exceedingly serious.[1] To name just a few of these effects, consider how increased pollution will force some people to spend more of their income on painting their houses or cleaning their clothes; how it will force them to spend more on medical doctors, drugs, or air-conditioners to preserve their health; how the noise will drive them to psychiatrists; how they

[1] This impact is described at length in Appendix A to Chapter 13.

will have to travel farther to find clean, quiet vacation spots; how they will have to buy more expensive food grown farther away and shipped in because plants won't grow in the polluted atmosphere near cities; and how their taxes go up when the run-off from salted roads poisons municipal water supplies.

Other effects. There is almost no end to the effects caused by the construction of highways to accommodate the desire for private car use. While businesses in some areas are physically destroyed or pushed on the way to bankruptcy, and their land values plunge, other businesses spring up and flourish near important new interchanges, and land values skyrocket there. The process is accelerated as every inch of new highway takes more land off the tax rolls and causes city governments to levy heavier taxes on remaining homes and businesses. (By 1980, Los Angeles will have 34 square miles of freeways, an area equal to the total size of Miami.) The tax hikes caused by highway building accelerate the exodus of people from central cities. One result among others is that the number of customers of mass transit companies becomes reduced and such companies find business unprofitable. As they reduce service, those dependent on mass transit are trapped in places where they live and cannot find jobs. This increases the city government's need for funds to pay unemployment or welfare benefits. The city then raises taxes some more, only to reinforce the vicious circle. Incidentally, the lack of mass transit facilities affects those living in suburbs as well. Note the growth of a new involuntary servant class, the suburban housewives. If they want their children to visit friends, make that dental appointment, or take their music lessons, there is no choice for the mothers but to become involuntary chauffeurs. Indeed, most of the chief new concerns of urban areas, such as the decline of central cities and the concentration of poor people in them, the mushrooming of suburbs with their peculiar life style, and the ruin of lovely countryside by them—all these have been caused in no small degree by auto and highway.[2]

THE ROOT OF THE PROBLEM

Now we must ask a question. *Why* do people prefer to use the private car over mass transit even though the social costs of that choice seem to outweigh the benefits? The answer is simple. *Users of transport facilities are not confronted with the social costs.* The private cost of automobile use, for instance, is far below the social cost. The use of roads, mass transit, and parking facilities is incorrectly priced. As a result, inefficient use is made of existing facilities.

Recall at this time some of the lessons of Chapter 2. To be correct, prices of all scarce things—fish, meat, or the services of roads or of mass transit facilities—must be such that all willing buyers can get and all willing sellers can get rid of all they wish at this price. *They must be equilibrium prices.* As was shown in Figure 2.3, "How a Market Discriminates," any price other than

[2] Many of these matters were discussed in Chapter 3.

this equilibrium price would be a mockery to some seller (who would find no buyer at an above-equilibrium price) or to some buyer (who would find no seller at a below-equilibrium price). More than that. For the sake of efficiency, *prices would have to equal marginal costs.* As was illustrated in Figure 2.6, "Efficiency through Selfishness," a rational household can be expected to allocate its income among various quantities of goods in such a way that the ratio of marginal benefits of any two goods equals the ratio of prices of those goods. If this equality did not exist, he would buy more of one good and less of another and be better off. Thus someone who wants to maximize his well-being, who is well-informed on market opportunities and is free to buy what he wishes (there are no artificial obstructions to his buying, and prices are not a mockery but at equilibrium), and who is observed buying (among other things) meat for $1 per pound and road services for 1 cent a mile can be assumed to get the same marginal benefit from a pound of meat as from using 100 miles of road. If he did not, but he preferred, say, 1 pound of meat to the privilege of driving over a 100-mile stretch of road, he would have driven 100 miles less, saved $1, spent it on 1 pound of meat and been better off.

Now observe the implications of relative prices that do *not* reflect marginal cost: Suppose the marginal cost of 1 lb of meat (priced at $1) equaled $1, but that of driving over a 100-mile stretch of road (priced $1) equaled $30. In this case it would be possible to save $30 of resources whenever someone chose not to drive 100 miles. These resources might be saved in a great variety of ways: less in labor, materials, and equipment used for road repairs ($1); less used for dealing with accidents ($7); less used for dealing with neighborhood breakup ($13); less used for coping with air pollution ($9). Thus driving 100 miles less would allow production of $30 of other goods, say 30 lb of meat. Our friend, who valued 1 lb of meat the same as a 100-mile drive, would clearly prefer 30 lb of meat to driving 100 miles. Yet as long as he is asked to pay (correctly) $1 for 1 lb of meat as well as (incorrectly) $1 for the 100-mile drive, he has no reason to change his behavior. Even if objectively there is a way to make him better off, the price system—working imperfectly—fails to tell him about it. Thus the opportunity is lost. Resources are inefficiently allocated, leaving some people worse off than they have to be.

There are further consequences tending to reinforce the inefficiency. When people consuming goods make inefficient choices (because prices lie to them about true social costs and thus about the rates at which one type of good can be transformed into another), suppliers tend to make wrong decisions, too, for example on the question of investing in new facilities. Their providers have no guidance for investment, as would be provided in a perfectly working price system. If all transportation services were correctly priced, profits or losses would indicate which service should be expanded or contracted.[3] When

[3] Recall the discussion of this point in Chapter 2 in the section dealing with the short-run and long-run consequences of an increased demand for bread.

users do not pay correct prices that cover the marginal social cost of providing the service in question, however, no such guidance for investment exists. Indeed, such decisions have been made on the basis of considerations other than market profitability. Let us pursue this in more detail.

Incorrect Pricing of Road Use

Consider the costs imposed on society when a highway is produced and put into use.

Types of costs. First, there is the original cost of construction, including acquisition of land, purchase of materials, and use of equipment and labor during construction. The sum involved typically is borrowed by the party constructing the road and the value of this typically is amortized, together with interest, over a long period, perhaps forty years. But there are other costs that occur year after year as long as the highway exists. There is, second, the obvious one of maintaining and repairing the road, as vehicle use and weather begin to produce wear and tear. There are, third, further costs of associated services for assuring the usefulness of the road, ranging from cleaning, snowplowing, and lighting to policing and highway administration. Fourth, as long as the road exists, society is forgoing the use for other purposes of the land on which the road is built (except, perhaps, for laying water, gas, electric and telephone lines under or along it). Society ought to make a proper rental charge equal to the best alternative output value that might have been obtained on this land. Fifth, the existence of the road is imposing all the external costs, as discussed in the preceding section.

How users pay. Do road users pay for all this? They typically do not pay for external costs. Thus individual road users see no reason to refrain from doing what obviously hurts lots of people in lots of ways. They also do not pay rent. Thus individual road users see no reason to refrain from asking for ever more highways gobbling up ever more precious land. This cost is not brought to their attention. Road users do not directly and fully pay all of the operating expenses. For example, note how policing costs are defrayed out of general taxes levied on users and nonusers alike. Thus road users are not aware—as they use roads—of these costs they (and others) pay for road use. This is exceedingly bad. Even the costs that users (and users alone) do pay are paid *indirectly* and are typically levied on all users *uniformly*, regardless of time and place of use, even though costs vary with time and place of use.

Highway users *as a group* do pay for the construction and maintenance of road systems as a whole. Although some direct payment is exacted from road users on occasion in the form of tolls (especially where bridges, tunnels, and ferries are involved), most highways are offered free to users at the time of use. The government monopoly providing these facilities collects typically construction and maintenance funds indirectly, as by license fees, vehicle taxes, and taxes on gasoline. In 1971, state and federal taxes on gasoline amounted to 10 cents per gallon. Since cars drive well over 10 miles per gallon, this tax translates into an indirect payment of less than 1 cent a mile for road use.

How users should pay. One can argue that, first, road users ought to pay for *all* the costs associated with the provision of road services. That is, they should bear not just construction and repair costs but also the other costs mentioned above. Just as buyers of meat pay a price containing a component of rent for the use of scarce land as pastures, so road users should pay a price containing a component of rent for the use of scarce land for roads. The same reasoning holds for the other costs we enumerated. There is no more justification for consumers of road services passing on the costs of snowplowing or police or hospitals to the general taxpayer than for consumers of meat passing on the costs of cattle ranchers or meat cutters or refrigerated railroad cars to the general taxpayer. Equally unjustified is the refusal by anyone, whether road user or general taxpayer, to pay certain costs at all, such as the costs of air pollution that others have to bear.

There is, second, a good reason for making road users pay the costs *directly* (at the time and place of use), rather than indirectly (at the time of purchasing gasoline, licenses, and so on), the reason being that these costs are not uniform. If urban highways were used at a uniform rate in all areas and at all times, a uniform price per mile would be justified. However, over 20 percent of urban road travel occurs in a few peak hours in a few dominant directions. The size of urban highway systems is planned so as to be capable of meeting a normal weekday's peak-hour demand on the assumption that no direct toll is charged. The planning implies that a reduction or increase in the number of peak-time users would allow a reduction, or require an increase, in the size of the highway system and its total construction cost. A change in the number of off-peak users would have no such effect. Because of the necessity for accommodating peak demand, the numbers of roads, lanes, ramps, traffic control devices, policemen, snowplows, lights, and even traffic courts would have to be the same even in the absence of *any* off-peak users. The opportunity cost of land tied up in road systems and many of the externalities of the system would be the same, too. There follows an important conclusion.

Since total road costs are (essentially) unaffected by adding or subtracting non-peak users (except perhaps only some costs of wear and tear, accidents, and pollution) the marginal opportunity cost of road use by non-peak drivers is *close to zero.* So also should be the price they pay. By the same token, peak users as a group should pay close to the *entire* cost involved—because correct pricing must indicate to any user the *marginal* opportunity cost of his action. Such correct price, in effect, says to the potential buyer: "This is what people throughout society must give up if you buy another unit of this good. If you are willing to reimburse them all for their added losses, you may get that extra unit." Since peak users should pay close to 100 percent of the cost and since they constitute 20 percent of users, correct pricing in effect requires that 20 percent of urban road users pay close to 100 percent of costs. Since they now pay 20 percent of a *fraction* of the total cost (covering construction, maintenance, and some operating expenses only), they should pay well over five times the amount now paid. Non-peak users should pay substantially less than peak users, but possibly more than they are now paying.

Since at present everyone using highways pays practically the same amount, whether driving at night or during the day, in the country or in the city, during the rush hour or not, some drivers are effectively subsidizing other drivers. Those driving a country road at night and those using urban roads in off-peak hours or directions (and who should pay no part of construction and associated costs), support, via license, vehicle, gasoline, and general taxes, others who drive urban roads during the rush hour (and should pay all of these costs). Those who suffer from the externalities of roads (and who should be compensated by road users) similarly subsidize peak road users a great deal and others somewhat less—because the actions of peak users determine the size of road systems and most of their associated externalities. Thus the price for using roads during the rush hour in dominant directions should include not only money for the cement and equipment and labor used to construct, maintain, and operate the roads, but also compensation for the loss of alternative land uses, for the loss of limbs and life and income, for the loss of neighborhoods, for extra cleaning bills and costlier vacations, for more expensive grocery bills, and for loss of jobs! Similarly, the price of using roads during other times should come to reflect the lower marginal social costs of additional wear and tear, accidents, and air pollution. Only then would auto users know the true costs of their actions. Quite possibly, urban road use would come to 30 cents a mile during peak hours and 3 cents a mile at other times! Nor is this the whole story.

Incorrect Pricing of Parking Space

Most cities treat parking space on public land, notably on streets, as a free good or something close to it. Public off-street parking lots and garages are typically subsidized from general tax revenues either directly or by being tax-exempt. The principle is incorrect, as evidenced by the demand for parking space that in many areas and at many times greatly exceeds the supply at current prices (which are zero or very low).

Bad effects. Residents, workers, shoppers, and delivery trucks alike scramble for the too few spaces. In urban areas, as much as a third of traffic consists of *mobile parking* (cars circling the block for a parking space). Many who claim a superior need (such as doctors, diplomats, press correspondents, and delivery trucks) habitually end up parking illegally. This increases traffic congestion, causes accidents, and hampers street cleaning and fire fighting. Under the system of first come–first served, early arrivals and long-term parkers (that is, workers) are given an advantage, but they do not necessarily need parking space the most and might better be encouraged to use mass transit. Some cities try to discourage longer-term parking by posting time limits for parking, but this is neither helpful nor wise. It is not helpful because it tends to increase the turnover on any given parking spot, thereby increasing traffic congestion in the streets. It is not wise because not all longer-term parkers are undeserving. The refusal to correctly price public on-street parking facilities, the supply of which is practically unchangeable, has further repercussions on off-street parking facilities, the supply of which could be increased. Private enterprise is at least discouraged from providing such facilities in the face of low-price public competition. As in the case of roads, one can expect a solution to parking congestion only after people change their behavior when confronted with correct prices.

Incorrect Pricing of Mass Transit

What has been said about pricing of road use and parking can in many ways also be said for the pricing of services provided by mass transit facilities.

How users pay. Mass transit users as a group, unlike private road users, pay for only 80 percent of expenditures for constructing, maintaining, and operating the facilities involved, the difference being made up by public subsidies or private company losses. As in the case of roads, mass transit users ignore externalities associated with this mode of transport. Users of mass transit typically pay a fare that is *uniform* regardless of time and place of use. This can again be shown to be unjustified.

How users should pay. As much as 80 percent of urban mass transit use occurs in peak hours and in dominant directions. The size of facilities is planned so as to accommodate a normal weekday's peak-hour demand at the current fare. Since the total number of tracks, vehicles, stations, crews, and so forth would have to be the same even if all off-peak travelers disappeared, the marginal cost of their use of the system is near zero (except perhaps only costs of wear and tear and fuel). Also near zero should be their fare. What about peak users? They now pay 80 percent of 80 percent of a fraction of total cost (since they make up 80 percent of riders, riders as a group pay only 80 percent of costs other than external ones). If 80 percent of users cause almost 100 percent of the cost, these peak users should pay close to 1.56 times present fares. This would make them pay for 100 percent of construction and maintenance, and most operating costs. But additionally charging users for land and external costs imposed on society might require raising fares three- to fivefold during peak times, and leaving them perhaps at present levels at other times.[4]

[4] It is generally believed that the opportunity cost of land tied up in mass transit and undesirable externalities caused by mass transit are lower than for highways. For instance, highways cut a wider swath across the countryside than railroad tracks, and railroad stations take less space than parking places. Similarly, the pollution caused by oil or electric power production (used to drive railroads) is likely to be smaller than that by the private cars needed to transport any equal number of persons.

Unequal competition. From this analysis it is clear that both peak-hour highway users and peak-hour users of mass transit facilities are now being subsidized in a variety of ways. The former, however, are being subsidized *more* than the latter. The same can be said for nonpeak users, although they are being subsidized less. As a result, the competition between the private car and mass transit is biased toward the former. Correct marginal cost pricing would raise the price of highway use much more than that of using mass transit, and this would be true for peak as well as non-peak use. Peak-hour road use would cost perhaps 30 times as much as now; peak-hour mass transit use, perhaps 5 times as much. Non-peak-hour road use might cost 3 times more than now; non-peak mass transit use might cost the same. This could be expected to change people's behavior substantially from what it now is.

Consequences of correct pricing. There can be little doubt that many present road users, if they were to be thus confronted with the true social costs of their choice would considerably alter their behavior. Under present circumstances, rational people use roads as long as the private benefit of this activity at least equals or exceeds the private cost. Since social costs greatly exceed private costs, it is not surprising that the traffic volume exceeds the socially desirable. If people had to pay the social marginal cost, there would be far-reaching consequences. Many people would use roads less or at different times: People who are now living in the suburbs and commuting to city jobs by private car would have the incentive to avoid rush-hour driving. They might look for jobs elsewhere, decide to live in the city instead, or travel in car pools. They might ask employers to stagger working hours or they might choose other modes or routes of transportation. Commercial truck deliveries would be fewer and differently timed. Shoppers and sightseers would stay off the roads during the rush hour when they are most expensive. Everyone would observe changes. General taxes, to the extent that they earlier supported road operating expenses, would be lower because road users would now pay for such expenses. Those previously affected by the undesirable externalities of road use would now find that there are fewer of such effects, and they would find that they could get compensation out of the funds paid by road users. For instance, to the extent that former commuters decided to live in the city, the decline of the city would be halted (together with suburban sprawl). To the extent that commuters teamed up in car pools or used mass transit, there would be less auto traffic, and there could be fewer roads. To the extent that commuters did not change their behavior, they would pay heavily for road use, and government would have funds to compensate all those harmed by former externalities.

Lack of Investment Criteria

If all transport services were priced at their marginal social cost, the providers of such services could get a clear indication of consumer preferences. If consumers, in spite of correct (and high) prices for road use and parking, continued to prefer private car use over mass transit, the providers of road services would make high profits (even after damages to third parties had been paid). The providers of mass transit services would make losses. This would enable and encourage the former to expand and improve the road system. It would force the latter to contract and liquidate transit facilities. On the other hand, if roads remained empty after correct pricing was introduced, while mass transit facilities were more congested than ever, the opposites would occur. In reality, there is no such guide to investment.

Past policies. Investment decisions have been made rather arbitrarily, often influenced by the incorrect picture of consumer preferences revealed by behavior based on incorrect price signals. Given the relatively underpriced road services, consumers have preferred road use. So governments have given rather lavish support to highway construction, but until recently, only niggardly aid to mass transit. They have made matters worse by restricting the numbers, ways of operation, and prices of private mass transit companies.

The source of funds. Until 1916, highway construction was a matter of state expenditures. Since that time, however, the federal government has paid 50 percent of the construction cost of roads routed, designed, constructed, and maintained by states with federal approval. The dollar spending by the federal government rose to over $1 billion a year after World War II and the initiation of the ABC program. It supported construction of (A) major highways, (B) farm to market and feeder roads, and (C) roads within built-up urban areas. While state gasoline and vehicle taxes were a primary source of highway construction funds from the 1920's, general tax collections were the source of federal funds until 1956. Funding changed at the time of approval of the interstate highway program, which proposed to link every city of over 50,000 people by a continuous system of modern, uniform-quality, limited-access roads. The system was to be paid for by new federal taxes on gasoline, tires, and truck tonnage. The law specified a 90 percent federal share in construction costs, the gathering of the new taxes in a newly formed "highway trust fund," and their automatic allocation to highway construction. The result has been a golden annual flow of many billions of dollars for highway construction. Just as the trust fund has grown inexorably (at a rate exceeding $5 billion in recent years), so has the network of highways.

In the meantime, mass transit until the early 1960's has been barely replacing its capital stock, financed as it was by private transit and railroad companies and an occasional city government. The 1961 Housing and Urban Development Act eventually provided for mass transportation demonstration grants, and the Urban Mass Transportation Act of 1964 ushered in federal aid in the form of matching grants for the "preservation and improvement of mass transit." This was followed by 1968 amendments that established the Department of Transportation, whose purpose was to promote "greater comfort, safety, speed, efficiency, and reliability in all modes of transportation." Federal aid for mass transit has been augmented by some state aid (in the Northeast) and some metropolitan areawide aid (in San Francisco and Washington, D.C.). As a result, there have recently occurred improvements in some suburban railroads (notably in New York and Chicago), some rapid transit system extensions (Boston), and even construction of entirely new systems (San Francisco and Washington, D.C.). However, while highway aid has been automatic through the use of earmarked gasoline tax funds, federal mass transit aid has to come from special and reluctant congressional appropriations.

Another bias. Furthermore, aid has been offered in such a way as to bias investment decisions toward highways. The federal government contributes 90 percent of interstate highway costs, and in fiscal 1972 the federal government paid out $4.9 billion for highway construction.[5] The federal government, however, paid only 66 percent of mass transit facilities construction costs until 1972 (when the maximum percentage was raised to 80), and its aid in fiscal 1972 was only $327 million. This is because states have preferred 90 percent highway aid over 66 percent mass transit aid. Not surprisingly therefore, in fiscal 1972, 63 percent of federal transportation aid went for highways, 23 percent for aviation, 9 percent for water transport, and only 5 percent for railroads and mass transit. Interestingly, in mid-1970, the Federal Highway Administration had 5,000 employees, the Federal Urban Mass Transportation Administration had 55. Since states stop highway construction at city limits, cities have gotten stuck with building access roads. (In 1961, the forty-three largest cities ended up spending twice as much on motor vehicle facilities as they received in tolls or grants for this purpose.) Frequently, they would much prefer enlarging mass transit facilities, which are cheaper to construct and operate, and are believed to involve lower social costs and to have a number of external *benefits* such as helping the young, old, poor, and disabled, who do not have cars, to follow jobs to the suburbs (*reverse commuting*). The incorrect pricing of transportation services, and the arbitrary investment decisions made as a result, keep making this impossible.

SOLVING THE PROBLEM

There has been no dearth of proposals to solve the urban transportation problem. These proposals can be grouped into three categories. Some focus attention on the demand for transportation services and recommend decreasing it *at current prices.* Others recommend increasing the supply of such services *at current prices.* Still others propose *correcting prices.* The nature of these strategies will be illustrated with respect to roads with the help of Figure 12.1,

[5] Additional federal aid is given for other programs, such as the ABC system of primary and secondary roads, TOPICS (Traffic Operations Program to Increase Capacity and Safety), and highway beautification.

"The Market for Road Services." On the vertical axis the price of road use is measured. If we assume that road users are uniformly charged, as they are in reality, 1 cent per mile of road use (even though indirectly), we can draw a horizontal supply curve of road services at this price. People are in effect given the impression that at this price (which is mainly paid via gasoline taxes) the supply of road service is infinite at all times. Anyone who wants to can use the road "free" whenever he wishes. He will burn gasoline when he does and thus pay the 1 cent tax per mile. However, the supply is not really infinite, for there is a definite *technical* limit to the number of cars that can be on the road *and still move* at any one time. We consider a one-mile stretch of one lane of a road on the horizontal axis. This provides exactly 5,280 feet of road. If we assume that cars must travel at a minimum speed of 1 mile per hour, are on the average 16 feet long, and cannot be closer than 1.6 feet to each other at a 1-mile-per-hour speed, it becomes clear that there is a maximum number of cars that can be on this portion of road at any one moment. That number is 300, for

Figure 12.1 **The Market for Road Services**

Price of road use (cents per mile)

$D_{8\ \text{a.m.-9 a.m.}}$

$D_{1\ \text{a.m.-2 a.m.}}$

$D_{3\ \text{p.m.-4 p.m.}}$

Number of cars in one lane and on 1 mile stretch of road at any time	0	30	60	90	120	150	180	210	240	270	300
Average speed in miles per hour		70	45	27	18	12	8	6	4	2	1
Number of cars traversing 1 mile stretch of road in one lane per hour		2,100	2,700	2,430	2,160	1,800	1,440	1,260	960	540	300

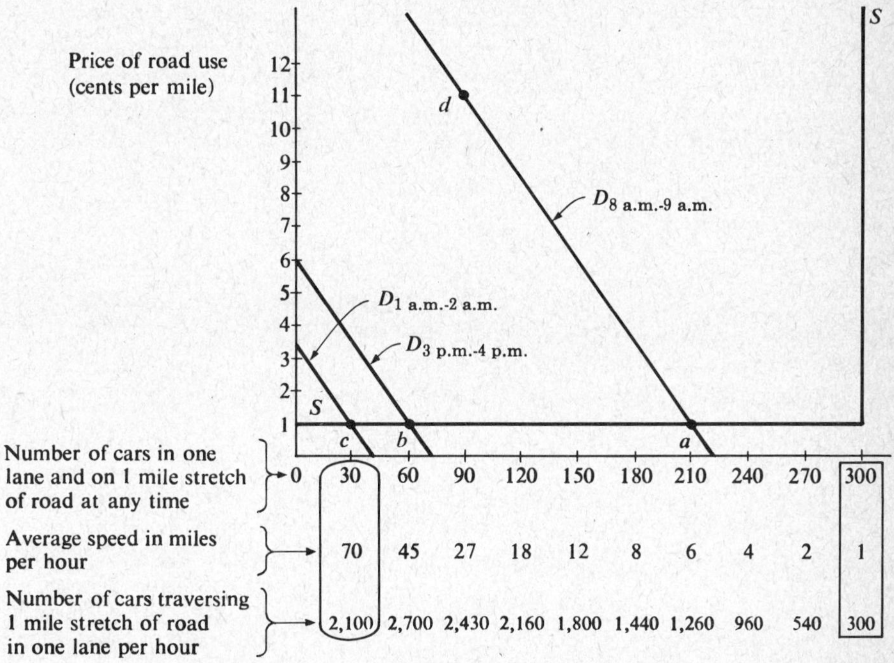

If road services are offered to all who desire them at a low and uniform price (as illustrated by the horizontal portion of line *S*), differences in demand at various times of the day (lines labeled *D*) cause a road to be used with varying degrees of efficiency. (Note the legend under the horizontal axis.)

16 + 1.6 = 17.6, and 17.6 times 300 = 5,280. Thus the supply curve must become vertical at this point. Hence the shape of supply curve *SS*. As indicated at the right-hand edge underneath the horizontal axis (boxed figures), if 300 cars should be on this 1-mile stretch of 1-lane road at all times, and if they should travel at 1 mile per hour, only 300 cars will be traversing that stretch of road per hour. A literal case of bumper-to-bumper traffic!

If there were fewer cars on the road at any one time, things would look different. Let us go to the other extreme. If there were only 30 cars on our 1-mile stretch at any one time, they would cover 30 × 16, or only 480 of the 5,280-foot total length. Thus the distances between cars could be 5,280 — 480 divided by 30, or 160. Certainly, cars could then travel as fast as 70 miles per hour. Thus 30 cars would get across our 1-mile stretch in 1/70 of an hour, and a total of 30 × 70, or 2,100 cars could traverse the road in one hour. All this is shown in the encircled portion of the legend at the left-hand edge of the horizontal axis. It is fairly easy to figure out what happens in between. Sixty cars on the road can only go at 45 mph, since a spacing of only 72 feet would exist between them. Yet a total of 2,700 cars could now traverse the road in 1 hour.

All other figures have been similarly calculated, always assuming that 1 car-length of distance is required between cars for each 10 mph of speed. Interestingly, the greatest number of cars (2,700) can traverse the road when 60 cars are on the road at any one moment traveling at 45 miles per hour.

Yet the number of cars that actually go on the road is another matter. At the 1-cent-a-mile charge, the number of cars on the road at any one moment may be 210 during the rush hour at from 8 to 9 A.M. (point *a*), it may be 60 during the afternoon offpeak period from 3 to 4 P.M. (point *b*), it may be 30 between 1 and 2 A.M. (point *c*). At higher prices, each of these quantities of road service demanded might drop, as along the three demand curves shown in the graph and labeled *D*.

The result of incorrect uniform pricing (at our assumed 1 cent a mile) is immediately obvious. From 1 A.M. to 2 A.M., only 30 cars will be on the 1-mile stretch of road at any one time. They will go 70 miles an hour. From 3 P.M. to 4 P.M., there will be 60 cars at any one moment, going 45 miles an hour. From 8 A.M. to 9 A.M., there will be 210 cars at any one moment, going 6 miles an hour. These hypothetical figures only serve to illustrate the nature of the situation found in reality. (However, the figures are not totally fanciful. A 1972 study showed the average speed of vehicles in Manhattan to be 4 mph.) We can now use this graph and these figures to illustrate the nature of proposed solutions.

Decreasing the Demand for Certain Transportation Services at Current Prices

One might leave prices for transportation services unchanged but decrease the quantity of such services demanded at any given price. In terms of Figure 12.1, "The Market for Road Services," if somehow 180 of the 210 cars on the road at any one time between 8 A.M. and 9 A.M. could be made to stay away, one could move from point *a* to point *c*. Cars could go 70 mph, instead of 6 mph; and lo and behold, a much *larger* number of cars could traverse our stretch of road than before! There are several ways of going about this.

Positive entry control. For instance, a positive entry control might be set up on urban roads during periods of congestion. That is, instead of allowing anyone to enter any road at any time, entries to a piece of road that can only accommodate 30 cars at some desired speed (perhaps, 70 miles an hour) might be regulated so as never to have more than 30 cars on this piece of road at any one time. Some potential entrants would be made to wait at the entry points. This would encourage the use of alternative routes or means of transport. It might encourage, in the long run, alternative residential and business locations. Above all, it would decrease the average travel time and increase, as Figure 12.1 shows, the number of cars getting across this distance in a given time period. Even a car that was made to wait for 45 minutes at the entry point, if it were assured of then being able to travel at 70 miles an hour to its destination 7 miles away, would get to its destination 9 minutes faster than entering at once and driving at 7 miles an hour in bumper-to-bumper traffic!

This type of thinking has been put to use at Chicago's Kennedy Expressway. It handled 267,000 vehicles a day in early 1973 and is probably the world's busiest road, easily topping the traffic volume of the Santa Monica Freeway at Los Angeles, the Ford Freeway at Detroit, or the Long Island Expressway at New York. At Chicago, electronic sensors have been buried every half mile in each lane of the city's seven expressways. A computer questions each sensor continually, translates the information into colored lights on a control room map (red for traffic speeds up to 30 mph, green above 45 mph, yellow in between), and adjusts the entrance ramp lights to decrease traffic flow to any congested area.

Promoting bus travel. Another approach to reducing the number of cars on the road at any one moment involves persuading people to switch from private cars to buses. A bus carrying 80 people (who previously used 80 private cars) might take the space of only 3 of these cars. This would be a 96 percent reduction in the number of cars on the road at any given moment without any loss in the number of passengers moved. The question is how to "persuade" people to make the switch. Some have suggested that urban roads during peak hours be exclusively allocated to buses, or that buses be given an exclusive lane on such roads or priority access to them. This would assure buses of high average speeds and lure private motorists into switching their form of transportation. In a few places, federal government aid has been given to encourage this. A half-million-dollar federal grant, for example, helped convert one of the Lincoln tunnel lanes in New York City into an exclusive bus lane during the rush hour. The aid was used to create special lane markings, changeable overhead signs, special access ramps for buses, and new parking lots at the bus starting points to encourage private motorists to switch. This program has cut bus travel time between New Jersey to mid-Manhattan by 15 minutes. In 1971, a test was made to ascertain the feasibility of similar exclusive bus lanes on the Long Island Expressway. Such lanes have also been introduced in San Francisco (where *filled* private cars may also use them) and in the approaches to Washington, D.C. Other cities have also experimented with luring private motorists into buses or railroads, thereby increasing the passenger-carrying capacity of existing roads. For instance, Milwaukee has created a two-lane "mini-freeway" restricted to buses that could move at 70 miles per hour between the suburbs and downtown. Ithaca has experimented with free bus service, other cities with greatly improved bus service.

But these experiments have given little indication that Americans are willing to forgo the comfort, convenience, guaranteed seating, independence of schedule, privacy, and storage capacity of private cars for the small public transportation subsidy offered in these experiments. The Flint, Michigan, experiment is indicative. In 1968, a "maxicab" service was introduced there. It consisted of luxury door-to-door bus service taking people from their homes to their places of work and back, very much like school buses taking children to and from school. The buses provided soft, spacious seating, stereophonic music, air conditioning, newspapers, even bus bunnies serving coffee and doughnuts. The cost was low: $18 per month for the longest ride (of one hour). In spite of all this, people stayed away in droves. By 1970, 3 of 1,000 commuters had been lured away from their own cars. A similar project at Hempstead on Long Island, New York, was abandoned in 1970 because of poor patronage after a two-year trial. Indeed, bus service has completely collapsed in 250 communities since 1954. In many places, as in Denver, it only survives because residents have voted to have the city take over and subsidize failing private companies.

Radical innovations. No wonder that some transportation planners believe that nothing but radically new ideas can get people to have fewer cars in cities. Thus the Department of Transportation has been studying the feasibility of moving sidewalks for Boston and New York. These would carry people at 25 miles per hour around town. But the technical problem has been how to get people on and off such a fast moving beltway without accidents. Indeed, in 1972, a private corporation (Dunlop) announced the development of the "speedway," a refinement of the 2-mile-per-hour moving sidewalks already in use at many shopping centers, fairs, and air and bus terminals. The speedway would move at 10 mph, thereby raising the people-carrying capacity of the 2-mph version from 7,200 per hour to 30,000. Dunlop developed a variable-speed integrator, which works like an access road to a high-speed freeway. One gets on the integrator when it is going at 2 mph; it accelerates to 10 mph; one steps off it and onto the 10-mph belt. The procedure is reversed for getting off. Dunlop claimed that people could profitably be moved across Manhattan on such speedways for a 5-cent ride, enclosed in a controlled environment at that.

Another radical-type proposal involves building roads on which electric mini-cars linked to each other travel on tracks at high speeds under central control. In terms of Figure 12.1, it would obviously be best if no space could be wasted on the road and if all 300 cars could travel on the road at 70 miles an hour, even though only 1.6 feet from each other. Such an arrangement is impossible with individually controlled vehicles for reasons of safety. In Denver, a "personal rapid transit vehicle" has been in the design stage. According to one version, the vehicle would make the first part of a suburb-to-city trip independently, then hook into a remotely operated rapid transit system for the longest part of the trip, then detach itself and proceed independently to the destination. Another version involves something like a horizontal elevator that travels at 50 mph along guideways and is controlled by a computer. People would push a button at a station; the next car coming along would stop there and stop again at the destination that would be indicated by pushing another button inside. Such things are understandably far in the future with regard to large-scale application. In the meantime, others have suggested, it would be expedient to use less of the carrot and to use more of a stick.

Banning cars. One could proceed to the outright banning of cars. It has been suggested that some public authority ban all vehicular traffic entirely, including parking, in some areas, or ban low-priority users. In the latter case, the sorting of users into priority groups would not be easy. It would involve many hair-splitting decisions on whose needs are "urgent" (for trade, businesses, and industry?) and whose are "slight" (for private pleasure and convenience?). But banning of cars could be done, even though such a policy would be cumbersome and unpopular and quickly turn into an administrative nightmare—the reason that it has not been used a great deal.

The complete banning of (nonemergency) vehicles has been tried, usually in a few selected streets only, which were thus turned into "bikeways" or "pedestrian malls." In 1971, limited street use was tried in Boston, Chicago, New York, Philadelphia, San Francisco, and Washington, D.C. The policy has typically been resisted by merchants and parking interests, however. Still, some city planners dream of future inner cities without *any* traffic at all, a pedestrian paradise covered by huge plastic domes, and air-conditioned at that!

Increasing the Supply of Certain Transportation Services at Current Prices

One might leave prices for transportation services unchanged but increase the quantity of such services supplied at present prices. In terms of Figure 12.1, "The Market for Road Services," if somehow the vertical part of curve *S* could be shifted over to the right for the reason that more road is available, even 210 cars on the road from 8 A.M. to 9 A.M. might not be disastrous at all. Suppose the one lane of road were converted, magically, into ten lanes. Then there would be not 5,280, but 52,800 feet of road space in a 1-mile stretch. Cars could be spaced so as to travel 235 feet apart. They could safely go 80 miles an hour!

Reversible lanes. This type of result might be achieved by making lanes on roads *reversible*. Picture a six-lane urban expressway during the rush hour. Typically, traffic will be moving bumper to bumper on three lanes in one direction, with practically no traffic moving on three other lanes going in the opposite one. Clearly, the road's capacity to move traffic quickly could be increased by two-thirds if lanes could be quickly reversed so that five lanes are always available for travel in the dominant direction rather than three.

Smaller cars. Another strategy to increase the car-carrying capacity of roads would involve inducing people, perhaps by heavy taxation of large cars, to use small ones. Just consider Figure 12.1 and note what would happen if the average car had a length of 8 feet rather than the assumed 16 feet.

Rerouting buses. The same general idea can be used to increase efficiency of use of other types of facilities. For instance, existing bus service might be rerouted. Traditionally, most bus lines converge on the central business district like spokes of a wheel. Therefore poor central city residents cannot get to suburban jobs except by traveling indirect routes involving frequent transfers. Some cities have subsidized auto ownership for the poor by renting or leasing cars at a subsidy, pressing for auto insurance reforms to reduce premiums, and decreasing credit costs to low-income car buyers. The aim was to enable central city poor to travel to suburban jobs on the empty lanes opposite the main travel direction of suburban residents. But others have pressed for more flexible bus service. Newark has paved the subways to make them usable for buses, which could have more convenient routing. Other cities have subsidized a reoriented bus service to increase the frequency of service or to create new lines of connection between the ghettos and outlying job locations. Others still are dreaming of nonscheduled bus service based on a computerized call system. As an MIT–Commerce Department study revealed, in most large cities individuals could get a bus within 6 minutes under such a system, and more people could be transported in a smaller number of buses than are now being used.

Increasing entry into bus and taxi industry. Besides improving existing facilities, one can try to expand them. A first step might involve eliminating some existing restrictions to entry into the public transport market. For instance, the supply of public transport services is often artificially restricted by governmental licensing. Archaic franchise regulations restrict entry into the bus business. As a result, lack of alternatives force private cars to clog roads that could more efficiently be used by buses.

With the notable exception of Washington, D.C., most cities also restrict the supply of taxis. This has resulted in high fares, monopoly profits of taxi companies, and the nonavailability of this means of transportation to the poor. Since anything that restricts the mobility of those poor who are capable of working increases their chances of not finding jobs and of remaining poor, the social costs of this policy are high. Slowly this type of policy is being changed. In New York City, for instance, in mid-1972, some 11,787 Yellow Cabs were licensed to cruise for passengers. This license consists of a transferable "medallion," which sells for a sum in the range of $20,000 to $30,000. This high price reflected the high profitability of the taxi business under conditions of restricted entry. Yet this profitability also attracted some 9,000 illegal, or "gypsy," cabs. They were not legally allowed to cruise for passengers, and they typically operated in the slums where Yellow Cab drivers refused to go for fear of robbery or personal injury. Obviously, "gypsies" were uncontrolled as to car standards, insurance, and driver qualifications. As of 1972, the city legalized them for a $100 license fee and an annual $10 street use fee. However, it restricted the operation of these cabs to telephone dispatch, disallowing cruising, yellow color, fare meters, and roof signs. To no one's surprise, the licensing of the gypsies was violently resisted by the Yellow Cab owners whose profits (and medallion values) would be depressed. In the meantime, another 4,400 totally illegal cabs were believed to be operating (so called "gypsy gypsies," or *jitneys*, so named after the slang expression for *nickel*, which referred to the fare charged in the 1920's). Frequently run by poor people using their family cars, these outlaws defied a possible $500 fine and were fought tooth and nail by Yellow Cabs and gypsies alike.

Clearly, such monopolistic restrictions are pointless and could be eliminated to increase the supply and reduce the price of this type of public transport service significantly. Such a move would, in turn, eliminate a much greater number of private cars now used in the city. (And it would have the added benefit of allowing poor people to earn income whenever needed by working as cab drivers, part-time with the family car perhaps.)

Building new rapid transit systems. City rail, subway, and streetcar systems can be expanded, too, or new ones be built. The creation of brand new facilities, other than more urban highways, has been slow in recent decades. Perhaps the most elaborate try has been made in San Francisco. It has built the first wholly new mass transit system in the United States in 50 years. San Francisco began to operate in 1972 the first third of a fully automated and air-conditioned electric rail system running almost inaudibly at an average speed of 45 miles per hour equally on the surface, underground, and elevated, over a 75-mile course. It involved the largest bond issue ever voted for mass transit—and voted by auto owners! The whole system is handled by a few men inside a control tower. Electronic fare collection devices admit passengers on the basis of magnetically coded cards.

By mid-1972, new rapid transit systems were being considered, in the planning stages, or under construction in a number of other cities. Work was under way on a 98-mile, 53-station, 556-car Washington, D.C., subway system. This $3-billion project is the largest public works undertaking in U.S. history. It is to link, by 1979, downtown Washington with Maryland and Virginia suburbs. Also under construction was an automated rapid transit system in Morgantown, West Virginia. This 3.2-mile elevated system is to have 100 rubber-tired electric vehicles and is expected to carry 3,300 passengers an hour by 1976. Produced by Boeing and Bendix, the system was billed as the forerunner of hundreds of its kind in other cities by the U.S. Department of Transportation.

Atlanta is planning a 56-mile rapid transit system plus 14 exclusive busways, financed by a new regional sales tax. Baltimore is planning a new 28-mile rapid transit system. Honolulu is planning an 18-mile subway and elevated rubber-tired train for 1979, plus "people movers." Los Angeles, long committed to the auto, now plans a 14-mile rapid transit system on the freeway median for 1978. Dade County (Greater Miami) has plans for a 45-mile, 48-station elevated rapid transit system to be built by 1985. Electric rubber-tired trains are expected to run on a monorail erected 15 feet above ground. Similar systems for Jacksonville and Tampa are planned for the late 1980's. Pittsburgh is counting on the Westinghouse *skybus*, trains running on rubber tires and concrete guideways. San Francisco is planning on new cable cars and the first American streetcar extension in 25 years. The list can be extended: Boston, Buffalo, Chicago, Dallas–Fort Worth, Detroit, Houston, Minneapolis–St. Paul, Philadelphia, St. Louis, San Juan, Seattle—all are planning on new transit systems.

Visions of the future. Some advanced thinkers, inspired by research from the Northeast Corridor (Boston–Washington) high-speed trains, dream of "gravitrains" in the city of the future. Propelled by their own weight and gravity, these trains would move through deep underground tunnels, then roll up on their own momentum at average speeds of 90 miles an hour despite frequent closely spaced stops. Some even dream of land and water vehicles riding at speeds of 300 miles per hour on cushions of air.

Federal aid. In the meantime, a number of urban mass transportation assistance acts have been passed (in 1964, 1966, 1970, and 1972) to help implement some of the more down-to-earth programs. The funds allocated, however, have remained small: $80 million in 1970, to rise to $1.86 billion by 1975, for a total of $10 billion over 12 years. In 1972, for the first time, Congress approved *operating* subsidies for local mass transit companies ($400 million over two years) in addition to construction subsidies, but this was done reluctantly and in the belief that the president would not spend the funds anyway. Earlier recommendations by the Department of Transportation to divert highway trust funds to mass transit were rejected by Congress, although precedents exist for such a move in state and city programs (Illinois, Maryland, Virginia, New York City Triborough Bridge and Tunnel Authority). Congress also rejected a proposal to set up a mass transit trust fund similar to the highway trust fund, although it did, in 1970, pass a trust fund bill for aviation. To finance air traffic control, airways, and airports, it legislated a variety of user charges on aircraft users. These include an international travel head tax of $3, a 5 percent tax on the value of air freight services, airplane registration fees, a tax on aviation tires, and higher taxes on domestic passengers (8 percent of fares) and general aviation fuel (7 cents a gallon). By early 1973, President Nixon urged a diversion of $3.65 billion from the highway trust fund in favor of urban mass transit construction during fiscal years 1974–1976. The Senate had passed such a bill by March 1973, but the House rejected it.

Correct Pricing of All Transportation Services

One can make a good case, finally, for a third strategy: solving the urban transportation problem by introducing a well-thought-out system of correct pricing for all transportation services. All the solutions discussed so far are painkillers more than cures of the disease. The cure is incomplete because no plan directly confronts individual decision makers with the costs of their actions. None gives guidance to investors. Correct pricing would do both. Little doubt exists that changes in the prices of transportation services would affect both the quantities demanded and those supplied and would eventually eliminate the traffic problem. If each user were to be charged the marginal social cost resulting from his use, not, as is now the case, *a fraction of* the current *average* cost of the system, he would be aware of the opportunity costs of his actions. The raising of total revenue on this basis in excess of total costs would signal an expansion of the facilities. If the total revenue did not exceed total costs, the reverse would be true. In the long run, revenues would cover costs exactly. In terms of Figure 12.1, "The Market for Road Services," the marginal social cost of, say, 11 cents a mile (hypothetical figure) might be charged for road use during the peak hours (and nothing during other times). This would change the horizontal portion of the supply curve to the 11-cent level. (You might wish to draw it in.) As a result, quantity demanded during the peak hour would fall from *a* to *d*. Only 90 cars would be on the road at any one time, traveling at 27 mph. The road authority would take in from users of this 1-mile stretch of 1 lane 2,430 × 11 cents, or $267.30, during this hour. This would contrast with 1,260 × 1 cent, or $12.60, taken in from peak users indirectly under the uniform gasoline tax system. After paying all expenses, including damages, the authority would make a profit or a loss, indicating to it whether it should expand or contract the road system.

Let us consider, in turn, policies of correct pricing for roads, mass transit facilities, and parking space.

Road use: Objections raised to correct pricing. People confronted with the idea that roads, like oranges, are scarce and therefore should be properly priced typically voice a number of objections. First, some claim that the *freedom of the road* is a traditional right that must be preserved for all. This is an irrational objection that denies the objective fact that with increased population the freedom to move about anywhere at any time has been abridged by scarcity of space.

Second, some object that such use of the price mechanism would be *unfair to the poor,* and propound that therefore roads must be provided for all as a free public service. This overlooks the fact that discrimination between those who get something and those who do not is an unavoidable phenomenon in a world of scarcity.[6] Either this task is carried out by a price system or it must be done by direct rationing. Abolishing the price system won't abolish the need to discriminate in this way. Under either system, people's claims to scarce goods can be distributed equally or unequally. One may deplore poverty as a sad phenomenon in that it means that some people are restrained more than others from having what they want, but this is no reason to paralyze the price system. Since one can take other countermeasures against poverty if one wishes, there is no reason why roads should be provided free any more than oranges or houses. Positive prices for oranges and houses also discriminate. Thus the argument of those who oppose correct road pricing as unfair to the poor is one about income distribution and has nothing to do with the efficient use and provision of roads. Furthermore, present roads are predominantly used by the nonpoor. In New York City, in 1971, for example, the income of drivers of private cars entering Manhattan was 50 percent above average.[7]

Third, people object that marginal-cost road pricing, although desirable in principle, would be *too expensive to administer.* One could neither calculate the correct charge, nor collect it, goes the argument. For instance, it is argued, it is easy to calculate construction, maintenance, and operating costs, but impossibly difficult to find proper charges for rent and external costs. To be sure, studies have been made to find correct charges, but experts have failed to agree. Thus the value of commuter time lost by congestion has been estimated anywhere from 75 percent of a worker's pay to a multiple of his pay (equal to his *net overtime* pay on the grounds that people would work overtime unless they valued their leisure at least this much). But actually, a correct charge could be found by trial and error. The charge for road use could be raised until congestion is reduced to a desirable level and until enough revenue is raised to compensate third parties for damages, for instance. This leaves the other half of the problem, which is not so much concerned with the size of the charge, but with the method of charging. Existing methods of charging for roads are usually bad because they are incapable of meeting some of the criteria a marginal social cost-type charge would have to meet.

Such a charge would have to be levied on the user *directly* whether he were a frequent user or an occasional one, and would have to be *variable* with

[6] Recall the discussion of this point in Figure 2.3, "How a Market Discriminates."
[7] Even the income of subway riders was slightly above average. Many of the poor were not using mass transit facilities at all or were using them during *off-peak* hours or in directions *opposite* to the main flow of traffic (for instance, cleaning women with nonstandard hours of work). They might get *cheaper* rides under a system of correct pricing!

respect to the amount of use (the distance traveled or time spent on a road) and with respect to the place and time of use. Most current financing methods are bad: license fees and vehicle taxes are a function of ownership, not of road use. Gasoline taxes are invariant with respect to place and time of use. Furthermore, in order to influence people's decisions, the charge would have to be *ascertainable in advance*. To avoid an administrative nightmare, the method of enforcing and collecting proper user charges would have to be simple and easy. It could not possibly involve placing a human monitor on every road and issuing millions of invoices every day.

The requirements suggest immediately some kind of nonhuman monitor or meter. It could be part of each vehicle (as in taxis) or it could be situated in a central place and actuated by the activities of vehicles. Provided the equipment is capable of withstanding rough usage and difficult to tamper with, either arrangement could be used. Charges could be made either at the time vehicles pass fixed pricing points or continuously as long as the vehicles are within certain pricing zones. The technology for metering exists.[8]

The on-vehicle point pricing system. Under a point pricing system, motorists incur charges when passing designated points at certain times. Under an on-vehicle system a meter, perhaps the size of a car's number plate, would be attached to each car. It could be a solid-state counter, without any moving parts, without any outward sign of counting. It could consist of a number of segments that can be electrically charged and discharged. At chosen pricing points, electric cables could be laid across the road, perhaps in groups of ten. Depending on the price one wanted to charge on this road at any one time, the number of cables energized could be centrally varied. The number of cables could also be varied at bridges or tunnels, where tolls for these facilities also might be imposed by this method. When a car with a meter crossed such a pricing point, the meter could count in binary numbers the electrical impulses generated by the cables.

Meters could be sold for various capacities and might indicate by a change of color when they were close to exhaustion. Then they might be exchanged at meter stations. Or they might be permanently affixed and read and reset at intervals. As long as charges were popularly regarded as necessary and fair, furthermore, there would be no reason to think that tampering with such meters would be any more widespread than in the case of electric, water, or gas meters now found in people's houses.

The on-vehicle continuous pricing system. As an alternative, special pricing zones might be designated, within which vehicles would be charged in accordance with time or distance traveled. If based on time, charges could be made from the moment of entry to the moment of exit from a pricing zone (very

[8] The technical information in the following sections is based on Gabriel Roth, *Paying for Roads: The Economics of Traffic Congestion* (Harmondsworth, England: Penguin, 1967).

much like a telephone charge is made from the moment of connection to that of disconnection). Electric impulses could switch meters within cars on or off as the zone borders were crossed. These impulses might be varied by time of day, week, or year within any given zone. Drivers (as well as policemen in the street) could ascertain by a light whether the meter had been activated. The light might be red for a high price and blue for a low price, and remain off for a zero price. Such meters might be run with batteries that would have to be purchased at meter stations and inserted.

This method would have its drawbacks, however. If pricing were based on time, it would encourage fast driving. The fast driving problem might be countered by metering distance only or by using an alternative to meters, such as differential stickers. These could be color-coded by area or time of day and monitored by traffic policemen. Cars driving in certain areas during certain times might be required to display a red sticker. Such sticker might be sold annually and made transferable. To eliminate cheating, stickers for each day of the year might be produced (with the date being conspicuous on each). These might be sold in booklets with unused ones being returnable. Although this method would be simple, it would not allow differentiation of pricing by length of trip.

There would be another problem with zone pricing. If people moved across a boundary from one zone into another, rather than through a zone completely, there would be no easy way to determine a charge. Nor could stickers eliminate the boundary problem. Similarly, it would be impossible to charge for trips originating and ending within a zone unless every private driveway were monitored. This would raise the danger of the police state, since every move by every car would be precisely recorded (not to mention the wife's finding out about her husband's trip to his old girl friend's town). Finally, the zone pricing method would be more liable to serious error (than the point system): if an exit had gone unrecorded, the bill could be infinite.

Off-vehicle pricing systems. Any off-vehicle pricing system would require a method of automatic vehicle identification at certain points or within certain zones, a method of transmitting this information to a central computing station, and a method of analyzing the information received and billing the vehicle owner.

For identification, black and white codes might be painted on the side of vehicles. These codes might be scanned by light beams from optical units mounted on posts at the side of the road at pricing points or the border of pricing zones. Or instead, use could be made of the Link tracer: static electromagnetic elements could be embedded in a plastic block attached to each car. This would require no batteries, no power connections. At pricing points or zone boundaries, an interrogator apparatus could be located. It could scan the road with electromagnetic waves. The element on the car would react and identify the car.

The information so received could be transmitted continuously to a computing station. Preferably, to avoid the need for a big computer capable of handling peak traffic flows, the information could be stored on tapes in the interrogating units and transmitted at intervals to the computer by human messenger or electrically on signal. The computer could then be of the smaller size needed to handle average traffic flows.

The central computer would then have to sort the gathered information by vehicle number and compute the debt of each vehicle in accordance with the places and times traveled.

Correct road use pricing and investment policy. The on-vehicle point pricing system seems to be the best pricing method available. If it were used and marginal social costs were charged, some roads would produce a profit, others losses, just as if road services had been produced under conditions of perfect competition. And just as under perfect competition, the road authority could be required to expand roads where profits were being made and to contract where the opposite occurred. Profits made on a particular street would not necessarily be usable to widen that particular street (this might destroy all the stores in the area and eliminate the demand for this road entirely), but they might be used to improve the road system in that general area so as to benefit the group who paid the charges. A road might be maintained even in the face of losses if the cost of abandoning it exceeded the losses being made.

Correct mass transit pricing. There is no technical problem associated with correct pricing of mass transit. Suppose it were introduced by adjusting the current flat-fare system up or down to make fares at any place or time cover marginal social costs. Then the quantity of mass transit services demanded during congestion would decline. But if at the same time correct road pricing were instituted, *relative* prices of transportation services could be expected to change markedly *in favor of* mass transit. This would raise the demand for mass transit. And it would in the long run materially help reduce traffic congestion by stimulating expansion or improvements of present systems. Imagine people switched to buses, for example. Although each bus would take the space of 3 cars on the road, it could carry 80 passengers and so replace 80 single passenger cars. Thus it could move faster than before and be filled rather than empty. All this would reduce fuel, equipment, and labor costs per passenger carried, since buses could go faster and any given operating expenditure would correspond to more revenue. Bus company deficits would disappear, allowing improvements in and expansion of service and stimulating, in turn, even greater demand.

Correctly pricing on-street parking. The idea of charging for parking space is in most cities nothing new. Novel, however, is the idea of making imaginative use of a variety of parking meters. Charges could vary with the area, length of parking, time of day, week, and year in such a way as to assure the availability in all areas at all times of a few empty parking spots. The correct charge would eliminate congestion and ration available spaces to those most in need of them (as measured by their willingness to pay the correct price).

Such meters could be of the *conventional type*, affixed to a pole by the side of the road. However, charges would have to be correct, that is, zero at times and places of an abundance of space, but very high at times and places of extreme congestion. The difficulty would be the finding and punishing of violators. But the cost of the required staff could be minimized by imposing heavy fines for violations, including revocation of drivers' licenses.

To avoid the unsightly clutter of conventional meters, alternatives might be used. One *ticket-issuing meter* might be placed on each street with time-stamped tickets valid for this street. Such meter would have the added advantage of allowing the driver a choice of any length of parking time.

Instead, a *personal parking meter* might be used. This could be a clock inside the car, visible to outsiders, that could be set to variable running speeds and could be started and stopped at will. It might be wound up for a fee for a certain number of hours at a special station. The driver could set it ticking at a metered parking area, but at a designated running speed depending on the price in use.

Parking fees could also be collected as part of a *general road pricing system*. In the case of on-vehicle point pricing systems, the meter on the parked car might be energized by a *moving* pricing point attached to a police car cruising each street at stated intervals. Where a continuous pricing scheme existed, special equipment in the parking area might activate the meter on the car.

Still another alternative would involve *frontager monopoly*. That is, one could allow those whose property fronts a street to monopolize the parking space along their property in return for an annual fee paid to the government. These property holders could, in turn, set up private meters to recover the fee paid the government. They could also hood these meters, thereby preserving the parking space for themselves or designated others (such as special customers or delivery trucks). This would assure parking space to those interested in a *specially placed* spot and willing to pay for it. It would also set up the incentive to charge what the traffic will bear at any given time and place without requiring any complicated government machinery to administer the system. Clearly, the fee charged by government could, by trial and error, be equalized to the sum a frontager would earn if he never hooded his private meter and always charged equilibrium prices.

Correctly pricing off-street parking. Correct pricing of on-street parking facilities could be combined with correct pricing of off-street facilities. Here, too, public parking lots and garages, instead of being subsidized out of general tax revenue, could charge the actual users such prices that at all times and places just a few empty spaces remain. If this pricing scheme produced profits, a clear indication would exist that facilities should be expanded. The reverse would be true where losses were made. Depending on the strength of demand for facilities in any given area, private producers would then also be induced to provide such facilities. Where profits were small, existing facilities might just be maintained. Where profits were larger, new open-site lots and open-walled structures might be erected. Where profits were huge, costlier underground garages and mechanical car parking facilities (that could pack cars together an inch apart) might be constructed.

The first steps. Cities have taken only a few hesitant first steps in the directions just described. After near paralysis of traffic in Manhattan, the mayor of New York City in 1970 proposed 25-cent tolls on four East River bridges. He was turned down, although existing tolls were raised on seven other bridges and two tunnels in 1972. Others have suggested tolls on all cars entering Manhattan, ranging from 25 cents for cars with one empty seat to $1 for those with three empty seats, to encourage people to team up. Yet there has been no action. But the idea of user charges that vary with time and place is beginning to sound familiar to many, and its popularization constitutes the first step to action.

Summary

1. In spite of unprecedented outlays on highway construction, considerable spending on mass transit, and revolutionary advances in transportation (such as the advent of the jet), cities have serious transportation problems. They are choking in vehicular traffic, have unsatisfactory mass transit systems, and suffer from undesirable external effects of transportation systems.
2. Road congestion develops when there are so many cars on a road at any one time that average speed has to drop for reasons of safety and the number of cars traversing the road in any given time period falls below its possible maximum. The congestion problem is not confined to roads. It also engulfs parking areas and public transit facilities ranging from subways to airports.
3. A study of travel patterns in cities reveals that public transport is used by low-income people for all purposes and by some middle- and high-income people for trips to and from work. But over 90 percent of urban vehicular travel involves use of the private car by middle- and high-income people for work and nonwork trips. Essentially, it is only work trips (that during a few hours each day account for more than half of urban travel) that cause congestion of roads and public transport facilities.
4. No less serious than congestion at certain times each day are the externalities associated with transportation: accidents, neighborhood breakup, environmental damages, and many others.

5. The root of these problems lies in incorrect pricing of transportation services. Individual decision makers are not confronted with the social costs of their choices. Providers of transport services have no guidance in investment decisions.
6. Road users, for instance, do not pay for external costs, nor the opportunity cost of land, nor some of the road operating expenses. Costs they do bear are paid by them indirectly and uniformly (without regard to time and place of use). Thus some drivers and many nondrivers are effectively subsidizing other drivers. A correction of this situation would require peak-hour users to pay perhaps 30 times more than they do now, while other users would pay, say, 3 times more.
7. Users of parking space are similarly paying incorrect prices. So are users of mass transit. The latter should pay perhaps 3–5 times more during peak hours than they do now and the same as they do now at other times. There is a pricing bias in the competition between private car transportation and mass transit in favor of the former. Charging correct prices could be expected to induce considerable behavior changes, with resulting reduction of congestion and elimination of uncompensated undesirable externalities.
8. Incorrect pricing leads to incorrect investment. In the past, transportation investment has been made on the basis of consumer preferences as expressed on the basis of incorrect prices. As a result of the deck having been stacked in favor of private car use, governments have given lavish support to highway construction, niggardly aid for mass transit. Federal aid has not only come in very different amounts, but also been offered in biased fashion.
9. To solve urban transportation problems some would like to decrease the demand for certain transportation services at current prices. To decrease the rush-hour use of private cars, they have proposed positive entry controls to roads, promotion of bus travel (by faster, cheaper, and higher quality service), a variety of radical innovations (like fast-moving sidewalks, and centrally controlled mini-cars on high-speed roads), and the outright banning of cars in city centers.
10. Others would prefer increasing the supply of certain transportation services at current prices. They propose the introduction of reversible lanes and smaller cars and rerouting bus lines to get more service out of existing facilities. They propose to eliminate entry restrictions in the bus and taxi industry or to build new rapid transit systems. They dream, finally, of entirely new types of rapid transit.
11. A third strategy for dealing with urban transportation problems involves correct pricing of all transportation services and subsequent investment based on profitability. Objections to correct road-use pricing are either untenable (freedom of the road, hurting the poor) or can be overcome (expensive administration). The expense in administration could be overcome by use of a point or continuous pricing system that could be on-vehicle or off-vehicle. Correct pricing of mass transit and parking facilities would present no technical difficulties. Both would tend to eliminate congestion and improve service in the long run. However, correct pricing schemes have not been introduced anywhere.

Terms[9]

- continuous pricing system
- gravitrain
- gypsy cab
- jitney
- mass transit
- mobile parking
- off-vehicle pricing system
- on-vehicle pricing system
- point pricing system
- public transport
- reverse commuting
- road congestion
- skybus

Questions for Review and Discussion

1. "The urban transportation problem arises from a struggle among the large capitalist corporations: Auto and oil and construction companies on the one hand push private-car ownership and highways; big city banks (holding central city land and transit bonds) push public transport, but only so wealthy suburbanites can come downtown to shop. There would be no such problem in socialism." Discuss.
2. "Urban transportation problems are caused in no small part by the construction of skyscrapers, each of which requires thousands of people to be in one spot at the same time. Therefore, the transportation problem should be solved with the help of special taxes on high-rise buildings or by closing off the top stories of towering buildings, or by letting wrecking crews shear them off physically." Discuss.
3. If you were in the business of producing cars or wheat (rather than highway services), which of the production costs corresponding to those listed in the section on "incorrect pricing of road use" would you make part of the price charged your customers? Which would you leave out and why? Show why it would lead to an inefficient use of society's resources if you left out any of these costs. How could society assure that you don't leave out any of them?
4. In the introduction to this chapter, the text says, "The construction of highways in and around cities appears to invite a situation of road congestion." Shouldn't it reduce the problem? Isn't that sentence just as absurd as one saying that the increased production of apples invites a shortage of them? What is it that, together with new highway construction, really invites congestion?
5. Mr. A: It is naive to believe that railroads could ever again rival the private car for urban transportation. The fixed investment in tracks and rolling stock is so expensive that only the most intensive utilization could bring prices down low enough to compete with

[9] Terms are defined in the Glossary at the back of the book.

the private car. You just aren't going to get such intensive utilization.

Mr. B: You are right. There is nothing, but nothing, that could ever make Americans give up the private car. One can't have a decent living without one. Just look at any suburb and how it is built. One needs a car, even for small errands. Even if one wanted to take a subway downtown, one would need a car to get to the station. After having shelled out money for buying and insuring a car, one might as well drive it all the way into town.

Discuss.

6. "If necessary, we should *pay* people to use mass transit facilities instead of private cars." Discuss. Show why it may well be cheaper for a city government to do this than to charge a positive price.

7. Mr. A: To get rid of the rush hour, government should induce firms by tax concessions to stagger working hours.

   Mr. B: No, lower taxes do nothing. The way to get rid of road congestion is to raise the gasoline tax.

   Comment.

8. San Francisco has legalized jitneys. Shouldn't all cities?

9. "The French have come up with the perfect scheme for keeping too many cars out of cities: a fleet of drive-yourself taxis. Whoever wants to can join a club and get a key fitting any of these cars. They are parked all over town. However, they will drive only with a plastic slug that can be bought at $1.80 for 12 miles. It must be inserted in a special meter that chews up the rim of the slug over a 12-mile trip. This avoids tempting thieves with coin boxes. Anyone who wants to just picks up the nearest car, drives it wherever he wants to go and leaves it there. No need to bring one's own car into a city." Do you think this is a good idea for American cities? Why or why not?

10. In late 1972 Congress passed a bill providing over two years $400 million of federal subsidies for *operating* mass transit companies. (However, the president was not expected to spend the money.) Previously, Congress had voted subsidies only for *building* mass transit facilities. Do you think operating subsidies are a good idea? Why or why not?

11. Mr. A: An operating subsidy for transit systems is insane. It would reward the worst systems, the worst management, the worst operation, the worst overloading of personnel.

    Mr. B: On the contrary. It would lead to increased transit use, better service, lower fares. Transit system failures would cease, and operators would get breathing room for developing innovative services.

    What do you think and why?

12. "Correct road pricing would be a disaster, for commuting workers would still pass on to others the high social cost of driving private cars. They would demand higher wages, this would lead to higher prices for everything, and this would offset any cut in general taxes or any compensation payments from government." Evaluate.

13. What do you think of the practice of giving quantity discounts on tolls to commuters? Why?
14. Suppose your town installed computers and closed-circuit TV to help control rush hour traffic.
    Who should pay for this? Why?
15. Transportation Secretary Volpe said: "We ought to get rid of the idea once and for all that public transportation must make a profit. Public transportation is so important that we must look at its financing much like [that for] any other public service. We don't expect the Army to make a profit." Evaluate.

Selected Readings

Edel, Matthew, and Rothenberg, Jerome. *Readings in Urban Economics.* New York: Macmillan, 1972. Part 6. Discusses urban transportation problems and presents technical papers, for example, on optimum transportation systems, and the measurement of congestion costs. Note the bibliographies on pp. 411, 436, 437, 485, and 486.

Gordon, David M. *Problems in Political Economy: An Urban Perspective.* Lexington, Mass.: D. C. Heath and Co., 1971. Pp. 408–50. Presents conservative, liberal, and radical views on the urban transportation problem, including an excellent bibliography.

Hirsch, Werner Z. *Urban Economic Analysis.* New York: McGraw-Hill, 1973. Ch. 4. Discusses interrelations among urban transportation, housing, and labor markets; the government role in transportation; the demand for transportation services and their supply in the short run and in the long run.

U.S. Bureau of the Census, *Statistical Abstract of the United States, 1972.* Washington, D.C., 1972. Lists some statistics on transportation (Sections 21 and 22) and—more important—sources to other statistics: Note the listing of statistical abstract supplements (p. v); and the guide to general sources of statistics (pp. 908–9, 946, 952–53), to recent censuses (p. 960), and to state statistical abstracts (pp. 961–64).

NOTE: The *Journal of Economic Literature* lists recent articles on the economics of transportation in general (section 615) and urban transportation in particular (933).

The *Index of Economic Articles* catalogs, in sections beginning with the indicated numbers, articles on transportation in general (15.8), and on highway finance (15.85) and urban transport and parking (15.86).

13 The Pollution Problem

Economists, who are professionally concerned with the important problem of scarcity, devote much of their attention to the process of production. This is the set of activities that uses human labor and natural resources ("land") and man-made goods ("capital") to create goods that either are used in further production or are made available to people for consumption. It has long been held that a society's success in conquering scarcity can be properly measured by its *real gross national product per person*. This measures the share of new capital and consumer goods each person would receive if output were equally distributed among the population. The maximization of the real gross national product per person has long been viewed as a desirable goal to strive for. But recently some have questioned whether the maximum possible real GNP is a pure boon to mankind. Have Americans really "made it big," having pushed per capita real GNP to unprecedented levels? Critics have pointed out that, first, the processes of production and consumption inevitably withdraw resources from nature. This cannot be done without limit, for many resources are exhaustible and possibly irreplaceable (such as coal, oil, and ores). Second, production and consumption at the same time discard waste products into nature, and there are no unlimited reservoirs to receive them. If waste disposal occurs at a sufficiently high rate, it can permanently change the character of the recipient natural environment (such as the air, the waters, and the land). Then the *benefit* of having more goods (which is measured by the real GNP) is at least in part offset by the *cost* of destroying the original state of the natural environment, namely rendering the environment subsequently useless or harmful to life. A GNP created by the exhaustion of irreplaceable resources and accompanied by the production of indestructible wastes might better be regarded as a source of shame than of pride, it is said.

SPACESHIP EARTH

Indeed, one might view mankind as travelers on a crowded spaceship called *Earth* that has embarked on a long voyage, with no end in sight. When life is viewed in this way, a natural corollary is that mankind should be proud whenever it is able to keep the spaceship (and all the human bodies traveling on it) in perfect shape with a minimum of effort. Maintaining a high-quality spaceship that has high-quality physical and human capital, and doing so with a minimum of investment and consumption, might be regarded as the most important long-run goal. Therefore, a maximum real GNP would be a true source of pride only if it had not been bought at the cost of environmental destruction. Unless the GNP could be produced each year with *renewable* resources and *recyclable* wastes, the human space travelers would do better to *minimize* the production of goods. Otherwise they would be destroying the ultimate source of their lives. They would be acting no differently than the mad bomber who is about to blow up the airplane in which he is flying.

Man has for millennia been taking the short-run view—and with no apparent harmful effects. He has been trying for millennia to improve his lot by conquering and exploiting nature, by destroying his spaceship a little bit at a time. For millennia he has gladly produced goods and thoughtlessly discarded wastes. But there has been no serious problem of pollution, on a worldwide basis, until recently. The reason is simple. Until quite recently, the number of people on earth has been small relative to the vastness of the earth. The whole earth was more akin to a frontier settlement than to a spaceship. Wherever resources were exhausted or nature had been despoiled, man could move on to virgin territory. This has ceased to be true in most places on earth. Thus man is for the first time becoming conscious of living as on a spaceship. He suddenly finds himself in cramped quarters and cannot help but notice how all of life is a continuous flow: Life takes mineral, vegetable, or animal materials from its environment, uses them, and discards other materials into the environment. This is inevitable. People are no exception. But where there are many people living closely together, as in our urban areas, the law of the conservation of mass becomes suddenly very noticeable. It reminds us that the quantities of materials taken in by living beings equal the quantities retained or discarded in one form or another. For example, in the United States, the average city dweller uses, among other things, 150 gallons of water per day, 4 pounds of food, and 19 pounds of fossil fuels (coal, motor fuel, natural gas, oil). He releases, among other things, 120 gallons of sewage, 4 pounds of refuse, and about 2 pounds of air pollutants. In principle, this discard of wastes deposited on the land or in water, or released into the air, need not cause any problem. There are, happily, counterforces at work. Animal and vegetable matter can be degraded by bacteriological action in the soil or in water. In a matter of a few weeks or months, waste material can disappear. Unless the level of new discarding exceeds the capacity to "take care of things" of the body into which wastes are discharged, they need cause no concern. The case is different with inorganic wastes. They are not self-purifying. Metal wastes are broken down gradually by rusting. Glass and plastics stay with us forever in their manufactured form. Many chemicals also remain. The phosphates from our detergents, the hydrocarbons and nitrogen oxides emitted from our cars, just accumulate in ever increasing quantities in soil and water forever. In short, *excessive* waste disposal and the disposal of *particular types* of wastes is the crux of the problem. It turns waste disposal into *pollution*, a serious change in the character of the environment so that its subsequent uses are impaired. Appendix A to this chapter describes in detail the main types of wastes dumped into the environment, the quantities involved in the United States, and also the effects of excessive dumping.

BASIC TRUTHS TO BE REMEMBERED

Many approaches might lead to dealing with the problem of pollution. Before we consider any of them, however, it is worthwhile to recall the lessons from the first two chapters of this book.

People want many things. These include clean air and water, beautiful scenery, and a peaceful environment. But they also include good food and housing, clothing, and electric light. To get more of the first-mentioned group, some of the second must be traded in. The avoidance of waste disposal into the environment, or the avoidance of the harmful effects of such disposal, has an opportunity cost. Resources are needed for such avoidance, and this means that some other goods must be forgone.

Opportunity Cost

For example, if all electric power plants were to install 100-percent-efficient filters in their smokestacks, the air pollution engendered by these plants would disappear, but surely some resources would have to be diverted from other uses to produce, install, and maintain the filters. As a result, someone in society would receive fewer goods. This would be the *inevitable* price to be paid for cleaner air. The people who paid this price might be the owners of electric power companies, who might have lower profits. It might be the users of electric power, paying higher prices for electricity. It might be the suppliers of fuel and labor to power companies, who might receive lower prices for fuel or lower wages. In this way someone would have less money to spend on other goods, and the resources that might have made those other goods would be diverted to making smokestack filters and thus cleaner air.

Alternatively, suppose that power companies were to discard wastes into the air freely and that every car and every building were air-conditioned to avoid the health effects of polluted air. In this case, resources would be needed to produce, install, and maintain air-conditioners. Again resources would have to be diverted from the making of other goods and someone would have fewer of those goods.

Optimum Pollution

Since the avoidance of waste disposal into the environment and the avoidance of its ill effects are not costless, any rational society must compare the costs of avoidance with the benefits it expects to receive. If the costs exceed the benefits—if for example, society values those other goods more highly than clean air—it would be foolish to avoid pollution. If the benefits exceed the costs—that is, if society values clean air more highly than those other goods—it would be foolish not to avoid pollution. Most likely, most societies will encounter diminishing returns as they travel along either of these routes, and their best course of action will involve some pollution as well as some pollution avoidance. That is, where there is no or little pollution avoidance, the extra benefit (marginal benefit) of avoiding at least some pollution is likely to exceed the extra cost (marginal cost) of doing so. The more a society travels on the path of lessened pollution, however, the more likely that the marginal benefit of pollution avoidance declines or its marginal cost (the pain of giving up other goods) rises until the two have become equalized. At the equalization point, it would not pay to carry pollution avoidance any further. Similarly, a society that avoided all pollution would probably find that the marginal benefit of allowing some pollution (that is, getting more of other goods) exceeds the marginal cost of doing so (that is, getting a dirtier environment). In any progression along the path of increased pollution, however, the marginal benefit of pollution will eventually decline, or the marginal cost rise, until the two have become equal. At some point, the place at which the marginal benefit and marginal cost of pollution are just equal, society is using its resources most efficiently.

In short, pollution is a problem only when there is obviously too much of it, when it is clear that the extra benefit from avoiding at least some of it exceeds the extra cost in other goods forgone that must be paid. Solving the pollution problem, therefore, does not necessarily mean stopping all harmful waste disposal. Rather, it means bringing about that *optimal* level of pollution at which marginal benefit just equals marginal cost. Going beyond this point would put society in a position wherein further reductions in pollution would bring less extra benefit than they would take away through the sacrifice of other goods, which alone makes reductions in pollution possible. The question is by what mechanism can society determine and bring about the proper degree of pollution avoidance.

POSSIBLE APPROACHES TO SOLVING THE POLLUTION PROBLEM

Some people seem to think that solving the pollution problem calls for nothing more than *persuading* polluters to desist from their actions.

Voluntary Sacrifice by Polluters

"If the owners of businesses," goes the argument, "were less eager for profits and had more of a social conscience, they would voluntarily stop smokestack emissions and clean up waste water and build quieter products, and they would finance the cost by paying themselves lower dividends. If the residents of a town were less selfish and had more of a social conscience, they would voluntarily stop dumping raw sewage and nonreturnable bottles and detergents, and finance the cost by paying higher taxes or higher prices." People who argue this way believe that man is indifferently exploiting nature not because he is fundamentally evil, but rather because he has been brainwashed by centuries of Judeo-Christian teachings. Consider Genesis 1:28: "Be fruitful and multiply, and replenish the earth and subdue it, and have dominion over the fish of the sea and the fowl of the air and over every living thing that moves upon the earth." Such statements, together with the rejection of earlier beliefs in the divinity of nature, are seen to have conditioned man's outlook against preserving nature. They have made him look at himself as an antagonistic exclusive exploiter of nature rather than as its friend and steward. Therefore, the proponents of persuasion feel that it is now just a matter of getting people to think otherwise, through a well-organized campaign of moral suasion; that it is just a matter of making good people aware of the harm done, perhaps inadvertently, to the environment by their particular kind of production or consumption; or that it is a matter of talking indifferent or greedy people into changing their behavior that they know full well to harm the environment.

Drawbacks. Yet one may seriously doubt that this call for self-sacrifice can be successful. Altruism is a notoriously weak force for social change. Asking for large-scale self-restraint is calling for nothing less than an ethical revolution, which we cannot hope to achieve in the near future. It is important to see the reason for this. Even if everyone in the population agreed that all would gain from reducing pollution, no rational individual would voluntarily act to stop his part of pollution. This is so because in most cases any one producer or consumer contributes an infinitesimal amount to total pollution; therefore, he can be certain that by itself any sacrificial action of his, though costly to him, will have no noticeable effect overall. It will appear as a futile, pointless effort, akin to holding back a flood with a pail.

By the same logic it follows that any one individual would still have the incentive to pollute (and thus save the cost to him of abatement) even if he were certain that everyone else would act to stop their pollution. The result when one person cheats would be indistinguishable from that when all were complying with antipollution measures! Thus the moral suasion approach amounts to asking each individual to act against his own interest. Indeed, a person who heeded the call for "responsible citizenship" could hardly expect to be admired as a saint by his fellow citizens. More likely they would look at him as some kind of fool, sucker, or crank.

Besides being impractical, the voluntary approach to pollution reduction has another drawback. It contains no mechanism to determine and achieve the correct amont of pollution, that is, the level at which the marginal benefit of further reductions is just balanced by the marginal cost of bringing them about. This difficulty might be overcome by another approach.

Victims Bribe Polluters

Instead of relying on people's altruism, one might appeal to their self-interest. Rather than try to change the nature of man, one might accept it as it is and try to harness people's very greed and avarice for the purpose of reducing pollution by offering them a bribe for doing so. One can imagine cases in which this would work very well indeed.

The nature of the private bribe. Suppose a family lives next to an orchard. Every spring morning, the orchardist burns hundreds of tar "smudgepots" to protect the blossoms from frost. This creates a thick local concentration of black smoke that, let us suppose, adversely affects only two things: the health of our family nearby and also the outward appearance of its house. Clearly the damage done could be assessed by figuring what it would take for our family to offset the effects of this annual event. It could spend, for example, $1,000 every year to have its house painted cach July. It could also spend $2,000 once to have its house air-conditioned. Then it would be able to filter out the smoke enveloping it every spring morning by running the system full time during those months. This may involve an additional maintenance and electricity cost of $60 a year. If the family expected to live in this neighborhood for the next 30 years, it would spend a total of $30,000 on painting the house and an additional $3,800 on installing, maintaining, and operating the air-conditioning system. The present discounted value of this expenditure would come to $22,178 if we assume an interest rate of 3.5 percent per year. That is, if our family had this sum now, invested it at 3.5 percent per year, and were to make the pollution-offsetting expenditures just described each year, it would just be able to cover its expenses.[1] Thus we can say that the orchard-caused pollution imposes over the next 30 years damages on our family equivalent to present purchasing power of $22,178. Theoretically, therefore, our family might be willing to pay a bribe to the orchardist up to this amount on the condition that the burning of smudgepots be stopped. Our family could be totally indifferent between paying this sum now (and never having to worry about this pollution again) or offsetting the pollution effects by spending $3,060 now, investing the rest at 3.5 percent, and spending $1,060 a year for another 29 years.

Now that we know the damage done by pollution, or the benefit harmed parties would reap if it were stopped, it is time to consider the opportunity cost of stopping pollution. Suppose it is less than the damages, or $15,000. That is, the orchardist may be able to install, for a one-time expenditure of $15,000, a water-sprinkler system that with equal effectiveness protects his blossoms from spring frost. Suppose the annual operating costs of this system are identical with the tar-pot alternative. Clearly, our orchardist would gladly

[1] On the nature of discounting, note also footnote 4, Chapter 10.

accept a bribe of $22,178 to switch his system. He would be $7,128 better off as a result, while our family would be no worse off than before. Alternatively, he might accept a $15,000 bribe. This would leave him equally well off, but make our family $7,128 better off.

On the other hand, if the opportunity cost were to exceed the damages (if it were, $30,000, let us say), even our family's maximum bribe could not move the orchardist to cease his pollution activities and switch to the sprinkler system.

All this is just as it should be. If the marginal benefit of pollution avoidance exceeds the marginal cost, pollution should be avoided. That was our first case. If the marginal cost exceeds the marginal benefit, pollution should not be avoided. This was the second case.

Problems with the private bribe. There are a number of reasons why this approach to pollution control is also unlikely to work in practice. First, it is quite possible to impose upon someone damages that far exceed the party's ability to offset. Our family, for instance, may have an annual income of $1,500. Under these circumstances, it would simply have to suffer the effects of pollution. It would have to live in a filthy-looking house and with whatever ill health befalls it as a result of the annual springtime catastrophe. It could neither afford to paint its house once a year nor escape the health effects by buying air-conditioning. Hence it could not afford to make the bribe contemplated above.

Second, even if a victim were able to pay, he might not be willing to. The whole idea of bribing a polluter not to victimize you smacks of buying protection from the Mafia. It is like paying tribute to a criminal (who has great power to harm you) for the privilege of not being harmed! Many people would find this a morally unacceptable course of action.

Third, even if the approach is acceptable and the victims are able and willing to pay a bribe up to the amount of damages experienced, there will appear additional concerns. There will probably be high costs associated with the very arranging of the bribe. Perhaps the polluter is unwilling or unable to disclose the cost of pollution avoidance (in our case, the cost of the sprinkler system). Perhaps he is, like a genuine criminal, out to rob his victim of every last cent and does not hesitate to exaggerate the cost of pollution avoidance and even to blackmail his victims by threatening to increase the level of pollution. Perhaps his workers or suppliers join the battle against change. Like the flunkies of a crime boss, orchard workers and the suppliers of tar may fear for their jobs. Like recipients of cheap stolen goods, even customers may oppose the change. Fearing higher prices of apples, they may join orchard workers in their battle against automated sprinklers!

Finally, and this is probably the most important practical obstacle to the private bribe approach, where there is more than one victim, any one of them can hope that someone else may offer the bribe first. This would enable all others to reap the benefit without any cost. As everyone waits for others to act, no one acts at all. The purchase of clean air in this case involves the purchase of a pure public good, the benefits of which cannot be withheld for nonpayment.

The nature of the public bribe. The idea of getting together and offering a bribe jointly through the agency of government suggests itself. If a majority of pollution victims should so vote, the government might collect a portion of the bribe through taxes from each family and subsidize the polluter sufficiently to alter his behavior. To use our earlier example, if a hundred families were affected in the way described, each might be willing to tax itself up to a maximum of $22,178. If a government inquiry (which in itself would be costly) determined the cost of the alternative sprinkler system at $15,000, it would clearly be socially desirable to avoid the pollution with collective damages far larger. Voters might vote a tax of $200 per family (of which $50 might cover the administrative cost of the whole arrangement). The arrangement would vastly improve the well-being of each family while not affecting that of the orchardist. He would receive a $15,000 subsidy to install a $15,000 sprinkler system. (A variant of this approach involves the merger whereby polluters and victims are merged into one unit. In our case, the citizens might expropriate the orchardist and run his firm as a public enterprise. Seeing the opportunities of bettering themselves, they would simply tax themselves $150 per family and install the sprinkler system in the new government enterprise.)

Disadvantages. This approach, though workable, may be inequitable. The distribution of pollution damage may not be equal, as postulated. Some families may not be affected by pollution at all. Suppose that of our 100 families, only 51 experienced the calculated damage while 49 experienced none. The 51 may vote for the bribery scheme, each expecting to get rid of a $22,178 burden at a $200 cost. Yet 49 may vote against the scheme, since they have no burden from pollution but a clear burden from additional taxes. As the majority wins, some citizens will end up subsidizing other citizens.

Finally, all bribe approaches have the disadvantage of providing no incentive to polluters to find a cheaper method of pollution avoidance. Our orchardist, for example, might discover a revolutionary method of frost protection that costs a lot less than the sprinkler system. But he has no particular reason to look for one if he is assured that whatever cost he incurs in avoiding pollution will be covered by the private or public subsidy.

Victims Sue Polluters

The approaches to pollution avoidance discussed so far have one legal implication. They imply that polluters somehow have property rights in the environment (therefore, the legal right to pollute) and that others who dislike the consequences therefore must buy polluters off. But it is not at all clear that polluters do have that right.

Ill-defined property rights. Property rights in the natural environment or the right to exclusive use of such things as the air or waterways have to this day remained ill-defined. For long periods, the natural environment was a free good, since its availability by far exceeded the demand people made on it. But the relationship has changed. The demand made on natural resources—for instance, bodies of water, for such purposes as drinking, fishing, recreation, navigation, waste disposal, and cooling—frequently exceeds the supply. If under such conditions use remains unrestricted, overuse occurs. Eventually, those users who deteriorate the resource (like polluting factories or municipalities) will win over other users who don't (like swimmers or fishermen). Those users who can harm other users will tend to crowd out the others who harm no one. But obviously, the act of exclusion has in no way bestowed an exclusive *legal* right to use on the former. Only a law could do that.

Defining rights in favor of polluters. If a law gave the right to the exclusive use of a river to a factory, then it would be clear that no one else had any business using that river at all. The factory could use it for whatever purposes it saw fit. If the property right were transferable, the factory could also rent or sell the river to someone else, just as a landlord can rent or sell a house. Then others, such as swimmers or fishermen, might acquire the right to exclusive use until the rental period expired or they, in turn, decided to sell the property right. Under such circumstances, when polluters hold the exclusive right to a natural resource, paying polluters to not exercise that right for waste disposal purposes would make sense. If our orchardist held the exclusive legal right to the use of the air over the town, nothing but the citizens' "bribe" could take that right away from him.

Defining rights in favor of victims. But, one may argue, since property rights in such things as air and water are so ill-defined, it would be just as possible for the government to now define such right in favor of the victims of pollution. And such a law might be regarded as more just. Each family, for example, might be given the exclusive right to use the airspace above the lot on which its house is built. Under these circumstances, the shoe would be on the other foot. A would-be polluting orchardist would have to buy off families living nearby, rather than the other way around. *He* would have to pay *them* whatever they required before he could dump particles into their airspace. Similarly, his son who might want to ride his noisy snowmobile through the orchard on winter nights might have to pay people for the right to dump unwanted sound into *their* air! Polluters who failed to pay would then be just as guilty before the law as someone who without your permission dumped a load of trash on your front lawn or who appeared on your land one fine morning and began to cut down all the trees. Such polluters could be sued for damages by their victims.

The outcome. Note that the end result of either form of clarification of the law (in favor of polluters or in favor of victims) would be very much the same so far as pollution levels are concerned, although it would differ with respect to income distribution. Consider again our earlier example, wherein an orchardist imposes $22,178 of damages on a single family while he could avoid the pollution for $15,000. If the property right in the air is given to the orchardist, the victimized family must buy him off. If the family pays any sum between $15,000 and $22,178, pollution will be stopped. If the property right in the air is given to the family, the situation is the other way around. The orchardist must buy off the family. He can choose to pay $22,178 or more for the right to pollute, or he can spend $15,000 to avoid pollution. He will prefer the latter. So again, pollution will be stopped.

If victims of pollution, however, are poor, while polluters are not, one might prefer giving them the environmental rights. They would be assured of zero pollution (as in our example, where avoidance cost is smaller than the required damage payment) or of full compensation with pollution (should avoidance cost exceed the required damage payment). By the same token, should polluters be poorer than their victims, one might prefer giving them environmental property rights. They would be assured of full compensation for pollution avoidance costs (as in our example) or of the right to pollute (should avoidance cost exceed the damages from pollution).

Direct Government Regulation of Polluters

A variant of the approach just described, which gives property rights in the natural environment either to victims of pollution or to polluters, would involve placing these rights in *government* hands. Unless it had received compensation payment, the government could then sue any polluter for infringing upon *public* property. Indeed, the implicit assertion that the natural environment is public property to be protected by the government is inherent in another set of antipollution proposals.

The ban. Many people argue that the government should simply ban outright all types of pollution on the grounds that no private individual or group of them has any right at all to use the environment as a waste-disposal site. The driving by households of cars emitting exhausts, the dumping of sewage by municipalities, the heating of rivers by industry, all these things should simply be forbidden.

Disadvantages of the outright ban. The problems with this strict approach are obvious. First, it is simply not possible to outlaw all these activities at once without inviting extreme chaos. Imagine the effects of suddenly outlawing all vehicles with polluting internal combustion engines.

Second, this approach cannot reach an optimum. It leads to a waste of resources to the extent that the natural environment has the capacity to assimilate *some* quantities of pollutants without ill effects. This approach would avoid even that part of waste disposal that does no harm at all, and it would avoid that part that causes harm smaller than the avoidance cost. Reason points to a less strict alternative, the setting of pollution standards.

Standards. Three types of standards have been proposed as a means of reducing pollution levels. First, the government might set *input standards,* specifying the types of inputs polluters may use (for example, fuel with specified sulfur content) or the manner in which they must be used. However, this controls pollution only most indirectly and without certainty because the quantities of inputs used are not regulated. Clearly, 10 tons of low-sulfur fuel burned may emit as much sulfur dioxide as 5 tons of high-sulfur fuel. Therefore, the setting of *emission standards* is to be preferred. They specify maximum quantities of pollutants that may be released by a polluter. Since, however, the number of polluters can change, this approach still does not assure the objective, which is, presumably, a certain quality of environment. Only an *ambient standard* can do that, for it specifies the quantity of pollutants the environment may contain.

The trouble with standards. The regulation-by-standards approach has one serious drawback. Since pollution control costs differ among polluters, the overall pollution-avoidance cost can only be minimized if standards are carefully tailored to the special circumstances of each polluter. That is, emission standards must be toughest for those who can avoid pollution at lowest cost. Often this would also be desirable for reasons of equity, since just those polluters who have already voluntarily avoided some pollution are likely to have the highest marginal cost for further reductions in emission. Yet the equitable and least-cost achievement of a given ambient standard by setting *differentiated* emission standards would spell an administrative nightmare. Thus government can almost certainly be relied on to set *uniform* emission standards for all polluters. This would be both inequitable and unnecessarily expensive.

Table 13.1 illustrates how uniform emission standards cannot be expected to minimize the pollution-avoidance cost. There are assumed to exist three firms in an area emitting initially quantities of pollutants given in row 1. Then emission standards are set requiring reductions by all firms to 50 percent of former emissions (row 2). Thus the emissions avoided are shown in row 3. Suppose the marginal and average costs of pollution abatement are constant for each firm as given in row 4.[2] Then the total costs of pollution abatement are those of row 5 of our table. Society is achieving a 50 percent reduction of pollution by incurring an opportunity cost of $480 million a year (encircled).

[2] This assumption is only made to simplify the illustration. The more realistic assumption of eventually *rising* marginal and average cost would complicate the illustration, but not alter the final conclusion reached with its help.

Table 13.1 Air Pollution Abatement: Uniform Standards vs. Differential Treatment

		Firm A	Firm B	Firm C	Total
(1)	Quantity of particulate matter emitted prior to antipollution law (million tons per year)	100	20	80	200
(2)	Quantity of particulate matter emitted after 50 percent standards are adopted (million tons per year)	50	10	40	100
(3) = (1) − (2)	Quantity of particulate matter emission that is avoided (million tons per year)	50	10	40	100
(4)	Unit cost of pollution avoidance (dollars per ton per year)	7	1	3	—
(5) = (3) × (4)	Total cost of pollution avoidance using standards law (million dollars per year)	350	10	120	(480)
(6)	Quantity of particulate matter emitted after selective decree (million tons per year)	100	0	0	100
(7) = (1) − (6)	Alternative quantity of particulate matter emission that is avoided (million tons per year)	0	20	80	100
(8) = (7) × (4)	Alternative total cost of pollution avoidance using selective decree (million dollars per year)	0	20	240	(260)

NOTE: If unit costs of pollution avoidance differ among firms, society cannot minimize the opportunity cost of a given amount of pollution avoidance by issuing uniform pollution standards.

Yet society could have gotten the same result at a much smaller sacrifice of other things. Only rarely is the unit cost of pollution avoidance uniform for all polluters. In our hypothetical case, there are indeed great differences. As shown in row 4, the unit cost of pollution avoidance is exceedingly high for firm A, less so for firm C, least so for firm B.

Had government known this detail, it could have issued a *selective* decree, treating different firms differently. For instance, it could have allowed firm A to dump as much as ever, while forcing firms B and C to reduce dumping 100 percent. The results are shown in rows 6 through 8. The same 100-million-ton-per-year reduction in pollution would have cost society only $260 million of other goods (encircled).

Another drawback of a scheme of standards would be the high administrative cost. The quality of the environment would have to be monitored. Standards would have to be agreed upon on the basis of scientific evidence concerning emission toxicity and persistence. Pollution would have to be traced to its sources and polluters be made aware of the standards applying to them. Most expensive would probably be the enforcement cost. Unlike traffic violations, which can bring harm to the violator (an accident), the violation of emission standards would bring pure pleasure to the violator (lower costs); people therefore would be very much inclined to break such rules.

Establishing a Market for Pollution Rights

There is, finally, one additional alternative. One could charge a positive price for the use as waste disposal sites of presently free natural resources, such as air or water, and thereby force every individual to bear financial responsibility for his actions.

As every student of economics quickly learns, and as we have noted on several occasions earlier in this book, charging too low or too high a price can cause all kinds of trouble. Since we are now charging a zero price for the use of air or water, people get the wrong signal. They are in effect told that pure air and water are available in infinite amounts (and that is why they cost nothing). They are told that everyone can take all he wants and then some. The truth is that the supply of pure air and water and space is limited. As people in the aggregate try to take more than there is, they end up polluting the limited amount that exists. If society charges too low a price for anything, people will make profligate use of the items in question. *Pollution of the environment is simply an indication that the charge made for using the environment is incorrect.* In other words, if people had to pay a positive price for the privilege of dumping wastes into the environment, they would think twice before doing it! The higher the monetary price or user charge, the less they would do it, for they would become aware (and painfully so) of the full social costs of their actions.

Now suppose that government did the following: Instead of attempting to achieve a given ambient quality of the natural environment through direct regulation of polluters, it establishes a market for pollution rights. As we shall see, this would achieve the same result in the way of pollution abatement but would have the advantage of assuring the desired reduction in pollution levels *at minimum cost.* We can use the numerical example just discussed to illustrate the scheme.

Pollution rights. Suppose that a study of the costs and benefits of reducing air pollution in a given region reveals that a halving of current emission levels to 100 million tons per year is socially desirable at an annual cost of $260 million. This may be so because the health effects on humans, animals, and plants are exceedingly high for higher pollution levels relative to their avoidance cost. By the same token, it may be clear that further reductions in pollution below the 100-million-ton annual level bring negligible improvements in health and would not be justified economically unless additional pollution avoidance costs were equally negligible. In short, we suppose the society is willing to tolerate pollution to the tune of 100 million tons a year. The government could therefore issue 100 million pollution licenses or "rights," each being a certificate allowing the holder to dump one ton of particulates into the air per year. These rights could be transferable in the same way that stock certificates are. Instead of any household or firm being invested with the private right to a piece of airspace, it could acquire the right to use the public air as a waste disposal site by buying a pollution right. Without such a certificate in its possession for every ton of particles it wishes to dispose of, no household or firm would be allowed to dump anything into the air *at all.* Such a solution may be considered vastly preferable to one that gives property rights in the environment to either polluters or their victims on the grounds that one or the other would be more just. Under the market scheme, *any* party that wants rights to nature's assimilative capacity to receive wastes and wants them badly enough to pay the equilibrium price can acquire such rights. In some cases, this may be would-be polluters. But the purchasers could also be special-interest groups such as conservationists, who—disagreeing with the government's decision to allow *some* pollution—could buy up pollution rights for the purpose of *not* using them, of keeping them out of the hands of potential users.

The market at work. It can easily be shown why use of the market mechanism would achieve a given pollution avoidance in the most efficient way. Consider Figure 13.1, "The Pollution Rights Market." We agreed that the government would issue 100 million pollution rights per year. This is the meaning of supply curve S. How many rights would firms want to buy at alternative prices? We already know from row 1, Table 13.1, that they would dump wastes to the tune of 200 million tons a year if everyone left them alone, that is, charged them nothing. Thus the demand curve for pollution rights cuts the horizontal axis at 200 at a zero price. We can argue that demand would be the same up to a price of $1 per right. All of the firms would rather pay $1 or less for the right to pollute than avoid dumping, which would cost them, as row 4 in Table 13.1 shows, $1 or more. Once a pollution right costs more than $1 (but less than $3), firm B would have the incentive to drop out of the pollution game. It would rather avoid dumping (at a cost of $1 per ton per year) than pay more than $1 for the right to pollute. Since firm B's total emissions amounted to 20 million tons per year, the quantity of rights demanded between the $1.01 and $3 prices drops to 180 million.

Once a pollution right costs more than $3 (but less than $7), firm C

Figure 13.1 The Pollution Rights Market

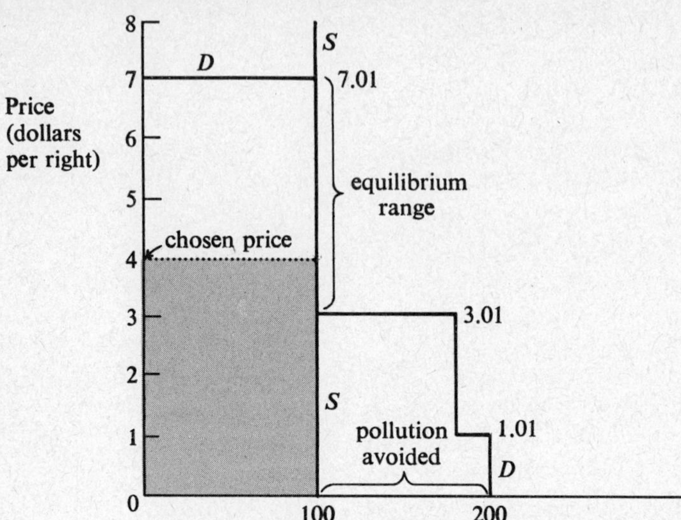

Given demand for pollution rights *D* and supply *S*, a perfectly competitive market would set an equilibrium price anywhere between \$3.01 and \$7 per right. Each year, 100 million such rights would be bought and sold. In this case, it would cut pollution in half from the 200-million-ton-a-year level that would prevail in the absence of such a market. The opportunity cost of pollution avoidance, furthermore, would be minimized, since the firms that can avoid pollution most cheaply would be the first to do so.

drops out of the game, too. It would rather avoid dumping (at a cost of \$3 per ton per year) than pay more than \$3 for the right to pollute. Since firm C's total emissions amounted to 80 million tons per year, the quantity of rights demanded between the \$3.01 and \$7 prices drops to 100 million.

Once the pollution rights cost more than \$7, firm A drops out, too. It would rather avoid dumping (at a cost of \$7 per ton per year) than pay more than \$7 for the right to pollute. Since firm A's total emissions amounted to 100 million tons per year, the quantity of rights demanded above the \$7.01 price drops to zero. From the graph it is clear that the demand and supply curves are identical between the prices of \$3.01 and \$7. The equilibrium price is indeterminate; that is, it could be anything in this range. Had our example included more firms, however, the demand curve would have taken on more of its usual shape, cutting the supply curve at a unique point.

Price setting by trial and error. What then should government do? It is fairly simple. After having fixed the total quantity of pollution rights to be sold (that is, after having decided on the amount of pollution it is willing to accept), it can set any tentative price for the rights concerned and invite offers to buy. If the offers exceed the supply (as they would at any price below $3.01 per right, in our example), government should raise the price. If the offers fall short of the supply (as they would at any price above $7 in our example), it should lower the price. By trial and error, it can find an equilibrium price, at which offers to buy rights equal the supply. In our case, this would be true at any price between $3.01 and $7 per right.

The result. Suppose that government set the price at $4 per right. What would be the result? Firms B and C would find it cheaper to avoid dumping 100 percent than to buy rights and dump wastes. Firm A would continue to dump as much as before. In short, without having had any detailed knowledge of who pollutes, how much, or what the individual firms' avoidance costs would be, without having issued orders to anyone, the government would exactly achieve the efficient result. It would achieve, that is, a given amount of pollution avoidance at minimum opportunity cost shown to be possible in rows 6 to 8 of Table 13.1. Society would give up $260 million of valuable things to buy the necessary equipment to avoid half the pollution. No other arrangement could have achieved this at lower cost.

Note the detailed implications of all this for prices, profits, and resource allocation. For example, the people who buy electric power from firms B and C (which now avoid pollution) pay higher prices, or the owners of firms B and C have lower profits, to cover the pollution avoidance cost. Costs formerly borne by others have now been made visible to customers and owners of polluting enterprises! As a result, they spend less on other things, perhaps less on furniture and cars. The resources that would have made these other things are diverted to make the pollution avoidance equipment instead. Society has reallocated resources from the production of furniture and cars to the production of cleaner air! At the same time, the customers of firm A pay more also (or the owners of firm A suffer lower profits) to cover the pollution permits costing $400 million a year (shaded area in graph). Note that this is simply a money transfer from some electric power consumers and producers to government. The former have less control over resources, the government has more. Although it will give firm A an incentive to find a pollution avoidance method that costs less than $4 per ton per year (so it can escape the need to spend $4 on dumping rights), at the moment this does not affect the degree of pollution by A. The government might use the revenue in any way it pleases, including the policing of the whole arrangement. Thus, again, the resources released in one place (as electric power consumers or producers spend less) are used elsewhere (as government spends more).

The important thing to note is this: *All those individual consumers or producers whose decisions (to consume or produce) affect the environment are personally made aware of their effect on the environment through higher prices or lower profits.* Thus they are made acutely aware of the scarcity of nature's resources. They can pay the higher prices, or receive the lower profits, or they can cease consuming or producing the good in question. If they opt for the former, they are either paying for resources to avoid harming nature or they are paying for the scarce waste-disposal capacity of nature, just as they are used to paying for labor and materials and equipment, which also are not available in infinite amounts. In the long run, furthermore, should population growth raise the number of firms and thus the demand on nature's waste-disposal capacity, we could expect this increased scarcity to be reflected in higher prices for pollution rights. Thus there would be given increasing incentives for pollution avoidance schemes.

Figure 13.2 illustrates what is involved.

The scheme generalized. If pollution rights markets were introduced foı all kinds of pollutants, all kinds of product prices would be higher and come to reflect the manifold expenses for pollution avoidance or the costs of acquiring pollution rights. Groceries in disposable containers would cost more to

***Figure 13.2* The Market for Pollution Rights in the Long Run**

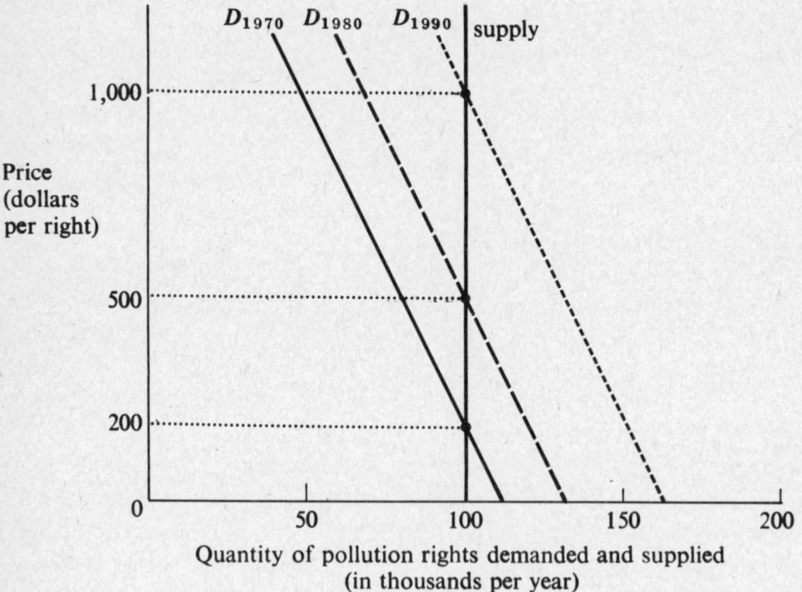

Demand for and supply of pollution rights might determine a short-run equilibrium price of $200 in 1970. Since the quantity supplied never rises, the price can be expected to rise over time with demand. By 1980, it may reach $500, by 1990 $1,000, and so on. Only those polluters who find it cheaper to purchase pollution rights than to engage in pollution prevention on their own will buy the rights and pollute. Thus nature's assimilative capacity is always reserved for those who need it most because their alternatives are costlier than paying the equilibrium price for pollution rights. (Each "right" allows the owner to dump one ton per year.)

cover the fees for dumping containers. Electricity would cost more to cover the costs of avoiding water and air pollution or of acquiring the rights to continue it. Airline tickets would cost more because airline companies would have to buy quieter planes with no exhausts or pay fees for dumping noise and fumes. Automobiles would cost more to buy if automakers had to make them quiet and exhaust-free, and because the steel they use would cost more if steel companies had to avoid dumping wastes or pay for pollution rights. Or automobiles would cost more to run, because households would have to pay fees for dumping noise and exhaust or buy costlier gas that gives out fewer exhausts. Apples would cost more because orchardists would have to replace tar smudgepots with sprinkler systems or buy pollution rights in the air.

After the creation of pollution rights markets, everywhere buyers turn they will be confronted with the true opportunity costs of their actions. Those who benefit from goods involving waste disposal in production or consumption must pay for such disposal in full. No individual is told by government what he may or may not produce or consume. Each individual household or firm can adjust its behavior to the extent and in a manner best suited to its particular circumstances. Yet while individual freedom is maximized, social control is exercised. The prices of various pollution rights will be high enough to assure overall control of pollution levels because they will be raised until they encourage sufficient numbers of would-be polluters, like firms B and C above, to prefer pollution avoidance to continued waste disposal. Because of the generally higher prices (or lower profits), the real income of households in terms of *man-made goods they get* would be lower, but in terms of *environmental quality* would be higher. This would be the whole aim of this policy: to achieve a cleaner environment at the unfortunate, but inevitable, price of forgoing other things.

A SURVEY OF U.S. ANTIPOLLUTION POLICIES

Every one of the *public* policies just discussed as potential antipollution weapons has been tried in the United States. However, these attempts have been made at various levels of government and have not been part of a well-designed overall strategy.

The Public Bribe

Various levels of government have offered a variety of economic incentives to private and public polluters to reduce their waste disposal.

Among these types of programs were the following in the early 1970's:

1. The federal government and six states granted income tax credits to businesses that bought pollution control equipment or introduced new, less polluting production methods. The federal law allowed businesses to deduct from 33 percent to 44 percent of their cost from their income tax liability. The New York law allowed a 1 percent deduction.

2. The federal government provided grants to state and local governments to construct antipollution facilities. In the case of liquid-waste-treatment facilities, the grants amounted to half of the cost. It has also provided research and development grants for antipollution demonstration projects, such as recycling solid waste.[3]
3. Twenty-four states exempted pollution control devices from property taxes.
4. Thirteen states exempted pollution control devices from sales taxes.
5. The federal government and 11 states allowed accelerated depreciation of pollution control equipment. The Federal Tax Reform Act of 1969 allowed such write-off over a five-year period, provided that the equipment conformed to state standards. As always, this method only postpones income taxes to later years. It is nothing more than the provision of an interest-free loan, since income taxes that would have been paid in one period will not have to be paid until later. In the short run, when depreciation charges are high, reported profits and income taxes go down. Later, when depreciation charges have been exhausted, reported profits and income taxes are correspondingly higher.
6. The federal government has granted low-interest loans for the purchase of pollution abatement equipment.
7. Businesses have been allowed by Congress to finance 100 percent of pollution control equipment through the sale of long-term industrial development revenue bonds. These are sold on behalf of firms by state-created local or state agencies. Income from such bonds is tax-exempt and these bonds carry lower interest rates than bonds in the private securities market. They are often bought by insurance companies and banks that would never agree to make privately such low-interest loans and loans covering 100 percent of the cost of pollution control equipment.

Drawbacks. As we noted earlier, all public bribes are bound to be inequitable as nonpolluters through their taxes subsidize polluters. In addition, none of the programs listed above offers coverage of 100 percent of pollution avoidance costs. They all offer *partial* bribes. As a result, these programs are highly ineffective because they still require a substantial voluntary sacrifice on the part of the polluters. They can do better by not controlling pollution at all. To consider again our earlier example, it is as if the orchardist (who could stop smoke emissions by installing a $15,000 sprinkler system) were offered government aid of $5,000 to do so. Clearly, this is equivalent to asking him to spend $10,000 of his own funds on pollution control. Why should he accept $5,000 on the condition that he throw away $10,000? He would be better off if he continued burning his smudgepots. One *advantage* of the partial bribe is that

[3] In the first of these projects in Franklin, Ohio, 50 tons of municipal wastes per day were being processed in 1972. They were being ground down by a huge pulping machine to a water-based slurry. Sifters, sorters, and separators then extracted from the waste stream metals, glass, and paper. The rest was cleanly incinerated to produce electricity. However, the managers of the project, while selling the paper at $25 a ton, were unable to sell the reclaimed glass and nonferrous metals, and these were buried in a nearby landfill. Other projects involved firing boilers with a mixture of pulverized garbage and coal (St. Louis), turning garbage into a low-sulfur fuel (San Diego), and reclaiming arid soil by spreading ground garbage on it to hold water (Oregon).

it provides an incentive to find the cheapest avoidance method. However, many of the above actual programs are undesirable for creating a bias in favor of pollution control *equipment*. Possibly other methods of pollution control such as the use of less polluting fuel or of different production methods, or the making of different products (unbleached rather than white paper), would be cheaper. Finally, even the partial bribes offered cannot help all polluters. Income tax credits, for instance, do not help firms with zero or negative incomes at all. Nor do they help state and local government units.

Assigning Property Rights to Victims as a Basis for Lawsuits

In 1971, two states (Michigan and Connecticut) allowed individuals to bring "class suits" against polluters. Under their laws any citizen can sue any polluter for harm done to people or the natural environment, even without having experienced personal damage. Courts can impose injunctions on the polluter or force him to comply with abatement standards. Implicitly, therefore, the law vests the right to the use of the environment in pollution victims. A similar *federal* bill (the Hart-McGovern bill) was opposed by President Nixon in 1971. Others have used the ninth amendment to the Constitution to sue polluters. It states that the listing of rights in other amendments (such as the freedoms of religion and of speech) does not eliminate other rights. Surely, it has been argued, people must have a right to a decent environment, for if they did not, all the other rights listed become illusory. One cannot enjoy them if one is dead. Reasoning in this way, a Long Island woman in 1969 filed a $30 billion damage suit against the manufacturers of DDT for having spoiled her living environment. The Elizabeth, N.J., board of education filed suit on the grounds that noise from Interstate Highway 278 had made classes impossible in one of its schools. Although the school board in 1971 was awarded $164,119 in damages, few such suits have been successful in the past. This has inspired proposals to change the United States Constitution by adding to it a *Conservation Bill of Rights*. This would guarantee to each citizen the right to an unimpaired environment. Unlike present laws, it would assure access to federal courts and create a powerful weapon for fighting encroachments, whether they were wastes in the air, in the water, or on the land. However, the U.S. Supreme Court ruled in 1972 that under the common law of nuisance federal courts already have the power to grant reprieve to pollution victims. In 1973 it promised to rule on whether people not having a personal stake in a pollution case could sue on behalf of citizens in general, as the Sierra Club has done.

There have also been some steps taken to change international law for the same reason. In 1969, for example, 40 nations agreed on a new maritime convention to protect their coastlines from oil pollution. The agreement places a monetary liability of up to $14 million per disaster on shipowners. It allows threatened nations to destroy the vessels involved on the high seas. In 1972, 12 European countries signed an antidumping agreement covering the northeastern Atlantic, while 91 nations agreed on a global convention ending or restricting the ocean dumping of poisonous wastes, such as radioactive materials, biological and chemical warfare agents, oils, pesticides, plastics, and mercury.

Direct Government Regulation

Recently, government has moved on a broad front to regulate polluters directly.

The ban. A few governments have moved to ban certain types of waste disposal or activities leading to it. In 1970, the federal government, following a similar move by the state of Wisconsin, banned the use of DDT on 50 types of vegetables and fruits, on tobacco, livestock, and shade trees, and on marshes, forests, and buildings. (It did not ban the use of DDT on citrus fruit, cotton, peanuts, soybeans, and certain minor crops, however.) As of 1973 the ban was made almost total, allowing only emergency use (as after floods) and use on minor crops (like green peppers, onions, and sweet potatoes).

In 1972, the federal government banned uses of mercury accounting for 20 percent of domestic consumption (notably in pesticides and mildew-proofing and antifouling paints).

The states have also gotten into the act. In 1970, there were some 70 proposals before 26 state legislatures to ban disposable beverage containers. In 1971, Bowie, Maryland, actually banned cans. Oregon banned detachable tabs on metal cans (effective 1972). Connecticut and New York banned phosphates in laundry detergents (effective mid-1973). Vermont banned non-returnable beverage containers as of 1973. In a much publicized move, Delaware passed its Coastal Zoning Act of 1971. Within two miles of the coast, it totally banned heavy polluters, including oil refineries, steel plants, paper mills, and offshore oil and iron ore transshipment terminals.

Finally, city governments have acted also. In 1972, several big cities, including Boston, Chicago, New York, and Philadelphia, banned the spraying of fireproofing asbestos.

Standards: The governmental machinery. Mostly, though, governments have gone the route of setting standards. This was done exclusively at the state and local level at first, at the federal level more recently. The first exhaust emission standards on cars were set by California in 1961; federal standards for all (new) U.S. cars did not appear until 1968. The first general noise control codes were set in Chicago in 1971 and in New York City in 1972. Later many states and the federal government adopted such codes also. While there was no such code on the federal books, the New York code specified decibel A-scale standards for a variety of equipment, for example, for compressors a maximum of 90 in 1972 was to be reduced to 75 or less by 1974. Although ambient noise levels (the all-encompassing noise that is a composite of sounds from many sources near and far) are associated with a given localized environment, most types of pollution are not very easily dealt with at the local level. Most pollutants can travel long distances and are no respecter of local political boundaries. Thus it has become increasingly clear that federal action is required in any meaningful antipollution effort.[4]

The concern at the federal level has become obvious since the inauguration of President Nixon. Recognizing that "we have become victims of our own technological genius," he first established the cabinet-level Environmental Quality Council in 1969. It was to guide the pollution fight. It consisted of the president, his science adviser, the vice president, and the secretaries of agriculture; commerce; health, education, and welfare; housing and urban development; the interior; and transportation. A citizens' advisory committee was attached to the council. Before the year was over, however, Congress passed the National Environmental Policy Act of 1969. It declared that it is the policy of the United States government "to create and maintain conditions under which man and nature can exist in productive harmony." The act required all federal agencies to take into account the environmental impact of all actions they propose. It created in the office of the president the permanent three-member Council of Environmental Quality, to recommend environmental policies to the president. When he signed the act on January 1, 1970, the president thought it particularly fitting as a first act of the new decade. He said, "I have become . . . convinced that the nineteen-seventies absolutely must be the years when America pays its debt to the past by reclaiming the purity of its air, its waters, and our living environment. It is literally now or never." Early in 1970, President Nixon established an advisory body, the National Industrial Pollution Control Council. It consisted of 63 top executives of big companies and industry associations. Late in 1970, President Nixon established the Environmental Protection Agency (EPA). Its purpose is to coordinate all federal antipollution efforts and to set and enforce environmental standards. As a consequence, the new agency took over many other agencies or some of their former concerns. It swallowed up the Water Quality Administration from the Interior Department and the National Air Pollution Control Administration and the Bureau of Solid Waste Management from the Department of Health, Education, and Welfare. It appropriated the control of pesticides from the Food and Drug Administration and the Department of Agriculture, and the control of radiation from the Atomic Energy Commission. Since then, the EPA has carried forward the standard-setting policies begun earlier at the federal level. Another agency, created at the same time, was the National Oceanic and Atmospheric Administration (NOAA). It consolidates the main federal oceanic and atmospheric

[4] Actually, the same argument would lead one to prefer worldwide to federal action. Indeed, a 113-country United Nations conference on the human environment was held in Sweden in 1972. As a first step, it established Earthwatch, a global monitoring system of the conditions of the atmosphere and the oceans. In the same year, a number of bilateral agreements on environmental cooperation were also signed, as, for example, between the United States and the Soviet Union.

research and monitoring programs (besides operating the Weather Bureau and the Coast and Geodetic Survey). It is supposed to establish ecological baseline data and models.

Standards concerning the air. The first federal act dealing with air pollution, the Clean Air Act, was passed in 1963. It was amended by the Air Quality Act of 1967. It enabled the Secretary of Health, Education, and Welfare, first, to establish 8 atmospheric areas in the 48 contiguous states plus 5 other areas outside. These areas, shown in Figure 13.3, "Atmospheric Areas and Air Quality Control Regions in the United States," were based on long-term meteorological factors affecting pollution transport and diffusion. Second, the secretary designated 57 air quality control regions for air pollution control programs. They are also shown in Figure 13.3. These covered more than 70 percent of the urban population. Air quality control regions were designated on the basis of such factors as meteorology, location and amounts of pollutant emissions, social and governmental aspects, and patterns of urban growth.

***Figure* 13.3 Atmospheric Areas and Air Quality Control Regions in the United States**

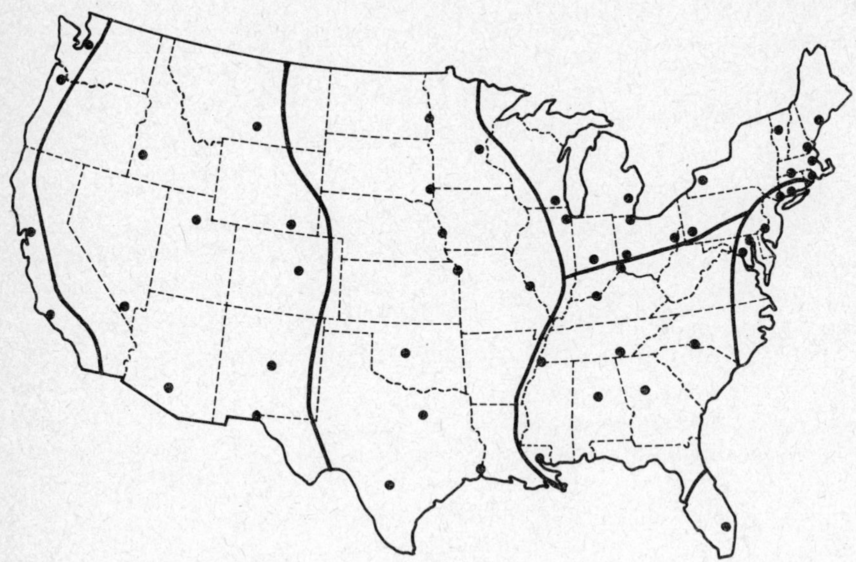

SOURCE: *U.S. Department of Health, Education, and Welfare.*

The first step in controlling air pollution on a regional basis was the designation of atmospheric areas. The lines on the map show the boundaries of the eight atmospheric areas designated by the Department of Health, Education, and Welfare in the contiguous states of the U.S. The next step was to designate air quality control regions. The dots on the map show the regions designated in the contiguous states.

Finally, a National Air Pollution Control Administration was established to publish air quality criteria for specific pollutants and material on the cost and effectiveness of control systems. On this basis, the *states* were to develop and implement air quality standards. The criteria were to cover sulfur oxides, particles, photochemical oxidants, carbon monoxide, atmospheric fluorides, nitrogen oxides, hydrocarbons, beryllium, hydrogen sulfide, odors, lead, asbestos, organic carcinogens, aldehydes, ethylene, pesticides, and rocket fuel.

However, federal criteria were published for only a few of these. The states were slow in publishing and enforcing their own standards. In many cases, fines imposed for violations of regulations were as low as $10, nothing more than a wrist slap for the offender. Under such circumstances, it paid to continue to pollute, for pollution abatement is costly business.

In 1971, however, the EPA moved to set and enforce tough standards using the authority of the new 1970 Air Quality Standards Act. The act requires the EPA to establish national air quality standards as well as national standards for significant new pollution sources and for all facilities emitting hazardous substances.

The EPA sets two types of standards. *Primary standards* specify concentrations of pollutants low enough "to preserve human health." *Secondary standards* are stricter and also "preserve soil, water, vegetation, animals, property, and human comfort." Primary standards must be met by 1975, secondary ones in a "reasonable" time thereafter. States may set their own (stricter) standards, but these must be approved by the EPA. If states do not set their own standards or do not set them in time, federal standards apply. (By late 1972, 17 states had received EPA clearance for their primary standards.)

The 1970 act required a 90 percent reduction from 1970 levels of automobile-caused hydrocarbon and carbon monoxide emission for 1975-model cars and of nitrogen oxides for 1976-model cars. (Manufacturers are required to guarantee performance of their equipment at these levels for 5 years or 50,000 miles. However, a 1972 ruling allowed replacement of equipment after 25,000 miles if longer-lasting equipment were not available.) The Environmental Protection Agency originally set emission regulations to implement these requirements. However, in 1973—after a court challenge by the auto companies which claimed that their catalytic converters could not do the job by 1975—the EPA granted a one-year extension of the 1975 auto emission deadline. It also indicated that it would ease the 1976 nitrogen oxide emission rule. In the meantime, the National Academy of Sciences urged the adoption of a simpler, cheaper, and more effective auto emission control technology, namely use of the dual-carbureted, stratified-charge Honda engine that was already meeting the 1975 standards in 1973.

Under the 1970 Air Quality Standards Act, the EPA has also set national air quality standards for particulate matter, sulfur oxides, and photochemical oxidants (in 1971), for newly built or modified older plants manufacturing nitric acid, sulfuric acid, and portland cement large incinerators, and fossil-fuel steam generators (in 1972), and for asbestos, mercury, beryllium, and seven other types of stationary sources (in 1973).

The act also allowed the banning of all polluting activities in emergencies. This authority was first used in 1971 in Birmingham, Alabama, when 23 companies, including U.S. Steel plants, were temporarily shut down as air pollution reached double the alert level. Under the same authority the EPA in late 1972 prepared a preliminary plan for gasoline rationing in the Los Angeles basin. During May to October, gasoline consumption might be cut 87 percent by this device if necessary to reach the 1975 standards.

In 1973, the EPA took further steps to assure that air quality standards would not only be reached but also maintained. It ordered the states to submit plans for regulating so-called complex sources of air pollution. States must prevent interference with national air quality standards by regulating the construction or modification of traffic-generating projects, as shopping centers, sports complexes, drive-in theatres, amusement parks, recreational areas, highways, and residential, commercial, and institutional developments. Thus the Clean Air Act of 1970 has the ultimate effect of regulating land use.

Noise standards. The federal government in 1971 proposed to set federal noise standards on new transportation and construction equipment, engines, and electrical equipment, and to require the labeling of noise characteristics on all consumer goods. Late in 1972, a general federal noise code was passed. It supplemented earlier standards for aircraft only. Under the earlier law, the Federal Aviation Administration was empowered in 1968 to set aircraft noise limits, and it ruled that in 1972 and thereafter new jets must be 50 percent quieter on takeoff and landing.

Meanwhile, the nation's most densely populated and noisiest state, New Jersey, passed the nation's first statewide noise law in 1972 (providing $3,000 fines for violators). We already noted the existence of city noise codes earlier in this chapter.

Standards concerning water. Legislative concern with water pollution goes back to the Water Pollution Control Act of 1948. There have been many amendments, including the Water Quality Act of 1965, the Clean Water Restoration Act of 1966 and the Water Quality Improvement Act of 1970. The 1965 act established the Federal Water Pollution Control Administration. It could set water quality criteria that were supposed to be implemented by federal-state cooperation. In many cases, the federal government could call a conference, hold hearings, and sue offenders. Hearings could be a strong weapon. They spotlight offenders and stimulate public pressure. However, only 40 states established federally approved standards and no state enforced them by 1971.

The EPA has concentrated not on emission standards but on setting ambient water quality standards and achieving them by requiring would-be industrial polluters to apply for dumping permits. This policy has been pursued under the authority of the 1899 Refuse Act. It forbids the dumping of harmful materials into navigable waters or their tributaries without a permit. The Secretary of the Army may issue permits only when the Corps of Engineers determines that anchorage and navigation will not be impaired.[5] But a presidential order (that all federal agencies must take into account the effect of their actions on the environment) has been used, together with the 1899 act, to limit dumping harmful to nature even if not to navigation.

Applicants for dumping permits in 1971 were required to give details on the types and quantities of intended discharges and to make periodic follow-up disclosures. If the discharges were found to be harmless, they were allowed. Otherwise applicants were forced to clean up their effluents. (In 1971, for example, Anaconda was fined $200,000 for dumping copper into the Hudson River; and a number of executives, including some from U.S. Steel, were criminally convicted and fined under the 1899 act.) To strengthen the legislative basis for this kind of policy, however, Congress passed the Water Pollution Control Act of 1972 (over President Nixon's veto). The bill also requires dumping permits. It specifies that effluent must be treated by use of the "best practicable" control technology by mid-1977 and of the "best available" technology by mid-1983. It sets a zero discharge goal for 1985. To help local governments achieve these goals the act authorized $24.6 billion in federal aid to pay for 75 percent of the cost of building or modernizing local sewage treatment plants (it was this portion of the bill that the president called "budget wrecking" and "unconscionable"). Almost immediately, however, the president ordered the EPA to spend no more than $5 billion of the $11 billion authorized for fiscal years 1973 and 1974. This provoked a major constitutional crisis, and it caused some cities, such as New York, to sue the federal government. A 1973 deadline for the issue or denial of dumping permits to tens of thousands of industrial, agricultural, and municipal polluters passed without fulfillment of the new law.

Enforcement problems. The enforcement of standards so far has proven very difficult indeed. State laws concerning automobiles have been enforced by roadside spotchecks of post-1966 cars (in California), or regular measuring of emissions on every car (in New Jersey).[6] The federal government has attempted to get information on emissions from polluters themselves and has, understandably, run into solid opposition. For example, Union Carbide, whose Alloy, West Virginia, plant alone is believed to emit particles equal to a third of New York City's particle pollution, has refused to give information, has refused access to officials, and would not attend a conference with control agency officials. United States Steel has challenged the water dumping permit

[5] In addition, ruled a court in 1971, the 1899 act implicitly forbids any discharges into nonnavigable waters.

[6] In California in 1972, 41 percent of 1970- and 1971-model cars failed the tests. The failure rate under the more lenient New Jersey standards was 30 percent for 1970-model cars and 25 percent for 1971-model cars.

policy as an invasion of privacy (as it required the publication of trade secrets), and as unconstitutional (as it required someone to give information to be used against himself). This reluctance on the part of polluters to provide information is easy to understand. Punishment for not meeting emission standards, or for dumping without a permit, have become increasingly stiff in recent years, although they are a lot less so than they might be. In London, in 1306, a man was "hanged by the neck until dead for burning coal and defiling the atmosphere." Nowadays, conviction for a first time carries fines ranging up to $25,000 per day as well as jail sentences up to two years. The federal government can also withhold contracts, grants, and loans from violators.

User Charges

To a limited extent, government has also gone the route of charging would-be users of the environment directly for purposes of waste disposal. Vermont followed the highly successful system in France, Germany, and Great Britain and introduced in 1971 fees for waste disposal in waterways if discharges were out of compliance with water quality standards. The fees were to reflect the cost of environmental damage. Fees of somewhat different nature were also charged in Maryland and Michigan for water discharges. As of 1972, Oregon requires a 2-to-5-cent deposit on every beer and soft-drink container sold in the state (depending on their size), and Vermont imposed a 0.4-cent tax on nonreturnable beverage containers for one year (to be followed by a ban).

President Nixon in 1971 proposed a tax on the sulfur content of coal, oil, and natural gas, which would be rebated to those who prevented sulfur from escaping during fuel use. The proposed tax of 1 cent per pound of sulfur in 1972 was to rise to 10 cents by 1976. Another tax (of 1 cent per gallon) was proposed by the president for leaded gasoline. In 1972, the president proposed an Environmental Protection Tax Act that would, for instance, discourage the development of coastal wetlands. He also urged a variable sulfur emission tax as of 1976. It would be zero in areas meeting primary and secondary air quality standards, 10 cents per pound in areas violating secondary standards only, and 15 cents per pound in areas violating both standards.

Within Congress, other taxes (on detergents, pesticides, and disposable goods) were talked about. Senator Proxmire urged a 1-cent-per-pound disposal fee for all goods requiring disposal within 10 years of origin. (This would come to 5 cents for the Sunday *New York Times* and $35 for a 3,500-lb car.) New York City imposed a 2-cent tax on plastic containers, but the New York State Supreme Court voided it.

These are no more than the first hesitant steps toward the establishment of markets for pollution rights—markets that would confront individuals with the costs they impose on others and give them the incentive to avoid waste-generating activities or to avoid waste disposal into the environment.

WHY THE ANTIPOLLUTION EFFORT IS MOVING SO SLOWLY

All in all, the movement to abate pollution in the United States has not exactly caught on like wildfire. Some people argue that "this is inevitable in the framework of capitalism. Only socialism can stop pollution." As shown in Appendix B to this chapter, that contention can be doubted. If things have been moving slowly in the antipollution field, a number of factors can be cited as causes.

Technical Difficulties: "There Is No Way"

One reason for continued high pollution levels is technological. Many polluters simply do not know how to reduce or avoid waste disposal short of ceasing their activities completely. Take disposal of human sewage. Unless you are willing to get rid of people, you will have to dispose of it somehow. As shown in Appendix A to this chapter, disposal of raw sewage into waterways causes trouble, but so does the disposal of sewage that has received first- or even second-stage treatment. This has given rise to the use of waste-disposal wells: A typical well is a 6-inch hole drilled in the ground to the depth of a sandstone or a limestone layer, perhaps at a level of 3,000 feet below the surface. These porous formations, resembling a petrified sponge, soak up the liquid wastes. The hole is encased in steel to prevent seepage of the waste on its way down. Such wells have large capacities. They can absorb sewage at a rate of 500 gallons a minute. Under these circumstances, it takes 200 years to saturate even a small 20-square-mile formation of sandstone that is 100 feet thick. Many actual formations cover 20,000 square miles and are 2,000 feet thick. In addition, the construction of such a well is cheap, costing at most $100,000 as compared with five times that for the smallest sewage treatment plant. In 1970, there were about 150 such wells in the United States, gobbling up everything from sewage to pesticides, from poison gas to acids. Yet most of these wells caused trouble, mainly by creating small earthquakes and unexpected geysers in nearby areas! After having had no earthquakes for 80 years, Denver recorded 1,500 of them from 1962 to 1966 after such wells had been drilled. In Lake Erie and in such diverse places as the post-office parking lot and the basement of homes in Port Huron, nearby wells "blew their tops."

Or take another case. How is one to stop the noise inevitably associated with the many power instruments used by man? Shall we just go back to human muscle?

Private enterprise has found one way of dealing with the problem: building devices to mask unwanted sound by other sound, by spreading "acoustical perfume." Acoustical engineers argued that continuous and uniform pleasant background noise could be used in homes, churches, schools, and hospitals to "achieve a comfort situation." As a result, in 1970 you could buy a noise-making machine called "Sleep Mate" for about $14, making a "soothing swoosh." For about $20, you could buy "Sleep Sound," making "a hum like trees in a breeze." If that were not good enough, you could get "Sleepatone" for $120, which would provide you with the sound of rain falling on a wood-shingled roof or of rustling wind or of ocean surf.

If you really wanted to live it up, you could spend $600 on an egg-shaped contraption (the "Sound Chair"), equipped with six stereophonic speakers, which would envelop you like a womb! Needless to say, medical authorities don't think too highly of fighting noise by making more noise. They think it about as useful as fighting brain tumors with aspirin.

High Cost: "There Is No Cheap Way"

The kind of problems just described are ubiquitous when *cheap* pollution avoidance schemes are used. They simply do not work. But this is not to say that pollution problems cannot be tackled. On the contrary. The emphasis in the above sentence is on *cheap*, and for a good reason. Much more costly schemes typically do work. This is probably the real reason for the slow pace of antipollution efforts.

Avoiding water pollution. Consider the case of human sewage. Most of it is dumped raw or after having received inadequate first- or second-stage treatment.[7] Yet there is such a thing as third-stage treatment of sewage. By chemical and mechanical processes, such as precipitation, coagulation, and filtration, the impurities remaining after second-stage treatment can be removed. This is very costly and few municipalities have it. For instance, the most advanced treatment plant at Lake Tahoe uses each day 7.5 million gallons of sewage that has received secondary treatment, treats it with lime (to remove phosphates), sprays the remainder from a 50-foot tower (to allow ammonia gas to escape), filters the remainder through coarse coal, sand, fine garnet, and finally, granulated activated carbon, and chlorinates it. This produces drinking water at a cost of 32 cents per 1,000 gallons (11 cents of which is the cost of secondary treatment). Similarly sized seawater distillation plants have a 65–85-cents cost per 1,000 gallons. To introduce third-stage treatment everywhere would be very costly. In comparison, the billions of dollars spent in recent years on municipal and industrial waste-treatment plants are a drop in the bucket. To supply all U.S. cities with second-stage sewage treatment would cost $29 billion more. To provide them with third-stage treatment facilities would cost more than the annual federal budget!

With similarly huge expenditures, atomic power plants could build cooling towers to dissipate waterborne waste heat. Paper mills could convert black liquor into activated carbon and use it to filter wastes from the mills' effluent. Similarly, the technology of really suppressing noise undoubtedly exists. For front-line combat vehicles, for instance, completely inaudible

[7] These processes are explained in Appendix A to this chapter, in the section dealing with wastes dumped into bodies of fresh water.

motors have been built. The roar of an airplane can be suppressed by spending about 5–10 percent more on it, not a negligible figure. The same seems to be roughly true for many other types of equipment, such as lawn mowers, trucks, and even air compressors. All it takes is careful choosing of materials. But in 1970, achieving even a 12-decibel decrease in the noise of all U.S. jets would have cost $1 billion. Since 1973, even sonic booms can be avoided.

Avoiding air pollution. Cost figures for dealing effectively with air and solid-waste pollution are equally impressive. For example, to avoid the air pollution associated with a single open-hearth steel furnace (of the type producing 43 percent of U.S. steel in 1969) would cost $1 million. The achievement of the 1975 automobile exhaust standards will cost $350 per car initially and raise operating costs: Gasoline mileage will be cut 15 percent. Frequent inspection will be necessary (since a single dead sparkplug could raise exhausts over the legal limit). Gas will cost more if present types are phased out. Since gas now contains too much tetraethyl lead (which makes gas burn more evenly) and too much butane (which facilitates the evaporation of gas in the carburetor), we must convert the refineries. Conversion to nonlead gas production in 1969 was estimated to cost $4.25 billion initially, raising production costs by 2 cents per gallon thereafter. Cutting out butane was said to raise cost by another 2 cents per gallon.

Or consider the expense of installing highly efficient electrostatic precipitators (against fly ash) and catalytic oxidation processes (against sulfur oxides) for fuel-burning units in every single residence. But it would not be impossible. Possibly, centralized production of heat would be preferable so that air pollution can be controlled at relatively few sites. Tests conducted in 1969 in New York have shown that it is possible to avoid pollution on demolition sites by enclosing them with a plastic skin, with the clouds of dust being drawn out by giant vacuum cleaners.

Avoiding soil pollution. The technology for dealing effectively with solid wastes exists also. Again, the cost is high. To have gotten rid of New York City's solid waste in 1970 by pyrolysis would have required an initial investment of $220 billion and annual operating costs of $60 million.[8] To have controlled the wastes from animal feedlots in 1970 would have required $75 million initially and $25 million annually.

Overall costs. The Environmental Protection Agency estimated in 1972 that from 1971 to 1980, a minimum total of $287.1 billion will have to be spent to meet standards set by it effective *for this period.* Of this total, 37 percent would have to go for air pollution control, 30 percent each for water pollution control and for solid-waste management, and the rest for radiation control and land reclamation from surface mining. See Table 13.2, "Expected Pollution

[8] Pyrolysis and other methods of solid waste disposal are discussed in Appendix A to this chapter.

Table 13.2 **Expected Pollution Control Expenditures in the United States, 1971–80**

Type of Pollution	Operating Costs Plus Interest and Depreciation on Investments in Environmental Controls: Billions of 1971 Dollars		Percent	
Air[a]	106.5		37.1	
Public		7.9		2.8
Private				
Automobiles[b]		61.0		21.2
Other		37.6		13.1
Water	87.3		30.4	
Public[c]		46.4		16.2
Private				
Manufacturing		26.1		9.1
Utilities		8.7		3.1
Feedlots		3.7		1.3
Vessels		1.4		0.5
Construction[d]		1.0		0.3
Solid waste[e]	86.1		30.0	
Other	7.2		2.5	
Surface mining[f]		5.1		1.8
Radiation		2.1		0.7
Total	287.1		100.0	

[a] Excludes noise.
[b] Excludes heavy-duty vehicles.
[c] Excludes separating combined sewers.
[d] Housing and highways only.
[e] Excludes interest and depreciation.
[f] Excludes reclamation of past damage.

SOURCE: Environmental Quality, the Third Annual Report of the Council on Environmental Quality (*Washington, D.C.: Government Printing Office, 1972*), *pp. 276–77.*

Control Expenditures in the United States, 1971–80." That is, by the end of this decade, the average American can expect to pay (via higher prices, higher taxes, or lower profits) at least $145 a year for pollution control.

However, the EPA total *excluded* a number of items for lack of knowledge. Among these were a possible $58.7 billion additional expenditure for separating combined sewers and meeting jet aircraft noise standards. Furthermore, the listed expenditures for investing in and operating environmental controls were estimated on the basis of standards set by 1972. Possibly stricter standards might emerge over the decade. And such tightening of standards can be expected to become ever costlier. The EPA estimates, for instance, that an 85 percent removal of municipal and industrial water pollution by 1982 would cost $60 billion; a 95 percent removal would cost $120 billion; and a 100 percent removal, $320 billion.

The predominant use of inefficient *standards*, rather than pollution rights, as a means of enforcing lower pollution suggests, however, that these costs are higher than they have to be. A study of the Delaware Estuary showed that the achievement of a 3-ppm-dissolved-oxygen level would cost twice as much with uniform standards on all firms as with differential standards that demanded the largest waste-load reductions from firms with low abatement costs and smaller reductions from firms with higher costs. However, although the above costs estimated by EPA may be unnecessarily high, a reduction in all types of pollution, including those for which standards have not been set, would increase this figure even more. Furthermore, one must not forget other costs.

In addition to abatement costs themselves, one must reckon those of *administering* any pollution control policy. Among these is the high cost of environmental monitoring. One cannot detect environmental changes, desirable or undesirable, natural or man-made, and one cannot formulate and assess policies, without established base lines and repeated observations. A recent study contracted by the EPA showed the need for 100 environmental indices, but it is expected to take several years before reliable data can be attained for them. In the meantime, some 56 main monitoring programs are in effect in 16 federal agencies. In fiscal 1971, direct federal spending on these programs for understanding, describing, and predicting the environment amounted to $850 million. (There were other nonfederal expenditures, for there are local and state government and private monitoring systems.) Since the selection of indices and of monitoring sites and instrumentation, and the determination of the frequency of samples taken, are only in their infancy, future expenses can be expected to be much higher. To high monitoring costs we must add further administrative costs for enforcement. There are millions of polluters to be supervised, some 40,000 industrial water polluters alone. All this leads to another criticism commonly voiced.

Fear of Hurting the Poor

Any scheme of pollution reduction will not only lower some profits, but also raise prices or taxes, and it is said that this would hurt the poor. They are held unable to afford any reduction in their real incomes that would come with the inevitable price or tax increases; therefore, antipollution efforts should not be pursued too vigorously. This can be answered in two ways.

Pollution avoidance helps the poor. First, it is true that the ability of the poor to buy man-made goods would be reduced (as the ability of everyone else would be also). However, the poor (like everyone else) also gain from a higher-quality environment. Indeed, it is quite likely that they would gain proportionately much more than the nonpoor. The nonpoor can often escape, because of their higher income, the consequences of pollution. They can live in nonpolluted areas, or travel more easily to them; they can afford home, car, and office air-conditioners, good medical care, and so on, to escape the effects of pollution even in polluted areas. The poor typically have to suffer with pollution. They cannot fight back. Hence the poor may well gain more than they lose. Consider some of the recent evidence.[9]

How air pollution affects the poor. Air pollution generally hangs more heavily over the inner city where the poor live than over the rest of the urban area, and far more heavily than over most suburban and rural areas. In some cities the central business district absorbs the most severe air pollution; in other cities close-in industrial areas bear the heaviest pollution loads. The largest concentrations of the urban poor often live near these two areas. A 1969 study conducted for the National Air Pollution Control Administration (NAPCA, now a part of the Environmental Protection Agency) confirmed that concentrations of particulate matter, carbon monoxide, and sulfur oxides decline steadily out from urban areas (urban measuring points are all located in downtown areas). This may be seen in Table 13.3, "Selected Particulate Constituents in the Air, United States, 1966–67."

Based on samples collected over a two-year period, the study shows that average concentrations of particulates in nonurban areas are between 10 and 50 percent of the average in urban areas. Moreover, within metropolitan regions, similar variations hold between suburbia and the central city.

A study of the St. Louis area made in 1966 by NAPCA reported that suspended particulates, dust fall, and concentrations of sulfur dioxide were higher in the predominantly poor black neighborhoods of St. Louis and East St. Louis than elsewhere in the metropolitan area.

A recent air pollution computer model of the Chicago region, when correlated with census data, indicates that the lowest-income neighborhoods are in the areas of highest pollution concentrations (see Figures 13.4 and 13.5). Similar conclusions surface in data drawn from Kansas City and St. Louis in Missouri, and Washington, D.C. (see Table 13.4, "Air Pollution Exposure Indices by Income").

Another survey, conducted by NAPCA concerning 22 other metropolitan areas including Cincinnati, Dallas–Fort Worth, Denver, Indianapolis, Louisville, New York City–Northern New Jersey, Pittsburgh, Providence, San Antonio, and Seattle, substantiates unequal geographical distribution of certain pollutants within metropolitan areas. Emissions of carbon monoxide, sulfur oxides, and particulate matter in these areas were measured by source and

[9] See *Environmental Quality: The Second Annual Report of the Council on Environmental Quality* (Washington, D.C.: August 1971), pp. 191–97, from which the following sections (on how air, water, and solid waste pollution affect the poor) are taken.

Table 13.3 **Selected Particulate Constituents in the Air, United States, 1966–67**

	Urban (217 stations)		Nonurban Proximate (5)[a]		Nonurban Intermediate (15)[b]		Nonurban Remote (10)[c]	
	μg/m³	Percent	μg/m³	Percent	μg/m³	Percent	μg/m³	Percent
Suspended particulates	102.0	....	45.0	....	40.0	....	21.0	....
Benzene soluble organics	6.7	6.6	2.5	5.6	2.2	5.4	1.1	5.1
Ammonium ion	0.9	0.9	1.22	2.7	0.28	0.7	0.15	0.7
Nitrate ion	2.4	2.4	1.40	3.1	0.85	2.1	0.46	2.2
Sulfate ion	10.1	9.9	10.0	22.2	5.29	13.1	2.51	1.8
Copper	0.16	0.15	0.16	0.36	0.078	0.19	0.060	0.28
Iron	1.43	1.38	0.56	1.24	0.27	0.67	0.15	0.71
Manganese	0.073	0.07	0.026	0.06	0.012	0.03	0.005	0.02
Nickel	0.017	0.02	0.008	0.02	0.004	0.01	0.002	0.01
Lead	1.11	1.07	0.21	0.47	0.096	0.24	0.022	0.10

[a] Technically in nonurban areas, but conspicuously influenced by proximity to city, e.g., Cape Vincent, N.Y.; Kent County, Del.; Washington County, Miss.
[b] Closer to urban areas, usually with agricultural activity, e.g., Jackson County, Miss.; Humboldt, Calif.
[c] Farthest from large population center, e.g., Glacier National Park; White Pine County, Nev.
NOTE: Percent shows indicated quantity in relation to the quantity of gross suspended particulates.
SOURCE: *Environmental Protection Agency.*

proximity to heavy population centers. Emissions of carbon monoxide result from vehicles; sulfur oxides and particulate emissions come from residential and commercial burning of coal and oil. For each of the three pollutants, the pattern is the same: Emission densities are highest in the core city and diminish with distance outward. Overall, the areas of highest emissions within the tested cities coincide with the areas of highest population density.

Other pollutants confirm this pattern. Lead, for example, is commonly found in the atmosphere and in the soil near heavily traveled roadways. Data vary widely for different sampling sites, but lead levels in the blood appear particularly high among urban-area dwellers.

Blood specimens of three groups of persons in the Philadelphia area were taken to determine the amount of lead in their systems. The groups were divided into those who had lived and worked within a 25-block radius of City Hall for five years, those who commuted regularly from the suburbs to work in the downtown area, and those who lived in the same neighborhood as the suburban commuters and also worked in the suburbs. For men and women both, lead was significantly highest in the city dwellers. Among the subur-

Figure 13.4 **Current Expected Mean Concentrations of Sulfur Dioxide, Chicago, Ill., and Gary, Ind. (In Micrograms per Cubic Meter)**

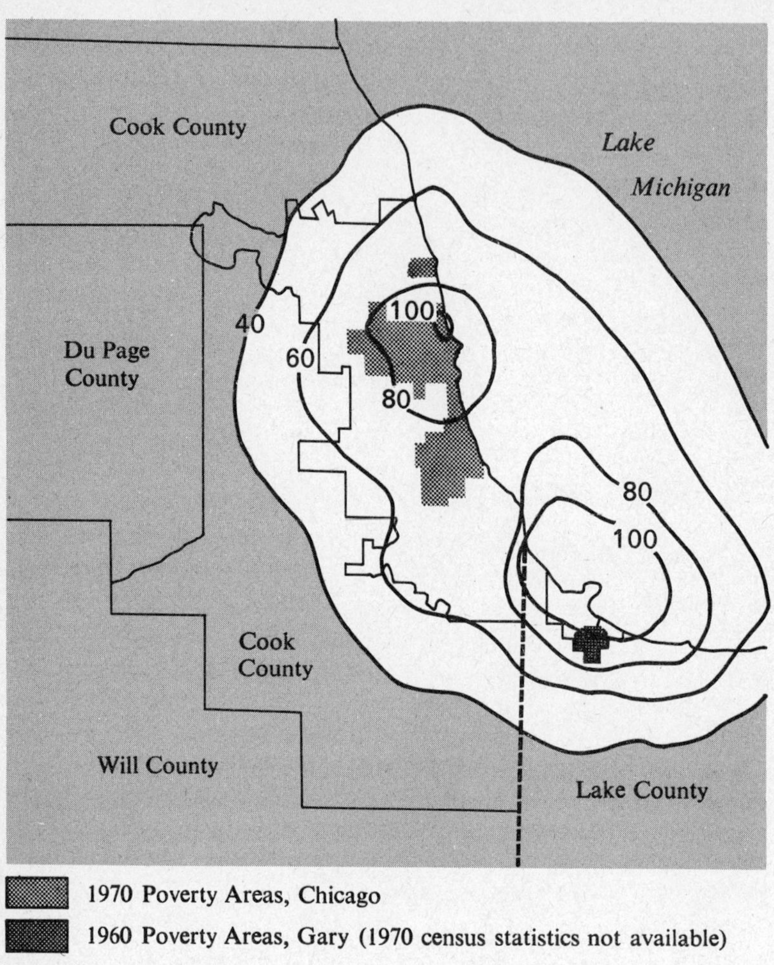

SOURCE: *See footnote 9. Based on computer simulation model of data from Atomic Energy Commission and Argonne National Laboratory, and on U.S. Department of Commerce, Bureau of the Census data.*

banites, those who worked in the city showed higher lead concentrations than those who lived and worked in the suburbs.

How water pollution affects the poor. Inner-city residents are delivered the same water as any other urban residents. But they frequently face added problems. Water pipes in inner-city housing are sometimes old and ill-kept and often contain pipe or joint cementing compound made of lead (no longer used

Figure 13.5 **Current Expected Particulate Concentrations for Chicago, Ill., and Gary, Ind. (In Micrograms per Cubic Meter)**

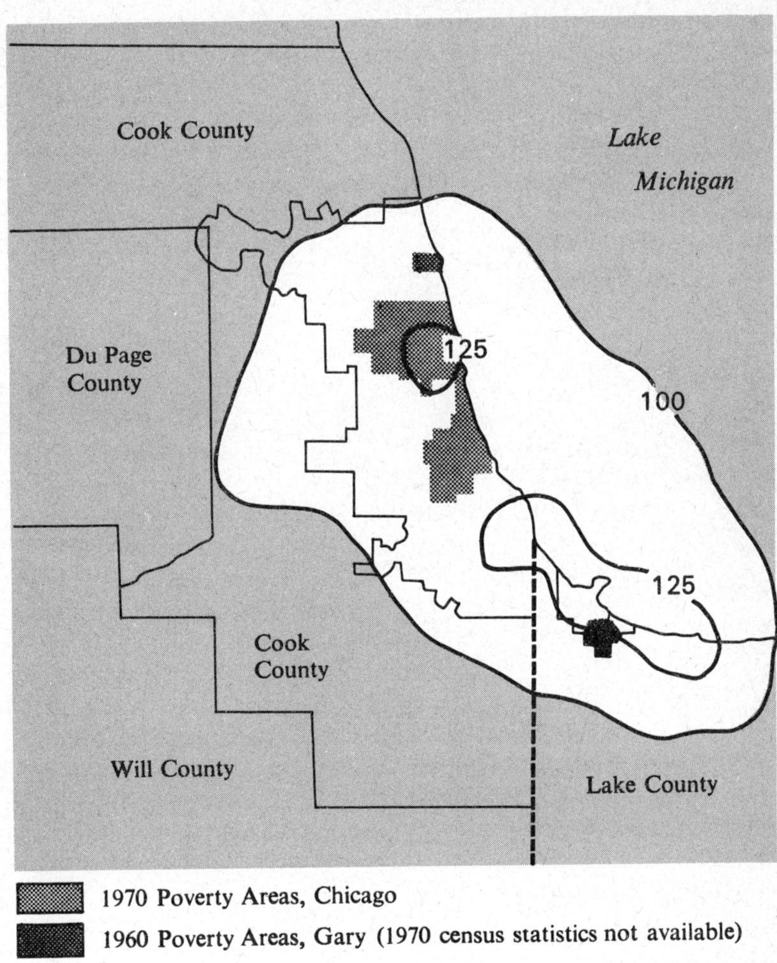

1970 Poverty Areas, Chicago

1960 Poverty Areas, Gary (1970 census statistics not available)

SOURCE: *See footnote 9. Based on computer simulation model of data from Atomic Energy Commission and Argonne National Laboratory, and on U.S. Department of Commerce, Bureau of the Census data.*

in construction). Under such conditions, water in inner-city areas has been found to contain as much as 920 micrograms of lead per liter, a contrast to the average of 20 micrograms per liter elsewhere.

Inner-city residents have limited access to water recreation. Conclusive data are lacking on how often the urban poor use nearby water bodies. River courses and harbors located within and next to large cities often contain dangerously high levels of bacteria and other pollutants. Yet they often constitute

Table 13.4 Air Pollution Exposure Indices by Income

Income	Suspended Particulates	Sulfation	Mean
Kansas City			
$0–$2,999	76.7	0.22	1.16
$3,000–$4,999	72.4	.20	1.09
$5,000–$6,999	66.5	.18	.93
$7,000–$9,999	63.5	.17	.93
$10,000–$14,999	60.1	.15	.86
$15,000–$24,999	57.6	.14	.80
$25,000–over	58.1	.12	.76
St. Louis			
$0–$2,999	91.3	.97	1.19
$3,000–$4,999	85.3	.88	1.10
$5,000–$6,999	79.2	.78	1.00
$7,000–$9,999	75.4	.72	.93
$10,000–$14,999	73.0	.68	.89
$15,000–$24,999	68.8	.60	.82
$25,000–over	64.9	.52	.74
Washington, D.C.			
$0–$2,999	64.6	.82	1.19
$3,000–$4,999	61.7	.82	1.16
$5,000–$6,999	53.9	.75	1.04
$7,000–$9,999	49.7	.69	.96
$10,000–$14,999	45.5	.64	.88
$15,000–$24,999	43.2	.58	.82
$25,000–over	42.0	.53	.77

SOURCE: *See footnote 9. Based on U.S. Department of Commerce, Bureau of the Census, and U.S. Department of Health, Education, and Welfare, Public Health Service data.*

the only source of water recreation easily accessible to the urban poor. The cleaner waters are, for many inner-city dwellers, more distant than a convenient one-day round trip will allow, and thus out of reach for those not able to afford overnight accommodations.

How solid waste pollution affects the poor. Junk and litter accumulated in streets, on sidewalks, and in vacant lots and doorways are a familiar sight in poverty areas and cannot help having a psychological effect on those who live there. The resident often despairs of keeping his small living space clean when all around him are litter and garbage. Residents in nine of twenty cities surveyed by the National Advisory Commission on Civil Disorders listed inadequate sanitation and garbage removal as significant grievances. Many cities able to set their own priorities with federal funds have placed emphasis on sanitation services such as collecting garbage, buying trash and garbage containers for the city poor, removing abandoned automobiles, cleaning up littered vacant lots, and increasing the number of sanitation workers.

Solving the problem involves more than merely upgrading municipal services. Some New York City poverty areas have garbage pickups six times a week, compared with three times a week elsewhere in the city. In Chicago, inner-city poor are served by three collections a week, compared with one collection in the rest of the city. Yet inner-city littering and unsanitary conditions continue, and there is widespread disenchantment at the failure of cleanup campaigns to have any lasting effect.

The reasons for this failure to maintain sanitary conditions in the inner city are complex and interrelated. Frustration over limited opportunities for housing, employment, and education can lead residents of the inner city to withdraw from active efforts to improve conditions around them. This psychological impact is worsened by physical conditions that work against sanitation. Buildings designed in earlier days have been subdivided into numerous crowded living units, with little provision for storage areas, common spaces, or refuse collection systems. Receptacles are often nonexistent, makeshift, or in poor condition—all leading to a situation in which wind, animals, and vandals spread litter throughout houses and neighborhoods. The abundance of vacant lots and abandoned structures, already strewn with refuse, encourages further junk, garbage, and other debris. Together these forces frustrate even the most willing city sanitation department in their attempted cooperation with residents toward a cleaner neighborhood. Also, sanitation collection services have been criticized as perfunctory in some poverty areas. Often such services are confined to curbside collection of packaged refuse, ignoring litter in lots, sidewalks, and gutters.

Strewn garbage, besides being unattractive and malodorous, also invites rodents. Rats feed on easily accessible garbage and present a health problem to inner-city residents. Greater than the danger of the diseases they carry is the insecurity and fear they inspire, especially in parents with small children.

An estimated 60 to 90 percent of rat bites occur in inner-city neighborhoods. Eighty percent occur after midnight, when most victims are asleep. The problem is intensified by large-scale building demolition in old, inner-city areas, where rats are dislodged and then flee to other parts of the city. The presence of rats in an apartment often has nothing to do with the particular building's cleanliness. Substandard housing often is replete with holes in basement walls or around windows and pipes, giving rats entry points from which they fan out through a building. Obviously, therefore, a vigorously fought antipollution battle can help the poor greatly.

Efficiency should not be confused with equity. Second, it is bad to confuse the issue of income distribution with that of efficient resource use. Antipollution policies such as the pollution rights market scheme can greatly improve the efficiency with which society uses its scarce resources. It would be foolish to give up efficiency, especially since other policies (such as redistributive taxation) could easily be devised to take care of the issue of income distribution. The same argument applies in general with respect to all those who oppose antipollution efforts for fear of the personal consequences of the implied economic adjustments.

Fear of Economic Adjustments

The widespread changes in taxes, profits, or prices that can be expected as a consequence of antipollution policies, will occasion widespread changes in quantities demanded and in resource allocation. Some firms and their employees—particularly those that must absorb large pollution-abatement costs—will be hard hit. But other firms will benefit; and new firms, industries, and professions will emerge and flourish.

For example, some households may buy less furniture because their income is lower (taxes are up or they earn lower dividends on stock they own) or because they have to pay higher prices for other goods (for example, electric power). This will put furniture workers out of work. Yet new workers will be needed to provide pollution control equipment that is bought with higher tax collections, retained profits, or greater revenues from higher prices. Similarly, households who buy imported bananas rather than costlier domestic apples will put orchardists out of work. But more jobs will open up in the freight and import business. Automakers who substitute relatively cheap plastic for relatively more expensive steel will put steelworkers out of work. But jobs will open in the plastics industry. Bottlers who use returnable containers (now that fees for nonreturnable ones make these more expensive) may put canmakers out of work. But new jobs will open up in glass-recycling plants.

Some people think that this makes the whole idea of standards or user charges for disposing wastes into the environment undesirable. They do not wish to see *any* such effects on employment. Indeed, they tend to see only the employment-decreasing, not the employment-increasing, part of antipollution policies. This fear of economic adjustments explains the recent industry offensive against the EPA. In 1971, industrial interests, allied with the Department of Commerce, introduced legislation to restrict the standard-setting power of the EPA where these actions were "not economically feasible and harmed the development of productive capacity or employment." All over the country, labor unions teamed up with business against the "hysteria" of conservationists, whose programs were interpreted as "banning jobs, not litter." Some extremists even have seen in the antipollution effort a foreign-directed plot to sap the strength of the U.S. economy. Noting that Earth Day 1970 coincided with Lenin's birthday, the Richmond *News-Leader* commented: "The date was not selected by chance. Here we have a classic example of how the Communists pervert idealism and worthwhile causes to their own purpose."

By such attitude, people show that they do not wish to see any pollution abatement. Any pollution abatement scheme *necessarily* involves a reallocation of resources. Indeed, a joint EPA–Commerce Department study on the expected impact of pollution standards in 14 industries for the period 1972–76 confirmed theoretical expectations. The industries studied were autos, baking, cement, electric power, fruit and vegetable canning and freezing, iron foundries, leather tanning, petroleum refining, pulp and paper mills, smelting and refining of aluminum, copper, lead, and zinc, and steelmaking. Because of the availability of substitute products and of foreign sources of supply, and the lower abatement costs of some firms in each industry, it is expected that many firms' pollution control costs can be passed on only in part in higher prices. Prices might rise, the study noted, anywhere from 0 to 10 percent, causing a fall in quantity demanded, but profits must also fall.[10] As a result, some firms will cut output, others close altogether. The study predicted 300 plant closings in connection with the antipollution effort, and perhaps as many as 125,000 job losses, mostly in smaller towns where offsetting employment opportunities are least likely to open up. Yet there will also be in each of the industries studied new jobs in firms with low pollution-abatement costs. There will be new jobs and new firms in other industries producing low-pollution products or pollution-abatement equipment. Clearly, further governmental policies can be devised to ease the movement of resources from one use to another. Programs that provide income maintenance, retraining, or labor market information, to name a few, could help to minimize the impact of a significant redirection of resources on any one individual.

Summary

1. It can be questioned whether the production of a large GNP is desirable if it is accompanied by exhaustion of irreplaceable resources and wholesale dumping of indestructible wastes. Earth, like a spaceship, has very limited resources, and it is foolish to destroy a spaceship on which one must continue to ride.
2. Nature has a certain capacity to absorb wastes, but this capacity is strictly limited. Excessive dumping of wastes changes the character of the environment so as to impair its subsequent use. This is pollution.
3. Pollution avoidance has opportunity costs. Therefore, any rational society must compare the costs of avoidance with the benefits it expects to receive. It must find the optimum level of pollution, which is unlikely to be equal to the actual level of pollution but equally unlikely to be zero.
4. Theoretically, the problem of pollution—greater-than-optimal waste disposal into the environment—can be solved in a number of ways. These include voluntary sacrifices by polluters, the bribing of polluters by victims (privately or jointly), the suing of polluters by victims, direct government regulation of polluters, and establishing pollution rights markets.

[10] Recall the analogous discussion in Chapter 9 (in the section on the theory of tax incidence) about the possibility of passing on a sales tax via higher price. Only if the buyer is totally inflexible can it be done.

5. Many of these approaches have drawbacks. The voluntary sacrifice requires an irrational act by the individual and does not assure optimal pollution. The private bribe method could assure optimal pollution, but is not available to the poor, is morally unacceptable to some, is administratively difficult, is unlikely to be used, and provides no incentives to polluters to find cheaper avoidance methods over time. The public bribe method can overcome some but not all of these drawbacks. It may, in addition, create inequities. The suing of polluters would be administratively very expensive. Outright banning of pollution cannot assure an optimum. Uniform emission standards are inequitable, impose unnecessarily high abatement costs, and are expensive to administer.
6. The pollution rights market, on the other hand, could at a fairly low administrative cost assure that an optimal level of pollution is reached in the cheapest way. Through it, all those responsible for pollution would be made personally aware of their responsibility by higher prices and taxes or lower profits. Thus they would be confronted with the choice of ceasing or reducing these polluting activities or personally bearing the opportunity cost.
7. In the United States, many of the above approaches have been tried. Public bribes, however, have been partial bribes, have not been available to all, and have been biased in favor of a single method of pollution control. Lawsuits in general have not been too successful, but there has been much activity in legislatures and the courts concerning environmental property rights.
8. The recent frontal attack on pollution has involved government regulation, especially via standard setting. Most of the requisite governmental machinery has been established since the late 1960's. Most important standards have been set by the Environmental Protection Agency since 1971. The establishment of pollution rights markets via user charges is in its infancy.
9. The U.S. antipollution effort has been moving slowly for many reasons. These include technical problems and an unwillingness to bear the high costs of workable avoidance schemes (some of these costs being, unfortunately, unnecessary costs). These also include the fear of hurting the poor and of having to make economic adjustments.
10. It can be shown that the poor more than others would gain from pollution avoidance. Furthermore, there is no reason why efficiency-raising antipollution policies cannot be pursued simultaneously with antipoverty policies. Indeed, such antipoverty policies are very important also for easing people over the inevitable economic adjustments accompanying any antipollution effort.

Terms[11]

ambient standards
class suit
emission standards
input standards
optimum pollution
pollution
pollution right
primary standards
secondary standards
third-stage sewage treatment

[11] Terms are defined in the Glossary at the back of the book.

Questions for Review and Discussion

1. "If production and population were evenly spaced over the U.S. land surface, we might have no pollution at all, even though we were discarding the same quantities of wastes that are now being discarded." Comment.
2. "Zero pollution would mean either close-to-zero production of goods or 100 percent capture and reuse of wastes. Both are unlikely to be optimum positions for society." Explain.
3. What would you do about the following externalities imposed on you by your neighbors:
   (a) Someone builds a house next door the shade of which ruins your favorite sunbathing spot (the City of Palm Springs forbids the building of houses that cast a shadow on other people's land between 9 A.M. and 3 P.M.).
   (b) Someone opens a restaurant, the smells of which drift into your home.
   (c) Your neighbor's trees grow, and ruin your magnificent 100-mile view.
4. In 1968, 5 billion pounds of detergents were sold in the United States. Most of these contained substantial quantities of phosphates (typically over 20 percent of the volume, but as much as 43.7 percent in one case). These phosphates end up in rivers and lakes stimulating algal growth and eutrophication. Similarly, some detergents contain enzymes that are complex proteins obtained from spore-forming bacteria. They are supposed to destroy binding agents in such things as milk and blood, which make stains adhere to fabrics. However, in high concentrations, enzymes also cause dermatitis and flu-like and asthmatic conditions. How would you deal with this type of pollution?
5. In 1969, construction was halted on a nuclear power plant at Cayuga Lake, New York, because people protested the thermal pollution danger. How do you think this problem should be handled? What are the reasons for your recommendation?
6. In 1969, Vahlsing, Inc., a potato processor, was the target of a nationwide boycott because of its pollution of the *Prestile Stream* in Maine. Do you think this is a good way to solve the pollution problem? Why or why not?
7. "The best approach to pollution avoidance is an all-out antilitter campaign, wherein litter is broadly defined to include all types of wastes dumped into the environment." Comment.
8. As of 1973, Vermont banned nonreturnable beverage containers. Is that a good idea? (Consider such benefits of a deposit-bottle system as less litter and dumping, but such disadvantages as more handling and storing by households and firms.)
9. "The doctrine of 'freedom of the seas' is pernicious. It leads to an inefficient use of the ocean's resources. (Note how whales are in danger of becoming extinct.) What we should do is extend each country's territorial waters to the middle of the ocean it borders and then sell off pieces of ocean to individuals." Discuss.
10. Under the 1965 Water Quality Act, the fifty states submitted to the Department of the Interior proposals for cleaning up interstate waterways. Iowa was the only state that refused to require secondary treatment of sewage (dumped into the Missouri and Mississippi rivers). If you had been the responsible federal official, what would you have done about this?

11. "We should not ban cars from city streets. Nor noisy airplanes from airports. We should simply force those who hurt others to pay fully for all the consequences of their actions." Explain.
12. If a pollution rights market is established, should it be a national market for each pollutant (with a uniform price throughout the nation for the privilege to dump it) or a set of several localized markets (with different prices, perhaps)? Justify your answer.
13. MR. A: The way to solve the pollution problem is to shoot all pollutants into outer space.

    MR. B: You are silly. Technology right here on earth will solve the pollution problem. It is already busily doing so. Consider how sawdust, which used to be a waste, is now pressed into boards. Consider how smelter gases are turned into fertilizer, how cinders become building materials, scrap turns into new steel, ground bottles pave streets and parking lots as 'glasphalt,' and shredded rubber tires become resilient surfaces for playgrounds. Even plastic can be made photodegradable and consequently self-destructible in direct sunlight.

    Discuss.
14. "The whole antipollution effort is an elitist thing, good mainly for the rich. Pollution avoidance costs ultimately show up in higher prices of consumer goods or in more unemployment. Since the poor consume a greater proportion of their incomes than the rich and they will be the ones thrown out of work, the poor will bear these costs disproportionately. Thus well-to-do ecology crusaders are driving the poor people right up the wall." Evaluate.
15. We can't stop pollution, for it would put people out of work.

    Example 1: PPG Industries, Inc., said that meeting Ohio's limit on discharge of calcium chloride into the Tuscarawas River (an Ohio River tributary) would force it to close its Barberton, Ohio, soda ash plant. Twenty-six hundred workers would lose their jobs.

    Example 2: State governments are keenly aware that differences among states of antipollution laws affect industrial location. A few years ago, Union Carbide decided against building a chemical plant in West Virginia and built it in Louisiana instead for this reason.

    Example 3: In 1969, the Portland Cement Company closed its plant in Egypt, Pennsylvania, where it had produced one-third of its output. It had been ordered to stop spewing cement dust and sulfur into the air, but that would have cost $1 million (annual profits were $1.2 million).

    Discuss.

Selected Readings

Boulding, Kenneth E. "The Economics of the Coming Spaceship Earth." In *Environmental Quality in a Growing Economy*, edited by Harry Jarrett. Baltimore: Johns Hopkins Press, 1966. First presentation of earth as a spaceship and thus a closed system.

Council on Environmental Quality. *Environmental Quality*. Washington, D.C.: Government Printing Office. Published annually since 1970. Deals with all aspects of environmental problems and policies. Presents many useful data otherwise unattainable.

Dolan, Edwin G. *Tanstaafl: The Economic Strategy for Environmental Crisis.* New York: Holt, Rinehart and Winston, 1971. A superb introduction to antipollution policies.

Edel, Matthew, and Rothenberg, Jerome. *Readings in Urban Economics.* New York: Macmillan, 1972. Part 5. Presents technical articles on the economics of congestion and pollution, measuring the cost of pollution, and devising incentives for pollution control. Note the bibliography on pages 344, 397, and 398.

Gordon, David M. *Problems in Political Economy: An Urban Perspective.* Lexington, Mass.: D. C. Heath and Co., 1971. Pp. 451–55 and 459–78. Presents conservative, liberal, and radical views on the causes of pollution and possible remedies, including an excellent bibliography.

Hardin, Garrett. "The Tragedy of the Commons." *Science* (1968), pp. 1243 ff. Discusses the problems arising when property rights in scarce resources are not assigned.

NOTE: The *Journal of Economic Literature* lists recent articles on natural resources, conservation, and pollution (sections 720–22).

The *Index of Economic Articles* catalogs in section 17 articles on natural resources, land economics, and conservation.

APPENDIX A TO CHAPTER 13
The Wastes Dumped into the Environment: Types, Quantities, and Effects

This appendix provides background material for those not familiar with the sources of pollution or its effects. It describes the principal types of wastes dumped into the environment in the United States, notes the quantities involved, and assesses the effects of such waste disposal.

WASTES DUMPED INTO THE AIR

The two main sources of airborne wastes in the United States are (in this order) the automobile and industry. The plight of Los Angeles is well known. It has the dubious honor of having been called "the city where one is awakened by the sound of birds coughing." Young fatal-car-accident victims in Los Angeles show four times more lung damage than similar victims who have been living in clean air communities. In 1968, sixty faculty members of UCLA medical school recommended that "anyone not compelled to remain in Los Angeles should leave immediately for the sake of his health." But don't think the problem is confined to Los Angeles. Look at any large city (especially the next time you fly in an airplane). You will find a yellow brown dome of hydrocarbons and carbon monoxide, soot, fly ash, and sulfur dioxide covering the city, reaching perhaps as high as 10,000 feet. Above that is the crisp blue sky, hidden to any observer on the ground by thousands of tons of particles suspended in the air. Auto exhausts, industrial smokestacks, heating units, city dumps, and private incinerators continually add to the supply. Once in a while, a rainstorm will bring it all to the ground (causing water pollution or soil pollution instead). Or strong winds will push the materials over hundreds of miles of countryside. (Persistent southwest winds during the summer push New York air pollution right up to Vermont, blanketing much of rural New England.)

Quantities Involved

Table A13.1 gives a summary of the quantity, sources, and composition of airborne wastes in the United States in 1970. Note, however, that the rankings in weight shown in Table A13.1 do not necessarily parallel the rankings of these pollutants in effects. Some pollutants are more dangerous than others. Also, they interact to create secondary pollutants. For instance, during temperature inversions in Los Angeles, a stinging smog develops from the interaction of sunlight with hydrocarbons and nitrogen oxide. This produces irritating nitrogen dioxide (plus ozone). The disparity in effect can be taken account of in

Table A13.1 Air Pollutant Emissions, United States, 1970 (In Millions of Tons)

Source	Total	Carbon Monoxide	Hydro-carbons	Particles	Sulfur Oxides	Nitrogen Oxides
Transportation	144	111	20	1	1	12
Fuel combustion (stationary)	38	1	1	6	22	9
Industrial processes	37	11	6	13	6	...
Refuse disposal	11	7	2	1	...	...
Other (e.g., forest fires)	30	18	7	4	...	1
Total[a]	260	149	35	26	29	22

[a] Detail may not add to total due to rounding.
SOURCE: Statistical Abstract of the United States, *1972, p. 175.*

Over half of airborne wastes in the United States has come from the use of automobiles in recent years.

calculating *pollution indexes*, which weight tons of different pollutants differently. For example, in an air pollution index a ton of sulfur dioxide (or of *fine* particles) might be weighted more heavily than a ton of carbon monoxide (or of *large* particles) because the effects on health differ. Several indexes have been developed. Among these are the Mitre Air Quality Index (MAQI), the Extreme Value Index (EVI), and the Oak Ridge Air Quality Index (ORAQI).

The MAQI first relates measured pollution levels to the EPA secondary air quality standards and then combines the values for individual pollutants. If a combined index for all pollutants is 1 (or less), all types of pollution equal (or fall short of) the maxima allowed by the standards.

The EVI measures the extent of very-high-level pollution for short periods of time. Thus it measures the conditions most directly related to personal comfort and well-being. It is first computed by comparing, for each individual pollutant measured, values that exceed the EPA's *extreme* standard (for 1–24-hour concentrations) with that standard. Then these ratios are aggregated for all pollutants. If a combined index for all pollutants is zero, all types of pollution equal or fall short of the maximum standard.

The ORAQI, finally, is also based on EPA secondary standards. If the index value is 100 (or less), all pollutant concentrations equal (or fall short of) the established standards.

Table A13.2, "Selected Air Pollution Indexes, United States," lists selected values of these indexes and provides further detail on their calculation.

It should be noted that total air pollutant emissions for the United States

Table A13.2 Selected Air Pollution Indexes, United States

City	Year	MAQI[a]	EVI[b]	ORAQI[c]
26 Cities with over 400,000 people	1968	4.03	11.56	
	1969	3.48	7.99	
	1970	3.06	6.66	
38 Cities, 100,000–400,000 people	1968	3.04	6.61	
	1969	2.56	4.10	
	1970	2.51	3.34	
18 Cities, under 100,000 people	1968	3.34	10.35	
	1969	3.00	7.68	
	1970	2.71	6.41	
New York	1968	6.07	20.06	246
	1969	5.01	13.39	181
	1970	3.48	7.38	116
Detroit	1968	4.01	17.90	145
	1969	3.68	12.11	138
	1970	3.39	9.17	102
St. Louis	1968	3.82	18.07	157
	1969	5.35	27.24	163
	1970	4.41	13.15	125
Milwaukee	1968	4.27	20.82	119
	1969	3.17	10.17	89
	1970	2.69	6.41	70

[a] The Mitre Air Quality Index shown here is based on sulfur dioxide, nitrogen dioxide, and total suspended particulates only. Secondary ambient air-quality standards allow an annual mean concentration of no more than 0.02 ppm (parts per million) for sulfur dioxide and of no more than 0.05 ppm for nitrogen dioxide, and an annual geometric mean of no more than 60 $\mu g/m^3$ (micrograms per cubic meter) for total suspended particulates. For the indexes shown in this table a value of less than 1 indicates that all secondary ambient air-quality standards have been met for the pollutants included in its computation. Values between 1 and 2.24 do not necessarily imply that any standard has been exceeded, but a value in excess of 2.24 guarantees that at least one standard has *not* been met.

[b] The Extreme Value Index is calculated for only those pollutants for which secondary "maximum values not to be exceeded more than once per year" are defined. These allow maximum concentrations of 35 ppm for 1 hour and 9 ppm for 8 hours for carbon monoxide; of 0.5 ppm for 3 hours and 0.1 ppm for 24 hours for sulfur dioxide; of 150 $\mu g/m^3$ for 24 hours for total suspended particulates; and of 0.08 ppm for 1 hour for photochemical oxidants. For the indexes shown in the table a value of zero indicates that all standards based upon the "maximum value not to be exceeded more than once a year" have been met for the pollutants included in its computation. If any standard is surpassed, the index will be 1 or larger.

[c] The Oak Ridge Air Quality Index is based on the same data as the MAQI, but standards are normalized to a 24-hour average basis. For sulfur dioxide this means 0.1 ppm; for nitrogen dioxide, 0.2 ppm, and for particulates, 150 $\mu g/m^3$. A value of 10 describes the condition naturally occurring in unpolluted air; a value of 100 is equivalent to pollutant concentrations reaching the secondary standards; larger values show heavier concentrations.

have been increasing rapidly in recent years. However, the ambient air quality in most urban areas has improved, due partly to the outward move of manufacturing, partly to increased efforts to control emissions. The air quality in U.S. nonurban areas has been declining correspondingly. The trouble with air pollution goes far beyond the obvious, such as eyes that burn, higher cleaning costs, and loss of scenic views. It also damages property. It interferes with the life of plants and animals. It has subtle effects on the human life span. On occasion, it kills people. Possibly, it may end all life on earth.[1]

Effects on Property

Air pollutants damage property physically and in value terms. By reducing visibility, air pollution has caused airplane accidents. Less dramatically, it can literally eat up property. The *physical* damage to structures has been estimated in the billions of dollars each year. It is not just a matter of dirt and paint, either. This is most dramatically illustrated by the fate of Europe's art treasures and ancient architectural heritage. Experts have concluded that in the last 20 years, damage to them exceeded that of the previous 2,000 years. Even marble statues crumble to dust, as if hit by leprosy. First the surface darkens, then pollutants combine with the calcium carbonate in the marble, producing calcium sulfate. The latter takes twice the volume of the former, so expansion occurs that breaks the stone. (A UNESCO commission seriously recommended putting the entire Acropolis under glass.)

Visitors to the Lincoln Memorial claim that they can hear the entire building fizz like a giant Alka-Seltzer in Washington's sulfuric rains. In New York City's Central Park stands a 224-ton granite obelisk (Cleopatra's Needle). Carved in 1600 B.C., it was given to the city in 1882, with hieroglyphics clearly visible on all four sides. By 1970, none were visible on the south and west sides, because prevailing winds had eaten off several inches of granite.

In addition to such physical destruction, which is worldwide, property *values* in heavily polluted U.S. cities have been shown to decline from $300 to $700 per house, or by over $5 billion annually. Off-color paint, sooty surfaces, unpleasant odors, and hazy views are simply not very inviting to potential buyers. Only lower price can make them buy under the circumstances.

[1] Most of the information in this appendix on the effects of pollution comes from reports on scientific studies which were summarized during the past decade in the *New York Times* or the *Wall Street Journal.*

SOURCE: Environmental Quality: The Third Annual Report of the Council on Environmental Quality (*Washington, D.C.: Government Printing Office, 1972), pp. 9–10 and 34–44.*

Concentrations of gaseous contaminants are continuously measured throughout the United States to provide basic data on the nature and extent of urban air pollution. All indexes in recent years have shown improvements in urban areas.

Effects on Plants

Plants are seriously affected by air pollution. Either their exterior is damaged directly, or their water intake is suppressed, stunting their growth. This, too, costs billions of dollars each year. Alfalfa, barley, cut flowers, celery, lettuce, onions, radishes, spinach, and tomatoes cannot be grown any more in the Los Angeles basin. Citrus fruit yields there have been cut in half. So has the output in vineyards. California forests are silently dying. Ever since 1955, ponderosa pines have been turning yellow, losing vigor, and then their needles. In 1970, in the San Bernardino Mountains alone 1.3 million trees on 161,000 acres were dead or dying. Pollutants destroy chlorophyll in leaf tissue; then bark beetles finish off the trees. The situation was similar in the San Francisco Bay area, the Sequoia National Park, and at Point Loma. Nor is this destruction confined to California. In 1969, when the sulfur dioxide level reached twenty times "normal," chrysanthemums and snapdragons on New York's Staten Island died by the thousands. Virginia tobacco leaves are up to 40 percent smaller. Michigan potatoes suffer, and so do Florida citrus crops.

Effects on Animals

Animals are also affected. More than 80 percent of sulfur oxide emissions come from man's use of sulfur-containing fuels, the rest from smelting of nonferrous metals, from petroleum refining, and from volcanic gases. The gases are absorbed by rain and snow, which then become more acid. The increased acidity affects bodies of water, in turn, and tends to kill aquatic life. Salmon are among the first to die.

Effects on Man

The most advanced animal of all, man, is no less affected. Billions of dollars of his medical bills each year can be traced to air pollution. The possible linkage between cigarette smoking and lung cancer is a warning sign. High incidence of chronic bronchitis has been traced to air pollution in Great Britain. In California, the death rate from pulmonary emphysema (the destruction of air sacs in the lungs) has quadrupled, possibly because of air pollution. Air *particle* pollution, for instance from asbestos fibers of auto brake linings and construction sites, has been linked to cancer of the esophagus, and stomach, and lungs, as well as to heart attacks caused by the inability to breathe properly with scarred lungs. Medical experts reported in mid-1972 that of 250,000 U.S. asbestos industry workers, 95,000 would eventually die of occupational cancer. In Germany's Ruhr, particle pollution has been blamed for the circumstance that children weigh less, are shorter, and have higher incidence of rickets, of eczema, and of asthma.

Carbon monoxide pollution is almost entirely the result of auto use. In New York City alone, 8 million pounds of it are released every day. It is significant that the concentration in New York City is 15–30 ppm (parts per million) from 9 A.M. to 7 P.M. (100 ppm in the Lincoln Tunnel), but less than 2 ppm from 1 A.M. to 2 A.M. This odorless, colorless poison affects people's ability to concentrate and think. It causes headaches, nausea, dizziness, and surliness (New York City drivers!). It harms vision and slows reactions, and has been linked with auto accidents. It damages human arteries (and can cause heart attacks). It harms the development of unborn children by causing mutations.

Well over 90 percent of air *lead* pollution is attributable to cars also. Lead additives are used to fuel high-compression engines to avoid destructive knocking. By 1970, 105 million cars were on U.S. roads that could not run on lead-free fuel. As a result, lead concentrations in the air of large U.S. cities were 20 times those in rural sparsely populated areas and 2,000 times those in the mid-Pacific. Compared with the condition that would exist in the absence of man, lead concentrations in the Northern Hemisphere were 1,000 times larger. In 1970, the life span of test animals given the amount of lead then taken in by people was reduced 20 percent because lead disturbed the oxygen-carrying capacity of the blood. Urban children were found to have twice as much lead in their blood as rural children. To this fact were linked colic, nausea, constipation, anemia, headaches, and occasional coma and death. Adults were shown to become subject to sterility and damage to nervous system, liver, and kidney. Pregnant women were more likely to have spontaneous abortions or brain-damaged, retarded, and otherwise abnormal babies.

Air pollution may have less obvious effects, too. Perpetual grayness, the inability to see the blue sky, are known to have a *psychological effect* on people, causing serious emotional and mental disease.

On occasion, the seriousness of air pollution is brought home to us more dramatically. In 1930, 63 deaths were directly attributed to air pollution in the Meuse valley in Belgium. In 1948, a choking smog from smelter fumes killed 22 persons in Donora, Pennsylvania. An eerie smog, containing a large percentage of *sulfur dioxide*, killed 4,000 people in London in 1952, 1,000 more in 1956, and 300 more in 1962. New York City has had similar incidents (220 deaths in 1953, 325 in 1963, and 168 in 1966). In addition, experiments in 1972 showed sulfur dioxide to disrupt normal genetic mechanisms.

Effects on Climate

In addition to people dying as individuals, in the long run air pollution may well eliminate man as a species. This may happen because air pollution affects the climate.[2] Some of these effects are localized and less serious than others. Air pollution may increase or decrease rainfall, for example. Particles get into the air from erosion, grinding, spraying, industrial dusts, and burning. Typically, they are removed from the air by gravitational settling. Depending on

[2] The remainder of this section is based in part on Richard D. James, "Changing Climate: Scientists Charge That Increased Air Pollution Is Altering the Weather," *Wall Street Journal*, December 31, 1969, pp. 1 and 10.

the height at which they are introduced, they can remain airborne from days to weeks. Particles may be invisible, measuring only 1/25,000 inch in diameter. They are good cloud-forming agents in that they attract water vapor, which condenses and freezes on them. This creates ice crystals and eventually clouds. As a result, interesting phenomena have been observed. La Porte, Indiana, located downwind from Chicago and the Gary steel mills, has 47 percent more rain than communities upwind. From 1923 to 1962, its rain has peaked with peaks in steel production! Similarly, Belleville, Illinois, located downwind from St. Louis, has more rain than upwind communities. On the other hand, where there is too much dust, no particle can attract enough moisture to grow raindrops. As a result, very thick particle pollution cuts rainfall. This has been observed in Queensland, Australia. When sugarcane leaves are burned off at harvest time, downwind communities receive 25 percent less rain than upwind ones. A similar drought effect is produced in the Northeastern United States.

As you might expect, where particle pollution creates more rain, it also creates more fog and more violent weather. Downtown Chicago and St. Louis have significantly more thunderstorms than surrounding areas. La Porte has four times as much hail.

The global effects of particles in the atmosphere are even more important. The turbidity of the air (the dustiness of the atmosphere) has increased everywhere, not just around big cities. It has increased tenfold over the past 40 years in such unlikely places as Arizona, Yellowstone National Park, and the Adirondack Mountains, nineteenfold in Central Asia, by 30 percent over the Pacific. This is being worsened greatly by high-flying jets nowadays. Every pound of fuel they burn releases 1¼ pounds of water and dust. At altitudes of 20,000 to 40,000 feet, because it is cold, this amount can saturate large bodies of air (in the manner of exhaling on a cold morning). Consider that one jet crosses the North Atlantic every six minutes. No wonder that we observe increasing high-cloud cover over such well-traveled routes as New York–London or New York–Chicago. (The supersonic transports, scheduled to fly between 45,000 and 150,000 feet, would reinforce this effect.) As a result of increased scattering of sunlight by clouds and particles, less sunshine reaches the earth. (A specific case: Before London's 1956 smoke control laws, the city had 64 hours of sunshine per winter, the surrounding areas had 268.) A decrease in sunshine reduces the average temperature. The global mean temperature has already declined by 0.5 °C from 1940 to 1967. If the change sounds unimportant, consider that the last ice age was brought about by nothing more than a 4–5 °C fall in temperature. A change can happen very fast. The end of the ice age took less than 100 years! Any permanent cooling of the earth would have disastrous consequences; it would take much of present agricultural land out of production and cause worldwide starvation.

Any permanent *increase* in the earth's temperature would have similarly disastrous effects. A warming trend would melt the ice caps of Greenland and

Antarctica and the resultant flood would affect most big cities over the earth. Forces effecting atmospheric increase in heat exist even now. Consider carbon dioxide, which is not listed in Table A13.1. We give off into the air a greater quantity of carbon dioxide than of any of the pollutants listed there. But carbon dioxide is not normally considered a pollutant, since it is thought to be harmless to human health. Furthermore, it is uncontrollable, being an inevitable by-product of combustion, at least until a new source of energy is harnessed (besides coal, oil, and gas). However, this does not mean there are no effects. Compared with 1958–68, the rate of increase of atmospheric carbon dioxide nearly doubled during 1969–70. It is estimated that the global concentration of carbon dioxide will have increased eighteenfold by the year 2000 from its 1890 levels. By itself, this would *increase* the global temperature markedly because of the so-called *greenhouse effect:* carbon dioxide acts as a one-way filter. It absorbs the long-wave infrared radiation from the earth and radiates it back to earth, while the energy from the sun arrives as short-wave radiation and passes right through the gas. There are many local examples of this effect. In some U.S. cities (like downtown Chicago), the frost-free season has been extended by as much as 60 days, while one would have to go south by hundreds of miles to find anything comparable in rural areas. On weekdays, when air pollution is greatest, temperatures in Washington, D.C., and New Haven, Connecticut, are higher than on weekends. On a worldwide basis, however, things are different. Apparently so far the temperature-lowering effect of suspended particles has more than offset the greenhouse effect. So the world temperature has been declining.

The Nature and Extent of Noise Pollution

A special kind of "air pollution" is the creation of *unwanted sound.*[3] It is no less dangerous than physical substances. In the United States, the noise level has become persistent and intense. It has doubled since 1955. And it continues to rise. Although there is no necessary relationship between noise and the use of power, the former has been rising with the latter. The total energy generated in the United States is equal to the muscular energy that would be generated if every American owned 500 slaves! These modern slaves make a lot of noise. We are surrounded by washing machines, refrigerators, exhaust fans, cars and trucks, sirens, clanking garbage cans, air compressors, jack-hammers, pile drivers, wrecking balls, riveting equipment, airliners, and so on. The noise they make is measured on a special yardstick, the *decibel scale.* Table A13.3 gives you some idea how this scale measures sounds. It expresses the sound values of the so-called A-scale, which assigns more weight to annoying

[3] This section is based in part on John M. Mecklin, "It's Time to Turn Down All That Noise," *Fortune* (October 1969), pp. 130–33, 188, 190, 195, and on Richard R. Leger, "If You Can't Shut Out the Racket, Drown It With Your Own Noise," *Wall Street Journal,* January 28, 1970, pp. 1 and 33.

Table A13.3 The Decibel A-Scale—Selected Values

Type of Sound	Decibels
Breathing	10
Rustling leaves	20
Soft whisper	30
Rural night	30
Window air-conditioner	55
Speech	60
Sound level where hearing damage begins after prolonged exposure	85
Heavy city traffic	90
Lawn power-mower	98
Shout at 0.5 ft	100
150 cu-ft air compressor	100
New York City subways	100
Roof air-conditioner	100
Jet airliner 500 ft overhead	115
Auto horn at 3 ft	115
Pain threshold, immediate hearing damage occurs	120
Rock music	130
Artillery blast	150
Saturn V moon rocket at takeoff	180

high-pitched sounds than to low-pitched ones. Zero decibel equals the weakest sound that the human ear can pick up. Other sounds receive increasingly higher values on the scale.

Effects. What are the effects of the cacophony around us? Sonic booms have caused landslides and damaged old buildings, but noise affects man mostly. According to the American Health Foundation and other authorities, noise affects every bodily function: It increases the heartbeat, constricts arteries, raises the blood pressure, dilates the pupils, causes sweating, pales the skin, and tenses the muscles. Noise has been linked with stomach ulcers, allergies, involuntary urination, spinal meningitis, indigestion, excessive cholesterol in the arteries, loss of equilibrium, impaired vision. Noise is a likely cause of emotional ailments. Just as any unexpected noise creates in us fear and the impulse to flee, continual high noise levels create psychic havoc: hypertension, inability to sleep, vertigo, hallucination, paranoia, suicidal and homicidal impulses—all these have been linked with noise. In Great Britain, a two-year study of 124,000 people showed a significantly higher incidence of admissions to mental hospitals among residents near London's Heathrow Airport with recurrent 100-plus-decibel noise levels.

Furthermore, persistent exposure to high noise levels (above 85 decibels) leads to permanent deafness. Deafness is created because noise deteriorates the microscopic hair cells that transmit sound from ear to brain. We often don't notice this, but some comparisons are striking: Aborigines in isolated African villages can easily hear each other in low conversational tones at 100 yards, even at old age! The U.S. surgeon general has estimated that perhaps as many as 16 million Americans are going deaf from occupational noise alone. Recently, noise generally has been increasing at the rate of one decibel a year. If it were to continue at this rate, all Americans would be deaf by the year 2000. And note: These effects work also during sleep. The ears cannot shut out the noise as the closed eyes can shut out light.

The American Association for the Advancement of Science noted in 1969 that violent noise can harm babies even before birth. By creating emotional stress in the mother, noise makes infants more active in late pregnancy, they cry more often after birth, suffer gastrointestinal tract problems, and greater anxiety generally in early childhood. Animal studies have confirmed all these observations, plus others: Animals subjected to noise were slower to develop emotionally and slower to learn, lost fertility, ate their young, and died of heart failure. Noise is truly a slow agent of death!

WASTES DUMPED INTO BODIES OF FRESH WATER

One of the perpetual concerns of man is a sufficient supply of clean water. In 1971 in the United States, over 338 billion gallons a day were needed. This figure is expected to rise to 443 billion by 1980 and, perhaps, double that by the end of the century. The dependable fresh water supply, on the other hand, is essentially unchanging at 650 billion gallons a day. Thus we can foresee severe shortages. Anything we do to destroy our water supply is an extremely short-sighted policy. Yet man has long been busy doing just that.

Types of Wastes

Rivers and lakes have been used to dispose of *human sewage* for as long as recorded history.

In early 1969, the sewage of 32 million urban Americans got no treatment at all. It was dumped raw into the ocean, rivers, or lakes. However, many cities give sewage *first-stage* treatment. This involves, prior to dumping, the settling out of the coarser solids in holding ponds. Nothing more.

Many other cities have more costly *second-stage* treatment. Benign bacteria break down over 80 percent of the organic material (that is, most human wastes plus the predominantly organic material from garbage disposals). This is broken down into chemical compounds innocuous for people. A special oxygen process can even break down over 90 percent. The resultant liquid is often used for irrigation. When chlorinated, it is even drinkable. Municipal wastes, however, are not the main source of fresh water pollution. *Industry* is a worse offender. In 1970, it used ten times more water than municipal systems, either for the dumping of physical wastes or for cooling purposes.

Additional water pollution comes from *agriculture*. It is responsible for soil, fertilizer, and pesticide runoff into bodies of water. Agriculture is also responsible for runoff from some 221,000 livestock feedlots that sustain 11 million cattle at any one moment. Overall, the wastes produced by farm animals exceed by 20 times those produced by people.

Additional water pollution stems from the operation of mines and watercraft. Sediment and acid drainage from mines, which occupy 11 million acres, pollute some 10,000 miles of U.S. streams. Seventy percent of this comes from abandoned mines.

Finally, more than 8 million watercraft in the U.S. discharge anything from human wastes to oil, ballast, bilge waters, and litter, providing us with the typical picture of rivers with miles of iridescent splotches—green, blue, and red—topped with floating debris, from trash and boards to steel drums, tires, and old rubber boots!

Quantities Involved

Table A13.4 gives a summary of the quantities and sources of some important water pollutants in the United States in 1963.

An estimate of the seriousness of water-discharged wastes is provided in column 2 by data on *standard biological oxygen demand*, commonly referred to as BOD. This is a measure of the amount of dissolved oxygen that would be used in five days by the biological processes involved in degrading organic matter. In recent years, due to increased waste treatment, the BOD level of wastes actually discharged has remained roughly constant. The ratio of the BOD of industrial discharges to the BOD of municipal discharges, however, is believed to have increased so that it is now 5:1. Since industrial pollution is generally much more toxic than municipal pollution, the overall quality of U.S. waters has deteriorated. This has been accelerated by increased discharges of toxic materials by agriculture. As a result, less than 10 percent of U.S. watersheds were estimated by the Environmental Protection Agency as unpolluted or slightly polluted in 1970.[4] Table A13.5 gives detail by region.

The evidence of excessive dumping of wastes into natural waters is everywhere. In 1969, a study of eight metropolitan areas and Vermont was conducted by the Department of Health, Education, and Welfare. It showed that 2 million people received inferior drinking water that was safe, but bad-tasting, bad-looking, or malodorous. It also showed that 900,000 people received dangerous water that contained excessive fecal bacteria, arsenic, and lead.

Effects of Sewage Dumping

There was a time when the dumping of raw sewage made people subject to the ravages of typhoid fever, cholera, and dysentery epidemics. In relatively recent times, public health measures (such as chlorination of drinking water) have

[4] In 1972, the EPA was working on the development of a "prevalence-duration-intensity" index for water pollution. It would indicate how badly a body of water was polluted, the types of pollutants, and the length of time during the year it was in violation of the standards.

Table A13.4 **Water Pollutant Emissions, United States, 1963**

	Wastewater (Billion Gallons)	Standard Biological Oxygen Demand (Million Pounds)	Settleable and Suspended Solids (Million Pounds)
Industry			
Food and kindred products	690	4,300	6,600
Textile mill products	140	890	.....
Paper and allied products	1,900	5,900	3,000
Chemical and allied products	3,700	9,700	1,900
Petroleum and coal	1,300	500	460
Rubber and plastics	160	40	50
Primary metals	4,300	480	4,700
Machinery	150	60	50
Electrical machinery	91	70	20
Transportation equipment	240	120	.....
All other manufacturing	450	390	930
All manufacturing	13,121	22,450	17,710
Domestic			
Served by sewers (120 million people)	5,300[a]	7,300[b]	8,800[c]

[a] Number of persons × 120 gallons per person per day × 365.
[b] Number of persons × 1/6 pound per person per day × 365.
[c] Number of persons × 1/5 pound per person per day × 365.

Source: *U.S. Department of the Interior, Federal Water Pollution Control Administration,* The Cost of Clean Water, Vol. I, Summary Report *(Washington, D.C., January 1968).*

Industry and municipal wastes are the main sources of water pollution in the United States.

reduced some of the health dangers to man, but other dangers have remained and new ones have appeared on the scene. Most obviously, unabated pollution cuts down the supply of drinking water. The cost of getting clean water is increased. For example, in New York City, 150 gallons are needed per person per day. The city is often short of clean water. In the summer, its lawns must die, its pools remain empty. All the while, billions of gallons of fresh water flow past the city each day into the sea. As it is, this polluted water is unusable. New York City now must get its clean water from reservoirs at the headwaters of the Delaware River. There are plans to extend the conduits into the Adirondack Mountains. Boston gets its water from western Massachusetts. Los Angeles had to build a 440-mile aqueduct to the Sacramento River. Santee, Southern California, even reclaims sewage (which is 99 percent water) for drinking purposes. This idea is repugnant to many. They do not think one

Table A13.5 **Estimated Prevalence of Water Pollution, by Region, United States, 1970**

Region	Percentage of Stream Miles Polluted	Percentage of Watersheds Polluted: *Predominantly Polluted*[a]	*Extensively Polluted*[b]	*Locally Polluted*[c]	*Slightly Polluted*[d]
Pacific Coast	33.9	14.8	59.3	22.2	3.7
Northern Plains	40.0	37.5	33.3	25.0	4.2
Southern Plains	38.8	27.3	51.5	18.2	6.1
Southeast	23.3	14.3	41.1	16.1	28.6
Central	36.6	23.2	51.8	21.4	3.6
Northeast	43.9	36.1	55.6	5.6	2.8
East of Mississippi River	31.6	23.0	48.7	15.5	12.8
West of Mississippi River	35.5	24.1	47.1	20.7	4.6
United States	32.6	23.7	48.5	17.7	9.9

[a] Predominantly polluted: ⩾ 50% of stream miles polluted.
[b] Extensively polluted: 20–49.9% of stream miles polluted.
[c] Locally polluted: 10–19.9% of stream miles polluted.
[d] Slightly polluted: ⩽ 10% of stream miles polluted.

SOURCE: *Environmental Protection Agency, Water Quality Office.*

should do anything with sewage except get rid of it. Many cities do just that. However, even those providing second-stage treatment of sewage continue to cause serious damage. The "innocuous" chemicals (mostly nitrogen and phosphorus) that result from second-stage treatment act as a fertilizer in rivers and lakes. Algae begin to grow faster than Jack's beanstalk. They clog city water intakes and strangle boat traffic, and when they die, they do more than ruin waterfront property and recreational facilities. They also help use up the dissolved oxygen supply in the water. (Algae use eighteen times as much oxygen as an equal quantity of organic raw sewage.) Bacteria feed on raw sewage, and they also feed on dead algae. They break these materials down into such inorganic components as nitrogen, phosphorus, and carbon. This process of *aerobic degradation* consumes oxygen dissolved in the water. If this oxygen consumption occurs at a faster rate than new additions of oxygen at the water-air interface or by the photosynthesis of water plants, all the dissolved oxygen in the water may become exhausted. This kills fish, shellfish, and other animals feeding on fish.

Effects of Industrial Dumping

Damage to water is accelerated by the activities of industry that use natural waters for dumping or cooling purposes.

Organic wastes. Some of these industrial wastes, namely organic ones dumped by the food, pulp, and paper industries, have the same effects on the recipient waters as the dumping of raw or partially treated sewage. Indeed, the wastes of a single pulp mill can affect a body of water exactly as if all the sewage of a large city had been dumped into it. Paper companies dump their "black liquor," a dark smelly mixture of acids and residue from the breakdown of wood pulp into paper fibers. They dump "white water," a discharge of tiny fibers that escape the machines that press fibers into paper. Bacteria feed on these wastes, as they do on raw sewage and dead algae, with the same ultimate result.

Waste heat. The process of *eutrophication* (the killing of marine life by oxygen being used up in water) is further enhanced by *thermal* pollution. The growth of algae is stimulated by a slight warming of the water temperature by the hot-water emissions from power plants and steel mills. In the Haverstraw Bay area north of New York City, a cluster of nuclear power plants use a million gallons of water *per minute* for cooling, leaving the river 15 degrees warmer. (In 1969, such power plants were using 100 billion gallons of water per day in the United States for cooling. This figure is expected to quadruple in fifty years.) The Federal Water Resources Council sees thermal pollution as the most serious long-range water problem. While only 1 percent of electric power was produced in the late 1960's in nuclear plants, one-third of all power is expected to be so produced by 1980. Lake Michigan, for example, received over 40 billion Btu per hour in 1968 from power plants (75 percent), steel mills (16 percent), and sewers (9 percent), an input that was expected to increase tenfold by the end of the century and if unchecked, to ensure the degeneration of the lake into a swamp.

Eventually all the dissolved oxygen would be used up. In the process, any accumulating organic wastes are degraded *anaerobically*, with the occurrence of gaseous by-products such as methane or hydrogen sulfide. The water becomes a witch's brew: black, bubbly, foul-smelling, and bad-tasting. Before long, it turns into a swamp. Northern pike, blue pike, and sturgeon give way to suckers and carp. The number of wild birds sharply declines. Once beautiful beaches and the voices of happy children are replaced by mounds of decaying algae and "No Swimming" signs. A once flourishing fishing industry dies. Eventually, there is left a putrid sludge, inhabited by worms and maggots and nothing else.

Inorganic chemicals. The possibilities for causing disease in man through the dumping of inorganic chemicals are legion. Take *mercury*, one of the biggest of industrial pollutants. In Minamata, Japan, its dumping has caused many fatalities among people living on fish since 1953. In the United States, it was first discovered in 1970 in fish in Lakes Erie and Saint Clair. At that time, U.S. and Canadian firms producing caustic soda, plastics, batteries, seed dressings, and fungicides were dumping over 750,000 lb of mercury per year into the Great Lakes alone in the belief that it would lie quietly at the bottom and harm nobody. Yet anaerobic bacteria convert mercury very slowly into methylmercury, which dissolves in water and enters the food chain. In man it accumulates in the brain and slowly destroys the central nervous system. Thus it can cause blindness, paralysis, and insanity. (Remember the Mad Hatter in Alice in Wonderland? His shaky and incoherent behavior represented that of hat makers whose work with mercury-processed felt made them subject to mercury poisoning.) Mercury also breaks up chromosomes and can deform the unborn. It associates itself with the red blood cells and attacks the liver. Since 1970, mercury has also been found in the oceans in exceedingly high concentrations. The Alaska fur seals, tuna, and swordfish have ingested huge quantities.

Other industrial nondegradable pollutants are no less serious. These include long-lived *radionuclides* from atomic power plants. They include *synthetic chemicals* with complex molecular chains, such as detergents, cleansers, pesticides, and phenols (the latter coming from the distillation of petroleum and coal products). All these degrade only slowly, if at all, and can cause serious harm in victims of prolonged exposure at even low concentrations.

Take *detergents*. Since the 1950's, they have taken over a large share of the market for soap previously held by flakes and powders. There was an obvious reason. Soap flakes and powders when used in water of high mineral content (hard water) left a dirt scum on clothing (the famous "ring around the collar"). Detergents contained phosphates that softened the water and avoided the problem. But eventually, they contributed to the eutrophication of bodies of water into which they were released. Worse still, the "new, improved and amazing" ingredients in detergents created billowing suds in the waterways, engulfed entire sewage treatment plants in heaps of foam, and caused tap water to suddenly have a head on it. Some of these ingredients were shown to cause cancer.

Effects of Agricultural and Mining Activity

Increased *arsenic* levels in fish have been traced to the use of contaminated phosphate fertilizer by agriculture. The arsenic entering waterways is converted by microorganisms into dimethylarsine, which enters the food chain. Over half of the nitrogen found in fresh water is also traced to fertilizer use. It is believed that it might be converted into cancer-causing nitrosamines. And consider the use of agricultural chemicals other than fertilizer. In 1972 in Iraq, over 500 people died and 7,000 were injured from mercury-based fungicides. Over 730 million pounds of *fungicides, herbicides, insecticides, fumigants, and rodenticides* were used in the United States in 1969. Among these were chlorinated hydrocarbons (such as DDT) and organophosphates (such as parathion), both of which have caused much worry in recent years. People have died due to exposure to parathion, and they might die from the less acutely toxic DDT. As with radioactive wastes, we do not really know its ultimate effect on life on earth. When it was discovered, it was hailed as a great miracle. Its developer received the Nobel Prize for Medicine: Before DDT, India had 100 million cases of malaria, with 750,000 deaths per year. Now it has 15,000 cases and 1,500 deaths per year. DDT, by killing the malaria mosquito, did it. Can one quarrel with that?

Now consider this: DDT (and its relatives) have been widely used in agriculture as pesticides. In a process of "biological magnification," DDT has entered higher life forms in large quantities. Through runoff from the fields, minute quantities enter algae. Smaller water organisms feeding on algae take in larger quantities. Little fish that eat these water organisms take in more. Large doses of DDT are found in larger fish that feed on the little fish. And the American eagle, which eats the larger fish, is dying out. DDT affects its calcium metabolism. As a result, it lays eggs with thin shells or none. The embryos die. Mallard ducks, pelicans, and falcons are affected similarly. In plants, DDT slows the rate of photosynthesis, the source of a large fraction of the world's oxygen. In laboratory animals, DDT attacks sex hormones, and the central nervous system. It causes mutations. It incites cancer. But by now DDT is spread all over the world. It has been found in such unlikely places as on rocky islets off Bermuda, in petrels living there; off Virginia, in oysters and shrimps; on the West Coast, in pelicans; and in Antarctica, in the fat of penguins. It is in you. The average American child contains about 5 ppm DDT. The content in older persons is slightly higher.

Breast-fed infants throughout the world in 1969 were ingesting double the quantities of DDT recommended by the World Health Organization as the maximum daily intake. At this range of exposure, laboratory animals are showing biochemical changes. The effect on human health is uncertain, although there are danger signs. Soviet scientists report that workers exposed to DDT for ten years show stomach and liver trouble. The University of Miami medical school reports that persons dying of liver cancer, leukemia, high blood pressure, and carcinoma (a cancer form) have two to three times more DDT in their bodies than persons dying accidental deaths.

Feedlots also do their share of harm. In Arizona, California, Colorado, Indiana, Iowa, Kansas, Minnnesota, Montana, Nebraska, and South Dakota, these lots have contaminated water with nitrates. The contamination has caused deaths among infants and massive fish kills.

Finally, acid pollution from mines can make the water's taste unbearable, besides killing the fish.

WASTES DUMPED INTO OCEANS

In spite of their vastness, the oceans of the world are thoroughly polluted with a coating of tar and oil. Whether you go to the beach in New Jersey, in Bermuda, on the Riviera, or along the Red Sea, you are likely to run into gooey black lumps that take the fun out of it all. According to a study by the Oceanographic Institute at Woods Hole, Massachusetts, even far from heavily traveled shipping lanes, as over the Sargasso Sea in the mid-Atlantic, the tar-oil coating persists. Besides killing many seabirds, the petroleum constituents are entering the oceanic food chain and may thus end up on people's dining room tables. Since these substances have been suspected of causing cancer, man may end up losing the ocean as a source of food.

Where does it all come from? According to the EPA and contrary to most people's preconceptions, more than 90 percent of the petroleum polluting the oceans comes from the vaporization of petroleum products ashore and reaches the oceans via the atmosphere. Other sources, more easily noted, include some 4,000 tankers that transport 60 percent of the annual world oil production of 1.8 billion tons. Their spillage due to leaks, accidents, and purposeful flushing of bilges and of tanks amounts to 1 million tons per year. And 50 gallons of oil can cover a square mile of ocean surface. A famous accident involved the Liberian supertanker *Torrey Canyon*, which ran aground between Britain and France in 1967. It spilled 30 million gallons of oil. When people tried to remove the oil by detergents, they only succeeded in breaking it up into tiny particles that more easily are taken in by tiny animals and thus enter the food chain. In addition, the smaller particles penetrated the beaches of the Cornish coast and the shores of Brittany more deeply and contributed to erosion by wave action. On the land, this single accident killed 50,000 birds. In 1969, the U.S. Coast Guard reported 1,007 large oil spills in U.S. coastal waters alone (each spill involving over 100 barrels).

In addition to shipwrecks, there are production accidents. Among these was the blowout of offshore wells in Santa Barbara, California, in 1969. It spilled 18 million gallons. A presidential panel set up after the incident concluded that by 1980 the United States can expect a big pollution incident like this from offshore wells every year. It noted how offshore production was increasing at 10 percent a year. Also the expected drilling in Northern Alaska, subject to earthquakes and the hazards of ice and great distance, made the potential of spills greater.

Finally, in recent years some 7.4 million tons annually of industrial wastes, sewage sludge, construction and demolition debris, and other solid wastes were dumped by barges coming from U.S. coastal cities alone. In addition, the dumping into rivers and harbors eventually reaches the oceans. The sewage of Albany, Troy, and New York City, for example, eventually escapes into the ocean (1.6 billion gallons a day from New York alone). Or take San Francisco. San Francisco Bay stinks. Each day 600 million gallons of sewage are released into a stagnant bay. Only a tiny portion of it has received treatment, and that rudimentary. In 1969, a $1 billion plan by twelve counties called for shifting the emission farther out into the ocean, where it could be "flushed out by the tides." At this time, it is only a memory that up to 300,000 lb of soft-shell crabs were commercially harvested in the bay each year before 1935. Similarly, the annual commercial harvest of shrimp from all U.S. coastal areas has dropped from over 6.3 million lb before 1936 to 10,000 lb in 1965.

This is not all. Increasingly, radioactive wastes have been dumped in the oceans, either deliberately in "safe" containers or as part of the operation of coastal atomic power stations and atomic vessels. Accidents, such as the

Table A13.6 Average Solid Waste Collected, Pounds per Person per Day, 1967

Solid Wastes	Urban	Rural	National
Household	1.26	0.72	1.14
Commercial	0.46	0.11	0.38
Combined	2.63	2.60	2.63
Industrial	0.65	0.37	0.59
Demolition, construction	0.23	0.02	0.18
Street and alley	0.11	0.03	0.09
Miscellaneous	0.38	0.08	0.31
Totals	5.72	3.93	5.32

SOURCE: *R. J. Black, A. J. Muhich, A. J. Klee, H. L. Hickman, Jr., R. D. Vaughan, "An Interim Report. 1968 National Survey of Community Solid Waste Practices," presented at 1968 annual meeting, Institute for Solid Wastes, American Public Works Association, Miami Beach, Fla., October 1968, Bureau of Solid Waste Management, U.S. Department of Health, Education, and Welfare, Washington, D.C.*

sinking of the atomic submarine *Thresher*, have contributed to this also. As a result, found a Soviet study in 1970, embryo fish in the Irish Sea had deformed backbones. Governments have also dumped chemical and biological weapons in the oceans.

If you combine spillage by ships, production accidents, and deliberate private industrial and governmental dumping, you get a grand worldwide total of at least 100 million tons of ocean pollutants per year.

WASTES DUMPED ON THE SOIL

Wastes that are not dumped into air or water remain with us on the land.[5] Some of these solid wastes come from animals. Others come from people. One single statistic can illustrate the size of the problem: A year's rubbish of 200 million Americans now covers 20,000 acres of ground, seven feet deep.

Quantities Involved

All this included in 1971 an estimated 1.1 billion tons of solid livestock wastes, 71 billion used cans, 38 billion bottles and jars, 35 million tons of wastepaper, 7 million junked cars, and 100 million tires. As shown by Table A13.6, excluding animal wastes, an average of 5.32 pounds of solid wastes per person per day was collected in 1967. If current trends continue, this might double by the end of this century. The total in 1967 amounted to 190 million tons, a figure likely to rise to 340 million tons by 1980. Note, however, that the data of Table A13.6 refer to quantities *collected* by collection agencies. In the

[5] Some of the materials in this section are based on American Chemical Society, *Cleaning Our Environment: The Chemical Basis for Action* (Washington, D.C., 1969).

late 1960's, the total quantities *dumped* were estimated at 360 million tons a year already. Table A13.7 shows the composition of the materials involved.

Most of these materials end up in *open dumps* (73 percent in 1970). On occasion, these are located in isolated areas, such as in open strip mines that have been abandoned. It is possible, however, to dispose of them differently: by *incineration*, by *sanitary landfill*, by *recycling*, or by *composting*.

Some 15 percent of the material was incinerated in 1970. However, incinerators were not always properly designed and operated to prevent air pollution. Proper incineration can involve *pyrolysis* (shredding, baling, and charring of materials in an oxygen-free environment) or high-temperature burning. (Both methods reduce the volume of materials by over 94 percent.)

Another 8 percent of materials went to sanitary landfills in 1970. This involves spreading the refuse in thin layers, compacting it with bulldozers up to 10 feet, covering it with 3 feet of compacted clean earth, then repeating the process. Eventually, such sites can be converted to recreational areas, such as parks or golf courses. They can also be turned into mountains and ski areas. For example, in 1970, New York City proposed to create a 2,500-foot "Grand Teton" of compacted refuse in the Pelham Bay Park. Virginia Beach has created somewhat less spectacular 80-foot Mt. Trashmore. European cities have created similar mountains, for example, Mt. Junk in West Berlin.

Three percent of materials were recycled in 1970, that is, salvaged for reuse. Recycling involves such projects as Goodyear's making new tires from carbon black extracted from old ones or the Glass Container Manufacturers Institute's attempt to collect discarded bottles for reuse in glass manufacture.

Table A13.7 **Sample Municipal Refuse Composition—U.S. East Coast (Weight Percentage)**

Physical		Rough Chemical	
Cardboard	7%	Moisture	28.0%
Newspaper	14	Carbon	25.0
Miscellaneous paper	25	Hydrogen	3.3
Plastic film	2	Oxygen	21.1
Leather, molded plastics, rubber	2	Nitrogen	0.5
Garbage	12	Sulfur	0.1
Grass and dirt	10	Glass, ceramics, etc.	9.3
Textiles	3	Metals	7.2
Wood	7	Ash, other inserts	5.5
Glass, ceramics, stones	10	Total	100.0
Metallics	8		
Total	100		

SOURCE: E. R. Kaiser, "Refuse Reduction Processes," in Proceedings, The Surgeon General's Conference on Solid Waste Management for Metropolitan Washington, *U.S. Public Health Service Publication No. 1729, Government Printing Office, Washington, D.C., July 1967,* p. 93.

Finally, 1 percent of materials was composted in 1970. Composting reduces materials by about 50 percent and yields a humuslike product that can be used as fertilizer or construction material.

Effects

No definite relationship between solid wastes and human health has been established. The problem is rather one of aesthetics and of air and water pollution caused by improper disposal of these wastes. For instance, 8 percent of *municipal* solid waste disposal involves incineration, 70 percent of this without air-pollution control. The carbon dioxide and other products of anaerobic decomposition in landfills can pollute groundwater. Methane, another by-product, can get trapped in buildings and cause explosions. However, this is not inevitable. As has been demonstrated in Tullytown, Pa., polluted water from a landfill can be prevented by a membrane barrier at the base of the landfill from penetrating to underground water supplies or from running off to nearby streams. Water that filters down to the membrane can be made to flow to collection points and treated there.

SOME FINAL THOUGHTS ON MAN AND NATURE

The foregoing sections should have made one thing clear. Pollution of the environment has reached significant proportions. It is like a time bomb hanging around our neck. Unless we defuse it, it will go off, and this will mean the end of mankind. For it is a fact that man cannot live without nature. The earth is a single vast system of interrelationships among plants and animals and climatic forces, an "ecosystem." As man cuts down and paves over huge tracts of forest, as he poisons air, water, and land with numerous chemicals, he slowly kills one species of plant and animal life after another. But each depends on the other, often in ways we do not even understand. Therein lies the danger. For example, should plants cease to produce enough oxygen (a possibility discussed above in connection with DDT), the ultraviolet rays of the sun would cease to be filtered out and *all* life on earth would come to an end. Because there are many interrelated dangers, man must come to change his basic outlook. The world has not been put here for man's sole benefit, to be despoiled at his pleasure. Man cannot forever evade the truth that he is only part of nature. He must strive to live in harmony with nature.

This issue was brought home by the great Everglades jetport controversy of 1969.[6] There had been plans to build in the Florida Everglades a new giant jetport serving Miami, together with industrial and residential developments. Thirty-nine square miles had been purchased, $13 million spent on one landing strip, when federal funds for the jetport were withdrawn and an agreement was reached to locate it elsewhere. All this, furious critics pointed

[6] This section is based in part on Philip Wylie, "Against All Odds, the Birds Have Won," *New York Times*, February 1, 1970, section 10, pp. 1 and 11.

out, to save a 5,000-square-mile superswamp full of alligators, poisonous snakes, clouds of mosquitoes, and huge biting flies! Why *not* pave it all over?

The reason given by ecologists was simply this: Here, south of Lake Okeechobee's 700 square miles of shallow fresh water, was a vast wetland composed of three swamps. At first sight, this area may indeed seem useless. First, there is the Big Cypress Swamp. Second, there is the sawgrass region of prairie of brownish "grass" standing in shoal water (really consisting not of grass but of an abrasive sedge that quickly strips a visitor of clothing and then of skin). Third, there is the largest and impenetrable mangrove forest on earth, where tentaclelike roots and stiff entwined branches stand in slow moving water that becomes brackish, then salty, and then the sea. This area harbors more than alligators and mosquitoes. It is the home of egrets and ibises, of ducks and turkeys, of panthers and foxes, of deer and bears, of herons and otters, of orchids and flowers. Because of its uniqueness, Congress established part of the area in 1934 as Everglades National Park. The construction of the jetport and its satellite developments would doom the area because it would change the flow of water and would pollute. And this is the problem, ecologists pointed out. Since we do not know what life forms are essential for man's survival, we cannot afford to let the Everglades die. Since we know so little about the intricate living understructure supporting man, we cannot risk losing *any* form of life. A single break in the planetary, life-sustaining system can become fatal for all life. We have already mentioned the possible effect of DDT pollution on the oxygen supply. This supply is not there for all time, but rather continuously produced, 70 percent of it by planktonic diatoms in the oceans that are so freely used as dumping grounds. There are many similar examples. All organisms build protein basically from hydrogen, oxygen, sulfur, carbon, and nitrogen. If man were to destroy any of half a dozen types of bacteria involved in, say, the nitrogen cycle, all life on earth could end.

When these arguments won out over commercial interests, for the first time in U.S. history man's dependence on nature, however indirect, was explicitly recognized to have priority over economic development.

Summary

1. Over half of airborne wastes in the United States come from the automobile. The rest come mainly from stationary fuel combustion, industrial processes, and refuse disposal. Air pollutants seriously damage property (both physically and in value terms). They injure plants, animals, and man (both physically and psychologically). They affect the climate.
2. A special kind of air pollution, namely, the dumping of unwanted sound, has equally serious effects on human and animal health.
3. Fresh-water supplies are being polluted heavily by human sewage. They are being polluted even more by industrial wastes (physical substances and heat),

agricultural activities (soil, fertilizer, pesticide, and feedlot runoff), and the operation of mines (sediment and acid drainage) and watercraft.

4. Although the BOD level of wastes discharged has remained roughly constant in recent years, toxic industrial and agricultural pollution has risen relative to less dangerous municipal pollution. In 1970, less than 10 percent of U.S. watersheds were unpolluted or slightly polluted.
5. Due to modern public health measures, the effects of sewage dumping into potential drinking-water supplies have ceased to be epidemics of typhoid and similar diseases. Rather they are increased cost of getting clean water and outright shortages of it. Even the dumping of wastes after second-stage treatment causes serious effects: by stimulating algal growth, it damages property; by the increase in algal decay (that uses up dissolved oxygen), it kills aquatic life.
6. Eutrophication is accelerated by the industrial dumping of organic wastes and heat. Industrial dumping of inorganic wastes (such as mercury and certain synthetic chemicals) and of radionuclides worsens the situation by adding serious health hazards for man.
7. Human and animal health hazards are further increased by agricultural fertilizer, pesticide, and feedlot runoff (bringing, for example, arsenic, DDT, and nitrates into the food chain).
8. Ocean pollution is widespread. The chief pollutants are tar, oil, industrial wastes, sewage sludge, construction debris, radioactive wastes, and chemical and biological weapons. The main sources are vaporization of petroleum products ashore, spillage by tankers, production accidents, and deliberate dumping by municipalities and governments. The effects are spoiled recreational areas, partial loss of the oceans as a source of food, and health dangers for man and lower animals.
9. Soil pollutants consist mainly of livestock wastes plus human trash and garbage. Most of the latter two end up in open dumps, some are disposed of via incineration, sanitary landfill, recycling, or composting. The main problem here is an aesthetic one plus the danger of air or water pollution by improper disposal.
10. The dumping of wastes has reached such significant proportions as to endanger the very existence of life on earth. Therefore, man must change his outlook on the matter of freely using his environment as a dumping ground.

Terms[7]

aerobic degradation
anaerobic degradation
composting
decibel scale
eutrophication
first-stage sewage treatment
greenhouse effect
noise
pollution index
pyrolysis
recycling
sanitary landfill
second-stage sewage treatment
standard biological oxygen demand
thermal pollution

[7] Terms and symbols are defined in the Glossary at the back of the book.

Symbols

BOD
EVI
MAQI
ORAQI

Questions for Review and Discussion

1. In 1971, Los Angeles exceeded on 218 days the state's maximum limit for photochemical air pollution. Why do people keep living there?
2. "The use of lead should be *banned,* especially in gasoline, paints, and printing inks. Most lead gets into the air (and into people) through the use of leaded gasoline. But additional lead gets into the air by the burning of newspapers and magazines made with lead-based printing ink. Much gets into children who eat chipped lead-base paints off the walls in slum housing and who chew newspapers into spitballs. As a result, 400,000 children had lead poisoning in 1969. There is no excuse for such suffering." Consider the benefits *and the costs* of this proposal.
3. In 1972, only 2.6 percent of glass, 3.7 percent of aluminum, and 2.3 percent of ferrous containers were made from recycled materials. Among other things, this was blamed on generally higher freight rates for scrap than for new materials and on tax advantages given to mineral mining operations (such as the depletion allowance). Another factor discouraging recycling was the requirement to label products: consumers are reluctant to buy clothing or furniture advertised as made from "waste" materials. Shouldn't recycling be *encouraged?* If so, how would you do it?
4. Ever since the 1820's, people have wanted to build a barge canal across Florida from Palatka (south of Jacksonville) to Yankeetown (on the Gulf of Mexico). In 1969, when it was 27 percent complete, someone sued to stop construction on the grounds that the canal, by changing water flows, would ultimately destroy the Everglades. How would you decide if you were the judge? Explain.
5. Some 10–30 miles above the surface of the earth is a layer of ozone, consisting of triple oxygen atoms. The lethal wavelengths of the sun's radiation are absorbed by ozone as they split ozone into paired and single oxygen atoms (which then recombine into ozone). Without this mechanism, searing ultraviolet rays would cause skin cancer and kill all plants exposed to the atmosphere. Unfortunately, methane gas reacts with those single oxygen atoms, thereby depleting the life-preserving ozone layer. Some of this methane comes from natural sources, such as swamp decay, but most comes from human activities. These include the flying of supersonic transports (SST's) at high altitudes, coal mining, growing rice in paddy fields, fertilizing fields with human and animal wastes, and plain flatulence associated with food digestion by humans and animals (notably the cattle raised by people). We can stop the SST, but we *can't* stop most of these other polluting activities. What should we do to preserve life?

Selected Readings

Council on Environmental Quality. *Environmental Quality*. Washington, D.C.: Government Printing Office. Published annually since 1970. Deals with all aspects of environmental problems and policies. Presents many useful data otherwise unattainable.

Gordon, David M. *Problems in Political Economy: An Urban Perspective*. Lexington, Mass.: D. C. Heath and Co., 1971. Pp. 456–59 and 476–78. Discusses briefly the sources and extent of pollution and presents an excellent bibliography.

U.S. Bureau of the Census. *Statistical Abstract of the United States, 1972*. Washington, D.C., 1972. Lists some statistics on pollution (Sections 6 and 25), and—more important—sources to other statistics: Note the listing of statistical abstract supplements (p. v); and the guide to general sources of statistics (pp. 926–28), and to state statistical abstracts (pp. 961–64).

APPENDIX B TO CHAPTER 13
Would Socialism End Pollution?

Some people reject altogether the idea that the natural environment could possibly be saved within the framework of the capitalist market economy. This system, they argue, inexorably drives society to despoil and uglify nature. It is hopelessly beyond redemption, for all is keyed to producing goods. Everybody is oblivious to the meaning and purpose of life. This type of economy cannot be patched up by standard setting or pollution rights markets or similar devices, goes the argument. Only a complete change in the *system*—to wit, toward central planning or socialism—could reverse this trend. This Appendix considers this argument at some length. It does so by presenting the available evidence from the Soviet and Chinese economies.

THE SOVIET CASE

The Soviet economy is indeed characterized by collective ownership of land and capital. Until the mid-1960's, *markets* and *profits* were dirty words, and complete central planning of all economic activity was the ideal toward which government leaders were striving. Ideally, they would direct, in physical terms, each factory and farm manager to use designated quantities of inputs (labor, land, and capital) to produce specified minimum quantities of outputs or more. The central plan would make sure that the marching orders issued to all firms fitted neatly together and that was that.

The Obsession with Growth

But what has been the goal of this economy since the beginning of the plan era and is still the goal today? The goal of overwhelming importance has been the most rapid possible economic growth. By the device of agricultural collectivization, the Soviet state placed the rural population in the status of dependent factory workers, forcing them, as Stalin put it "to sell without purchasing." In return for a subsistence diet, the peasants delivered to the state a huge agricultural surplus. Part of it was used to provide a similar subsistence diet for urban workers. Most of it was used as industrial raw material or as the export price for importing capital. The "tribute" paid by the Soviet peasant, as Stalin put it, was the cost of industrialization. In his own words, the goal was stated thus:[1]

[1] J. Stalin, *Voprosy Leninizma* (Moscow, 1952), pp. 362–63. Italics supplied by the author.

> To slacken the tempo would mean falling behind. And those who fall behind get beaten. But we do not want to be beaten. No, we refuse to be beaten! One feature of the history of old Russia was the continual beatings she suffered for falling behind, for her backwardness. She was beaten by the Mongol khans. She was beaten by the Turkish beys. She was beaten by the Swedish feudal lords. She was beaten by the Polish and Lithuanian gentry. She was beaten by the British and French capitalists. She was beaten by the Japanese barons. All beat her—for her backwardness: for military backwardness, for cultural backwardness, for industrial backwardness, for political backwardness. . . . Do you want our socialist fatherland to be beaten and lose its independence? If you don't want this, you must liquidate our backwardness and develop a real Bolshevik tempo in building our socialist economy. There is no other road. . . . We lag behind the advanced countries by 50 to 100 years. *We must make good this distance in ten years.*

Stalin was absolutely pitiless in carrying out his policy. Though his people were groaning, his ears were deaf and his eyes were fixed to the stars. Through Stalin, the Soviet Union was on her way, "starving to glory." There being assured a source of food for the urban population as well as a means of payment for record-breaking imports of machinery from the West (then in the midst of the Great Depression and eager for business), it now became simply a matter of coordinated central planning to assure the production by the nonagricultural sector of the economy of the types of goods most conducive to economic growth. And the goal was achieved, even if not in ten years.

The Incentive System

Now consider in what kind of a position this put the individual Soviet peasant, industrial worker, or manager. Each received input and output quotas—work so many hours at such and such a place doing this or that: use so much fertilizer, land, machinery, and labor (or less) to produce so many tons of potatoes (or more); use so much machinery, labor, iron ore, coke, and lime (or less) to produce so many tons of steel (or more). If a person fulfilled his quota, he was assured an income sufficient to fulfill his minimum food, clothing, and housing needs, but practically no more.

After 1934, however, new additional incentives were added. Peasants could produce additional output on private plots of land and sell the product in free "collective farm markets." Industrial workers could work hard and earn bonuses for *overfulfilling* output targets. They might earn as much as 50 percent extra income this way. And this could be translated into all kinds of agricultural goods (in the collective farm markets) or into industrial consumer goods and even vacations at the Black Sea.

All were affected by this system: workers on the production line, foremen, engineers, the managerial staff, party supervisors, and up the planning hierarchy —local, regional, and national administrative and planning officials. No wonder output plan overfulfillment was attention-getter number one. Everywhere there was tremendous pressure for intense operations. Everyone was constantly exhorted to increase his output. There were always others spoiling for a chance at your job if you did not live up to expectations.

Among socialist managers, this system led to a number of well-known behavior traits. They would try to hide the true capacity of their firms from central planning officials (in the hope of being assigned low output quotas that could easily be overfulfilled). They would overstate their input needs (in the hope of being assigned sufficient quantities to overfulfill their output targets). They would produce low-quality output (if this enabled them to produce a larger quantity in terms of which output fulfillment was determined). They would ignore the production of spare parts and the provision of servicing (for the material, personnel, and machinery so tied up could be used to produce more output for plan overfulfillment). They would resist technological change (for this would require reassigning and retraining workers, installing new equipment, and making all kinds of changes likely to interrupt the accustomed flow of production and thus endanger plan fulfillment). Typically, managers were shielded in these activities by local and regional party and planning officials, whose careers and incomes, in turn, depended on smooth fulfillment and preferably overfulfillment of output plans in their area.

The View on Pollution Avoidance

Now consider how pollution avoidance might be viewed under such circumstances: Producing, installing, and operating antipollution devices or changing production processes to avoid dumping would be equivalent to wasting resources (from the standpoint of achieving output plan overfulfillment). From the personal standpoint of the workers and managers of a tractor factory, those men, materials, and machines used to prevent water or air pollution would better be used to make a few more tractors. And higher officials would agree! Pollution avoidance by introducing new production processes would be viewed with similar distaste. Like technological change, it would upset the applecart. Workers would have to learn new jobs and get used to different equipment, time would be lost, spoilage would be high, and—for a while—output would be sacrificed.

As a result, introducing pollution-avoidance schemes have been viewed by Soviet workers and managers as courting disaster, as a sure road to lower income. Thus they have resisted; and higher officials, far from protecting the broad interests of society, have consented.

The Extent of Pollution

As a result, pollution in the Soviet Union is widespread.[2] Any horror story one can tell about the United States could be matched by one from the USSR.

Fish-kill incidents in the Belaya, Irtysh, Kama, Ob, Oka, Ural, Vetluga,

[2] The remainder of this section on the Soviet case is based in part on Marshall I. Goldman, "The Convergence of Environmental Disruption," *Science* (October 2, 1970), pp. 37–42, and in part on a variety of Radio Free Europe Research Reports.

Volga, and Yenesei rivers are constant news. Most rivers in the Ukraine have been declared "dead," as the lakes of Gorky oblast have. The Iset River in Sverdlovsk, like the Cuyahoga in Cleveland, catches fire on occasion (being coated heavily with oil).

The reasons are the same as in the U.S. Only 40 percent of Soviet cities have any sewage treatment at all. About 65 percent of Soviet factories discharge their wastes raw. Oil spills from wells, ships, and pipelines are frequent occurrences in the Baltic, Black, and Caspian seas, as well as in the big rivers. The northern Caspian is reported to be one huge oil slick. In the country, sewage and chemicals from factories and mines have spoiled the ground water. The thoughtless construction of dams and hydroelectric and irrigation facilities along tributaries has reduced the water level of the Aral and Caspian seas and threatens to turn them into salt marshes by the end of this century. Already, a third of the fish spawning area has become dry land. The yield of fish from the Aral Sea has fallen by 80 percent. The Sea of Azov now supplies only 9 percent of the fish it produced at its peak because water withdrawals along its Don and Kuban tributaries have laid dry spawning ground and also caused an influx of saltier Black Sea water. Lake Sevan in the high Caucasus has shrunk by a third, and its water level lost 52 feet as the result of power-station construction and irrigation. Recently, it has become the object of a campaign to save it by diverting water from other rivers to it through canals. In general, though, the Soviet fondness for canals has caused ecological trouble. Seepage from a network of unlined canals across the USSR has raised water tables and led to salination in dry areas.

Worst of all is the story of Lake Baikal. It is the largest and deepest fresh-water body on earth, containing twice the volume of Lake Superior. It is 20 million years old, and its highly transparent water harbors 1,200 species, 700 of which (including the celebrated omul and fresh-water seals) are found in few places on earth or nowhere else.

Yet the bulk of numerous factories along the Selenga (Baikal's chief tributary) discharge wastes raw into the river. These range from sulfates to chlorides, from nitrates to magnesium hydroxide. In addition, the farming of ever steeper slopes in the mountainous region has led to disastrous earth crumblings and landslides and increasing silt flow. In 1966, the first of several pulp and paper mills along the lake was constructed at Baikalsk and began dumping into the lake. Logs were rafted on the lake, and since 10 percent sink on the way, began rotting in it. Huge alkaline sewage islands began appearing on the lake. Although the lake and its basin were a "protected zone" from 1950, economic considerations won out. In spite of much publicity, a second mill was constructed in 1971 at Selenginsk. In mid-1971, the Soviet government, following a directive issued in early 1969 (which had not been implemented) ordered new deadlines for the installation of treatment facilities at the two mills and along the Selenga River, which empties into the lake. Yet scientists argued that no existing waste-treatment system could protect the unusual purity of the lake and preserve its distinctive plant and animal life.

Soviet *air pollution* is equally ubiquitous. Tbilisi, the capital of Georgia, has problems like Los Angeles. Chemical plants around Tula are killing a prime oak forest. Large cities like Alma Ata, Chelyabinsk, Leningrad, Magnitogorsk, and Moscow have all the problems found in the West. (During the 1960's, 200 factories were closed or moved out of Moscow to alleviate air pollution.)

The *solid-waste* problem in the USSR has been less serious. Some goods, such as disposable bottles or diapers, are simply not produced. Many others are recycled. There is much more emphasis on collecting junk and on making goods last as long as possible. (In contrast with New York City, where people abandon 50,000 cars a year, no one abandons cars in the streets of Moscow.)

Antipollution Activities

True enough, there *are* antipollution activities in the Soviet Union. But Party officials have protected violators of such laws and economic commands. A 1960 Law on the Protection of Flora and Fauna established liability on polluters, but it was not enforced. In 1970, the Supreme Soviet approved the draft of the Foundations of Water Legislation for the USSR and Union Republics. This law forbade the use of industrial plants and houses without purification equipment, ordered the recycling of industrial effluents, and allowed their discharge only with the approval of local water boards and on the condition that this does not lead to an increase in pollution above authorized levels. Polluters were made criminally liable and made subject to the payment of damages. In 1973, the Soviets set up a national environmental protection service to monitor air and water pollution; and as of 1974 annual and long-term plans are to be set up for the optimal use of resources and *conservation of nature*.

This announcement was preceded, in 1972, by another one, involving a billion-dollar cleanup project for the Volga and Ural river basins, both of which drain into the Caspian Sea. By 1975, said that announcement, 421 industrial-waste-treatment plants plus 15 municipal ones would be built, and by 1980 all untreated discharges would be banned. In addition, a dam is planned at the Kerch Strait to prevent Black Sea water going into the Sea of Azov.

Yet one cannot help being skeptical. Even in mid-1972, a year after the latest Baikal cleanup order, nothing had been done. In general, the courts, themselves not independent agents but an arm of the very government that has elevated rapid economic growth above all else, have imposed exceedingly small fines and stated that "one must not forget the greater task," namely, the increase of output. Reports indicate that resources allocated in the central plan for antipollution activities have not been used. Existing waste-treatment equipment is typically reported out of order, working intermittently, or below capacity. The reason is easy to see: Every bit of resources used for antipollution activities could also be used for raising output; and the entire fabric of economic decision making is biased in favor of the latter choice.

Conclusion

There is no evidence that socialism, as found in the USSR, has been conducive to pollution avoidance. Workers, managers, and planners alike have displayed a strong incentive to divert or withhold resources from pollution avoidance; they have primarily been interested in something that promised personal rewards, namely, high and rapidly growing output of goods. These people, who have the power to do something about pollution, have no reason whatsoever to listen to the clamor of Soviet newspapers that are fond of championing the conservationist cause.

Nor can any group of conservationists in the Soviet Union hope to change this state of affairs by any of the means open in the United States. Voting will not work, for Communist party officials are not responsive to the wishes of an aroused electorate. Going to court will not work, for courts are agents of the very officials whose actions would have to be challenged. Furthermore, there are few *private* property rights on the basis of which court action might be initiated. Discouraging waste disposal by privately charging polluters for the use of natural resources as waste disposal sites will not work, for the air, water, and soil, like all capital, are unquestionably owned by the state.

Thus pollution is seen related not to the character of ownership, private or public, but to the process of industrialization itself. The ugly by-products of growth—foul air, noise, poisoned water, and despoiled land—are not endemic to capitalism and attributable to the private greed of capitalist "tycoons." The wholesale rape of the environment can also be found in a socialist country—led by party bureaucrats. In either case, only the introduction of incentives that would lead decision makers to respect the natural environment could change this outcome. As we have seen, private producers and consumers in a capitalist economy might change their rapacious behavior if personally confronted with the monetary costs of their actions. This awareness can be brought about only if an aroused public elects a government that is willing to set up the proper framework of incentives. In the Soviet case, a similar reaction is needed. The government must become willing to modify its growth-at-all-costs policy and tell its managers so (as it did, for example, by banning DDT). Otherwise pollution will not be reduced. That willingness is as difficult to bring about in the Soviet Union as it is in the West.

This leads to another argument often encountered. The Soviets, it is said, are not really socialists at all. True socialists are not selfish men who must be given personal rewards for acting in the interest of society. Rather they are selfless creatures, new kinds of men, who driven by internal forces will naturally act in the social interest. The Chinese are often cited as a society of men fitting this definition.

THE CHINESE CASE

Extraordinary things have happened in China, especially since 1957. During the First Five Year Plan, from 1952 to 1957, the Soviet model of rapid industrialization had been copied on a large scale. Agriculture was collectivized, and resources were allocated primarily to heavy industry, education, health, and research and development, to lay the basis for rapid economic growth. All the trappings of material self-interest were there: wages, bonuses, and private peasant plots.

The Great Leap Forward

Then came the "Great Leap Forward" (1957–1962). The people were admonished to lay aside selfishness, to stop dreaming of grimy pay or fame or power. They were urged to be guided, as Mao's guerrilla fighters had been earlier, by purity of motive, by a true Communist enthusiasm to work for the good of all. In truly Marxist fashion, each was asked to "give according to his ability, and take according to his need." This was the time when a hundred million people organized to work on mass irrigation projects, digging canals and building dikes and reservoirs in unceasing day and night shifts and under incredibly harsh conditions. This was the time when 60 million students and women stoked their backyard furnaces to raise steel production to unprecedented levels. This was the time when the family unit was abolished and all the peasants found themselves in communes, without any private property at all.

The Great Proletarian Cultural Revolution

The economic consequences of this policy (measured in terms of output growth) were less than admirable, but the social ones were truly revolutionary. After a short period of "consolidation and readjustment," the "Great Proletarian Cultural Revolution," which began in 1966, took up where the Great Leap Forward had left off. Economic development, argued the Red Guards, is not to be considered a process of turning inputs into outputs as massively and as fast as possible, but a matter of changing people. Man must not be deemed an input, a means to an end, but the end itself. If every man is to "give according to his ability," he must be made as able as possible. Every person must be enabled to fully realize his manifold creative powers. That means that everyone must be enabled to participate in everything on an equal basis, for it is from participation that ability is born. Therefore, a classless society must be created, wherein distinctions disappear between leaders and followers, experts and laymen, the skilled and the unskilled, mental and physical work, worker and manager, urban resident and farmer, the rich and the poor, teachers and students. "The lowly are the most intelligent," argued the Red Guards, "the elite are most ignorant." With that they moved through cities and countryside and turned worker into manager, student into teacher, manager into farmer, and farmer into doctor. The idea was to break down specialization, even if it meant a decrease in productivity.

Even Adam Smith, the great proponent of specialization, had observed how specialized work is alienating: "The man whose life is spent in performing a few simple operations . . . generally becomes as stupid and ignorant as it is possible for a human creature to become." It is better, argued the Red Guards, for most men to be able to perform many jobs reasonably well, to have universal men, men who are fully aware of and participating in the world and who therefore are happy. Quite possibly, argued the Red Guards, this approach will achieve what neither capitalist nor Soviet-style economies have ever achieved: the release of a huge reservoir of enthusiasm, energy, and creativeness, "an atom bomb of talent" that will pay off in "volcanic economic growth."

As long as scarcity stalks the earth, "to each according to his need" cannot mean that everyone gets everything. Therefore, argued the Red Guards, material incentives that develop man's desires must be done away with. "Material incentives look attractive, but like rat poison, they are fatal to the system." People must find joy in giving as much as possible. They must be selfless enough to take as little as possible.

The View on Pollution Avoidance

It is easy to see how this Chinese attitude is likely to dispose people to give up goods in favor of preserving nature.[3] Indeed, the Chinese have a long history in this regard. As early as the first century B.C., the Record of Rites of the Elder Tai warned against man's polluting his environment. Throughout history, down to the teachings of Mao Tse-Tung, Chinese writers have emphasized sensitivity to nature and curative measures of afforestation, land reclamation, and water conservancy by those who would exploit nature. One of the "black deeds" of Liu Shao-chi, former president of the People's Republic of China, was the stress on economic growth and the treatment of industrial wastes as so much garbage to be thrown out. This has been branded a "counter-revolutionary, revisionist approach."

The Extent of Pollution

But these are words. Is China really a showpiece of a nonpolluting society? Although data are scarce, China's pollution problems at present do seem relatively minor, but this may well be due to its underdevelopment and not due to the presence of "new men." Most of China's wastes are still agricultural and organic, as is typical in the underdeveloped world. The country has not yet reached the stage of chemicals, plastics, and car cemeteries. Where there is pollution, it is concentrated around industrial plants. There is very little pollution connected with the transportation system. In 1969, for instance, China had only 0.007 miles of railroads per square mile and it had only 0.8 vehicles (counting trucks, buses, and cars) per mile of roads. What is likely to happen as industrialization proceeds? Past policies give us some hints.

[3] The remainder of this Appendix is based in part on L. A. Orleans and R. P. Suttmeier, "The Mao Ethic and Environmental Quality," *Science* (December 11, 1970), pp. 1173–76.

Antipollution Efforts

Consider these actual policies of the Chinese Communists with respect to the environment. In the 1950's, there were ten "comprehensive expeditions" to explore and inventory the natural environment and to plan for exploitative and curative environmental management. This was followed by great efforts to improve the health conditions of workers. Emphasis was placed on vaccination and environmental sanitation, with the aim of stamping out typhus, typhoid fever, cholera, plague, and dysentery; thus the disposal of human wastes into lakes and rivers was reduced, the proper construction of latrines and wells was emphasized, and sewage was transported to the country for fertilization and irrigation.

So far as industrial wastes are concerned, two types of policies have been pursued, recycling and relocation. Recycling has been stressed as "a serious political assignment," notably a transformation of industry's "four wastes" (materials, water, gas, and heat) into "treasures." Many plants make multipurpose use of wastes. Take the Kiangmen sugarcane plant, for instance. It processes its cane scrap into paper, and the waste from that is used to fire a small blast furnace to make crude steel. It ferments syrupy remnants from sugar refining into alcohol or turns them into animal fodder and even growth hormones. The carbon dioxide given off by the production of alcohol is, in turn, chilled into dry ice. Another waste from refining sugar (lime) is turned into cement.

As an alternative, there has been much emphasis on transporting industrial wastes, together with sewage, to the country also—for fertilization and irrigation or just to get them away from cities. This has been done by tying their disposal into vast irrigation systems and by relocating industry downwind and downriver from cities. Both of these are not pollution avoidance measures at all but rather a design to relocate pollutants. Ecologically, the use of industrial wastes for fertilization and irrigation may have catastrophic consequences, since there is no evidence of any scientific analysis of these wastes prior to such use. The policy of discrediting of "experts" in China tends to discourage such activity.

Overall, therefore, the Chinese case is interesting and well worth watching, but it is certainly too early to come to any lasting conclusions.

A FINAL WORD

There is no evidence that introduction of a socialist centrally planned economy would magically end the problem of pollution. Abandoning the capitalist market economy with that thought is rather like abandoning a car because it has a flat tire. There is much to be said for restructuring incentives in the market economy to solve the pollution problem while preserving its clear advantage of decentralized decision making. A scheme such as the pollution rights market is exceedingly simple and closest to the present state of affairs in the West. Therefore, it can be expected to solve the pollution problem more rapidly than any alternative such as changing the nature of all men away from selfishness or completely changing the economic system. Even so, the best remedy might take a generation. As Max Planck, the physicist Nobel laureate, has said: "A new scientific truth does not triumph by convincing its opponents and making them see the light, but rather because its opponents eventually die, and a new generation grows up that is familiar with it."

Summary

1. Some people argue that socialism and central planning would avoid pollution. The Soviet Union is a socialist and centrally planned economy, but its example does not bear out this claim. In the Soviet Union, the economic goal of overwhelming importance has been the most rapid possible growth. For this reason, workers, managers, and party officials have been given incentives to overfulfill economic plans concerned with the production of goods. This has led to a number of behavior traits, among them the viewing of pollution avoidance as a waste of resources.
2. Not surprisingly therefore, the extent of pollution in the Soviet Union is widespread, especially water and air pollution. The solid-waste problem is less serious.
3. There are antipollution laws and projects in the USSR, but they are not strictly enforced or carried out. Thus pollution seems more related to the existence of industrialization than to the economic system under which it occurs.
4. Some argue, however, that the Soviets are not true socialists. True socialists are not selfish men who must be given personal rewards for acting in the interest of society, it is said; they are selfless creatures, like the Chinese.
5. It is true that the Chinese have stressed the changing of people into universally skilled men who selflessly give "according to their ability," take as little as possible, and are thus uninterested in material incentives. This approach would predispose people to favor pollution avoidance over producing more goods.
6. It is somewhat difficult to judge at this point whether Chinese deeds measure up to words. Many antipollution measures taken so far in China have only spread out wastes over the countryside. Furthermore, most wastes in this still underdeveloped economy are organic, and it is impossible to judge how this society would deal with pollution once heavy industrialization is a reality.
7. Overall, there is no evidence that changing the entire economic system is a better way to avoid pollution than restructuring economic incentives within the capitalist market economy.

Questions for Review and Discussion

1. "Under capitalism, pollution is bound to rise without limit because capitalists are driven to ever higher levels of production by the profit motive. Furthermore, they prefer to produce goods with high waste components so that people have to come back to them to buy more goods. Note the priority given to such

goods as bombs and rapidly obsolescing cars. This would not happen in socialism." Discuss.

2. "To stop pollution, the Russians closed a Riga superphosphate factory in 1967 and a Leningrad coke-gas plant in 1972. Such a move could never be taken in the United States." Comment.
3. "The Soviet government is recultivating strip-mining areas once mining ceases. This was done with oil shale mines in Estonia, with brown coal mines near Moscow, and with manganese mines in the Ukraine. Such thoughtful dealing with nature could never happen in the United States." Comment.
4. "If there is any difference in the view on pollution, the capitalist U.S. rather than the socialist USSR shows more concern. Note how Americans worry about the environmental impact of the Alaska pipeline (while the Russians boast of having the world's longest pipeline), how Americans agonize over the construction of every nuclear power station (while the Russians freely build them), how Americans have rejected the building of the SST (while the Russians have not)." Evaluate.
5. Mr. A: Basically, the Chinese got it all wrong and the Americans and Russians got it all right. There is only one way to persuade people to act in the social interest: *economic incentives.* The trick is to shape these incentives so they give people the right signals. If somebody just *tells* people that using phosphate detergents is harmful, they might shrug it off. But if somebody makes those detergents very expensive (as by taxing them), most people will stop using them.

   Mr. B: I see no difference. Both approaches involve dictatorship. In one case, Mao or some great leader orders people directly what to do. In the other case, Congress (as by levying a tax) tricks people indirectly into doing what it considers right. In fact, I prefer the former approach. It is more honest.

   What do you think? Why?

Selected Readings

Goldman, Marshall I. *The Spoils of Progress: Environmental Pollution in the Soviet Union.* Cambridge, Mass.: MIT Press, 1972. The best study available on Soviet environmental problems. Discusses Soviet environmental protection laws, the extent of their enforcement, and all types of pollution. Includes a very comprehensive bibliography (pp. 333–57).

Kohler, Heinz. *Economics: The Science of Scarcity.* Hinsdale, Ill.: The Dryden Press, 1970. Chs. 25 and 26. Discusses economic growth in the USSR and China.

Radio Free Europe. The following research reports, and others, discuss all aspects of pollution in the Communist countries. They are published at irregular intervals.

China Battles Growing Pollution (6-6-1972)

Environmental Problems in Bulgaria (5-18-1972)

Environmental Problems in Czechoslovakia (5-17-1972)

Environmental Problems in the GDR (6-5-1972)
Environmental Problems in Hungary (5-23-1972)
Environmental Problems in Poland (5-26-1972)
Environmental Problems in Rumania (5-18-1972)
Steps Towards Pollution Control in the USSR (4-6-1972)

NOTE: The *Journal of Economic Literature* lists recent articles on socialist and communist economic systems in section 052. The *Index of Economic Articles* catalogs them in sections beginning with 3.2.

Part Four
Budget Matters

In one way or another, all the solutions to urban problems examined in this book require action by government. Thus they require the spending of funds and inevitably their collection by taxation or borrowing. Without exception, city governments in recent decades have run into serious budgetary problems when attempting to tackle the growing problems encountered within their jurisdictions. In part, they have been helped by state and federal aid. Yet some believe that the solution to the urban governments' fiscal crisis—which is nothing but a monetary reflection of urban problems—must lie elsewhere. Only a complete restructuring of the responsibilities now carried by the various levels of government, it is argued, can solve the urban fiscal crisis and in doing so set up the proper machinery for dealing with urban problems. These are the matters discussed in this final section of the book.

14 On the Proper Division of Labor Among Governments

In a thousand different ways, the problems that beset the American city cry out for government action. Whatever the form this action takes, it costs money. That is exactly what city governments have been spending in rapidly increasing amounts in the recent past.

During the fiscal 1955 to fiscal 1971 period, when the GNP rose 2.7-fold, and federal spending rose 3.1-fold, that of cities rose 3.7-fold from $10.5 billion to $39.1 billion.[1]

The rapid rise during this period of overall city government spending has been matched by an equally impressive rise in revenues (from $10.2 billion to $37.4 billion). Still, city debts outstanding at the end of fiscal years rose from $16 billion in 1955 to $45 billion in 1971. Many city governments were in serious financial difficulties. A close look at their budgets will help explain why.

CITY GOVERNMENT BUDGETS

Figure 14.1, "The Makeup of City Government Spending," shows budget allocations for fiscal 1971. Note how the greatest chunk went for utilities. Of this portion 8 cents went for sanitation (refuse disposal and street cleaning) and sewage, 6 cents for pure water, and 5 cents for electric and 1 cent for gas supply systems. Police and fire protection took 14 cents of each spending dollar; education, another 14 cents. Transportation took 11 cents per dollar, of which almost 7 went for highways, almost 3 for mass transit, over 1 for airports, and less than 1 for water transport and terminals. Expenditures for housing, parks (including recreational facilities), and urban renewal accounted for 8 cents on the dollar, public welfare for 7 more. Of the 6-cent-per-dollar health expenditures, 5 cents went for city-owned hospitals. The "other" category, finally, comprised a multitude of items. These ranged from financial control and maintenance of public buildings (3 cents) to interest payments on the public debt (3 cents), and from so-called insurance trust expenditures (such

[1] Most of the statistical data used in this chapter come from U.S. Bureau of the Census, *City Government Finances* and *Governmental Finances* and from U.S. Office of Management and Budget, *The Budget of the United States Government*.

Figure 14.1 The Makeup of City Government Spending

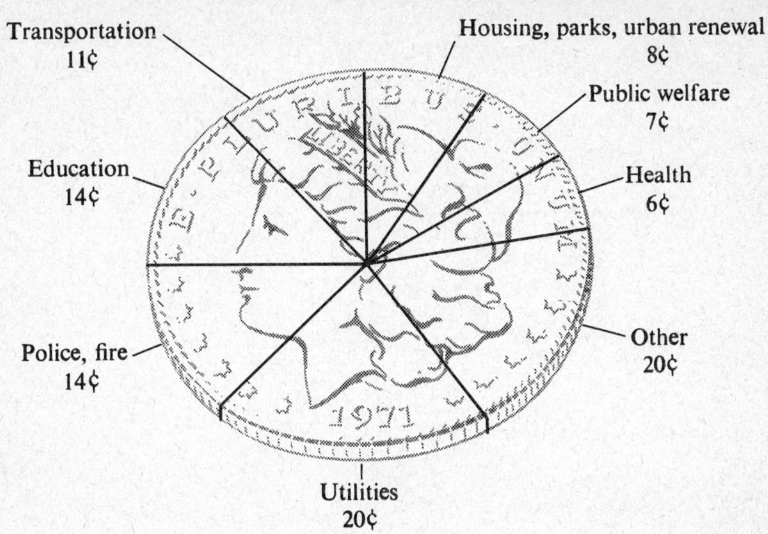

SOURCE: *U.S. Bureau of the Census,* City Government Finances in 1970–71 *(August 1972).*

City government spending in fiscal 1971 amounted to $39.1 billion in the United States. Here we see the purposes to which each dollar was put.

as 3-cent-per-dollar public employee retirement, life insurance, and unemployment benefits) to the operation by local governments in four states of liquor stores (less than 1 cent).

It is interesting to compare this breakdown with a corresponding one for all state and local government units. The cities spend relatively much more on utilities, police, fire protection, and housing, parks, and renewal (42 cents vs. 15 cents). Cities spend relatively much less on education (14 cents vs. 39 cents). Spending is just about relatively equal in all other categories. The spending pattern reflects the special problems cities face. The needs to get enough pure water, electric power, and gas; to get rid of garbage, trash, sewage, and urban blight; to fight disorder, crime, and fire are so urgent that education budgets are slighted. The cost of insufficient education is long-run, that of uncollected garbage is immediate!

Figure 14.2, "The Makeup of City Government Revenue," reflects the revenue situation in fiscal 1971. Twenty-seven cents of each revenue dollar came from the property tax. The sales tax brought in 7 cents per dollar of revenue, licenses issued by city governments and other taxes brought an additional 6 cents. Employee retirement contributions and similar "insurance trust fund" taxes brought in 3 cents per dollar. A variety of charges made to users of city government services brought in 31 cents per revenue dollar. These included 7 cents for water, 6 cents for electricity and gas, 2 cents for mass transit.

Figure 14.2 The Makeup of City Government Revenue

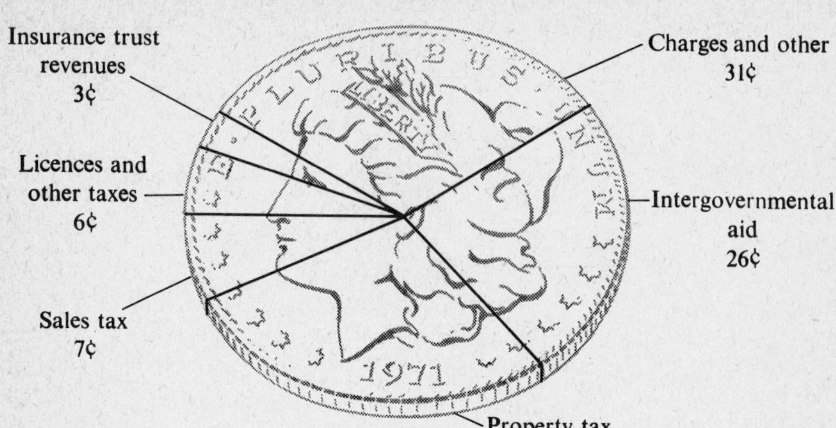

SOURCE: *U.S. Bureau of the Census,* City Government Finances in 1970–71 *(August 1972).*

City government revenue in fiscal 1971 amounted to $37.4 billion in the United States. The typical revenue dollar shows clearly the relative importance of the various types of revenues.

The remaining 16 cents came from innumerable smaller sources, such as parking fees and city liquor store revenues.

Note how unimportant income tax revenues are. (They are hidden in Figure 14.2 in the category labeled "licenses and other taxes.") City income taxes have been rising in importance. While covering 12.2 percent of the city population in 1957, they reached 37.8 percent a decade later. Still, income taxes are completely negligible overall. They play a role only in a few places, such as New York, Philadelphia, St. Louis, and a number of Ohio cities. The effect of reliance on nonincome taxes is this: each 1 percent rise in the GNP raises federal revenues by 1.5 percent, but city revenues by only 0.5 percent. With city spending rising so much faster than the GNP, this spells financial trouble. It is therefore not surprising that an increased portion of city revenues has had to come from state and federal aid. While this percentage was 14 in 1955, it was 26 by 1971. Of the 26-cent-per-dollar intergovernmental aid share in fiscal 1971, 19 cents was state aid. Most of the remainder was federal aid, although a small amount of aid was received from other local governments.

THE NATURE OF THE CITY FISCAL CRISIS

The large share of state and federal aid in city revenues is highly significant. It has resulted from two simple facts.

Rapid Yet Insufficient Spending Increases

First, city governments have raised spending rapidly. However, some of the higher spending has not gone for additional services but for the higher costs of given service levels. From 1960 to 1971, the local government services price index rose twice as fast as the consumer price index. Much of this was due to higher employee costs from higher wages, pensions, health benefits, and the granting of shorter workdays, longer vacations and lunch breaks, paid holidays, and sick leave. The upswing in benefits has been the result, in part, of the fact that city government employees have become increasingly unionized and their unions increasingly militant. In 1970, 28 percent of the nation's government employees were union members, but in the large cities of New York, Los Angeles, Philadelphia, and Detroit the percentage was 93. While in 1960, there were 36 public worker strikes, there were 327 in 1971 (and that was a decrease from 414 in 1969). Among the strikers were notably teachers and sanitation workers. But even without union activity, city government employees could not have been kept on their jobs without wage hikes comparable to those in private industry. Since the opportunities for corresponding productivity increases are much more limited in the government service sector, higher wages per hour typically mean spending more dollars for the same quantity of services.

Yet after adjusting for price increases, real city government spending has still gone up. Cities have provided many additional services. Ironically, though, in spite of their tremendous spending effort, city governments have not been able to make great progress with the problems inside their borders. In view of the overwhelming dimensions of their problems, they could easily have spent twice as much as they did on health and education, on employment services and job training, on welfare and crime prevention, on housing and transportation and pollution control—and they still would not have solved those problems. Thus city governments have raised their spending in a valiant effort and have yet provided totally inadequate levels of services.

Insufficient Rise in Own Revenues

Second, city governments have not raised spending enough because they could not raise sufficient extra funds of their own to support sufficient extra spending. This is easily explained. The potential revenue yield of traditional sources (property and sales taxes, licenses and charges) is strictly limited. For reasons shown in Chapter 3, the property tax base of many cities has been shrinking. Consider the effect on property valuations as businesses move out. Where there was a bustling manufacturing plant one year, there is an empty building the next. The effects of housing abandonment and deterioration, of highway construction, and of crime on property tax collections are equally bad. Where riots have replaced former businesses and apartment houses with block after block of burned ruins, the effect on the property tax base is most obvious. Where there is less property left, you cannot tax as much as before. The same factors have caused an erosion of the sales tax base, too. Where there was a white family earning and spending $10,000 a year, there now lives a black one barely subsisting at $1,800. As less is spent, sales taxes bring in less revenues.

Nor can city governments easily make up for shrinking tax bases (like property or sales values). In many cases, tax rates are already at legal maximums set by state governments; cities are legal creatures of states, and their taxing powers have been delegated by the states through special legislative actions, often reluctantly. Typically, city taxing power is restricted as to allowable tax rates and base. Thus Pennsylvania allows its cities to tax anything not taxed by the state.

Even where tax rate increases are legal, they have recently encountered heavy voter resistance. (In the early 1970's, voters turned down half of all proposals to raise property tax rates to finance current school expenditures, as well as half of all school construction bond issues.) Even where tax rate hikes can be carried out, the result may be far from salutary. Often, higher property or sales tax rates speed up the departure of higher-income families and businesses (and the erosion of the tax base); and the plight of the poor (who spend such a large part of their income on housing) is noticeably worsened.

Nor can a city avoid raising tax rates by slashing "inessential" services. Many have tried. In 1971, Boston closed playgrounds; Toledo, swimming pools; Portland, symphonies and theatres; and Detroit, museums. Indianapolis, Kansas City, and Los Angeles cut the school teaching staff; New York City, that of police, firemen, and sanitation workers. Ironically, the result is the same: The tax base shrinks as industry and higher-income families move out to escape traffic congestion, bad schools, inadequate police and fire protection or lack of sanitation services, and recreational and cultural facilities. Poor families stay behind and suffer.

Plugging the Gap

No wonder many cities end up with deficits. Even borrowing is not easy. Often it is restricted by state-imposed limitations or the requirement for referenda. Some cities have to do it in cumbersome and expensive ways. Take East St. Louis. It has had a deficit in every year since 1950. Its assessed property value dropped from $188 million in 1962 to $166 million in 1972. Its tax rates and debts are at their ceilings. Except for one thing. If sued and found guilty, the city may borrow and raise tax rates to pay off such debt. So the city has assigned the wage claims of city employees to the Illinois State Trust Company, which borrows in its own name and pays the wages. Ten days later, it sues the city to recover the money. The city pleads no contest, and the court orders a judgment against the city. The city orders the sale of "judgment fund bonds" that may be paid off with special taxes not covered by the legal ceiling.

Many cities are spared this type of maneuvering by outside aid. Increased state and federal aid has enabled most cities to avoid bankruptcy in the face of rising spending and limited ability to raise revenues on their own. This dependence on outside aid has also prevented them, however, from raising spending sufficiently to grapple with their problems successfully. There are three obvious solutions to this dilemma, each of which is discussed in the remainder of this chapter: Cities can spend more if they raise more revenue on their own. Cities can spend more if they can get more revenues from other governments than heretofore. Cities can spend less if someone else takes care of their problems for them. The latter approach is usually suggested on the grounds that city problems have been dumped onto cities by others, and that others are much more able to deal with them. To a large extent, both of these assertions are true.

Cities are victims of spillovers. Problems that require government action have been concentrating within cities. Yet, as should be clear from our discussion in Chapter 3, more often than not city residents or their governments cannot be blamed for this development. They have become the involuntary victims of the harmful external repercussions of the actions of millions of rural and suburban residents, the effects of whose decisions have *spilled over* onto the cities.

The century-old neglect of health and education in the countryside has presented the city with hordes of adult immigrants lacking health and skills. The simultaneous movement of manufacturing and of trade out of the city has changed the demand side of the city's labor markets toward higher skills. Thus the resident population is increasingly unsuitable for city jobs. Together with the refusal of the suburbs to allow the unemployed, low-skilled poor of the city to settle near suburban jobs, this accounts for much of the city's need to spend in areas of health, education, job training, welfare, crime prevention, and housing.

The insistence of suburban residents on living outside but commuting to the city, on the other hand, contributes greatly to the city's problems with traffic and air pollution. It accounts ultimately for the need for making expenditures designed to deal with these problems.

Richer revenue sources elsewhere. Yet those who present the city with problems are out of reach of the city's tax collectors. A city cannot tax the rural areas whence its recent immigrants have come. It cannot easily tax the manufacturing plants and higher-income residents who remove themselves into outlying areas that quickly incorporate themselves under separate governments.

The richest revenue source of them all, the income tax, has largely been unavailable to city governments. It has been monopolized by the state and federal governments.

Let us consider in turn each of the proposed solutions to the city fiscal crisis.

INCREASING THE CITIES' OWN REVENUES

Cities can attempt to support high service levels by raising revenues on their own. In 1971, there were on the average 91 separate governments in the standard metropolitan statistical area. Chicago had 1,113; Philadelphia, 871; New York, 551. The multitude of existing governments has the drawback of restricting the ability of any one of them to impose taxes. If property taxes are higher in one jurisdiction, households and businesses can move to another one nearby. If excise taxes are imposed (as they often are on cigarettes, liquor, gasoline, amusements, insurance, hotel-motel occupancy), people can buy in a nearby locality without such tax. General sales taxes suffer from the same disability. A local income tax, not matched by a similar tax in nearby localities, similarly drives people away. Therefore, one obvious method allowing a significant increase in tax revenues and in city efforts to deal with city problems involves greater cooperation between central city and surrounding area governments. This would allow, for example by city taxation of suburban dwellers, the pushing back onto the private offenders of the external costs of their actions.

Expanding the Tax Base

If the many governments in a metropolitan region would just cooperate, one could make it impossible for households and businesses to escape, as they now do, unattractive public actions by moving to another jurisdiction. Such cooperation is not easily achieved, but it has been attempted in a number of ways.

First, the city can annex the surrounding territory. (This has been successful in the Southwest due to favorable state laws. Cities such as Knoxville, Phoenix, and Houston simply expand steadily so that the city limits take in the entire metropolitan area.)

Second, the surrounding territory can annex the city (Dade County, Florida).

Third, two or more governments can be consolidated (Nashville and Davidson County, in Tennessee; Columbus and Muscogee County, in Georgia; Indianapolis and Marion County, in Indiana; Jacksonville and Duval County, in Florida; and the city and borough of Juneau, Alaska.

Fourth, municipalities can form a federation (Toronto).

Fifth, regional authorities can be formed to deal with a particular areawide problem (Port Authority of New York and New Jersey, the Delaware River Port Authority).

Sixth, cities can leapfrog their own suburban rings and annex territories *beyond* them, thereby forcing on the suburbs a new two-tier system of government (for example, decentralized schools, but centralized transportation and environmental policies).

Changing the Tax Base

Another approach involves changes in the types of revenues collected by cities so as to increase their yield.

Property tax to land-value tax. Cities could, for instance, place less reliance on the property tax, which on the average takes annually 2 percent of the market value of urban taxable property. Mostly, it is only real property (land and buildings) that is taxed. In some instances, however, the tax also applies to such tangible household property as furniture, paintings, jewelry, books, and clothing; to tangible business property like tools and equipment; and even to intangible personal property like stocks, bonds, and bank deposits. On occasion, some people (such as the aged or veterans) are exempt from the tax, but mostly it is applied across the board at a flat rate on the estimated value of such property. The disabilities of this important tax are legion.

It is highly regressive in that it falls heavily on poor renters, but less heavily on better-off home owners (who get a federal income tax deduction for property taxes paid) and on businesses (who pass on at least part of the tax in higher prices). Since a major portion of city spending is on welfare, designed to help the poor, this type of financing is particularly grotesque. The tax also discourages housing improvements, which inevitably raise the assessed value of improved buildings. Reliance on this tax in the suburbs has given rise to fiscal zoning, which is in part responsible for some of the city's problems. Administratively, the tax, by requiring assessment, causes inequities and hostility. (In 1973, thirty states required no training or certification of local assessors.) The true value of property is never known, except when it changes hands between willing and well-informed parties. Therefore, any given piece of property is assessed subjectively on the basis of similar sales, of income received from the property, or of construction costs. Frequently, assessments are out of date. Always, they lack consistency. Now suppose cities taxed not buildings, but only the bare sites on which they may or may not stand. Such a *land value tax* was first proposed by Henry George, who almost was elected mayor of New York in 1886. Such a tax has been promoted as equitable, since it taxes the totally unearned increase in land values that occurs as a consequence of population growth and community development, not as the result of any efforts by any owner. Thus, goes the argument, it is only fair that the community recapture the unearned increments for public purposes. Furthermore, this type of tax, which is widely used in Western Canada, Australia, and New Zealand, does not discourage investment in buildings. The construction of a building, or the improvement of an existing one, is not punished by imposing a higher tax. Since the tax would remain the same, regardless of land use, it would encourage the intensive development of any given lot and discourage the hoarding of vacant urban lots for speculation.

Property taxes to nonproperty taxes. Many would prefer to get completely away from reliance on property taxes. "Just as in Western Europe," they argue, "city governments in the United States should rely more on local income and sales taxes rather than allow the federal and state governments to monopolize them." At present, less than a tenth of local revenues come from these taxes. Many governments, such as counties and school districts, use them not at all.

In only 17 states do local governments impose sales taxes, in only 7 do they impose income taxes. Local sales and income taxes have significant advantages over the property tax: They require no arbitrary assessment, since sales and income are objectively determinable quantities. They can be levied on nonresidents, such as visiting shoppers (in the case of the sales tax) or commuting workers (in the case of the income tax). They are less regressive. By exemption of food and housing or by a flat per capita refund to everyone, the sales tax can be made proportional. By the inclusion of all types of income (including wages, interest, rent, and profits) and by exemptions for low-income recipients, the income tax can become progressive. Neither of these taxes discourages housing construction or improvement.

However, as with all taxes, income and sales taxes affect locational choices if tax rates differ among localities. For example, prior to 1965, when New York City was a sales tax island (there was no such tax in New Jersey), 25 percent of retail trade and employment in furniture and clothing was lost to New Jersey.

One simple way for local governments to collect income taxes would be for them to "piggyback" state or federal income taxes. The state or federal tax authorities could simply collect for them a surcharge on the state or federal levy and remit it to them. Local governments in Maryland are allowed to piggyback their state income tax in this way. Some congressmen proposed in 1971 a similar system for the federal tax.

Taxes to user charges. There is, finally, the obvious possibility of directly linking government services with the collection of revenues from those served. This idea has gradually been catching on. Recently, the city of Milwaukee installed coin meters for the lights on municipal tennis courts. Oakland, California, charges interested citizens $1 a page for police and fire reports and the city council agenda. Ravenna, Ohio, charges a fee for the recovery of stolen vehicles.

There are limits to this approach. It would be inappropriate to charge welfare recipients for their welfare checks, or to charge the poor for public health or elementary school services. It would be infeasible to charge any particular beneficiary for street lighting or crime prevention. It may even be undesirable to make such charges, if the widest possible use of a public service (for example, a library) is desired. Yet often, correct charges can and should be applied in cases where they are now not applied or badly applied. Equilibrium charges for the use of roads, parking facilities, or the waste disposal capacity of the environment may be wholly appropriate, feasible, and desirable. As a result, certain government services would not have to be provided at all (if people changed their behavior when confronted with the costs of their actions) or could be financed from money provided by the beneficiaries who may or may not be city residents.

INCREASING FEDERAL AID TO CITIES

"If city governments cannot help themselves because their problems are national in origin and too overwhelming in size to be tackled with local revenues," some have argued, "the federal government can and should step in." There is no dearth of suggested solutions.

Maintaining Prosperity

The federal government could help city governments by pursuing proper monetary and fiscal policies to assure full employment. The rise in incomes, sales, and property values resulting during prosperity would automatically tend to fill city coffers at a faster rate, *without any change in their tax rates.* The reduced incidence of unemployment and poverty would tend to reduce necessary city expenditures. Thus the cities' fiscal crisis, though far from being eliminated, would be eased.

Interest Subsidies

The federal government can help cities finance long-term borrowing for construction projects by subsidizing interest payments. The subsidizing has been done indirectly, by exempting interest received from municipal bonds from federal income taxes. This tends to depress the rates cities must pay on their bonds. However, in periods of generally rising interest rates, the policy is of little help, since cities cease all borrowing when municipal bond rates exceed certain legal limits. (One occasion was the period between 1962 and 1970, when such rates rose from 3.18 to 6.5 percent.)

The federal government, however, has also subsidized interest payments directly, as by paying half the difference between 5 percent and higher market rates. In 1968, a presidential task force recommended for this purpose the creation of an urban development bank. The bank would issue its own federally guaranteed, taxable bonds. It would lend to cities funds for up to 40 years for capital construction purposes, and do so at rates below municipal bond rates, with the federal government paying the difference. The idea is to increase the flow of funds to cities and to free them from certain disadvantages not faced by other borrowers. For example, corporate borrowers pay low rates because they have many banks to choose from and recover some of their interest expenses through lowered income taxes. Cities, even with excellent debt service records, pay high rates because they are faced with local banking monopolies and do not recover their interest costs either in lower taxes paid or, like the U.S. government, in higher taxes collected. President Nixon in 1970 proposed a similar institution (the Environmental Financing Authority), which would lend to cities for waste treatment plants only.

Tax Credits

The federal government might encourage states to allow cities to levy income taxes (or to levy higher income taxes if they already have such a tax). It might then encourage cities to introduce income taxes (or to raise those already in existence) by granting taxpayers, *in addition to* the deductions for state and local taxes already allowed from taxable income, say a 20 percent federal *tax credit* for such tax paid. For example, a family paying $200 of city income tax and now owing $2,000 in federal income taxes, would under the tax credit plan have its federal tax liability reduced by $40 (which is 20 percent of $200) to $1,960. The knowledge that their residents pay less in federal taxes would presumably encourage cities to levy higher city income taxes on their residents, which they now hesitate to do in light of existing high federal taxes. In this case, the city could raise its income tax by 25 percent (from $200 to $250) without raising the total of taxes paid by our family. (It would then pay $50 more to the city, but 20 percent of $250, or $50 less to the federal government.) In cases where city income taxes are newly introduced, residents would pay higher taxes overall, but their total tax bill would rise less than their city taxes—another comforting thought for city fathers.

Such a 20 percent tax credit proposal was made in 1971 by Representative Byrnes. He proposed similar federal tax credits for state and local estate taxes. If enacted, his proposals would allow state and local governments to raise an additional $3.5 billion per year at the expense of the federal treasury. Others have criticized, however, that this federal tax money would, in the first instance, go to individuals and flow into state and local government coffers only after they changed their tax laws. The critics would therefore rather stimulate state and local income taxation by promising these governments additional federal grants equal to a percentage of such taxes collected. In this way, federal funds would flow to city governments, but directly, while the net effect on taxpayers would be to pay more rather than the same.

However, both of these proposals suffer from the fact that they would help richer states and cities more than poorer ones. This is so because of two areas with identical tax rates, the one with the higher total income would have the highest tax collections and collect the biggest federal subsidy.

Occasional Categorical Grants

The potentiality for inequity in the tax credit proposals leads one naturally to the obvious alternative of making outright federal grants to specified cities for specified purposes. In 1971, over $30 billion in such grants were made to state and local governments. Their purpose ranged from Medicaid to vocational rehabilitation, from crime prevention to compensatory education. In 1971, there were 1,089 types of grants available. These grants required matching funds from local governments ($4 billion in 1971). They were designed to assure a minimum level of some services nationwide. But many have criticized them for forcing expenditures in directions that may be inappropriate in some cities, however appropriate they may be elsewhere. For example, the Crime Control and Safe Streets Act of 1968 provided for $800 million of federal money to be spent over three years on police, the prison system, and the courts. This was to supplement the $6 billion annual expenditure by state and local governments in these areas. But the federal guidelines were held too detailed. They specified spending on personnel testing techniques for potential new policemen, on salaries, on new jails, and on equipment, ranging from riot guns to tear gas to new powerful walkie-talkies, from night-vision devices for probing dark alleys to computerized intelligence systems for keeping track of organized crime. Many cities, although in need of all these things, felt that greater needs existed elsewhere.

Occasional Block Grants

Block grants could avoid the problems of categorical grants. The federal government would turn over, whenever it seems desirable, funds to cities and states that could be used, within broad federal guidelines, at the discretion of the recipient governments. Thus the different relative needs and preferences of different cities could be best served.

Permanent Assumption of Local Program Costs

Finally, it has been argued, the federal government could simply take over completely the financial responsibility for some of the current programs of cities. An added advantage of such federal control would be the assurance of a uniform quality of certain services and their provision to all without discrimination. The most frequently mentioned fields for federal takeover have been public welfare and public education. President Nixon in 1972 proposed a new 3 percent federal *value-added tax* (which would be rebated to the poor and some middle-income families). The $13 billion a year proceeds of this tax (as of 1972) would go to the states to pay for public primary and secondary education, provided that all residential property taxation now supporting schools were eliminated. By 1973, nothing had come of this particular proposal. However, Congress has enacted legislation authorizing federal takeover (as of 1974) of assistance programs for the aged, blind, and disabled.

Systematic Revenue Sharing

The fiscal crisis of the cities was no less obvious in 1964 than today. Yet the federal government had large and growing surpluses thanks to a booming revenue from the fairest of all taxes, the progressive federal income tax. It looked as if massive federal tax cuts would squander this precious chance to help the cities by the obvious method of turning over surplus federal revenues to them. Walter Heller, economic adviser to President Johnson, at that time proposed a permanent system whereby federal funds equal to a given percentage of the federal income tax base would be *automatically* turned over to the states each year with the provision that local governments receive a specified portion of these funds. Thus the idea of *systematic revenue sharing* was born. Foreseeing similar federal surpluses after the end of the Vietnam War, President Nixon embraced the idea. In 1971, he proposed a general and a special revenue-sharing plan.

The general plan. Under the general plan, 1.3 percent of federally taxable personal income (an estimated $5 billion by 1973) would be channeled to state and local governments. Each state would receive funds on a population basis with a small adjustment to reward those making a bigger tax effort on their own. States would be asked to agree with their local governments on the appropriate formula for subdivision. In cases where such agreement could not be reached, 10 percent of the funds would be lost, and Washington would divide the rest.

The special plan. Under the special plan, the federal government would dismantle a third of its categorical grant programs (many from the days of the "Great Society"). The $10 billion currently spent on them, plus another $1 billion of new money, would be also turned over to state and local governments. These governments would be "liberated" from federal regulations on these programs and not required to continue to supply matching funds. The funds would simply be allocated to six large categories: "Urban development" would take the place of Office of Economic Opportunity community action, urban renewal, model cities, rehabilitation loan, and water and sewer grant programs ($2 billion). "Education" would take the place of old school lunch, compensatory education, vocational education, library, and handicapped education programs ($3 billion). "Transportation" would take the place of urban mass transport, airport, highway safety and beautification, and noninterstate highway grants ($2.6 billion). "Rural development" would swallow up the Appalachian aid, extension service, conservation, tree planting, environmental aid, and water bank programs ($1 billion). Finally, funds for "manpower training" ($2 billion) and "law enforcement" ($.5 billion) would be distributed.[2]

The alleged advantages. President Nixon has called his proposed program "a historic and massive reversal of the flow of power in America," a "new federalism," and a "new American revolution" that would return the "power to the people." Behind these words lies the belief that federal programs inevitably involve massive waste in a federal bureaucracy. Secretary Romney once likened the Washington guidance of proliferating federal programs to a "20-mule team being harnessed in the dark by a one-eyed idiot." As evidence for his assertion, he produced a single city's application for an urban renewal grant; this application weighed 53 pounds and was stacked 30 feet high, the result of having to satisfy 134 federal and 17 state agencies with as many sets of different regulations.

[2] In 1973, President Nixon revised his special plan. He proposed ending seventy narrow categorical grant programs, replacing them with four broad-purpose special revenue-sharing programs that would pay out $6.9 billion in fiscal 1974. These programs would cover education (specifically, disadvantaged and handicapped children, vocational education, impact aid, and support services—all noted in the discussion of Table 7.2), law enforcement, manpower training, and urban community development.

Further, the Nixon plan reflects the belief that spending decisions are too far removed from the people ultimately affected by them. Therefore, the federal government, which happens to have such massive taxing power, should untangle its bureaucracy, give up some of its programs, and enable the state and local governments, *which are so much closer to the people*, to spend some of these funds for purposes best seen by the people on the spot. By presumably easier access to local officials than to those in Washington, the people would thus have increased influence.

The drawbacks. For a long time, however, the Nixon revenue-sharing plan has been blocked single-handedly by Representative Mills in Congress. He has substituted a plan of his own: providing a modest $1.5 billion a year to state governments on a permanent basis, with no strings attached, and $3.5 billion a year to local governments for a few years only, provided that none is spent on education and 20 percent of the local funds are used at the discretion of states for regional programs. Mills and others have serious reservations about revenue sharing in principle, for these reasons.

First, they are not so sure that state and local governments are "closer to the people." They see local governments rather as insensitive, especially to the needs of poor people who are more likely to have friends in Washington than in the mayor's office. Local governments exist in such abundance that no citizen can pick his way through the long list of officeholders in townships, counties, and school districts to control them effectively. Typically, local officials are chosen by an apathetic citizenry (a quarter of whom turn out on the most important issues), serve one brief term, along with independently chosen, unresponsive, disloyal fellow officials who hold wholly uncoordinated mandates. These are the very officials who habitually tax those least able to pay and who wall off the people with the most income from those with the most problems. Will more money in their hands make them likely to redress these age-old grievances?

Second, critics note, local governments in the past have neither attracted nor been able to afford expertise and administrative skill. They are likely to be incompetent, and quite possibly dishonest. The actions of any one local government are certainly hobbled hopelessly by the lack of cooperation of many others. Does this make them best suited to administer programs of regional and national importance? Therefore, these critics would prefer a drastic reordering of the responsibilities of all three levels of government to the blind acceptance of their present ones.

Congress acts. In late 1972, Congress enacted a version of the *general* revenue-sharing plan, but it cut simultaneously and substantially the funding of categorical grant programs. The plan provides for $33.5 billion in general revenue sharing over five years, retroactive to January 1, 1972. While a third of the funds will be channeled to the states, two-thirds will go to local governments. The distribution formula takes into account not only an area's population and tax effort but also its per capita income. As a result, poor rural and central city areas are favored.

RESTRUCTURING THE RESPONSIBILITIES OF GOVERNMENTS

In fiscal year 1971 all levels of American governments combined spent $369.4 billion. This figure excludes duplications; that is, the payments of funds by one level of government to another and the subsequent re-spending of these funds by the recipient government are only counted once. Let us consider what types of domestic responsibilities were taken on by the three levels of government—federal, state, and local—by examining their patterns of domestic spending for civilian purposes.

As a first step, we deduct from the $369.4 billion total any spending—all on the federal level—on international affairs and defense. This deduction comes to $111.9 billion. It covers spending on foreign affairs (including "food for freedom" and economic and military aid), on atomic energy and space programs, on military and defense-related activities, on interest for the national debt (mostly war-related), and on programs providing compensation payments, pensions, life insurance, health care, education, and cash assistance to veterans. The small amounts of state and local government spending on civil defense, the National Guard and armory activities have not been deducted. Thus we are left with a total domestic government spending for civilian purposes of $257.5 billion.

If we always count intergovernmental aid as having been spent by the originating rather than the recipient government, then the federal government spent 44 percent of this total, the states spent 30 percent, and local governments 26 percent. We can classify the activities among which this spending was distributed in a manner reflecting three types of objectives generally sought by government.[3] First, governments seek economic stabilization, that is, they attempt to counteract fluctuations in the overall level of economic activity. Second, they redistribute income among people on the grounds that the distribution of income that would otherwise exist is somehow unfair. Third, they seek to influence the allocation of resources by demanding the production of certain types of public goods. Table 14.1, "Government Civilian Spending by Major Objective, United States, Fiscal 1971," indicates the extent to which governments took on one or all of these responsibilities.

It turns out that of the $10.4 billion spending for economic stabilization purposes the federal government spent 55 percent, state governments were a close second with 45 percent, while local spending was negligible. In the field of income distribution, local government spending becomes much more important while the relative shares of federal and state government spendings are lower than for stabilization. Of the $149.4 billion spent, the federal government provided 48 percent, states 30 percent, and localities 22 percent. The relative role of local governments increases further as we move from income

[3] This classification was first introduced by Richard A. Musgrave, *The Theory of Public Finance* (New York: McGraw-Hill, 1959), Ch. 1.

distribution to resource allocation activities. Of the $97.7 billion total, the federal government spent only 37 percent, the states 27 percent, and the localities 36 percent. Considering all civilian domestic programs, the federal government spent 44 percent of the $257.5 billion total, the states 30 percent, and local governments 26 percent. One can make a good case for the argument that this division of labor among governments is foolish indeed, and that this faulty allocation of tasks is, in turn, ultimately responsible for the urban governments' fiscal crisis and the continued existence of urban economic problems.

A Proper Distribution of Tasks

To distribute governmental tasks properly, one might follow some rule like the following:

Since the scope of problems that are addressed by governmental services differs, all governmental services that clearly benefit mostly the people present in a single locality (for example, street lighting in New York City) should be supplied by local government and financed by local taxes or charges. Governmental services that clearly benefit mostly the people of a single state (for example, a state flood control system) should be supplied by state government and financed by state taxes or charges. Governmental services that clearly benefit people in many states (for example, national defense) should be supplied by the federal government and financed by federal taxes or charges.

Often we act according to this rule. For example, we recognize that the need for national defense or economic security in old age is not confined to a single locality or state. Therefore, we peg the burden of supplying the appropriate services and of financing them on the federal government. It would not occur to us to let Alaskans worry about national defense because they alone border the Soviet Union. It would not occur to us to let Floridians worry about old age security because that is where so many old people spend their later years. Yet equally often we do just such silly things. We refuse to recognize that the educational and health services provided or not provided in one community will ultimately, in view of the mobility of today's population, benefit or harm mostly other communities. Thus the neglect of education and health in Puerto Rico, Appalachia, and the South ends up as the problems of the large cities of the East, North, and West, and we expect *them* to take care of "their" problem. But local governments cannot be expected to cope with spillovers from larger areas. They could do so only by taxing residents of the larger areas. But they cannot undertake such taxing.

One can argue clearly that only the federal government should engage in *economic stabilization* policies. The origin of the unemployment problem can be found neither in any one locality nor in any one state. Policies to combat unemployment if pursued by any one locality or state would most likely be insufficient in scope, and their benefits would almost totally spill over into other localities or states.[4]

[4] Note the discussion of this in Chapter 3 in the section dealing with the stage of export specialization.

Table 14.1 **Government Civilian Spending by Major Objective, United States, Fiscal 1971 (In Millions of Dollars)**

	Federal Spending		State Spending		Local Spending	
Objective	*Direct*	*Via Aid to State and Local Governments*	*Direct, Excludes Spending Financed by Federal or Local Funds*	*Via Aid to Local Governments*	*Direct, Excludes Spending Financed by Federal or State Funds*	*Via Aid to State Governments*
1. Economic stabilization	5,729	...	4,692	...	16	...
farm price supports	5,227	...	...	...	...	...
unemployment insurance benefits	502	...	4,692	...	16	...
2. Income redistribution	54,721	17,470	19,209	25,803	31,892	338
health	1,757	787	4,475	751	5,055	138
education[a]	3,595	6,783	10,489	19,292	23,573	38
social security[b]	47,107	...	3,635	...	1,450	...
public welfare[c]	2,262	9,900	610	5,760	1,814	162

3. Resource allocation	26,404	9,959	19,341	6,837	34,875	263
police, correction, fire[d]	613	...	1,991	...	7,424	...
housing, urban renewal, local parks and recreation	1,936	1,611	...	143	2,908	1
land transport[e]	301	4,987	7,287	2,507	5,462	30
air and water transport	3,761	70	274	42	1,178	1
utilities[f]	...	475	...	...	10,269	...
natural resources[g]	5,700	563	1,915	64	533	6
postal service	8,683	...	...	...	...	...
liquor stores	...	...	1,395	...	230	...
administration	4,315	721	2,536	...	4,392	...
other[h]	1,095	1,532	3,943	4,081	2,709	226
Total	86,854	27,429	43,242	32,640	66,783	601
	114,283		75,882		67,384	

[a] Includes, besides spending on schools and higher education, spending on libraries, museums, and manpower training.
[b] Includes old-age, survivors, disability and health insurance, and public employee and railroad retirement programs.
[c] Includes old-age assistance, aid for families with dependent children, aid to the blind and disabled, vendor medical payments (as Medicaid), general public welfare, public employee compensation payments, and disaster relief.
[d] Includes, at the federal level, spending on the FBI, Immigration and Naturalization Service, Bureau of Narcotics, Secret Service, and Law Enforcement Assistance Administration.
[e] Includes spending on highways, streets, bridges, tunnels, ferries, mass transit, and parking facilities.
[f] Includes spending on refuse collection and disposal, street cleaning, sewage systems, and water, electricity, and gas supply.
[g] Includes, among others, spending on agricultural research, irrigation, drainage, conservation, power and reclamation projects, national and state parks, forestry, mineral resources, the Army Corps of Engineers, and the National Oceanic and Atmospheric Administration.
[h] Includes, among others, federal interest on tax refunds and interest on state and local government debt.

SOURCE: *U.S. Bureau of the Census,* Governmental Finances in 1970–71 *(October 1972).*

The picture is not much different with *income redistribution*. The origins of inequality and poverty are not confined to any locality or state. Redistribution policies if pursued by any one locality or state would most likely not solve the problem. The benefits from such policies would most certainly spill over to other localities and states to a large degree. For example, only 20 percent of those educated in one locality live there as adults. Forty percent move to another locality in the same state. Forty percent move to other states.[5] Thus local governments might be called upon to pay for only 20 percent of public school expenditures, the rest being paid for by the state or by the federal government (to the extent that people educated in one locality finally settle in another one in the same state or in other states, respectively).

On the basis of corresponding estimates for the geographic incidence of health, other education, social security, and public welfare benefits, one may argue that the federal government should finance 70 percent, the states 20 percent, and local governments 10 percent of income redistributive policies.

Thinking, similarly, about *resource allocation* policies suggests that, perhaps, 27 percent of their benefits remain confined to a single locality; 40, to a single state; and 33, to the nation. Thus, ideally, the three levels of government ought to finance such policies in these same proportions. All this is summarized in Table 14.2, "The Structuring of Government Responsibilities." The table also contains a summary of the actual division of government spending.

A study of Table 14.2 pinpoints the problem. Considering where the benefits of these policies accrue, the federal government ought to spend much more, states much less on economic stabilization (line 1). The federal government ought to spend much more, the states slightly less, and local governments much less on income redistribution (line 2). The federal and local governments ought to spend less, the states more on resource allocation (line 3). Overall, local governments ought to spend a lot less, the federal government a lot more for the objectives now pursued (line 4). Local governments are in trouble precisely because the federal government is not living up to its responsibility to deal effectively with problems that are larger in scope than any one state or locality. It must relieve local governments of obligations that local residents have not created. Only in this way can there be a rational sharing of the costs of desirable and necessary government programs.

Redrawing Boundaries?

One further matter should be noted. There is no reason why political boundaries must be accepted as they now are. The definition of local and state government might well have to be changed as the country continues to be covered by huge webs of urbanization. The governmental unit that most effectively can deal with certain problems (because it has jurisdiction of the entire

[5] On this point see Dick Netzer, *Economics and Urban Problems* (New York: Basic Books, 1970), pp. 177–181, on whose analysis the ideal apportionment of government responsibilities is based.

Table 14.2 **The Structuring of Government Responsibilities: Percentage of Civilian Domestic Spending Total by Level of Government, Fiscal 1971**

	Federal		State		Local	
Objective	*Ideal*	*Actual*	*Ideal*	*Actual*	*Ideal*	*Actual*
1. Economic stabilization	100	55	0	45	0	0
2. Income redistribution	70	48	20	30	10	22
3. Resource allocation	33	37	40	27	27	36
All civilian programs	53	44	29	30	18	26

SOURCE: *Table 14.1 and source cited in footnote 5 to this chapter.*

area affected by the problem) may well exceed the size of present localities and exceed or fall short of the size of present states. If, according to the above type of analysis, local governments should take care of, say, garbage collection, this does not necessarily refer to local governments as now constituted. Possibly it would be wiser to let a metropolitan areawide agency take care of this matter, thereby being able to take advantage of *economies of scale*, that is, a reduction in the average cost of providing a commodity or service due to the larger scale at which production takes place. Similarly, if the states seem to be the proper providers of air pollution control, this might well mean that the necessary policies should be carried out by a government that has jurisdiction over an entire air shed, which possibly would encompass several existing states in whole or in part (see Figure 13.3, "Atmospheric Areas and Air Quality Control Regions in the United States"). Thus one can make a good case for an imaginative redrawing of governmental boundaries. Better yet, one might think of future governments being set up for dealing with specific problems, such as garbage disposal, air pollution, or poverty. Each of these governments might have jurisdiction over a differently sized *problem shed*, a geographic area inhabited by all the people who potentially receive benefits from policies dealing with a given problem. Naturally, these "problem sheds" would overlap and each citizen might be a member of as many as two dozen of these jurisdictions. Such imaginative governmental machinery would eliminate the spillover problem and allow in each instance the taxation of all those and only those who potentially benefit from a public service. It would also allow the production of this service on an efficient scale, thus assuring the greatest benefit from each tax dollar spent. There can be no doubt that such political reforms would be difficult; yet neither can there remain any doubt that urban governments as now constituted will never solve urban economic problems by themselves.

Summary

1. In one way or another, the solution to urban problems requires government action—and spending. This requires the collection of sufficient funds by taxation or borrowing. The spending by city governments has been rising rapidly in recent years; so has their revenue collection and debt.
2. A closer look at city government budgets shows the allocations of spending and the sources of revenue. Of city spending in fiscal 1971, 20 percent went for utilities, 14 for police and fire protection, 14 for education, 11 for transportation, 8 for housing, parks, or renewal, 7 for public welfare, and 6 for health. Cities spent relatively much more on utilities, police, fire, housing, parks, and renewal than all state and local governments did. Cities spent relatively much less on education.
3. Of city revenues in fiscal 1971, 27 percent came from the property tax, 7 percent came from the sales tax, 6 from licenses and other taxes, 31 from charges, and 26 from state and federal aid. It is significant that income taxes, collections of which rise faster than the GNP, play a negligible role in city finances. Since city spending has risen faster than the GNP but their own funds (revenues exclusive of intergovernmental aid) have not, state and federal aid has become increasingly important.
4. The rapid city spending rise has partly reflected the higher costs of given service levels, partly the real provision of extra services. Yet the latter has not risen fast enough to make a dent in city problems. This is so because cities have been unable to raise their own funds sufficiently fast: Tax bases have been shrinking. Tax rates have often reached legal maximums, or voters have resisted tax-rate hikes, or such hikes have accelerated the erosion of the tax base. (Ironically, failure to hike taxes and provide sufficient services has the same effect. Cities are damned if they do and damned if they don't.)
5. All cities have had to fill the gap between spending and their own revenues with outside aid. This has seriously restrained their ability to raise spending sufficiently to really tackle their problems. Thus their choices are: finding new ways of raising revenue from sources other than other governments, getting more outside aid or getting someone else to handle so-called city problems. The latter makes sense on the grounds that cities suffer from externalities imposed by outsiders and that outsiders have better revenue sources.
6. Cities have attempted to increase their own revenue-raising capability by replacing political fragmentation of local governments with cooperation. This enables them to expand the tax base or change the tax base. The latter approach has involved proposals to change the property tax to an exclusive land-value tax, to give up property taxes in favor of other types of taxes, and to rely more heavily on user charges.
7. It has also been suggested that cities be helped by more massive federal action. This might involve a determined federal effort to maintain prosperity, subsidization of municipal borrowing costs, tax credits for individuals paying local income taxes, occasional categorical or block grants to municipalities, permanent federal assumption of local program costs, or systematic revenue sharing.

8. The most promising way out of city fiscal problems, and out of urban economic problems in general, lies in a restructuring of the responsibilities of present governments. To distribute governmental tasks properly, one might follow some rule like the following:

   Since the scope of problems that are addressed by governmental services differs, all governmental services that clearly benefit mostly the people present in a single locality should be supplied by local government and financed by local taxes or charges. Governmental services that clearly benefit mostly the people of a single state should be supplied by state government and financed by state taxes or charges. Governmental services that clearly benefit people in many states should be supplied by the federal government and financed by federal taxes or charges.
9. When these guidelines are followed, it becomes clear that the federal government ought to spend more, states less, on economic stabilization. The federal government ought to spend much more, the states slightly less, and local governments much less, on income redistribution. The federal and local governments ought to spend less, the states more, on resource allocation. Overall, local governments ought to spend a lot less, the federal government a lot more, for the objectives now pursued.
10. Possibly, future governments might be established on the basis of problem sheds. Such imaginative governmental machinery would eliminate the spillover problem and allow in each instance the taxation of all those, and only those, who potentially benefit from a public service. It would also allow the production of this service on an efficient scale.

Terms[6]

block grant
categorical grant
cost assumption
economies of scale
excise tax
insurance trust fund
judgment fund bonds
land value tax
matching funds
piggyback tax
problem shed
revenue sharing
spillovers
tax base
tax credit
tax rate
value-added tax

Questions for Review and Discussion

1. "City budgets are far larger today than what would have been considered more than adequate a decade ago. Yet all cities are threatened by serious disruption of their vital services. Candidates for mayor like to blame it all

[6] Terms are defined in the Glossary at the back of the book.

on corruption and inefficiency. But when they take office, they cannot do better either. Cities are in deep fiscal trouble." Can you explain it?

2. "The only way cities nowadays can attract business is by tax relief and that is the last thing they can afford to do." Comment.
3. "Cities are being exploited by suburban and rural dwellers and that is why they have fiscal problems." Comment.
4. "To get large cities out from under state control (and rural-suburban domination) they should be chartered by the federal government as independent national cities." Discuss.
5. The local property tax is a wonderfully rich revenue source for local governments. Why does everybody criticize it?
6. In many cities, many factors have tended to shrink the tax base. One is the increase in tax-exempt property. In New York City these include properties of religious, charitable, and educational institutions as well as of governments (city, state, federal, foreign, United Nations), plus a great variety of others, such as hospitals, cemeteries, fallout shelters, railroads, and the homes of veterans. In 1957–58, 28.6 percent of total New York City real estate was tax-exempt. By 1969–70, the percentage had climbed to 33.8 percent. How would you deal with the problem this creates?
7. In 1969, there was a drive in California to put on the ballot an initiative measure to eliminate the property tax on buildings and improvements while taxing *land alone*. What effect would such a law, if passed, have on slum formation?
8. "Just as users of oranges pay for them in our society, users of schools, and highways, and streets should pay for these. Local governments would have no fiscal problems if they relied exclusively on *user charges*." Evaluate.
9. Mr. A: Mayor Cavanaugh of Detroit has claimed that $250 billion is needed for the rebirth of America's cities. Mayor Lindsay of New York put the figure at $50 billion for his city alone. If we can spend $70 billion to put a man on the moon, and $43 billion on the interstate highway system, we can certainly spend this kind of money to save our cities. The federal government should simply hand it over to the nation's mayors.

   Mr. B: Are you kidding? You can't hand out money without strings. It would be spent recklessly and solve little.

   Evaluate.
10. President Nixon favors federal aid to the cities given through state governments. The mayors of cities want money given directly to them. They fear that rural and suburban interests would dominate the state government's dispensing of the money. Which approach would you favor? Why?
11. In 1971, at least 34 states withdrew from federal cost-sharing programs or restricted the extent of their participation. Can you imagine why?
12. "If President Nixon's value-added tax proposal were to become law, it would not help future buyers of property. The decreased property taxes would simply show up as higher land prices. Only the present owners of real estate would make a one time gain. Here is why: Suppose the gross income from a piece of real estate minus expenses is $1,000 a year when property

taxes are $200. If comparable investments yield 5 percent, the real estate in question would sell for $1,000 divided by 0.05, or $20,000. Elimination of the property tax would change the figures to $1,200 divided by 0.05, or $24,000. Thus future buyers of real estate would pay in higher prices what they don't pay in higher taxes!" Comment.

13. "There is no need to wipe the slate clean and get rid of all local and state governments as now constituted. If efficient production of a public service requires a larger scale than any of these present units would need, several of them could provide a service jointly or they could pool their funds and let a private firm produce it for all of them." Evaluate.
14. "Problem-shed government is a terrible idea, for it takes away much of people's ability to escape the dictates of any one government by their moving into the jurisdiction of another government nearby. Furthermore, it would be administratively too expensive, probably requiring each person to vote in 30 separate elections." Comment.
15. "Redrawing political boundaries can never help with urban problems. Any metropolitan areawide government or any larger regional government would be dominated by rural and suburban interests. These would have the funds, but not the will, to tackle urban problems." Comment.

Selected Readings

Edel, Matthew, and Rothenberg, Jerome. *Readings in Urban Economics.* New York: Macmillan, 1972. Part 7. Discusses many aspects of urban public finance, including intergovernmental fiscal relations, the theory of local expenditures and of optimal government, and the fiscal crisis of the state. Note the bibliography on p. 504.

Fusfeld, Daniel R. *Economics.* Lexington, Mass.: D. C. Heath and Co., 1972. Chs. 39 and 40. An elementary discussion of the public sector of the economy.

Hirsch, Werner Z. *Urban Economic Analysis.* New York: McGraw-Hill, 1973. Chs. 10–13. A detailed discussion of the urban public sector in general, and of four major services in particular (police protection, fire protection, recreation, cultural activities).

Mushkin, Selma J., ed. *Public Prices for Public Products.* Washington, D.C.: Urban Institute, 1972. A collection of articles dealing with economic efficiency and pricing. Discusses the theory of public prices and numerous applications (effluent charges, congestion tolls, pricing hospital services, pricing education, and other public services).

Thompson, Wilbur R. *A Preface to Urban Economics.* Baltimore: Johns Hopkins Press, 1968. Ch. 7. A thorough discussion of the urban public economy and its problems of scale and choice.

U.S. Bureau of the Census. *Statistical Abstract of the United States, 1972.* Washington, D.C., 1972. Lists some statistics on government finance—federal, state, and local (Sections 14, 15, and 33), and—more important—sources to other statistics: Note the listing of statistical abstract supplements (p. v); the guide to general sources of statistics (pp. 921–23 and 950–52), to recent censuses (pp. 958–59), and to state statistical abstracts (pp. 961–64).

NOTE: The *Journal of Economic Literature* lists recent articles on federal government expenditures and taxes (sections 322 and 323), on state and local government finance (324), on intergovernmental financial relations (325), and on urban economics and public policy (931).

The *Index of Economic Articles* catalogs, in sections beginning with the indicated numbers, articles on state and local public finance (10.02, 10.3–10.5), intergovernmental finances (10.03), federal expenditures (10.3), all types of taxes (10.4), and the public debt (10.5).

Glossary

Terms

This Glossary contains brief definitions of the most important terms used throughout this book. It may be used, therefore, as a convenient study guide for the terms found at the end of each chapter.

The economic definitions found in this Glossary are those with which most economists would agree. Yet definitions are by nature arbitrary, and some people may at times prefer to use a term in a way slightly different from the one given here. This Glossary only shows the sense in which terms have been used in this book. The reader can thereby understand what the book is trying to say. If then he should prefer to use different terms from those that have been used here, he can always do so.

Finally, note that new terms have often been defined with the help of other terms newly learned in this book. Then the reader might also want to look at their definitions.

Above-normal profit Profit larger than normal; see **Normal profit.**

Absolute definition of poverty The specification of a certain dollar family income as the poverty line (for example, $3,000) without regard to the actual distribution of income among families; disregards size of incomes earned by people above this line.

Aerobic degradation The breakdown by bacteria in the presence of oxygen of organic material (such as sewage) into inorganic material such as nitrogen, phosphorus, and carbon.

Affirmative action plan A plan whereby employers promise to change the racial, ethnic, or sexual composition of their work force, or even of individual job categories within the work force, in such a way as to reduce over time the incidence of discrimination in hiring or promotion.

Aggravated assault Assault with intent to kill.

Aggregate demand The amount of money people in the aggregate are able and willing to spend on an area's new output in a period; the sum of consumption (private and public) and investment expenditures plus exports minus imports; in equilibrium, equal to the level of income and output.

Ambient standards Governmental standards designed to reduce pollution and specifying maximum allowable waste concentrations in the recipient environment (such as 100 units of sulfur dioxide per million units of air).

Anaerobic degradation The breakdown of organic material (such as sewage) when no oxygen is present, resulting in gaseous by-products such as methane and hydrogen sulfide.

Asset Anything of value held by someone.

Black capitalism A scheme to create a whole spectrum of black-owned and black-run businesses to eliminate the poverty of black people.

Block grant A grant that can be used at the discretion of the recipient.

Building codes Laws prescribing the types of materials and methods that have to be used in constructing buildings.

Burglary Actual or attempted unlawful entry, regardless of whether followed by a felony or a theft.

Business transfer payments Values given up by businesses in return for nothing, like gifts made or thefts suffered.

Capital The total of man-made resources existing at a moment in time; includes all buildings, all types of equipment, and all inventories of producers (raw materials, semifinished, and finished goods).

Capital consumption allowances A dollar estimate of the wear and tear of capital during a period; also called depreciation.

Capital gains Income derived from the appreciation of property held for more than six months.

Capitalism In its pure form, a society wherein all resources are privately owned and privately used.

Capitation system A system under which medical personnel providing health services are paid in advance a fixed sum per head and then provide all services as required without further charges.

Categorical grant A grant for specified purposes, usually requiring matching funds of the recipient.

Centers strategy A strategy of land-use planning that envisions clusters of offices, colleges, hospitals, and shopping and cultural facilities in a few planned centers of architectural distinction with residential areas in between.

Centrally planned economy An economic system wherein decisions on what is produced, where production is carried on, and who carries it on and how, and also decisions on who receives the output, are made by a central human authority and then carried out in accordance with a central economic plan issued by it.

Child nutrition programs Some of several government programs to combat insufficient or improper diets, involving direct commodity distribution, and special milk and school lunch programs.

Children's allowances A system of government payments for children designed to eliminate poverty associated with youth.

Chronic unemployment A situation wherein the numbers of job openings and job seekers may well coincide but their types are seriously mismatched.

Class suit A suit brought by any one member of a group (such as all urban residents) on behalf of the entire group, without the necessity of personal damage having been experienced by the party bringing the suit, for example against a polluter for harm done to some members of the group.

Command economy An economy in which all or most economic transactions are guided by a central human authority; a centrally planned economy.

Commodity distribution program One of several government programs to combat insufficient or improper diets, involving the distribution of 22 basic farm commodities.

Community development corporations Authorized by the 1970 Housing Act to aid in the development of new towns via loan guarantees, loans, grants, and demonstration projects.

Compensation principle The principle by which society at large reimburses a crime victim for damages suffered.

Competitive economy See **Market economy.**

Composting A method of solid-waste disposal yielding a humuslike product that can be used as fertilizer or construction material.

Consumption expenditures The spending by an area's households or governments on new goods that are typically used up within a year, such as bread or policeman's services.

Continuous pricing system A system of road-use pricing whereby motorists incur charges as long as they stay or travel within designated zones.

Corporate profits Sales value (after rebates and discounts) minus costs attributable to goods sold by corporations.

Cost assumption The takeover by a higher level of government of all the costs of certain programs of lower governments.

Crime of passion Murder, rape, or aggravated assault.

Crime rate Number of crimes per 100,000 population.

Crowded dwelling unit A dwelling unit with more than one person per room.

Culturally biased IQ tests Intelligence tests that do not measure the degree of a person's intellectual development because they require a person from one culture to take a test on experiences of another cultural environment.

Culture of poverty The set of beliefs, customs, habits, morals, and so forth shaping the life of many poor people.

Decibel scale A yardstick for measuring noise.

Dilapidated dwelling unit A dwelling unit in such a bad physical condition as to endanger the health, safety, or well-being of its occupants, for example, having holes in the exterior walls or roofs or furnaces that do not work.

Discounted value The present value of an amount of money available at a given future date; equals that amount of money which, invested at the current interest rate would at that future date yield the future amount involved.

Discouraged workers Involuntarily unemployed persons who want a job but have stopped looking for one because they consider it hopeless to find work; officially counted under *voluntary* unemployment.

Diversification stage The stage in a city's growth at which its original export industry has generated a host of complementary industries that provide its inputs, process further its outputs, and become exporters, in turn.

Dollar votes The expenditures by buyers of goods that ultimately determine, in a capitalist market economy, which goods continue to be produced.

Dual market An artificially split market (for example, for labor or housing) in which some sellers or buyers (for example, females or blacks) are compelled to deal in a segment of the market only, while others (for example, males or whites) are not so constrained or have a different but larger share of the market available.

Dwelling unit A group of rooms or a single room intended for occupancy as separate living quarters, having direct access from the outside or through a common hall and having complete kitchen facilities for the exclusive use of the occupants.

Economically motivated crime Robbery, auto theft, larceny, or burglary.

Economic efficiency A situation in which the allocation of resources among producers or of goods among households is such that it is impossible to reallocate resources or goods and thereby make someone better off without making anyone else worse off.

Economic justice A situation in which the apportionment of scarce goods among people is considered fair; that is, because it is believed that the potentiality no longer exists for increasing social welfare by the taking of goods from one person and the giving of them to another.

Economic order A state of coordination of the specialized activities of households and firms so that the activity of each fits in neatly with that of all others.

Economic system The set of institutions designed to work out a rational social program of resource use.

Economic wants Human desires that can be satisfied by the provision of economic goods, that is, scarce commodities or services that can be produced by man.

Economies of scale A situation in which a given percentage increase in all inputs leads to a greater percentage increase in output, hence to a reduction in unit costs as a result of large-scale production.

Educational vouchers Certificates akin to food stamps, allowing the holder to buy educational services wherever and of whatever type he chooses.

Emission standards Governmental standards designed to reduce pollution and specifying maximum allowable waste concentrations in the effluents of polluters (such as 100 units of sulfur dioxide per million units of stack gases).

Equilibrium price (or quantity) A price (or quantity) that has no innate tendency to change because quantity demanded equals quantity supplied in this market.

Equity See **Economic justice.**

Eutrophication The killing of marine life as a consequence of water fertilization, rapid plant growth and decay, and thus the using up (for example, by aerobic degradation) of oxygen dissolved in the water.

Exclusive franchise The granting by government to a firm of the exclusive right to sell a good, such as bus service, in a given area.

Excise tax A tax on the purchase of specific domestically made goods.

Exploitation A situation in which a resource is paid less than what it contributes to production, that is, less than its marginal value product.

Exports The sale of newly produced goods by an area to households, firms, and governments outside the area.

Export specialization stage The stage in a city's growth wherein most of its production is exported (sold beyond city limits) and most of the goods it uses are imported (bought beyond city limits).

Externalities See **External repercussions of consumption** and **External repercussions of production.**

External repercussions of consumption The cost or benefit imposed on parties other than the consumer of a good because of and for no other reason than his consumption of this good.

External repercussions of production The cost or benefit imposed on parties other than the producer of a good because of and for no other reason than his production of this good.

Fee-for-service system A system under which medical personnel providing health services are paid a fee for each separate service as it is performed.

Filtering process The process by which older, but standard, housing is passed on to lower-income families as higher-income families acquire new units.

Firm The legal and administrative entity in charge of the process of production.

First-stage sewage treatment The settling out in holding ponds of coarse solids from raw sewage.

Fiscal policy The deliberate exercise by the federal government of its power to tax and spend in order to influence the levels of output, employment, and prices.

Fiscal zoning Legislating zoning laws with an eye to the fiscal implications of land uses, notably with an eye to encouraging high tax yield while minimizing government spending requirements.

Fixed cost Cost independent of output volume; occurs even at zero output, as long as a firm exists.

Food stamp program One of the several government programs to combat insufficient or improper diets; involves the distribution of food stamps that allow the recipients to buy food in regular stores.

Frictional unemployment A situation wherein the numbers and types of job openings and job seekers roughly coincide, but the two are temporarily mismatched.

Functional income distribution The distribution of income according to the "function" for which income was paid (how much payment was for labor, how much payment for land, how much for capital).

General unemployment A situation in which the number of job seekers in all or most fields exceeds that of job openings.

Ghetto A blighted city area inhabited by members of racial or ethnic minority groups under conditions of involuntary segregation and poverty.

Goods Want-satisfying commodities or services.

Gravitrain A futuristic means of urban transport, propelled by its own weight through underground tunnels and pulled up by its own momentum.

Gray area Areas of aging and unattractive, but nonslum housing, typically the suburbs of the past, located between central cities and the new suburbs.

Greenhouse effect The increase of global temperatures as a result of increasing global concentration of carbon dioxide.

Gross national income The gross incomes earned by resource owners in a period in the process of production; or the sum of wages, salaries, and supplements plus net indirect business taxes plus business transfer payments plus capital consumption allowances plus the rental income of persons plus net interest plus proprietors' income plus corporate profits, including inventory valuation adjustment.

Gypsy cab Taxis that are not allowed to cruise for passengers, and are limited to dispatch by telephone.

Health maintenance organization Group practice by medical personnel based on the capitation system and emphasizing preventive rather than crisis care.

Health vouchers Certificates akin to food stamps, allowing the holder to buy medical services wherever and of whatever type he chooses.

Household One person living alone or more persons living together and making economic decisions independently from other such individuals or groups with the aim of maximizing the well-being of all who compose the household unit.

Housing service unit A hypothetical bundle of satisfaction derived from a dwelling unit, its size depending on the size, physical condition, equipment, and environment of the unit.

Imports The spending by an area's households, firms, and governments on new goods produced outside the area.

Imputed food and fuel income An estimate of the amount farmers could have earned if they had sold the food and fuel they produced and used up personally.

Imputed interest income An estimate of the amount of interest owner-occupiers of residential and institutional buildings could have earned if they had lent out the money actually sunk into these buildings, plus an estimate of the interest depositors would have received from financial intermediaries if these institutions had not netted out such amounts against the costs of services provided to depositors.

Imputed rental income An estimate of the net amount home owners could have earned if they had rented out rather than lived in their homes; equals current rental charges minus costs such as depreciation, taxes, interest.

Incidence of poverty The percentage of people within a given group (such as "all Americans" or "all urban Americans" or "all urban black Americans") who are below the poverty line.

Income-producing wealth Land and capital.

Input standards Governmental standards designed to reduce pollution and specifying the use of particular inputs (such as low-sulfur fuels) by polluting firms.

Insurance trust fund A fund into which employee and employer contributions for retirement and unemployment insurance are made and from which benefits are paid.

Internal consistency (of resource allocation) See **Economic order.**

Inventory valuation adjustment A correction applied to corporate profits to eliminate apparent profits or losses resulting not from producing but from the valuation of inventories at changing prices.

Investment expenditures The spending by an area's households on new residences and by the area's firms and governments on new capital.

Involuntary unemployment Category assigned to all members of the civilian labor force not working *at all* during the survey week (in which statistics are gathered) if they are currently available for work (even if perhaps temporarily ill), and if they (1) have looked for work in the preceding four weeks or (2) have not looked for work because they are (a) temporarily laid off subject to recall or (b) scheduled to begin a new job within thirty days.

Jitney Gypsy "gypsy cabs," that is, totally illegal taxis, usually operated by poor people in family cars.

Job banks Collections of data on jobs and job seekers providing computerized job placement services.

Judgment fund bonds Bonds issued to collect the funds necessary to pay a legal judgment of damages.

Labor All types of human effort put forth in the process of production, physical as well as mental.

Land Natural resources in their original state, or nonhuman gifts of nature.

Land-value tax A property tax on land only, excluding the value of buildings on it.

Larceny Theft, other than auto theft, of property in excess of $50 value without the use of force, fraud, and violence.

Law of diminishing marginal effectiveness If the level of any benefit-producing activity is increased successively by equal units during a fixed time period (while the levels of other activities are held constant), the additional activity units will after some point lose effectiveness and produce declining marginal benefits (that is, successive units will raise the total benefit by less and less). For example, the activity might be the consumption of apples (or of labor services), the benefit might then be the enjoyment derived from consuming apples (or the output produced by using labor services).

Law of diminishing returns A specific case of the law of diminishing marginal effectiveness; the technical fact that, with at least one input fixed, and technical know-how unchanged, equal increases in one or more other inputs will add less and less to output.

Liability Anything of value owed by someone.

Line of actual inequality See **Lorenz curve.**

Line of perfect equality A line indicating the position of the Lorenz curve if income (or wealth) were distributed perfectly equally.

Line of perfect inequality A line indicating the position of the Lorenz curve if income (or wealth) were distributed perfectly unequally, that is, if all went to one family and nothing to all others.

Long run A period of such length that a producer can vary all the inputs he is using in the productive process and so have the choice of many plant capacities.

Lorenz curve A graphical device measuring the extent of inequality of income (or wealth) among persons or families.

Marginal benefit The change in total benefit associated with a unit change of an activity (such as consuming or producing a good or supplying or using a resource) other things being equal. Examples: the change in total satisfaction when eating eleven rather than ten apples; the change in total output when using eleven rather than ten workers.

Marginal (opportunity) cost The change in total cost associated with a unit change of an activity (such as consuming or producing a good or supplying or using a resource) given all else. Examples: the change in total cost when producing eleven rather than ten apples, or when working eleven rather than ten hours.

Marginal physical product The physical change in output associated with a unit change in the use of one input, other things such as other inputs and technical know-how being equal.

Marginal revenue The change in total revenue associated with a unit change in output sold.

Marginal revenue product Marginal physical product multiplied by marginal revenue.

Marginal value product Marginal physical product multiplied by output price.

Market The framework within which potential buyers and sellers of goods or resources make contact with one another for the purpose of transferring ownership of goods or resources.

Market demand A series of price-quantity combinations showing the amounts of a good (or resource) that households (or firms) as a group are able and willing to buy at alternative prices; the sum of individual demands.

Market economy An economic system wherein decisions on what is produced, where production is carried on, and who carries it on and how, and also decisions on who receives the output, are made in decentralized fashion; owners of resources sell them for money to firms in resource markets, with firms producing the kinds and quantities of goods recipients of money income demand in goods markets, while market prices guide self-seeking households and firms to act in such a way as to assure economic order.

Market supply A series of price-quantity combinations showing the amounts of a good (or resource) that firms (or households) as a group are able and willing to sell at alternative prices; the sum of individual supplies.

Mass transit Buses, subways, streetcars, and railroads.

Matching funds An amount of money a grant recipient must put up on his own for a specified purpose as a condition of receiving the grant.

Maturation stage The stage in a city's growth at which a significant portion of its production is locally consumed and of its consumption is locally produced.

Medicaid A federal grant program to the states supporting health services for the poor who are not covered by Medicare insurance.

Medicare A government health insurance program mostly for those aged 65 and over.

Mesbic Minority enterprise small business investment company.

Minimum wage The minimum wage that can legally be paid to certain groups of the labor force, as defined by the Fair Labor Standards Act; in general, an above-equilibrium wage.

Minorities advancement plan A specific affirmative action plan proposed by John Kenneth Galbraith, aimed at assuring nondiscriminatory promotions.

Minority capitalism A scheme to create a whole spectrum of businesses owned and run by members of minority groups (blacks, Puerto Ricans, Orientals, American Indians) in order to eliminate the poverty of these groups.

Mobile parking Cars circling the block while looking for a parking space.

Mobility The freedom of anyone to become a buyer or seller in any market.

Modular house A factory-produced house.

Monetary policy Regulation of the supply and cost of money in the United States by the Federal Reserve System in order to influence the levels of output, employment, and prices.

Monopolist The only seller of a good or resource having no close substitutes.

Monopolistic exploitation Exploitation resulting from imperfections in the goods market causing the marginal revenue to be below the price of goods (and hence the marginal revenue product to be below the marginal value product of resources).

Monopsonist The only buyer of a good or resource for which the seller has no alternative outlets.

Monopsonistic exploitation Exploitation resulting from imperfections in the resource market causing the marginal cost of acquiring a resource to be above its price.

Natural monopoly A situation wherein competition among producers, although possible, is deemed undesirable for technical reasons or reasons of public safety. Examples: the provision of drinking water or of telephone service.

Negative income tax A scheme to eliminate poverty according to which persons with low or zero income receive payment from, rather than make payment to, the government.

Net benefit Total benefit minus total cost.

Net indirect business taxes All taxes not levied on income (such as sales, excise, and property taxes) plus the current surplus (or minus the current deficit) of government enterprises minus government subsidies to private businesses.

Net interest Net interest payments to Americans by U.S. businesses and foreigners plus imputed interest earned by owner-occupiers of nonfarm and farm dwellings and of institutional buildings plus imputed interest earned by depositors from financial intermediaries.

Net worth Assets minus liabilities.

New towns Settlements created from scratch on totally undeveloped land according to a long-range master plan.

Noise Unwanted sound.

Normal profit The minimum return necessary to keep a firm in existence in the long run; represents the maximum amount the owner of a firm could earn in alternative pursuits from the resources he owns and uses in his firm.

Off-vehicle pricing system A system of road-use pricing relying on side-of-the-road meters that identify passing vehicles.

On-vehicle pricing system A system of road-use pricing relying on a meter attached to each vehicle.

Open admissions A policy whereby any high school graduate is guaranteed admission to some college.

Opportunity cost Of producing a good: the quantity of another good that might have been made with the resources that were used to make the first good. Of anything: the next best thing that could have been done instead.

Optimum pollution Since the avoidance of waste disposal into the environment is costly, the level of pollution is optimal when the marginal cost of pollution (the extra harm done by another unit of it) just equals the marginal benefit of pollution (the extra avoidance cost saved by another unit of it).

Organized crime The production and sale of goods that are demanded, but the supply of which has been declared illegal, for example, narcotics, loan sharking, prostitution, gambling.

Perfect competition A hypothetical market economy that fulfills certain strict conditions: all market participants are fully informed on exchange opportunities; all are perfectly mobile; there are so many buyers and sellers that none of them, acting alone, can influence the terms of exchange (that is, the price); and prices are perfectly flexible.

Performance contracting The subcontracting by government to private firms of the production of educational services, with payment being a function of the students' performance at the end of the contract period.

Piggyback tax A local tax added ("piggyback") onto an existing state or federal tax.

Piggyback transport The carrying of truck trailers on railroad flat cars specially designed for this purpose.

Point pricing system A system of road-use pricing whereby motorists incur charges when passing designated points.

Political fragmentation In the government of metropolitan areas, the existence of a multitude of uncoordinated and partially overlapping governmental units.

Pollution Waste disposal into the natural environment that so changes the character of the environment that its subsequent uses are impaired.

Pollution index An aggregative measure of the seriousness of air pollution that weights equal quantities of different pollutants in accordance with their effects.

Pollution right A certificate, part of a proposed anti-pollution strategy, allowing the holder to dump a specified quantity of specified wastes into the environment per period.

Potential labor force Everyone 16 years old or more, outside institutions.

Poverty income deficit The difference between the actual aggregate personal income of the poor and the total income required to give each family the poverty-line income.

Poverty line The income level below which a family is counted as poor by the government.

Price fixing The fixing of a price above or below equilibrium, usually by government.

Price system The totality of interdependent prices in goods and resource markets to which self-seeking households and businessmen respond and which, in turn, change with their combined actions; the governor, or "invisible hand," of the market economy.

Primary standards Governmental standards designed to reduce pollution sufficiently to preserve human health.

Principle of optimization Anyone desiring to maximize the total net benefit of an activity should expand that activity up to the point at which the extra benefit from another unit of that activity (the marginal benefit) just equals the extra cost of another unit of that activity (the marginal cost).

Problem shed A geographic area inhabited by all the people who potentially receive benefits from policies dealing with a given problem.

Process of production Any activity by firms that helps make economic goods available to people when and where wanted; includes manufacturing, but also transportation, storage, insurance, selling, etc.

Production possibilities frontier A listing or graphing of all the alternative combinations of two goods or groups of goods a producer is capable of producing in a given period by fully and carefully using a given total of resources, under conditions of existing technical know-how.

Production quota A law that producers may not produce more than a specified maximum quantity of a good during a period; notably applies to agricultural commodities in the U.S.

Progressive tax A tax that takes a larger *percentage* of higher than of lower incomes.

Property right The right to exclusive use of something.

Proportional tax A tax that takes the same *percentage* of everyone's income.

Proprietors' income The income of professional people and of unincorporated firms, the latter including the imputed net rental return to owner-occupants of farm dwellings plus the imputed value of food and fuel produced and consumed on farms.

Public transport Taxis and mass transit.

Pure public goods Goods demanded by government and paid for from general taxes because private demand is nonexistent or very small since the goods cannot be withheld from anyone once produced for even one person. Examples: national defense, some types of knowledge.

Puritan ethic A set of beliefs held originally by Puritans on religious grounds that prescribes a life led by certain austere and strict principles, including hard work; includes the belief that the poor are primarily personally responsible for their condition and should be helped by others as little as possible.

Pyrolysis Shredding, baling, and charring of solid-waste materials in an oxygen-free environment.

Recycling Salvaging solid-waste materials for reuse.

Red capitalism A scheme to create a whole spectrum of businesses owned and run by American Indians to eliminate the poverty of American Indians.

Regressive tax A tax that takes a larger *percentage* of lower than of higher incomes.

Relative definition of poverty The setting of the poverty line in a specified relation to above-poverty incomes, for example at 80 percent of the median family income.

Rental income of persons Earnings from renting real property (including natural resources), royalties from patents and copyrights, and the imputed net rental returns to owner-occupants of nonfarm dwellings.

Rent controls The fixing of rents for dwelling units by government, typically below their equilibrium levels.

Resources Labor, land, or capital; that is, ingredients used in the process of production.

Revenue sharing The making of systematic block grants, for example, by the federal government to the states and localities, perhaps calculated as a percentage of federal income tax receipts.

Reverse commuting Traveling to suburban jobs from central city homes.

Road congestion A situation in which there are so many cars on a road at any one time that average speed decreases, and then the number of cars traversing the road in any given time period falls below its possible maximum.

Robbery The taking or attempted taking of anything of value by force or threat of force.

Sanitary landfill A method of solid-waste disposal, involving spreading in thin layers, compacting with bulldozers, and covering with clean earth.

Satiation The situation in which the marginal benefit of an activity is zero and the total benefit is maximized.

Scarcity Condition existing when people's desires for economic goods exceed, in general, the availability of such goods.

Secondary standards Governmental standards designed to reduce pollution beyond the level specified by primary standards so as to protect not only human health, but also soil, water, vegetation, animals, property, and human comfort.

Second-stage sewage treatment The breaking down of over 80 percent of the organic material remaining after first-stage treatment by the work of benign bacteria.

Self-fulfilling prophecy The fact that believing in something leads to its happening (perhaps because this belief shapes action): for instance, if you believe you are inferior, you are likely to turn out inferior because you will not try hard enough to prove otherwise.

Serious crimes As defined by the FBI, include murder, rape, aggravated assault, robbery, auto theft, larceny, and burglary.

Shortage A situation in which quantity demanded exceeds quantity supplied at the given price.

Short run A period of such length that a producer is unable to vary at least one of the inputs he is using in the productive process; this fixed input defines plant capacity.

Skybus A train running on rubber tires and concrete guideways.

Slum Any area where dwellings predominate that, by reason of dilapidation; overcrowding; faulty management or design; lack of ventilation, light, or sanitation facilities; or any combination of these factors, are detrimental to safety, health, and morals (from the 1937 Housing Act).

Socialism In its pure form, a society wherein all nonhuman resources (capital and land) are collectively owned and collectively used.

Spillovers See **Externalities.**

Standard biological oxygen demand A measure of the amount of dissolved oxygen that would be used in five days by the biological processes involved in degrading a given quantity of organic matter.

Standard metropolitan statistical area A county or township, or a group of contiguous ones, containing one central city (or twin cities) with at least 50,000 people.

Substandard dwelling unit A dwelling unit that is dilapidated or lacks such plumbing facilities as inside hot and cold piped water, flush toilet, and bathtub or shower for the exclusive use of the people in the unit.

Success insurance Government insurance offered to businesses in cities against losses incurred in private job training of the chronically unemployed in slum-based plants.

Surplus A situation in which quantity supplied exceeds quantity demanded at the given price.

Tax base The thing that is taxed, such as income, property value, purchase value.

Tax credit The granting by a higher level of government to its taxpayers of a reduction of their tax liability equal to a given percentage of the taxes paid to a lower level of government.

Tax incidence Where the burden of a tax ultimately rests.

Tax loopholes A set of legal tax preferences and exemptions resulting in different taxation of different types of income recipients and spenders.

Tax rate Percentage of tax applied to the tax base.

Thermal pollution A warming of the water temperature by hot-water emissions into a body of water.

Third-stage sewage treatment The removal of impurities remaining after second-stage treatment by chemical and mechanical processes such as precipitation, coagulation, and filtration.

Total benefit The entire benefit (with costs ignored) associated with a given level of an activity. Examples: the total satisfaction from eating ten apples, the total revenue from selling ten apples, the total income from working ten hours, the total output from employing ten workers.

Total cost The entire cost (with benefits ignored) associated with a given level of an activity. Examples: the total cost of eating or producing ten apples, the total cost of working ten hours or of employing ten workers.

Transactions costs Costs incurred to bring about exchange, such as transportation and communications costs.

Transfer payments Payments made without currently receiving commodities or services in return.

Urban renewal A systematic program of slum eradication by tearing down or rehabilitating buildings and redeveloping the affected area.

Value-added tax A tax on the value added by each producer to the value of goods purchased by him from other firms.

Variable cost Cost that is zero at zero output volume and varies with the volume of output; it equals at any output volume the sum of marginal costs of production up to the output volume in question.

Voluntary unemployment Category assigned to all members of the potential labor force who do not want to work at the wage currently paid for the skill and experience they have to offer (as evidenced by the fact that they are neither working nor looking for work); hence the category includes discouraged workers as well as genuinely retired persons, housewives, and so on.

Wage supplements Employer contributions to social security, unemployment, and health insurance, retirement funds, and employer compensation payments for injuries.

Wealth Household assets minus liabilities secured by these assets.

Weight-gaining industry An industry producing bulky products by adding huge quantities of some ubiquitous material, such as water, to small quantities of other inputs; tends to locate near customers (for example, breweries).

Weight-losing industry An industry using bulky raw materials to make less bulky products; tends to locate near raw material sources (for example, iron and steel).

Zoning laws Laws governing the types of uses to which land may be put.

Symbols

The following list gives the meaning of all symbols and abbreviations used in this book. If you wish, you can turn to the Glossary of Terms for more exact definitions.

AFDC Aid to Families with Dependent Children
AFL–CIO American Federation of Labor–Congress of Industrial Organizations
AMA American Medical Association
B as subscript: business
BOD biological oxygen demand
C consumption expenditures
CORE Congress of Racial Equality
D demand
EPA Environmental Protection Agency
EVI Extreme Value (air pollution) Index
FBI Federal Bureau of Investigation
FHA Federal Housing Administration
FNMA Federal National Mortgage Administration
G as subscript: government
GNMA Government National Mortgage Association
GNP gross national product or income
H as subscript: household
HMO Health Maintenance Organization
HUD U.S. Department of Housing and Urban Development
I investment expenditures
IQ intelligence quotient
JOBS Job Opportunities in the Business Sector program
M imports
MAQI Mitre Air Quality Index
MB marginal benefit
MC marginal cost
μg microgram
MIT Massachusetts Institute of Technology
mph miles per hour
MRP marginal revenue product
MVP marginal value product
NAPCA National Air Pollution Control Administration
NOAA National Oceanic and Atmospheric Administration
OASDHI old age, survivors, disability, and health insurance
ORAQI Oak Ridge Air Quality Index
ppm parts per million

S supply

∑ the Greek letter sigma, denoting "sum of"

SMSA standard metropolitan statistical area

SSA Social Security Administration

SST supersonic transport

VA Veterans Administration

WIN Work Incentive program

X exports

Y aggregate demand, equal to the GNP in equilibrium

Index

1 2 3 4 5 6 7 8 9 10